EXPERIENCE AND ENVIRONMENT

Major Influences on the Development of the Young Child

VOLUME I

EXPERIENCE

Major Influences on the

VOLUME I

AND ENVIRONMENT

Development of the Young Child

BURTON L. WHITE and JEAN CAREW WATTS

with

ITTY CHAN BARNETT

BARBARA TAYLOR KABAN

JANICE ROSEN MARMOR

BERNICE BROYDE SHAPIRO

Preschool Project
Laboratory of Human Development
Harvard Graduate School of Education

PRENTICE-HALL, INC., Englewood Cliffs, New Jersey

Library of Congress Cataloging in Publication Data

WHITE, BURTON L
    Experience and environment.

    Bibliography: p.
    1. Child study. 2. Education, Preschool.
I. Watts, Jean Carew, joint author.
II. Title.
BF721.W43   155.4'13   72-10354
ISBN 0-13-294843-5

BF
721
.W43
v. 1

EXPERIENCE AND ENVIRONMENT
Major Influences on the Development of the Young Child

Burton L. White and Jean Carew Watts
with Itty Chan Barnett, Barbara Taylor Kaban,
Janice Rosen Marmor, Bernice Broyde Shapiro

Printed in the United States of America

10   9   8   7   6   5   4   3   2   1

PRENTICE-HALL INTERNATIONAL, INC., *London*
PRENTICE-HALL OF AUSTRALIA, PTY. LTD., *Sydney*
PRENTICE-HALL OF CANADA, LTD., *Toronto*
PRENTICE-HALL OF INDIA PRIVATE LIMITED, *New Delhi*
PRENTICE-HALL OF JAPAN, INC., *Tokyo*

Contents

Preface *xiii*

part I
INTRODUCTION AND BACKGROUND, 1

1 Background of the Project *3*

BURTON L. WHITE

The State of Knowledge at the Outset of the Project, *5*

2 Evolving a Strategy *9*

BURTON L. WHITE

What, Specifically, Is Human Competence at Six?, *9*
  Social Abilities: Labels, Definitions, and Examples, *10*
  Nonsocial Abilities: Labels, Definitions, and Examples, *13*
  A Basis for Evaluation of Our Hypotheses about Early Experience, *16*
  A Source of Direction for Etiological Early-Education Research, *17*
  A Potential Description of the Goals of Any Early-Education Program, *18*
The Etiology of Competence in Young Children, *18*
Narrowing the Focus, *20*
The Plan of Attack, *22*

v

part II

THE LONGITUDINAL NATURAL EXPERIMENT, 23

3 The Design of the Study 25

BURTON L. WHITE AND JEAN CAREW WATTS

Design Considerations, *25*
  Testing Schedule, 26
Subjects, *27*
  Description of Subject Sample, 29
  Instruments to Screen Out Handicapped Children, 38

A. The Development of Competence

4 The Development of Competence 39

BURTON L. WHITE, BARBARA KABAN, JANICE MARMOR, AND BERNICE SHAPIRO

Introduction, *39*
Quantitative Methods for the Study of the Development of Competence, *40*
Assessing the Development of Social Competence
During the Second and Third Years of Life, *41*
  Social Competence: Results and Discussion, 43
Assessing Receptive-Language Development
During the Second and Third Years of Life, *47*
  Receptive Language: Results and Discussion, 49
Assessing the Capacity to Sense Dissonance
During the Second and Third Years of Life, *54*
  Sensing Dissonance: Results and Discussion, 56
Assessing the Capacity for Abstract Thought
During the Second and Third Years of Life, *60*
  Abstract Thought: Results and Discussion, 61
Tests of General and Intellectual Development, *65*
  General and Intellectual Development: Results and Discussion, 65

B. The Child's Stream of Experience

5 An Instrument for the Quantitative Analysis of the Stream of Experience of One- to Six-Year-Old Children 68

BURTON L. WHITE, BARBARA KABAN, JANICE MARMOR, AND BERNICE SHAPIRO
Social Tasks: Labels, Definitions, and Examples, *69*
Nonsocial Tasks: Labels, Definitions, and Examples, *81*

6 **Patterns of Experience During the Second and Third Years of Life: Results and Discussion** *84*

BURTON L. WHITE, BARBARA KABAN, JANICE MARMOR, AND BERNICE SHAPIRO

Task Data—General, *86*
Task Data—"A" versus "C" Children, *91*
   1A vs. 1C Children, 91   2A vs. 2C Children, 95
Subanalyses, *95*
   Language Experience, 95   Mastery Experience, 98   Discussion, 100
Frequency Analyses, *100*
Initiation Data, *102*
   Initiation Data—Social vs. Nonsocial Tasks, 103
   Initiation Data—Specific Social Tasks, 104
   Initiation Data—Specific Nonsocial Tasks, 105

7 **Case Studies in the Light of the Competence and Experience Data** *111*

BURTON L. WHITE, BARBARA KABAN, JANICE MARMOR, AND BERNICE SHAPIRO

Subject #1, *111*
   Background Data, 111   Discussion of Test Performance, 112
   Social Competence, 112
Subject #3, *114*
   Background Data, 114   Discussion of Test Performance, 115
   Social Competence, 116
Task Data, *116*
   Social Tasks, Subjects 1 and 3, 116
   Nonsocial Tasks, Subjects 1 and 3, 117   Task-Initiation Data, 120
Subject #32, *122*
   Background Data, 122   Discussion of Test Performance, 123
   Social Competence, 124
Subject #34, *126*
   Background Data, 126   Discussion of Test Performance, 126
   Social Competence, 127
Task Data, *128*
   Social Tasks, Subjects 32 and 34, 128
   Nonsocial Tasks, Subjects 32 and 34, 131   Task-Initiation Data, 131
Subject #22, *134*
   Background Data, 134   Discussion of Test Performance, 134
   Social Competence, 135
Subject #28, *137*
   Background Data, 137   Discussion of Test Performance, 137
   Social Competence, 138   Social Tasks, Subjects 22 and 28, 139
   Nonsocial Tasks, Subjects 22 and 28, 142   Task-Initiation Data, 142

Subject #7, *143*
  Background Data, 143   Discussion of Test Performance, 145
  Social Competence, 146
Subject #21, *146*
  Background Data, 146   Discussion of Test Performance, 147
  Social Competence, 149
Task Data, *149*
  Social Tasks, Subjects 7 and 21, 149
  Nonsocial Tasks, Subjects 7 and 21, 149   Task-Initiation Data, 154

C.   The Child's Environment

8   Observing the Child's Environment   *156*

JEAN CAREW WATTS AND ITTY CHAN BARNETT

Conceptual Framework, *156*
Scales for Measuring the Child's Environment, *159*
  Human Interaction Scale, 160   Object Interaction Scale, 172
  Questionnaires, 173
Summary, *174*

9   Environments Compared   *176*

JEAN CAREW WATTS AND ITTY CHAN BARNETT

Observation Schedule: When, Who, and Where We Observe, *177*
Method of Observation: Who Observes and How They Observe, *180*
Preliminary Data Analysis: Activities and Techniques, *182*
Differences Between "A" and "C" Children from One to Three Years, *186*
  The Mother's Role in Encouraging, Initiating, and Controlling the Child's
  Activity, 193
  Interaction with Other People in Addition to the Mother, 195
  The Influence of Socioeconomic Factors, 195
  Interaction with the Physical Environment, 197
Summary, *199*

10   Four Children: Four Environments   *201*

JEAN CAREW WATTS AND ITTY CHAN BARNETT

The Children of the Case Studies, *202*
Sandra, a One-Year-Old "A" Girl, *202*
  Sandra's Background: Physical Environment, 202
  Human Environment, 203   Observations on Sandra, 204
  Commentary, 206, 208, 209

Cathy, a One-Year-Old "C" Girl, *211*
  Cathy's Background: Physical Environment, 211
  Human Environment, 212
  Observations on Cathy, 212   Commentary, 215, 217, 218, 220

Nancy, a Two-Year-Old "A" Girl, *221*
  Nancy's Background: Physical Environment, 221
  Human Environment, 222
  Observations on Nancy, 222   Commentary, 224, 225

Robert, a Two-Year-Old "C" Boy, *225*
  Robert's Background: Physical Environment, 226
  Human Environment, 226
  Commentary, 228, 229

part III

INTEGRATION AND TENTATIVE INTERPRETATIONS, 231

11   Discussions and Conclusions 233

BURTON L. WHITE

Introduction, *233*
  The Critical Period of Development, 234
The Child at One Year of Age, *234*
The Child at Two Years of Age, *236*
The Special Importance of the 10- to 18-Month Period of Life, *237*
Important Characteristics of Primary Caretakers, *240*
Mothering, a Vastly Underrated Occupation, *242*
Best Guesses About Most Effective Child-Rearing Practices, *242*

12   Ramifications for Society 245

BURTON L. WHITE

Informal Early Education—Child-Rearing Practices, *245*
Infant-Education Programs for Children Less Than Three Years of Age, *246*
Preschool Education Programs for Three- and Four-Year-Olds, *247*
Epilogue, *248*
References, *249*

appendix I

MEASUREMENT TECHNIQUES:
MANUALS AND RELIABILITY STUDIES, 252

A   **Auditory Screening Techniques** *254*

B   **Visual Screening Techniques** *256*

Language Test

C   **Manual for Testing the Language Ability of One- to Three-Year-Old Children** *257*

Abstract Abilities Test

D   **Manual for Testing Abstract Ability** *291*

Sensing Discrepancies Test

E   **Manual for Assessing the Discriminative Ability of One- to Three-Year-Old Children** *323*

Task Instrument

G   **Manual for Quantitative Analysis of Tasks of One- to Six-Year-Old Children** *360*

Social Competence Checklist

F   **Manual for Assessing Social Abilities of One- to Six-Year-Old Children** *334*

appendix II
INDIVIDUAL SUBJECT DATA, 391

appendix III
ENVIRONMENTAL INSTRUMENTS AND
SUPPLEMENTARY TABLES, 465

Human Interaction Scale

A **Manual for Human Interaction Scale** *468*

Object Interaction Scale

B **Manual for Object Interaction Scale** *506*

C **Typical Day of the Week** *510*

D **Preliminary Home Interview** *511*

E **First Home Interview** *512*

F **Final Home Interview** *524*

G **Supplementary Tables** *533*

Index *543*

Preface

This book was written by two teams of authors, one consisting of Burton L. White, Barbara Kaban, Janice Rosen Marmor, and Bernice Broyde Shapiro; and the other of Jean Carew Watts and Itty Chan Barnett. This division of authorship reflects a major division in research responsibilities within the Preschool Project from about the summer of 1969. At that time we began work on the longitudinal experiment described in Part II. In that experiment, White directed the research on the child's development of competence and the stream of experience while Watts directed the research on the child's human and physical environment. Their two research teams worked collaboratively and harmoniously within the organizational and conceptual framework of the Preschool Project, studying the same children over the same period of time. But they also worked in considerable independence of each other and so far as this writing is concerned, did not always agree on questions of style, emphasis, or interpretation or feel equally ready to commit themselves to conclusions derived from these preliminary results. Therefore, it seems only fair that each team of authors should be held responsible only for the chapters ascribed to it, and not for any other parts of the book.

PURPOSES

This book is concerned with the psychological development of preschool-aged children. The research it describes was designed to produce dependable information on the question of how to raise children so that their basic abilities might develop as well as possible during their first years of life. Though our research has been underway for over five years, and though the equivalent of ten people have been working continuously on the project during this time, we are quite some distance from the completion of our studies. Nevertheless, for several reasons, we feel the time has come for us to report to our colleagues and also to the public.

There are several important consequences of the fact that our work is not complete as we are writing this book. First of all, none of our statements about the effects of various child-rearing practices and experiences of children have been put to experimental test. We plan this testing as the next phase of our work; and, of course, without experimental confirmation we cannot have ultimate confidence in our observations on this central topic. However, our information on what one- to three-year-old children actually experience in their daily lives, our studies of natural behaviors during this age period, and our work in plotting the development of various dimensions of competence during that time all appear to be valid and of potential use. Our assessment techniques are admittedly less than perfect; however, we believe that they are either as good as or better than any others available for the study of the one- to three-year-old child.

Although our judgments about the effects of various child-rearing practices have not been tested experimentally, they do emerge from a form of experimentation. While we have not yet seen mothers rear their children according to our recommendations, we have been conducting a "natural" experiment. We have been observing how families manage to produce very competent three-year-olds. Simultaneously, we have been observing other families produce much less able three-year-olds. Though our comparative analysis can only yield correlational data which must be confirmed by experimental test, we believe this design allows us to place more stock in our hypotheses about the effects of various child-rearing practices than we might on the basis of exclusively theoretical ideas or observations of a random sample of families.

We are preparing this document for several audiences: parents and others responsible for rearing children; undergraduate and graduate students; and research personnel. To cope with this situation, we have kept to a minimum the amount of technical information presented in the body of the book. A full presentation of assessment techniques, manuals, reliability test results, and detailed data can be found in the appendix section.

ACKNOWLEDGMENTS

We wish to extend our gratitude to the present research staff of the Preschool Project: Mrs. Nancy Apfel, Miss Martha Carroll, Mrs. Kitty Riley Clark, Mrs. Mary Comita, Miss Anna DiPietrantonio, Miss Christine Halfar, Mrs. Sandra Lin, Miss Maxine Manjos, Mrs. Ingrid Stocking, Mr. Paul Weene, Miss A. Elise Weinrich, and Dr. Melvin Zolot. In addition, we wish to thank all those who have helped us in the past: Mrs. Jacqueline Allaman, Miss Frances Aversa, Mrs. Ellen Cardone Banks, Mrs. Martha Bronson, Mrs. Barbara Rich Bushell, Mrs. Cherry Collins, Mr. Andrew Cohn, Mrs. Virginia Demos, Mrs. Marjorie Elias, Dr. John Guidubaldi, Miss Geraldine Kearse, Dr. E. R. LaCrosse, Jr., Dr. Patrick C. Lee, Mrs. Frances Litman, Mrs. Mary Meader Mokler, Dr. Daniel M. Ogilvie, Mrs. Meridith S. Pandolfi, Mrs. Sylvia Skolnick Staub, Dr. Susan S. Stodolsky, Mrs. Jolinda Taylor, Mrs. Eleanor Wasserman, and Mrs. Louise Woodhead. Particular gratitude is owed to Drs. Theodore Sizer and Gerald Lesser of the Harvard Graduate School of Education, and to Dr. Edith Grotberg of the Office of Economic Opportunity, and to Mrs. Barbara Finberg of the Carnegie Corporation of New York, who were willing to take risks for this project. In addition, this study has been made possible by the cooperation of several hundred families and many school personnel from nearby public and private institutions. Special thanks must go to Dr. Miriam Fiedler of the Maternal Infant Health Project.

The research and development reported herein was performed in part pursuant to a contract (OE 5-10-39) with the United States Office of Education, under the provisions of the Cooperative Research Program as a project of the Harvard University Center for Research and Development on Educational Differences, the Carnegie Corporation of New York, and the Office of Economic Opportunity, Head Start Division. The statements made and views expressed are solely the responsibility of the authors.

part **I**

INTRODUCTION
AND BACKGROUND

1

Background of the Project

BURTON L. WHITE

This report was begun in late 1970. It is important to highlight that fact, because it will be some time before this book is in print and because the subject of this study is currently being literally assaulted by scores of research personnel. We believe that our approach to the problem of early human development is quite rare in spite of that massive research effort; for unlike most current studies, ours is not oriented toward a single developmental process, such as the acquisition of language or intelligence, nor have we begun by executing intervention studies with underdeveloped children. We have instead begun by studying the development of *overall* competence in children who have gotten off to a superb start in their early years. Another way of characterizing our work is to describe its goal as optimizing human development rather than removing developmental deficits. We are in the business of prevention rather than remediation.

Our project was christened the Harvard Preschool Project. It began in September 1965 with funds provided by the U. S. Office of Education. Ours was one of several projects in the School of Education's Research and Development Center. Accumulating evidence suggested that although most educators were concerning themselves with the educational process of children age six and older, much of a child's crucial development was

3

over by the age of six. By that age, so it seemed, it might already be too late to prevent stunted development and to insure full growth. Thus the Preschool Project was designed as a cornerstone for the whole research and development effort with older children. The object was to find out as much as possible about the preschool-age child and, in particular, to study the attributes and development of the successful or educable child. The phrase we used then was, we were concerned with the development of educability.

Our mandate was maddeningly simple to express: to learn how to structure the experiences of the first six years of life so that a child might be optimally prepared for formal education. Though the problem was easily stated, the solution was not likely to be achieved with ease. Not only was the research task a formidable one, but in addition, good strategies of approach were not obvious. Our knowledge of the literature suggested that none of the then-current theoretical orientations toward early human development were adequately rooted in directly relevant empirical data—with the exception of Piaget's theory of intelligence (LaCrosse et al., 1970).* We were not committed to any particular theory. We saw this latter point as an advantage. Instead of bending children to fit a particular theoretical approach, we decided, we could immerse ourselves in preschools, observe the behavior of young children, and *evolve* a strategy for tracing the etiology of educability. Under the shelter of the Research and Development Center, we were in a position to develop a reality-based strategy.

When we began our work, Project Head Start was only a few months old. Parent–child centers were not yet conceived and the focus of those in early education was on the "disadvantaged" four-year-old. Our project director, Burton L. White, was offered the opportunity to begin the project partly on the basis of his work with young infants (White, 1971).† For the preceding seven years, he had worked on the problem of the role of experience in the development of adaptive abilities during the first six months of life. Those studies seemed to indicate that young infants could enjoy and apparently profit from exposure to experiences specifically designed to match their rapidly changing interests and abilities.

White was quite ambivalent about beginning the project. On the one

---

* Piaget's theory of the development of intelligence during infancy grew out of extensive research on the intellectual development of his own three children. No other major theory of early human development is similarly based on extensive direct studies of children. An example of an influential theory of infancy is the well known work of Sigmund Freud. Freud's theory of infantile sexuality was developed from studies of adult neurotic patients.

† From 1958 to 1965, Burton L. White had been studying the role of experience in the development of adaptive abilities in the first six months of life of human infants. That work is reported in a volume called *Human Infants: Experience and Psychological Development* (Englewood Cliffs, N.J.: Prentice-Hall, Inc., 1971).

hand, a scientific approach to such a problem could obviously aspire to only limited success, owing to the awesome complexity of the problem and the primitivity of available research methods. On the other hand, the possibility of making a significant contribution to the development of children of future generations was too attractive to turn down. In addition, it looked at that time as if resources would be no problem. Ample funds were available, and that fact, along with the prestige of Harvard University, seemed to assure that the project would be able to hire a sizable well-trained staff and that we would have quite a few years to pursue its goals.

We have enjoyed the full support of the school's administration, especially from Dean Theodore Sizer and from Dr. Gerald Lesser, director of the Laboratory of Human Development. Two factors have hampered us somewhat: In 1968, funds for behavioral research suddenly became scarce for the first time in years. We have survived; but an inordinate amount of energy has had to be devoted to fund raising. Second, the field of early education has been mushrooming spectacularly, thereby putting pressure of various kinds on our personnel. In spite of such difficulties, we believe we have made good progress toward our goal. Watching a human life being shaped and feeling that you are beginning to understand how a child can be helped to realize his potential is a most exciting way to earn a living. Until we test our current judgments via experimental studies, we can offer our ideas only tentatively, but we do believe we have learned a significant amount about early human development.

THE STATE OF KNOWLEDGE AT THE OUTSET OF THE PROJECT

In 1965, there were many points of view among concerned professionals about the state of knowledge of how to prepare children for formal education. A few believed that the laws of early human development were well understood and that all that was needed was an effort to apply that knowledge. Richard Wolf, a colleague of Benjamin Bloom at the University of Chicago, expressed that point of view in a seminar at the Harvard Graduate School of Education. A few others either had been writing about the problems of disadvantaged preschool children or were actually operating experimental programs. Martin Deutsch and David Weikart were already operating compensatory preschool elementary programs. Deutsch stressed the problem of inadequate sensory-discrimination capacity (among other presumed deficits), whereas Weikart was less sure of what the root problem was and was designing eclectic programs at that time.

Carl Bereiter was performing the first dramatically successful compensatory preschool program (Bereiter and Engelmann, 1966). His work was a form of high-quality educational engineering. Bereiter concluded that the core abilities that were deficient in disadvantaged six-year-olds were cognitive and linguistic. He therefore devised a highly focused remedial curriculum that aimed at rapid improvement in those areas.

In addition to those pioneers in the field, there were numerous professionals who had been working in the field of early education long before the problem of preschool education for the disadvantaged became fashionable. Shirley Moore, at the University of Minnesota; Barbara Biber, at the Bank Street College of Education; Louise Bates Ames and Frances Ilg, at the Gesell Institute—these were some of the leaders of a large group of people who could justly be called "the Establishment" in the field of early education. What these people believed about the total problem of early education is hard to say. They did apparently feel that they knew enough to train teachers and direct preschool education programs for middle-class three- to five-year-olds.

Another group of professionals operated a small number of preschool programs for low-income children. Such programs were usually called "day-care" programs rather than nursery schools. Day-care programs would look after young children for as much as ten hours a day while their parents worked, whereas nursery schools usually operated on a half-day basis. Many day-care operators felt that they were preschool educators, while others only claimed to provide custodial care. Day-care operators were not often consulted on the problem of early education, and their views have really never been fully heard.

Yet another type of professional came from the ranks of developmental psychology. J. McV. Hunt, from the University of Illinois, the senior author of this study, had been interested in the role of early experience in human development for many years. Hunt's interest covered the entire span of early human development, whereas White had been concentrating on the first six months of life. Others, such as Lewis Lipsitt at Brown University and Yvonne Brackbill at the University of Colorado, had been studying conditioning processes in infancy and therefore felt a professional interest in the problem of early education. Hunt and White, at least, were quite sure that we were unprepared to cope immediately with the problem of early education. They shared the point of view that early education for *all* children, not merely those judged disadvantaged, was a societal goal of paramount importance. They also shared the view that basic knowledge about early human development, and especially about the role of experience in the development of abilities, simply was not available in any but grossly inadequate amounts.

It was against this background of diversity of opinion and lack of data that the Preschool Project began. We invested an enormous amount of energy in checking our judgment on the state of existing knowledge during the first two years of the project. Any empirical investigation starts with an analysis of what is known about the phenomena in question. The magnitude of this phase of a project is largely a function of two factors—the scope and complexity of the problem and the amount of previous relevant research. Because human abilities are diverse and apparently dependent on the almost infinite number of events of the individual's past, the library research of this project was a major endeavor. Library research served conventional *instrumental* functions; it was not an end in itself. The instrumental functions were (1) to determine the baseline of knowledge from which to proceed with new work, and (2) to serve a heuristic purpose as a reservoir of ideas of varying potential.

One way to organize this portion of our effort, we thought, was to simply assimilate *all* serious relevant research. This possibility was feasible. In the spring of 1966, we made a preliminary survey of publications and research projects concerning children three to six years of age. We determined that we could, given a few years, digest most of the material written in English and available since 1900. We also concluded that we could assimilate all comparable new information as it appeared.

By the end of the first academic year of the project, the core staff was familiar with the behavior of children in the preschool environment, an effective observational technique had been devised, much of the past work in the field had been assimilated into the project's thought, and preliminary taxonomies of tasks and coping abilities were being suggested.

It was decided that the technique of taking behavioral protocols was sufficiently powerful to provide the raw material for inducing the components of educability. It was thus resolved that the project would move toward systematic collection of protocol data in order to amass a strong base from which induction could proceed.

We organized and expressed our ideas on what the literature contained in position papers that summarized each of the several fields, such as studies of language, intellectual development, and assessment techniques. We combined all the information into a lengthy report (LaCrosse et al., 1970).

The pessimism with which we began the literature search was not dispelled by the two-year effort. True, many first-rate studies of elements of the problem of early education had been made, but the question of how to structure early experience to assure the optimal development of a preschool child remained mostly unanswered. An impressive corroboration of this judgment can be found in an editorial by Alberta Siegel, which appeared in *Child Development* in December 1967.

What to do? Given a strong suspicion that preschool-age children could be helped significantly by the provision of more suitable sequences of experience, but given also an inadequate knowledge base for designing such experiences, what does one do? There seemed to be two positive directions to take: One could plunge right into intervention work and try whatever seemed reasonable with children less than six years of age. In fact, many people did just that—often in Head Start programs, at times in field research operations such as those of Bereiter, Susan Grey, Glen Nimnicht, and David Weikart, to name a few of the better-known projects. The other obvious approach would be to work on the problem of building the knowledge base. The first approach had the virtue of offering hope for children growing up then, in 1965. At the same time, it seemed clear that even if hastily conceived programs were occasionally partly successful, they were designed only to serve the emergency function of eliminating severe developmental deficits. Optimal development for each child was not their concern. The second approach could be oriented toward the problem of understanding the laws of optimal development (which might simultaneously aid in solving the compensatory-education problem). The second approach would not, however, help a single child for several years. We chose the second approach.

2

Evolving a Strategy

Burton L. White

We are concerned with the problem of how to structure the experiences of the first six years of life so as to encourage maximal development of human competence. Such a goal leads naturally to a consideration of two problem areas: (1) what is human competence in six-year-old children, and (2) how do we learn the details of the interactions between early experience and the development of such competence?

WHAT, SPECIFICALLY, IS HUMAN COMPETENCE AT SIX?

Nowhere in the literature could we find detailed descriptions of healthy, well-developed six-year-old humans. We decided therefore to attempt to follow the lead of the European ethologists (Lorenz, Tinbergen, etc.). Initially, we selected as broad an array of types of preschool children as we could. Our original sample consisted of some 400 three-, four-, and five-year-old children living in eastern Massachusetts. We reached the children through seventeen preschool institutions (kindergartens and nursery schools). These children varied in at least the following dimensions:

(1) residence—from rural to suburban and urban; (2) SES (socioeconomic status)—lower-lower to lower-upper class; and (3) ethnicity—Irish, Italian, Jewish, English, Portuguese, Chinese, and several other types. On the basis of extensive, independent observations by fifteen staff members and the teachers of these children, and also on the basis of their performance on objective tests such as the Wechsler and tests of motor and sensory capacities, we isolated fifty-one children. Half were judged to be very high on overall competence, able to cope in superior fashion with anything they met, day in and day out. The other half were judged to be free from gross pathology but generally of very low competence. We then proceeded to observe these children each week for a period of eight months. We gathered some 1,100 protocols on the typical moment-to-moment activities of these children, mostly in the institutions, but also in their homes. At the end of the observation period, we selected the thirteen most talented and thirteen least talented children. Through intensive discussions by our staff of twenty people, we compiled a list of abilities that seemed to distinguish the two groups. These abilities were divided into social and nonsocial types. It should be noted that not all abilities of such children were included. We concluded, for example, that differences in motor and sensory capacities between children of high and low overall competence were generally quite modest. The resultant list of distinguishing abilities represents an observationally based differentiated description of what we mean by competence in preschool children. The list, along with short definitions and examples, follows.

Social Abilities: Labels, Definitions, and Examples

(1) *To Get and Maintain the Attention of Adults in Socially Acceptable Ways*
Definition: The ability to get the attention of an adult through the use of various strategies (e.g., moves toward and stands/sits near A; touches A; calls to A; shows something to A; tells something to A.)*

Examples:

(*Five-year-old boy*) S stands up and walks out of the closet, walking only on his heels.† S yells, "Hey, Miss T!" (T doesn't answer.) S talks to PM. He shouts, "Hey!" but no one pays attention. S walks over to T and says, "Hey, Miss T, look," and holds out his hand, which is holding the piece of ice. (T says something.) S says, " 'cause it's hot in here," and laughs.

(*Five-year-old boy*) S looks at PM, listens to T, and utters something under his

---

* These examples were taken directly from the protocols recorded by the observers in the schools. Consequently, they are often brief descriptive phrases rather than complete sentences.

† Several abbreviations are used throughout the text to refer to the following: S = subject; M = mother; T = teacher; AT = assistant teacher; PF (or FP) = female peer; PM (or MP) = male peer; and O = observer.

breath. He looks at his long line of letters—rocks his chair. Standing, smiling, calls out, "What's this, T? What's this?" while looking toward front of room and T. S repeats, "T, what's that?" indicating his picture and rocking on his chair. T guesses, "A lamp post?"

(*Five-year-old girl*)   (T is sitting on a chair, and most of the children are sitting around her discussing the things they did on their vacation.) S stands up on her knees. She calls out, trying to get T's attention. S talks to PM next to her (he shows her pencils in a pencil case that he has). S sits and looks at the pencils. S holds the pencil case and gives it back to PM. They talk. S pushes her hair back with both hands. She bites her nails, stands on her knees, and raises her hand trying to get T's attention. (T calls on S.) S says, "Guess what! Natalie is such a pig, she ate everybody's Easter eggs, she's a pig." (T comments that Natalie is a pig.) S repeats again, "She's a pig."

(2) *To Use Adults as Resources*

Definition: The ability to make use of an adult in order to obtain something by means of a verbal request or demand or a physical demonstration of his need. His object may be to gain information, assistance, or food, and he may demonstrate this by declaring what he wants, making a request, making a demand, or by gesturing, acting out, or pointing.

Examples:

(*Four-year-old boy*)   S sees a new crayon box. He gasps as if excited, takes the new crayon box, and then takes a piece of paper (written or scribbled on back). He looks up at AT, and tries very hard to open the box. He places his tongue out and tries harder to open it but can't. (AT passes and taps him affectionately on the head.) After she passes, he touches his head a few times. He then watches T put up pictures along the wall, looks at O, smiles at O (O smiles back), looks again at O, and smiles at O. He then tries to open the crayon box again. It still will not open. For the next minute he tries again and again. Finally, he says loudly, "I can't open it." He looks at T, but she does not hear and just walks into the porch room to dry some pictures. (It is raining outside.) He says to T, "This screen is wet." T walks back into room and passes S. He looks up at T, and puts his face on her apron. (She just walks away.) He then watches the boy opposite him crayon. (AT comes near.) He says to her, "I can't open this." (AT opens it for him.) He smiles.

(*Five-year-old boy*)   S glances at T and asks, "Teacher, how do you make a letter that goes like girl and helicopter? I forgot the letter that goes with helicopter and little girl." He looks at T while he grasps his pencil and moves it about. He continues to move the pencil about and slides around his chair. Then he calls again, "Miss T, how do you make a little girl and a helicopter?" (T walks over to his table and points to the girl. She asks, "What's this?") S responds, "A little girl." (T asks, "What sound does it have?") S responds with the correct sound of *g*. (T then asks the same questions about *helicopter*.) S answers all these questions correctly. (T then asks, "What's the problem?") S responds, "I don't know how to write it." S stands, his pencil drops, he bends down to pick it up. (T turns his paper over and prints *H*. She then turns it back to its original position and indicates that he should try to print one.) He looks at a girl, looks at the other side of the paper, then at the teacher, and succeeds in printing an *H*. (T then points to the picture of the girl and asks, "How do you make this letter?")

(3) *To Express Both Affection and Hostility to Adults*

Definition: The ability to express affection and/or hostility through verbal and/or physical means (e.g., friendly statements, such as "I like you," "You're nice," or hugging A; statements of dislike, such as "I hate you," "You're bad," hitting A, or physically resisting A).

Examples:

(*Three-year-old boy*)   T pulls S and says, "Do some work." S hangs down limp while T pulls him. He does not stand or move his legs. S says, "No, I don't want to." T continues to pull him up and yells, "Stand on your feet!" S just hangs and slides back and forth. (T drags him to work room and to a table where another T is. The other T says that she should give him the cylinders, since they are new—he may be interested in them.) T drags him to the shelf to get the set of cylinders. T takes set and S follows T to the table.

(*Four-year-old boy*)   In library time, children at different times kept on saying, "I would like this book. I would like *Swimny*. I would like *Red Riding Hood*," etc., etc. AT kept on saying, "Yes, here it is, what would you like?" S then said in a loud, angry voice, "Would you like to be quiet, then I'll read the *Fire Engine Book*."

(*Four-year-old girl*)   T sits down at table where S is working. S looks up at T and smiles warmly.

(4) *To Lead and Follow Peers*

Definition: The ability to assume control in peer-related activities; e.g., to give suggestions, to orient and direct, to set oneself up as a model for imitation. The ability to follow the lead of others; e.g., to follow suggestions.

Examples:

(*Three-and-a-half-year-old boy*)   S comes into view with several other children. They all appear to be excited about something. He is hopping and jumping as he enters the playroom, goes over to the AT talking excitedly, and says something about the window being stuck. He talks some more and then says something about "we saw fire trucks." PM1, who is sitting next to the AT, says, "What did they come for?" S says, "To put out the fire." S turns to walk out of the room, then turns back and comes back and says to PM2, "Come on, let's go." S starts to walk away. He turns back and says again, with more irritation in his voice this time, "Come on. Let's go." PM2 and the other children follow him out into the hallway, out of sight.

(*Four-year-old boy*)   PM walks over to S. S makes a funny face at him. PM copies S. Imitation game with S as leader. S, always first, hits his face, then head, etc., while the other boy follows.

(*Four-year-old boy*)   S is drawing a picture. He says, "I'm making a clown." PF looks up and says, "Make his hat red." S picks up the red crayon and draws a red hat.

(5) *To Express Both Affection and Hostility to Peers*

Definition: The ability to express affection and/or hostility to peers through verbal or physical means.

Examples:

(*Five-year-old girl*)   S walks across the playground with her arm around PF1, who in turn has an arm around S. In this manner they walk together to far side of yard where the swings are.

(*Four-and-a-half-year-old boy*)   S notices peer taking S's letter from the floor area. S yells, "Hey, put that back, put it back—supposed to be over there." (The child is still picking up the letters.) S walks over to him and says sternly, "Put that back."

(6) *To Compete with Peers*

Definition: The ability to exhibit interpersonal competition.

Examples:

(*Four-and-a-half-year-old girl*)   Attaching sequins to styrofoam balls for Christmas decorations. Says to PF, "I'm the first one done."

(*Three-year-old boy*)   Children are punching holes in paper. S asks PM if he can have some red pieces of punched-out paper. PM says, "OK." S picks up some red and blue pieces of paper out of PM's bowl. S then drops the pieces on the table, picks up a larger piece of red paper, and asks PM if he can punch holes in that piece. (PM says, "Yeah.") S says, "I'll punch more holes than you ever dreamed up."

(7) *To Praise Oneself and/or Show Pride in One's Accomplishments*

Definition: The ability to express pride in something he has created, owns, or possesses at the moment, or something he is in the process of doing or has done.

Examples:

(*Four-and-a-half-year-old girl*)   Children are making Christmas decorations by pinning sequin beads onto styrofoam balls. S says (to PF), "I need them too. How do you stick these on?" (PF replies, "I'll show you how I put the other color in.") S says, "I know how." (At this point S refuses to follow the advice of PF and concentrates on accomplishing her task.) After having successfully attached some sequins to the ball, she looks up and says to PF, "Look what I did!"

(*Four-year-old boy*)   Upon T's instructions, S traces over the *G*, turns the page over, and writes. He looks up and loudly states, "I did my best." (T says, "That's a better improvement.")

(8) *To Involve Oneself in Adult Role-Playing Behaviors or to Otherwise Express the Desire to Grow up*

Definition: To act out a typical adult activity or verbally express a desire to grow up.

Example:

(*Four-year-old girl*)   S sits down on the floor with the phone beside her. She pushes her hair in back of her right ear, takes the receiver with her right hand, and puts the receiver on top of her hair—which has now fallen over the right ear. She kicks her foot on the chair to the left of her and then whispers into the receiver. She says "Yes" and laughs and twists cord around her fingers. S sits on her knees and continues to do this. (Observer comments that S is play-acting as if a teen-age girl.)

Nonsocial Abilities: Labels, Definitions, and Examples

(1) *Linguistic Competence; i.e., grammatical capacity, vocabulary, articulation, and extensive use of expressed language*

Definition: Self-explanatory.

[*No examples.*]

(2) *Intellectual Competence*

a) The ability to sense dissonance or note discrepancies

Definition: This is a critical faculty on the part of the child, an ability to indicate one's awareness of discrepancies, inconsistencies, and other forms of irregularity in the environment. It is almost always expressed verbally, but occasionally takes nonverbal forms as well. It is observable whenever a child comments upon some noticed irregularity. The effect that generally accompanies it usually involves mild confusion, a look of discovery, or a display of righteousness, in pointing out and correcting the irregularity.

Examples:

(*Three-year-old girl*) S is sitting at a table working with Play Doh and glancing up periodically from one peer at the table to another. S turns to an FP beside her and asks, "Is your name Margot? Do you have a haircut?" (The FP has had her hair cut from shoulder- to ear-length.)

(*Three-year-old boy*) S is coloring at a table with several peers. An MP holds up his picture, announcing that it is the moon. S looks at the picture and remarks, "A moon doesn't have hair," noting that the moon in the drawing seems to have hair.

b) The ability to anticipate consequences

Definition: This is the ability to anticipate a probable effect on, or sequence to, whatever is currently occupying the attention of the child. It is usually expressed verbally, but also takes nonverbal forms. It can take place in a social context or in relative isolation. It is not simply an awareness of a future event— e.g., "Tomorrow is Thursday"—but must somehow relate that event to a present condition. The relationship may be either causal—e.g., "If X, then Y"—or sequential—e.g., "Now 1, next 2." The second half of each relationship *must* be an anticipated future outcome. It cannot actually occur until after the child anticipates its occurrence.

Examples:

(*Three-year-old girl*) S has been waiting for her turn at the juice table and checks on it periodically. MP is sitting there now. S comes and observes MP for a few seconds, then says, "He's finishing his cracker and after him I'm going to eat, okay?"

(*Three-year-old girl*) S has just finished washing her hands of paint and is drying them in a room with T and several peers. FP asks what time it is, and S then asks, "Is it time to go home now?" T answers that it is only 10:20 and not time to go home. S then says, "Just one more hour then it's time to go home, right?" About five minutes later, S refuses a task with the rationale that that particular task will take too long to do by the time she finishes the task with which she is presently occupied. S says, "I'll match them next time, okay?"

c) The ability to deal with abstractions; i.e., numbers, letters, rules

Definition: To use abstract concepts and symbols in ways that require building upon what is concretely present, and showing mental organization of what is perceived. The term *concept* means "a mental state or process that refers to more than one object or experience"; the term *symbol* means "an object, expression, or responsive activity that replaces and becomes a representative substitute for another."

Examples:

(*Five-year-old boy*)   In a spelling game with Scrabble tiles, S asks, "Does she get two turns?" "I have 5 tiles—supposed to have 7." Asks T what his letters spell and repeats this (a nonsense word). S asks, "Does anybody have an A?" Attentive to others' moves as well as his own.

(*Four-year-old boy*)   Class is doing a number exercise with collections of fingerprints on the board. Tasks are selecting the set that corresponds to a number, subtracting and adding ("How many more?" "How many too many?"), and making correct numbers of prints. S answers the counting questions, says, "I know where six is"; sometimes answers with others but seems to answer more questions than the rest of the class.

d) The ability to take the perspective of another

Definition: To show an understanding of how things look to another person whose position in space is different from the subject's, or to show an understanding of a person's emotional state or mental attitude when they are different from the subject's. (The opposite of egocentricity.)

Examples:

(*Five-year-old boy*)   In a word game, another child is having difficulty deciding where to place a letter. S watches her and smiles reassuringly, in a way that convinces the observer that he understands the girl's problem.

(*Five-year-old boy*)   S is given the job of passing out cookies. He checks carefully to see that all are served, watches their selections, and assures a child, who is worried, that he will get a cookie.

e) The ability to make interesting associations

Definition: When presented with visible scenes, objects, or verbal descriptions, a person with this ability shows a capacity to produce related kinds of objects or themes from either his own realm of past experience or some imagined experience. These productions are characterized by the ingenuity of the relationships or the elaborateness of the representation. Another form is the ability to build upon these events by assigning new and interesting labels or building coherent stories around the presented elements.

Examples:

(*Four-year-old boy*)   "Miss T, this is the simplest work, simple as a bee can fly."

(*Four-year-old boy*)   T suggests building pictures with letter squares, and makes a circle. S immediately builds a "Prudential Building" and asks T, "What's that?" She asks for a clue. "It stays in the same place." She gives up, and he tells her, "A Prudential Building." Peer: "What are you building now?" S: "Same thing, not a Prudential Building, a giant building." P: "Empire State?" S: "It's pretty big anyway. There's something wrong with this building. Supposed to stand up, not supposed to fall down . . . I gonna make the biggest American building in the whole wide world . . . outta these blocks."

(3) *Executive Abilities*

a) The ability to plan and carry out multistep activities

Definition: This designation applies to largely self-directed activities, rather than activities in which the child is guided. At earlier ages, it would develop through gradual refinement of the use of means–ends relationships and the ability to plan and execute longer sequences.

Examples:

(Five-year-old girl) S fills a jug with water in another room, carries it back to main room, and carefully waters all the plants.

(Four-year-old girl) S sets up various materials in order to play store, getting others to participate and playing roles of storekeepers.

b) The ability to use resources effectively

Definition: The ability to select and organize materials and/or people to solve problems. An additional feature is the recognition of unusual uses of such resources.

Examples:

(Four-year-old girl) Some drinking glasses and a box of crackers have been brought into the classroom in a paper shopping bag. S and PM use them to set up a store game, moving a table, arranging the glasses on a shelf, deciding on prices, and imitating storekeepers.

(Four-and-a-half-year-old girl) S is having trouble blowing up a balloon. She tries and fails, then takes her problem to another girl. S takes over her friend's job, setting out napkins for snack time, while her friend blows up the balloon.

(4) *Attentional Ability—Dual Focus*

Definition: The ability to attend to two things simultaneously or in rapid alternation; i.e., the ability to concentrate on a proximal task and remain aware of peripheral happenings; the ability to talk while doing.

Examples:

(Three-year-old girl) S is sitting at table pasting. S glances frequently at MP across table and 2 MPs standing by the door. S is obviously listening to their conversation while she works, and occasionally makes a brief comment to one of them.

(Three-year-old boy) S is cutting paper into a bowl with a scissors. S talks incessantly to both MP and FP while continuing to cut.

A Basis for Evaluation of Our Hypotheses about Early Experience

Gathering anthropological information on preschool-age children, especially during their sixth year of life, was a fundamental necessity for the project. It was our way of determining both the goals and the direction of our work. The distinguishing abilities of well-developing preschoolers constitute one form of specification of desirable outcomes of early education. Another form might have been produced by asking experienced kindergarten teachers to describe excellent development at six. Yet another could have been based on performance by six-year-olds on tests of academic readiness, social maturity, and personality. Our literature search ruled out the simplest approach, which would have been to locate authoritative information on the well-developed six-year-old from the results of previous research. Hard to believe as it may be, virtually no such material was available. A conspicuous and excellent exception is the report on Colin, a "normal" preschooler (IQ in the 130's but free from clinical symptoms) by Lois Murphy and associates (1956). In that study, a multidisciplined team of professionals gathered systematic and diverse data on Colin over a three-year span, beginning during his third year, when he entered the Sarah Lawrence nursery school. Only one child, however, is described.

We didn't choose to rely exclusively on the opinions of teachers (although we did extensive interviewing with them) to help acquaint ourselves with preschoolers and their environments. We were not satisfied with the degree of specificity about good development that the teachers were providing. Their descriptions were most often at a fairly global level, such as, "Johnny was so much brighter than any average child, so eager to learn," or, "Mary was a sheer delight in the classroom, and very imaginative." Of course, there was more to what each teacher provided during a one-hour interview, and often the observations were very perceptive; but the need for a description of the characteristics of optimal development was too fundamental for us to rely solely on information generated this way.

The possibility of piecing together a useful picture of optimal development from data from the various types of existing tests turned out to be nil. Data from tests of social and personality development were often not useful due to very low reliability. Further, the more reliable academic-readiness tests provided a very spotty, incoherent picture of a child, simply because they were designed for a rather special narrow purpose, from our point of view. Since our concern was with general or overall development, we needed more kinds of information than tests such as the Stanford-Binet could provide. Put another way, the designers of such tests were not aiming for a quantitative assessment of the full range of a child's abilities, but rather for an assessment of a child's likelihood of success in school, based upon a sampling of his linguistic and cognitive skills. Leadership and other social qualities, planning abilities, imagination, resourcefulness, and many other human abilities were outside the scope of such tests.

A Source of Direction for Etiological Early-Education Research

Once we had our working definition of the competent six-year-old child, we knew we had a basis for evaluating our eventual hypotheses about the role of experience in early development. Without a clear position on this issue of specific goals, no program of educational research can have coherence or good prospects for success. In addition to this basic role, our definition of competence could also serve a vital guiding function for our etiological research. If you start with an item from the Stanford-Binet, such as success in solving maze problems, you could, of course, then plot the growth of this capacity by testing children at younger ages. However, the child of less than two and a half years of age is not really testable on such an item; and furthermore, you would be hard pressed to identify factors in the child's early experiences that might influence the development of that skill. Our observationally generated dimensions of competence seem to be more suitable for an etiological early-education study. For example, *using an adult as a resource* is an ability that almost all children engage in repeatedly in one way or another from birth, and therefore the growth of each child's ability in that area can be monitored and assessed throughout the early years. Furthermore, and of even greater importance, such an ability suggests where to look for salient experiences and influences on development. In this case, one is obliged to study the early social experiences of the child, and as you might guess, the role of the mother as she behaves in this *particular* regard (as a potential resource) appears to be of central importance. *Getting and maintaining the attention of an adult* is another competence dimension with such advantages, as are most of our target abilities.

A Potential Description of the Goals of Any Early-Education Program

Aside from the general lack of dependable knowledge about rearing children, the most serious problem early educators face is a lack of clarity about their goals.

We would like to suggest that the aforementioned description of distinguishing attributes of highly competent three- to six-year-old children may be one acceptable, though tentative, definition of the goals of early child-rearing or early formal education. Surely that list is not necessarily the best possible, but it does go beyond a deficiency-oriented concentration on preacademic skills, and in addition, it is more specific than most "whole-child" program aspirations.

THE ETIOLOGY OF COMPETENCE IN YOUNG CHILDREN

The next step in our strategy, like most of the process, was obvious. Once we had decided to gamble on the validity of our description of the distinguishing qualities of the very competent six-year-old, we began to study the growth of these abilities. This process overlapped and extended beyond the process of isolating and refining the dimensions of competence. It should be noted that we were not yet investing in the problem of measurement, although we were committed to a scientific form of investigation. The question of what was worth measuring and when we should go beyond subjective rating techniques in assessing competence was a chronic concern. We decided to develop instruments to assess competence levels and maternal behaviors, but to do so with caution. We were not sure what age range (of preschool children) we would be concentrating on, and we knew that designing new assessment techniques would be a very large task.*

Again, using the method of group discussions of each child based on extensive observational records and objective test scores, we examined the issue of the growth of competence as we had defined it. We considered all the three- to six-year-old children we had come to know well over a two-year period. This number was now well over a hundred, about 75 percent of whom were developing either very well or rather poorly, with perhaps 20 to 25 percent (the remainder) developing in average fashion. Our staff (numbering some twenty people by now) came to a rather remarkable conclusion. Our well-developed three-year-olds (called 3A's) looked more like four- to five- and six-year-old A's on our target abilities than did our older but poorly developing (C) children. If we had to guess which group would have done better in first grade had 3A's and older C's entered the following year, we would have chosen the 3A's over the 5 and 6C's. Even though this judgment was clearly made on less-than-ideal grounds, as a group we were most impressed by its probable truth.

Now, this judgment does not mean that 6A children do not have better language and intellectual skills than 3A's. Nor does it mean that 6C's have no abilities of any consequence. In the absence of quantitative data on the several dimensions of competence, we were unable to say more than that the general thesis seemed valid to us. In the area of social competence, for example, we found 3A's routinely using adults as a resource as did 6A's, in contrast to C's of all ages, who acted this way far less often. Dual focusing was a regular characteristic of A's regardless of age, and was rarely seen in C children. In other ability areas, differences, although impressive, were less striking; for example, the language of 3A's was not necessarily superior to that of the 6C's and was clearly considerably less developed than that of the 6A's.

The implications of this judgment of the remarkable level of achievement of some three-year-olds were most important for the project, and

---

* We did develop ways of assessing *dual-focusing* ability and social competence for the three-to-six age range.

potentially for the field of early education. If most of the qualities that distinguish outstanding six-year-olds can be achieved in large measure by age three, the focus of the project could be narrowed dramatically. We rather abruptly found ourselves concentrating on the zero-to-three age range.

Narrowing the study immediately finessed a large amount of work. We reasoned that our first priority was to examine the early growth of human competence in its optimal form. Our judgment about 3A's meant that much of what we wanted to learn could probably be found if we examined the processes of development during the first three years of life. If so, then we could concentrate our instrument construction work and data gathering and analysis effort on that period, and set aside work with three- to six-year-old children for the time being. It also meant that some of the work we had invested in the three-to-six age range was wasted. We counted such waste as part of the price you pay when you attempt to break new ground in a problem area.*

NARROWING THE FOCUS

The literature on human development during the first three years of life was the source of another judgment that has shaped our efforts. Although all signs indicated that developmental divergence was a major national problem with six-year-olds (and so, Project Head Start), it does not begin until sometime during the second year of life. The number of American children undergoing severe physical or psychological abuse from, for example, being kept in the attic for several years, or being beaten or starved regularly, is mercifully a fraction of 1 percent of all young children. Such children do very poorly on developmental tests at one year of age. Aside from such extreme pathological cases, studies of infants from various socioeconomic backgrounds seem to indicate that those many four-, five-, and six-year-old children we are worrying about now looked no different from the best of their peers until some time during their second year of life (Florence Halpern, 1969, and E. S. Schaefer, 1968, among many). Now, some will vigorously argue this point. T. D. Wachs, Uzgiris, and Hunt (1967) seem to have found very modest but possible significant deficiencies in "disadvantaged" eleven-month-old children in Piagetian sensorimotor intelligence development. On the other hand, M. Golden and Beverly Birns (1969) found none all the way up to twenty-four months of age.

---

* Interestingly, compensatory early-education efforts were moving down the age ladder in parallel as their focus shifted (in part) a year or so later, from the four-year-old to the three-year-old, and then in 1968 to the zero-to-three age range.

It appeared then that *under the variety of early-rearing conditions prevalent in modern American homes,* divergence with respect to the development of educability and overall competence first becomes manifest sometime during the second year of life, and becomes quite substantial, in many cases, by three years of age. We therefore resolved to focus our effort on the process of the development of competence during the second and third years of life. Nothing that we have learned since has changed our confidence in that judgment. In fact, what we have learned has suggested a reasonable explanation.

Two major factors that underly the effectiveness of early child-rearing practices have suggested themselves in our recent work; the development of locomotor ability (walking), and the emergence of language. For the better part of the first year, the infant's ability to move about is very limited. For the first eight months he usually cannot even crawl. Even when he begins to crawl and then walk about while holding on to a support (cruise), he is considerably less mobile than the fourteen- to eighteen-month-old, who can usually walk, and climb both furniture and stairs. This increased mobility, combined with the curiosity typical of a child this age, produces a very real stress on the caretaker (usually the mother). After all, even though he can move about, he is still clumsy and unsure of his large-muscle skills; and even though he is curious, he is inexperienced, so that razor blades and electric outlets are perceived simply as additional objects to explore. His clumsiness and lack of practical judgment mean that he is prone to personal injury and also likely to damage breakable household items. None of these factors confront the infant's mother until the end of his first year of life, and they become most pressing during the second and third years. Families adopt a variety of methods of dealing with the toddler. Some "childproof" the home, others follow the child everywhere, others restrict the child's range of mobility, and some use various combinations of these techniques. It appears from our work that part of the answer to why some children develop better than others during this age period lies in the manner of response of the mother to the emergence of locomotor mobility in her child.

The second major factor is language. In a manner virtually parallel to locomotor ability, language ability is essentially nil during the first eight or nine months of life, then moves ahead dramatically (especially *receptive* language) during the second and third years of life. What families provide in the way of elaborate or simple, clever or dull, voluminous or sparse language during the first eight months of life is far less likely to influence development than what they do in regard to language in the second and third years of a child's life.

Add to these two factors the impression that few mothers (as yet) have clear ideas about the particular psychological needs of very young infants in cribs, and the result is at least a reasonable explanation of why developmental divergence seldom becomes clear until the second year of life.

THE PLAN OF ATTACK

Once the prime focus of the project had been achieved, the shape of our succeeding efforts seemed clear. We prepared the following plan:

1. Develop measuring instruments for the one- to three-year-old child for:
   a. The dimensions of competence
   b. The stream of experience
   c. Salient environmental factors such as maternal behavior and physical circumstances
   d. Screening out handicapped children
2. Study the process of optimal development of competence where it is currently occurring naturally.
3. Simultaneously study the process of restricted development of competence where it is currently occurring naturally.
4. Find the major apparent differences in the patterns of experience across the two sets of children.
5. Find the major apparent environmental causes for the differences in experience most likely to influence the development of competence.
6. Isolate those environmental causes that might be amenable to change.
7. Test our ideas experimentally about the influence of experiences on the development of competence by providing optimal patterns of experience for one- to three-year-old children who would ordinarily develop average levels of competence.
8. Refine our ideas in the light of the results of our experiments, adjust our hypotheses, and retest. Repeat the cycle until we feel we have done as much as we can to solve the problem.

THE LONGITUDINAL
NATURAL EXPERIMENT:

studying the processes of optimal
and restricted development
of competence under natural conditions

In Part II we shall describe in detail the methods and findings of the longitudinal natural experiment that we began in the summer of 1969 and plan to complete in 1972. In Chapter 1 we shall describe the methodology of the natural experiment as a whole, including the manner in which we procured children for the study and the background characteristics of our subjects. The remaining chapters of Part II are organized to reflect major divisions in day-to-day research responsibilities. From summer 1969, Dr. White took the major responsibility for research on the child's development of competence and on the stream of experience. The methods and findings pertaining to these two areas of investigation will be described by Dr. White in Chapters 2 and 3. Simultaneously, Dr. Watts took the major responsibility for research on the child's human and physical environment. The methods and findings pertaining to her research on environmental factors will be described in Chapters 4 and 5.

3

The Design of the Study

BURTON L. WHITE/JEAN CAREW WATTS

DESIGN CONSIDERATIONS

Our first longitudinal study is a natural experiment. We want to learn the details of excellent child-rearing practices for the second and third years of life. We are therefore observing two sets of families as they rear their children during those years. One set of families has been selected because we have reason to believe that their children will attain high levels of competence as defined by our project. The other set has been selected because we believe their children will achieve a less-than-average level of general competence. Of course, our predictions may for any number of reasons turn out to be wrong at times (as indeed they have), and we have acknowledged this likelihood in our plans.

The primary purpose of our planned longitudinal natural experiment was to search for environmental factors that play important causal roles in the early development of human competence. It should be noted that the major causes of developing competence need not involve the environment in any significant way. Indeed, some students of the problem (including Jensen, 1969) seem to hold the view that our search would be fruitless. Our view was, and is, that there was good reason to believe that environmental factors do play an important role in early human development, and further, that the possibility was far too vital an issue to leave untouched by direct inquiry.

After screening each subject for assurance of physical normality, we conduct an interview with the child's mother to gain a general understanding of household routines, schedules, and other information relevant to the child's everyday experience. Within a few days of his birthday— usually about a week after the interview—we begin formal data collecting.

We need to monitor the development of competence to validate the usefulness of both data on the experiences of the child and data on environmental influences on those experiences. Further, if we have guessed wrong about an infant's likelihood for outstanding growth (either positive or negative), we need to know as soon as possible, so as to avoid a continuing investment in a family that would be less useful to us than another. Fourteen tests for the development of various aspects of competence are administered during the second year of life. Fifteen or eighteen such tests are administered during the third year of life, depending on whether a child started in the project at one or two years of age.

Testing Schedule

The first assessment measure given to the subjects is the Bayley IQ Test. This is administered once to each age group, the younger children at 12 months, and the older at 24 months.

Three other tests, on language ability, capacity for abstract thinking, and ability to sense discrepancies, are always administered within the same one- or two-week period. The sequence is begun at twelve and a half or twenty-four and a half months for the respective age groups, and the three tests are repeated approximately two and a half months later, at 15 and 27 months respectively.

Beginning at about 15 months of age, and extending into the 20th or 21st month, there arises a period during which testing becomes even more difficult than usual with young children. The child is apt to be unusually shy or stubborn and fussy. This type of behavior is often attributed to the newly developing "age of autonomy," when the child has discovered the word *no* and has little hesitation in using it. He is no longer the generally friendly, cooperative child of 12–14 months and has not yet reached the stage where sociability and curiosity make him eager to try the games the experimenter introduces. Naturally, there are many exceptions of all ages, but we have found it best to postpone testing during these months, and to resume at about 21 months of age. This problem occurs far less often for the two-year-olds, and their testing schedule continues at three-month intervals, the 22–27-month testing being followed by another sequence at 30 months.

Another problem that arises as the one-year-olds approach 24 months is that they begin to outgrow the 12–24-month version of the tests and are often ready for the 24–36-month-old adaptation. The experimenter must use his discretion as to the appropriate time to introduce the more difficult material. Many of the subjects can master the more advanced tests to some degree by the 21-month age level. This pertains to the language and abstract abilities tests, which differ for younger and older subjects, but not to the discrepancies test, which has increasingly difficult steps ranging from the 12- to the 36-month-old level of development.

We gather data on the typical experiences of our subjects once every three weeks, six months out of each year. Since we collect three ten-minute continuous records on each visit, we accumulate thirty such protocols each year for one child. Correspondingly, we gather data on the child's social experience, his mother's interactions with him, and his utilization of the physical environment (toys, furniture, areas of rooms, etc.) once every three weeks for six months of the year. The result is a very substantial amount of systematically interrelated data on each child. The schedule of observation and test sessions is illustrated in Figures 3.1 and 3.2.

Special note should be taken at this point of the danger of drowning in information. Each ten-minute task record may involve as many as forty or more separately coded and analyzed events. We collect thirty a year for each child. The numbers involved are very large. On the one hand, such an amount of data helps to insure the validity of our findings. On the other hand, many a longitudinal study has collected (at great expense) masses of data, much of which was subsequently not used.

SUBJECTS

Originally we planned to study 48 children as they developed during the second and third years of life. Twenty-four children would have been

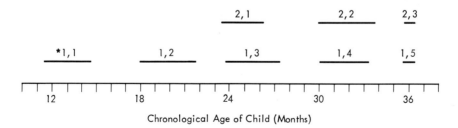

Chronological Age of Child (Months)

* First number is the starting age of child,
  second number is the run number

Figure 3.1   Schedule of runs

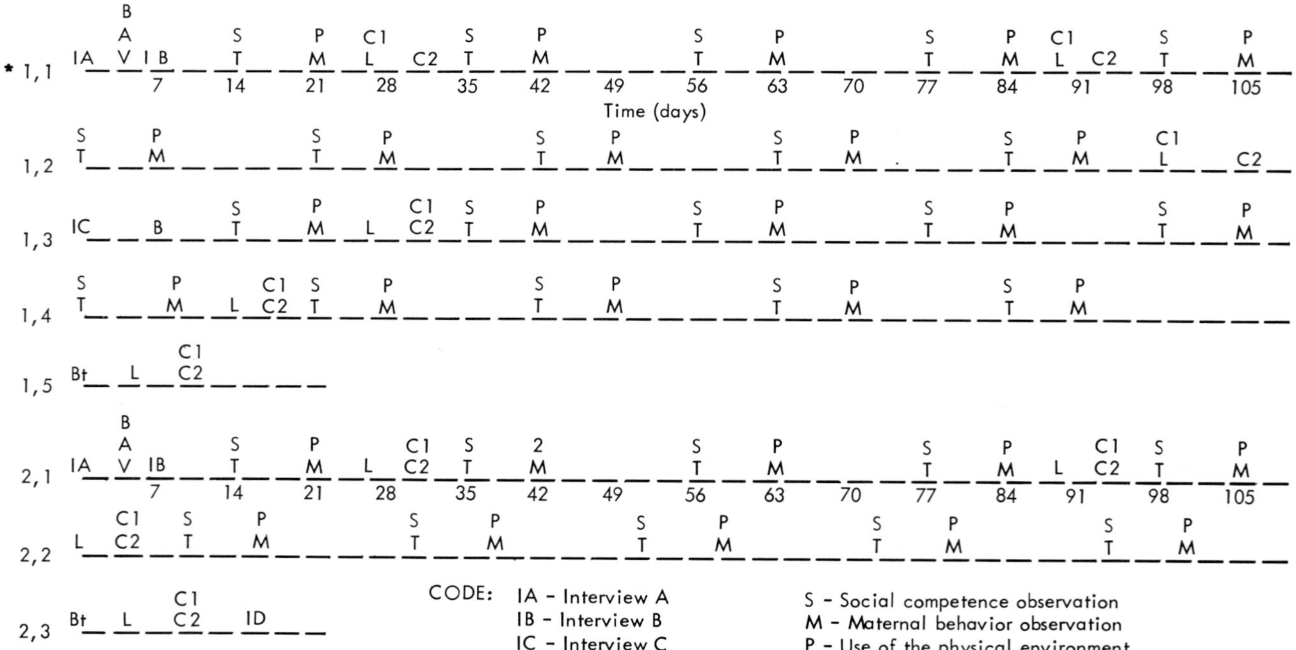

Time (days)

```
        A   S    P    C1   S   P    S   P    S   P    S   P    S   P    C1   S   P
* 1,1  IA V IB T   M  L  C2 T  M   T  M   T  M  T  M   M  L  C2  T  M
        7  14   21  28  35  42  49  56  63  70  77  84  91  98  105

        S   P    S   P    S   P    S   P    S   P    S   C1   S   P
1,2    T   M   T  M   T  M   T  M   T  M   L    L  C2
                                                          91  98

        S   P    C1   S   P    S   P    S   P    S   P    S   P
1,3    IC  B  T  M  L C2 T  M   T  M   T  M   T  M   T  M
                                                          M   T

        S   P    C1   S   P    S   P    S   P    S   P    S   P
1,4    T  M  L C2 T  M   T  M   T  M   T  M   M   T

        C1
1,5   Bt  L  C2

        B
        A   S    P    S   C1   S   2    S   P    S   P    S   P    C1   S   P
2,1   IA V IB T   M  T  L C2 T  M  T  M   T  M   T  M   T  M  L  C2  T  M
        7  14   21  28  35  42  49  56  63  70  77  84  91  98  105

        C1   S   P    S   P    S   P    S   P    S   P
2,2   L C2  T  M  T  M   T  M   T  M   M   T

        C1
2,3   Bt  L  C2  ID
```

* First number is the starting age of the child,
  second number is the run number

CODE: IA – Interview A
       IB – Interview B
       IC – Interview C
       ID – Interview D
       L – Language
       A – Auditory screening
       V – Visual screening
       T – Task observation

S – Social competence observation
M – Maternal behavior observation
P – Use of the physical environment
B – Bayley
Bt – Binet
C1 – Discrimination test
C2 – Abstract abilities (Hunt-Uzgiris for 1-year-old;
                          Meyer for 2-year-old)

Figure 3.2 Details of observations and tests within runs

one year old when we began. Half would have come from families that had previously reared children who had attained very high levels of competence; the other half from families whose older children had developed lower-than-average levels of competence. We planned to follow that group for two years. The remaining 24 children would similarly have been divided among A and C families but would have been started at two years of age and followed for one year, in order that we might learn something about third-year phenomena sooner than if we had to wait for our one-year-olds to turn two.

We knew, of course, that we would probably lose some of our subjects due to illness, family disruptions, relocations, and the like. We also expected that some of our predictions about how well children would develop would turn out to be false. And, of course, unless a child did develop as either an A or a C, data on his history of experiences would weaken the usefulness of our pool of information on excellent and poor child-rearing practices. We therefore planned to start with 60 families. That plan turned out to be totally unrealistic.

First of all, since we wanted to start all the children in the study within the space of a few months time and at about their first or second birthday, we could not use children whose birthdays fell at other times of the year. Second, we were planning to deal with special kinds of children, who constituted a small minority of all children. Third, we were fairly sure we would have trouble working with families who were doing a poor job of rearing their children. And finally, since we fully intended to gather extensive data on the average of once a week for at least 26 weeks of each year, we would simply have drowned in the sheer volume of work and information. We have therefore resigned ourselves to an upper limit of 35 to 40 children, with more A's than C's.

Description of Subject Sample

The subject sample to be reported on consists of 31 children grouped by age, sex, socioeconomic status, and competence ratings (A versus C). These children are from a variety of religious and ethnic backgrounds, including Irish, Italian, Jewish, and several others. The sample includes one Afro-American and one Puerto Rican child. The number of children in each subgroup can be seen in Table 1-2.

Our subjects can be grouped according to the widely used Index of Social Position developed by Hollingshead and Redlich (1958), which employs occupation, education, and residence as class criteria. Table 1 shows that in terms of this index, ten of our subjects are in Class I, five in Class II, nine in Class III, six in Class IV, and one in Class V. The fathers of children in Classes I and II are nearly all professional men: lawyers, doc-

TABLE 1-1. Source of Recruitment, Competence Ratings and IQ Information on Siblings of Subjects

Class I and II
1-Yr. A's

	Source[a]	Rating Made by[b]	Sibling Intel. Comp.	Sibling Socl. Comp.[c]	Sibling IQ	Sibling Age	Subject MO 12 (Bayley DQ)	Bayley DQ MO 24
031211	N-Sch	Teacher	A	B	—	4	102	143
311111	N-Sch	Teacher	A	A		5	112	
081111	NO*	PSP	—	—	—	—	106	123
201211	PSP	PSP	A	A		4	134	132
171211	PSP	PSP	A	A		5	100	137
241111	Sch	Teacher	A	B		7	107	116
111211	Coll	PSP	High	High	163	6	119	119
191211	Coll	PSP	High	High	121	6	102	127

Class I and II
2-Yr. A's

	Source[a]	Rating Made by[b]	Sibling Intel. Comp.	Sibling Socl. Comp.[c]	Sibling IQ	Sibling Age	Subject MO 24 (Bayley DQ)	Binet IQ MO 36
122111	Sch	Teacher	A	A		6	102	133
102211	Sch	Teacher	A	B	125	8	106	135
212111	Sch	Teacher	A	A		5	111	138
052111	N-Sch	Teacher	A	A		5	97	142
022111	N-Sch	Teacher	A	A		4	137	140
092211	NO*						109	150
132111	N-Sch	Teacher	A	A		5	102	128

Class III and IV
1-Yr. A's

	Source[a]	Rating Made by[b]	Sibling Intel. Comp.	Sibling Socl. Comp.[c]	Sibling IQ	Sibling Age	Subject MO 12 (Bayley DQ)	MO 24
161121	Coll	PSP	High	A	123	5	102	127
321121	PSP	PSP	High	A		4	94	

TABLE 1-1. (continued)

		Rating Made by	Sibling Intel. Comp.	Sibling Socl. Comp.	Sibling IQ	Sibling Age	Subject MO 24	Bayley DQ MO 36
Class III, IV 2-Yr. A's								
372121	Sch	Teacher	High	High	132	7	94	
352221	Coll	PSP	High	High	119	5	104	
182221	Sch	Teacher	High	High	133	9	100	116
222221	Coll	PSP	High	High	143	5	140	145
362121	Coll	PSP	High	High	142	5	119	
							Bayley MO 12	DQ MO 24
Class III, IV, V 1-Yr. C's								
341123	Coll	PSP	Low	Low	86	7	109	
381123	Sch	Teacher	C	C		5	50	
011223	PSP	PSP	C	C		4	134	112
061223	Sch	Teacher	C	C	87	11	89	109
							Bayley DQ MO 24	Binet IQ MO 36
Class III, IV, V 2-Yr. C's								
002223	Coll	PSP	Low	Average	78	5	77	92
072123	Coll	PSP	Low	Low	83	5	69	85
282223	Coll	PSP	Low	Low	67	5	94	99
142123	PSP	PSP	C	C		5	86	92
272123	Sch	Teacher	C	C	86		88	99

[a] Sch = Elementary School
N-Sch = Nursery
Coll = Collaborative Study Files
PSP = Sibling Participation in Previous Preschool Study Project
Ad = Response to Newspaper Advertisement
Clinic = Well Baby Clinic
NO = No Sibling—* PSP staff judged mother to be highly likely to possess outstanding childrearing capacities
[b] PSP = Preschool Project Staff
[c] A rating of B indicates average social competence

31

TABLE 1–2.   **Distribution of Subjects with Respect to Age at Which Observations Were Started, Social Class (SES), Sex and Predicted Competence Ratings**

		1-Year-Olds					2-Year-Olds			
SES Score	I	II	III	IV	V	I	II	III	IV	V
A's Boys	1	2	1	1	0	4	1	2	0	0
Girls	3	2	0	0	0	2	0	3	0	0
C's Boys	0	0	0	1	1	0	0	1	2	0
Girls	0	0	0	2	0	0	0	2	0	0
TOTAL	4	4	1	4	1	6	1	8	2	0

All Subjects	= 31		
One-Yr.-Olds	= 14		
Boys	= 17	Two-Yr.-Olds	= 17
A's	= 22	Girls	= 14
		C's	= 9

tors, university professors, scientists, and so on. The fathers of children in Class III include an elementary school teacher, a laboratory technician, a city planner, an accountant, two small shop owners, two salesmen, and a court officer. The fathers of children in Classes IV and V include a repairman, a truck driver, a bus driver, a steelworker, a baker, a maintenance man, and a soldier.

The education of fathers in these groups is appropriate to their occupations. All fathers of children in Classes I and II have had graduate professional training, while the education of fathers in Class III, IV, and V ranges from college (B.A. degree) to graduation from elementary school. Typically, fathers of Class III children have had some college, while fathers in Classes IV and V have not finished high school. The family income of children in Classes I and II ranges from about $3,000 (in the case of two university students) to well over $20,000, the median income being about $20,000 per annum. Income for families in Class III is typically between $7,000 and $12,000 per year, and income from seven of the families in Classes IV and V is between $7,000 and $12,000; and for five of these families, it is between $3,000 and $7,000. Some families in Classes I and II live in large, expensively furnished houses in suburban neighborhoods, while several live in smaller houses or apartments in urban areas near a university. The typical family in Class III lives in a medium-sized, well-maintained apartment in an urban location, while the typical family in Classes IV and V lives in a smaller apartment in a similar urban location that is often part of an ethnic neighborhood (in Boston, most often Irish).

Table 1-3 supplies the details of occupation, education, residence, income, and ethnic and religious background of the family of each child. It should be noted that although we planned to recruit both A and C children from many social classes, we were not very successful in doing so. Among our nine C children, six are from Classes IV and V, three from

TABLE 1–3. Class I and II A's

Sub. ID	Sex	Hollings-head–Redlich Code	Family Income	Mother Education	Father Education	Mother Occupation[a]	Father Occupation[b]	Mother Ethnic[c]	Father Ethnic[c]	Mother Religion[d]	Father Religion[d]	No. Children in Household
03	F	II	$20,000 or over	College graduate	Post-col. graduate	Secretary	Chemist	Caucas.	Jewish	None (Prot.)	None	2
31	M	II	$12,000–$20,000	Post-col. graduate	Post-col. graduate	Restaurant manager	Restaurant owner	Italian	Italian	Catholic	Catholic	3
08	M	II	less than $3,000	Post-col. graduate	Post-col. graduate	Teacher	Ph.D. student	Caucas.	Caucas.	Prot.	Prot.	1
20	F	II	$12,000–$20,000	Post-col. graduate	Post-col. graduate	(Teacher)	Architect	Jewish	Caucas.	Jewish	Jewish	4
17	F	I	$20,000 or over	College graduate	Post-col. graduate	None	Physicist	Caucas.	Caucas.	None	None	2
24	M	I	$20,000 or over	Post-col. graduate	Post-col. graduate	None	Univ. professor	Italian	Jewish	Prot.	Jewish	4
11	F	I	$12,000–$20,000	College graduate	Post-col. graduate	None	Univ. professor	Italian	Caucas.	None	None	2
19	F	I	$12,000–$20,000	Partial/jr. coll.	Post-col. graduate	None	Univ. professor	Caucas.	Caucas.	Prot.	Prot.	—

a Parentheses denote mother's occupation prior to our study.
b Parentheses used when parents are divorced and mother is head of household.
c Caucasian used to mean of European background other than Irish, Italian, Jewish, or Spanish.
d Parentheses denote the religious background where parents no longer profess a religious faith.

33

TABLE 1-3. (continued)

Sub. ID	Sex	Hollings-head–Redlich Code	Family Income	Mother Education	Father Education	Mother Occupation[a]	Father Occupation[b]	Mother Ethnic[c]	Father Ethnic[c]	Mother Religion[d]	Father Religion[d]	No. Children in Household
12	M	I	$12,000–$20,000	Post-col. graduate	Post-col. graduate	Prenatal teacher	Physician	Jewish	Jewish	Jewish	Jewish	4
10	F	I	$20,000 or over	Post-col. graduate	Post-col. graduate	Teacher	Lawyer	Jewish	Jewish	Jewish	Jewish	3
21	M	I	$12,000–$20,000	College graduate	Post-col. graduate	None	Lawyer	Caucas.	Caucas.	Prot.	Prot.	2
05	M	I	$20,000 or over	Part./jr. coll.	Post-col. graduate	Nurse	Psycho-analyst	Caucas.	Caucas.	Catholic	Episcopal	3
02	M	II	$3,000–$7,000	Part./jr. coll.	Post-col. graduate	None	Medical student	Caucas.	Caucas.	Prot.	Prot.	2
09	F	I	$7,000–$12,000	Post-col. graduate	Post-col. graduate	Social worker	Univ. professor	Caucas.	Spanish	None (Unit.)	None (Catholic)	1
13	M	I	$20,000 or over	Post-col. graduate	Post-col. graduate	(Teacher–college)	Physician	Caucas.	Jewish	Prot.	Jewish	3

[a] Parentheses denote mother's occupation prior to our study.
[b] Parentheses used when parents are divorced and mother is head of household.
[c] Caucasian used to mean of European background other than Irish, Italian, Jewish, or Spanish.
[d] Parentheses denote the religious background where parents no longer profess a religious faith.

TABLE 1–3. (continued) Class III and IV A's

Sub. ID	Sex	Hollings-head–Redlich Code	Family Income	Mother Education	Father Education	Mother Occupation[a]	Father Occupation[b]	Mother Ethnic[c]	Father Ethnic[c]	Mother Religion[d]	Father Religion[d]	No. Children in Household[d]
16	M	III	$7,000–$12,000	Partial/jr. col.	Partial/jr. col.	None	Physical ed. teacher	Caucas.	Caucas.	Catholic	Catholic	3
32	M	IV	$3,000–$7,000	High sch. graduate	Partial high sch.	None	Small repair shop	Irish	Italian	Catholic	Catholic	8
38	M	III	$3,000–$7,000	Partial/jr. col.	High sch. graduate	None	Travel agent	Latin Amer.	Latin Amer.	Catholic	Catholic	6
35	F	III	$7,000–$12,000	Partial/jr. col.	Partial/jr. col./voc. sch.	(Lab. techn.)	Sr. lab. techn.	Caucas.	Caucas.	Catholic	Catholic	6
18	F	III	$7,000–$12,000	Part./jr. col.	Part./jr. col.	None	TV repair shop owner	Italian	Italian	Catholic	Catholic	7
22	F	III	$3,000–$7,000	Part./jr. col.	College graduate	Cocktail waitress	(City reg. planner)	Caucas.	Caucas.	None (Cath.)	None (Cath.)	3
36	M	III	?	High sch. graduate	Part./jr. col./voc. school	None	Industrial tool salesman	Italian	Italian	Catholic	Catholic	2

[a] Parentheses denote mother's occupation prior to our study.
[b] Parentheses used when parents are divorced and mother is head of household.
[c] Caucasian used to mean of European background other than Irish, Italian, Jewish, or Spanish.
[d] Parentheses denote the religious background where parents no longer profess a religious faith.

TABLE 1–3. (continued) Class III, IV, V C's

Sub. ID	Sex	Hollings-head-Redlich Code	Family Income	Mother Education	Father Education	Mother Occupation[a]	Father Occupation[b]	Mother Ethnic[c]	Father Ethnic[c]	Mother Religion[d]	Father Religion[d]	No. Children in Household[d]
34	M	IV	$7,000–$12,000	Partial high sch.	High sch. graduate	None	Truck driver, liquor deliverer	Caucas.	Caucas.	Catholic	Catholic	3
37	M	V	Under $3,000	Partial/jr. col.	?	None	(Prof. soldier)	Caucas.	Caucas.	Catholic	?	3
01	F	IV	$7,000–$12,000	High sch. graduate	High sch. graduate	None	Maintenance man	Italian	Italian	Catholic	Catholic	13
06	F	IV	$7,000–$12,000	Less than 6 yrs. sch.	Elementary sch.	None	Restaurant baker	Afro-Lat. Amer.	Afro-Lat. Amer.	Jehov. Witness	Jehov. Witness	5
30	F	III	$12,000–$20,000	Jr. high graduate	Partial high sch.	Maintenance ct. house	Ct. officer	Irish	Irish	Catholic	Catholic	7
07	M	IV	$3,000–$7,000	Partial high sch.	Jr. high graduate	Waitress	Steelworker	Caucas.	Caucas.	Prot.	Prot.	6
28	F	III	$3,000–$7,000	Jr. high graduate	Part./jr. col./voc. school	None	Accountant	Italian	Italian	Catholic	Catholic	2
14	M	IV	$3,000–$7,000	Partial high sch.	Partial high sch.	(Hairdresser)	MBTA bus driver	Irish	Irish	Catholic	Catholic	2
27	M	III	$7,000–$12,000	Part./jr. college	College	None	(Antique dealer)	Greek	Irish	Greek Orthod.	None (Cath.)	3

[a] Parentheses denote mother's occupation prior to our study.
[b] Parentheses used when parents are divorced and mother is head of household.
[c] Caucasian used to mean of European background other than Irish, Italian, Jewish, or Spanish.
[d] Parentheses denote the religious background where parents no longer profess a religious faith.

Class III, and none from Classes I and II. In contrast, among our twenty-two A children, fifteen are from Classes I and II, six are from Class III, and only one from Class IV. Similarly, all but two mothers in our A group have had some education beyond high school graduation, while only three of the nine mothers of the C's have had such education. Parallel differences also exist on religious background, size of family, and so on, which may have some bearing on the environments and experiences of the subjects. This failure to locate A's and C's of exactly comparable social-class background should be remembered when interpreting the preliminary results of the natural experiment, which are given later in this book.

To further illustrate the socioeconomic status characteristics of our sample, the following section describes one family in our study for each of the five Hollingshead and Redlick levels.

Five Modal Families (Class Positions I–V)

CLASS POSITION I (20–31 POINTS)

Family I—20 points. Family I is a well-to-do family with four children and a live-in housekeeper. The father is a physician (occupation = 1; education = 1) with an income over $20,000 per year. The mother has a master's degree in nursing and works part time on occasion. Their residence is a large three-story house, located on a lovely tree-lined street in the Chestnut Hill area of Brookline (residence = 1). The children attend a private nursery school and a Brookline public school.

CLASS POSITION II (32–55 POINTS)

Family II—41 points. Family II is a young student couple with one child, presently residing in a tiny but well-equipped and modern apartment on campus in married student's housing in Cambridge (residence = 3). The father is a graduate student in physics (occupation = 2; education = 1). The mother has a master's degree in education and is presently working parttime. Their combined income is in the $3,000–7,000 range.

CLASS POSITION III (56–86 POINTS)

Family III—75 points. Family III is a family of four (two children), living in a clean but modestly furnished apartment in fair condition, located in a residential neighborhood of East Boston (residence = 4). The father earns in the $3,000–7,000 range as a clerk-accountant (occupation = 4). He is a high school graduate with additional vocational training in accountancy school (education = 3). The mother has an eighth-grade education and does not work outside the home.

CLASS POSITION IV (87–115 POINTS)

Family IV—104 points. Family IV is a family of fifteen (thirteen children), living in their own overcrowded seven-room cottage, which until recently was in quite poor condition, with only the barest of shabby but utilitarian furnishings. It is located on a cul-de-sac in a working-class area of West Newton (residence = 5). (The house is presently undergoing much-needed expansion and renovation and should eventually rate a 4.) Both parents are high school graduates (education = 4). The father is a maintenance man in a public school and earns $8,000 a year (occupation = 6).

CLASS POSITION V (116–134 POINTS)

Family V—117 points. The mother in Family V is a divorcee with three children,* living on welfare (no occupation = 8) in a public housing project. Her apartment is in very poor condition—shabbily furnished and in a state of filth and disrepair. The building has some grassy areas but is mostly surrounded by pavement. It is located in a residential area dotted with construction projects in Cambridge (residence = 5). The mother is a high school graduate with one year of college (education = 3).

Instruments to Screen Out Handicapped Children

We needed to be confident that the development of competence in our subjects was not significantly influenced by physical abnormalities in any of our children. If a child was developing poorly, part of the source of poor development might lie in his history of experiences. On the other hand, if he had an undetected physical handicap such as poor vision or hearing or other such anomaly, our search would be confounded.† Our problems were complex enough without adding such extraneous factors. We therefore decided to test for general maturational status, hearing, and vision prior to admitting a subject to our study.

We selected the Bayley scales of infant development (1936) for assessing general maturational status. Not only would we learn whether a child was markedly underdeveloped, but in addition, such data would help us compare our subjects with those of other studies and with the national population. The Bayley is one of several widely used, up-to-date, standardized tests. We administer the Bayley at 12 and 24 months of age. For vision and hearing, we developed two brief sets of procedures which are described in Appendix I. These tests are administered with the Bayley at 12 months of age.

* Mother is "head of household."
† The development of the visual screening procedures was achieved by Dr. Melvin Zolot, O.D., a practicing optometrist with several years of experience with infants and preschool children. The hearing test was developed by Janice Marmor with the aid of Kathy Tennican, an experienced audiologist.
‡ A physical handicap might be the primary source of a child's poor development, rather than his family's inadequate child-rearing practices.

4

The Development of Competence

Burton L. White/Barbara Kaban/Janice Marmor/Bernice Shapiro

INTRODUCTION

We have accumulated a great deal of data on our subjects. It is grossly divisible into three types: (1) the development of competence, (2) patterns of experience, and (3) environmental factors as they influence the experiences of the child. Our plan was to execute a "natural experiment." We hoped to learn something about how to rear a child well from that minority of families doing an extraordinarily effective job. Families doing a poor job were to be studied as a contrast group, to help us sift out those elements of the child-rearing practices of successful families that were most useful. Were we to study only successful families, we would be no better off than those who, for example, study abnormal behavior exclusively. The clinical psychologist has to be able to tell the difference between a behavior that is truly symptomatic of a pathological state and an aberration that means nothing. If a normal population exhibits a potential "symptom" from time to time, it is less likely to be worthy of examination than are other behaviors not exhibited by normals. It may very well be the case that many of the experiences and environmental factors of successful children are common to poorly developing children as well. Such similarities and differences must be identified if we are to focus on the truly important processes in the development of competence.

We selected families that we thought would rear their one- or two-year-olds either very successfully or rather poorly. It would be incautious to assume that our selections would all turn out to be correct. There are numerous reasons why some of the children we are studying may not turn out to be either A or C children. We have depended heavily on the level of development achieved by the older siblings of our subjects (see Table 1-1), but a family's child-rearing capacity may not always be accurately revealed by its first or first few children. A family may do a fine job with three children, and then do markedly less well with the fourth, if the children are too closely spaced, if the parents begin to dissolve their marriage, or for any other of a variety of reasons.

Conversely, a child may develop very well, in spite of less-than-ideal family-rearing practices. Nevertheless, the most useful indicator of the quality of a family's child-rearing practices is likely to be the level of achievement of the child. It is for this reason that our information on the developing competence of the child is most important for our study.

We had no reason to expect that our A and C children would differ markedly in competence at one year of age. According to performance on the Bayley scales of general development, the groups did not differ. We designed our testing effort partly around the need to identify misclassified children as soon as possible so as to avoid a continual investment of time and energy in gathering irrelevant data. We were confident that two-year-olds would reveal their A, B, or C status rather readily. One-year-olds were another matter, since we had reason to expect that developmental divergence would not even begin to reveal itself clearly until the middle of the second year of life. It is against this background that the data on the development of competence in our subjects should be reviewed.

QUANTITATIVE METHODS FOR THE STUDY OF THE DEVELOPMENT OF COMPETENCE

The usefulness of our data on the environments of the young children in our first longitudinal study depended on the levels of competence our subjects achieved. Dependable yardsticks for assessing competence levels were therefore necessary. We faced several difficult problems in respect to the assessment of competence. First of all, we had described some twenty-one dimensions of competence. Second, children between one and three years of age are extremely difficult to test, particularly when language is an element in the procedure. In addition, our early efforts at test development confirmed the widespread belief that children are inclined to be negativistic during their second year of life. When you consider that a test situation often involves a direction to a subject to, say, point to a picture or operate a mechanism, you can see that negativism is incompatible with valid test results. Preliminary data indicates that the likelihood that a child will comply with a request by his mother is quite variable during this age range, reaching a probability of less than 50 percent during the 18- to 24-month age range. When someone other than the child's mother administers tests during that period, the likelihood of compliance is often even lower. We have therefore avoided such testing during the 15- to 21-month age range.

Another serious problem for us was that our strength did not lie in the area of the development of assessment techniques. Such skills constitute a difficult specialty in which our staff has only modest competence. We tried to find existing assessment techniques but found very few for this age range. In receptive language development, for example, virtually all previous investigators had simply asked mothers what language their children understood. We were not content with this method. For social skills, there were no existing methods for assessing the processes we were interested in. We attempted to subcontract with the nation's leading test specialists. We visited with them and described what we wanted to measure. After several months, we learned that they were quite unable to help us. We therefore began the process on our own.

We invested two years in developing assessment techniques of various kinds. For the development of competence, we selected the following processes from our large list: all the social skills, two facets of receptive language development, the capacity to sense dissonance or note discrepancies, and the capacity for abstract thinking.

ASSESSING THE DEVELOPMENT OF SOCIAL COMPETENCE DURING THE SECOND AND THIRD YEARS OF LIFE

The group working on social development having discovered that roughly eleven social abilities were found to differentiate well-developed from poorly developed six-year-old children, it became their goal to devise an instrument for measuring these abilities in children aged one to three years. This section sets forth the steps we took in developing such an instrument.*

Analysis of the observations and intensive case-study discussions of the thirteen "most able" and thirteen "least able" children on our original

* The development of this assessment device was the work of Daniel Ogilvie, Bernice B. Shapiro, and Jolinda Taylor.

group of subjects (fall 1966 to spring 1967) led to the compilation of the following list of eleven classes of behavior that seemed to discriminate these two groups:

1. To get and maintain the attention of adults when such attention is appropriate
2. To use adults as resources
3. To express affection and hostility to adults
4. To assume control (leadership) in peer-related activities
5. To follow the lead of others
6. To express affection and/or hostility to peers
7. To compete
8. To resist distractions
9. To empathize
10. To praise oneself and/or show pride in one's accomplishments
11. To involve oneself in adult-role-playing behaviors or to otherwise express the desire to grow up

In the fall of 1967, an additional 50 children (aged two and a half to six years) were observed in nursery schools, and 35 children aged one to three years were observed in their homes. "Spot" recordings of effective and ineffective social behaviors were gathered on children from a wide range of socioeconomic, ethnic, and racial backgrounds. The purpose of these observations was to collect as many descriptive examples as possible of the eleven classes of behaviors in order to develop a scoring instrument for field observations. For example, whenever a child tried to get the attention of an adult, we described the situation and the form of the behavior. When we were satisfied that nearly all major forms of behavior that could be clustered under each of the eleven labels had been described, we began to construct a checklist instrument using these descriptions as our data base.

For our purposes, a checklist seemed preferable to more standard rating scales because (1) we wanted to categorize ongoing behavior, (2) we wanted to stay as close to actual behavior as possible, and (3) we wanted to keep inferences at a minimum. We aimed for an instrument that could be used in homes and schools of children in the one-to-six age range. Finally, our efforts were directed toward classifying those interpersonal dimensions isolated during the exploratory stages of our research. An exception to this general strategy was the inclusion of a few categories intended to capture behaviors observed in the homes of one- to three-year-olds, behaviors seen as precursors to more mature forms of interpersonal relationships.

After two months, the first version of the Social Behavior Checklist was ready for field testing. Sadly, after a few observations it was realized that scoring 79 categories represented ambitiousness beyond attainment. For example, although it was sometimes difficult to remember if a certain form of behavior was one of the 79 scorable acts, the mental strain of remembering was simple compared to the physical task of locating the category on the scoring sheets.

As we became familiar with the realistic boundaries of the task, we began to develop more usable instruments. Finally, an instrument made up of 31 categories was completed by early spring 1968. After several weeks of training five observers, a reliability study was initiated. Paired observers scored the behaviors of 20 children (each possible pair observed two children). Each child was observed for half an hour. Correlations were computed for these joint observations. The average correlation was .87, with a range of .69 to .99.

It should be pointed out that by the time the final form of the checklist was completed, the initial list of discriminating behaviors had been partially revised. For example, empathy had been dropped, because very few instances of such behaviors had been observed. Several of the other eleven classes of behavior had been expanded for the purpose of scoring different forms of the behavior in separate categories. For instance, "Leading in Peer Activities" was divided into the following three categories:

1. Giving direction in a positive or neutral manner
2. Giving direction in a negative manner
3. Serving as a model for imitation without giving specific directions to that effect.

Descriptions of all the categories, scoring instructions, and reliability findings are provided in the Appendix.

Social Competence: Results and Discussion

After having observed 14 one-year-olds and 17 two-year-olds over the course of one year, we derived social competence scores for each child separately, by age group. The group medians for 1A's, 1C's, 2A's, and 2C's appear below.

Although we hadn't expected one-year-old A's to outweigh C's quite so much in social competence, this early trend suggests that significant differences in competence may, in fact, exist at this early age. Even though none of the group medians were significantly different when the Mann–Whitney U test was applied, we came closest to significance with a U of 10 for 1A's and C's on adult competence. (7 is needed for statistical

TABLE 2.   **Comparison of Social Competence of A vs. C Subjects**

		Scores					
		w/adults		w/peers		overall	
Age	Group	A	C	A	C	A	C
1 year (12–15 months)	N	10	4	10	4	10	4
	Median score	17.3	10.6	**	**	17.3	10.6
2 years (24–27 months)	N	12	5	11	5	11	5
	Median score	17.1	11.2	6.2	4.3	22.5	15.5

Significance Levels

Mann–Whitney U test (two-tailed for one-year-olds,
one-tailed for two-year-olds)

1 year*	U obtained	10	**	10
	U needed	7 for .10 level	—	7 for .10 level
2 years	U obtained	26	25	21.5
	U needed	13 for .05 level	12 for .05 level	12 for .05 level

* At 12 months, we expected no difference between 1A and 1C children. These scores for one-year-olds are based on their performance on five occasions at three-week intervals between 12 and 15 months of age. Since we predicted that superior performance by 1A's would emerge sometime after 12 months, there is some justification for using a one-tailed test. On that basis, the difference between 1A and 1C scores would be very close to statistical significance.
** The opportunity for interacting with peers (children less than seven years old) was too infrequent with one-year-olds to enable us to gauge their social abilities with peers.

significance.) For 2A's and C's on adult competence, we obtained a U of 26, while 13 was needed for significance. For 2A's and C's on peer competence, we obtained a U of 25, while 12 was needed for significance; for 2A's and C's on the combined index, we obtained a U of 21.5, with a U of 12 being necessary for significance. Since there was only a single one-year-old with a peer-competence score, it is not really possible for us to discuss peer competence among our one-year-olds, from a statistical point of view.

Table 3 presents comparative information on the separate dimensions of social competence for all groups of subjects.

Among one-year-olds in general, A's received higher scores on gaining the attention of an adult, using the adult as a resource, and showing pride in product, while the C's showed more ability in expressing affection and hostility. This is possibly due to the maternal style of C mothers, which is

TABLE 3. Group Medians: One-Year-Old and Two-Year-Old A's and C's

	Social-Competence Dimensions			
	Ones' Adult dimensions		Twos' Adult dimensions	
	A (n = 10)	C (n = 4)	A (n = 12)	C (n = 7)
Gain adult attention	6.3	1.5	4.3	3.5
Use adult as resource	5.5	4.0	5.5	2.5
Express affection and hostility to adult	2.2	4.6	3.6	4.6
Role play	0	0	0	0
Pride in product	.7	0	1.2	0

	Twos' Peer dimensions	
	A (n = 11)	C (n = 6)
Competition with peers	.3	.7
Express affection and hostility to peers	1.7	1.3
Leading and following peers	2.0	.7

to confine their social interactions to playfulness and occasional affectionate interchanges.

Two-year-old A's and C's have surprised us by looking slightly more alike in their social-competence scores than we might have expected. This is in part due to the increase in social awareness that occurs for all two-year-olds, coupled with their added ability to promote social interaction through increased verbalization. It may be that early differences in abilities are masked during this period by the two-year-old's general burgeoning as a social, verbal being, and that true differences will appear at a slightly later age, when the children have stabilized in their behavior to a greater extent. Despite close group medians for two-year-old A's and C's on the dimensions of social competence, the A's continue to maintain a small but probably reliable superiority in their ability to get an adult's attention, to utilize adults as a resource, to show pride in product,* to show hostility and affection to peers, and to lead and follow peers. (See Table 3.) Around

* Mann–Whitney: $U = 12.5$ signifies .025 level.

TABLE 4. Two-Year-Old Medians and Significance Levels—Mann–Whitney U Test

	A	C	Significance Level (two-tailed)
Compliance/noncompliance ratio	3.2	1.4	.02
Pride in product	1.2	0	.02

age two, we find some children who are so tied to their mothers that they strive endlessly for help, attention, and affection, so much so that they show a deceptively high score on these dimensions. We feel that this type of ability may be so exclusively mother-oriented that it will not be transferred easily to other adults, such as teachers, in the child's later life.

In looking at the other visible dimensions of social behavior among two-year-olds, we found that two areas in particular seem to differentiate the predicted "more able" from the predicted "less able" children. The two-year-old A's show a higher compliance-to-noncompliance ratio than do the C's (3.2 versus 1.4). In addition, A's show more frequent imitation of adults in their environment—most frequently their mothers (9 versus 6). These scores would seem to indicate that even as early as age two, some children evidence a stronger desire to grow up and to be like an adult model. Although this age group is still rather young to demonstrate role-playing ability, the two-year-old A's nevertheless are already showing an early trend toward surpassing the C's in leading and following peers, expressing hostility and affection to peers, showing pride in product, expressing affection and hostility to adults, and utilizing adults as a resource.

The subanalysis shows two-year-old A's also higher on controlling

TABLE 5. Subanalysis of Additional Social Behaviors

	ONEs		TWOs	
	A N = 10	C N = 4	A N = 12	C N = 7
Compliance/noncompliance ratio	2.3	2.6	3.2	1.4*
Controls adult	4	2.5	8.5	6
Imitates adult	7	5.4	9	6*
			N = 11	N = 6
Gains peer attention			7	13
Uses peer as a resource			3	4
Refuses to follow peer			4	5
Imitates peer			7	5

* See discussion.

adults, imitating adults, and imitating peers. These results would all indicate to us a desire on the part of these children to grow up and master their social environment.

In view of the striking differences manifested in the development of nonsocial competencies, we may question the smaller differences in social development seen among our one- and two-year-old A's and C's. Some of the problem arises from part of our sample having been selected mainly on the basis of differences in nonsocial competence. Apart from the gathering of information on social behavior of older siblings in school settings, other sources of subjects such as the MIH study provided no opportunity for predicting social competence. In addition, some children among our C's have a great many siblings to interact with and thus have an advantage in having more opportunities for social learning. Finally, as stated earlier, we suspect that much of the social ability our C children show vis-à-vis the mother may be a situation- or person-specific phenomenon, which will show little carryover to a teacher in a classroom setting.

ASSESSING RECEPTIVE-LANGUAGE DEVELOPMENT DURING THE SECOND AND THIRD YEARS OF LIFE

As a starting point, we examined lists of language norms such as that compiled by McCarthy (Carmichael ref., 1954). Although spoken language is often taken as the index for all language development (it is the form of verbal behavior most readily obtained), a listing of norms made it clear that verbal understanding always precedes verbal expression. This was indeed fortunate, because with subjects 12 to 24 months old, spoken language could rarely be measured. Because the relationship between productive (spoken) and receptive (understood) language is not really known, it was deemed safest to concentrate on receptive language for the 24- to 36-month-old as well as with the younger children. Once these decisions had been made, what remained was to devise the content of the language tests.

Our tests of linguistic competence deal with the child's ability to understand rather than produce language. Because of the wide variation in linguistic ability of one-year-olds versus two-year-olds, separate tests were devised for each group. The first, directed toward 12- to 24-month-olds, consists of simple object labelling and the ability to understand instructions. We have found it best, in most cases, to have the mother conduct the "testing," since the child is likely to be more responsive to her than to a stranger.

The first part of the test of 12- to 24-month-old children deals with object labelling.* On the simplest level, this consists of gathering together five or six objects that his mother says are *familiar* to the child (bottle, cup, child's blanket, a favorite toy, a sister, or a pet, etc.) and asking the child, "Where is your cup?" or "Find the kitty." A more advanced child is asked to identify several *unfamiliar* objects that the experimenter brings along with her. These items include a ball, cup, spoon, pencil, toothbrush, eyeglasses, and keys. For the most advanced child in the 12- to 24-month-old group, the task is to identify *classes* of the same unfamiliar items as listed above: "Where is the ball; can you find *another* ball?" In this case, the experimenter has two samples of each item—for instance, a small red ball and a larger blue ball. Again, the task is to indicate an understanding of the class label.

The second part of the test deals with the comprehension of instructions. Here too, there are three levels of difficulty appropriate to different ages and abilities. The simplest is a one-step familiar instruction such as "Wave bye-bye; come here; sit down; kiss me." The next most difficult type of instruction is also one with which the child is familiar (according to mother), but that requires a sequence of behavior. For example, "Bring me the keys," "Turn off the light," and so on. The child must know what keys are and also how to get them and bring them to mother. The most difficult type of instruction is the unfamiliar sequence involving familiar elements. Some examples are "Put the diaper under the table," "Take the keys up the stairs."

The language test for children 24 to 36 months of age can also be given by the mother, but at this age, many children enjoy the novelty of a stranger as long as mother is close at hand. Often the child prefers sitting on mother's lap. This test consists of two parts, vocabulary and grammar, and also assesses receptive rather than expressive language. The vocabulary items are taken from the Ammons Full-Range Picture Vocabulary Test and consist of a set of cards, each with four different pictures printed on it. One card is held up before the child and he is asked to point first to the horse, and then to the wagon. (The four pictures on this card are of a bird, a dog, a horse pulling a wagon, and an insect.) The words vary in difficulty and sometimes may be guessed by the process of elimination. A second vocabulary test is included to be given only if the child will not respond to the Ammons pictures. This test is taken from Meyer's vocabulary items and consists of actual objects rather than pictures. The objects are the same as those used in the most difficult labelling task for the 12- to 24-month-olds. These include two types of balls, cups, spoons,

---

* The rationale for this test is based on the work of David McNeil. The development of this assessment technique was the work of Mary Meader Mokler, Janice Rosen Marmor, and Burton L. White.

pencils, toothbrushes, eyeglasses, and keys. The child is asked, "Where is the pencil; where is another one?" and so on.

The second part of this test is an assessment of the child's under standing of grammar.* The child is asked to act out a number of phrases with materials the experimenter provides. These consist of balls, cups, and so forth. The grammar items range from the simplest prepositional relationships—for example, "Put the ball *in* the cup; take the ball *out* of the cup; where's your *head*; where's *my* head?"—to such complex verbal and plural forms as "Show me how the *doll walks*; show me how the *dolls walk*," and "Give me a stick that is *longer and thinner* than this one." These grammar items are based on studies by Ursula Bellugi-Klima on the grammatical development of very young children.

Receptive Language:
Results and Discussion

Table 6, below, contains the results for all groups on the tests of linguistic competence.

TABLE 6. **Comparison Data on Language Ability**

		Age at Testing			
		12 months	*15 months*	*21 months*	*24 months*
1 yr. A	N	10	10	10	10
	Range	10–21 mos.	14–24 mos.	18–42 mos.	21–51 mos.
	Group median	15 mos.	17 mos.	31.5 mos.	36 mos.
1 yr. C	N	4	4	4	3
	Range	10–16 mos.	10–21 mos.	10–27 mos.	10–40.5 mos.
	Group median	11.5 mos.	13 mos.	19 mos.	30 mos.

		Age at Testing			
		24 months	*27 months*	*30 months*	*36 months*
2 yr. A	N	12	12	12	11
	Range	18–42 mos.	27–54 mos.	18–51 mos.	39–60 mos.
	Group median	36 mos.	40.5 mos.	48 mos.	51 mos.
2 yr. C	N	5	5	5	5
	Range	18–30 mos.	18–36 mos.	21–42 mos.	33–39 mos.
	Group median	18 mos.	27 mos.	27 mos.	39 mos.

* A complete description of these tests, methods of scoring, and reliability find-ings will be found in the Appendix.

Table 7 summarizes the results of tests of statistical significance, based on the Mann–Whitney U, for the data presented in Table 6.

TABLE 7. Significance Levels for Table 6

Comparison	Significance Level (Mann–Whitney U Test) (two-tailed)			
1A	12 months	15 months	21 months	24 months
vs.	n.s.*	n.s.	<.05	n.s.
1C	A > C	A > C	A > C	A > C
2A	24 months	27 months	30 months	36 months
vs.	<.01	<.01	<.05	<.01
2C	A > C	A > C	A > C	A > C
1A	12 vs. 24 months	12 vs. 36 months		24 vs. 36 months
vs.	<.001	<.001		<.01
2A	2 > 1	2 > 1		2 > 1
1C	12 vs. 24 months	12 vs. 36 months		24 vs. 36 months
vs.	.003	.067		n.s.
2C	2 > 1	2 > 1		2 > 1

* A two-tailed test was utilized here, since we had no reason to expect divergent test scores at 12 months.

Figure 4.1 provides another view of these same group median differences obtained on the language tests. There, it can readily be seen that A's score higher than C's, and two-year-olds higher than one-year-olds, as would be expected. The difference between A and C scores increases with increasing age: 3.5 months difference between A's and C's at 12 months; 4 months difference at 15 months; a difference of 12.5 months between one-year A's and C's by 21 months. In all cases, the A subjects obtained the higher scores.

Our data suggest the following picture of the language capacities of high-achievement children. At 12–15 months, a typical high-competence child understands a number of words and phrases that relate directly to him and to his immediate world. Typically, he can say several words, such as "mommy," "bye-bye," "ball," and "cookie," but ability in productive (spoken) language varies widely, particularly at this age, so the present discussion will be based primarily on receptive (understanding) language.

The following list of words and phrases, based on language-test results, gives some indication of the child's level of comprehension:

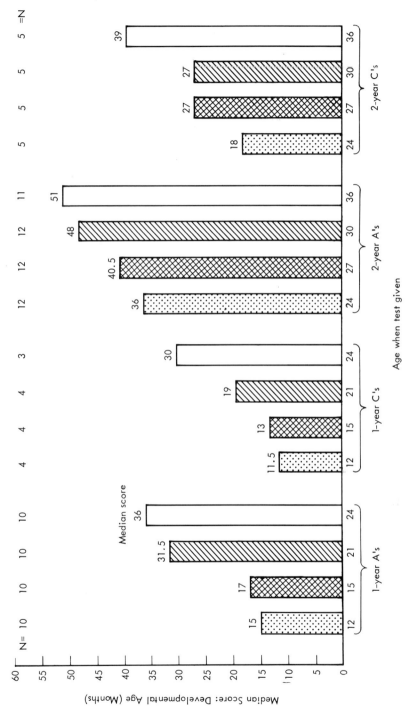

Figure 4.1 Language development data—A vs. C children

8–12 MONTHS

mommy	juice	names of family members
daddy	no-no	and pets—often known
bye-bye	wave bye-bye	idiosyncratically (*doody*
baby		for *Judy*)
shoe		cookie (sometimes idio-
ball		syncratically)

12–14 MONTHS

hi	ears	book
kitty (or *cat*)	feet	socks
dog (or *doggy*)	hair	dance
cup	hug	patty-cake
cracker	water	peek-a-boo
car	drink	kiss
eyes	chair (or *high chair*)	

14–18 MONTHS

milk	bottle	where is, are . . .
spoon	horse	turn on, off the light
telephone (or *phone*)	hat	open, close the door
	coat (or *jacket,*	go get . . .
keys	*sweater*)	let's go . . .
blanket	apple	find
bed	teeth	do you want (a cookie;
cereal	brush your hair,	to get up . . .)
	teeth	don't touch
		show me . . .

In addition to vocabulary, our outstanding 12- to 15-month-olds both understand and can carry out a sequence of familiar instructions. By "familiar" we refer to those events that occur repeatedly in a child's life—commands such as "Come here," "Sit down," "Give Mommy. . . ." Under everyday circumstances, such verbal communications are accompanied by gestural and contextual cues. These are eliminated, however, when we administer our language test, in order to determine the child's understanding of the words and phrases themselves. By a "sequence" of instructions, we mean commands that involve more than a single piece of behavior; for example, "Give Mommy the shoe." Such an instruction requires the child to get the shoe (part one) and to bring it to his mother (part two), implying an understanding of the words "give," "shoe," and "Mommy."

The next language test takes place when subjects are 21 months of age. The reasons for not testing children between 15 and 20 months will be discussed in a later section. By 21 months, receptive-language ability has increased enormously (see Table 6). Sixteen of the seventeen subjects tested have completely mastered the 12–24 month version of our language test. That is, they are able to label unfamiliar objects by class—for example, both a yellow toothbrush and a green toothbrush they have never seen before, as "toothbrush"—and can readily follow instructions consisting of an unfamiliar sequence of familiar elements, such as "Put the diaper on your head." These children are ready for the language test for 24- to 36-month-olds, which includes the Ammons Full-Range Picture Vocabulary and a test of understanding the use of grammatical constructs.

The typical performance of the superior 21-month-old child would include the ability to point out a range of pictures from the Ammons vocabulary cards, including such items as pie, window, horse, clock, numbers, telephone, bed. The median number of such vocabulary words recognized at this age is twelve. Understanding of syntactic construction typically includes the first level of difficulty on the grammar section of the language test* and often all or part of the next most difficult level. These items are predominantly tests of understanding of prepositional relationships (in, out, on, in front of, behind, toward, away from). Successful comprehension of the grammar items implies an understanding of the entire sentence, including the various grammatical constructions (i.e., "Stand *in front of* the chair," "Touch the daddy *of* the boy"). Coping with such instructions is considerably beyond the capacity of the 15-month-old child.

By 27–30 months, A subjects are averaging sixteen Ammons vocabulary words and are showing an understanding of such grammatical constructions as size comparison (bigger, smaller; longer, shorter); more difficult prepositions, such as "between"; negatives such as "can–can't," "is–isn't"; and connectives such as "either–or," "neither–nor." The most outstanding subjects are able to act out little stories, showing accurate comprehension of such time designations as "before" and "after." The C subjects, on the other hand, remain at about the 21-month-old level of performance.

Any discussion of test results for children as young as 12–36 months would be incomplete without a word about "confounding variables." By this we mean those factors that have little to do with the child's language ability, but that nevertheless have an influence on the test results. This would include such things as noise and confusion in the home while the test is being conducted, interference by a sister or brother, the child's being tired or having a temper tantrum, and so forth. The most important of these variables are those that are specific to certain age groups. For example, the 12- to 14-month-old child is usually cooperative, but may be quite dependent on mother, in which case her presence would be an important factor in eliciting the best test results. Between 15 and 20 months, roughly,

---

* See Language Manual in the Appendix.

a difficult period arises from the standpoint of testing. This has already been mentioned as a time when children are just entering the "age of autonomy"; they have discovered the word no and have very little hesitation in using it. Also, at this age they may tend to cling to mother in the presence of strangers, or are stubborn about complying with requests. Since the entire language test (like many other tests) consists of a series of requests, an uncooperative child would be seriously penalized for noncompliance even though his language-comprehension ability might be excellent. For this reason, we have ruled out testing between the ages of 15 and 20 months. However, these factors are occasionally relevant for younger and older children as well. Although it is believed that negativism continues into "the terrible twos," these older children are more sociable than the 15- to 20-month-old child, and are often eager to do the game-like tests with an experimenter. However, negativism does occur as a confounding variable among the 24–36-month group as well, diminishing with increasing age.

Another problem with which the experimenter must contend is the occasional limited interest in test situations of 12- to 36-month-old children. This isn't as great a problem with the 12- to 14-month-old because the testing is very casual and is largely incorporated into the child's spontaneous play. For example, if the child is playing with a ball, the experimenter might ask him to "throw the ball to mommy" (without any gestural clues). For the older children, however, the testing situation is more structured and requires that the child sit down at the table and concentrate on specific questions. Consequently, the results will be somewhat influenced by the child's ability to sit still and pay attention, and this ability, although perhaps related to competence, is not a central attribute of language ability. All these factors are taken into consideration when assessing the overall validity of a child's language-test performance. If the interfering factors are too predominant, a retest is arranged. Nevertheless, test-taking ability is a by-product that also contributes to the overall picture of a child's competence or incompetence.

ASSESSING THE CAPACITY TO SENSE DISSONANCE DURING THE SECOND AND THIRD YEARS OF LIFE

Another way of describing this competence dimension is to say that children with high levels of this ability are acute observers. They are good observers of several kinds of phenomena. They notice when something is "different" or "wrong" in a visual display—for example, a sketch of the moon with hair, or the new haircut of a peer. They are quick to notice when a sequence of events has not gone as it should—for example, when another child has gone out of turn in a group game. They notice inconsistencies in abstract realms—when, for example, an adult tells a story with elements of nonsense, or when an error has been committed in spoken simple arithmetic exercises.

Our problem was to develop a way of measuring the growth of this ability during the one-to-three-year age range.* As a preliminary step, we tried to piece together a sketch of the growth of this ability and its several forms from birth through the first years of life. This process proved difficult and complex. For example, the eight-month-old who smiled at his mother's face and cried at a stranger's was apparently noting a discrepancy in a visual display in the sense that the stranger's face was perceived as different from his mother's. It appeared that, fundamentally, we were talking about simple discriminative ability. When does a child first make discriminations? The answer would appear to depend on the type of discrimination. Clearly, the earliest discriminations in the abstract realm come a good deal later in life than those in respect to sensory arrays. When a hungry two-month-old infant ceases to suck an object that does not yield nutriment, he is exhibiting a capacity to sense dissonance or note discrepancies. On the other hand, Piaget's work on the roots of intellectual development (1952) suggests that the ability to sense dissonance in abstract realms hardly develops before the child is two or three years of age. Furthermore, to the extent that language is usually the medium through which such circumstances are brought to the child's attention, the young child's inadequacies in that area preclude the existence of the ability. Sensing dissonance in situations involving violations of rules, as in, for example, taking turns in a game, probably emerges in the third or fourth year of life for similar reasons.

We were left then with the most primitive form of ability, sensing dissonance in immediately present sensory arrays. Although this form of the ability may appear in simple form very early in a child's life, it does have a developmental course and it does have an upper limit for all human beings; witness, for example, the growth and limits of visual acuity. We could then design items to test this ability for any age.

Our first thought was to use a situation designed in 1949 by Harry Harlow with rhesus monkeys, the "oddity" test. In order to obtain a reward, the subject has to select the one object of three that is different from the others. Presumably, a young child who succeeded on such a test was exhibiting his ability to note discrepancies. We designed such a test for one- to three-year-old children, using small containers of various shapes

* The development of this assessment technique was the work of Barbara Koslowski and Burton L. White.

and colors, and found after extensive testing that the "oddity" test was too difficult for all our children. This came as something of a shock to us, as in Harlow's work, adult rhesus macaques handled these and far more complicated problems with great skill. Nonetheless, we could find no reports about human subjects less than three years of age solving "oddity" problems.

We therefore shifted our ground to a two-choice situation. A reward, usually a small piece of marshmallow, a raisin, or a piece of sugared cereal was hidden (in view of the child) under one of two cups. These cups were identical eight-ounce white plastic models with patterned cards appended to the surface that faced the child. On these cards were line drawings of squares, circles, and the like, which were to serve as cues for the child. Again to our surprise, we found that children under 15 months failed almost every time. We finally succeeded by dropping the use of identical white cups with line drawings for our youngest subjects and substituting containers that varied in color, size, and shape. Our easiest item then involved two containers of different size, shape, and color. Our next item involved two containers that differed in size and shape; and our most difficult items of this series involved two containers that differed only in color. We then proceeded to use line drawings and diamonds stuck directly on the cup, with differences at first very gross, then succeedingly more subtle (see illustrations).*

Sensing Dissonance:
Results and Discussion

Table 8 contains the results for all groups on the test of capacity to sense discrepancies.

Table 9 summarizes the results of tests of statistical significance, based on the Mann–Whitney U, for the data presented in Table 8.

Figure 4.3 provides another view of these same group median differences on the discrepancies test. These results do not present as clear a picture of A versus C and two-year versus one-year group differences as do the language and abstract-abilities tests.

Although the overall test results are in the predicted direction (A's scoring higher than C's at all age levels and two-year-olds scoring higher than ones), some unexpected outcomes within groups occur. Among the 1A's, both 12- and 15-month-olds achieve the same Level 2 score. Among 2C's, subjects show a drop in performance from 24 to 27 months (from Level 3 to Level 2).

---

* Figure 4.2 illustrates the items and their order of difficulty. Administering this test takes about twenty minutes. A complete description of this test, methods of scoring, and reliability findings will be found in the Appendix section.

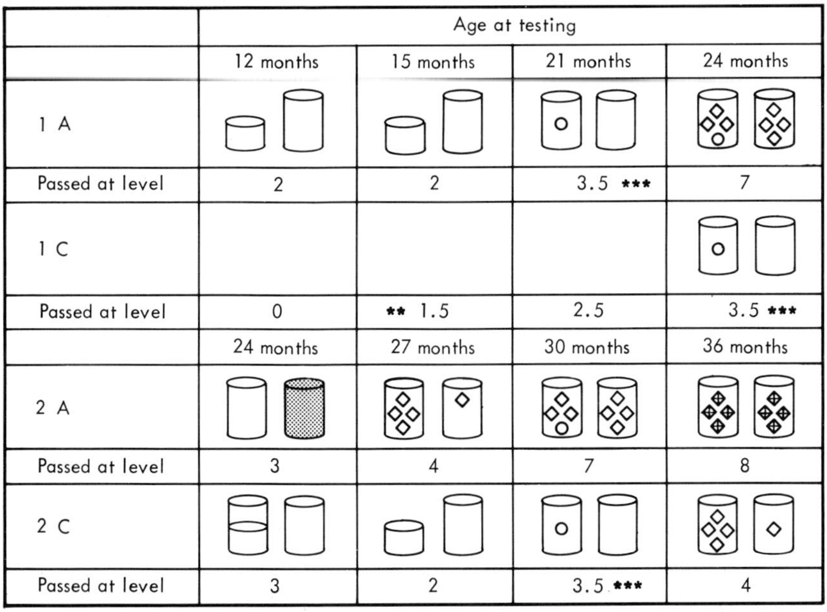

	Age at testing			
	12 months	15 months	21 months	24 months
1 A				
Passed at level	2	2	3.5 ***	7
1 C				
Passed at level	0	** 1.5	2.5	3.5 ***
	24 months	27 months	30 months	36 months
2 A				
Passed at level	3	4	7	8
2 C				
Passed at level	3	2	3.5 ***	4

* Median score for group 1C at 21 months; no test item for this score

** Median score for group 1C at 15 months; no test item for this level

*** See footnote to text, below

Figure 4.2   Typical items passed by various groups at different ages

An interesting but not unexpected finding is that the one-year-old starters tested at 24 months with previous testing experience perform considerably better than do the two-year-old group who are tested at the same age, but for the first time (see Figure 4.3). This is especially true for the A subjects (1A's = L.7; 2A's = L.3), who seem to benefit more from their experience than do the C's (1C's = L.3.5;* 2C's = L.3).

Among the one-year-old subjects, none of the A-versus-C comparisons are significant, although in all cases, A's perform better than C's. Among two-year-old subjects, differences are significant at 27 and 36 months. In addition, the size of the A-versus-C difference increases as subjects get older, so that by 36 months, C's score four levels lower than A's.

The ability to sense discrepancies is rather narrowly defined by the test under discussion. The levels represented by test scores are presented

---

* Level 3.5 is a full step above Level 3 and a full step below Level 4; therefore the difference between Levels 3 and 3.5 is of one level.

TABLE 8.   Comparison Data on the Capacity to Sense Discrepancies

		Age at Testing			
		12 months	*15 months*	*21 months*	*24 months*
1 yr. A	N	10	10	10	10
	Range (levels)	L.0–L.3	L.0–L.3	L.2–L.8	L.2–L.8
	Group median	L.2	L.2	L.3.5	L.7
1 yr. C	N	4	4	4	3
	Range	L.0-L.2	L.0–L.4	L.0–L.5	L.3.5-L.4
	Group median	L.0	L.1.5	L.2.5	L.3.5

		Age at Testing			
		24 months	*27 months*	*30 months*	*36 months*
2 yr. A	N	12	12	12	11
	Range	L.0–L.7	L.2–L.8	L.0–L.8	L.2–L.8
	Group median	L.3	L.4	L.6.5	L.8
2 yr. C	N	5	5	5	5
	Range	L.2–L.4	L.2–L.4	L.2–L.7	L.3.5–L.6
	Group median	L.3	L.2	L.3.5	L.4

TABLE 9.   Significance Levels for Table 8

Comparison	*Significance Level (Mann–Whitney U Test)*			
1A	*12 months*	*15 months*	*21 months*	*24 months*
vs.				
1C	n.s.*	n.s.	n.s.	n.s.
2A	*24 months*	*27 months*	*30 months*	*36 months*
vs.				
2C	n.s.	.05	n.s.	<.05
1A	*12 vs. 24 months*	*12 vs. 36 months*		*24 vs. 36 months*
vs.				
2A	<.01	<.01		p = .14 (n.s.)
1C	*12 vs. 24 months*	*12 vs. 36 months*		*24 vs. 36 months*
vs.				
2C	p = .02	p = .07		<.05

* Two-tailed test was utilized here, since we had no reason to expect divergent test scores at 12 mos. All others are one-tailed.

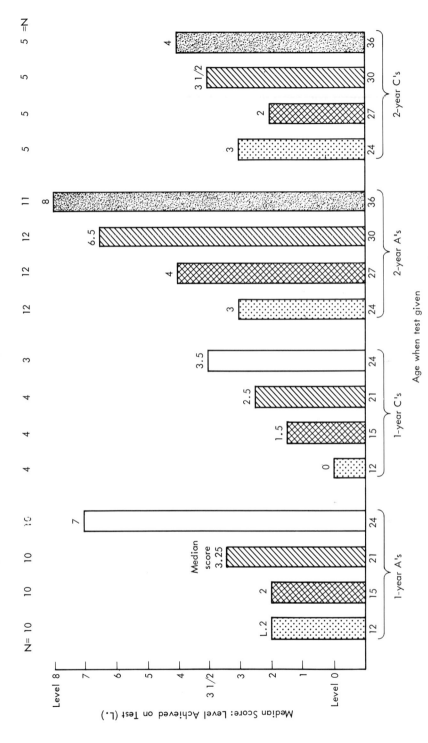

Figure 4.3 Discrepancies test data—A vs. C children

in terms of the stimulus characteristics pictured in Figure 4.2. Our data suggest that high achievement children at 12 to 15 months of age are able to discriminate between objects that differ grossly in size and color (Level 1: small red cup versus larger green cup) and between those that are quite different in size but are alike in color (Level 2: two white cups, one small and one large). They cannot, however, use color alone as the differentiating factor between stimuli; this is the level achieved by the competent 21- to 24-month-old child.

Sometime between 24 and 27 months, the presence or absence of a black circle on two otherwise identical stimuli (Level 3.5) becomes a meaningfully differentiating feature. The outstanding 27-month-old child can also note the discrepancy between two cups that are identical, except that one cup has one diamond while the other has four; this child is attending to a difference in number of markings (or perhaps a difference in configurations), when this difference is as great as one diamond versus four diamonds (see Figure 4.2). However, the high-achieving 27-month-old child cannot consistently discriminate between four circles and two circles

(Level 5: ○ ○ ○ ○ versus ○ ○), or four diamonds versus four circles.

(Level 6: ◇ ◇ ◇ ◇ versus ○ ○ ○).

By 30 months, Levels 5 and 6 are readily distinguished, and Level 7, which presents a more subtle distinction (Figure 4), is also mastered by the competent child. At 36 months, the high-achieving subject can sense the most subtle discrepancy available in the present test—Level 8 (see Figure 4.2). In contrast, the 36-month-old C subject has not progressed beyond the recognition of differences in numbers of circles or diamonds (Levels 4 and 5).

ASSESSING THE CAPACITY FOR ABSTRACT THOUGHT DURING THE SECOND AND THIRD YEARS OF LIFE

As is the case with certain forms of the ability to sense dissonance, the capacity for abstract thought is quite limited in all children less than three years old, regardless of their level of development. Rudimentary development has begun, for example, as language develops, in the sense that any such symbolic function is a form of abstract thought. Nonetheless, our focus had to be mainly on prerequisite phenomena—if, in fact, such could be identified. Fortunately, in this topic area, Piaget's monumental work on the origins of intelligence was of central relevance. Presumably, the several processes of sensorimotor intelligence that develop during the first two years of life are the foundations of the capacity for dealing with abstractions. Also, fortunately for us, several investigators had been recently establishing scales for assessing the developing of sensorimotor intelligence. The two most advanced products were those of Uzgiris and Hunt (1966) and Escalona and Corman (1968). We chose to use the best-developed portions of the work of Uzgiris and Hunt, since they seemed to have been more advanced in their work at that time than were Escalona and Corman.

For the 12- to 21-month period, we use the Uzgiris and Hunt object-permanence and spatial-relations scales. For the 21- to 36-month period, we use a test made up mostly of pattern or picture completion items from Meyer's Pacific tests of intellectual abilities.*

Abstract Thought:
Results and Discussion

Subjects 12 to 15 months of age were given the Hunt–Uzgiris Object Scale, which consists of various items that measure the child's conception of the world of objects and the child's awareness of how objects perform in the physical world (gravity, balance, trajectories, reversals). Although we did not expect our A subjects to perform better than C's as early as 12 months of age, there is, in fact, a sizable developmental spread at this early point, with A's already attaining the maximum developmental stage of 15.5 months and C's achieving only 9.5 months. (See Table 10 and Figure 4.4.) Although the differences are not statistically significant (see Table 11), this early trend is interesting to note, since it suggests that the object concept may be more advanced among one-year-old A's, possibly due to their increased opportunity to deal with objects in their natural environment. C subjects, by contrast, do not attain the maximum score on this scale during this age range, reaching only the 11-month level when they are 15 months old. At 21 months, the Meyers Pacific Test Series was administered. This test involves considerably more mature manipulation of three-dimensional materials. In Table 10 it can be seen that at 21 months of age, the 1A's outperform the 1C's. This difference is statistically significant (see Table 11).†

Among the two-year-old group at 24 months we witness continued

* The test takes about 25 minutes to administer. A complete description of this test, methods of scoring, and reliability findings will be found in the Appendix section. The development of this assessment technique was the work of Ellen Cardone Banks and Burton L. White.

† At the time of the publication we are reporting data on only three 1C subjects at 36 months of age.

TABLE 10. Comparison Data on the Capacity for Abstract Thought

		Age at Testing			
		12 months	15 months	21 months	24 months
1 yr. A	N	10	10	10	10
	Range (levels)	8.0–15.5 mos.	all 15.5 mos.	16.5–24.5 mos.	16.5–28.5 mos.
	Group median	15.5 mos.	15.5 mos.	20.5 mos.	22.5 mos.
1 yr. C	N	4	4	4	3
	Range	8.0–15.5 mos.	11.0–15.5 mos.	all 16.5 mos.	16.5–20.5 mos.
	Group median	9.5 mos.	11.0 mos.	16.5 mos.	16.5 mos.

		Age at Testing			
		24 months	27 months	30 months	36 months
2 yr. A	N	12	12	12	11
	Range	16.5–28.5 mos.	20.5–32.0 mos.	16.5–32.0 mos.	24.5–60 mos.
	Group median	20.5 mos.	24.5 mos.	24.5 mos.	54 mos.
2 yr. C	N	5	5	5	5
	Range	all 16.5 mos.	16.5–18.0 mos.	16.5–20.5 mos.	20.5–28.5 mos.
	Group median	16.5 mos.	16.5 mos.	16.5 mos.	24.5 mos.

TABLE 11. Significance Levels for Table 10

Comparison	Significance Level (Mann–Whitney U Test) (one-tailed)			
1A vs. 1C	12 months	15 months	21 months	24 months
	n.s.*	<.05	<.05	.05
2A vs. 2C	24 months	27 months	30 months	36 months
	<.001	<.001	<.01	<.01
1A vs. 2A	12 vs. 24 months	12 vs. 36 months		24 vs. 36 months
	<.001	<.001		<.001
1C vs. 2C	12 vs. 24 months	12 vs. 36 months		24 vs. 36 months
	p = .003	p = .07		<.05

* A two-tailed test was utilized here, since we had no reason to expect divergent test scores at 12 months.

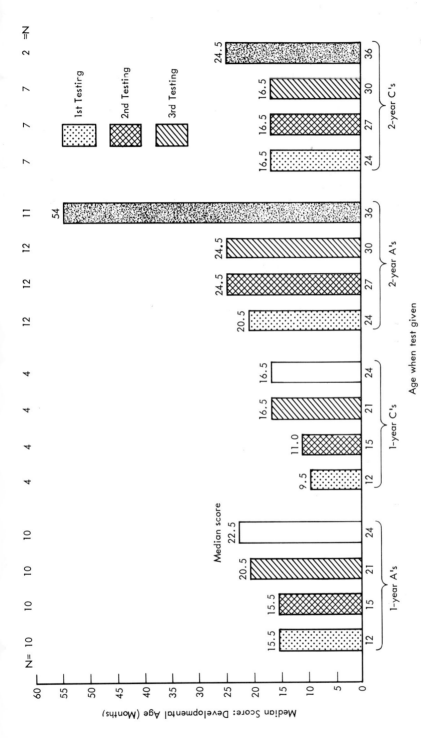

Figure 4.4 Tests of abstract abilities (consists of two different tests: the Hunt–Uzgiris, given at 12 and 15 months, and the Meyer Pacific Test Series, given at 21, 24, 27, 30, and 36 months)

developmental divergence between our A and C children. At 24 months, the 2A's score 20.5 months, versus 16.5 months for 2C's. The difference between the groups grows steadily greater, so that at 27 and 30 months the scores are 24.5 months for the A's and 16.5 months for the C's. The Meyers Test Series, which is the instrument in question, requires the subjects to perform with abstract shapes such as cutouts and puzzles using pictures of real objects, where they must recreate objects from their parts.

At 36 months, those children who achieved a sufficiently high score (32.0 months) on the Meyers test were given additional items dealing with abstract thinking abilities taken from the Stanford–Binet test. The performance of C subjects at 36 months was not good enough to warrant the administration of these additional items. This accounts for the large spread between A and C medians, 54 months for A's and 24.5 months for C's.

As would be expected, there is a significant difference between the performance of two-year-olds and one-year-olds of similar competence levels, with 2A's performing better than 1A's and 2C's better than 1C's. It should be noted that the 2A's are different children from the 1A's and were not tested when they themselves were 1.

The following presentation will help the reader understand more fully what types of exercises the competent 12-, 15-, 21-, 24-, and 36-month-old child was able to perform successfully. A full description of each item in each test will be found in the Appendix.

On the Hunt–Uzgiris Object Scale, the 12-month-old is basically expected to search for an object hidden before him beneath a screen. As the test progresses, the searches become more difficult and more involved; after successfully retrieving a partially hidden object, the infant will search actively for a completely hidden object, and by the age of 12 months should at least be able to master retrieval of an object after observed displacements of that object. By 15 months, not only can the child perform all the previous operations, but should also master invisible displacements of objects, such as when the examiner hides an object under three screens in sequence and leaves it hidden under one of the screens.

AGE 12 MONTHS

Series I, items 8, 9, 10; Series V, items 6, 7
> The child will find an object such as a toy after it has visibly been successively hidden under various screens; he will find an object under three superimposed screens; he will find an object hidden in a container that is covered by superimposed screens; he will understand the relationship of the container and the contained; he will understand equilibrium.

AGE 15 MONTHS

Series I, items 11, 12, 13, 14, 15, 16; Series V, items 8, 11
The child will find an object after it has gone through hidden displacements with several screens; he will follow an object through a series of invisible displacements in sequence and find it; he will demonstrate an understanding of gravity; and he will recognize the absence of familiar persons.

AGE 21 MONTHS

The child will be able to perform some or all of the following exercises: selecting the correct geometric form to complete a pattern; putting together two pieces to form a whole geometric figure; matching geometric figures; completing simple puzzles consisting of two or three pieces.

AGE 24 MONTHS

The child will perform the operations above with increased accuracy.

AGE 36 MONTHS

The competent child of this age will perform, mainly verbally, a series of exercises, some of which may involve questions about three-dimensional or two-dimensional materials designed to determine his level of understanding of abstractions; for example, items involving opposite analogies, pictorial identification, discrimination of forms, and similarities and differences are some of those he will be able to deal with successfully at this age.

TESTS OF GENERAL AND INTELLECTUAL DEVELOPMENT

We test all subjects for general development at 12 and 24 months of age with the Bayley test. We test all subjects for intellectual function at 36 months with our preschool project tests and also with the Stanford–Binet.

General and Intellectual Development: Results and Discussion

Figure 4.5 and Tables 12 and 13 contain data obtained to date with the aforementioned tests on the 31 subjects in question. Our 1A and 1C subjects score at or about normal at 12 months (group medians: 1A, 104; 1C, 99 N.S.). At 24 months, 1A's do considerably better than 1C's (group medians: 1A, 125; 1C, 109, $p = <.05$). The comparatively high

TABLE 12.   Comparison Data on Bayley and Stanford–Binet Tests

		Age at Testing	
		12 months	*24 months*
1 yr. A	N	10	10
	Range	94–134	108–143
	Group median	104	125
1 yr. C	N	4	3
	Range	50–134	66–112
	Group median	99	109

		Age at Testing	
		24 months	*36 months*
2 yr. A	N	12	11
	Range	94–140	101–150
	Group median	105	138
2 yr. C	N	5	5
	Range	69–94	85–99
	Group median	86	92

scores of the 1C group at 24 months seem to us to be due to test sophistication, although it is possible that the various effects of our study have produced positive benefits for the children. We will learn more on this subject as these children grow.

For subjects starting with us at two years of age, scores on the Bayley test indicate a clear superiority of our 2A group (group medians: 2A, 105; 2C, 86, $p = <.001$).

Of especial interest are the initial scores on the Bayley at 12 and 24 months. Our 1A children look about the same as our 1C group, and

TABLE 13.   Significance Levels for Table 12

Comparison	Significance Level (Mann-Whitney U Test) (two-tailed)	
1A	*12 months*	*24 months*
vs.	n.s.	<.05
1C	A > C	A > C
2A	*24 months*	*36 months*
vs.	<.001	<.001
2C	A > C	A > C

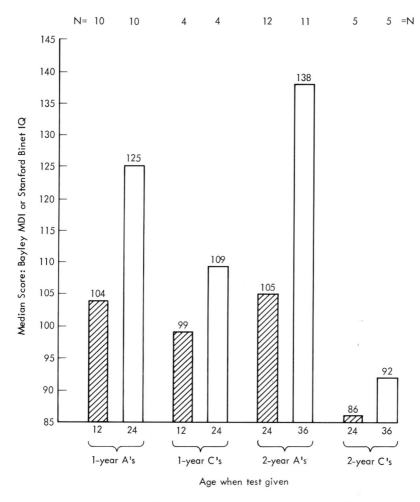

Figure 4.5 Bayley MDI and Stanford Binet scores: A vs. C children

our 2A children don't score remarkably high. The differences in group performance at 36 months give the reader another indication of the kinds of children we are studying.

5

An Instrument for the Quantitative Analysis of the Stream of Experience of One- to Six-Year-Old Children

BURTON L. WHITE/BARBARA KABAN/JANICE MARMOR/BERNICE SHAPIRO

Nowhere in the literature could we find information about the ongoing experiences of infants and toddlers, nor could we find many analytic techniques for gathering such data.* The approach that seemed most promising to us was the work of Roger Barker and Herbert Wright and their associates at Kansas. In their attempts at building a quantitative inquiry into human ecology, we believed there was the potential for gathering adequately detailed information on the moment-to-moment experiences of young children.

The approach we have taken is not a conservative one in many respects. We observe children as they go about their normal activities. We tape-record a continuous series of remarks designed to include our best commonsense judgments as to what the child is trying to do from moment to moment, along with other relevant information about stimulating factors, impediments, and his success or failure. After ten minutes of such recording, with the duration of tasks timed to the second with stopwatches, we play back the tape and code the record during the next twenty minutes. Three such cycles are a normal half-day's work.

---

* Since that time two articles on analyzing the stream of behavior have appeared—Caldwell (1968), and Schoggen and Schoggen (1971).

We constructed a coding scheme *inductively* from such running records. The preliminary scheme was field-tested and revised more times than we would care to mention over a period of about twelve months; at first with three- to six-year-olds, then with one- to three-year-olds. The result is an instrument with thirty-five individual and several combination classes, plus a wastebasket category for those times when no purpose is even remotely discernible in the behavior of the subject.* The categories are illustrated in the series of illustrations, pp. 70–80.† The definitions of the categories are as follows:

SOCIAL TASKS: LABELS, DEFINITIONS, AND EXAMPLES

1. *To Please*

   Def.: To attempt to obtain another's good favor by means of a sustained display of affection, or by offering an object to the other person.

2. *To Cooperate*

   Def.: To comply with another's directive when there is little evidence that the compliance is unwilling. To listen, when brief demands are made on one's attention.

3. *To Gain Approval*

   Def.: To ask (verbally or nonverbally) for favorable comment on a piece of work or on behavior.

4. *To Procure A Service*

   Def.: To try to obtain aid from another.

5. *To Gain Attention/To Achieve Social Contact*

   Def.:   a. to join a group
   b. To initiate social contact
   c. To maximize the chance of being noticed.

6. *To Maintain Social Contact*

   Def.: To be absorbed in ensuring that a social contact continues, or to be interested in the social pleasantry rather than in the content of a conversation or other activity.

7. *To Avoid Unpleasant Circumstances*

   Def.: To do something for the purpose of evading actual disapproval, possible disapproval, or simply a clash.

8. *To Reject Overtures and Peer Contact, to Avoid Attention*

   Def.: To refuse to allow a peer to join one's group or become sociable with oneself. Rarely: To act in order to minimize the possibility of being noticed.

---

* The development of this instrument was the work of Kitty Riley Clark, Andrew Cohn, Cherry Wedgewood Collins, Barbara Kaban, and Burton L. White.
  † These drawings were made by Kitty Riley Clark.

SOCIAL
To please/cooperate

SOCIAL
To gain approval

SOCIAL
To procure a service

SOCIAL
To achieve social contact/To gain attention

a. To join a group

b. To initiate
   social contact

c. To maximize
   the chance of
   being noticed

CLACKITY
YAK
CLICKITY
CLACK

SOCIAL
5. To maintain
   social contact

SOCIAL
To avoid unpleasant
circumstances

SOCIAL
To reject overtures, peer
contact, to avoid attention

SOCIAL
To annoy

SOCIAL
To dominate,
to direct or lead

SOCIAL
To compete,
gain status

SOCIAL
To resist domination, assert self

a. Resistance to demands,
   orders or any trampling
   under foot

b. Protection of property

SOCIAL
To enjoy pets

SOCIAL
To provide
information

SOCIAL
To converse

uh
uh
um...

SOCIAL
Production of
verbalizations

NONSOCIAL
To eat

NONSOCIAL
To relieve oneself

NONSOCIAL
To dress/undress
oneself

NONSOCIAL
To ease discomfort

NONSOCIAL
To restore order

NONSOCIAL
To choose

NONSOCIAL
To procure
an object

NONSOCIAL
To construct
a product

NONSOCIAL
To engage in large
muscle activity

NONSOCIAL
Non-task behavior

NONSOCIAL
To pass time

NONSOCIAL
To find something
to do

NONSOCIAL
To prepare for
an activity

NONSOCIAL
To explore

NONSOCIAL
To pretend to
be someone or
something else

NONSOCIAL
To improve a developing
motor, intellectual, or
verbal skill

NONSOCIAL
To gain information

a. Auditory and Visual

b. Visual only

NONSOCIAL
To gain pleasure

NONSOCIAL
To imitate

NONSOCIAL
To operate
a mechanism

9. *To Annoy*

   Def.: To disturb another. To act in a manner designed to displease; to provoke by means of irritating teasing.

10. *To Dominate, to Direct or Lead*

    Def.: To play the leader role or to demonstrate a process to others or advise others; in short, to direct a specific activity of others.

11. *To Compete, Gain Status*

    Def.: To contend for something (e.g., in games involving competition), to make comparisons between own "superior" product (possession, etc.) and other's product (possession, etc.), or to try to elevate one's standing (in one's own eyes or in the eyes of an audience) by appealing to an authority figure.

12. *To Resist Domination, Assert Self*

    Def.: To oppose any intrusion on one's personal domain, including both
    a. Resistance to demands, orders, or any trampling underfoot, and
    b. Protection of property.

13. *To Enjoy Pets*

    Def.: Affectionate play with animals.

14. *To Provide Information*

    Def.: To indicate or communicate, in a public way, one's affects, desires, needs, or specific intelligence.

15. *To Converse*

    Def.: Any give-and-take of verbalization, when there is mutual interest in the conversation rather than a social or some other overtone, or where the communications cannot be heard.

16. *Production of Verbalizations*

    Def.: The actual production of communication; that is, when a child is engaged in the give-and-take of exchanging communications and he is deficient in language skills and cannot get across what he wants to say.

NONSOCIAL TASKS: LABELS, DEFINITIONS, AND EXAMPLES

1. To *Eat*

   Def.: To ingest food or drink.

2. *To Relieve Oneself*

   Def.: To void or to eliminate.

3. *To Dress/Undress Oneself*

   Def.: Self-explanatory.

4. *To Ease Discomfort*

   Def.: Purposeful behavior to alleviate physical or psychic discomfort, in contrast to apparently aimless or habitual behavior.

5. *To Restore Order*

   Def.: To return things to a previously acceptable state but not for the purpose of easing discomfort, pleasing another, or preparing for an activity.

6. *To Choose*

   Def.:   To choose a specific object from an array.

7. *To Procure an Object*

   Def.:   To get something, not as an instrumental task for constructing a product, but as a task per se. If procuring an object in order to use it for constructing a product, or for any purpose, takes longer than 15 seconds, it is coded as focal.

8. *To Construct a Product*

   Def.:   Involves the whole complex of behavior of procuring materials and using the materials (e.g., glue, pencils, piece of puzzle), oriented toward the end product as a consequence of the use of the materials.

9. *To Engage in Large-Muscle Activity*

   Def.:   To engage in large-muscle activity as an end in itself, not as a means of getting attention, being a member of a group, etc. To use gross motor muscles to propel all or some part of the body or to perform other motor activities that require unusual physical effort and coordination. Working hard to do something with the body that is out of the ordinary—e.g., bike riding up a hill (after the skill has been mastered).

10. *Non-Task Behavior*

    Def.:   To remain in place and not dwell on any specific object (e.g., desultory scanning, sitting with eyes closed, or holding a blank stare), or to wander aimlessly from one location to another.

11. *To Pass Time*

    Def.:   To occupy oneself with some alternative task in a situation where one is captive (i.e., must remain in the field) and where the prescribed activity holds no appeal for one. To occupy oneself while waiting for a prescribed activity to begin.

12. *To Find Something to Do*

    Def.:   To move around, sampling objects and activities in a purposeful fashion, but not settling in on anything specific.

13. *To Prepare for an Activity*

    Def.:   To perform the socially prescribed activities or sequence of actions that a child carries out almost automatically owing to previous experience and/or practice, in order to prepare for something that the child anticipates.

14. *To Explore*

    Def.:   To explore materials, objects, activities, people. To investigate the properties or nature of materials, objects, activities, or people through touch, taste, vision, etc. Experimenting with an object or material's possibilities by adding to it or taking something away from it as the primary concern, rather than for the purpose of constructing a product or because of interest in the process per se, as is evident in *to pretend*.

15. *To Pretend/Role Play*

    Def.:   To fantasize in any of the following ways: to pretend to be someone or something else; to pretend to be doing something one really isn't; to pretend an object is something other than it really is; to pretend to be in an imaginary situation.

16. *To Improve a Developing Motor, Intellectual, or Verbal Skill*

    Def.: To improve a developing motor, intellectual, or verbal skill is typically distinguished by the redundancy of S's behavior (i.e., repeats the same sequence of actions again and again) and by less-than-masterful skill in performing the activity in question.

17. *To Gain Information (Visual)*

    Def.: Sustained visual inquiry directed toward a specific object or person.

18. *To Gain Information (Audio and Visual)*

    Def.: To attend to language from any source. To gain information through looking and listening when the prime interest is on the context of information being made available.

19. *To Gain Pleasure*

    Def.: To engage in a task for no other reason than to achieve a state of gaiety, excitement, or amusement.

20. *To Imitate*

    Def.: The immediate reproduction of the behavior of another person.

21. *To Operate a Mechanism*

    Def.: To attempt to use or manipulate a mechanism. Operating a mechanism is, by definition, instrumental but becomes focal because it takes 15 seconds or longer to execute.

Let us emphasize one point. Neither the task labels nor the extended definitions in our manual constitute airtight behavioral descriptions. We have attempted to keep our inferences as closely tied to behavior as is humanly possible. It is true that one could be considerably less inferential than we have been in recording ongoing behavior. There were two major reasons for proceeding as we did. First, we felt that more literal descriptions of behavior would have resulted in a totally unmanageable number of classes; and second, we thought that this system of labeling the units of experience would prove useful in unraveling the interrelations among environmental factors and developing abilities. At any rate, we do not pretend that this is the only, or necessarily the wisest, way to attack the problem, but one has to start somewhere.

Informal tests of interobserver reliability were an integral part of the evolution of the instrument. The uniqueness, complexity, and precision of timing involved in this venture argued for modest aspirations regarding reliability. We set ⅔ or 66.7 percent agreement as our goal. If, for example, a two-year-old engaged in 30 tasks in ten minutes, both observers had to have labeled at least 6.67 minutes of behavior identically to within five seconds before we considered the instrument to have minimally acceptable reliability.

Our several tests of reliability produced percentage agreements which range from 67 to 71 percent. Although we would prefer scores above 85 percent, we will have to live with lower reliability for the time being.

6

Patterns of Experience During the Second and Third Years of Life: Results and Discussion

BURTON L. WHITE/BARBARA KABAN/JANICE MARMOR/BERNICE SHAPIRO

In the following sections, we will present various kinds of information on the types of everyday experiences undergone by our children. These data were gathered on five separate days, each three weeks apart, during the child's twelfth to fifteenth month or his twenty-fourth to twenty-seventh month, depending on whether he was one or two years of age. On each observation day, three ten-minute records were collected over a two-hour span. We observed at various times between 9 A.M. and 5 P.M., Monday through Friday. We attempted to distribute observation times throughout the day for each subject, but were not always successful. Occasionally, especially among one-year-olds, long naps interfered with our plans. Other uncontrollable factors prevented a totally balanced schedule. By and large, however, we were successful.

We did not observe on weekends, nor before 9 A.M. or after 5 P.M. As a result, we very probably missed out on a fair amount of experience our children had with their fathers. We doubt that we missed much of such experience during the week, since few fathers have time for their infants between 6 A.M. and 9 A.M., and such children are pretty much ready for bed when their fathers return from work. However, we must acknowledge some probable loss of information, especially with regard to weekend life.

Another important factor affecting the quality of our data is the previously mentioned effect of the observer in the home. Our presence in the home unquestionably alters the behaviors of the people we are observing. Furthermore, there is reason to believe that such alterations vary across children and adults. We take pains to keep this source of error as small as possible. We instruct all our data collectors to try to establish an orientation in the adults who may be present, to the effect that they should try to continue with their normal routine as if we are not there. Small children seem to be less of a problem, in that after an initial brief period, almost all one- to three-year-olds seem to accept readily the notion that the observer is there to "work" and cannot "play" with them. Another precaution is built into our design. We spend two hours or so in each home once each week for twenty-six weeks out of each year. We hope that mothers will be unable to maintain atypical behavior for such a length of time. Of course, we do not expect these precautions to eliminate observer effects, and we are obliged to consider this problem in our interpretations of the data.

An additional consideration to keep in mind is the imperfect reliability of the observational instrument. All such defects must be acknowledged when interpreting our results.

We will present information on patterns of experience for one- versus two-year-old children. We will then present information on patterns of experience for 1A versus 1C and 2A versus 2C children in the following categories:

1. All tasks of all groups (social and nonsocial) that occur at least 1 percent of the time
   Initiation of tasks:

   | self- vs. other-initiated experiences | self- vs. mother-initiated experiences |

   for social and nonsocial tasks
   and for all tasks

2. Live vs. mechanical language experiences
3. Gross vs. fine motor mastery experiences
4. Mastery and exploratory tasks, according to physical objects used
5. The frequency of gain-attention, prepare-for-activity, and procure-object tasks.

We will also present information on the following predictions we had made about possibly important differences in the patterns of experience of A and C children.

One-year-Old A's vs. one-year-old C's

One-year-old C's will have more social tasks than one-year-old A's.

One-year-old C's will have more pass time than one-year-old A's.

One-year-old C's will have more gain attention and will maintain social contact more than one-year-old A's.

One-year-old A's will have more explore and more mastery than one-year-old C's.

One-year-old A's will have more procure an object than one-year-old C's.

Two-year-old A's vs. two-year-old C's

Two-year-old C's will have more social tasks than two-year-old A's.

Two-year-old C's will have more assert self, annoy, and avoid unpleasant circumstance than two-year-old A's.

Two-year-old C's will have more initiate social contact and maintain social contact than two-year-old A's.

Two-year-old C's will have more non-task than two-year-old A's.

Two-year-old C's will have more procure object and procure service than two-year-old A's.

Two-year-old A's will have more prepare for activity than two-year-old C's.

Two-year-old A's will have more construct a product than two-year-old C's.

Two-year-old A's will have more mastery than two-year-old C's.

Two-year-old A's will have more role play than two-year-old C's.

Two-year-old A's will have more prepare for activity and construct a product than two-year-old C's.

Two-year-old A's will have more cooperate than two-year-old C's.

Two-year-old C's will have more explore than two-year-old A's.

One-year-old C's vs. two-year-old C's

One-year-old C's will have more pass time than two-year-old C's.

One-year-old C's will have less non-task than two-year-old C's.

One-year-old C's will have less assert self, avoid unpleasant circumstances, and annoy than two-year-old C's.

One-year-old C's will have less maintain social contact than two-year-old C's.

One-year-old C's will have less mastery and explore than two-year-old C's.

Two-year-old C's will have more social tasks than one-year-old C's.

One-year-old A's vs. two-year-old A's

One-year-old A's will have more explore than two-year-old A's.

One-year-old A's will have more procure object than two-year-old A's.

Two-year-old A's will have more prepare for activity and construct a product than one-year-old A's.

Two-year-old A's will have more mastery than one-year-old A's.

Two-year-old A's will have more role play than one-year-old A's.

Two-year-old A's will have more gain approval than one-year-old A's.

Two-year-old A's will have more converse and provide information than one-year-old A's.

One-year-old A's will have more social tasks than two-year-old A's.

TASK DATA—GENERAL

Figures 6.1 and 6.2 represent stream-of-experience or task data on one- and two-year-old children. Table 14 contains the data from which the figures were constructed. There are quite a number of interesting points to be noted within this information.

First of all, note the predominance of nonsocial tasks. Regardless of whether a child is developing very well or very poorly, he spends far more

TABLE 14. **All Tasks, Comparative Data**

Social tasks	1	2	1A	1C	2A	2C
To please	0.2	0.3	0.2	0.1	0.2	0.4
To cooperate	1.5	2.8	1.4	2.5	3.2	1.4
To gain approval	0.0	0.0	0.0	0.0	0.3	0.0
To procure a service	0.9	2.1	1.3	0.4	2.1	2.1
To gain attention	2.6	2.6	3.1	1.9	2.1	3.9
To maintain social contact	2.3	5.6	2.0	2.6	4.7	7.2
To avoid unpleasant circumstances	0.0	0.1	0.0	0.0	0.0	0.3
To annoy	0.0	0.1	0.0	0.0	0.0	0.4
To direct	0.0	0.1	0.0	0.0	0.3	0.1
To assert self	0.6	1.7	0.6	1.0	1.2	2.6
To provide information	0.0	0.3	0.0	0.0	0.3	0.3
To compete	0.0	0.0	0.0	0.0	0.0	0.0
To reject overtures	0.0	0.0	0.0	0.0	0.0	0.0
To enjoy pets	0.0	0.0	0.0	0.0	0.0	0.0
To converse	0.0	0.2	0.0	0.0	0.3	0.0
To produce verbalizations	0.0	0.0	0.0	0.0	0.0	0.0
Nonsocial tasks						
To eat	4.3	5.7	4.3	4.2	5.8	5.3
To gain information (visual)	18.6	13.8	20.1	16.2	13.6	14.0
To gain information (visual and auditory)	7.4	10.0	7.2	10.3	12.7	6.5
Non-task	10.9	10.7	10.7	11.2	8.1	14.3
To pass time	2.1	2.3	2.1	4.2	2.4	0.3
To find something to do	0.1	0.0	0.2	0.0	0.1	0.0
To prepare for activity	1.8	1.8	1.8	1.1	2.5	1.2
To construct a product	0.0	0.0	0.0	0.0	0.1	0.0
To choose	0.0	0.0	0.0	0.0	0.0	0.0
To procure an object	3.1	1.6	3.3	2.8	1.5	1.9
Gross motor activity	0.0	0.6	0.0	0.1	0.3	2.0
To gain pleasure	0.6	0.8	0.3	0.8	0.9	0.8
To imitate	0.1	0.5	0.1	0.0	0.4	0.6
To pretend	0.0	0.8	0.0	0.1	0.9	0.6
To ease discomfort	0.6	0.4	0.7	0.6	0.3	0.8
To restore order	0.6	0.8	0.8	0.2	0.8	0.8
To relieve oneself	0.0	0.0	0.0	0.0	0.0	0.0
To dress	0.0	0.1	0.0	0.0	0.1	0.2
To operate a mechanism	0.3	0.2	0.3	0.3	0.2	0.3
To explore	13.2	4.4	13.5	11.8	4.2	7.9
Mastery	8.1	10.1	8.1	6.7	9.9	10.1
To eat and gain information (visual)	4.8	2.1	5.1	1.6	1.7	2.3
To eat and gain information (visual and auditory)	0.4	0.4	0.3	0.4	0.9	0.4
Mastery and miscellaneous	0.0	0.0	0.0	0.0	0.2	0.0

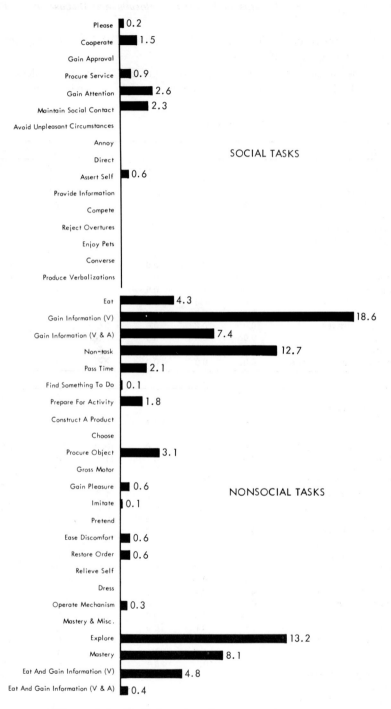

Figure 6.1 Task data for all one-year-olds (N = 14)

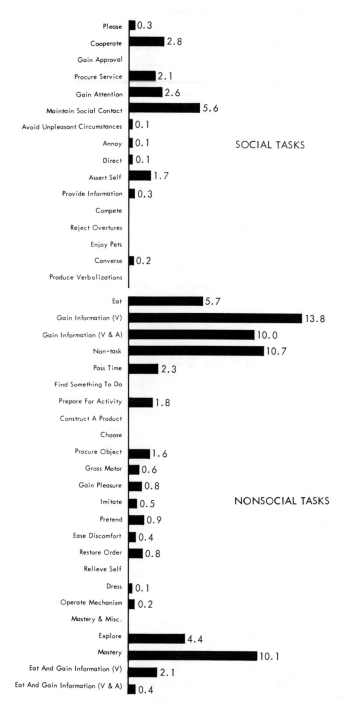

Figure 6.2 Task data for all two-year-olds (N = 17)

TABLE 15. Social vs. Nonsocial Tasks, Comparative Data

Group	All 1-yr.-olds	All 2-yr.-olds	1A	1C	2A	2C
Social tasks (median % duration)	10.6	17.7	10.6	9.3	17.2	20.6
Nonsocial tasks (median % duration)	89.4	82.3	89.7	90.7	82.8	79.4
N =	14	19	10	4	12	7

time oriented toward interactions with physical reality than he does trying to affect people during these age ranges. For one-year-olds, the figures are 89.4 percent for nonsocial tasks versus 10.6 for social tasks (see Table 15). For two-year-olds, the figures are 82.3 percent for nonsocial tasks and 17.7 percent for social tasks. There is a near doubling of social tasks between the first and second birthdays. (Later we will dwell on the rather striking fact that very good mothers apparently spend very little time in direct interaction with their children during this period.)

A second rather unexpected finding is that the most frequent experience of most children in this age range is what we call *gain information—visual,* which is staring steadily at one object or scene for at least three seconds. Only one of many child psychologists guessed correctly that visual inquiry was the most frequent activity of this age range. Little wonder, however, when you realize how few professionals have studied the one- to three-year-old child, especially under natural circumstances.

Other general points are:

Exploring objects is a common activity with one-year-olds, and seems to decrease during the next year (13.2 percent for one-year-olds vs. 4.4 percent for two-year-olds).*

Mastery behavior (i.e., practicing simple skills such as putting small objects in and out of receptacles, putting lids on and off containers, etc.) seems to be a more mature form of behavior as it increases from the second to the third year of life (8.1 percent for one-year-olds vs. 10.1 percent for two-year-olds).

Non-task behavior (desultory scanning or wandering) is quite common among most one- and two-year-old children (10.9 percent for one-year-olds vs. 10.7 percent for two-year-olds).

Cooperation tasks increase during the third year of life, reflecting increased demands made by others (usually the mother) on the growing child (1.5 percent for one-year-olds vs. 2.8 percent for two-year-olds).

* All figures are medians of percent of total duration.

Achieving and maintaining social contact are the most common social tasks of one-year-olds, and they increase during the second year (4.9 percent for one-year-olds vs. 8.2 percent for two-year-olds).

Procuring the services of another (usually the mother) is an emergent during the second year (0.9 percent for one-year-olds vs. 2.1 percent for two-year-olds), as is *to annoy* (another person) 0 percent for one-year-olds vs. 0.1 percent for two-year-olds).

Asserting oneself or resisting domination is most frequent in homes where other young children are nearby a good deal of the time—although older siblings generally spend very little time with one- and two-year-olds (0.6 percent for one-year-olds vs. 1.7 percent for two-year-olds).

Gaining information through looking and hearing relevant language (*gain information—audio* + *visual*) increases during the second year of life (7.4 percent for one-year-olds vs. 10.0 percent for two-year-olds).

TASK DATA—"A" VERSUS "C" CHILDREN

The strategy of our project is to look for differences of potential importance in the everyday experiences of young children. We cannot be sure of our current judgments on that issue, since we are discussing only some 33 percent of the data we will ultimately have from our natural experiment. Nonetheless, we can make some educated guesses. I repeat, the following are *educated guesses.*

Figures 6.3 and 6.4 present comparative task data for 1A and 1C children. Table 14 presents the information on which Figures 6.3 and 6.4 are based. Table 28 provides data on the statistical significance of differences in important experiences.

1A vs. 1C Children

At twelve to fifteen months of age, the social tasks of A and C children look rather similar. There seem to be more overtures toward the mother by A children, either to gain her attention briefly (*achieve social contact,* 3.1 percent for 1A's vs. 1.9 percent for 1C's) or to ask for help (*procure a service,* 1.3 percent for 1A's vs. 0.4 percent for 1C's). C children seem to assert themselves more often than A's (0.6 percent for 1A's vs. 1.0 percent for 1C's), usually with siblings (who are more likely to be around). C children seem to try to cling to their mothers more (*maintain social contact,* 2.6 percent for 1C's vs. 2.0 percent for 1A's). Mothers of C children seem to make more demands of their one-year-olds (*to cooperate,* 2.5 percent for 1C's vs. 1.4 percent for 1A's).

In the realm of nonsocial tasks, the difference in *pass time* experience

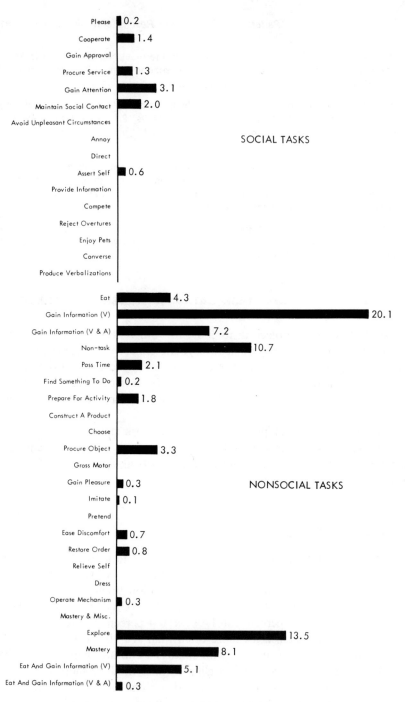

Figure 6.3 Tasks data for 1A's (N = 10)

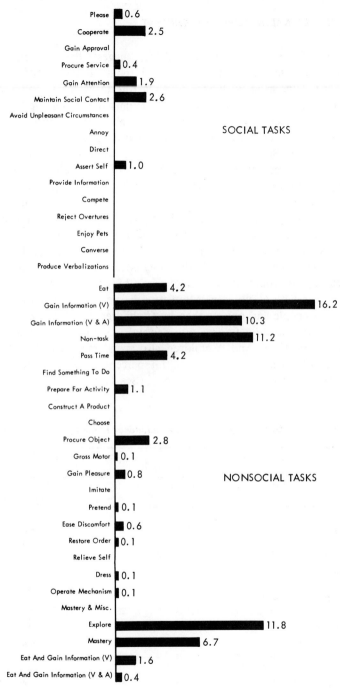

Figure 6.4 Task data for 1C's (N = 4)

(4.2 percent for 1C's vs. 2.1 percent for 1A's) suggests that C mothers may be more restrictive than A mothers at this point in their children's lives. This idea is supported by higher *to cooperate* tasks for C children at this stage. Remember, our *N,* for these data, is only four C children and ten A children; nevertheless, this difference is probably real. Furthermore, there seem to exist reasonable and obvious bases for such differences, which we shall discuss later. Suffice it to say that our C mothers seem to use playpens and gates to restrict the *gross* movements of their children much more than A mothers, especially if the child is not physically precocious.

Children who are A's seem to show more interest than do C children in exploration and mastery experiences with physical objects (21.6 percent for 1A's vs. 18.5 percent for 1C's). Although C children attend to more language than A's (10.3 percent for 1C's vs. 7.2 percent for 1A's), Table 16 shows that the language to which the A child attends is much more often from people than from a mechanical device (TV or records), whereas the opposite is true with C children. More time is spent by A children in staring steadily at people and objects than by C children (*gain information —visual* and *to eat and gain information—visual,* 25.2 percent for 1A's vs. 17.8 percent for 1C's). And A children also spend more time preparing for activities (1.8 percent for 1A's vs. 1.1 percent for 1C's), such as looking at magazines or playing with small toys. (See Table 14.)

TABLE 16. Task Data—Subanalysis, Live vs. Mechanical Language Experience

	Sample Size		Duration of Experience	Mann–Whitney Significance Data		
	N_1	N_2	Median %	U obtained	U needed	Level of Sig. 2-tailed test
Live Language						
1- vs. 2-yr.-olds	14	17	5.9 vs. 7.8	77.5	67	n.s.
1C vs. 1A subjects	4	10	2.8 vs. 6.0	8.5	5	n.s.
2C vs. 2A subjects	5	12	5.5 vs. 8.6	7.0	11	<.02
Mechanical Language						
1- vs. 2-yr.-olds	14	17	0.2 vs. 1.3	78	67	n.s.
1C vs. 1A subjects	4	10	4.9 vs. 0.0	3	5	<.02
2C vs. 2A subjects	5	12	3.1 vs. 1.8	25.5	11	n.s.
Live vs. Mech. Lang.						
1C subjects	4	4	2.8 vs. 4.9	6	<2	n.s.
1A subjects	10	10	6.0 vs. 0.0	3	23	<.002
2C subjects	5	5	5.5 vs. 3.1	9	43	n.s.
2A subjects	12	12	8.6 vs. 1.8	26.5	37	<.02

Note: The task categories involved in this analysis are all those including a primary language emphasis. The predominant category is *gain information—audio and visual.* Also included are the few instances of *to eat and gain information—audio and visual,* and other, rarer multiple categories that include *gain information—audio and visual.*

2A vs. 2C Children

Figures 6.5 and 6.6 present comparative task data for 2A and 2C children. Table 14 presents the information on which Figures 6.5 and 6.6 are based. Table 28 provides data on the statistical significance of differences in important experiences.

When children are 24 to 27 months of age, A mothers seem to make more demands than do C mothers (*to cooperate* and *to pass time,* 5.6 percent for 2A's vs. 1.7 percent for 2C's). As at one year of age, although both groups experience comparable total amounts of language (*gain information—audio and visual*), the A child's language input comes mostly from people, whereas the C's comes from television sets (see Table 15). C children make many more overtures to their mothers (*to please,* 0.4 percent for 2C's vs. 0.2 percent for 2A's); and *to achieve social contact,* 3.9 percent for 2C's vs. 2.1 percent for 2A's). Finally, C children seem to assert themselves more than A children (2.6 percent for 2C's vs. 1.2 percent for 2A's).

With respect to nonsocial tasks, both A and C children now engage in more *mastery* than *explore* activities with physical objects (mastery 9.9 percent, explore 4.2 percent for A's; mastery 10.1 percent, explore 7.9 percent for C's).* C children are now exhibiting more sustained looking behavior than A children (*gain information—visual,* 14.0 percent for 2C's vs. 13.6 percent for 2A's). Now A children attend to more language overall than do C children (*gain information—looking and listening,* 12.7 percent for 2A's vs. 6.5 percent for 2C's). Furthermore, 2A children as a group rarely watch television, getting their language primarily from people (8.6 percent live vs. 1.8 percent mechanical); 2A children spend more time than 2C's *preparing for activities* (2.5 percent for 2A's vs. 1.2 percent for 2C's). They also engage in more *pretend* or fantasy experiences than do 2C children (*role-play,* 0.9 percent for 2A's vs. 0.6 percent for 2C's); 2C children spend more time than 2A children idling (*non-tasks,* 14.3 percent for 2C's vs. 8.1 percent for 2A's).

SUBANALYSES

Language Experience

Our subjects, like all children, are exposed to language in varying degrees and fashions throughout the day. We do not measure the language environment directly when sampling the stream of experience. In many

---

* Note that A's spend proportionately more time than C's at mastery rather than exploratory behaviors, although C's engage in more of both such experiences combined than do A's.

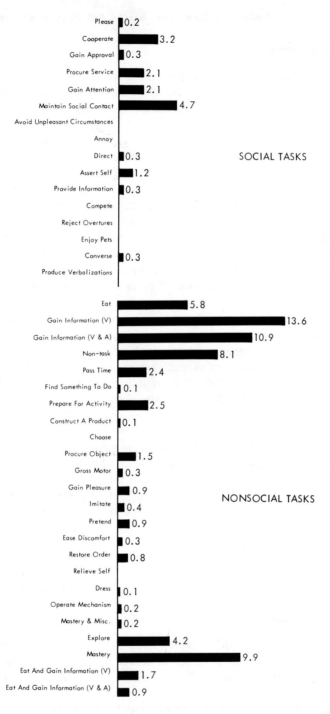

Figure 6.5 Task data for 2A's (N = 12)

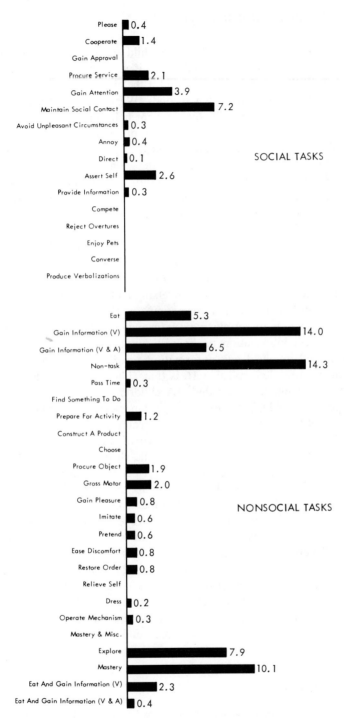

Figure 6.6 Task data for 2C's (N = 5)

instances, a few words will be attended to by a child and the event will not be coded as linguistic experience. For example, if a mother should point to a mitten and say, "Please pick that up," and if the child did so promptly, the episode would take only five to ten seconds. We would code such an experience as *to cooperate*. If a child should want help and his mother or peer should say a few words while agreeing or disagreeing, the episode would again usually be brief and would be coded as *to procure a service*. In addition, when we think a child is interacting with another, primarily to hold the other person's attention, although there may be protracted (more than fifteen seconds) language involved, we code such episodes *to maintain social contact*. In all the aforementioned situations, we lose information about linguistic input to the child.

The categories in our task system that bear the burden of directly assessing language input are *gain information through looking and listening* (*gain information—audio and visual*) and *to converse* and *provide information*. Since our subjects do very little conversing and providing information up to 27 months of age, *gain information—audio and visual* and a few multiple tasks, such as *to eat* plus *gain information—audio and visual*, contain the best direct information on linguistic input. Table 16 presents data on all tasks that involved *gain information—audio and visual*.

What is clearly revealed in Table 16 is that although 1C children, if anything, have more language input than 1A children, they get much less *live* language. One-year-old C's, for example, get language by watching television 4.9 percent of the time, whereas A's as a group do not watch television at all (0.0 percent, signif. <.02). Only two of the ten one-year-old A subjects had any television watching at all, while all four C subjects had some. When television language is eliminated, 1A children had 6.0 percent live-language scores (language spoken directly to the child or nearby), whereas 1C children had 2.8 percent of such input (n.s.).

For two-year-olds, the story is similar with respect to live versus mechanical language, although overall language input is now greater for the 2A's (2A = 12.7 percent, 2C = 6.5 percent); 2A's have more live language than 2C's (8.6 vs. 5.5 percent, signif. <.02), whereas C's have more mechanical language (3.1 vs. 1.8 percent, n.s.). (See Table 14.)

While these findings are not unexpected, they are useful, in that, unlike most reports about language experience, these are based upon extensive, directly obtained data gathered in homes and over a three-month period.

Mastery Experience

In our system, mastery experiences are those tasks a child seems to be trying in order to improve a developing skill. They are characterized

TABLE 17.   **Types of Mastery Experiences***
                Comparison Data

Group	Gross Motor Mastery**	Fine Motor Mastery**	Verbal Mastery	Unspecified Mastery	Total Mastery Experiences
1C % Time (Median)	3.2	4.1	0	0.3	6.7
1A % Time (Median)	5.4	3.5	0	0.4	8.1
2C % Time (Median)	1.6	2.2	0.4	0.3	10.1
2A % Time (Median)	3.6	3.9	0	0.3	9.9

* To improve a developing skill.
** *Fine motor mastery* refers to fine hand-eye coordination experience. All other motor mastery is classified as gross motor.

by redundancy or practice. Since important A-versus-C differences seemed to involve exploratory and mastery behaviors, we did a subanalysis of mastery experiences, to determine whether fine motor activities (mainly involving hand–eye coordination) as opposed to gross motor activities (e.g., mastering tricycle riding, etc.) would distinguish our groups. The answer in a word is no. The data are presented in Table 17.

THE IMPORTANCE OF DIFFERENT TYPES OF PHYSICAL OBJECTS.   We coded whatever objects were involved in exploratory or mastery behaviors, so we could see what types of objects were utilized by the children. More data of this sort is presented in the section dealing with environmental factors. Tables 18 and 19 present the data on object use for both *mastery* and *explore* experiences.

TABLE 18.   **Types of Objects Used in Mastery Tasks**
                (Median of % Total Duration)

Object	2-Yr.	1-Yr.	1A	1C	2A	2C
Self	0.0	0.2	0.2	0.7	0.0	0.0
Food	0.0	0.0	0.0	0.0	0.0	0.0
Clothes	0.0	0.0	0.0	0.0	0.0	0.0
Toys—small portable	1.0	2.2	1.9	2.2	0.8	1.1
Toys—large portable	0.0	0.0	0.1	0.0	0.0	0.5
Toys—large nonportable	0.0	0.0	0.0	0.0	0.0	0.0
Household—small portable	0.8	0.9	1.1	0.1	0.7	0.2
Household—large portable	0.3	0.3	0.2	0.4	0.5	0.0
Outdoor—small portable	0.0	0.0	0.0	0.0	0.0	0.0
Outdoor—large portable	0.0	0.0	0.0	0.0	0.0	0.0
Not specified	0.5	0.3	0.3	0.3	1.1	0.0
Other	0.2	0.1	0.2	0.0	0.2	0.7

TABLE 19. **Types of Objects Used in Exploration Tasks (Median of % Total Duration)**

Object	2-Yr.	1-Yr.	1A	1C	2A	2C
Self	0.0	0.0	0.0	0.0	0.0	0.0
Food	0.0	0.0	0.0	0.6	0.0	0.0
Clothes	0.0	0.0	0.0	0.0	0.0	0.1
Toys—small portable	1.5	3.9	3.9	6.0	1.6	1.4
Toys—large portable	0.0	0.0	0.1	0.0	0.0	0.0
Toys—large nonportable	0.0	0.0	0.0	0.0	0.0	0.0
Household—small portable	0.9	2.2	2.3	1.8	0.3	1.3
Household—large portable	0.4	0.2	0.2	0.4	0.5	0.3
Outdoor—small portable	0.0	0.0	0.0	0.0	0.0	0.0
Outdoor—large portable	0.0	0.0	0.0	0.0	0.0	0.0
Not specified	0.9	2.0	2.0	3.1	0.8	1.0
Other	0.0	0.2	0.3	0.1	0.0	0.0

Discussion

There are no differences across the A and C groups with regard to the various kinds of objects used for exploratory or mastery experiences. Perhaps a finer view of the events would reveal different qualities of interaction, but for the moment all we can say is that A children engage in somewhat greater amounts of such activity with physical objects during the 12-to-15-month period, and that they seem to *shift from exploration to mastery activities more rapidly than C children.* We do see, however, that small toys and small household objects are the objects that are most often used for mastery and exploration by all children.

FREQUENCY ANALYSES

GAIN ATTENTION.   The task category *to gain attention* is potentially quite important as an index of a young child's orientation toward others, especially his mother. Because of the way we gather our data, the many brief (15 seconds), successful instances of such behavior get buried. We consider such brief efforts as part of the child's larger purpose—for example, *to eat* or *to procure an object.* When, however, a young child is unusually interested in monopolizing his mother's time, such episodes are often longer in duration and fairly frequent. The duration scores tell part of the story, and, for example, 1A children seem to exhibit more of this behavior than 1C's (3.1 vs. 1.9 percent, n.s.), whereas 2C children seem to exhibit more than 2A's (3.9 vs. 2.1 percent, signif. $<.025$).

The frequency analysis (see Table 20) seems to confirm this situation, with 1A's engaging in such behavior more often than 1C's, although nonsignificantly (25.5 vs. 11 percent, n.s.), and 2C's engaging in more such attempts than 2A's (26 vs. 18 percent, n.s.).

PREPARE FOR ACTIVITY.   The task category *prepare for activity* seems to reflect a child's interest in organized, fairly goal-oriented behavior, such as procuring objects, getting something to sit on, and so on. We did a frequency analysis on this category. The results are presented in Table 20. There appear to be trends favoring A over C children and two-year-olds over one-year-olds.

PROCURE AN OBJECT.   This category would appear to reveal something about the interest that a young child has in the small physical objects of his world. It also might reflect his growing ability to procure objects rapidly as he matures; that is, if a child is able to procure an object in less than fifteen seconds it is not coded, since it is instrumental to the task he is trying to perform. It may also reveal something about the ease of avail-

TABLE 20.   Frequency of Selected Tasks, Comparison Data

| Task | Group Score (Median) | | | | Significance Data | | |
	Group	Score	Group	Score	Mann–Whitney U Value	U Needed	Significance Level
To gain attention	1A	25.5	1C	11.0	8	7 for .10 level (2-tailed)	n.s.
	2A	18.0	2C	26	17.5	12 for .05 level (1-tailed)	n.s.
	1A	25.5	2A	18.0	46	34 for .10 level (2-tailed)	n.s.
	1C	11.0	2C	26	0	>3	$p = .004$
To prepare for an activity	1A	6	1C	2.5	9	7 for .10 (1-tailed)	n.s.
	2A	9	2C	6	28.5	13 for .05 (1-tailed)	n.s.
	1A	6	2A	9	54	34 for .05 (1-tailed)	n.s.
	1C	2.5	2C	6	4.0	>3	$p = .095$ (n.s.)
To procure an object	1A	18.0	1C	6.5	7	7 for .05 (1-tailed)	$p = <.05$
	2A	7.5	2C	11	29	13 for .05 (1-tailed)	n.s.
	1A	18.0	2A	7.5	18	24 (2-tailed)	$p = <.01$
	1C	6.5	2C	11	9	>3	n.s.

Note: Frequency analysis made from fifteen 10-minute observations (9000 seconds).

ability of such items in his world. Table 20 presents data on the frequency of this task.

1A's attempt to procure objects more frequently than 1C's (18 vs. 6.5, signif. <.05). 1A's show more of such behavior than 2A's (18 vs. 7.5, signif. <.01). There were no other differences found.

INITIATION DATA

We were very much interested in the question of who initiated which experiences in the lives of our subjects. Certain categories of tasks are by definition, always initiated either by the child or by another person. These tasks are presented below:

Always self-initiated		*Always other-initiated*	
Social tasks	*Nonsocial tasks*	*Social tasks*	*Nonsocial tasks*
to please	non-task	to cooperate	pass time
to gain approval	to ease discomfort	to avoid unpleasant	
to procure a		circumstances	
service		to assert self	
to gain attention			
to maintain social			
contact			
to annoy			
to direct, dominate,			
or lead			
to reject overtures			

The remaining tasks may be initiated by the child or a variety of other people. Others who may initiate tasks are classified as mother, other adult (over seven years of age), other child, and peer (not more than one year older than a one-year-old or two years older than a two-year-old). Unfortunately, we were not careful enough about distinguishing peers from other children; therefore, we present those data in combined form. Peer-initiated tasks were very rare, except with a few two-year-old A children.

Table 21 presents comparative data on the initiation of all tasks for all groups of children.

The most striking finding in Table 21 is that over 80 percent of all experience is self-initiated. This finding will probably surprise a lot of people. Mothers initiate more tasks for one-year-olds than for two-year-olds, with 1C children having the most direct maternal influence and 2C children having the least. If a person other than the child or his mother initiates a task for a child, it is likely to be another child rather than another adult.

TABLE 21. All Tasks, % Self- vs. Other-Initiated

Group	Self-Initiated	Mother-Initiated	Other Adult-Initiated	Child-Initiated
All 1-yr.-olds	84.4	15.0	0.1	0.5
All 2-yr.-olds	89.4	9.3	0.3	1.0
1A	85.8	13.7	0.2	0.3
1C	80.3	18.8	0.0	0.9
2A	88.5	9.8	0.4	1.3
2C	91.4	8.2	0.1	0.4

Initiation Data—Social vs. Nonsocial Tasks

Table 22 presents comparative data on the initiation of social tasks. The table indicates that children initiate fewer numbers of their social tasks than of their nonsocial tasks. The direct role of mothers is of about equal magnitude for both one- and two-year-olds. Mothers of 1C children initiate more social tasks (*to cooperate* and *to assert self*) for their children than is the case with any other group. In addition, other children initiate more of the social tasks of 1C children than of any other group. One-year-old A and two-year-old C children are the most self-directive groups with regard to social tasks.

Table 23 presents comparative data on the initiation of nonsocial tasks.

Table 23 reaffirms the notion that one- and two-year-old children initiate the major portion of their own experiences. The most striking group in this respect are the 2C children, with 96.0 self-initiation of nonsocial

TABLE 22. Social Tasks, % Self- vs. Other-Initiated

Group	Self-Initiated	Mother-Initiated	Other Adult-Initiated	Child-Initiated
All 1-yr.-olds	65.2	32.0	1.1	1.8
All 2-yr.-olds	71.0	25.7	1.0	2.2
1A	67.1	30.4	1.5	1.0
1C	59.9	36.2	0.0	3.9
2A	70.0	25.7	1.3	3.0
2C	73.1	25.8	0.3	0.7

TABLE 23. **Nonsocial Tasks, % Self- vs. Other-Initiated**

Group	Self-Initiated	Mother-Initiated	Other Adult-Initiated	Child-Initiated
All 1-yr.-olds	86.7	13.0	0.0	0.3
All 2-yr.-olds	93.4	5.7	0.2	0.7
1A	88.1	11.6	0.0	0.2
1C	82.8	16.7	0.0	0.5
2A	92.3	6.6	0.2	0.9
2C	96.0	3.7	0.0	0.3

tasks. Laissez-faire is the order of the day with all groups except the 1C children, whose mothers are more intrusive in regard to nonsocial tasks than any other group (16.7 percent). A large factor in this situation is likely to be the use of playpens and cribs by mothers of physically immature 1C children, which results in high *pass time* scores. People other than the child himself and his mother initiate fewer of the child's nonsocial than social tasks. There is a trend toward greater self-initiation of nonsocial tasks with increasing age.

Initiation Data—Specific Social Tasks

Unlike the case with nonsocial tasks, the only social tasks that occur in any great amounts (0.9 percent or more) that are not by definition self-initiated are *to cooperate* and *to assert self,* both of which are, by definition, always other-initiated. The only interesting questions about those categories are how often they occur and who initiates them. We have already shown how often they occur in Table 14. Who initiates them can be seen in Tables 24 and 25.

The first point to be made about Table 24 is that most *to cooperate* tasks of these one- and two-year-olds were initiated by their mothers. The second point is that the older the child, the more people other than his mother began to make more requests of him. A third point is that other children initiated more *to cooperate* tasks with 1C children than with any other group.

Comparable data on *assert self* tasks is presented in Table 25.

To *assert self* is the child's task when another person invades his territory or tries to dominate him somehow, and the child resists. Such experience is always initiated by his mother in the case of our one-year-old subjects, whereas other children are occasionally the instigators with our

TABLE 24. **Source of Initiation of *To Cooperate* Tasks**

Group	Mother-Initiated	Other Adult-Initiated	Child-Initiated
All 1-yr.-olds	92.8	2.0	5.2
All 2-yr.-olds	88.9	4.9	6.3
1A	94.3	3.0	2.7
1C	89.8	0.0	10.2
2A	88.0	5.6	6.4
2C	92.3	1.9	5.8

two-year-olds, especially with 2A children. This is probably because a few more of our 2A children are in regular contact with children than is the case with our 2C children.

Initiation Data—Specific Nonsocial Tasks

There are many more types of nonsocial than social tasks that can be initiated by others in our system and probably in the life of the child in general. Table 26 presents information about the source of initiation of all such tasks.

Mothers of 1A children initiate more of the following types of experiences than mothers of 1C children: *to eat* (12.6 vs. 5.4 percent); *to gain information—visual* (2.6 vs. 1.0 percent); *to gain information—visual and auditory* (19.9 vs. 6.8 percent); *to eat and gain information—visual* (15.3 vs. 0.0 percent); *to explore* (5.9 vs. 2.4 percent); and *to improve a developing skill* (8.5 vs. 1.8 percent). Mothers of 1C children initiate,

TABLE 25. **Source of Initiation of *To Assert Self* Tasks**

Group	Mother-Initiated	Other Adult-Initiated	Child-Initiated
All 1-yr.-olds	100.0	0.0	0.0
All 2-yr.-olds	96.0	0.4	3.6
1A	100.0	0.0	0.0
1C	100.0	0.0	0.0
2A	94.0	0.7	5.3
2C	98.6	0.0	1.4

TABLE 26. The Source of Initiation of Nonsocial Tasks for 1A vs. 1C Children

	1A				1C			
Task	Self-Initiated	Mother-Initiated	Other Adult-Initiated	Child-Initiated	Self-Initiated	Mother-Initiated	Other Adult-Initiated	Child-Initiated
To eat	86.1	12.6	0.0	1.2	92.8	5.4	0.0	1.8
To gain info (visual)	97.4	2.6	0.0	0.0	97.3	1.0	0.0	1.7
To gain info (visual and auditory)	79.7	19.9	0.0	0.4	93.2	6.8	0.0	0.0
To prepare for activity	91.7	8.3	0.0	0.0	93.9	6.1	0.0	0.0
To procure an object	95.6	4.3	0.0	0.2	87.7	12.3	0.0	0.0
To eat and gain info (visual)	84.7	15.3	0.0	0.0	100.0	0.0	0.0	0.0
To explore	93.5	5.9	0.0	0.5	97.2	2.4	0.0	0.3
To improve a developing skill (mastery)	91.3	8.5	0.0	0.3	98.2	1.8	0.0	0.0

more than mothers of 1A children, more of the following type of experiences: *to procure an object* (12.3 vs. 4.3 percent). We remind the reader, however, that in general, mothers of 1C children initiate more of the non-social tasks of their children than do mothers of 1A children (16.7 vs. 11.6 percent).

Of all the tasks above, when they are other-initiated, it is usually the mother rather than anyone else who precipitates the experience. Perhaps the most important findings are the higher number of *to gain information— auditory and visual, to explore* and *to improve a developing skill* tasks initiated by mothers of 1A children.

Comparable data for two-year-old subjects are presented in Table 27.

Mothers of 2A children initiate more than mothers of 2C children of the following activities: *to prepare for activity* (14.2 vs. 1.5 percent); *to improve a developing skill* (3.3 vs. 2.2 percent); and *to procure an object* (3.7 vs. 2.9 percent). Mothers of 2C children initiate more than mothers of 2A children of the following activities: *to eat* (5.5 vs. 3.4 percent); *to gain pleasure* (9.2 vs. 0.0 percent); and *to pretend* (2.8 vs. 0.0 percent). Here again, we must remind the reader that 2C children initiate 91.4 percent of their own experience vs. 88.5 percent for 2A children. We saw other children initiating more tasks for our two-year-olds than for our one-year-olds, especially in the case of our 2A children (*to prepare for activity,* 4.3 percent; *to gain pleasure,* 6.0 percent). Even so, when tasks were other-initiated, it was more often by the mother than by anyone else.

Perhaps two points are worthy of special mention: the fact that mothers of 2A children seemed to encourage more activities that involved lengthy preparations; and the fact that mothers of 2C children initiated horseplay-type experiences for their children in noticeable amounts, whereas other children were the other-initiators of *gain pleasure* experiences for 2A children. Again, the reader must be reminded that he should refer to Table 14 for information on the total amount of each task for each group. For example, in the case of *gain pleasure* experiences, 2A children had 0.9 percent as an average total score for such experience, as contrasted to 0.8 percent for 2C children.

We designed our longitudinal natural experiment to uncover differences in experiences regularly associated with excellent or poor development. Our statistical analyses are therefore typically two-tailed, since we are seeking differences rather than predicting them. We were, however, in a position before we began collecting data to make some predictions about the probable direction of certain differences in experience. Those predictions were listed at the beginning of this chapter. Table 28 presents information on those predictions for all subjects, for the 12-to-15- and 24-to-27-month periods.

Generally, our predictions were borne out. The results were nearly

TABLE 27. The Source of Initiation of Nonsocial Tasks for 2A vs. 2C Children

Task	2A				2C			
	Self-Initiated	Mother-Initiated	Other Adult-Initiated	Child-Initiated	Self-Initiated	Mother-Initiated	Other Adult-Initiated	Child-Initiated
To eat	96.4	3.4	0.0	0.2	94.5	5.5	0.0	0.0
To gain info (visual)	99.0	0.9	0.0	0.1	99.0	1.0	0.0	0.0
To gain info (visual and auditory)	95.8	2.5	0.3	1.5	96.8	3.2	0.0	0.0
To prepare for activity	80.2	14.2	1.3	4.3	96.2	1.5	0.0	2.3
To procure an object	93.7	3.7	2.6	0.0	96.4	2.9	0.0	0.7
To gain pleasure	94.0	0.0	0.0	6.0	90.8	9.2	0.0	0.0
To pretend (role play)	100.0	0.0	0.0	0.0	100.0	2.8	0.0	0.0
To eat and gain info (visual)	100.0	0.0	0.0	0.0	99.6	0.0	0.4	0.0
To explore	98.3	0.5	0.0	1.3	98.4	0.7	0.0	0.9
To improve a developing skill (mastery)	96.1	3.3	0.0	0.6	96.8	2.2	0.0	1.0

TABLE 28. Task Data, Statistical Analysis of Hypotheses

Hypotheses	Sample Size		Duration of Experience	Mann–Whitney Significance Data		
	N_1	N_2	Median %	U obtained	U needed	Level of Sig. 1-Tailed
1-yr. A's spend more time than 1-yr. C's in:						
Explore	10	4	13.5 vs. 11.8	19	7	n.s.
Mastery	10	4	8.1 vs. 6.7	19	7	n.s.
Explore and master	10	4	21.6 vs. 18.5	18	7	n.s.
Procure an object	10	4	3.3 vs. 2.4	12.5	7	n.s.
1-yr. C's spend more time than 1-yr. A's in:						
All social tasks	4	10	8.25 vs. 10.5	18	7	n.s.
Gain attention and maintain social contact	4	10	4.65 vs. 5.1	14.5	7	n.s.
Pass time	4	10	4.2 vs. 2.1	19	7	n.s.
2-yr. A's spend more time than 2-yr. C's in:						
Prepare for activity	12	5	2.45 vs. 1.2	18	13	n.s.
Construct a product	12	5	0.1 vs. 0.0	15	13	n.s.
Prepare for activity and construct a product	12	5	3.3 vs. 1.2	16	13	n.s.
Mastery	12	5	9.9 vs. 10.1	23.5	13	n.s.
Role play	12	5	0.9 vs. 0.6	27	13	n.s.
Cooperate	12	5	3.2 vs. 1.4	17	13	n.s.
2-yr. C's spend more time than 2-yr. A's in:						
All social tasks	5	12	20.6 vs. 17.25	25	13	n.s.
Assert self, annoy, avoid unpleasant circumstances	5	12	4.3 vs. 1.25	8	13	$<.01$
Gain attention and maintain social contact	5	12	12.3 vs. 7.0	13	13	.05
Non-task	5	12	14.3 vs. 8.1	34	13	n.s.
Procure an object and procure a service	5	12	3.6 vs. 4.2	23	13	n.s.
Explore	5	12	7.9 vs. 4.25	19.5	13	n.s.
2-yr. C's spend more time than 1-yr. C's in:						
Non-task	5	4	14.3 vs. 11.2	11	>3	n.s.
Mastery and explore	5	4	14.6 vs. 22.9	7	>3	n.s.
All social tasks	5	4	20.6 vs. 8.4	3	>3	$p = .056$
Assert self, annoy, avoid unpleasant circumstances	5	4	4.3 vs. 1.1	6	>3	n.s.
Maintain social contact	5	4	7.2 vs. 2.75	2	>3	$p = .032$
1-yr. C's spend more time than 2-yr. C's in:						
Pass time	4	5	4.2 vs. 0.3	6	>3	n.s.

TABLE 28. (continued)

Hypotheses	Sample Size		Duration of Experience	Mann–Whitney Significance Data		
	N_1	N_2	Median %	U obtained	U needed	Level of Sig. 1-Tailed
2-yr. A's spend more time than 1-yr. A's in:						
Prepare for activity and construct a product	12	10	2.55 vs. 1.8	33.5	34	<.05
Mastery	12	10	9.5 vs. 8.1	55	34	n.s.
Role play	12	10	0.9 vs. 0.0	5	34	<.001
Converse and provide information	12	10	0.7 vs. 0.0	6.5	34	<.001
Gain approval	12	10	0.4 vs. 0.0	39	34	n.s.
1-yr. A's spend more time than 2-yr. A's in:						
All social tasks	10	12	10.5 vs. 17.25	22	34	<.01
Explore	10	12	13.5 vs. 4.25	12	34	<.001
Procure an object	10	12	3.3 vs. 1.55	34	34	<.05

always in the predicted direction (26 out of 31 predictions). Two of twelve differences were statistically significant for two-year-olds. For one-year-olds, none of the differences were statistically significant. The possible significance of these differences for good child-rearing practices is discussed in the last chapter of this book.

7

Case Studies in the Light of the Competence and Experience Data

Burton L. White/Barbara Kaban/Janice Marmor—Bernice Shapiro

In this chapter we will attempt to provide coherent portraits of nine of our subjects based upon the competence and task data. These subjects have been selected in order to illustrate major ideas that have emerged from our work. We will discuss these children in pairs—that is, a 1A boy will be compared to a 1C boy, and so on. In the next chapter, three of these nine children, subjects 1, 3, 7, will be described on the basis of data collected by the environment group. The final chapter consists of an overall discussion and summary.

The first pair of subjects to be discussed are number 1, a 1C girl, and number 3, a 1A girl.

SUBJECT #1

Background Data

Subject number 1 is a (Class Position IV) one-year-old C girl. She is the youngest of thirteen children who range in age from one to nineteen years. Both parents are high school graduates, and the oldest child is at present attending a state university.

The family lives in a small, well-worn seven-room house that is sparsely furnished. The major source of entertainment for the family seems to be the large color television, which is often on most of the day.

This subject is a sturdy little girl who is physically and socially mature for her age. In the mornings she is at home with her mother and two-and-a-half-year-old sister. The mother is a warm, loving woman who is usually busy with household chores. Most of her interaction with the subject is centered around food.

By noontime, different siblings and the father start arriving home. The subject is the recipient of a lot of affectionate hugging and kissing, but very little interaction of any other type occurs. She is usually left to roam freely around the house, and since there are very few toys available to her—and even fewer that are appropriate for a one-year-old—she spends most of her time watching television or wandering from room to room.

Discussion of Test Performance

Subject number 1 is a physically and socially mature one-year-old C child who consistently scores at the top of the one-year C group on most of our tests. Most of her test scores are above the group median for C subjects and, in fact, fall on or above the one-year A group medians, particularly at 12 and 15 months.* By 21 months, she still ranked highest among the C's, but she now scores below the A group median on two of the three tests (language and abstract thinking). On the discrepancies test she was still above the A group median of 3.25, with a score of 5. Her Bayley Mental Development Index clearly indicates her superiority at 12 months (MDI = 134), which then declined to a more average performance by 24 months (MDI = 112).

Subject 1's test scores reflect the fact that she excels in language comprehension and in the physical dexterity required in portions of the Bayley and abstract thinking tests. In addition, her social maturity and easy-going disposition allow for a smooth and comfortable testing situation. She is patient, attentive, alert, and eager to please. She is highly motivated by the praise of her mother and the examiner, and enjoys and understands the idea of "playing a game." She is able to understand and follow directions and takes much pleasure in the undivided attention of the examiner, all of which create an optimal testing situation.

Social Competence

Subject 1 is a child whose large family group has enabled her to develop a high degree of social competence with peers. Her score of 24.3

* See Appendix.

TABLE 29. **Summary of Test Scores**

Subject: No. 1   Group: 1-year C

Tests	S's Score	Group Median	S's Rank	No. of S's Rank of that Rank
Bayley (MD1) 12 m.	134	99	1/4	—
24 m.	112	110.5 (N = 2)	1/2	—
Language Test				
at 12 mos.	16	11.5	1/3	—
at 15 mos.	21	16	1/3	—
at 21 mos.	27	25.5	1/2	—
at 24 mos.	40.5	35.75 (N = 2)	1/2	—
Abstract Abilities				
at 12 mos.	11.0	9.5	2/4	—
at 15 mos.	15.5	11.0	1/3	—
at 21 mos.	16.5	16.5	1/2	—
at 24 mos.	20.5	18.5 (N = 2)	1/2	—
Discrimination				
at 12 mos.	L.0	L.0	2/2	—
at 15 mos.	L.3	L.3	1/2	—
at 21 mos.	L.5	L.4	1/2	—
at 24 mos.	L3.5	L.3.75 (N = 2)	2/2	—

The following tests are included in Summary of Test Scores tables:
   Bayley Scales of Infant Development
   Stanford–Binet Intelligence Scale
   Preschool Project Test of Receptive Language Ability
   Preschool Project Test of Abstract Thinking Ability
   Preschool Project Test of Ability to Sense Discrepancies

All scores are developmental ages expressed in months, with the exception of the Bayley score, which is expressed as a mental development index (MDI), and the Stanford–Binet, which is an IQ score.

S = Subject
L = Level

on this dimension is so outstanding that it puts her on the top of the list of one-year-olds in her ability to *lead* and *follow peers, compete,* and *express affection* and *hostility to peers.* However, the picture changes markedly upon examination of her adult competence score, 6.4. It appears as though the subject makes little attempt to interact with adults in her environment, except possibly for those times when only an adult can serve as a helper to a one-year-old child. Otherwise, she shows no ability either *to gain attention* or *to express affection* and *hostility to adults.* An inspection of her *compliance/noncompliance* ratio of 3.3, which is above average, shows that she tends to go along with what adults require of her; there is no evidence of unusual assertiveness or resistance to adults. The adult whom she interacts with most is her mother, although several siblings over seven years old are occasionally present.

```
                                    SOCIAL COMPETENCE FOR SUBJECT 1

        GAIN            0     C                         A
        ADULT           0     |                         |
        ATTENTION       0
                        0
        USE             0                    C        A
        ADULT           OXXXXXXXXXXXXXXXXXXXXXXXXXXXX
        RESOURCE        OXXXXXXXXXXXXXXXXXXXXXXXXXXXX  |
                        0
        HOSTILITY       0          A           C
        AFFECTION       OXXXXXXX   |           |
        TO ADULT        OXXXXXXX   |           |
                        0
        ROLE PLAY      A0C
                        |
                        0
                        0
        PRIDE IN       C0 A
        PRODUCT         |  |
                        0
                        0
        COMPETES        0    A                                           C
        WITH            OXXXXXXXXXXXXXXXXXXXXXXXXXXXXXXXXXXXXXXXXXXXXXX
        PEER            OXXXXXXXXXXXXXXXXXXXXXXXXXXXXXXXXXXXXXXXXXXXXXX
                        0
        HOSTILITY       0      A                  C
        AFFECTION       OXXXXXXXXXXXXXXXXXXXXXXXXXXXXX
        TO PEER         OXXXXXXXXXXXXXXXXXXXXXXXXXXXXX
                        0
        LEADS AND       0      A                                          C
        FOLLOWS         OXXXXXXXXXXXXXXXXXXXXXXXXXXXXXXXXXXXXXXXXXXXXXXXX
        PEER            OXXXXXXXXXXXXXXXXXXXXXXXXXXXXXXXXXXXXXXXXXXXXXXXX
                        0
                        0   1   2   3   4   5   6   7   8   9   10
```

	S#1	1A	1C
Adult Competence	6.4	17.3	10.6
Peer Competence	24.3	7.9	24.3
Overall Competence	30.7	20.1	30.7
Compliance/Non-Compliance Ratio	3.3	2.3	2.6

* These marks indicate central tendency scores for 1A and 1C children on each dimension of social competence.

Figure 7.1

SUBJECT #3

Background Data

Subject number 3 is a (Class Position III) one-year-old A girl. She is an active, alert little girl. Both parents are college graduates and the father has advanced degrees.

At the outset of the study, the family lived in a six-room apartment in a residential area. The apartment was functionally furnished but not elaborate. She shared a bedroom with her sister, and this room seemed to overflow with their toys. She was not restricted within the apartment, and her toys were usually scattered throughout. During the study, the family moved to a large private home with spacious grounds. In addition to their bedroom, the children now have a very large playroom, which seems to contain every toy imaginable. Again this child has access to the whole house but spends most of her time in the playroom. Her mother is easily available and will often spend time reading or playing with her.

Discussion of Test Performance

Subject 3 is a one-year-old A child whose test scores are just on or below the median at 12 and 15 months, including her Bayley MDI of 102 (median = 103). She ranks just below the middle of the A group on these tests and is quite unremarkable in test performance until she is tested at 21 months. At 21 and 24 months, she shows a marked improvement, particularly on the Bayley test (MDI = 143 at 24 months) and the discrepancies test (Level 8 at 21 months, versus group median of 3.25), and on the language test at 24 months (she scores at 51 months). By 24 months, this child has shown herself to be one of the outstanding one-year-old A subjects in terms of test results.

Her general behavior during test sessions reflects the change in her scores. At 12 and 15 months, subject 3 was a pleasant, cooperative, but unremarkable subject. By 21 months, however, she had become a mature

TABLE 30. Summary of Test Scores

Subject: No. 3   Group: 1-year A

Tests	S's Score	Group Median	S's Rank	No. of S's Tied at that Rank
Bayley (MDI) 12 m	102	103	7/9	3
24 m	143	127.5	1/4	—
Language Test				
at 12 mos.	14	16	4/7	2
at 15 mos.	16	17	4/5	4
at 21 mos.	36	36	3/4	3
at 24 mos.	51	40.5	1/4	—
Abstract Abilities				
at 12 mos.	11.0	15.5	4/5	2
at 15 mos.	15.5	15.5	6/6	—
at 21 mos.	24.5	22.5	2/6	2
at 24 mos.	24.5	24.5	1/2	3
Discrimination				
at 12 mos.	L.2	L.2	2/4	5
at 15 mos.	L.2	L.2	2/4	6
at 21 mos.	L.8	L.3.25	1/6	—
at 24 mos.	L.7	L.7	1/2	3

and verbal young lady who looked forward to "playing games" with the examiner and was happy to sit still and remain attentive for over an hour (at her request) during a testing situation. Her grasp of concepts such as color and form matching, understanding of "same" and "different," and comprehension of grammatical constructs (including negatives: "can, can't"; size comparisons: "long, short"; and time designations: "before, after") were clearly outstanding for her age level.

Social Competence

Subject 3 is a one-year-old whose social interactions are frequent and generally positive and successful in nature. She has attained the highest social-competence score of any of our one-year-old subjects: 38.1 for an overall competence score. Her social behavior is characterized by frequent attempts *to gain an adult's attention* and *to utilize adults as resources,* as well as by an ability *to express affection* and *hostility to adults and peers.* Compared to other one-year-olds of her general competence level, she shows an unusually high frequency on *competition with peers* and *expressions of pride in product.* At age one, she tended *to comply with adult directives* more than twice as often as she would resist them, which is average for one-year-olds, and tended *to imitate adult behavior* more often than did other one-year-olds. She is a child who as early as age one has shown a significant ability to master her social world, having shown above-average ability on six out of the eight dimensions of social competence. The adult she interacts with most frequently is her mother, and her peer contact is mainly with her older sister, aged four.

TASK DATA

Social Tasks, Subjects 1 and 3

Figures 7.3 and 7.4 present social-task data for subjects 1 and 3. The social experiences of these children appear rather similar. There are three differences of possible consequence. The 1A child made more *to please* overtures toward her mother than did the 1C child. These events involve the child either offering something to her mother or spontaneously expressing affection toward her. The 1C child, on the other hand, showed more of an interest in clinging to her mother or following her about (*to maintain social contact*). In addition, the 1C child showed a fair amount of resistance to suggestions or intrusions on her domain (*to assert self*) than our 1A child. This 1C child has twelve brothers and sisters, the youngest of whom is only one and a half years older than she. It is a very warm and happy family, but our subject has had to learn to stand

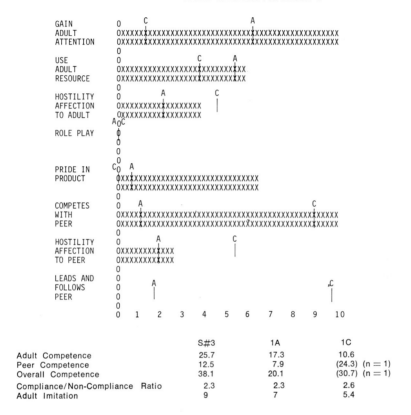

SOCIAL COMPETENCE FOR SUBJECT 3

	S#3	1A	1C
Adult Competence	25.7	17.3	10.6
Peer Competence	12.5	7.9	(24.3) (n = 1)
Overall Competence	38.1	20.1	(30.7) (n = 1)
Compliance/Non-Compliance Ratio	2.3	2.3	2.6
Adult Imitation	9	7	5.4

Figure 7.2

up for her rights at a very tender age. To us, this behavior represents precocity at this age. In general, this child is precocious in many ways, as is shown by her very high score on the Bayley test of general development.

In contrast, our 1A child who has only one sister and no brothers spent much more time alone with her mother.

Nonsocial Tasks, Subjects 1 and 3

Figures 7.3 and 7.4 present nonsocial-task data for subjects 1 and 3. In their nonsocial experiences, these children differed rather considerably. Our 1C child had almost no physical materials to play with. There were virtually no toys she could call her own, and she had only partial access

SUBJECT NUMBER 1   SUBJECT CLASS 1C   99.4 % OF OBSERVED TIME REPRESENTED

SOCIAL TASKS

```
TO PLEASE                               0==
TO COOPERATE                            0==
TO GAIN APPROVAL                        0=
TO PROCURE A SERVICE                    0===
TO GAIN ATTENTION                       0===
TO MAINTAIN SOCIAL CONTACT              0
TO AVOID UNPLEASANT CIRCUMSTANCES       0
TO ANNOY                                0
TO DIRECT                               0==
TO ASSERT SELF (PROTECT DOMAIN)         0
TO PROVIDE INFORMATION                  0
TO COMPETE                              0
TO REJECT OVERTURES                     0
TO ENJOY PETS                           0
TO CONVERSE                             0
TO PRODUCE VERBALIZATIONS               0
```

NON-SOCIAL TASKS

```
TO EAT                                          0===========
TO GAIN INFORMATION - VISUAL                    0===============
TO GAIN INFORMATION - VISUAL AND AUDITORY       0==================
NON-TASK                                        0=
TO PASS TIME                                    0==
TO FIND SOMETHING TO DO                         0==
TO PREPARE FOR AN ACTIVITY                      0=
TO CONSTRUCT A PRODUCT                          0=
TO CHOOSE                                       0===
TO PROCURE AN OBJECT                            0==
TO ENGAGE IN LARGE MUSCLE ACTIVITY              0
TO GAIN PLEASURE                                0
TO IMITATE                                      0
TO PRETEND (ROLE PLAY)                          0=
TO EASE DISCOMFORT                              0
TO RESTORE ORDER                                0
TO RELIEVE ONESELF                              0
TO DRESS/UNDRESS                                0
TO OPERATE A MECHANISM                          0
TO EAT AND TO GAIN INFORMATION (VISUAL)         0=====
TO EAT AND TO GAIN INFORMATION (VISUAL AND AUDITORY)  0
TO EXPLORE                                      0============
TO IMPROVE A DEVELOPING SKILL (MASTERY)         0=====
                                                0123456789012345678901234567890123456789 0
                                                    10        20        30        40      50
```

TASK DATA (% OF TOTAL TIME)

Figure 7.3 (These percents have been rounded off to the nearest whole percent.)

```
SUBJECT NUMBER  3                      SUBJECT CLASS 1A
                                                 100.0 % OF OBSERVED TIME REPRESENTED
              SOCIAL TASKS
TO PLEASE                                       0==
TO COOPERATE                                    0==
TO GAIN APPROVAL                                0=
TO PROCURE A SERVICE                            0==
TO GAIN ATTENTION                               0===
TO MAINTAIN SOCIAL CONTACT                      0==
TO AVOID UNPLEASANT CIRCUMSTANCES               0
TO ANNOY                                        0
TO DIRECT                                       0
TO ASSERT SELF (PROTECT DOMAIN)                 0
TO PROVIDE INFORMATION                          0
TO COMPETE                                      0
TO REJECT OVERTURES                             0
TO ENJOY PETS                                   0
TO CONVERSE                                     0
TO PRODUCE VERBALIZATIONS                       0
             NON-SOCIAL TASKS
TO EAT                                          0====
TO GAIN INFORMATION - VISUAL                    0===================
TO GAIN INFORMATION - VISUAL ANDAUDITORY        0======
NON-TASK                                        0=========
TO PASS TIME                                    0======
TO FIND SOMETHING TO DO                         0
TO PREPARE FOR AN ACTIVITY                      0=
TO CONSTRUCT A PRODUCT                          0=
TO CHOOSE                                       0
TO PROCURE AN OBJECT                            0==
TO ENGAGE IN LARGE MUSCLE ACTIVITY              0
TO GAIN PLEASURE                                0
TO IMITATE                                      0
TO PRETEND (ROLE PLAY)                          0
TO EASE DISCOMFORT                              0
TO RESTORE ORDER                                0
TO RELIEVE ONESELF                              0
TO DRESS/UNDRESS                                0
TO OPERATE A MECHANISM                          0=
TO EAT AND TO GAIN INFORMATION (VISUAL)         0========
TO EAT AND TO GAIN INFORMATION (VISUAL AND AUDITORY) 0=
TO EXPLORE                                      0=================
TO IMPROVE A DEVELOPING SKILL (MASTERY          0============
                                                012345678901234567890123456789012345678901234567890
                                                0         10        20        30        40        50

                                     TASK DATA (% OF TOTAL TIME)
```

Figure 7.4 *(These percents have been rounded off to the nearest whole percent.)*

to the rather sparse furnishings in the kitchen. She spent the bulk of her day wandering around the kitchen and living room of the home. The 1A child, in sharp contrast, had an incredible array of toys available to her, as well as a fully equipped kitchen, although her mother did not invite her to examine the contents of kitchen cabinets as often as did some of our mothers. The results seem to be reflected in the *explore, mastery,* and *non-task* categories, which are quite different. While our 1A child was very frequently engrossed in mastery experiences with small mechanical or stacking toys, our 1C child was more likely to be wandering about or eating. There was a remarkable amount of eating in the life of this 1C child. Even though both children have fairly equal amounts of language experience, our 1A child had 5.3 percent *live* language experience, versus 2.3 percent for our 1C child. Our 1C child had 0.9 percent television language, versus none for our 1A child. The mother of our 1A child controlled her daughter more than did the mother of our 1C child, as can be seen in the very large difference in *pass time* scores. In fact, our 1C child was left to her own pursuits far more often than our 1A child. This high 1A *pass time* score was predominantly due to regular auto trips in a car seat, when mother and daughter went to pick up the older child at the nursery school.

Task-Initiation Data

The source of initiation of tasks for subjects 1 and 3 is illustrated in Tables 31 and 32. It can be seen that both children initiated almost all their own experiences, especially the nonsocial experiences. With regard to social tasks, it may be notable that our 1C girl, with twelve siblings, had many of such tasks initiated by other children (8.0 percent), whereas our 1A child, with only one older sister, had none.

Turning to individual experiences, we find that our 1C's mother initiated the following tasks: to cooperate (44.4 percent), assert self (100.0 percent), gain information—visual (0.3 percent), pass time (100.0 percent), procure an object (21.7 percent), and mastery (3.3 percent). The mother of our 1A child initiated the following tasks: information—visual (4.1 percent), pass time (100.0 percent), to explore (0.3 percent), and mastery (3.6 percent).

The most interesting difference is that the 1A child's mother initiated more language experiences, more *cooperate* experiences, and much less *prepare for activity, explore,* and *mastery* tasks. In the case of the last two important areas, the mother of our 1A child had her influence by providing a rich, stimulating environment, but not apparently by actually directing her child to act on that environment.

TABLE 31. **Source of Initiation of Tasks**

Subject: No. 1   Group: 1C

		Source of Initiation (% Time)			
Task	Total Task Time, % Duration	% Duration Self-Initiated	% Duration Mother-Initiated	% Duration Other Adult-Initiated	% Duration Child-Initiated
All tasks		96.1	1.6		2.3
All social tasks		88.4	3.6		8.0
All nonsocial tasks		98.7	1.1		0.2
Social tasks					
To please	0.1	100.0			
To cooperate	1.5		44.4		55.6
To gain approval	0.0				
To procure a service	1.2	100.0			
To gain attention	2.7	100.0			
To maintain social contact	3.0	100.0			
To direct	0.0				
To assert self	2.0		100.0		
To converse	0.0				
Nonsocial tasks					
To gain info (v)	18.5	99.7	0.3		
To gain info (v and a)	4.4	100.0			
Non-task	20.7	100.0			
Pass time	0.9		100.0		
Prepare for activity	2.3	100.0			
Construct a product	1.1	100.0			
Procure an object	2.6	78.3	21.7		
Gross motor activity	0.0				
Gain pleasure	1.0	100.0			
Imitate	0.3	100.0			
Pretend	0.3	100.0			
Ease discomfort	0.7	100.0			
Restore order	0.2	100.0			
Eat and gain info (v)	5.2	100.0			
Eat and gain info (v and a)	0.3	100.0			
Explore	13.8	98.8			1.2
Mastery	3.5	96.7	3.3		
Eat	12.9	96.9			3.1
Mastery and misc.					

The next pair of subjects to be compared consists of two one-year-old boys, subjects number 32 (1A) and 34 (1C).

TABLE 32. **Source of Initiation of Tasks**

Subject: No. 3   Group: 1A

		Source of Initiation (% Time)			
Task	Total Task Time, % Duration	% Duration Self- Initiated	% Duration Mother- Initiated	% Duration Other Adult- Initiated	% Duration Child- Initiated
All tasks		96.6	3.3	0.1	0
All social tasks		86.8	12.5	0.7	0
All nonsocial tasks		98.3	1.7		
Social tasks					
To please	2.1	100.0			
To cooperate	1.9		100.0		
To gain approval	0.7	100.0			
To procure a service	1.6	100.0			
To gain attention	2.9	100.0			
To maintain social contact	1.6	100.0			
To direct	0.0				
To assert self	0.3		100.0		
To converse	0.2	100.0			
Nonsocial tasks					
To gain info (v)	18.9	95.9	4.1		
To gain info (v and a)	5.6	100.0			
Non-task	9.3	100.0			
Pass time	5.9		100.0		
Prepare for activity	0.6	100.0			
Construct a product	0.8	100.0			
Procure an object	2.3	100.0			
Gross motor activity	0.0				
Gain pleasure	0.0				
Imitate	0.1	100.0			
Pretend	0.0				
Ease discomfort	0.5	100.0			
Restore order	0.4	100.0			
Eat and gain info (v)	7.9	100.0			
Eat and gain info (v and a)	0.9	100.0			
Explore	17.5	99.7	0.3		
Mastery	12.3	96.4	3.6		
Eat	4.5	100.0			
Mastery and misc.					

SUBJECT #32

Background Data

Subject 32 is a (Class Position IV) one-year-old boy. He is the youngest child in a family of eight children ranging in age from one to nineteen years. The family owns their own home, a small house in South Boston that consists of seven rooms. Interior space is very limited. The house is nicely furnished and always neat. There is no yard. The neighborhood children play on the sidewalk. The first floor consists of three rooms: living room, kitchen, and bedroom. The kitchen is between the other two rooms, and it is the heart of the house. A large table takes up most of the space in the kitchen.

This subject is an ebullient little boy whose characteristic facial expression is one of good humor. He is very active. (He learned to walk at the age of 9 months.) He enjoys movement: climbing kitchen chairs, chasing his sister around the small living room, bouncing on the bed, walking up and down the kitchen table. Within the limits of the first floor, he is permitted maximum mobility. Both parents are permissive in regard to the subject's tendency to use family furniture for his own active purposes (the father has been observed twirling the subject on the lazy susan that is the centerpiece of the kitchen table). The major limitation on the child's freedom was a gate across the stairway, which prevents him from getting to the second floor whenever he wants to do so (usually in order to keep up with a sibling).

The child's mornings are spent alone with his mother (all siblings are in school). At lunchtime there is a high flow of people in and out: father, father's friends, brothers and sisters and their friends.

The atmosphere in this household is warm and congenial. The child's mother keeps an affectionate eye on him from the central vantage point of the kitchen. She checks up on him regularly but does not hover over him. Although she does not speak very much, she quietly encourages exploratory activities, such as finding out what's under the kitchen sink or what's behind the bed. When the child becomes overactive, his mother attempts to interest him in small toys (tops that spin, cars that wind) or quiet activities such as "reading" the newspaper on her lap. Although the child has been encouraged to watch "Sesame Street," so far he is not interested in sitting still and looking at a television screen.

Discussion of Test Performance

Subject 32 is a very active and friendly one-year-old A child whose test scores are rather inconsistent, but are generally on or below the medians for the one-year A group. On the Bayley MDI (94) and the discrepancies test (Level 0 at both 12 and 15 months), he ranks lowest among the one-year A's, while his abstract-thinking scores are fairly high (he ranks second of five and six subjects at both 12 and 15 months). Language test scores fall on the median at 12 and 15 months. It is interesting to note that he obtains the same scores at 15 months that he

TABLE 33. **Summary of Test Scores**

Subject: No. 32   Group: 1-year A

Tests	S's Score	Group Median	S's Rank	No. of S's Tied at that Rank
Bayley (MDI) 12 m	94	103	9/9	—
24 m				
Language Test				
at 12 mos.	16	16	3/7	2
at 15 mos.	16	17	4/5	4
at 21 mos.				
at 24 mos.				
Abstract Abilities				
at 12 mos.	15.5	15.5	2/5	4
at 15 mos.	15.5	15.5	2/6	3
at 21 mos.				
at 24 mos.				
Discrimination				
at 12 mos.	L.0	2	4/4	2
at 15 mos.	L.0	2	4/4	—
at 21 mos.				
at 24 mos.				

did at 12 months on all three tests. He has not yet been tested at 21 months.

The child's approach to the testing situation is characterized by a high level of physical activity, much cheerfulness, and a strong expression of independent thinking. These characteristics make him a difficult but challenging subject to test. The problem is to maintain his attention long enough to allow him to complete the task at hand. The language test presented the least amount of difficulty, because it is flexible and unstructured for one-year-olds. The discrepancies test is the most formal, and requires some patience on the subject's part. This child did not exhibit that patience, as his score reflects (Level 0 at both 12 and 15 months). He has very definite interests of his own and refuses to comply with the examiner if her interests conflict with his, which was the case with the discrepancies test. However, he did not become angry or unhappy, but merely ran off to carry on his busy activities beyond the examiner's reach.

Social Competence

Subject 32 is a one-year-old whose social interactions with adults are frequent and successful for the most part, with a particularly high frequency of successfully *utilizing an adult as a resource.* In addition, he shows an ability *to gain the attention of adults* when he desires, and can *express affection and hostility* toward them. He *complies with adults' directives* more than twice as often as he resists them, which is average for his age group. In addition, he shows an above-average ability to occasionally *control adults' behavior.* More significantly, he is the most frequent *imitator of adults' behavior* among our one-year-old subjects. Although he did not have much opportunity to interact with peers during our observations, we might predict a similarly high degree of successful encounters for him in his future peer interactions. The adult with whom he interacts most often is his mother.

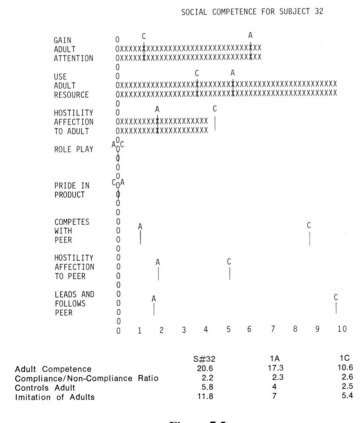

	S#32	1A	1C
Adult Competence	20.6	17.3	10.6
Compliance/Non-Compliance Ratio	2.2	2.3	2.6
Controls Adult	5.8	4	2.5
Imitation of Adults	11.8	7	5.4

Figure 7.5

SUBJECT #34

Background Data

Subject 34 is a (Class Position IV) one-year-old C boy. He is the youngest of three children. He has a seven-year-old brother and a four-year-old sister. The family lives in a seven-room apartment in a two-family house in a residential area of the city. The apartment is usually neat but the furniture is quite worn.

This subject is a well-developed, alert little boy who spends the majority of each day alone in a playpen that takes up most of the space in the living room. The television is left on for him, and usually there are several toys in the playpen with him. His mother rarely interacts with him, but when she does, it is in an affectionate and playful manner. Although his four-year-old sister is also home all day, she rarely pays any attention to the subject.

Discussion of Test Performance

Subject 34 is a one-year-old C child whose test scores generally fall below the group median for C's. An exception is his Bayley Mental Devel-

TABLE 34. Summary of Test Scores

Subject: No. 34   Group: 1-year C

Tests	S's Score	Group Median	S's Rank	No. of S's Tied at that Rank
Bayley (MDI) 12 m	109	99	2/4	—
24 m	66	109	4/4	—
Language Test				
at 12 mos.	10	11.5	3/3	2
at 15 mos.	10	16	3/3	—
at 21 mos.	10	19	4/4	—
at 24 mos.	10	30	4/4	—
Abstract Abilities				
at 12 mos.	8.0	9.5	3/4	—
at 15 mos.	11.0	11.0	3/3	—
at 21 mos.	16.5	16.5	all 16.5	—
at 24 mos.	16.5	16.5	all 16.5	—
Discrimination				
at 12 mos.	L.0	L.0	2/2	3
at 15 mos.	L.0	L.3	2/2	—
at 21 mos.	L.0	L.2.5	4/4	—
at 24 mos.	L.3.5	L.3.5	2/4	2

opment Index (109), which compares favorably with the group median score of 99. He ranks last or next to last among the four C subjects on all other tests and shows no improvement in test performance from 12 to 15 months, with the exception of his score on the test of abstract-thinking abilities. It should be noted, however, that this subject has not been tested at 21 months, and may yet show improvement.

His test performance is mainly characterized by his confusion and frustration. He is unable to understand the desires of the examiner and is interested in the testing materials (such as cups, balls, and wooden beads) only for primitive fingering and mouthing purposes. He screams with anger and frustration when a toy is removed, even though it is returned almost immediately.

In the less-structured testing situation, such as the test of receptive-language ability, he responds with passivity, merely ignoring all verbal commands made by his mother or the examiner.

It should be added that this child spends most of his time happily confined to a playpen or feeding table without protest. When a test situation requires his freedom of movement, as in the test of abstract-thinking abilities, a new complication is introduced. He seems to find his lack of confinement to be such a novelty that he completely ignores any attempts to involve him with the testing materials, and the examiner spends most of her time chasing him from room to room.

Social Competence

Subject 34 is a one-year-old whose social life is limited and confined. He spends much of his time enclosed in a playpen, and is thus entirely dependent on someone else's approach for social contact. Apparently his own rare attempts *to gain the attention of adults* meet with little success, for his score is far below even the median for one-year-old C subjects on the dimension; in addition, his extremely low score on *utilization of adults as resources* would further support the view that he is dependent on being a receiver of social stimulation rather than an initiator. Finally, the picture of his meager interaction is completed with the average score of one-year-old C's on *expressions of affection and hostility* toward adults. It appears that such children experience social interaction mainly as a series of random affectionate or hostile interchanges between themselves and their mother. There is little development of an awareness that adults can be helpful or act as an attentive audience, and certainly little encouragement is given this kind of child to develop optimally or to grow up mastering his social world.

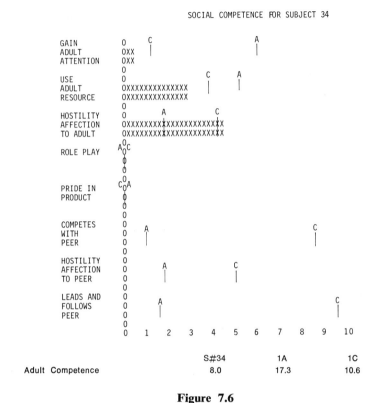

Figure 7.6

TASK DATA

Social Tasks, Subjects 32 and 34

Figures 7.7 and 7.8 present social-task data for subjects 32 and 34. Unlike our two one-year-old girls, these subjects had quite different patterns of social experience, even though both are from low-income, multichild families.

Our 1C child had a strikingly barren social life, with only one type of experience occurring more than 0.8 percent of the time (*maintain social contact,* 2.3 percent). In marked contrast, our 1A boy had six types of social experience, totalling some 21.7 percent of the time. He showed the most mature pattern of social experiences of any of these four one-year-olds, as exemplified by his use of others (*to procure a service*) and his attempts at controlling others (*to direct,* 1.9 percent). Like our 1C girl

SUBJECT NUMBER 32   SUBJECT CLASS 1A   98.7 % OF OBSERVED TIME REPRESENTED

SOCIAL TASKS

TO PLEASE   0
TO COOPERATE   0===
TO GAIN APPROVAL   0==
TO PROCURE A SERVICE   0===
TO GAIN ATTENTION   0===
TO MAINTAIN SOCIAL CONTACT   0=========
TO AVOID UNPLEASANT CIRCUMSTANCES   0
TO ANNOY   0==
TO DIRECT   0==
TO ASSERT SELF (PROTECT DOMAIN)   0==
TO PROVIDE INFORMATION   0
TO COMPETE   0
TO REJECT OVERTURES   0
TO ENJOY PETS   0
TO CONVERSE   0
TO PRODUCE VERBALIZATIONS   0

NON-SOCIAL TASKS

TO EAT   0====
TO GAIN INFORMATION - VISUAL   0===========
TO GAIN INFORMATION - VISUAL ANDAUDITORY   0===========
NON-TASK   0==
TO PASS TIME   0==
TO FIND SOMETHING TO DO   0==
TO PREPARE FOR AN ACTIVITY   0==
TO CONSTRUCT A PRODUCT   0
TO CHOOSE   0
TO PROCURE AN OBJECT   0=====
TO ENGAGE IN LARGE MUSCLE ACTIVITY   0==
TO GAIN PLEASURE   0
TO IMITATE   0
TO PRETEND (ROLE PLAY)   0
TO EASE DISCOMFORT   0==
TO RESTORE ORDER   0==
TO RELIEVE ONESELF   0
TO DRESS/UNDRESS   0
TO OPERATE A MECHANISM   0
TO EAT AND TO GAIN INFORMATION (VISUAL)   0==
TO EAT AND TO GAIN INFORMATION (VISUAL AND AUDITORY) 0===========
TO EXPLORE   0
TO IMPROVE A DEVELOPING SKILL (MASTERY   0========

0123456789012345678901234567890123456789012345678 90
0   10   20   30   40   50

TASK DATA (% OF TOTAL TIME)

Figure 7.7 (These percents have been rounded off to the nearest whole percent.)

129

```
                    SUBJECT NUMBER 34        SUBJECT CLASS 1C           99.6 % OF OBSERVED TIME REPRESENTED

                                             SOCIAL TASKS

TO PLEASE                                              0
TO COOPERATE                                           0
TO GAIN APPROVAL                                       0
TO PROCURE A SERVICE                                   0
TO GAIN ATTENTION                                      0==
TO MAINTAIN SOCIAL CONTACT                             0
TO AVOID UNPLEASANT CIRCUMSTANCES                      0
TO ANNOY                                               0
TO DIRECT                                              0
TO ASSERT SELF (PROTECT DOMAIN)                        0
TO PROVIDE INFORMATION                                 0
TO COMPETE                                             0
TO REJECT OVERTURES                                    0
TO ENJOY PETS                                          0
TO CONVERSE                                            0
TO PRODUCE VERBALIZATIONS                              0
                                             NON-SOCIAL TASKS

TO EAT                                                 0=
TO GAIN INFORMATION - VISUAL                           0=======
TO GAIN INFORMATION - VISUAL AND AUDITORY              0================
NON-TASK                                               0=
TO PASS TIME                                           0==============================
TO FIND SOMETHING TO DO                                0
TO PREPARE FOR AN ACTIVITY                             0
TO CONSTRUCT A PRODUCT                                 0
TO CHOOSE                                              0
TO PROCURE AN OBJECT                                   0==
TO ENGAGE IN LARGE MUSCLE ACTIVITY                     0
TO GAIN PLEASURE                                       0=
TO IMITATE                                             0
TO PRETEND (ROLE PLAY)                                 0
TO EASE DISCOMFORT                                     0
TO RESTORE ORDER                                       0
TO RELIEVE ONESELF                                     0
TO DRESS/UNDRESS                                       0
TO OPERATE A MECHANISM                                 0=
TO EAT AND TO GAIN INFORMATION (VISUAL)                0
TO EAT AND TO GAIN INFORMATION (VISUAL AND AUDITORY)   0
TO EXPLORE                                             0=========
TO IMPROVE A DEVELOPING SKILL (MASTERY                 0

                                                       0123456789012345678901234567890123456789012345678900
                                                       0         10        20        30        40        50

                                             TASK DATA (% OF TOTAL TIME)
```

Figure 7.8 *(These percents have been rounded off to the nearest whole percent.)*

(subject 1), he asserted himself fairly often, and there was evidence of a good deal of parental direction in his high *cooperate* score (3.5 percent).

Nonsocial Tasks, Subjects 32 and 34

Figures 7.7 and 7.8 present nonsocial-task data for subjects 32 and 34.

One is immediately struck by the enormous amount of *pass time* experience (37.1 percent) in the life of our 1C boy. The mother of this child placed him in a playpen for long periods every day. This child-rearing technique makes some sense when a twelve-to-fifteen-month-old child is physically immature (as this child is) and a mother is very busy. Over the years, however, with very few exceptions, none of our mothers of 1A children confined their children in playpens or cribs for more than very brief periods, whereas the majority of the mothers of our 1C children did.

Both these boys spent a great deal of time investigating objects, as reflected in high *explore* and *mastery* scores. Our 1A boy had a higher *gain information through looking* score but a lower overall language input score (*gain information—audio and visual* is 8.2 percent for 1A, 17.6 percent for 1C). Again, however, when we look at the source of language, we find our 1C child got 1.3 percent live language and 15.9 percent television language, whereas our 1A boy got 6.6 percent live language and 1.0 percent television language.

The larger amount of non-task behavior by our 1A child (13.5 vs. 1.0 percent) should be considered in the light of the reversed figures in regard to *pass time* experience (2.5 vs. 37.1 percent). A 13.5 percent score for our 1A child is only slightly higher than average for all our one-year-olds.

Finally, our 1A boy had more *prepare for activity, restore order,* and *procure object* experiences than our 1C boy. There is in general a good deal of similarity between the task profiles of our two 1A children, while those of the 2C children show less resemblance to each other's and to those of our A children.

Task-Initiation Data

Tables 35 and 36 present information on the source of initiation of tasks for subjects 32 and 34. Our 1C boy had far fewer self-initiated experiences than our other one-year-olds. This is due in large part to his mother's extensive use of the playpen. Our 1A boy selected his own experiences almost all the time, except for certain social tasks. Again, in both cases, these one-year-olds initiated more of their own nonsocial than

TABLE 35. **Source of Initiation of Tasks**

Subject: No. 32   Group: 1A

	Source of Initiation (% Time)				
Task	Total Task Time, % Duration	% Duration Self-Initiated	% Duration Mother-Initiated	% Duration Other Adult-Initiated	% Duration Child-Initiated
All tasks		93.8	5.3		0.3
All social tasks		88.5	9.2		1.0
All nonsocial tasks		96.2	3.4		
Social tasks					
To please	0.2	100.0			
To cooperate	3.5		82.4	9.8	7.8
To gain approval	0.0				
To procure a service	2.4	100.0			
To gain attention	3.3	100.0			
To maintain social contact	9.1	100.0			
To direct	1.9	100.0			
To assert self	1.5		100.0		
To converse	0.0				
Nonsocial tasks					
To gain info (v)	13.2	100.0			
To gain info (v and a)	8.2	94.9	5.1		
Non-task	13.5	100.0			
Pass time	2.5		88.9	11.1	
Prepare for activity	1.7	100.0			
Construct a product	0.0				
Procure an object	4.5	100.0			
Gross motor activity	1.5	100.0			
Gain pleasure	0.0				
Imitate	0.1	100.0			
Pretend					
Ease discomfort	1.0	100.0			
Restore order	2.1	100.0			
Eat and gain info (v)	2.4	100.0			
Eat and gain info (v and a)	0.0				
Explore	12.7	100.0			
Mastery	7.4	100.0			
Eat	4.9	100.0			
Mastery and misc.					

social tasks. In neither case did other children or other adults initiate any significant number of tasks for these subjects.

Looking at social tasks, we find our 1A boy was occasionally asked to do things by other adults and other children. Almost no one asked our 1C boy to do anything, and on the rare occasions when someone did, it was always his mother. The only other social task that occurred that was

TABLE 36. **Source of Initiation of Tasks**

Subject: No. 34   Group: 1C

		Source of Initiation (% Time)			
Task	Total Task Time, % Duration	% Duration Self-Initiated	% Duration Mother-Initiated	% Duration Other Adult-Initiated	% Duration Child-Initiated
All tasks		75.8	23.3		0.9
All social tasks		65.8	34.2		
All nonsocial tasks		76.2	22.9		0.9
Social tasks					
To please	0.0				
To cooperate	0.1	0.0	100.0		
To gain approval	0.0				
To procure a service	0.2	100.0			
To gain attention	0.0				
To maintain social contact	2.3	100.0			
To direct	0.0				
To assert self	0.0		100.0		
To converse	0.0				
Nonsocial tasks					
To gain info (v)	8.2	88.4	2.8		8.8
To gain info (v and a)	17.6	98.7	1.3		
Non-task	1.0	100.0			
Pass time	37.1		100.0		
Prepare for activity	0.0				
Construct a product	0.0				
Procure an object	3.4	100.0			
Gross motor activity	0.3	100.0			
Gain pleasure	0.6	100.0			
Imitate	0.0				
Pretend	0.0				
Ease discomfort	0.5	100.0			
Restore order	0.0				
Eat and gain info (v)	0.0				
Eat and gain info (v and a)	0.0				
Explore	9.8	96.6	3.4		
Mastery	16.2	100.0			
Eat	1.5	100.0			
Mastery and misc.					

not self-initiated was *assert self*. In the few instances involved, it was the mother in both cases whom the child was resisting.

The picture in regard to nonsocial tasks is a bit more complex. By and large (96.2 percent), our 1A boy determined his own nonsocial experiences. Only in two important categories did he experience direct control by others. In the important area of language, his mother initiated a fair amount of live-language experiences (*gain information—audio and visual,* 5.1 percent). He was occasionally obliged to *pass time* by adults other than his mother; these people were his father and fifteen-year-old sister.

Our 1C boy, in contrast, had much more of his nonsocial experience initiated for him by others (mainly his mother). By far the bulk of such time was in *pass time* situations (100.0 percent mother-initiated). Small amounts of three other tasks, *gain information—visual, gain information —audio* and *visual,* and *to explore,* were other-initiated, with other children rather than his mother initiating a modest amount of looking behavior (*gain information—visual*).

The next pair of subjects to be discussed consists of a 2A girl (subject 22) and a 2C girl (subject 28).

SUBJECT #22

Background Data

Subject 22 is a (Class Position III) two-year-old A girl. She is an attractive child who appears extremely capable. She is the youngest of three girls (ages five and a half, three, and two) in a father-absent home. The family lives with relatives in a fairly comfortable seven-room house in a semiresidential area. The mother, who has completed one and one-half years of college, takes care of the children during the day and has a job as a waitress in the evenings.

The general atmosphere in this home is warm and loving but not particularly child-centered. The mother encourages independence, although she will suggest activities for her daughter. The child has access to the whole house and is allowed to go out and play by herself with the neighborhood children.

Discussion of Test Performance

Subject 22 is a poised and mature two-year-old A child whose test scores are consistently above the median for her group. Of particular note is the mental development index of 140 obtained at 24 months on the Bayley Infant Development Scale; this is the highest score achieved by any subject. Her Stanford–Binet IQ score of 145, obtained at 36 months, continues to support the impression that she is an extremely capable young lady.

Her approach to the testing situation is a reflection of her general

TABLE 37. **Summary of Test Scores**

Subject: No. 22 Group: 2-year A

Tests	S's Score	Group Median	S's Rank	No. of S's Tied at that Rank
Bayley (MDI) 24 m	140	105	1/12	—
Stanford–Binet	145	138	2/12	—
Language Test				
at 24 mos.	39	36	2/7	—
at 27 mos.	48	40.5	3/9	—
at 30 mos.	51	51	1/4	6
at 36 mos.	60	51	1/12	2
Abstract Abilities				
at 24 mos.	28.5	20.5	2/9	3
at 27 mos.	28.5	24.5	4/9	2
at 30 mos.	28.5	24.5	2/8	—
at 36 mos.	60.0	54.0	1/12	2
Discrimination				
at 24 mos.	L.3	L.3	4/6	6
at 27 mos.	L.5	L.4	4/6	2
at 30 mos.	L.8	L.7	1/5	3
at 36 mos.	L.8	L.8	1/5	6

behavior style. She is remarkably calm and dignified for a two-year-child, but has the capacity for enthusiastic responsiveness as well. She always had an audience of sisters and friends during her test performance, but was never perturbed by their presence. She took great delight in correctly solving the problems presented to her, and always understood the goal to be achieved.

She was also unusual in her approach to the puzzles in the abstract-thinking abilities test. She focused on the picture content of the puzzle, rather than just trying to fit the contours of the pieces together according to shape. She referred to the sample picture as she proceeded, and when a puzzle was completed, she turned the finished product right side up and was the only subject to do so.

Social Competence

Subject 22 is a two-year-old who has attained the highest adult competence and overall competence score in the two-year-old group of A's. She is best described as a child who really desires to perform well and tries to model her behavior on adult models, despite the fact that she appears not to be unduly pampered or catered to by her mother. The extremely high *role play* and *pride in product* scores, combined with slightly below-average *gain attention* and *adult resource* scores, make her picture rather unique among our more competent subjects. Her *compliance/ noncompliance ratio* is the highest among our two-year-olds (6.2 percent), showing how cooperative and attuned she is to adults' wishes; yet her above-average expressions of *affection/hostility* show also that she is spirited in her interactions with adults. She has shown an above-average ability to deal effectively with peers in *leading and following,* although her *competitiveness* with them is only average, and she expresses neither *affection* nor *hostility* to them. In addition, she is above average on *refusing to follow peers' directions.*

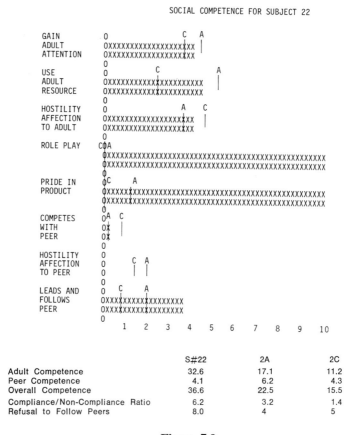

                    SOCIAL COMPETENCE FOR SUBJECT 22

	S#22	2A	2C
Adult Competence	32.6	17.1	11.2
Peer Competence	4.1	6.2	4.3
Overall Competence	36.6	22.5	15.5
Compliance/Non-Compliance Ratio	6.2	3.2	1.4
Refusal to Follow Peers	8.0	4	5

Figure 7.9

SUBJECT #28

Background Data

Subject 28 is a (Class Position III) two-year-old C girl. She is the younger of two children. The family lives in a five-room upstairs apartment in a two-family house in a residential working-class area. The apartment is furnished with care and is always spotless.

Subject 28 is a pretty child with blond hair and blue eyes, who seems large for her age. She has access to the whole apartment but spends most of her time in the living room watching the television, which is on most of the day. She rarely interacts with her mother except for brief instances when her mother checks on her whereabouts in the apartment. Her mother rarely initiates any activities for her and seems pleased as long as she is quiet.

Discussion of Test Performance

Subject 28 is a two-year-old C child whose test scores fall on the group median for the language and abstract-thinking tests (except for 27

TABLE 38. **Summary of Test Scores**

Subject: No. 28   Group: 2-year C

Tests	S's Score	Group Median	S's Rank	No. of S's Tied at that Rank
Bayley (MDI) 24 m	94	86	1/5	—
Language Test				
at 24 mos.	18	18	3/3	3
at 27 mos.	27	27	3/5	—
at 30 mos.	27	27	2/3	2
Abstract Abilities				
at 24 mos.	16.5	16.5	all 16.5	—
at 27 mos.	18.0	16.5	1/2	2
at 30 mos.	16.5	16.5	2/2	3
Discrimination				
at 24 mos.	L.3	L.3	2/3	2
at 27 mos.	L.2	L.2	3/3	2
at 30 mos.	L.6	L.3.5	2/4	—
Social Competence				
With Adults	5.3	11.7	6/6	—
With Peers	6.3	4.7	2/7	—
Overall	11.6	17.6	6/7	—

months) and the discrepancies test (except for 30 months). Her test scores improve, but only slightly, over the six-month period from 24 to 30 months. On the Bayley test she obtains a mental development index score of 94, which is the highest-ranking score among the two-year-old C's. On all other tests, however, she ranks near the middle of the C group.

Subject 28 is a difficult child to test because of three characteristics that combine to interfere with her test performance. These include, first, her ability to "tune out," completely ignoring examiner's attempts to interact with her. Second, she expresses a great deal of negativism and open hostility. And finally, her expressive-language ability is very limited. She babbles unintelligibly and cannot make her desires understood, a deficiency that probably contributes to her frustration and consequent hostility.

A typical test situation is characterized by quiet defiance on the subject's part, when she seems pleased to ignore the examiner's instructions. When she does cooperate, she shows much aggressive behavior toward the testing materials, biting the heads of the rubber dolls, spontaneously making the dolls "fight," bending puzzle pieces, or just manipulating them with an unusual amount of force. Every so often she yells "No!" very loudly when she does not want to cooperate.

The description above is especially applicable to her behavior at 24 and 27 months. By 30 months, her expressive language was improving and her hostility was less frequently expressed, allowing for a more effective and enjoyable testing situation. She has not yet been tested at 36 months, but one would expect even greater improvement at that time.

Social Competence

Subject 28 is a two-year-old girl whose social behavior is low-keyed and evenly distributed among six out of eight dimensions of competence. Although her scores are uniformly below average in interactions with adults (mainly her mother), she does show an encouraging ability to deal effectively with peers such as her older brother. She is able *to lead and follow peers* more frequently than others her age, and shows an average ability *to express affection and hostility* and *to compete*. It would seem as if her mother's lack of participation with her has kept her from developing any real effectiveness with adults. Her higher-than-average scores on *gaining peer attention* and *imitating peers* seem to indicate that she could develop stronger social abilities in a more supportive environment. She does in fact show an average ability to *comply with adult directives* and would probably enjoy additional social contacts with adults.

SOCIAL COMPETENCE FOR SUBJECT 28

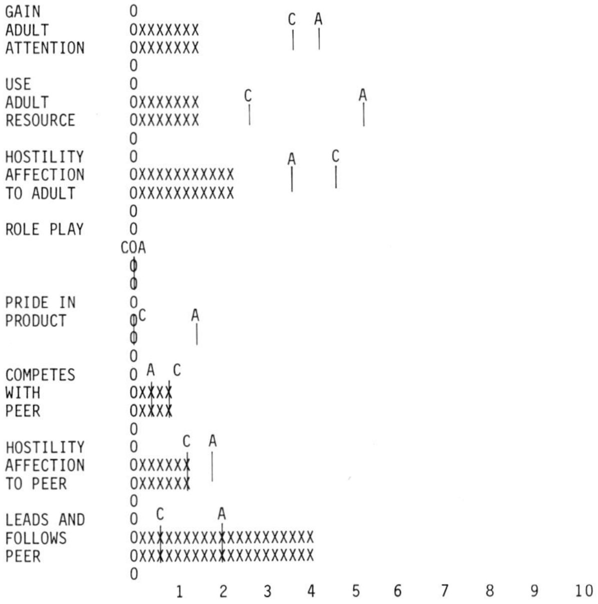

```
GAIN           0
ADULT          OXXXXXXX              C  A
ATTENTION      OXXXXXXX              |  |
               0
USE            0
ADULT          OXXXXXXX      C            A
RESOURCE       OXXXXXXX      |            |
               0
HOSTILITY      0                  A   C
AFFECTION      OXXXXXXXXXXX       |   |
TO ADULT       OXXXXXXXXXXX
               0
ROLE PLAY      0
               COA
               ⌀
               ⌀
PRIDE IN       0
PRODUCT        ⌀C    A
               ⌀     |
               0
COMPETES       0 A  C
WITH           OXXXX
PEER           OXXXX
               0
HOSTILITY      0    C  A
AFFECTION      OXXXXXX  |
TO PEER        OXXXXXX
               0
LEADS AND      0  C     A
FOLLOWS        OXXXXXXXXXXXXXXXXXXXX
PEER           OXXXXXXXXXXXXXXXXXXXX
               0
               1    2    3    4    5    6    7    8    9    10
```

	S#28	2A	2C
Adult Competence	5.3	17.1	11.2
Peer Competence	6.3	6.2	4.3
Overall Competence	11.6	22.5	15.5
Compliance/Non-Compliance Ratio	1.7	3.2	1.4
Peer Attention	14.0	7	13
Peer Imitation	7.0	7	5

Figure 7.10

TASK DATA

Social Tasks, Subjects 22 and 28

Figures 7.11 and 7.12 present social-task data for subjects 22 and 28. Perhaps the most striking difference in these social-task profiles is the virtual absence of *to cooperate* tasks in our 2C child and the comparable absence of *assert self* tasks in our 2A child. These scores indicate that the mother of our 2C child made very few requests of her, whereas the opposite was the case with our 2A child. *Assert self* situations are a joint function of people making unwanted intrusions into a child's domain, and

SUBJECT NUMBER 22   SUBJECT CLASS 2A

97.1 % OF OBSERVED TIME REPRESENTED

SOCIAL TASKS

```
TO PLEASE                               0
TO COOPERATE                            0======
TO GAIN APPROVAL                        0
TO PROCURE A SERVICE                    0==
TO GAIN ATTENTION                       0===
TO MAINTAIN SOCIAL CONTACT              0===
TO AVOID UNPLEASANT CIRCUMSTANCES       0
TO ANNOY                                0
TO DIRECT                               0
TO ASSERT SELF (PROJECT DOMAIN)         0=
TO PROVIDE INFORMATION                  0=
TO COMPETE                              0
TO REJECT OVERTURES                     0
TO ENJOY PETS                           0
TO CONVERSE                             0
TO PRODUCE VERBALIZATIONS               0
```

NON-SOCIAL TASKS

```
TO EAT                                          0=========
TO GAIN INFORMATION - VISUAL                    0==================
TO GAIN INFORMATION - VISUAL ANDAUDITORY        0=========
NON-TASK                                        0==========
TO PASS TIME                                    0==========
TO FIND SOMETHING TO DO                         0
TO PREPARE FOR AN ACTIVITY                      0===
TO CONSTRUCT A PRODUCT                          0
TO CHOOSE                                       0
TO PROCURE AN OBJECT                            0=
TO ENGAGE IN LARGE MUSCLE ACTIVITY              0
TO GAIN PLEASURE                                0===
TO IMITATE                                      0
TO PRETEND (ROLE PLAY)                          0
TO EASE DISCOMFORT                              0
TO RESTORE ORDER                                0=
TO RELIEVE ONESELF                              0==
TO DRESS/UNDRESS                                0
TO OPERATE A MECHANISM                          0=
TO EAT AND TO GAIN INFORMATION (VISUAL)         0=
TO EAT AND TO GAIN INFORMATION (VISUAL AND AUDITORY)   0
TO EXPLORE                                      0======
TO IMPROVE A DEVELOPING SKILL (MASTERY          0=====
```

```
0123456789012345678901234567890123456789012345678901234567890
0        10        20        30        40        50
```

TASK DATA (% OF TOTAL TIME)

Figure 7.11 (These percents have been rounded off to the nearest whole percent.)

SOCIAL TASKS   99.8 % OF OBSERVED TIME REPRESENTED

```
TO PLEASE                                              0
TO COOPERATE                                           0=
TO GAIN APPROVAL                                       0
TO PROCURE A SERVICE                                   0==
TO GAIN ATTENTION                                      0
TO MAINTAIN SOCIAL CONTACT                             0=====
TO AVOID UNPLEASANT CIRCUMSTANCES                      0=======
TO ANNOY                                               0
TO DIRECT                                              0
TO ASSERT SELF (PROTECT DOMAIN)                        0====
TO PROVIDE INFORMATION                                 0
TO COMPETE                                             0
TO REJECT OVERTURES                                    0
TO ENJOY PETS                                          0
TO CONVERSE                                            0
TO PRODUCE VERBALIZATIONS                              0
                            NON-SOCIAL TASKS
TO EAT                                                 0=======
TO GAIN INFORMATION - VISUAL                           0=============
TO GAIN INFORMATION - VISUAL ANDAUDITORY               0====
NON-TASK                                               0=================
TO PASS TIME                                           0
TO FIND SOMETHING TO DO                                0
TO PREPARE FOR AN ACTIVITY                             0
TO CONSTRUCT A PRODUCT                                 0
TO CHOOSE                                              0
TO PROCURE AN OBJECT                                   0=
TO ENGAGE IN LARGE MUSCLE ACTIVITY                     0==
TO GAIN PLEASURE                                       0
TO IMITATE                                             0
TO PRETEND (ROLE PLAY)                                 0=
TO EASE DISCOMFORT                                     0
TO RESTORE ORDER                                       0=
TO RELIEVE ONESELF                                     0
TO DRESS/UNDRESS                                       0
TO OPERATE A MECHANISM                                 0
TO EAT AND TO GAIN INFORMATION (VISUAL)                0==
TO EAT AND TO GAIN INFORMATION (VISUAL AND AUDITORY)   0
TO EXPLORE                                             0====
TO IMPROVE A DEVELOPING SKILL (MASTERY                 0====
                            0123456789012345678901234567890123456789012345678 90
                            0        10        20        30        40        50
                                     TASK DATA (% OF TOTAL TIME)
```

Figure 7.12 (These percents have been rounded off to the nearest whole percent.)

the child's being autonomous enough or perhaps testy enough to resist such behavior. The home of our 2A child was firmly run by a talented mother, who expects her children to act with maturity. The home of our 2C child is different, in that the mother appears clearly less capable and the subject's older brother (aged six years) seems less friendly to her than are the other children in child 2A's world.

The higher-than-average *gain attention* and *maintain social contact* scores of child 2C suggest "clinginess" and a general orientation toward her mother to a considerably greater degree than with our 2A child.

Nonsocial Tasks, Subjects 22 and 28

The nonsocial experiences of these children were at least as different as their social experiences. Perhaps the most telling differences were in the categories *non-task*—21.2 percent (2C) vs. 6.4 percent (2A)—and *gain information—audio plus visual*—10.0 percent (2A) vs. 5.4 percent (2C). Furthermore, when all sources of language are examined, our 2A child had 12.0 percent live language and 0.0 percent mechanical language, versus 1.6 percent live language and 3.1 percent mechanical language for our 2C child. These three comparisons appear to be of particular significance for the differential development of skills in these children.

As for other nonsocial task differences, child 2C exhibited a greater and more sophisticated interest in physical objects than child 2A. Child 2A exhibited more *prepare for activity* behavior (2.7 vs. 0.3 percent) and more *pass time* (10.8 vs. 0.3 percent). As in the case of the 1A girl, our 2A girl accompanied her mother on auto trips and generally spent more time with her mother than did our 2C girl.

Task-Initiation Data

Tables 39 and 40 present task initiation for Subjects 22 and 28. Among social tasks, all of our 2C child's *assert self* episodes were precipitated by her mother, whereas our 2A child frequently asserted herself with other children (31.6 percent). To a lesser degree, the same is true of *cooperate tasks,* with 8.8 vs. 0.0 percent involving other children. In several other instances, other children initiated the tasks of our 2A child, whereas this was never the case for our C child. Our 2A child lives with several other children, while our 2C child has a brother who is frequently nearby but is singularly remote from her. Of note also is the fact that the mother of our 2C child initiated much more *restore order* behavior (58.8 vs. 16.7 percent) than did the mother of our 2A child.

Finally, we shall discuss two two-year-old boys, one an A (subject 21) and one a C (subject 7).

TABLE 39. **Source of Initiation of Tasks**

Subject: No. 22   Group: 2A

Task	Total Task Time, % Duration	% Duration Self-Initiated	% Duration Mother-Initiated	% Duration Other Adult-Initiated	% Duration Child-Initiated
		Source of Initiation (% Time)			
All tasks		88.8	7.9		3.2
All social tasks		76.2	20.3		3.2
All nonsocial tasks		92.8	3.8		3.4
Social tasks					
To please	0.2	100.0			
To cooperate	5.7		91.2		8.8
To gain approval	0.0				
To procure a service	1.9	100.0			
To gain attention	3.0	100.0			
To maintain social contact	3.3	100.0			
To direct	0.1	100.0			
To assert self	1.1		68.4		31.6
To converse	0.4	100.0			
Nonsocial tasks					
To gain info (v)	20.2	98.3	1.7		
To gain info (v and a)	10.0	88.9	11.1		
Non-task	6.4	100.0			
Pass time	10.8		100.0		
Prepare for activity	2.7	81.6			18.4
Construct a product	0.0				
Procure an object	1.3	70.8	29.2		
Gross motor activity	0.2	100.0			
Gain pleasure	2.6	51.1			48.9
Imitate	1.2	100.0			
Pretend	0.2	100.0			
Ease discomfort	0.4	100.0			
Restore order	1.0	83.3	16.7		
Eat and gain info (v)	2.1	100.0			
Eat and gain info (v and a)	1.4	92.0	8.0		
Explore	7.2	92.2			7.8
Mastery	2.4	100.0			
Eat	9.6	98.8	1.2		
Mastery and misc.					

SUBJECT #7

Background Data

Subject 7 is a (Class Position IV) two-year-old C boy. This child is an average-looking boy whose most outstanding feature is his blank expression. He is the youngest of six children in a family that seems gen-

TABLE 40. **Source of Initiation of Tasks**

Subject: No. 28   Group: 2C

Task	Source of Initiation (% Time)				
	Total Task Time, % Duration	% Duration Self- Initiated	% Duration Mother- Initiated	% Duration Other Adult- Initiated	% Duration Child- Initiated
All tasks		97.5	2.5		
All social tasks		97.8	2.2		
All nonsocial tasks		97.3	2.7		
Social tasks					
To please	0.3	100.0			
To cooperate	0.6		100.0		
To gain approval	0.0				
To procure a service	2.1	100.0			
To gain attention	5.1	100.0			
To maintain social contact	7.2	100.0			
To direct	0.1	100.0			
To assert self	3.7		100.0		
To converse	0.2	100.0			
Nonsocial tasks					
To gain info (v)	16.7	100.0			
To gain info (v and a)	5.4	96.2	3.8		
Non-task	21.2	100.0			
Pass time	0.3		100.0		
Prepare for activity	0.3	100.0			
Construct a product	0.0				
Procure an object	2.5	88.9	11.1		
Gross motor activity	1.8	100.0			
Gain pleasure	0.8	100.0			
Imitate	1.9	100.0			
Pretend	0.4	100.0			
Ease discomfort	0.8	100.0			
Restore order	2.4	41.2	58.8		
Eat and gain info (v)	1.5	100.0			
Eat and gain info (v and a)	0.0				
Explore	4.0	100.0			
Mastery	10.6	100.0			
Eat	7.4	100.0			
Mastery and misc.					

erally overwhelmed by the daily problems of living. The father, a semiskilled laborer, was unemployed during the period under discussion. The mother worked several evenings a week as a waitress.

The family lives in a six-room duplex that is part of a public housing project. The living room is usually cluttered with large piles of laundry. The television is on most of the day and the child spends a good deal of his day watching it.

He is rarely encouraged to do anything and is often severely threatened for something he has done. Most of his mother's interactions with him are disciplinary in nature, although there is little consistency or follow-through in her approach. Even friendly exchanges are worded aggressively (for example, "Hey, bad boy, get over here," said with a smile).

Discussion of Test Performance

Subject 7 is a quiet and serious two-year-old C child whose test scores are characterized by inconsistency and fall at or below the group median for two-year C's. By inconsistency, we refer to the fact that his scores at 27 or 30 months are likely to be at or below those obtained at 24 months. For example, at 24 months, he obtains a developmental age equivalent score of 21 months (median = 18 months) on the language test, but at 27 months, his score drops to the 18-month level (median = 27 months). The same phenomenon occurs in the abstract-thinking test and the discrepancies test. His Bayley score is the lowest of all subjects, at MDI = 69. Although at 36 months, on the Stanford–Binet Test, he

TABLE 41. Summary of Test Scores

Subject: No. 7   Group: 2-year C

Tests	S's Score	Group Median	S's Rank	No. of S's Tied at that Rank
Bayley (MDI) 24 m	69	86	5/5	—
Stanford–Binet	85			
Language Test				
at 24 mos.	21	18	2/3	1
at 27 mos.	18	27	5/5	—
at 30 mos.	21	27	3/3	2
at 36 mos.	36			
Abstract Abilities				
at 24 mos.	16.5	16.5	all 16.5	—
at 27 mos.	18.0	16.5	1/2	2
at 30 mos.	16.5	16.5	2/2	3
at 36 mos.	20.5			
Discrimination				
at 24 mos.	L.2	L.3	1/3	2
at 27 mos.	L.3	L.2	2/3	3
at 30 mos.	L.2	L.3.5	5/5	—
at 36 mos.	L.4			
Social Competence				
With Adults	7.3	11.7	5/7	—
With Peers	0.7	4.7	6/7	—
Overall	7.9	17.6	7/7	—

had an IQ score of 85, he remained at the bottom of the two-year-old C group.

His approach to the testing situation is marked by general unresponsiveness and lack of enthusiasm. He is not uncooperative or openly negative toward the examiner or the test itself, but merely ignores all directions addressed to him. He has a remarkable ability to "tune out" requests, whether made by the examiner or by his mother, who is considerably more forceful than the examiner. He enjoys the testing materials, but in a reserved and rather lackadaisical manner. For example, his favorite objects are a cup and a ball, but his only play with these toys is the repetitive dropping of the ball into the cup and then spilling it out again, over and over.

Another striking feature of this subject's behavior is his limited speaking vocabulary. He appears to have very little expressive language, although he babbles unintelligibly to himself and to his toys. He uses one-word requests when he wants something. Because of his "tuning-out" ability, it is difficult to determine how much his test performance is being affected by inability to understand the directions. However, it seems clear from his interactions with his mother and siblings outside the testing situation that his comprehension falls within the normal range for two- to three-year-olds.

Social Competence

Subject 7 is a two-year-old boy whose social life aptly characterizes him as a poorly developed child. He makes little attempt to interact with adults such as his mother except on an emotional level; his extremely low adult-competence score is composed mainly of expressions of *affection* and *hostility,* with a below-average score on *gain adult attention*. Otherwise, his scores on the three other adult dimensions are 0. As for peer interactions, despite the potential for these to occur, he has a score of 0.7 percent on peer competence. Here is a child who is far below average, even when compared with others of below-average ability. Having developed a capacity to survive his somewhat chaotic, threatening environment, he has little energy or ability to participate successfully in social interactions. Even his compliance/noncompliance ratio is below average for his group.

SUBJECT #21

Background Data

Subject 21 is a (Class Position I) two-year-old A boy. The family lives in a lovely, spacious home with well-kept grounds. Both parents are college graduates and the father has advanced degrees. The mother, a busy, energetic woman, spends most of her time with her children.

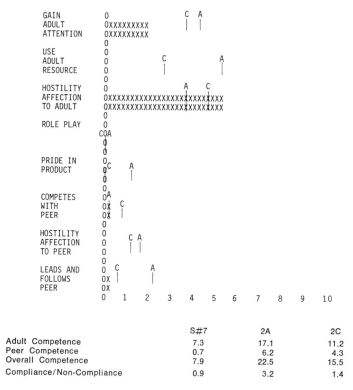

Figure 7.13

The child is a handsome, alert little boy who spends most mornings at home with his mother while his four-year-old brother attends nursery school. There are many toys, books, and puzzles for him to play with and he is usually busy with them. He has a playroom, but he usually plays in the general vicinity of his mother as she goes from room to room doing her chores. She is easily available to him and is often heard answering his questions or explaining something to him.

The child has access to all the rooms in the house but is not allowed to go outside unless someone is with him.

Discussion of Test Performance

Subject 21 is a charming and strikingly verbal two-year-old A child who performs well on tests, always ranking in the upper third of the 12

TABLE 42. **Summary of Test Scores**

Subject: No. 21   Group: 2-year A

Tests	S's Score	Group Medians	S's Rank	No. of S's Tied at that Rank
Bayley (MDI) 24 m	111	105	4/12	—
Stanford–Binet	138	139	4/6	—
Language Test				
at 24 mos.	36	36	4/7	4
at 27 mos.	51	40.5	2/9	2
at 30 mos.	51	51	1/4	6
at 36 mos.	60	51	1/5	—
Abstract Abilities				
at 24 mos.	28.5	20.5	2/9	3
at 27 mos.	28.5	24.5	3/9	—
at 30 mos.	24.5	24.5	4/8	—
at 36 mos.	54	54	1/2	5
Discrimination				
at 24 mos.	L.3	L.3	4/6	6
at 27 mos.	L.7	L.4	2/6	2
at 30 mos.	L.8	L.7	1/5	—
at 36 mos.	L.8	L.8	1/4	4

two-year-old A subjects. His Bayley MDI of 111, while not outstanding, is above the group median of 105. More impressive is his performance at 36 months on the Stanford–Binet Intelligence Scale, with an IQ score of 138, which we believe to be an adequate reflection of his level of development.

The most striking features of his behavior are his social maturity, his remarkable poise for a two-year-old, and his outstanding use of expressive language, including clear articulation and easy handling of compound and complex sentences. He thoroughly enjoyed participating in all testing situations, and exhibited excellent concentration and attention span. In fact, he would show disappointment when the test was completed; he was always ready for more. Another feature of this subject's test performance, and something that characterizes the behavior of several of the most outstanding subjects, was his manner of handling failure. He was aware of his limitations with amazing accuracy. When he did not know the solution to a problem, he would indicate by stating that he did not know the answer. If asked to guess, however, he would do so. Less capable children are often as satisfied with an incorrect answer as with a correct one. Other children constantly say they "can't" or "don't know," and then proceed to give the appropriate response.

Social Competence

Subject 21 is a two-year-old whose social interactions are balanced and evenly distributed among adults and peers, generally his mother and older brother. He is able *to gain an adult's attention* and can successfully *make use of adults' help,* as well as showing an ability to *express affection and hostility to adults and peers.* He is outstanding on his *role-play* score, lending further support to our feeling that he is a child who wants to grow up and enjoy the added success that comes with mastery of his social interactions. He shows an early precocity in *leading and following peers* and can successfully *compete* with them in play and in *gaining an adult's attention.* The fact that his scores are above the median on six out of eight social-competence dimensions convinces us that he is in all ways an outstanding child who is developing optimally. Furthermore, he shows above-average scores in *utilizing peers as a resource* and in *imitation of peers'* behavior, which are two dimensions of social behavior that we feel to be especially important in later childhood. He is, in general, a cooperative child around adults, *complying* slightly more than other children of his general competence level.

TASK DATA

Social Tasks, Subjects 7 and 21

Figures 7.15 and 7.16 present social-task data for subjects 7 and 21. Our lower-class 2C (subject 7) had a sparse social life in comparison to that of our middle-class 2A (subject 21). His mother has a lot to do, has many children, and is not a very contented woman. She tended to be harsh with this child when he was nearby, and she tried to keep him away from her as much as possible. He still tried *to gain and maintain* her *attention* fairly frequently, in spite of her best efforts to the contrary. However, some of his social tasks involved other children, of whom there were usually several nearby.

Our 2A boy, in contrast, had an apparently delightful relationship with his mother, who was almost always at home, and was rather quiet and generally indulgent. He also had a generally pleasant relationship with his older brother. He had a diverse social-task profile, which included occasional *conversing* (1.1 percent) and *seeking of approval* for some product or activity of which he was proud (1.0 percent).

Nonsocial Tasks, Subjects 7 and 21

Figures 7.15 and 7.16 present nonsocial task data for these children. Our lower-class 2C boy spent much more time idling than do most two-

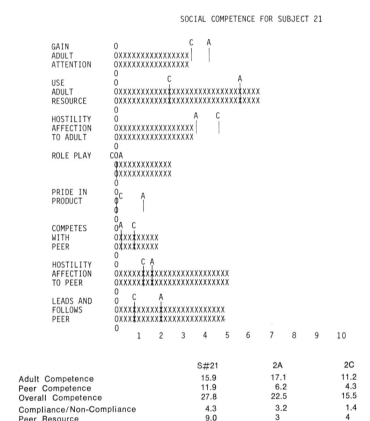

SOCIAL COMPETENCE FOR SUBJECT 21

	S#21	2A	2C
Adult Competence	15.9	17.1	11.2
Peer Competence	11.9	6.2	4.3
Overall Competence	27.8	22.5	15.5
Compliance/Non-Compliance	4.3	3.2	1.4
Peer Resource	9.0	3	4
Peer Imitation	29.0	7	5

Figure 7.14

year-olds. He had very few toys, and he was not allowed access to any-thing in the kitchen. He spent a lot of time watching television, or staring out the back door at a courtyard where other children played, or munch-ing on snacks between meals. His live-language total was surprisingly high (7.8 percent), reflecting a good deal of overheard language (he was rarely spoken to directly). His mechanical-language score was also high (7.1 percent), all as a result of watching television. His modest amount of in-teraction with physical materials was at a very immature level. He had almost no *pass time* experience (0.8 percent), reflecting his mother's suc-cessful attempts to simply get him out of her vicinity. Watching this child was a fairly depressing experience.

Our 2A boy had a rich, and apparently very healthy, set of non-

```
                                                              99.2 % OF ORSERVED TIME REPRESENTED
                    SOCIAL TASKS
TO PLEASE                                          0=
TO COOPERATE                                       0=
TO GAIN APPROVAL                                   0
TO PROCURE A SERVICE                               0=
TO GAIN ATTENTION                                  0===
TO MAINTAIN SOCIAL CONTACT                         0====
TO AVOID UNPLEASANT CIRCUMSTANCES                  0
TO ANNOY                                           0
TO DIRECT                                          0
TO ASSERT SELF (PROTECT DOMAIN)                    0=
TO PROVIDE INFORMATION                             0
TO COMPETE                                         0
TO REJECT OVERTURES                                0
TO ENJOY PETS                                      0=
TO CONVERSE                                        0
TO PRODUCE VERBALIZATIONS                          0
                  NON-SOCIAL TASKS
TO EAT                                             0========
TO GAIN INFORMATION - VISUAL                       0=======================
TO GAIN INFORMATION - VISUAL ANDAUDITORY           0=============
NON-TASK                                           0==============
TO PASS TIME                                       0=
TO FIND SOMETHING TO DO                            0
TO PREPARE FOR AN ACTIVITY                         0=
TO CONSTRUCT A PRODUCT                             0
TO CHOOSE                                          0
TO PROCURE AN OBJECT                               0=
TO ENGAGE IN LARGE MUSCLE ACTIVITY                 0====
TO GAIN PLEASURE                                   0====
TO IMITATE                                         0==
TO PRETEND (ROLE PLAY)                             0
TO EASE DISCOMFORT                                 0
TO RESTORE ORDER                                   0=
TO RELIEVE ONESELF                                 0
TO DRESS/UNDRESS                                   0
TO OPERATE A MECHANISM                             0
TO EAT AND TO GAIN INFORMATION (VISUAL)            0====
TO EAT AND TO GAIN INFORMATION (VISUAL AND AUDITORY) 0=
TO EXPLORE                                         0========
TO IMPROVE A DEVELOPING SKILL (MASTERY             0=
                                                   012345678901234567890123456789012345678901234567890
                                                   0         10        20        30        40        50

                                          TASK DATA (% OF TOTAL TIME)
```

Figure 7.15 *(These percents have been rounded off to the nearest whole percent.)*

SUBJECT NUMBER 21   SUBJECT CLASS 2A

97.4 % OF OBSERVED TIME REPRESENTED

SOCIAL TASKS

```
TO PLEASE                                          0=
TO COOPERATE                                       0======
TO GAIN APPROVAL                                   0=
TO PROCURE A SERVICE                               0=
TO GAIN ATTENTION                                  0=
TO MAINTAIN SOCIAL CONTACT                         0======
TO AVOID UNPLEASANT CIRCUMSTANCES                  0
TO ANNOY                                           0
TO DIRECT                                          0
TO ASSERT SELF (PROTECT DOMAIN)                    0
TO PROVIDE INFORMATION                             0
TO COMPETE                                         0
TO REJECT OVERTURES                                0
TO ENJOY PETS                                      0
TO CONVERSE                                        0
TO PRODUCE VERBALIZATIONS                          0=
```

NON-SOCIAL TASKS

```
TO EAT                                             0==
TO GAIN INFORMATION - VISUAL                       0=========================
TO GAIN INFORMATION - VISUAL ANDAUDITORY           0=========
NON-TASK                                           0=
TO PASS TIME                                       0
TO FIND SOMETHING TO DO                            0==
TO PREPARE FOR AN ACTIVITY                         0==
TO CONSTRUCT A PRODUCT                             0=====
TO CHOOSE                                          0
TO PROCURE AN OBJECT                               0=
TO ENGAGE IN LARGE MUSCLE ACTIVITY                 0
TO GAIN PLEASURE                                   0
TO IMITATE                                         0====
TO PRETEND (ROLE PLAY)                             0=
TO EASE DISCOMFORT                                 0=
TO RESTORE ORDER                                   0=
TO RELIEVE ONESELF                                 0=
TO DRESS/UNDRESS                                   0
TO OPERATE A MECHANISM                             0=
TO EAT AND TO GAIN INFORMATION (VISUAL)            0
TO EAT AND TO GAIN INFORMATION (VISUAL AND AUDITORY) 0
TO EXPLORE                                         0====
TO IMPROVE A DEVELOPING SKILL (MASTERY             0==
```

```
   0123456789012345678901234567890123456789012345677890
   0        10        20        30        40        50
```

TASK DATA (% OF TOTAL TIME)

Figure 7.16 *(These percents have been rounded off to the nearest whole percent.)*

152

TABLE 43. **Source of Initiation of Tasks**

Subject: No. 21   Group: 2A

Task	Total Task Time, % Duration	% Duration Self-Initiated	% Duration Mother-Initiated	% Duration Other Adult-Initiated	% Duration Child-Initiated
		Source of Initiation (% Time)			
All tasks		93.5	4.9		1.6
All social tasks		74.5	17.9		7.6
All nonsocial tasks		98.5	1.5		
Social tasks					
To please	0.6	100.0			
To cooperate	4.8		79.5		20.5
To gain approval	1.0	100.0			
To procure a service	2.4	100.0			
To gain attention	1.7	100.0			
To maintain social contact	5.9	100.0			
To direct	0.3	100.0			
To assert self	1.0		100.0		
To converse	1.1	100.0			
Nonsocial tasks					
To gain info (v)	17.6	98.7	1.3		
To gain info (v and a)	8.4	100.0			
Non-task	6.5	100.0			
Pass time	1.4		100.0		
Prepare for activity	1.8	93.5	6.5		
Construct a product	2.5	100.0			
Procure an object	1.4	100.0			
Gross motor activity	0.2	100.0			
Gain pleasure	1.4	100.0			
Imitate	2.9	100.0			
Pretend	1.3	100.0			
Ease discomfort	0.7	100.0			
Restore order	0.7	100.0			
Eat and gain info (v)	0.4	100.0			
Eat and gain info (v and a)	0.3	100.0			
Explore	4.2	100.0			
Mastery	23.2	96.8	3.2		
Eat	2.1	100.0			
Mastery and misc.	1.9	100.0			

social experiences. He had a marked and sophisticated interest in physical reality, as is reflected by his scores in the following categories: *mastery* (23.2 percent), *explore* (4.2 percent), *prepare for activity* (1.8 percent) and *construct a product* (2.5 percent). He engaged in *role play* tasks (1.3 percent) and was idle less than most two-year-olds (*non-task* 6.5 percent). Although his *gain information—audio and visual* score was not very high

TABLE 44. **Source of Initiation of Tasks**

Subject: No. 7   Group 2C

Task	Total Task Time, % Duration	Source of Initiation (% Time)			
		% Duration Self-Initiated	% Duration Mother-Initiated	% Duration Other Adult-Initiated	% Duration Child-Initiated
All tasks		94.6	4.5		1.0
All social tasks		84.2	13.8		2.0
All nonsocial tasks		96.8	2.5		0.7
Social tasks					
To please	0.6	100.0			
To cooperate	1.4		84.6		15.4
To gain approval	0.0				
To procure a service	0.9	100.0			
To gain attention	2.6	100.0			
To maintain social contact	4.2	100.0			
To direct	0.0				
To assert self	0.7		75.0		25.0
To converse	0.0				
Nonsocial tasks					
To gain info (v)	23.4	96.9	3.1		
To gain info (v and a)	12.9	99.1	0.9		
Non-task	14.3	100.0			
Pass time	0.8		100.0		
Prepare for activity	1.0	88.9	11.1		
Construct a product	0.0				
Procure an object	1.4	96.0			4.0
Gross motor activity	3.9	100.0			
Gain pleasure	4.5	92.6	7.4		
Imitate	1.6	89.3			
Pretend	0.0				
Ease discomfort	0.2	75.0	25.0		
Restore order	0.9	100.0			
Eat and gain info (v)	4.3	100.0			
Eat and gain info (v and a)	0.8	100.0			
Explore	7.9	97.9	2.1		
Mastery	1.5	55.6	22.2		
Eat	7.6	85.4	14.6		
Mastery and misc.					

(8.4 percent), he had 8.4 percent live language versus 0.0 percent mechanical language, and was quite a contrast in this regard to our 2C boy.

Task-Initiation Data

Tables 43 and 44 present task-initiation data for our two-year-old boys. Our lower-class 2C boy had more self-initiated tasks than most two-year-olds. Except for a few social tasks, all other-initiated tasks were mother-initiated. Our 2A boy initiated most of his tasks, especially the nonsocial ones (98.5 percent); however, his mother and older brother made a fairly substantial number of requests of him (*to cooperate* tasks), resulting in a high other-initiated social-task score.

In the area of particular social tasks, we find, in the two types of other-initiated activity (*to cooperate* and *to assert self*), that our 2C lower-class boy had very little of this experience. His siblings, as well as his mother, initiated few of such tasks. Our 2A boy had considerably more of such experience, but a fair number (20.5 percent) of his *to cooperate* tasks were initiated by his older brother.

The mother of our 2C lower-class boy rarely initiated nonsocial tasks for him. Although several entries are present in Table 44 for mother-initiated nonsocial tasks, the key item is a total score of 2.5% mother-initiated nonsocial tasks. Perhaps the most significant items initiated by his mother were looking steadily at something (gain information—visual), eating, and gaining pleasure (usually roughhousing).

As for our 2A boy, he, too, directed most of his own nonsocial experiences, except for four categories, *gain information—visual, pass time, prepare for activity* and *mastery*.

8

Observing the Child's Environment

Jean Carew Watts/Itty Chan Barnett

CONCEPTUAL FRAMEWORK

The major goal of the Preschool Project is to find out how the environments of highly competent and less competent children differ in early childhood. The basic hypothesis of our "natural experiment" is that differences in competence apparent in children by age three may to some extent be explained by systematic differences in the environments these children encounter before age three. The aim of this study is not to prove that differences in environments *cause* subsequent differences in competence (we could not make such a claim from a descriptive study), but to specify, first, which aspects of the environment actually are dissimilar for highly competent and less competent children, and second, to learn how the environment influences the day-to-day experiences of the child.

Our first problem was to define "environment." We were not satisfied with the customary definition, which refers to socioeconomic status, culture, family structures, or life-styles. Information of this type was useful to us in selecting subjects to represent the population at large, but was considered far too crude to explain individual differences in development. We wished to go beyond these gross classifications to the experiences that occur with greater or less frequency within different class, culture, or family groups, since our purpose was to learn about the detailed connections among environment, experience, and competence. With this idea in mind, we therefore defined environment somewhat unconventionally as "a set of human and nonhuman elements in the external world that are directly and observably connected with the child's experience and that may affect his development of competence either through participating in a developmentally pertinent experience, or by making such an experience more or less likely to occur, or more or less pleasurable for the child."

The main point to be noticed about this definition is that it does not consider environment and experience to be entirely separate concepts. The child, at least when he is awake, is always experiencing some part of his external environment, so that on any particular occasion some element in his environment is psychologically active or "functional" for him. The research method and scales that we use in this study focus predominantly on these active or "functional" elements of the child's environment. Thus, in describing the child's environment, we first designate the relevance of the child's *experience* to his development of intellectual and social competence, and then we characterize the elements of the external *environment* that enter into that experience.

As our definition states, the direct role played by environment in the child's experience may be participatory or nonparticipatory. By *participatory,* we mean that the environment, let us say a person, has actually shared in the experience that we have judged to be relevant in some degree to the child's development of competence. By *nonparticipatory*, we mean that the person has not actually participated in the experience itself, but has initiated it, facilitated it, reinforced it, restricted it, or influenced it in some observable way. For example, a mother may join with a child in playing with a toy. We may judge the child's experience, the game the child and mother play together, as highly likely, or moderately likely, or not at all likely to promote the child's intellectual development. Whatever may be our judgment, the mother is considered to have played a *direct participatory* role in promoting the child's development in accordance with our assessment of the intellectual or social value of the experience. Now, on another occasion, this mother may merely suggest that the child play with the toy. In this case, the mother's behavior is still directly connected with the child's experience (at least while she makes the suggestion), but she plays a *nonparticipatory* role in the child's subsequent play with the toy and consequently, a nonparticipatory role in an experience that may turn out to have much, little, or no developmental value for the child.

Here are two concrete examples to illustrate a mother's direct-participatory and nonparticipatory roles in a child's experience. Imagine we are observing a mother and child playing with a set of animal toys. The child grabs the animal shapes eagerly, while the mother tells him their names and makes appropriate roaring, mooing, and bleating sounds, bringing to life a miniature zoo. The child's experience in this illustration has to do with learning the names for the animals and the sounds they make, and this experience is judged as highly likely to promote his intellectual development. The mother's role, coupled with the role of the toy animals in the experience, is a direct, participatory one. She and the animals are functional parts of the child's human and material environment; they share in the child's experience, and they promote his intellectual development directly.

The mother's nonparticipatory role can be exemplified by changing the illustration a little. Suppose we observe the mother suggesting to the child that he play with his toy animals in the manner described above. The child accepts her suggestion and plays with the animals by himself, naming them and imitating their sounds while his mother is busy washing the dishes. The mother's role here is nonparticipatory as far as the experience that promotes his intellectual competence (actually playing with the toy animals) is concerned. By her suggestion she has made this experience more likely to happen (and perhaps also more enjoyable because of her encouragement), but her behavior is not an integral part of the experience as in the previous example, when she actually played with the child.

So far we have described two ways in which a mother or other person may directly influence a child's experience and so his development of competence. Our research method focuses predominantly on those roles that involve interactions between mother and child, but we also study two other, more *indirect* roles that a mother plays. One of these is called the mother's *managerial* role. This is the role she plays as organizer of the child's daily routine, designer of settings for his activities, and maker of rules governing his access to people, places, and things. This role overlaps with the mother's interactive roles discussed above, in the sense that if the mother is actually observed taking part in the child's activity, suggesting something for the child to do, or invoking a rule, these actions would be considered part of her direct, participatory or nonparticipatory roles. Perhaps the mother's managerial role is best thought of as the unobserved side of her direct roles. It refers to the whole framework of time, space, and rules with which the mother regulates the child's activity, including how much time she devotes to activities with him, how much television the child is allowed to watch, what places and objects in the home he is permitted to use, whether he has a play area and how it is equipped, and who his playmates and adult acquaintances are. The mother's managerial role is not fully observed in this study, but is constructed from interviews in which mothers are asked to recall the child's activities of the previous day and from descriptions of the child's toys and the design and furnishings of the home.

The fourth role of the mother that is evaluated in this research is her *diffuse* role. This is her role when she is considered as a totality, and not merely in relationship to her preschool child. This role consists of many factors, such as the mother's personality, values, and standards, her socioeconomic, cultural, and educational background, her responsibilities for other members of the family, her work obligations, her feelings toward young children, her awareness of their developing needs, and her beliefs regarding how these should be met. Like her managerial role, the diffuse role of the mother is not fully observed but gauged through interviews and incidental conversations.

Before going on to describe the scales we developed to study the child's environment,* a word should be said about the basis for judging experience in these scales as compared to that for the Task Scale described in Chapter 5. Both the task and environment scales use dictated descriptions of the child's activity and the surrounding context as their raw data for coding experience. However, from that point the perspectives of the two scales differ. An observer using the Task Scale focuses predominantly on the behavior of the child, interpreting what the child is trying to do from moment to moment. For example, the child's task may be interpreted as exploration, mastery of skill, gaining information, achieving social contact, and so on. In contrast, an observer using the environment scales is concerned with several other aspects of the child's experience, including the behavior of other people and the qualities of objects that enter into the experience, in addition to the child's own behavior. Information on all three aspects of the child's experience is used in judging the relevance of that experience for promoting the child's intellectual or social competence.

SCALES FOR MEASURING THE CHILD'S ENVIRONMENT

We developed two scales for measuring the child's environment as he experiences it. The first scale, the Human Interaction Scale, focuses on the active role played by people in the child's experience, and is ap-

---

* All scales and questionnaires described in Chapters 8, 9, and 10 were developed by Jean Carew Watts, Itty Chan Barnett, Nancy Apfel, and Christine Halfar, with the assistance of Geri Kearse, a former staff member. These instruments are described in detail in Appendix III.

plied only to those experiences of the child that involve interactions between the child and other people. The second scale, the Object Interaction Scale, focuses on the active role played by the child's nonhuman environment in the child's experience. This scale is applied to all the child's observed experiences, because some aspect of the material environment is nearly always functional for the child.

In both these interaction scales, the child's experience is labeled "activity" in order to distinguish it from "experience" as treated in the Task Scale, although the term "experience" may be more appropriate since the child need not play an active role in the interaction.

Human Interaction Scale

To use this scale, the observer starts by making a running commentary of the behavior of the child and others with whom he is interacting, then later codes each unit of interaction on six dimensions. The dimensions are (1) the person with whom the child is interacting; (2) the child's experience or activity (this may be ongoing, being prepared for, or being suggested to the child); (3) the technique of interaction used by the other person; (4) who initiated the activity; (5) whether the other person encouraged or discouraged the activity; and (6) whether the other person was successful in attempting to control the child, if such an attempt was made. Here are brief descriptions of the activity and technique dimensions of the Human Interaction Scale. The other dimensions are self-explanatory.

ACTIVITIES. This dimension encodes the child's activities or experiences in categories relevant to different aspects of intellectual and social development. For example, naming the pictures in a book is judged relevant to verbal development; building a tower with blocks is judged relevant to spatial, perceptual, and fine motor development; playing "Superman" is judged relevant to the development of imaginative skills.*

It may be helpful for the reader to think of the basis for our categories as similar to the learning goals an evaluator of a Head Start program might have in mind when she observes different types of activities scheduled in the classroom; story-book time (*verbal learning*), puzzle time (*spatial, perceptual* and *fine motor learning*), jungle-gym time (*gross motor learning*). If the child actually engages in the prescribed activity, then he may be assumed to be learning the skill which that activity is designed to teach. In our system, the observer is a bit like the Head Start evaluator. She does not prescribe activities for the child, but has in mind a set of

---

* In Appendix III are listed the categories that make up our Activity dimension, along with examples of typical activities that are coded in these categories.

developmental goals by which she judges his behavior. Using a complex and somewhat arbitrary set of criteria to be described later, the observer codes the child's activities according to the opportunity they present for the child to develop certain intellectual or social skills.

Of course, in making the analogy between school-evaluator and observer, we should not gloss over the fundamental differences that exist between the school and home settings. In the home, no one normally plays the role of the teacher, playthings are not usually designed to promote specific intellectual or social skills, and the child's activities are not scheduled in advance, they last only a short time, and they change character rapidly. Indeed, the most difficult aspect of the observer's task is to demarcate units of activity as they occur spontaneously, and to categorize these activities according to criteria that, in practice, are seldom unquestionably met.

Here is an example drawn from a real observation to illustrate the rapid and spontaneous changes in activities that typically confront an observer in the home.

Mark (2½ years) finds a tiny bead on the floor and runs to his mother holding it out and shouting, "Ma!" Mother looks at the bead and says, "Right. Put it in the box" (pointing to a sewing box on a shelf near her). Mark moves toward the box, but instead of putting in the bead, he takes out a narrow plastic tube filled with tiny beads. He sits on the floor and begins to tip the tube up and down, watching the beads roll down and back. He pulls out the stopper with his teeth (a feat requiring some dexterity), carefully tipping the mouth of the tube up and down as if experimenting with gravity, and tips all the beads onto the floor. Mother notices and says sharply, "Now, look what you've done. Put them all back in." Mark begins to pick up the tiny beads one by one and slide them into the tube. Mother looks and says, "Do it like this." She gets down on the floor, wetting the tip of her finger. Mark wets his finger in imitation. Mother begins to count the beads as they put them in alternately. Mark repeats the numbers she calls out: "One, two, three. . ." Mark says, "Red." Mother: "It's not red, it's purple. See it in the light." She holds up the bead to the window and Mark looks intently and smiles, saying, "Not red, purple!"

In terms of our scale, there are four changes in activity in this episode. At first the interaction is concerned with the mother unsuccessfully trying to get the child to carry out an instruction requiring *executive skill,* involving a sequence of steps (put the bead in the sewing box). The next interaction focuses on *concrete reasoning* (Mark initiates an experiment with gravity) of which mother disapproves, and she orders him to carry out another task (put the beads back into the small tube), which very likely involves the learning of *spatial, perceptual* and *fine motor skills.*

She observes Mark's attempts at mastering the fine motor task and then demonstrates how to do it. The activity then shifts to *verbal symbolic learning* (counting and labeling), which the mother initiates and teaches.

In this example, not only is the child's behavior rapidly changing, but the mother's actions in relation to each of these activities also change. She does not necessarily interpret the child's activity in the same way as the observer does. When the mother said, "Now look what you've done; put them all back in," she probably had no conscious intention of cutting off Mark's attempt at concrete reasoning, nor of launching him off on a fine motor sequence. However, this was the effect on the child, and these are the activities that are coded.

TECHNIQUES.   The technique dimension of our Human Interaction Scale gives basic information on the *direct* roles the mother and other people play, providing a means of coding their behavior when they interact with the child. For example, telling the child the name for an object is coded as "teaching"; suggesting that the child come indoors is coded as "positive control"; scolding the child for hitting his baby brother is coded as "restriction"; praising the child for eating up his food is coded as "positive reinforcement."

These techniques or forms of interaction may be classified in accordance with our analysis of roles discussed earlier in this chapter. The distinctions made in this analysis are vividly conveyed by cartoons that show an interactor sometimes playing a *direct, participatory* role in the child's activity (for example when the mother reads the magazine to the little girl in Figure 8.1); sometimes playing a *direct, nonparticipatory, but facilitative* role (for instance, when she provides the pots and pans to the little boy in Figure 8.2); sometimes playing a *direct, nonparticipatory, but restrictive* role (for example, when she scolds her daughter for reading the magazine in Figure 8.1); and sometimes playing a *neutral* role (for instance, when she observes her son's sweeping up in Figure 8.3 or having a tantrum in Figure 8.6).

Of course, a variety of techniques may be used to play any of these roles, and our considering different techniques within a role-category as equivalent for purposes of analysis is somewhat arbitrary. Thus, within our system of analysis, an interactor plays a *participatory* role when the person employs one of four techniques in interaction with the child: teaching, justifying, active joining in, or conversing. The common feature of these participatory techniques is that the interactor shares in the child's experience and is an integral part of it for him. The interactor plays a *nonparticipatory, facilitative* role when he suggests an activity, supplies materials for it, praises, or helps the child. The common feature of these nonparticipatory, facilitative techniques is that the interactor makes the child's experience more likely to occur or more pleasurable and likely to be repeated. The interactor plays a *nonparticipatory, restrictive* role when he prohibits or prevents the child from engaging in the activity, refuses to help, scolds him, or distracts him to another activity. The common feature of these nonparticipatory, restrictive techniques is that the interactor makes the experience less likely to occur or less pleasurable and likely to be repeated. Finally, the interactor plays a *neutral* role when he merely observes the child engaging in an activity.

Variations in the specific techniques used by an interactor to play a given role are illustrated in Figures 8.4 and 8.5. In Figure 8.4 a mother uses three different techniques to play a participatory role in the child's experience: she teaches her little girl how to draw, joins in the actual production of a drawing, and finally chats enthusiastically about their artistic creation. Similarly, the father in Figure 8.5 plays a nonparticipatory, restrictive role using three different techniques: he prevents the little boy from playing in the fish tank, scolds him for dropping in the Teddy Bear, and finally tries to distract him to a more acceptable activity.

VERBAL/SYMBOLIC

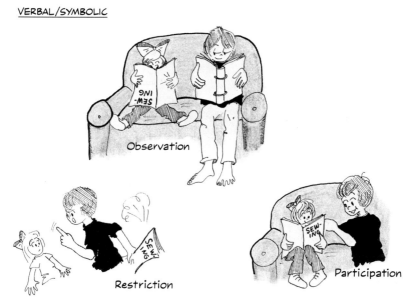

Figure 8.1 Mother uses techniques of observation, restriction and participation in a verbal/symbolic activity.

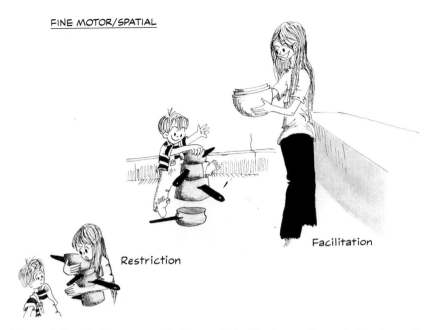

Figure 8.2 Mother uses techniques of facilitation and restriction in a fine motor/spatial activity.

Figure 8.3 Mother uses techniques of observation and facilitation in an executive skill activity.

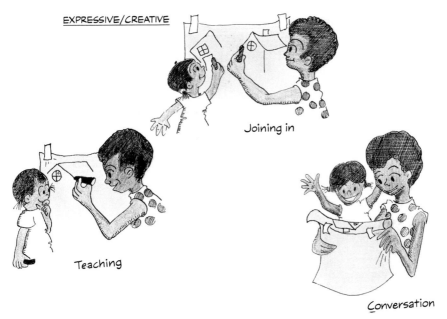

EXPRESSIVE/CREATIVE

Joining in

Teaching

Conversation

Figure 8.4 Mother uses participatory techniques of teaching, joining in, and conversation in an expressive/creative activity.

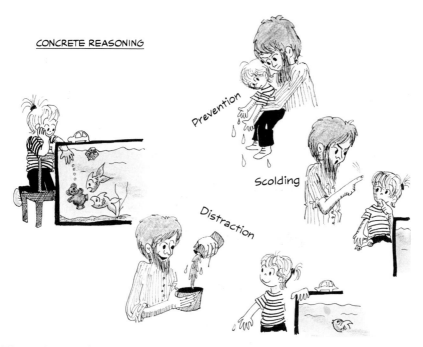

CONCRETE REASONING

Prevention

Scolding

Distraction

Figure 8.5 Father uses restrictive techniques of prevention, scolding, and distraction in a concrete reasoning activity.

Observation

Figure 8.6 Mother uses the nonparticipatory technique of observation in a negative social activity.

SOCIAL POSITIVE

Participation

Figure 8.7 Child using technique of participation in a positive social activity.

ACTIVITIES AND TECHNIQUES CONSIDERED SIMULTANEOUSLY. One of the real advantages of the Human Interaction Scale is that it codes simultaneously, yet separately, both the activity of the child and the technique used by the other person in the interaction. In real life, a given technique (e.g., mother restricts child) may be applied to many different types of activities (e.g., stops child from hitting baby brother, or from listening to "Sesame Street," or from falling off his high chair), and the different combinations of activity and technique may have quite different implications for the child's development.

To illustrate the connections among the activity, the technique, and the other three dimensions of the Human Interaction Scale (initiation, encouragement, and success in control), here is a description of how some fictitious episodes would be handled by that scale.

Susan (24 months) pulls down a magazine from a rack in the living room and begins turning the pages. Occasionally she babbles as if labeling the pictures she sees. Her fingers are sticky and the pages are getting messy. Mother comes in, sees her, and says, "No, no, no. Let's put this back." Mother takes away magazine and puts it on a high shelf. Susan begins to whimper and tries to pull the magazine down again.

There are five essential points in this episode that would be picked up by our scale.

1. Susan's activity (leafing through the magazine) is likely to provide her with an opportunity for intellectual development; in this case, verbal or representational learning.
2. Susan initiated the activity.
3. Mother discouraged the activity by
4. Taking away an object essential to the activity (thus playing a direct, restrictive role in Susan's experience).
5. Susan resists Mother.

Joey (15 months) is sitting on the floor and trying to put blocks of different shapes into the holes of a shape-box. Mother is washing dishes at the sink. She stops and watches Joey as he tries to put the square block into the round hole. She goes to him, saying, "Try it here," pointing to the square hole. Joey gets the block in and grins happily.

The essential points about this episode that are coded by our scale are these:

1. The child's activity (putting blocks into appropriate holes) is likely to provide him with an opportunity for intellectual development; in this case, perceptual and spatial learning.
2. The activity is initiated by Joey.
3. Mother encourages the activity, and
4. Teaches the child (thus playing a direct role in Joey's experience).
5. Child responds positively to mother's teaching.

Nancy (24 months) has been following her Mother around the kitchen as Mother does household chores. Mother suggests Nancy play with two pots on the floor and hands her the pots. Nancy sits on the floor and pushes the pots around.

The essential points about this episode are these:

1. The child's activity (pushing the pots around) is less likely than in the other cases described to provide her with an opportunity for intellectual learning. (If Mother had encouraged Nancy to stack the pots or transfer their contents, we would have coded this episode as providing a greater opportunity for intellectual development.)
2. Mother initiates the activity.
3. Mother encourages the activity by
4. Suggesting it to Nancy and providing the necessary materials (thus playing a direct, facilitative role in her experience).
5. Nancy carries out Mother's suggestion.

By simultaneously coding each episode on the five points listed above, the scale captures the fundamental differences among the cases, which are that Susan experiences an opportunity for intellectual development that is cut off by her mother; Joey has a similar experience in which his mother directly participates, and Nancy has an experience less "intellectual" than that of the others, which her mother encourages and helps to bring about.

CRITERIA FOR JUDGING ACTIVITIES. We have postponed a discussion of the criteria for judging activities until the reader could gain some idea of the meaning of the terms "activity" and "technique" in our scale. In coding an activity, the observer has to make two judgments. She has to decide, first, whether the activity is likely to promote an intellectual or social skill, and second, to what type of skill it is most relevant. In our system of coding, there are twelve categories of activities that are considered relevant to intellectual development, and three that are considered relevant to social development. Intellectual and social activities are arranged in separate hierarchies, reflecting the judgment that some categories are more likely than others in the same hierarchy to promote the child's development.

Table 45 shows the hierarchy of activities relevant to intellectual development. The second column shows that this hierarchy has three clusters, the categories of activities in each cluster having equal status. Activities judged *highly likely* to promote the child's development of a specific intellectual skill are coded in the first cluster; activities that are *moderately likely* to promote intellectual development are coded in the second cluster; and activities *least likely to promote* intellectual development are coded in the third cluster. An example for each cluster is given in Table 45.

TABLE 45. Hierarchy of Intellectual Activities

Cluster I = highly intellectual activities
Cluster II = moderately intellectual activities
Cluster III = nonintellectual activities

Series I. S uses a book.

Example	Cluster	Activity
1. M reads *Goodnight Moon* to S and they label pictures.	I	Verbal/Symbolic learning
2. M asks, "Can you find the little mouse?" S looks for the tiny mouse imbedded in the detail of the picture.	I	Spatial/Perceptual/Fine motor learning
3. S watches the shadows of her finger on the book. M moves S's finger and S watches the shadow move.	I	Concrete reasoning
4. S pretends to be the bunny in *Goodnight Moon*. S curls up on the couch saying, "Goodnight chair, goodnight comb, goodnight brush." M smiles.	I	Expressive skills
5. M asks S to put toys away. S takes the books and toys, a few at a time, to the toy box, closing the lid when they are all in.	I	Executive skills
6. M says, "Go find something to play with." S takes a book down from a bookshelf and puts it on the table. S touches the covers but says nothing.	II	Play with toys
7. S wanders about clutching a book, staring blankly into space.	III	Purposelessness

Series II. S is being changed on changing table.

Example	Cluster	Activity
8. M bends over S to change her. S touches M's hair, and babbles. M says, "Hair, that's hair."	I	Verbal/Symbolic learning
9. S gets hold of a shoelace and seems to be trying to lace her shoe. M looks on, saying, "It's hard, isn't it?"	I	Spatial/Perceptual/Fine motor learning
10. M plays peek-a-boo, hiding her face behind a diaper and saying, "Where's Mommy?" S chuckles.	I	Concrete reasoning
11. S makes a pouring motion on doll's head. S says to M, "Baby's crying." (S often cries when her hair is shampooed.)	I	Expressive skills
12. M suggests S powder herself. S shakes container of powder over her legs, then rubs it in. M looks on.	I	Executive skills
13. S takes container of powder and shakes it briefly, then throws it on the floor. M gives her a bottle to suck.	II	Explore or play with household objects
14. M changes S on changing table. S lies supine staring at ceiling.	III	Basic care
15. M finishes diapering S. She bounces and kisses her. S laughs and hugs M.	IV	Positive Social Emotional

Several criteria are considered in deciding whether an activity is likely to stimulate intellectual development in the child. The first set of criteria have to do with the child's own behavior in the interaction. (In the Human Interaction Scale only interactions between the child and other persons are coded.) If the quality of the child's own behavior indicates that the experience is highly likely to promote his intellectual development, the activity is automatically coded on that basis. However, if the child's own behavior is passive or primitive, the behavior of other people in the inter- action becomes crucial to the judgment of activity. For example, a clear- cut case for judging an activity as "highly intellectual" occurs when the interactor teaches the child conceptual or symbolic material. In this case, the child's role in the activity may be limited to looking and listening, but the opportunity for his intellectual development is clearly present.

Table 45 illustrates how two common situations for a young child, "S uses a book" and "S is being changed," can give rise to quite different activities as the level and purpose* of the child's behavior change and as the behavior of the interactor also changes. Some of the resulting activi- ties are considered as highly likely (examples 1–5 and 8–12), others as only moderately-likely (examples 6 and 13), and others as not likely (examples 7 and 14) to promote the child's intellectual development. One activity (example 15) is judged primarily relevant to the child's social and emotional development.

The examples of Table 45 should also make it clear that "highly intellectual" activities by no means typically involve "lessons" or educa- tional materials. On the contrary, almost any situation may become a highly intellectual activity, that is, an opportunity that is very likely to pro- mote the child's intellectual development, as long as the child's behavior is reasonably systematic, structured, purposeful, and attentive. There is really no one word to describe the essential distinction between the wide array of activities that the observer will judge to be of high intellectual promise and those she will judge to be of less intellectual value. Again, we have to fall back on the examples of Table 45. When the child in Series I listens to mother read *Goodnight Moon* or tries to find the tiny mouse in the picture or watches the shadow of her mother's finger on the book or tidies up, put- ting the books and toys away—she is performing activities judged to be of high intellectual value, although the specific intellectual gain for the child varies from one example to another. In contrast, when the child in example 6 simply transfers a book from one place to the other, we judge this experience as only moderately likely (at best) to promote his intellec- tual development and think of it as unstructured, unsystematic "Play with

---

* "Purpose" in this scale corresponds roughly to "task" in the task scale de- scribed in Chapter 5, but it is only one of several criteria taken into account in judging an activity.

Toys." A more extreme instance of relatively "empty" behavior is in example 7, where the child is wandering around with a book in hand, staring into space and essentially "doing nothing." This behavior is coded as "Purposelessness" and considered to be least conducive to intellectual development.

More striking than the examples of Series I, Table 45, are the examples of Series II which presents a situation that is ordinarily far from educational in nature (see Figure 8.8 also). The scene is one with which observers of young children are familiar: the child lies supine on a changing-table while mother changes his diaper. Commonly, the child accepts the situation passively and whiles away the time staring or babbling at nothing in particular. This situation is coded as "Basic Care" and represents minimal intellectual stimulation. An enterprising mother, however, sometimes uses this time to entertain the captive infant with a peek-a-boo game, or an energetic child might get hold of his shoes and try to tie the laces, entertaining the mother with his antics. These embellishments on the mundane task of diapering provide the child with opportunities for intellectual development, so we code the peek-a-boo game as "Concrete Reasoning" (the child is learning the concept that a thing continues to exist although it is hidden from sight) and the shoe-lacing episode as "Spatial Perceptual Fine Motor Learning."

DISTINCTION AMONG HIGHLY, MODERATELY AND NONINTELLECTUAL ACTIVITIES

Figure 8.8 Mother and child interact in activities of high, moderate and low intellectual value.

In sum, the child's own behavior, his level of functioning, and the task he is trying to accomplish all have a major influence on the choice of code in the Activity column of our Human Interaction Scale, although these items are not explicitly coded in this scale. As its name implies, however, a major ingredient of the interaction scale is its *interactive* quality. Hence the behavior of other people interacting with the child may also determine the judgment of activity, and the form of their behavior is explicitly coded.

Finally, we must make the obvious point that we depend very much on what the child's and/or other person's behavior "is about" in order to decide what the child may be learning. As Table 45 shows, the same basic situation (such as using a book or diapering) may be the setting for activities that are judged quite differently. First, the overall intellectual level of an activity is judged as high, moderate, or low, depending on the child's or other person's behavior, and second, the activity is judged to be relevant to one of several intellectual skills, depending on its content. Thus when the mother in Table 45 labels the pictures in *Goodnight Moon,* this activity is judged relevant to verbal learning, whereas when she asks the child to find the little mouse embedded in the picture, this activity is judged more relevant to spatial learning. Some degree of arbitrariness and imprecision enters into both types of judgment, of course. No one knows for certain whether the structured use of materials (an important element in the distinction between "highly intellectual" and "moderately intellectual" activities) promotes intellectual development more than the unstructured use of the same materials, or whether the building of block towers develops spatial skills more than it develops verbal skills. These assumptions are plausible but not necessarily correct. Their usefulness is seen in the ability of this coding system to organize our observation data and to relate the data to development in the child and to activities that will later go on in school.

Object Interaction Scale

The Object Interaction Scale is used to code the child's use of objects and of his physical environment. It was amazing that in our search of the literature we could find no scale that measured by direct and repeated *observation* the availability of objects in the child's home environment, much less the use he actually makes of them. We could find no study that observed systematically such things as the toys, household objects, furniture, and space to which the child has access; the communications media to which he is exposed; the noise level, crowdedness, order, or consistency of routine that surround him. All the information we could find on the effects of the physical environment of the home was obtained from studies using interviews, retrospective reports, or, at most, one-shot observation (e.g.,

Bing, 1963; Hess and Shipman, 1965; Wachs, Uzgiris, and Hunt, in press; Wolf, 1964).

We therefore decided to develop a simple scale of our own to assess the child's interaction with material aspects of his surroundings.* With this Object Interaction Scale, after each 15 seconds of observation, we describe and later code:

1. The room occupied by the child
2. Barriers and restrictions imposed upon him
3. The person to whom he is attending
4. The size and portability of objects to which he is attending or that he is using.

Questionnaires

We have described at length the two scales that are used in our study to measure those aspects of the environment that enter actively into the child's experience. In addition to these two scales, three questionnaires were developed to provide more general information on the child's external environment. The first, the Typical Day Questionnaire, is used to obtain information on the basic routine of the child's day and the child's range of experience, especially the amount of time regularly devoted to activities such as eating, sleeping, playing indoors, playing outdoors, and looking at television; the amount of time the child spent with certain people, such as his mother, father, siblings, other adults, and other children; and the amount of contact the child had with people and places in and out of his neighborhood.

The Typical Day Questionnaire provides basic information on the mother's *managerial* role; the role she plays as organizer of the child's routine, designer of settings for his activities, and maker of rules governing his access to people, places, and things. This questionnaire is administered each time we visit the child's home to make an observation for our interaction scales. Mothers are asked to recall as far as possible the child's activities during the 24 hours preceding the visit. Some mothers

* After the data reported in this book were collected, the Object Interaction Scale was extended to incorporate all the dimensions of the Human Interaction Scale and some new dimensions dealing with the design characteristics of objects used by the child; the child's mode, level, and purpose in attending to a person or object; and the absence or presence of verbal stimulation. The new dimensions just mentioned have all along influenced our coding of "Activities" but were not explicitly coded in either the Human Interaction or Object Interaction Scale described in this report. This new scale, the Human or Material Environment or HOME Scale, codes these dimensions explicitly, thereby taking account of all aspects of the environment that are active in a single unit of experience. Data collected with this scale will be reported in a later volume.

are able to do this with great facility, recalling changes in the child's activities, say, every fifteen minutes. Other mothers remember only landmarks, such as breakfast, lunch, and dinner, and describe most activities in between as "playing around." Differences in the specificity with which mothers are able to remember the child's activities are likely to be related to the mother's general awareness of her child's development and the degree to which she plans and structures his experience.

The other two questionnaires are loosely structured schedules for interviewing the mother. These questionnaires provide information on the mother's *diffuse* role, which we have previously discussed. Each mother in our study is interviewed before the first observation on her child and again when all observations are completed and the child is three years old. The first interview includes questions relating to the family's socioeconomic status, educational, cultural, and religious background, family routines, and so on. The second interview focuses on the mother's awareness of the child's development and of her own beliefs and behavior relating to him. This interview includes questions on the following points:

1. Division of responsibility for caring for and bringing up the child
2. Inventory of toys and playthings
3. Training in self-care—ages at which the child learned to feed himself, keep clean, etc., and problems associated with training
4. Mother's awareness of the value to the child's development of play with different toys, household objects, books, and TV programs
5. Mother's descriptions of the child's present personality and intellectual abilities and estimates of how he will have developed by the time he is five to six years old
6. Mother's beliefs that aspects of the personality or intellect can be modified by her actions
7. Mother's awareness of the effects of her own behavior on her child's development
8. Mother's own activities, interests, and outlook on life.

The main aim of the final interview is to give the mother an opportunity to talk about her child, her relationship with him, and how he is developing; and to give us a chance to compare data from our own observations with the mother's reports.

SUMMARY

We developed four instruments for measuring the effects of the child's human and material environment on his intellectual and social development. The first scale, the Human Interaction Scale, is applied to interactions between the child and other people. It codes the child's experience and specific aspects of the human environment that form part of that experience. The second scale, the Object Interaction Scale, codes the child's experience and various aspects of the nonhuman environment that enter directly into that experience. A third instrument, the Typical Day Questionnaire, provides information on the child's daily routine and range of experience, while a preliminary interview and a final interview with mothers give more general information on the mother's personality, background, responsibilities, and values.

9

Environments Compared

JEAN CAREW WATTS/ITTY CHAN BARNETT

In this chapter we shall report and discuss some preliminary findings about the effects of the environment on the child's development of intellectual and social competence. We shall focus primarily on findings from only one of our scales, the Human Interaction Scale, since data gathered with our other instruments have not yet been completely coded or analyzed. This means that we shall be discussing mostly those activities that occur when the mother or another person is interacting with the child, rather than when the child is alone or when no one is paying attention to him. These activities will be judged as having much, moderate, or little developmental value for the child; and we shall explore questions such as who initiates them, whether they are encouraged or discouraged, what particular form of behavior the other person in the interaction uses, and whether this other person successfully influences the child. The child's interaction with his physical environment will be only briefly discussed and will be limited to three aspects: restrictions on the child's movements, the amount of attention he pays to *things* rather than *people,* and characteristics of objects he uses in his activities.

OBSERVATION SCHEDULE:
WHEN, WHO, AND WHERE WE OBSERVE

The data on environment were gathered on five separate days approximately three weeks apart, in the child's own home or neighborhood. We plan eventually to observe twenty children, five times per period, during four periods between ages one and three (at 12–15 months, 18–21 months, 24–27 months, and 30–33 months), and twenty children during two periods between ages two and three (at 24–27 months and 30–33 months). However, since our study is still in progress and no child has yet completed more than two periods of observation, the following report of our findings includes some children who were observed at 12–15 months only, some who were observed at both 12–15 and 18–21 months, some who were observed at 24–27 months only, and some who were observed at both 24–27 and 30–33 months.

We also planned to balance the number of middle-class and lower-class children in our sample, the number of boys and girls, and the number of children who we predict will develop extremely well ("A" children) and the number who we predict will develop poorly ("C" children). However, a number of problems have so far prevented us from achieving these goals, and the sample on which this report is based is far from being perfectly balanced. Table 46 shows the distribution of children in our age, social class, and competence classifications. We expect that much of the present unevenness in our sample will be rectified by the time our study is completed.*

Our visits were made at various times of the day between 9 A.M. and 5 P.M., Monday through Friday. To ensure our observing a variety of activities and people interacting with the child, one of the five visits was always scheduled for lunchtime, two were scheduled for the morning, and two were scheduled for the afternoon. We also tried to make sure that our observations did not altogether coincide with the television program "Sesame Street," since some of our children were avid "Sesame Street" fans, and while they watched the program, real people were no match for Ernie, Oscar, or the Cookie Monster. In addition, we tried to schedule each child's observations to reflect the relative amount of time he was normally in the charge of his mother or some other regular caretaker, with the proviso that no child was recruited to our study if we knew that his mother was not normally at home at least three out of five weekdays. Actually, because of emergencies or last-minute changes in the mother's

---

* The data reported in this chapter are from a larger number of children and cover more periods of observation than the data reported in Chapters 5–7, pp. 68–155.

TABLE 46. Distribution of Subjects by Age at Which Observations Were Begun, Period during Which Subject Was Observed, Socioeconomic Status, and Predicted Level of Competence

| Observation Begun at: | Predicted A's | | | | Predicted C's | | | | Totals |
| | 1 yr. | | 2 yr. | | 1 yr. | | 2 yr. | | |
	At 12–15 Months	At 18–21 Months	At 24–27 Months	At 30–33 Months	At 12–15 Months	At 18–21 Months	At 24–27 Months	At 30–33 Months	
Upper to middle classes (I and II)*	8	7	7	7	0	0	0	0	29
Middle to lower classes (III, IV, V)*	2	1	5	2	3	2	6	4	25
Total observation periods	10	8	12	9	3	2	6	4	54
Total subjects	10	8	12	12	3	2	6	6	31

* Index of Social Position, from A. B. Hollingshead and F. C. Redlich, Social Class and Mental Illness (New York: John Wiley & Sons, Inc., 1958).

plans, we did not always know who would be taking care of the child when we made our visits. As it turned out, for over 90 percent of our observations, and for 23 out of the 31 children included in our preliminary analysis of data on the environment, the mother was always the child's caretaker. In the case of four children, someone else (usually a female babysitter) was in charge of the child during one of our observations, and in the case of another four children, someone else was in charge of the child during two of our observations (reflecting the fact that these particular children were regularly cared for by babysitters). More detailed information on the nature of the child's caretaker is given in Table 47. The facts presented in this table should be borne in mind when interpreting our data on interactions between mother and child, since, in this chapter, the term "mother" may refer either to the child's real mother or to some other person who was in charge of the child during our observations.

We have mentioned that we limited our observation to weekdays from 9 A.M. to 5 P.M. This limitation probably means that our data underrepresents the influence on the child of fathers and older siblings, who are not usually at home during this period. We probably also miss some of the more exciting and unusual places the child visits, since trips to such places are likely to be reserved for weekends. Despite these constraints, the range of people, places, and things we actually sampled in our observation is quite extraordinary.

We have seen children interacting with mothers and fathers, grandmothers and grandfathers, aunts and uncles, brothers and sisters, babies and pets; friends of parents, friends of older siblings, friends their own age; babysitters, cleaning women, deliverymen, repairmen, storekeepers, and strangers on the street. We have followed children into living rooms, bedrooms, bathrooms, kitchens, basements, attics, backyards and front gardens; into the homes of neighbors, community rooms, playgrounds, parks, down the block, and on busy highways; into offices, stores, museums, schools, cars, trailers, and on bicycles.

TABLE 47. Distribution of Subjects on Varying Percentages of Observations During Which Mother Was the Main Caretaker

% Observations in Which M Is Caretaker	A's Months				C's Months			
	12–15	18–21	24–27	30–33	12–15	18–21	24–27	30–33
100%	7	8	8	6	3	2	5	4
80%	2	0	1	0	0	0	1	0
60%	1	0	3	3	0	0	0	0

We have seen these children engage in an astounding array of activities. These include eating, bathing, dressing, and going to the potty; swinging, sliding, exercising, and dancing; playing with small toys such as books, blocks, trucks, dolls, and balls; with large toys such as tricycles, carts, motor scooters, and rocking horses; with small household items such as knives, ashtrays, pots, rice, and spaghetti; with large household items such as vacuum cleaners, record players, barrels, and boxes; with animals such as horses, dogs, cats, frogs, and cockroaches; and with natural objects such as grass, stones, mud, sand, and water. In view of this fantastic array of settings and stimuli we are almost thankful for the few constraints on data collection that we did reluctantly impose on ourselves. Without these limitations, comprehensiveness of coverage might easily have degenerated into chaos.

METHOD OF OBSERVATION: WHO OBSERVES AND HOW THEY OBSERVE

The observers in our environment group are five females with graduate degrees in Education and Psychology.* Their backgrounds are varied. One observer comes from a large city in China, and is of middle-class background; one is Protestant, American, from a large city in the Midwest, and of working-class background; one is Catholic, from a small city in the West Indies, and of middle-class background; one Protestant, American, from a small city in the East, and of middle-class background; and one is Catholic, from a rural area in the Midwest, and of working-class background. Two of our observers are black, one is Chinese, and two are white. We consider this diversity in the backgrounds of our observers a great asset, since it ensures that our data will be collected and interpreted from a variety of cultural perspectives.

In making our observations, we capitalized on cultural differences in our staff by rotating visits among our observers. Thus, the typical child is visited by four different observers and by one of them twice. When the observer visits the home, she usually stays approximately one hour and collects data relevant to three different scales: three 10-minute observations for the Human Interaction Scale, two 10-minute observations for the Object Interaction Scale, and one 10-minute interview for the Typical Day Questionnaire.†

For the Human Interaction Scale, the observers dictate into a small tape recorder a running commentary describing the behavior of the child and others who interact with him; this commentary is coded as soon as pos-

---

* The observers are Nancy Apfel, Itty Chan Barnett, Christine Halfar, Geraldine Kearse, and Jean Carew Watts.
† See Appendix III for details of the scales.

sible after the visit is completed. For the Object Interaction Scale, the observer uses a special coding sheet and tries to code on the spot; she observes the child's behavior for fifteen seconds, then writes and codes what she has observed during the next fifteen seconds, repeating this alternating sequence for 10 minutes. For the Typical Day Questionnaire, the observer interviews the mother and asks her to recall the child's activities of the preceding 24 hours. The observer probes the mother concerning each half hour or so of the preceding day—where the child was, whom he was with, what he was doing, and what she, the mother, was doing. The Human Interaction and Object Interaction observations in the visit are alternated, and the visit ends with the Typical Day interview.

POSSIBLE SOURCES OF ERROR IN OUR FINDINGS

Before presenting our findings, we must remind the reader of their preliminary and tentative nature and also point out some possible sources of error.

One major source of error is inherent in all observational research in which the observer is not concealed. This has to do with the effect of the observer himself on the data he gathers. Specifically in our own study, there is very likely a tendency on the part of mothers and other people to interact more with the child and to do so in more "suitable" ways when we are in the home than when we are not there. Admittedly, in our study it would be extremely difficult for a mother to keep up a totally artificial front, considering that she receives a visit from someone connected with our project almost every week for three months running, and that this cycle is repeated as many as four times over the course of two years. Nevertheless, it is still likely that she will try to make a good impression, and this distorts our findings to some degree. We have no way of knowing how much this distortion occurs or how it may vary from mother to mother, but our guess is that the true figures for such items as the quantity of mother–child interaction, the frequency of "intellectual" activities, and the amount of teaching that goes on are somewhat lower than the estimates derived from our study.

Another important source of error affecting our findings is the imperfect reliability of our scales. Agreement between pairs of observers, after observing the same child and coding their data, averages 76–87 percent for the dimensions of the Human Interaction Scale and close to 100 percent for dimensions of the Object Interaction Scale discussed in this report. This degree of agreement compares well to that reported by other researchers conducting similar observational studies, but is nevertheless far short of perfect. Fortunately, our method of rotating observations of each child among several observers mitigates this unreliability to some extent; no one child is victimized by the personal bias or other shortcomings of any one observer.

A third source of bias has to do with the conceptual basis of the scales themselves. We have made this conceptual basis quite explicit in Chapter 8. But here we want to acknowledge that there is nothing inherently correct about the scale categories we chose to use. With a different orientation, we might quite easily have developed a different set of scales, applied them to our data, and come up with a different set of results. In interpreting our findings, the reader should constantly bear in mind the value judgments implicit in our scales and our specific definitions of terms.

Finally, we are obliged to stress the preliminary and tentative nature of the present report of our findings. Our data are to be taken as tentative for several reasons:

1. We have not included in this report all the subjects necessary to complete the design of the study, and the subjects we have included are unevenly distributed on our classificatory variables of age, social class, and predicted competence levels ("A" versus "C" children). With small numbers of subjects, this sampling imbalance can substantially affect our results.

2. Subjects are classified in terms of *predicted* competence levels. In the final analysis of data, competence will be determined from *actual* test performance. Some children will no doubt have to be reclassified.

3. As previously discussed, our study is still in progress, and no child whom we started observing at 12 months has yet completed more than two phases of observations. This means that the data we will present for the second and third year of life come from two different groups of children, one group started at one year of age and another group started at two. Until we have completed our study, we cannot be sure that the longitudinal data on our one-year-old starters will replicate the data from our two-year-old starters.

4. The available data on our scales are incompletely analyzed. Practical considerations require that we concentrate on only the most obvious aspects and ignore subtleties, complexities, and contradictions. Plainly, our expectation is that many of these problems will resolve themselves when the study is complete, and there is little point in worrying ourselves or the reader with premature questions.

PRELIMINARY DATA ANALYSIS: ACTIVITIES AND TECHNIQUES

In reporting our findings, we shall first examine the data for interaction between the child and mother (or main caretaker) only, and then consider the data for interaction between the child and all people including the mother. Table 48 shows the average amount of observation time spent by mother and child in each group on "highly intellectual," "moderately intellectual," "nonintellectual" and "social" activities, which are coded according to the hierarchical categories of our Human Interaction Scale. Table 49 shows the average amount of observation time spent by mothers of each group using different techniques of interaction with the child. Important aspects of our findings are highlighted in Figures 9.1–9.8*

Let us start by describing the basic behavior of that fictitious figure, the "average" mother of our study. How much time does she spend interacting with her young child? When she is interacting with him, in what way is the child likely to be benefiting intellectually, or socially? Is he learning the names for things? Or how to perform some household chore? Or to be cooperative and share things with his friends? What form does her behavior usually take on during the interactions? Is she likely to do much direct teaching or simply behave in ways that generally encourage the child in his activity? Does she often restrict or scold him?

Preliminary answers to some of these questions are given in Tables 48 and 49 and in Figures 9.1–9.8, which show the amount of interaction time spent on different activities and techniques. Tables 48 and 49 give separate information on mothers with A children and mothers with C children. For the purposes of this discussion, the performance of the "average" mother may be thought to fall somewhere between that of mothers of A's and mothers of C's.

The first finding that stands out is that the average mother does *not* spend a great deal of time interacting with her child. During about 65–75 percent of our observation time, mother and child are typically not interacting at all. They may not even be in the same room, and if they are, the mother may not even be looking at the child. During the remaining 25–35 percent of our observation time, mother and child may be said to be interacting in some way, but this interchange may have little intellectual significance, either because the child's activity is unlikely to be intellectually stimulating, or, if it is, because the mother's behavior does not encourage or enhance its intellectual promise.

The last columns of Table 48 show that if we average the time spent on different types of activities over the two-year observation period, the average mother and child spend only 4–10 percent of observation time on activities that are highly intellectually stimulating (as for example, in labeling objects, building block towers, or teaching a child to perform a multistep household chore). This percentage is to be compared with the 11–12 percent of observation time devoted to activities that we assume are of only moderate intellectual value (such as unsystematic play with

---

* Parallel information on interaction between the child and all other people including the mother is given in Supplementary Tables 1 and 2 in Appendix III.

TABLE 48. Comparison of Age Groups among A and C Children on Percentage of Observation Time Spent with Mother on Different Types of Activities

| | A's[a] | | | | | C's | | | | |
| | Months | | | | All Phases | Months | | | | All Phases |
Activities[b]	12-15	18-21	24-27	30-33		12-15	18-21	24-27	30-33	
Highly intellectual	7.8	11.8[d]	3.8[c]	15.2[d]	9.6	4.5	3.8	1.5	4.8	3.6
Moderately intellectual	17.5	12.8	10.5	8.9	12.4	11.7	12.0	10.3	9.5	10.9
Nonintellectual	13.6[c]	10.7	13.3[c]	8.5	11.5	8.0	10.8	8.6	5.4	8.2
Social	2.2	1.4	1.9	2.5	2.0	1.3	0.4	1.7	1.5	.5
All interaction	41.1[d]	36.7[d]	29.5[c]	35.1[d]	35.6	25.5	27.0	22.1	21.2	24.0
Number of subjects	10	8	12	9		3	2	6	4	

Note: Each entry is a mean of percentages of total observation time during which mothers engage with their children in the listed activities. For each subject, the total amount of time spent with Mother on an activity is summed over the five observations of a three-month phase, and the percentage of total observation time (9,000 secs.) is calculated.
[a] Means of all A subjects considered as one group. This method of calculation was used because the N's for the working-class groups were too small for their means to be taken as reliable.
[b] Highly Intellectual Activities include activities likely to promote verbal, spatial, reasoning, expressive, and executive skills (categories 1–5 of the activities dimension of Human Interaction Scale); Moderately Intellectual Activities include unstructured play with toys, household objects, and living things, and routine conversation (categories 6–9); Nonintellectual Activities include basic care, gross motor activity, and nonspecific activity (categories 10–12); Social Activities include interactions concerning negative and positive social behavior (categories 31–33). See Appendix III for details.
[c] p = .05.
[d] p = .01. Two-tailed t's are calculated on the difference between the means of all A children versus all C children in the same three-month phase.

184

TABLE 49. Comparison of Age Groups among A and C Children on Percentage of Observation Time Mothers Use Each Technique in the Human Interaction Scale

Techniques[b]	A's[a] Months 12-15	18-21	24-27	30-33	All Phases	C's Months 12-15	18-21	24-27	30-33	All Phases
Teaching	3.2	5.8[c]	1.5	5.8[c]	4.1	1.0	1.5	0.7	1.6	1.2
Facilitation	23.3[c]	18.4	18.4[d]	17.2[d]	19.3	15.4	15.2	10.9	10.7	13.0
Routine talk	2.3	1.9	2.1	3.5[c]	2.4	1.1	2.5	0.8	0.5	1.2
Observation	6.9	7.4	4.7	4.5	5.8	4.4	5.8	4.4	3.1	4.4
Restriction	5.7	3.9	3.4	3.6	4.2	4.2	2.8	5.3	6.1	4.6
Number of subjects	10	8	12	9		3	2	6	4	

Note: Each entry is a mean of percentages of total observation time during which mothers use the listed techniques. For each subject, the total amount of time Mother uses a technique is summed over the five observations of a three-month phase, and the percentage of total observation time (9,000 secs.) is calculated.
[a] Means of all A subjects, middle-class and working-class, considered as one group.
[b] Teaching is category 21 of the technique dimension of the Human Interaction Scale; Facilitation includes all techniques that generally promote the activity in an interaction (categories 23, 25, 31, 35, 37, 38, 39, 40, and class-codes 1, 3, 5, 6); Routine talk is category 22; Observation includes category 33; Restriction includes all attempts to inhibit the child's activity (categories 24, 32, 34, 36, and class-code 4). See Appendix III for details.
[c] $p = .05$.
[d] $p = .01$. Two-tailed *t*'s are calculated on the difference between the means of all A children versus all C children in the same three-month phase.

185

toys and household items); 8–12 percent allocated to activities of low intellectual significance (such as eating, dressing, and engaging in gross motor activity); and 2 percent to social activities. We must conclude from these data that the average mother does not earmark much of the time she spends with her toddler for activities that the classroom teacher might deem important to his intellectual development. Most of the time she spends with him is focused on forms of play that are much less clearly "intellectual" in nature, or on basic care that may be irrelevant to his intellectual development but is essential to his physical well-being.

To round out the picture, let us now look at the mother's style of behavior when she *is* interacting with the child.* Is she likely to do much direct teaching? Does she generally encourage or discourage the child's activity? Table 49 gives the relevant information. The most surprising finding in these data is the small amount of time that mothers spend directly teaching their children anything. The term "teaching" here includes telling the child the names for things, showing him how things work, expanding, elaborating, and correcting his statements, and so on. During only 1–4 percent of observation time does the average mother use any of these direct-teaching methods. She is much more likely to employ strategies that generally encourage the child's activity, such as suggesting things for him to do, helping him when he is in difficulty, supplying needed materials, participating in his activity, admiring his achievements, and so on. Low-keyed facilitative techniques such as these are used most of the time (about 13–19 percent of observation time) in preference to patently didactic procedures. It is also interesting to note that the average mother is by no means always permissive. We find that during a fair amount of observation time (4 percent), our average mother is preventing the child from doing something, scolding him for what he has done, distracting him from what he would like to do, or refusing to help him do what he is trying to do. Sometimes the mother gives her child satisfactory reasons for restricting him, but usually the restriction is arbitrary and apologies are not forthcoming.

DIFFERENCES BETWEEN "A" AND "C" CHILDREN FROM ONE TO THREE YEARS

It is now time to examine the differences in the quantity and quality of interaction with the mother experienced by A and C children as they

---

* In the tables, two of the four techniques used by mothers in playing a direct participatory role in the child's experience are listed separately ("Teaching" and "Routine talk"). The other two techniques belonging to the mother's direct, participatory role ("Participating" and "Justifying") are grouped with techniques appropriate to the mother's nonparticipatory, facilitative role. The reason for this is that we wished to highlight the mother's *didactic* role rather than all forms of her direct, participatory role.

grow from babyhood to nursery-school age. The reader must bear in mind that A children are children who we predict will develop extremely well, and C children are children who we predict will develop below average, intellectually and socially

The data are quite straightforward. (See Table 48 and Figures 9.1–9.4.) First, A children experience much more interaction with their mothers than do C children, during each period of time at which we observed them. The difference in sheer quantity of interaction is quite large at 12–15 months (41 versus 26 percent) and holds almost steady through the three subsequent observation phases. The quality of interaction, interpreted both in terms of types of activities and of mother's style of interacting with the child, also differs profoundly.

Starting as early as 12–15 months, mothers of A children spend more time with them on activities that are "highly intellectual" than do mothers of C children. This difference in favor of the A's increases between 12–15 months and 18–21 months, and becomes very large at 30–33 months. At 30–33 months, the average mother of an A child devotes

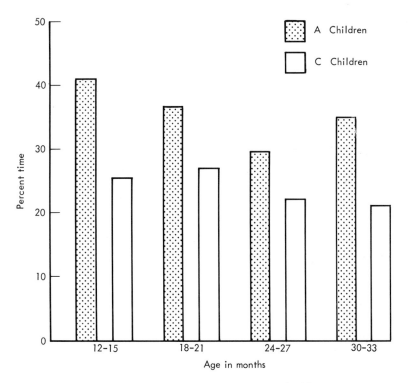

Figure 9.1 Comparison of age groups among A and C children on percentage of observation time spent with mother on all intellectual and social interactions.

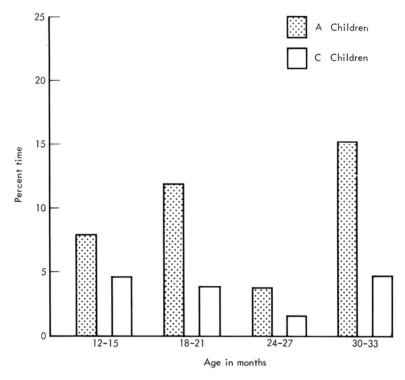

Figure 9.2   Comparison of age groups among A and C children on percentage of observation time spent with mother on highly intellectual activities.

about nine minutes (15 percent) of an observation hour to interaction focused on "highly intellectual" activities such as reading a book or working a puzzle, while the average mother of a C child spends only about three minutes (5 percent) on similar activities with her child.

This pattern of differences complements the pattern we find when we compare mothers of A and C children on time spent on activities of moderate intellectual promise (this difference is not statistically significant). Mothers of A children sharply *decrease* interaction time allotted to these activities as the child grows older (they shift to richer intellectual pursuits), while mothers of C children continue to spend about the same amount of time on these activities. To put it another way, when the A child is 12–15 months old, his mother spends about eleven minutes out of an observation hour interacting with him on activities of moderate intellectual significance; by the time he is 30–33 months old, this time is reduced to five minutes. The contrasting figures for the mother of the C child are seven minutes when the child is 12–15 months old, and six minutes when he is 30–33 months old.

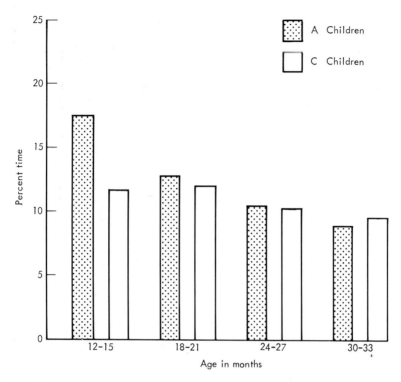

Figure 9.3 Comparison of age groups among A and C children on percentage of observation time spent with mother on moderately intellectual activities.

Finally, let us examine the pattern of differences between A and C children on interaction time spent with mother on activities of low intellectual value. The picture here closely resembles that for activities of moderate intellectual value that we have just discussed. Mothers of A children sharply reduce the proportion of interaction time allotted to activities of little intellectual promise as the child grows older, while mothers of C children do not consistently do so.

We can summarize the data we have so far presented on differences in the experience that A and C children receive from interacting with their mothers by referring to Figure 9.4. In this figure we can see that when the A child is very young (12–15 months), more of the time he spends interacting with his mother is allocated to activities of moderate intellectual significance than to activities of high intellectual promise. However, by the time he is two and a half, this ratio is reversed; at 30–33 months, his mother devotes the larger amount of time she spends with him to activities of high intellectual value. These findings are in contrast to those for C children in Figure 9.4. Whether the C child is one, one and a half, two, or two and a half, the larger part of his interaction with his mother is

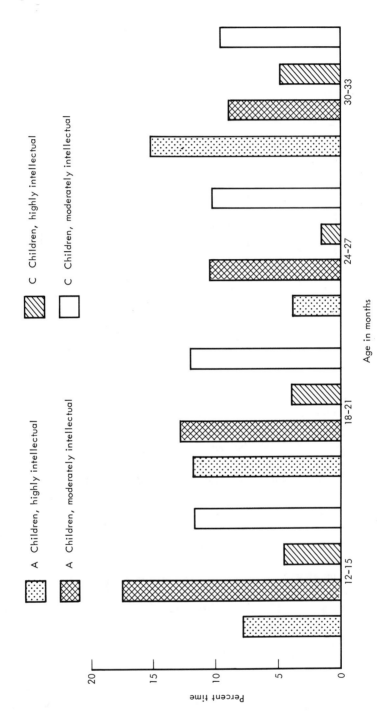

Figure 9.4 Comparison of age groups among A and C children on percentage of observation time spent with mother on highly intellectual activities versus moderately intellectual activities.

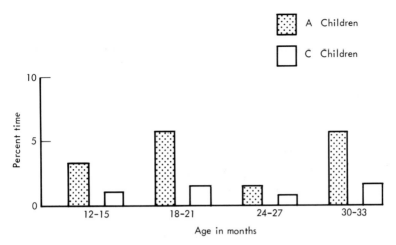

Figure 9.5 Comparison of age groups among A and C children on percentage of observation time mother uses teaching techniques.

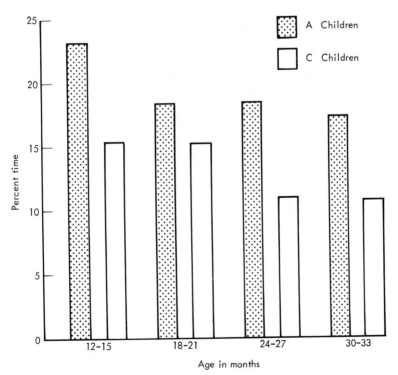

Figure 9.6 Comparison of age groups among A and C children on percentage of observation time mother uses facilitative techniques.

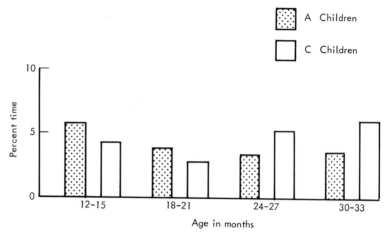

Figure 9.7   Comparison of age groups among A and C children on percentage of observation time mother uses restrictive techniques.

spent on activities of only moderate intellectual value. Although there is some increase in highly intellectual activities as the child grows older, at no stage do highly intellectual activities predominate in the interaction between mother and child.

What now of the mothers' use of different techniques of interaction with their children? Here, also, the pattern of differences between mothers of A and C children is simple and coherent. (See Table 49 and Figures 9.5–9.7.) From the first observation period, 12–15 months, mothers of A children use either teaching or facilitative techniques of interaction more often than do mothers of C children, and this difference holds steady throughout. (This difference is statistically significant at 12–15 and 24–27 months only on facilitation, at 18–21 months only on teaching, and at 30–33 months on both teaching and facilitation.) To put it more concretely, when the A child is 12–15 months old, his mother is likely to spend about two minutes out of an observation hour teaching him something; by the time he is 30–33 months old, she will have doubled this teaching time to four minutes. In contrast, when the C child is 12–15 months old, his mother is likely to spend only half a minute teaching him; by the time he is 30–33 months, his mother will have increased her efforts, but her total teaching will still only amount to one minute.

To complete this picture, we should note that the mother of the A child is somewhat more likely to use restrictive techniques when he is under two years old than is the mother of the C child, and less likely to use them when he is over two. (These differences are not statistically significant.) The mother of the A child *decreases* her use of restrictive

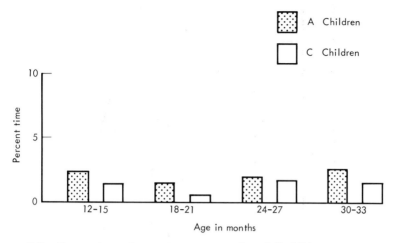

Figure 9.8 Comparison of age groups among A and C children on percentage of time spent with mother on social activities.

techniques as the child grows older, while the mother of the C child *increases* their use.*

The Mother's Role in Encouraging, Initiating, and Controlling the Child's Activity

In addition to coding the particular activities and techniques that occurred in mother–child interactions, we also noted whether the mother seemed to be encouraging the child's activity, who initiated the activity, and whether the mother was successful in controlling the child's behavior if she tried to do so. Data on each of these points are given in Table 50.

Consider first our fictitious entity, "the average mother." Our data show that *when the child is interacting with her,* the average mother initiates about one third of the child's activities, encourages twice as many activities as she discourages, and is successful in controlling the child twice as often as not. (Most of the time, control is not at issue, since the mother is not trying to change the child's behavior.) Note, however, that as with the findings for activities and techniques previously discussed, these data for the average mother mask some real differences between the behaviors of mothers of A children and mothers of C children. The most dramatic of these differences concerns encouragement and discourage-

---

* As Figure 9.8 shows, there were no important differences in total amount of social interaction from one observation period to another, or between A and C children, so these data are not discussed.

TABLE 50. Comparison of Age Groups on Frequency with Which Mothers Encourage, Initiate, and Are Successful in Controlling the Child's Activities

Techniques	A's[a]					C's				
	Months				All Phases	Months				All Phases
	12–15	18–21	24–27	30–33		12–15	18–21	24–27	30–33	
Encourages	58.3	57.6	60.9[c]	60.9[c]	59.4	59.1	56.6	47.2	46.3	52.3
Discourages	24.3	21.5	22.6[c]	21.1[c]	22.4	22.7	18.1	35.1	35.8	30.4
M initiates	41.4[b]	34.6	31.0[c]	36.4[c]	35.8	32.6	30.0	23.9	27.8	28.6
S initiates	54.6	58.5	54.3[c]	52.8[c]	55.0	51.0	56.8	69.3	64.4	60.4
Success in control	22.6	20.8	22.9	21.2	21.9	22.5	20.2	24.7	26.6	23.5
Failure to control	8.6	7.3	9.4	8.6[b]	8.5	8.5	10.0	13.2	13.4	11.3
Number of subjects	10	8	12	9		3	2	6	4	

Note: For each subject, the total number of mother–child interactions was found for the five observations of a three-month phase and percentages calculated of interactions that were encouraged by the mother, discouraged by the mother, etc. Entries are means of these individual percentages.
[a] Means of all A subjects, middle-class and working-class, considered as one group.
[b] p = .05.
[c] p = .01. Two-tailed t's are calculated on the difference between the means of all A children versus all C children in the same three-month phase.

ment. When the child is under two years of age, mothers of A and C children are identical in the percentage of the child's activities they encourage and discourage; they both encourage more than twice as many activities as they discourage. But once the child enters into the period aptly called "the terrible twos," these mothers react quite differently. The mother of the A child now encourages over three times as many of her child's activities as she discourages, while the mother of the C child doubles the occasions on which she discourages the child. To put it more vividly, at 24–27 and 30–33 months, about two thirds of the A child's experience is "encouraging" and one quarter is "discouraging," while at the same period of life, less than half of the C child's experience is "encouraging" and over one third is "discouraging."

Interestingly enough, it seems that mothers of C children meet with less success than do mothers of A children in controlling their "terrible twos." Could it be that they discourage the child's activities too often? Finally, we should note that there is a consistent difference between mothers of A and C children in the frequency with which they initiate activities for the child. In each observation period, mothers of A children are more likely to take the initiative (that is to suggest, prepare, or start off a child's activities), while mothers of C children are more likely to be reacting to situations that their children initiate.

Interaction with Other People in Addition to the Mother

The patterns of differences we have presented may be questioned on the ground that they may change substantially if we include in our data the child's interaction with people other than his mother. For example, it may be that C children receive significantly more intellectual stimulation from older siblings, which compensates for any shortcomings in their interaction with their mothers. The short answer to this question is "not so." When we include in our data the child's interaction with all other people in our observations, this increases the total amount of interaction but has no discernible effect on the patterns of differences we have discussed. Children who are A's continue to receive a richer intellectual diet, so to speak, and it is fed to them in a more structured and overtly didactic fashion.*

The Influence of Socioeconomic Factors

Another plausible objection to our comparison of A and C children lies in the fact that all the children in our C group are from Classes III,

---

* See Supplementary Tables 1 and 2 in Appendix III.

TABLE 51. Comparison of Age Groups among A and C Children on Percentage of Observation Time Spent Interacting with Different Classes of People

| | A's[b] | | | | | C's | | | | |
| | Months | | | | All Phases | Months | | | | All Phases |
	12–15	18–21	24–27	30–33		12–15	18–21	24–27	30–33	
Mother[a]	41.6	38.9	30.8	37.5	37.2	26.4	27.8	22.2	25.4	25.4
Adults	2.4	3.2	2.8	1.0	2.4	0.5	3.4	5.8	3.8	3.4
Children	2.2	3.9	6.5	5.7	4.6	9.2	6.9	3.4	3.1	5.6
Peers	0.2	0.1	2.1	1.9	1.1	2.3	0.0	0.3	0.9	0.9
Number of subjects	10	8	12	9		3	2	6	4	

[a] "Mother" refers to the child's true mother or main caretaker; other "Adults" are people over 7 years of age; other "Children" are children 4–7 years old (for the two-year-old subject), or 2–7 (for the one-year-old subject); peers are children 0–4 (for the two-year-old subject), or 0–2 (for the one-year-old subject).
[b] Means of all A subjects, middle-class and working-class, considered as one group.

IV, and V, whereas about two thirds of the children in our A group are from Classes I and II according to Hollingshead and Redlich's *Index of Social Position.** It may be that the differences between A and C children that we have been discussing are actually reflections of differences in ways mothers of different *social classes* interact with their children. This objection is best answered by referring to Tables 00 and 00 in Appendix III. In these tables the means for A children in Classes I and II, A children in Classes III and IV, and C children in Classes III, IV, and V are listed separately. The reader should compare the means for A's in Classes I and II to those of A's in Classes III and IV on the major items of our analysis. It is obvious that there are no consistent differences between these means in pattern. Where discrepancies exist, they sometimes favor lower class A's in the sense that, had we limited our original comparisons only to A's and C's of similar background (that is, Classes III, IV and V), we would have found larger differences between A's and C's on some items of our analysis and smaller differences on others. It must be stressed, however, that for this preliminary analysis of data we have very small numbers of lower class A's so that comparisons of these A's to other A's or C's are very risky. Since the time that these data were compiled, we have expanded our sample to include more Class III and IV A's, and data from these new subjects will allow us to make the necessary statistical tests to meet the objection. Until we do so, the reader may legitimately question whether the differences in mother-child interaction that we describe are reflections of class differences rather than pointing to necessary environmental antecedents of intellectual and social competence.

Interaction with the Physical Environment

In this section we shall examine only a few aspects of the child's interaction with his physical environment. Four aspects will be touched upon: the mother's use of physical barriers to restrict the child's movements, the relative amount of attention the child pays to *things* as opposed to *people* in his activities, and some physical characteristics of objects the child uses in his play. Data on each of these points are given in Table 52.

Consider first the use of physical restrictions. Essentially, these come in two varieties: high chair and playpen. (Other barriers, such as gates and cribs, were used less than 1 percent of the time by mothers in all groups.) Both types of restrictions are infrequently used during the child's third year, and the major difference between mothers of A and C children

---

* Classes I and II are upper to middle classes; Classes III, IV, and V are middle to lower classes. A. B. Hollingshead and F. C. Redlich, *Social Class and Mental Illness* (New York: John Wiley & Sons, Inc., 1958).

TABLE 52. **Comparison of Age Groups on the Mother's Use of High Chair and Playpen, and the Child's Attention to Objects and People in his Environment**

	Months			
	12–15	*18–21*	*24–27*	*30–33*
A subjects				
High chair	12.1[a]	8.8	6.4[b]	2.1
Playpen	5.1	2.7	0.0	0.0
C subjects				
High chair	5.0	12.5	0.0	0.0
Playpen	33.3[b]	0.0	0.0	0.0
All subjects				
Objects attended to:				
personal	14.1	13.3	12.2	12.7
toys	20.3	24.1	16.6	19.8
household	24.1	19.8	18.6	17.2
outdoor	0.9	1.8	4.4	1.3
all	59.4	59.0	51.8	51.0
Size/Portability				
small	34.1	33.6	23.4	28.7
large	11.2	12.0	16.2	9.7
portable	38.8	39.7	30.3	33.7
nonportable	6.5	5.9	9.3	4.7
People attended to:				
mother	19.1	21.9	19.3	23.2
other adults	4.8	3.8	5.4	3.2
other children	10.0	9.8	13.0	8.3
all people	33.9	35.5	37.7	34.8

Note: Data for this table are from the Object Interaction Scale. For each subject, percentages were found of the total number of 15-second time samples (1,000 in a three-month phase) in which the child was kept in a high chair, focused attention on his mother, etc. Entries are means of these individual percentages.
[a] $p = .05$.
[b] $p = .01$.

occurs when the child is between 12 and 15 months old. During this period, A children are more often kept in high chairs than are C children, while C children spend very much more time in playpens (during 33 percent of our fifteen-second time samples, we observed our C children in playpens, as compared to 5 percent for our A children).

We should note in passing that this finding is not a mere reflection of class differences, since our Class III and IV A children were identical to the Class I and II A children in the relative amount of time they were kept in high chairs and playpens. If we compare our working-class C children to our Class III and IV A children only, this differential use of high chairs and playpens still pertains: A children spend more time in high chairs and C children spend more time in playpens. The significance of this seemingly innocuous difference lies in the customary functions of high chairs and playpens. A high chair is a place in which to eat, and a playpen is a place in which to keep a child out of mischief. A high chair restricts the child's movements but does not necessarily interfere with his interaction with people, while a playpen can be like a cage, a safe place to put a child while his mother gets on with her work.

Our findings for the other aspects of the child's use of the physical environment are given in the bottom half of Table 52. In this section, only the means for all subjects together, both A and C, are given, since there were no consistent differences between A and C children on any of the items listed. These results are interesting in that they give details of the relative amount of time the child attends in his activities to different classes of people, such as mothers, other adults, and other children, and to different types of objects, such as personal items (food, clothes, toilet articles), toys, household articles, and outdoor objects. These toys, household, and outdoor objects that the child attends to or uses are further categorized into small versus large, and portable versus nonportable.

The salient points in these data are that the child spends much more time attending to things than to people; that he is just as likely to use household objects as to use toys in his activities; and that, not surprisingly, small and portable objects are his favorites.

SUMMARY

In this chapter we have presented some preliminary findings from two of the scales we use to measure the influence of the environment on the child's development of intellectual and social competence. We have presented only the most basic findings from the simplest analyses of our data, since the aim of this book is to describe the purpose and method of our study rather than its findings. We have postponed a more complex treatment of our data to a later volume, when our data collection will be complete.

We can summarize our preliminary findings by saying that as early as 12–15 months of life and increasingly thereafter, the environments of the A and the C child differ markedly. A major difference between them concerns their interaction with their mothers. Mothers of A children interact more with them, engage in more intellectually stimulating activities with them, teach them more often, encourage them more often, initiate activities for them more often, and are more successful in controlling their children.

The most important implication of these findings is that children who later grow up to be exceptionally competent intellectually do not seem to become so because of innate capabilities only. Starting as early as one year of age, these children have daily experiences in their homes that systematically promote their intellectual development much as if they were attending nursery school. The curriculum of the home is not hidden or unsystematic; it is observable and focused on intellectual development as an important goal for the young child.

Caution

The reader is cautioned that the conclusions are based on preliminary analyses of data in which the A group is predominantly upper and middle class and the C group is predominantly lower class. It follows that differences between A's and C's may be reflecting class differences to some extent, rather than pointing to necessary environmental antecedents of competence in young children. For our final data analyses we shall have a larger number of lower class A's to be compared to lower class C's, and shall determine the differences between A's and C's within this social class.

Four Children: Four Environments

JEAN CAREW WATTS/ITTY CHAN BARNETT

In the preceding chapters we have concentrated on describing the methodology and preliminary quantitative findings of our research on the environments of children who are developing exceptionally well, and those who are developing poorly. In this chapter we shall examine in a more qualitative fashion the human and physical environments of four of these children. We shall first describe in some detail the background and family life of each child, then we shall use excerpts from our actual observation records to give the reader as vivid a sense as we can of what each child looks like "in action."

The main theme our case studies will exemplify is the many roles the mother plays in influencing the child's development: her *direct* roles, as manifested in her observed behavior toward the child; her *managerial* role as designer of the child's physical and social environment and organizer of his daily routine; and her *diffuse* role embodied in herself as a total person with a history, a set of values, a certain degree of awareness of her effect on her child's development, and a certain set of socioeconomic and cultural constraints on her actions. For practical reasons, we focused our discussion of our quantitative findings almost entirely on the mother's direct and indirect roles expressed in her observed behavior toward the child. But in our case studies we shall provide information relevant to all of the mother's roles and point to instances where the mother's managerial or diffuse role seems particularly important in influencing her child's development.

THE CHILDREN OF THE CASE STUDIES

We shall include four children in our case studies: a one-year-old A, a one-year-old C, a two-year-old A, and a two-year-old C. These children are not necessarily typical of all A and C children at one and two years of age. Indeed, they could not possibly be typical, since there is no such thing as a single type of A or C child. Even a cursory examination of our data on individual children convinces us that there are many different environments in which A and C children live, and there is no one critical dimension that separates the two. Lack of space and the incomplete nature of our data force us to select only a few children from among those available, and the reader should not conclude that children of the case studies are the "best" or "worst" or even most representative of their respective groups.

SANDRA, A ONE-YEAR-OLD "A" GIRL

The first child we shall describe is Sandra.* Sandra was one year old when we first started observing her. Her only sibling, Rachel, was attending a locally well-known nursery school, and the teachers there recommended Rachel as a child who was developing especially well and who, conveniently for us, had a younger sister just turning one year old. On the basis of the teacher's ratings of her sister, we predicted that Sandra would develop into an A child. At the start of our observations, when Sandra was 12 months old, her test scores were only average, but her performance on tests improved tremendously over the next nine months, and by the time she was two years old, her test scores were among the top third of all children in our study. These scores validate our prediction of Sandra as an A child (a more complete description of Sandra's test results is included in Chapter 7 (Case #3).

Sandra's Background: Physical Environment

When we first started observing Sandra, the family lived in a six-room apartment in a residential area of Greater Boston. The neighbor-

---

* The names of the children in our case studies are fictitious, as are the initials of their families.

hood included some big mansions surrounded by spacious gardens, smaller, single-family houses, and oldish apartment buildings. Sandra's family lived on the first floor of an older apartment building, which was beautifully situated in terms of affording Sandra a rich, pleasant, and varied environment. Immediately adjacent was a park full of trees and a rolling meadow, a rose garden, and a well-equipped modern playground, while just a few blocks away was a busy commercial district, full of small stores, shoppers, and trolleys on the street. Sandra's apartment, too, was full of interesting variety. It was fairly small, consisting of a bedroom for her parents and one for the two girls, a kitchen and dining area, a small living room, and a tiny den out on the porch. But Sandra was free to roam wherever she wished in the apartment, as was evident from the childish clutter and masses of toys scattered about.

We visited Sandra in this location from the time she was 12 months to when she was 15 months old. However, by the time we began our second cycle of observations, when Sandra was 18–21 months old, her family had moved to the suburbs. They now live in an extremely large, beautifully furnished house set in spacious grounds, complete with a small hill for sliding and skiing, a hammock, swings, and sandbox. Sandra shares a bedroom, playroom, and bathroom with her sister, an arrangement obviously made by choice rather than necessity. The playroom is a delightful place, with a picture window in an adjoining sunporch overlooking the grounds, a playhouse, a child's kitchen area, shelves loaded with a fabulous array of small manipulable toys, books, dolls and puppets, a swing hanging from the doorway, a tiny-tot slide, and a full-length mirror. In addition, Sandra has the run of the house, which includes two sunny sitting rooms and an enormous kitchen decorated with her sister's artwork and mobiles hanging from the ceiling. Of all the children in our study, this child must be regarded as one of the most fortunate so far as having a varied, stimulating, and accessible physical environment is concerned.

Human Environment

What now of her human environment, the people with whom Sandra comes into contact?

When we first started observing Sandra, her family was classified in Class II. Both parents were college educated, her father had a Ph.D. and was doing postgraduate work in science, and their income was between $7,000 and $12,000 per year. However, a large financial windfall enabled the family to move into a wealthy neighborhood during the course of our study, and this family would probably be classified now in Class I.

The religious and ethnic background of Sandra's parents is Northern

European Protestant in the case of her mother and Jewish in the case of her father, but neither parent now professes a religious faith.

The person with whom Sandra spends most time is her mother. Except for one observation when a regular student babysitter was taking care of her, all our observations were done when Sandra was in her mother's charge. Not surprisingly, during these observations Sandra mostly interacted with her mother (or played alone), although often her four-year-old sister or a one-year-old playmate was present, and for short periods of time she played with them also. From time to time we caught glimpses of her father, grandfather, and other adults, but they seldom stayed more than a few minutes while we were there and entered only briefly into our recorded observations.

Observations on Sandra

Sandra is one of the one-year-olds in our study who we predict will develop exceptionally well intellectually and socially. Her interaction scores with her mother on such things as the amount of time spent on "highly intellectual activities" and teaching are in the top third of the range for all one-year-olds, and on the basis of test scores and "task" observations she is undoubtedly an intellectually superior child (see Chapter 7, Case #3).

Table 53 shows that when Sandra was 12–15 months old, her mother typically spent about 29 minutes out of an observation hour interacting

TABLE 53. **Number of Minutes per Observation Hour Spent by Children of the Case Studies in Various Types of Interaction with their Mothers**

	Case Study A's[a]				Case Study C's[b]			
	12–15	*18–21*	*24–27*	*30–33*	*12–15*	*18–21*	*24–27*	*30–33*
Total interaction time	29.4	18.0	17.4	10.0	10.8	13.8	12.6	12.6
Highly intellectual activities	5.9	3.8	2.8	0.9	1.3	1.4	1.1	1.7
Teaching	1.9	2.2	1.2	1.0	0.2	1.0	0.0	0.4
Restriction	3.5	1.4	1.1	0.9	1.3	1.4	3.5	3.8
Mother encourages	19.7	11.2	10.6	7.3	6.7	7.0	7.3	6.7
Mother discourages	7.0	2.0	1.3	2.2	1.4	1.6	3.8	4.4
Mother initiates	14.9	10.4	9.2	3.2	4.1	4.3	6.1	5.6
Subject initiates	14.3	7.3	4.9	6.7	6.7	9.5	6.4	6.9
Mother successful in control	4.4	2.0	1.7	2.3	1.9	1.9	3.5	3.2
Mother unsuccessful in control	2.0	1.9	1.1	0.6	0.2	0.5	1.1	1.1

[a] Sandra at 12–15 and 18–21 months; Nancy at 24–27 and 30–33 months.
[b] Cathy at 12–15 and 18–21 months; Robert at 24–27 and 30–33 months.

with her in some way, about six minutes engaging with her in highly intellectual activities, such as building towers with blocks or labeling objects, about two minutes in direct teaching, and about three minutes restricting Sandra's activities. Over this first three-month period, Mrs. S. encouraged three times as much of Sandra's activity as she discouraged, initiated about as much as Sandra herself initiated, and was more successful than not in her attempts to control Sandra.

In the second observational period, when Sandra was 18–21 months old, Sandra's interaction scores with her mother are still high relative to the group of C children, but are considerably lower than when she was 12–15 months old. In this second phase, Sandra's mother spent 18 minutes out of an observation hour interacting with her in some fashion, four minutes engaging in highly intellectual activities, two minutes in teaching and one minute restricting her. Over this three-month span, Mrs. S encouraged much more of Sandra's activity than she discouraged, initiated as much as Sandra initiated, and was successful in only half her attempts at controlling her.

What we would like to do in the remainder of this case study is to give as vivid a picture as possible of what Mrs. S. and Sandra look like "in action," by providing several verbatim excerpts from our minute-to-minute commentaries on their behavior. These excerpts come from various observations made when Sandra was 12–15 months old and when she was 18–21 months old. The picture we shall see is of a child who is obviously very bright and self-directed even at one year. She is very fond of small, manipulable objects that call for fine motor activity and, to an extent unusual for her age, is often involved in little prescientific experiments in which she appears to be struggling to understand the laws of nature. Equally indicative of intellectual talent is her interest in expressive role play and in verbal learning. Her ability to persist in an intellectually demanding activity is outstanding, and this persistence is associated, not at all paradoxically, with an intense dislike of being thwarted. On almost every single observation, Sandra spends some time whining or protesting frustrations, and she is quite skilled at getting her own way.

Mrs. S. should be characterized as a child-centered mother. During our observations she seemed always very readily accessible to the child, in the sense of being able to leave whatever she was doing and spend time with Sandra if she wanted her to. Mrs. S. characteristically adopts a nondirective approach in dealing with Sandra (especially so far as intellectual activities are concerned). She is less apt to suggest activities than are other A mothers, and more apt to merely observe Sandra (often with a wry and amused expression) as she busies herself on her little projects. On the other hand, she is not the most successful of mothers in dealing with Sandra's whining or tantrums. Possibly, as with many a mother of an obviously bright and determined child, she is a little afraid of conflict with her, viewing her as a near-adult whose desires must be respected and given considerable weight.

EXCERPT NUMBER 1

In this observation Sandra is about thirteen and a half months old. It is lunchtime, and Sandra has been quite cranky, presumably because mother was late coming home and she was hungry. Mother, too, is not at her best, having just tried to deal unsuccessfully with one of Sandra's tantrums. The scene opens with Mother at the door, welcoming home Sandra's sister, while Sandra sits in her high chair at the kitchen table. Sandra, on her own and quieting down after her tantrum, launches into one of her little "scientific" experiments: her topic, the law of floating bodies. [In this and the following excerpts, the times stated on the left are the number of minutes and seconds counting from the start of a 10-minute observation on the child. For example, 3:15 means 3 minutes and 15 seconds from the beginning of the observation.]

3:15 Sandra reaches for a glass of milk on the table, which is about one foot away.

3:20 Very carefully, Sandra slides the glass along the tabletop, apparently trying not to spill the milk. She spills only a little.

3:25 She sips the milk with a contented look.

3:30 She pushes the glass away, again sliding it along the tabletop.

3:40 Suddenly she drops a piece of meat into the glass and it sinks. She startles slightly and then deliberately puts a potato chip in and it floats. She looks puzzled.

4:00 Sandra puts her hand deep into the glass and seems to be searching for the piece of meat at the bottom.

4:15 Sandra lifts the glass toward her. Peers into it. Then pushes it away.

4:35 Sandra puts her hand in again and waves her fingers about in the milk several times as if trying to reach the meat.

4:50 Mother comes in with Sister. M: "Pretty good!" (She refers to the fact that Sandra has eaten some food.) "Do you want a drink?"

5:00 Mother holds glass for Sandra and she drinks.

5:20 As mother begins to take away the glass, Sandra starts to screech. M: "Oh, you are naughty today!" She goes to kitchen, leaving the glass on the table.

5:30 Sandra slides the glass over and drops a chip in, resuming her experiment. M returns, removes the glass well out of Sandra's reach, lifts her out of the chair, sits her on the floor, and leaves.

5:45 Sandra starts screaming and whimpering.

6:00 Mother comes in and wipes table, deliberately ignoring Sandra's tantrum, which continues for four more minutes.

Commentary

Sandra's experiment with flotation is a clear example of a "highly intellectual activity" for a child of this age. In this episode, Sandra's mother inadvertently cuts short this intellectual activity, thereby provoking a tantrum in Sandra. This behavior on the part of Sandra's mother is not particularly characteristic of her. Mrs. S. is no more prone to restricting her one-year-old than is the average mother of a one-year-old A child. She is much more likely to adopt a positive approach: a mixture of techniques to teach, facilitate, and observe her child's activities. Some of the ingredients in this mixture are illustrated in the following excerpt:

EXCERPT NUMBER 2

In this excerpt Sandra is about 15 months old. Once more, Sandra has been whining, this time because her mother refused to let her play with a pair of scissors. Mother has tried several distractions, and now starts to build a tower with blocks, an activity that from previous observations we know Sandra enjoys.

3:00 Mother builds a tower of three blocks. Sandra carefully puts on the fourth block. Mother says, "Hey, that's right, Sandra."

3:22 Sandra picks up the third one and drops the very top one. Mother says, "You dropped it."

3:28 Mother sits down on the bed and watches.

3:34 Sandra puts the one back on the top. Mother hands her another one.

3:40 Sandra looks at the three blocks on the tower.

3:46 Mother gives Sandra another block. Sandra puts it on top. Mother claps and says, "Hey, Sandra! Good."

3:49 Sandra says, "Dat," and laughs. Sandra takes the top two off and puts them on the floor.

4:04 Sandra puts the little one on top. Then puts the bigger one on top of the smaller one. Mother looks on.

4:19 The small one is pushed off on her leg. Sandra puts the big one on top. Then puts the little one on top. Then Sandra says, "Mama, Mama."

4:27 Mother says, "I see."

4:30 Mother smiles. Sandra drops the top two off and puts them on again.

4:45 Sandra drops the smallest one behind the tower. Sandra crawls around the tower to get it.

4:51 Sandra stands up and picks it up and puts it on the top.

5:00 Sandra takes up the two blocks and walks across to Mother. Sandra walks by Mother and goes to the small table.

5:10 Sandra sneezes and puts the blocks down on the chair.

5:13 Sandra picks up the other block and says, "Down." Sandra walks to tower, almost trips on the teapot. Mother looks on. Sandra goes to put the block on the tower.

5:22 Mother removes the teapot so Sandra won't trip on it.

5:30 Sandra goes to pick up the bigger one and puts it over the small one so the small one is hiding under the big one. Now Sandra moves the big one and puts the bigger one on the table. Mother looks on.

5:45 Mother picks up the little one. She says, "Go," and puts the little one on the table, too. Now Sandra goes after the second biggest one and puts it on the table, over a green cup, so it covers the cup completely.

6:00 Sandra goes to pick up the biggest one, but her attention is drawn to the street outside and she runs to the window. Garbage men are collecting garbage, and there is much clanging and banging of cans.

Commentary

This excerpt may seem rather long and repetitious. The point of including it, however, is to show Sandra's outstanding ability to persist at a task, and her mother's use of a variety of techniques that maintain the child's attention without being overintrusive. At the beginning, Mrs. S. introduces the blocks to distract Sandra from play with the scissors; she makes the task interesting by showing what a tower of blocks looks like, rather than merely suggesting that Sandra build one. Then, as soon as Sandra's interest is awakened, she reinforces it by immediately praising the child's efforts. Once Sandra's interest seems self-sustaining, Mrs. S. assumes a less active role, observing Sandra's efforts, assuring her of mother's continued interest in what she is doing, supplying her with blocks when needed, removing obstacles from her path, and finally, permitting her to cease this activity when, after a prolonged stint, her attention turns to something equally captivating—the garbage men clanging cans on the street.

EXCERPT NUMBER 3

This excerpt comes from our second observation period, when Sandra is close to 19 months old. True to form, Sandra has just had a small tantrum because her mother stopped her from playing with a chain of safety pins she had found. Mother now takes her into the playroom and distracts her with a safe substitute, a toy necklace and a barrette that Mrs. S. pins in Sandra's hair. This distraction, presumably intended by her mother to initiate a "dress-up" sequence, turns into another of the little "scientific" experiments that this little girl loves. Her topics this time are "reflections" and "gravity."

6:00 Mother clips a small barrette on Sandra's hair. Mother: "You can see it in the mirror." (There is a full-length mirror on the wall a few feet away.) Sandra looks around, puzzled. Mother repeats, "Look in the mirror!"

6:20 Sandra moves toward the mirror and Mother points to the barrette in her hair as Sandra looks in the mirror.

6:30 Mother says, "You have to get near to see it," and leads her nearer to the mirror. Mother: "See your barrette? See it?" Sandra pulls at her hair and at the clip. She still seems puzzled. It seems as if she can't reconcile the feel of the barrette in one location (her hair, which her hand is touching), and seeing it in front of her in another position.

6:45 Mother fixes the barrette in her hair and says, "You are not watching. Look there!" Mother points to the reflection in the mirror, and Sandra stands still, pulling at her hair, with a puzzled expression. Mother asks Sandra's one-year-old playmate, Tom, if he wants a barrette, too.

7:00   Sandra holds out her hand, gesturing for the can full of barrettes and little objects, which her Mother has taken down. Mother gives her the can and Sandra takes out a barrette.

7:15   Sandra takes the barrette to her friend and tries to clip it in his hair. She doesn't know how to do this and simply places it on his hair and it falls.

7:30   Mother observes, and says, "Here's a nice one to put on his hair." Mother slowly clips one on the boy's hair, demonstrating to Sandra how it works. Sandra looks on. Mother leaves the room.

8:00   Sandra tries to clip the barrette on her friend's hair, moving the clip a little, but again it falls off.

8:15   Sandra puts several clips back into the can, one by one.

8:30   She puts the cover on the can and screws it slightly. She takes off the necklace from around her neck.

8:45   Sandra puts a barrette on her hair, again not clipping it but placing it on her hair, and it falls off.

9:00   She repeats this action two or three times.

9:20   She turns her attention to taking the small barrettes and ornaments one by one from the can and putting them back in, examining each carefully, apparently still trying to understand how their clips work.

9:55   Sandra covers the can and screws on the top. (She continues with her exploration for several minutes after the end of this observation.)

Commentary

This episode is remarkable again for the topic of the child's interest, and also for the length of time she persists at the task of understanding, first, how an object in one place can be reflected in another, and second, how mechanisms operate to keep things from falling. In this episode, her mother takes a more assertive and directive approach, which actually doesn't work particularly well, since the child obviously did not seem to learn much from her mother's efforts about reflection or how to operate the clip. Nevertheless, by supplying the materials for the experiment (mirror and barrette), and showing enthusiastic interest, Sandra's mother has at least posed the question for Sandra, and she continues to grapple with it long after the mother quits the scene.

EXCERPT NUMBER 4

This final excerpt comes from an observation when Sandra was twenty-one months old. It provides a beautiful example of a "highly intellectual" activity involving verbal learning for Sandra and a mixture of direct teaching and active participation on the part of her mother and sister. It is again remarkable for the length of time that Sandra sustains interest in the task and the mother's enthusiastic approach.

5:25   Sandra takes out a plastic animal from a box and makes a noise.

5:29   Mother says, "Neigh, neigh—that's a horse." Sandra: "Horse." Mother looks on as Sandra labels and makes "moo" noise.

5:40 Sandra drops horse on the table and tries to reach for Mother's address file.

5:45 Mother: "No, no, you can't play with mommy's card. Find more animals. Find the cow."

5:50 Sandra looks through the box.

6:00 Sandra takes out another animal and says, "Moo-moo."

6:16 Mother: "You found it!" Sandra: "Moo." Mother: "Moo." They laugh. Mother and sib label for Sandra—"Cow."

6:32 Mother: "Can you stand it up?" Sandra complies.

6:37 Mother suggests Sandra go find more animals. Sandra goes back to the box.

6:44 Sandra takes out another one and says, "Neigh, neigh." Mother: "Yes, that's another horse."

7:00 Sib: "Black one." Mother: "Yes, that's a big black one." Sandra: "Black." Mother: "Yes, black horse."

7:08 Mother suggests dog. Sandra: "No," but goes to find it.

7:34 Mother: "No doggie? Look some more." Sib offers to help.

7:41 Sandra looks on as Sib rummages through the box.

7:50 Sandra glances at the rain and snow outside.

7:57 Sib hands Sandra another cow. Sandra looks at it. Sandra stands it on the table and says, "Moo."

8:13 Sandra looks on and waits. Mother also helps look for the dog.

8:34 Mother shows Sandra another animal—"What's that, Sandra?" Sandra: "Mew, mew." Mother: "What does a dog say?" Sib: "That's a dog."

8:46 Mother: "Yes." Sandra looks on as Mother rummages and takes out another animal and makes roaring noise. Sandra: "Lion!" Mother: "That's right. That's a lion."

9:05 Mother: "Here's another one," and puts a calf on the table. Sandra looks on and then says, "Moo-moo."

9:18 Mother smiles as Sandra says, "Moo-cow, Moo-cow!" in excitement.

9:22 Sandra looks at the lion and makes roaring noise.

9:30 Mother looks through box and takes out another animal. Sandra: "Baa-baa" noise at the lamb.

9:39 Mother looks on as Sandra makes "baa" then roaring noise at the lion.

9:42 Mother: "That's a lion," and makes roaring noise also. Sandra joins in. Mother: "That's right." Sandra makes "baa" noise.

9:52 Mother: "Which one says baa?" Sandra looks. Mother: "This one," and points. Mother and Sandra make "baa" noise. Sandra picks it up as Mother looks on.

We have now completed our picture of Sandra, a one-year-old A child from Class II background. Sandra is clearly an exceptional child. Are her talents mostly innate and their development intrinsically determined? Would they have bloomed so early or so luxuriantly in another environment? These questions are obviously unanswerable with respect to any particular child. In Sandra's case, as is often the case with most children from advantaged backgrounds, there are many things promoting her development simultaneously: Her parents are highly intelligent and well educated; her material environment is rich and exceptionally well designed from a child's point of view; her mother has the time and willingly spends it participating with her in intellectually promising activities; and her mother is knowledgeable enough and observant enough of her to be able to use those techniques of interaction that generally promote her intellectual and social development. It is impossible to point to any one of these factors as *the* determinant of Sandra's excellent development; they all enter into her experience, which, in turn, fundamentally molds her development. This happy coincidence of inherited abilities and a superior human and physical environment is not common in children from other socioeconomic backgrounds; a case in point is presented in our next case history.

CATHY, A ONE-YEAR-OLD "C" GIRL

Our next subject is Cathy. Like Sandra, Cathy was just one year old when we first started observing her. Cathy is the youngest child in a family of thirteen children ranging in age from one to nineteen years. Her mother is in her early forties and her father in his early fifties. Cathy is an appealing little girl who, at the beginning of our observations, was very advanced (her Bayley IQ was 134, higher than that of most of our A children). She was able to walk, run, and climb with relative ease, showed little shyness of strangers, and was socially very competent, especially in dealing with other children. Nevertheless, we predicted that Cathy would eventually become a C child. She would fail to realize her obvious intellectual potential, primarily because her environment would not provide her with the necessary intellectual focus and sustained stimulation. We made this prediction on the basis of the school records of her numerous siblings and our own observation of those closest in age to Cathy who were not yet in school. They seemed lethargic, uninterested in intellectual pursuits, and performed below average intellectually.

Cathy's Background: Physical Environment

When we first started observing Cathy, the family lived in a deteriorated, sparsely furnished seven-room house in a residential area of Greater Boston. Their house is situated on a dead-end street and is flanked by other small houses in mixed states of repair. Half a block away is a main street with somewhat more substantial houses, but the general impression is of a lower-middle-class area with families struggling to maintain a respectable appearance. The children on the block play in their small backyards and on the dead-end street in front.

Curiously, as was the case for Sandra, our one-year-old A, the family's living situation changed substantially during the course of our study. Sometime after the end of our second series of observations on Cathy, three bedrooms and one and a half baths were added to the house to alleviate the space problem. Despite these additions, Cathy still has to share a room, aptly termed a "dormitory" by the family, with four other siblings. Also, since this change did not take place till after Cathy was 21 months old, all the observations to be discussed in this case study took place when living quarters for the family were extremely cramped. At that time, the house consisted of one floor with two bedrooms and the "dormitory," a bedroom in the attic and one in the cellar, a kitchen, and a living room. All the bedrooms except the dormitory were off limits to Cathy, and she spent most of her time near the large central table in the kitchen, in front of the television set in the living room, and on the dead-end street in front of the house, where the family frequently congregated for entertainment and socializing.

Human Environment

In terms of income, residence, and education, Cathy's family is classified in Class IV. Her father worked at a semiskilled building-maintenance job, and their income, for a family of fifteen people, was about $8,000 per year. Neither parent has more than a high school education, but interestingly, their oldest child is now attending a state college, and Mrs. C. has recently started art lessons. The parents and children are all Catholics and their ethnic background Southern European. The people with whom Cathy spends most time are her siblings, particularly her four-year-old sister, a teen-age sister, and a pre-teen-age brother under whose supervision she is frequently left as her mother busies herself with the household chores.

During all our observations, Cathy was nominally in her mother's charge, but with brothers and sisters very often around, more than half her interaction took place with them.

Observations on Cathy

As we have previously noted, Cathy is a gifted one-year-old (so far as test scores are concerned) who we predict will not realize her intellectual potential because of a lack of intellectual stimulation at home. So the first question is, "What does her environment, intellectually speaking, look like?"

First, let us examine some statistics. Table 53 shows that when Cathy was 12–15 months old, her mother typically spent about eleven minutes out of an observation hour interacting with her in some way, about one minute engaging with her in "highly intellectual activities" such as teaching her how to perform a household chore, almost no time in direct teaching, and about one minute restricting her activities. Over this three-month period, Mrs. C. encouraged five times as much of Cathy's activity as she discouraged, initiated half as much as Cathy herself initiated, and was successful in the vast majority of her attempts at controlling her.

In the second observational period, when Cathy was 18–21 months old, her mother spent, on the average, 14 minutes out of an observation hour interacting with her in some fashion, less than two minutes engaging in "highly intellectual" activities, about one minute in direct teaching, and about two minutes restricting her activities. Over this span of three months, Mrs. C. encouraged five times as much of Cathy's activity as she discouraged, initiated half as much as Cathy initiated for herself, and was successful in the overwhelming majority of her attempts at controlling her daughter.

From these numbers we get a picture of Mrs. C. as a mother who has changed very little her style of interacting with her one-year-old during a period of her child's life when development is extremely rapid. Both at 12–15 months and at 18–21 months, Mrs. C. spends less than two minutes out of an observation hour engaging with Cathy in activities that could be construed as intellectually promising, and no more than one minute teaching her. A major reason for this is that with a large family to look after, Mrs. C. is a very busy woman, and it is a rare occasion when she literally has the time to devote undivided attention to her one-year-old. This situation would not be detrimental if Cathy got the intellectual stimulation she needed from her brothers and sisters. However, as Table 54 shows, Cathy engages in few intellectually stimulating activities with her siblings and they seldom try to teach her.

On the other hand, we should note that a truly outstanding feature about Mrs. C.'s home is the atmosphere of cheerfulness and sociability. Mrs. C. seldom seemed to raise her voice at the children, managed the home with efficiency, and demonstrated much love, patience, and good humor toward her family. Also, we observed very little fighting and squabbling among the children, and, like their mother, older brothers and sisters showed a great deal of patience and affection toward Cathy. Cathy's mother and mother surrogates must be characterized as positive and loving toward her, but intellectual stimulation of this one-year-old is not at the top of their list of priorities.

It is time now to present some excerpts from our actual observations on Cathy. It will be no surprise to find that a major point of contrast between Cathy and Sandra is in the materials that the two children play with. Sandra, you will remember, was among the most fortunate of

TABLE 54.   **Number of Minutes per Observation Hour Spent by Children of the Case Studies in Various Types of Interaction with All People**

	Case Study A's[a]				Case Study C's[b]			
	12–15	*18–21*	*24–27*	*30–33*	*12–15*	*18–21*	*24–27*	*30–33*
Total interaction time	31.8	19.8	22.2	16.4	19.8	18.0	20.4	15.0
Highly intellectual activities	6.1	3.8	4.1	2.7	2.2	2.6	1.2	1.6
Teaching	1.9	2.2	1.7	1.1	0.2	1.0	0.0	0.4
Restriction	4.1	2.2	2.2	3.2	2.7	2.4	4.7	4.3
Other encourages	21.5	11.5	13.1	10.4	14.0	9.6	13.5	8.4
Other discourages	7.6	2.8	2.2	3.5	2.8	2.4	4.6	4.8
Other initiates	16.0	8.5	6.6	3.4	8.0	11.2	10.6	7.8
Subject initiates	15.9	10.9	11.3	9.9	11.0	6.6	9.7	7.2
Other successful in control	5.2	2.4	3.0	3.3	2.8	2.8	3.7	3.5
Other unsuccessful in control	2.0	2.1	1.4	0.8	0.7	1.1	1.2	1.7

[a] Sandra at 12–15 and 18–21 months; Nancy at 24–27 and 30–33 months.
[b] Cathy at 12–15 and 18–21 months; Robert at 24–27 and 30–33 months.

our subjects in the number of well-designed toys she possessed. Cathy, in contrast, has far fewer than the average number of toys. We noticed her playing with a balloon, a party noisemaker, a hand-me-down robot, and a rocking horse, whereas Sandra had so many toys it would have taken several paragraphs to list them all. In comparison to Sandra, we are far more likely to find Cathy playing with household objects, such as juice cans, sponges, and wastebaskets than toys, and the "intellectual activities" she experiences usually concern learning how to carry out household chores.

EXCERPT NUMBER 1

4:00   Cathy falls at the doorway to the living room. She picks herself up and cries.

4:07   Mother turns around and asks, "What's the matter? What happened?" (Cathy walks to Mother.) "Did you fall?"

4:15   Mother bends down to hug Cathy, saying, "Okay, okay. You want the Kleenex?"

4:26   Mother hands Cathy a wet paper towel. Cathy takes it and starts to wipe the kitchen table.

4:31   Mother looks on and says, "Clean, clean."

4:33   Mother goes back to work at the sink. Cathy walks around the table, wiping it with short motions.

4:45   Cathy takes the wet towel to living room and goes to clean the chair, then the cabinet.

5:00   Cathy cleans the couch with the wet towel, then the chair on which a brother is sitting watching "Sesame Street." Cathy goes to a sister and wipes her chair, then Cathy wipes the couch again.

5:20 Cathy walks to kitchen and goes to wipe the high chair near the doorway.

5:35 Cathy goes to wipe the icebox.

5:43 Mother leaves. Mother comes back.

6:03 Mother looks at Cathy, saying, "Clean, clean, clean!" Mother walks to the hall.

6:10 Cathy walks around, wiping the stove, then the icebox again, then goes to wipe the TV screen in living room.

6:32 Cathy goes to wipe the chest of drawers.

6:40 She then wipes the window sill, then the chair.

7:00 Then she wipes the couch again.

7:15 Cathy goes to wipe her brother's chair, then walks to kitchen.

7:19 Cathy makes an "eh eh" sound. Mother is cutting some bread at the stove and looks at Cathy.

7:27 Cathy goes to wipe the stove with the wet towel.

7:36 Mother says, "It is clean, that's good."

7:39 Mother resumes cutting bread. Cathy walks back to the living room.

7:45 Cathy wipes the TV screen again.

8:00 Cathy walks around in living room and wipes the furniture in there.

8:28 She walks to kitchen, then down the hallway to the dormitory, where Mother is putting some clothes away in the drawers.

8:40 Cathy goes to Mother and babbles.

8:52 Mother looks up and asks, "What do you want?"

9:00 Cathy wipes the drawers.

9:04 Mother puts clothes away and then tidies up the beds. Cathy smiles at observer and wipes the dresser. She babbles to herself.

9:30 Cathy continues wiping with the wet towel and babbling to herself. Mother is tidying up at the other end of the room. Cathy kneels on the floor and wipes the dresser. Mother walks by Cathy.

9:58 Mother glances at Cathy, then walks out of the room. Cathy stays in the dormitory.

Commentary

This excerpt of Cathy's activities should be compared to excerpt Number 1 of Sandra. Both excerpts come from observations when the subjects are approximately 13½ months old. They are similar in that the child's activities are to a large extent self-initiated and self-directed, with minimal input from Mother or other people. Cathy's excerpt shows Mrs. C. in a characteristic light. She is ready to comfort Cathy when she falls, and skillful at distracting her from preoccupation with her hurt to a constructive activity (contrast Mrs. S.'s less-adept handling of Sandra's tantrums). Even with regard to intellectual stimulation, Mrs. C.'s behavior seems very well adapted to Cathy's activity. She lets her get on with the task of learning, yet helps to sustain her interest by appropriate words of encouragement and praise as she busies herself with household chores similar to those Cathy is undertaking. The problem for Cathy is that she experiences *so few* interactions of this type. Much more typical are the experiences exemplified in the next excerpt.

EXCERPT NUMBER 2

In this excerpt Cathy is in the living room. The drapes to the front windows are drawn even though it is full daylight, and the room is dark and very sparsely furnished. Her youngest sister, Sylvia (just over two years old), is in the living room playing with a ball.

0:00   Cathy gets onto rocking chair. Sister Sylvia (2½ years old) throws ball at her. Cathy tries to get it (after it had landed on a chair).

0:20   Cathy gets down from rocking chair. Puts out her arms as if to catch the ball. Sister picks up ball from chair and throws it, hitting Cathy lightly on face.

0:35   Cathy smiles and runs to window.

0:45   Cathy makes a noise. "Ca-aaa, Caaa."

1:00   Wanders to couch.

1:10   Wanders to door of living room.

1:20   Wanders around living room not looking at anything in particular.

1:45   Touches stroller near doorway to kitchen. Pushes it along from side. Another sister, Mary (three years old), comes in. Takes ball from younger sister, Sylvia.

2:00   Cathy climbs on couch and looks at sisters.

2:15   Mother comes in to arbitrate dispute between sisters. Takes Mary out into kitchen.

2:45   Cathy follows. Sits on floor.

3:00   Cathy looks around as Mother busies herself at counter.

3:30   She climbs onto chair near large table.

3:40   Mother bends over and ties Cathy's shoes. Mother: "OK?" and moves off.

4:00   Mother: "You want to play ball? What are they doing?" (Pointing to sibs.) "They play ball." (Said in a didactic tone.) Cathy laughs.

4:15   Cathy walks to living room, then crawls on floor.

4:30   Crawls to sibs, who are sitting on floor rolling ball to and fro between them.

4:50   Crawls to sibs, gets in way. Mary lifts her up from floor and gives her a plastic statue and says, "Play with the dolly," pushing her gently over to window side.

5:15   Cathy examines statue. Pushes it against chair (as if testing its resilience).

5:30   Kisses statue. Walks over to sisters and then gets in way. They say nothing.

5:40   Cathy continues over to couch. Then walks back.

6:00   She goes to window and looks out, moving the drapes aside. Cathy looks out (there is nothing much to see, as the window faces a dead-end street).

6:30   She walks back and gets in way of sisters' ball game.

6:35   She goes over to couch, then to sisters, looking at them.

6:45   Cathy goes to Sylvia, is in the way of the game. Sylvia: "Get out of the way!" Cathy moves off.

7:00   Cathy goes to window. Pushes plastic statue against chair.

7:15   Crawls about on the floor.

7:45   Again gets in way of her sisters. Sylvia pushes her firmly but gently to kitchen.

8:00   Cathy crawls under telephone table. Takes up transparent ball from floor.

8:30   Goes to living room entrance, which is blocked by sister. Moves back into kitchen. Picks up a baseball mitt from floor. Lets it drop. Doesn't observe it.

8:45   Wanders about kitchen. Goes to mother in living room. Says something, showing her the ball.

9:00   Mother: "What you got? A ball?" Mother's attention immediately turns to sibs. She shows them how to play with ball. Cathy looks ahead blankly.

9:10   Cathy comes over to stroller, babbling. Touches stroller.

9:35   Wanders over to couch, looking at nothing in particular.

9:40   Mother leaves the living room.

9:45   Cathy crawls around in living room, as sisters continue with their game.

Commentary

In this excerpt, we observe Cathy mostly wandering on the periphery of others' activities. Interaction with her mother consists of mother tying her shoes, two brief checks on what she is doing, and a very brief attempt to instruct. Throughout the episode, her sisters are intent on keeping her out of their game; each time she interrupts, they gently but firmly get her out of the way. Moreover, the physical environment is so monotonous that Cathy finds little to do on her own, apart from pushing the stroller, exploring the rigid outlines of the statue, and looking out of the window at a dead-end street. It takes little imagination to see the contrast between this and Sandra's Excerpt 2, in which Sandra receives her mother's undivided attention as she learns to build a tower of blocks, and leaves this activity only to observe the equally exciting spectacle of garbage men emptying huge cans into the enormous mouth of a garbage truck.

EXCERPT NUMBER 3

The next excerpt from Cathy's observations provides a sharp contrast to Sandra's Excerpt Number 3. Both observations were done when the children were 18–19 months old. In this excerpt, Cathy had found a paper bag full of sea shells that her brother had collected and brings them to her mother.

1:00   Cathy pulls down a paper bag from the bureau in the dormitory.

1:20   Cathy opens it, looks into it, then rolls up the top, closing it.

1:30   Cathy shakes the bag and smiles at the clatter inside it. She goes to the kitchen.

1:45   Says something to her mother. Mother: "What? What you got? What is it?"

2:00   Cathy says something (indistinct). Mother: "Are they Johnny's?" Cathy: "I want. . . ." Cathy runs in a circle shaking the bag and obviously enjoying the clatter.

2:15   She shakes the bag. Mother busies herself at the stove. Cathy babbles. Mother: "What?"

2:30   Cathy takes one or two shells out and throws them on the floor. Mother: "Those are shells."

2:35   Cathy sits on the floor and takes out one shell after another, throwing them on the floor. Mother is busy and doesn't observe.

3:00   Mother suddenly notices and says: "Don't throw them down there! Put them in here." Mother bends over Cathy and shows her how to put the shells in the bag. (Cathy obviously knows how to do this, and Mother's purpose seems to be to persuade her to do it rather than teach her.)

3:15   Mother: "Put them back in. There's another one, right here." (Pointing.) Cathy: "Another one." Mother: "Yes, another one." Mother moves off. Mother leaves the room.

3:30   Cathy puts the shells one by one into the bag.

4:00   Cathy takes the shells out of the bag one by one, putting them on the floor.

4:30   Cathy places the shells one by one on the seat of a chair that is next to her.

4:55   Cathy stacks one shell on another like two saucers.

5:00   She continues placing the shells on the chair, putting them on the floor, then putting them on the chair again. She handles the shells one by one.

6:00   She stacks some shells, one by one, like saucers on the floor (about six or seven in all).

6:45   Mother returns. Cathy holds out the stack of shells to her mother (holding the stack by the bottom shell quite carefully). Mother says, "Put them back, quick! Put the rest back in. You got one on the floor." Mother goes to the stove. Cathy puts a handful of shells (from the stack, which has now disintegrated) into the bag.

7:00   Cathy puts a few more shells into the bag, one by one, and squeezes together the mouth of the bag.

7:15   She looks around the floor obviously searching to see if any are left. She gets up, holding the bag, and walks to Mother. Mother: "Have you got them all?" Mother glances around at the floor, satisfying herself that there are no shells remaining there.

Commentary

The major point of contrast between the excerpts from Sandra and Cathy is in the mother's awareness of what the activity in question means to the child, what she might be learning from it. Sandra's mother makes a deliberate attempt to teach Sandra the concept of "reflection" with the mirror and is not conspicuously successful in doing it. But she poses the problem for Sandra and thereby sets off a train of exploration that, in a child as bright as Sandra, will very likely culminate soon in a rudimentary understanding of the concept. To use terms from Piaget's writing (1952), Sandra's mother pushes the child from assimilation to the brink of accommodation. In contrast, Cathy's mother seems to be unaware of the intellectual significance of Cathy's stacking the shells. We view this as a "highly intellectual" activity, which provides an opportunity for the child to learn spatial relationships, but clearly, Mrs. C. is concerned only with the housekeeping aspect—that the child should not clutter the floor or damage her brother's possessions. In a large family and small space, it is probably necessary to enforce rules of possession, but a price is paid, perhaps unwittingly, as this excerpt illustrates.

EXCERPT NUMBER 4

Our final excerpt comes from an observation when Cathy was 21 months old. It should be contrasted with Sandra's Excerpt Number 4, taken when Sandra was at a similar age. The activities described in both excerpts deal with the learning of names for things. Cathy's mother is more attentive to Cathy than is typical for her, yet there is a considerable contrast between her and Mrs. S. in both quantity and quality of interaction with their one-year-olds.

Mother has been feeding Cathy a bowl of noodles and prepares to clean up Cathy's messy face and hands.

6:00   Mother: "How about your face?" Mother wipes Cathy's hands with a wet towel. Cathy says something. Mother: "You want to hold it?" Mother gives Cathy the folded wet towel. Mother: "Wipe your face."

6:20   Cathy takes the towel and rubs her mouth. She opens up the towel and puts it on the tray.

6:25   Cathy: "Clean." Mother: "That's right, clean." Cathy: "Fold it," as she rolls the towel up, putting one end over toward the middle and pushing at the bulky end. Mother: "Fold it."

6:40   Mother goes back to the sink and starts doing the dishes. Cathy straightens out the towel on the tray by pulling at the edge nearest her, then crumples it up, squeezing it in the middle.

7:00   Cathy wipes her mouth with the towel. She babbles as she hangs the towel over the side of the highchair, holding it by one end.

7:20   Mother: "Wait a minute." (Apparently thinking Cathy wants to get out of the chair.) Cathy puts towel over her face.

7:30   Mother: "Do you want to get down?" Cathy says nothing and Mother lifts her out.

7:40   Cathy: "Water." Mother: "Do you want water on this (the towel) to get it clean?"

7:55   Mother gives Cathy the wet towel (without wetting it any more), saying: "What are you going to clean?"

8:00   Cathy: "Face." Mother: "You are going to clean up your face?" Cathy puts the towel over her face.

8:20   Mother watches her.

8:30   Cathy: "Wash face." Mother: "You are washing your face." Mother goes back to the sink. Cathy wipes the table with the towel, then her cheek.

8:50   Cathy blows her nose in the towel, and follows Mother to the door in the kitchen that opens to the backyard.

9:00   Cathy follows Mother back into the kitchen. She wipes her face. Goes into the living room. Wipes her hand, wipes her nose.

9:45   She stands staring into space, holding the towel.

Commentary

Cathy's mother is usually "at her best" when she is interacting with Cathy in the context of some household chore or basic-care activity—in this example, cleaning her up after a meal. It is on these occasions that Mrs. C. usually finds the time to instruct Cathy in attaining either some practical skill or in naming things, and Mrs. C. does both in this example. Nevertheless, Mrs. S.'s interaction may be contrasted with Mrs. C.'s in the length of time she spends teaching Sandra and the quality of excitement she imparts to the task as she dramatizes the animal sounds. It is true that Mrs. C. provides feedback to Cathy, telling her that her labels are correct ("clean"; "fold it"; and Cathy: "Wash face," Mother: "You are washing your face"), but the teaching aspect simply does not go very far. For Mrs. C. could have made a dramatic game out of washing different parts of the body reminiscent of the nursery rhyme ("This is the way we wash our face," etc.), but she doesn't do so. She picks up on the child's cue only and goes only as far as the child's limited language and imagination demand.

We have now completed our study of Cathy, a one-year-old girl who we predicted will become an intellectually average child. Our tests demonstrate that Cathy is now performing well above average, but our detailed observations suggest that she may fail to realize her potential because of an inadequate environment. In Cathy's case, there seem to be several factors simultaneously inhibiting her development: her mother's lack of time for her one-year-old in the face of enormous family responsibilities; her family's unawareness of the significance of certain intellectual activities for Cathy's intellectual development; the relative poverty of her material environment; and the need for rules restricting her access to places and things. On the other hand, Cathy is luckier than most children in having a family whose relationship with her, considered from a social and emotional point of view, is generally very good.

It may be that the counterbalancing good socio-emotional milieu of Cathy's home will offset the relative lack of intellectual stimulation we observed in her second year of life, and that our prediction for Cathy's intellectual development will not be confirmed. Several remarkable changes in Cathy's home situation during her third year of life point to this as a possibility. First, the family's economic situation has improved considerably. Her father now has a better paying job, an older brother has started work and contributes regularly to the family income, and the house has been greatly expanded and redecorated. Second, Cathy's two sisters closest to her in age are now in Head Start classes, and not only are their teachers' reports of their intellectual progress good, but the "spill-over" to Cathy is tangible. They are now more likely to engage in "intellectual activities" at home and to involve their little sister in singing nursery rhymes, playing school, and the like. Most important, with the improvement in their economic and physical circumstances and having fewer children to attend to at home, Cathy's mother now has more time to devote to her own intellectual development as well as to Cathy's. This mother of thirteen children is now taking art lessons and is producing delightful oil paintings of which her family is very proud. Asked what she "gets out of the lessons," Mrs. C. replied "two hours of rest!" In view of the striking changes that have taken place since this case history was written, we may eventually well be in the happy situation of having our original prediction for Cathy's intellectual development disconfirmed. The story of Cathy will be continued in a later publication.

NANCY, A TWO-YEAR-OLD "A" GIRL

A child can develop superbly under crowded house conditions and without well-designed toys if he is permitted a certain amount of freedom to move about and explore and has access to interesting household and natural objects. Similarly, his mother need not be highly educated nor well-off financially in order to use the time she spends with him interacting in intellectually and socially profitable ways; or to organize his routine so that a varied and stimulating range of activities is regularly included in his experience; or to make herself aware of his rate and stage of development and the effects of the child's home environment on his development. An example illustrating these points is given in the story of Nancy. Nancy is the youngest child in a family of six children, four boys and two girls, ranging in age from one to eight years. Her mother and father are both in their late twenties. We predicted Nancy would develop very well intellectually and socially, on the basis of the outstanding achievements of her older siblings. This prediction is being confirmed by Nancy's test scores on all intellectual tests, and especially those of abstract ability and sense discrimination. Nancy performed in the top third of all children on these tests every time she was tested.

Nancy's Background: Physical Environment

Nancy's family lives in an eight-room single-family house in a deteriorating residential area of Greater Boston. Their house is situated on a dead-end street and is flanked by other single-family houses, which, like their own, are in fair-to-poor states of repair. The children on the block play in the pocket-size backyards and in the dead-end street in front. A few blocks away is a mixed commercial–residential area, with small stores and considerable traffic.

There are eight rooms for eight people in Nancy's home. The rooms include a small front parlor, a living room, dining area, kitchen, two baths, and four bedrooms. Nancy shares her bedroom with her only sister. The front parlor and parents' bedroom are off limits to Nancy except under supervision, but her mother stressed that she is not scolded for breaking these rules, just reminded of them.

Human Environment

With respect to income, residence, and education, Nancy's family is in Class III. Both her mother and father have had a year or two of training in vocational school, and her father works as a technician in a research operation. Previous to her marriage, her mother also held a technical job in a laboratory. Their classification as Class III rests mainly on their income, which is between $7,000 and $12,000 for a family of eight, and their residence, which we have already described.

All our observations were done when Nancy was in her mother's charge. Most of Nancy's interaction with people is with her mother, but with a three-year-old brother nearly always around, and other siblings sometimes at home, about one third of Nancy's interaction is with them. It is important to note that the quality of Nancy's interaction with her siblings is exceptional and must be in part due to Mrs. N.'s expertise in handling her large family. We observed very little fighting or squabbling among the children, a great deal of joint participation in activities, and a large amount of help and instruction being given by older siblings to younger. Nancy is one of the few children whose interaction scores on such things as teaching and engaging in highly intellectual activities are significantly increased when we count interactions with all people, including siblings, and not just the mother. Mrs. N. is very skilled at organizing interesting activities for her brood. Often these take the form of practical projects to please specific people, such as making Christmas gifts, or creating posters and banners to welcome home a brother who had had his tonsils out, or making a cake and cookies. Consistent with her interest in having the children be active participators, she is one of the few working-class mothers who turned on the television only for selected programs like "Sesame Street," often sat and watched the program with her children, and discussed the program with them while or after it was on.

Observations on Nancy

Table 53 shows that when Nancy was 24–27 months old, her mother typically spent about 17 minutes out of an observation hour interacting with her in some way, about three minutes engaging in highly intellectual activities, about one minute in direct teaching, and about one minute restricting Nancy's activities. Over this three-month period, Mrs. N. encouraged ten times as much of Nancy's activity as she discouraged, initiated twice as much of Nancy's activity as Nancy herself, and was successful in half her attempts to control Nancy.

The remainder of this case study will be devoted to providing verbatim excerpts and interpretations of our actual observations on Nancy when she was 24–27 months old. The picture we shall see is of a more mature version of our A one-year-old, Sandra. Like Sandra, Nancy enjoys activities involving fine motor activity, and, in a development to be expected for her age, she sometimes uses these in an original fashion. Her persistence at a task is similar to that of Sandra, but in her case there is not the infantile tendency to give way to tantrums when thwarted.

EXCERPT NUMBER 1

When this observation was made, Nancy was just over 25 months. The situation is a familiar one to observers of two-year-olds. Mother is changing Nancy after she has had an "accident."

2:00   Mother rubs salve on Nancy's behind. Mother: "You've got a spot. There, you're all set. Do you want to put your pants on?"

2:10   Nancy picks up her pants and puts leg in. "I can do it." Mother: "I know, I'll watch you."

2:28   Nancy gets other leg in. Mother helps Nancy. Mother: "Okay?" Nancy: "I know how to do it." Mother: "I know you know how to do it."

2:45   Nancy struggles to lift pants over her behind. Mother gestures, offering help. Nancy struggles silently. Mother: "Do you want help?"

3:00   Mother: "Your nose is running, too. You're running from both ends!" Mother wipes her nose as Nancy struggles with pants. Mother: "They're hard." Nancy pulls at pants. Mother watches.

3:34   Mother offers help. Nancy: "Yes." Mother pulls pants up. Mother: "Oh, boy! That's a hard job."

3:50   Mother holds Nancy's outer pants and helps her into these. Mother: "One foot, then the other foot." Nancy almost falls. Mother: "Careful!"

4:00   Mother tucks in Nancy's shirt. Mother: "Sit down, I'll get your shoes on." Nancy sits. Nancy: "On floor?" Mother: "Yes, right on the floor."

4:10   Mother puts Nancy's socks on. Nancy tries to put her shoe on. Mother: "That goes on your other foot." Nancy: "This one." Mother: "Other foot."

4:30   Nancy pulls shoe off. Nancy: "I can get it." Mother watches Nancy put shoes on. Nancy holds laces.

4:55   Nancy: "Is this the *other* one?" Mother: "Yes, that's the *other* one (foot)."

5:00   Mother: "What a big girl!" Mother: "Can I help you tie them?" Nancy: "Okay." Mother: "You watch Mommy." Mother ties shoes quickly (not really demonstrating how to tie). Mother: "Okay." Mother ties other shoe. Mother: "All done."

Commentary

The excerpt describes a basic-care activity that all mothers have to perform several times a day. Mrs. N. is very skillful here in allowing her two-year-old to master the skill of dressing herself, in recognizing and praising her accomplishments ("I know you know how to do it"; "That's a hard job!"), in offering and giving help, and in using the opportunity to teach ("Your nose is running, too. You are running at *both* ends." Nancy: "Is this the *other* one?" Mother: "That's the *other* one").

EXCERPT NUMBER 2

When this observation was taken, Nancy was just over 27 months. She is playing with Play Doh with her 3½-year-old brother, Richard, a type of activity that Mrs. N. often encourages. Mother sits nearby with a cup of coffee, reading a paper and observing the children frequently.

3:00   Nancy watches Richard, who is using an inverted measuring cup on his dough.

3:10   Watches Richard, eats cookie. Richard takes measuring cup from play dough. Nancy: "You make a hat?" (Richard's cup on the dough looks like classic straw hat.)

3:21   He doesn't answer.

3:31   Nancy points to dough. "Hey, look what I made."

3:35   Richard looks but does not respond.

3:37   Nancy turns over dough, pats it, cuts it off with a plastic block.

3:49   Richard watches her.

3:55   Nancy cuts dough again.

4:00   Nancy pinches off a bit of dough and puts it in the middle of the square indentation she has made.

4:09   Drinks some juice, watches Richard.

4:23   Cuts on play doh with knife.

4:25   Mother sits down at table with book, observing Nancy.

4:38   Mother watches. Nancy punches fist into Play Doh and pounds it.

4:50   Makes another square indentation with block.

5:00   Repeats. Pounds block with fist.

5:10   Pinches off a bit of dough and places it in square. Places block again and pounds (trying to cut all the way through).

5:24   Kneeling on chair, she pushes again at block and dough, using her whole body.

5:30   Sits again and looks into glass of juice.

5:38   Picks up dough, square piece falls out.

5:44   Nancy: "Look what I made, Mommy."

5:50   Mother: "Ooh, that's a biscuit."

5:54   Some dough falls on floor. Nancy: "My biscuit fell." Mother: "I'll get it," and does. Mother asks, "Do you want to put it on a plate?" Mother puts it on plate.

6:03   Nancy moves it to middle of plate: "I'm going to make another one."

6:16 Mother sits down. "Okay." Nancy makes square indentation in dough.

6:25 Nancy: "Here, I'll make a piece." Mother, reading, doesn't hear.

6:35 Nancy looks under Play Doh. Makes another square. "I've made a muffin."

6:49 Makes another square. Nancy: "Two windows," counts them, "one, two."
(Nancy continues with this activity past the end of the observation.)

Commentary

This excerpt is remarkable for the length of time Nancy spends at
an activity that is relevant to the learning of spatial and fine motor skill
and also to the development of the imagination. Nancy makes an original
association to the materials ("You've made a hat") and enters into an
extended role-play sequence, which, at this age, is highly indicative of
superior cognitive development. In this episode, Nancy's mother for the
most part merely observes Nancy in an approving fashion, while her
brother participates in the activity with her. Her behavior is unusual compared to that of the average mother, in that she has suggested and provided the materials for Nancy to use with the Play Doh, and has taken
the time to sit with the children while they played. This seemingly trivial
detail indicates a significant characteristic in Mrs. N. Routinely, Mrs. N.
makes time to sit for half an hour or so with the children, reading, watching "Sesame Street," joining in some "intellectual activity," or merely
observing them. In this respect, Mrs. N. is outstanding among our mothers
in Classes III, IV, and V, and in her up-to-date knowledge of how Nancy
is developing, what activities interest her, and what she learns from them.
Among our mothers of two-year-olds, she was one of the few who could
describe in detail the several concepts that the program "Sesame Street"
attempts to convey, who had firm ideas about the educational value and
age-appropriateness of different types of toys, and who had an articulated
philosophy about how a mother should promote intellectual and social
development in a young child.

Nancy's excellent social and intellectual development should be contrasted with that of Robert, who is the subject of our fourth case study.

ROBERT, A TWO-YEAR-OLD "C" BOY

Robert was just two years old when we started observing him. He is
the youngest child in a family of six children. Robert's mother and
father are in their thirties. We predicted that Robert would develop below
average intellectually, on the basis of a Stanford–Binet IQ of 83 of the
sibling closest to him in age who was not yet in school, and the generally
poor performance in school of his older brothers and sisters. This predic-

tion is clearly being borne out by Robert's test performance. At 24 months, Robert's test scores were already below average, and through the period of our observations they became progressively worse, his test scores at 30 months being actually lower than at 24 months (see Chapter 7, Case #7).

Robert's Background: Physical Environment

Robert's family lives in a public housing project in a residential area of Greater Boston. The project is a small one, composed of four rows of adjoining houses, two stories high, around a central courtyard. The neighborhood is mostly residential, consisting of one-family and multiple-family dwellings generally in a poor state of maintenance, and a few small stores. The children in the project play mostly in the courtyard, which is equipped with swings, a slide, and a paved path for cycling.

Robert's house consists of five rooms—a living room and kitchen on the first floor, and three small bedrooms for parents, girls, and boys, on the second floor. Robert shares a bedroom with his brother, aged four. The interior is dark, for lack of windows, and is in a poor state of repair, with furnishings mostly old and shabby.

Human Environment

In terms of income, residence, and education, Robert's family is in Class IV. His father left school in the ninth grade and works as a semi-skilled operator in a steelworks. His mother left school in the tenth grade, and has a part-time job waitressing in the evenings. When we first started observing Robert, the family income was between $5,000 and $7,000, but during our second period of observations, when Robert was 24–27 months old, Mr. R. lost his job, and the family went on welfare until his father found part-time maintenance work.

All our observations were done when Robert was in his mother's charge, and most of his interaction with people is with her. Mrs. R. frequently put Robert out to play in the courtyard, and with a younger brother continually at home, and a father irregularly employed, Robert spent about a third of his interaction time with people other than his mother. Observed interactions between Robert and other children were seldom positive and never intellectually promising. Mostly they consisted of other children barely tolerating Robert's joining them in play out of doors, and not infrequently excluding him or teasing him. Robert nearly always seemed on the margin of other children's activities, and some children seemed to actively dislike him.

Robert's mother's personality is of great importance to our understanding of Robert's development and will undoubtedly play a large part in his predicted failure to become either intellectually or socially competent. Mrs. R.'s characteristic style of interacting with Robert is a mixture, extremely volatile, of bullying, teasing, restriction, and affection. In every observation she referred to him with phrases such as "you bad boy," "Mr. Mischief," "troublemaker," said sometimes with a smile, sometimes with a glare, sometimes with a slap or a shake. Without warning, a tickling or horseplay activity would turn into an occasion for threats ("I'll kill you"; "I'll beat you") or shaming. Occasional attempts on Robert's part to master some skill were often summarily interrupted, and Mrs. R. was seldom observed trying to teach Robert. Indeed, Robert is one of the few children for whom interaction with his mother often seemed intellectually deleterious. For example, although Table 53 shows that one or two minutes out of an observation hour were devoted to "highly intellectual" activities in which both Robert and his mother were in some way involved, Mrs. R.'s mode of behavior on these occasions almost never included teaching, and often took the form of restricting or interfering with his activity. As an index of opportunity for learning, Robert's score on highly intellectual activities is therefore quite misleading—it should be much lower.

These points are best illustrated by excerpts from our actual observations on Robert.

EXCERPT NUMBER 1

This observation was done when Robert was 25½ months old. At the start of the observation, Robert was outdoors in the project courtyard, where a group of children were playing on the swings and slide.

0:00   Robert wanders through curtains hanging on a line. Mother: "Get out of there right now."

0:05   Robert walks away from curtains. Mother: "Go get your car, go ride your car. Where is your car?"

0:15   Mother returns to kitchen. Robert walks with finger in mouth, falls down, gets up.

0:29   Walks to sidewalk.

0:54   Robert goes to back porch of another apartment, hides from observer.

1:00   He follows another child (male, older). Sib brings car over to Robert (on Mother's orders). Robert walks by it, falls on it.

1:21   He sits on the car.

1:30   Robert pushes car with his feet.

1:41   He rides car under curtains.

2:00   He then rides between the curtains.

2:30   He climbs off car to go to steps to his apartment.

2:45   He climbs up stairs.

3:02   Robert looks into the kitchen. Mother: "What do you want?"

3:04   Robert looks in.

3:15   He looks at the observer. Mother comes to door.

3:19   Mother: "What do you want? Get down off the stairs, smart guy."

3:27   "Get down the stairs."

3:30   Mother takes hood from his head, pats Robert. Mother: "Hold on."

3:39   Robert goes down stairs, walks along sidewalk area.

3:50   Mother keeps watching.

3:55   Robert gets behind car and pushes it.

4:00   Mother: "Give me a ride." Robert looks at her, puzzled.

4:07   Mother: "Bad guy."

4:11   Robert looks at observer, goes to steps. Mother: "No, get down the stairs and play."

4:22   Mother opens door and points down stairs.

4:30   Robert looks at Mother, eases self down stairs.

4:40   He sits on bottom step. Mother stops watching him.

4:44   Robert stares ahead.

5:00   He stands, walks along walk, wanders, looks at other children playing.

Commentary

This excerpt shows Robert in a typical light. For the most part he spends his time wandering about or engaging lethargically and by himself in unstructured play, carrying, pushing, or pulling toys about. Instead of trying to engage and sustain Robert's interest in an activity, his mother seems intent on getting him away from her by issuing commands ("Go get your car"). On the one occasion when she shows an interest in his activity, her behavior is inappropriate and has the effect of puzzling and threatening Robert ("Give me a ride"—obviously she doesn't mean it—"Bad Guy").

These particular events may seem inconsequential taken in isolation, but repeated over and over again they become a significant factor in Robert's human environment. A more extreme but by no means isolated example of Robert's interaction with his mother and other children is seen in the next excerpt.

EXCERPT NUMBER 2

In this observation Robert is again in the courtyard and there are several children running about or talking to each other.

0:00   Robert looks at children, thumb in mouth. Wanders about with a blank look.

1:00   He spits (makes a spitting gesture) at a small girl (probably younger than he is). The girl ignores him.

1:20   Robert babbles to the little girl. She ignores him. Robert wanders.

2:00   Robert leaves his pull toy on the path. Mother comes to door and talks to the neighbor about stray cats. Robert wanders over to slide (large) in the court-yard.

2:30   He goes up the ladder of the slide.

2:55   Mother sees him. "You better stay down off there, you hear! Get off! Off!"

3:05   "Get over here! C'mon!" Mother goes over. Robert starts down the stairs.

3:15   He walks toward Mother.

3:20   "You better move a little faster!" Mother holds and slaps him firmly. "If I walk away and you go up that slide, I'll pull your pants down and give you a licking! You have your train and toys! Stay off that slide! You hear!" (She holds him by the shoulders as she says this.)

4:05   Mother leaves. Robert hangs on to the pole of the slide with his head down watching his mother leave.

4:10   Small girl (no older than Robert) goes up the ladder a little way to show off to Robert that *she's* allowed.

4:30   Robert hides in back of slide with his head hanging down and rubbing his head against the slide. Small girl teases, "I can go up!"

4:40   Small girl whirls around the pole supporting the slide. Robert imitates (but they are not really interacting). He does this distractedly and seems to be preoccupied with what has happened with Mother.

5:00   Robert babbles to self (as if he were muttering angrily).

Commentary

Of the ten observations our environment group made on Robert, there were several in which Mrs. R. physically or verbally assaulted Robert in the extreme way depicted here. This excerpt therefore describes a scene with which Robert is familiar (probably more familiar than our observations suggest, considering that his mother probably restrains herself in our presence). Other notable features in this excerpt are the extent to which Robert is excluded from the activities of other children and the way he is taunted by the little girl no older than himself. She clearly senses from observing Robert and his mother that Robert is an easy victim. Robert's interaction with other children in this excerpt is characteristic. We seldom observed Robert in friendly play with children, and in several observations he was teased, assaulted, or deliberately ignored by peers.

INTEGRATION AND
TENTATIVE INTERPRETATIONS

11

Discussions and Conclusions

BURTON L. WHITE

INTRODUCTION

In this final chapter we will describe our current best sense of how some families seem to do a superb job of rearing their children during their second and third years of life. We shall also look at some of the consequences of our work for early-education programs. The reader must understand that *nobody* has definitive information on how to optimally rear children. Our information and our interpretations must also be considered nondefinitive. In spite of the pressing demand for answers, we must state that it will be many years (if at all) before a full, scientifically valid picture can be drawn. We can state, however, that our interpretations are based on a very intensive study of the development of 31 young children. We have been in their homes gathering information at the rate of once each week for six months out of each year. After we collect the balance of the data on this natural experiment, we shall refine our ideas and present a modified discussion of excellent child-rearing practices. Presumably, each modification will bring us somewhat nearer to the truth.

Another point to bear in mind in reading what follows is that our subject group, although diverse, is limited in several important ways. First of all, it numbers only 31 families at this time (ultimately that figure will be somewhat higher). Then, too, we are studying only families from eastern Massachusetts; there are many other families in this country alone, to say nothing of those in other parts of the world, living in far worse conditions than do the least fortunate of our subjects. In addition to such economic considerations, our study is clearly culture-bound by virtue of the population we work with. Finally, there are methodological problems. To some extent, our data and our judgments are in error owing to less-than-perfect data-collecting instruments, and also to the distorting effects on the natural home scene caused by the presence of an observer.

The Critical Period of Development

Many people who study the development of children have made statements about the special importance of particular age ranges. In this regard, we are no different. Our study, even though incomplete at this writing, has convinced us of the special importance of the 10- to 18-month age range for the development of general competence. At this time of life, for most children, several extremely important developments seem to coalesce and force a test of each family's capacity to rear children. The primary burden in most cases falls upon the mother.

Let us first characterize children during the second and third years of life, to help set the stage for explaining why we believe so strongly in the unique importance of the 10- to 18-month period. We will then summarize what we think we are learning about desirable child-rearing practices.

THE CHILD AT ONE YEAR OF AGE

Most one-year-olds appear to resemble each other in a few interesting and fundamental ways. First of all, perhaps the hallmark of this age is curiosity. The one-year-old seems genuinely interested in exploring his world throughout the major portion of his day. Aside from mealtimes and the need to relieve various occasional physical discomforts, his consuming interest is in exploration. This fact is confirmed by our task data, especially in the predominance of the *explore, mastery,* and *gain information —visual* experiences. Unfortunately, not all situations are optimal for nurturing that curiosity, nor are the rules governing exploratory behavior equivalent across homes. Nonetheless, the one-year-old is primed for expending enormous amounts of energy exploring and learning about his world.

The curiosity of the one-year-old is aided by his newly acquired ability to cover space. Whereas, at 6 months of age, he was limited to the places his mother kept him (i.e., crib, high chair, playpen, changing-table, bath, carriage, etc.), he can now either crawl, cruise, or walk wherever he wishes, subject to his mother's approval and the physical layout of the home. Unfortunately, he is not yet very skillful with his body, nor very knowledgeable about danger or destruction. On the one hand, he is capable of enormous amounts of intellectual and social learning and development of motor skills such as walking, climbing, and especially the use of his hands. On the other hand, razor blades, broken glass, and electrical equipment are to him only additional opportunities for exploration. In addition, fragile objects that are precious to other people engender no special treatment from him. This combination of factors alone places considerable stress on most mothers. But there is more.

The one-year-old is poised for fundamental development in social and language development as well. During the first year of life, there is little to suggest that infants are self-conscious or particularly thoughtful creatures. During the second year, however, one can observe the emergence of a sense of self. Increasingly, the child seems to assimilate ideas of who he is. His name comes to produce an appropriate and a special response from him. Gradually, he begins to use the terms "me" and "mine." Also during that second year, he begins for the first time to seriously engage in interpersonal contests. As many have noted before, a sense of autonomy begins to manifest itself during this period.*

Along with a growing sense of self and independence, the child during the second year of life seems to be learning a great deal about his mother and her reactions. He studies her and approaches her often during this period and seems to develop a very strong attachment to her. Other human beings count, but not much compared to his mother, in most cases. Peers ordinarily spend very small amounts of time with him. Fathers may spend a bit more when we do not observe, but they still probably do not compare with the mother as centers of continuing interest (except in rare cases). During the second year, unlike any other time in his life, the child seems to develop in these directions in a manner that may produce a vigorous, secure, loving, and healthy social animal, or else may take other paths. By two, he may become a modest form of social tyrant whose major orientation during his waking hours is clinging to and dominating his mother,† or he may learn that his mother is rather unpredictable—sometimes, someone to fear, while at other times, someone who will protect him.

---

* For a graphic illustration, see our section on the ratio of compliance/noncompliance responses between one and three years of age. The one-year-old is largely compliant, as are most two- to three-year-olds. The 1½- to two-year-old is considerably more likely to refuse a request than he was when younger or than he will be when he is older.

† A major casualty of such a development is that normal intrinsic interest in exploring physical reality and mastering skills becomes subjugated to the social orientation. This division of interest may have profound importance.

Before 8 or 9 months of age, there is little reason to believe that infants understand words. By 36 months of age, they seem (in most cases) to be able to process most simple language. It is clear that a remarkable amount of language development is taking place beginning at about one year of age (see section on language development). Certainly, no analysis of the effects of child-rearing practices during this age period should ignore this fact.

A further point on one-year-olds concerns the issue of physical maturity. At one, some children look and behave very much like the average 9- or 10-month-old, while others appear several months advanced. The fact that walking ability emerges at about this time helps accentuate differences in maturity at this age. We suspect that part of the reason one cannot predict future development from a one-year-old's behavior is this factor. The commonly seen, striking differences in physical maturity become much less marked by the time the child reaches two years of age, but at one they hinder prediction and also complicate the problem of effective child-rearing techniques.

THE CHILD AT TWO YEARS OF AGE

Data about the two-year-old (24 to 27 months) are slightly less interesting to us than data about the one-year-old. The reason is that it appears the two-year-old has already taken shape, to a degree that suggests that many basic formative experiences are already behind him. Our test data, like that of many other studies, indicate that children who are going to develop well or poorly (during the preschool period, at least) begin to reveal which course they are on at about the middle of the second year of life.

The two-year-old is usually just emerging from a rather dramatic phase, the aforementioned emergence of his sense of agency. This has been manifest in many ways, but perhaps the most dramatic is reflected in our compliance/noncompliance data (see section on social competence). As we discussed earlier, the one-year-old is generally an agreeable child, as are most three-year-olds, but sometime during the second year of life, our subjects begin asserting themselves, rejecting suggestions, ignoring commands, testing limits, and generally flexing their muscles. Some mothers cope well with this normal phenomenon, others not so well. Not all children have left this stage behind at two, and in many cases, children seem to carry the related conflicts along for many years.

Two-year-olds usually maintain a high level of intrinsic curiosity, but not as uniformly high as among one-year-olds. They are much more sophisticated about social relations, although their prime area of knowledge concerns their own family. They seem to have developed a standard inventory of social-interaction patterns to use with the family, and are usually more shy with strangers than one-year-olds. Their language capacities have increased dramatically, such that most everyday simple language is usually understood, if not expressed. They may now exhibit the capacity for "pretend" or fantasy behavior, and you may see signs of a budding sense of humor. They are now slightly more interested in television but still spend (on the average) no more than about one-half hour a day really attending to the screen. Their body control is now much advanced over the one-year-old, and they have moved on to practicing advanced motor skills like tricycle and wagon riding and climbing. Their play with objects involves more practicing of skills than exploration of object qualities, but they have not yet ordinarily begun to *construct products,* such as drawings, puzzles, or playhouses. Their capacity for sustained conversation is very limited, although they will listen to language for fairly long periods. Finally, their direction of interest still shifts rapidly, with typical units of experience lasting only twenty to thirty seconds or so, with the exception of occasional long periods of viewing television.

THE SPECIAL IMPORTANCE OF THE
10- TO 18-MONTH PERIOD OF LIFE

At the beginning of this section we remarked that the 10- to 18-month period of life was of peculiar importance for the development of overall ability in children. In addition, we believe that families first reveal their level of capacity for child-rearing during this period. What follows is an explanation of why we think this way.

First of all, the development of the capacity for receptive language begins to become substantial at about 8 or 9 months of age. Our subjects developing *very well* (and those of other studies) first show fairly clear precocity, as compared with children developing poorly, at about 18 months. Variations in the language milieu prior to 8 months of age are far less likely to affect language and related development than are those occurring subsequently. Second, the emergence of locomotor ability in the form of crawling at about 9 or 10 months of age combines with several factors to place a great deal of stress on the primary caretaker. Locomobility plus intense curiosity, plus poor control of the body, plus ignorance of common dangers, plus ignorance of the value of things, plus ignorance concerning the rights of others, spells trouble. Third, sometime toward the end of the first year of life, two social developments of significance begin to undergo rapid development. Babies begin to reveal a growing awareness of themselves as agents, as beings with separate identities. The

form of this identity appears to be shaped largely through social interactions with the primary caretaker. These interchanges also appear to
shape the infant's basic orientation toward people in general. He typically
reveals a very strong orienting tendency toward his mother and initiates
very sizable numbers of overtures in her direction. He seems to be ac-
quiring his basic style as a social animal.

To the degree that we are correct, then, most of the basic foundations
of educational and general development will receive their shape and quality
during this short interval. Now, we do not mean to say that the first 10
months of life are of no importance at all, nor that every child enters and
leaves the critical stage at the same time. Certainly, a child has to be well
nourished and well loved from birth. Furthermore, previous research by
the senior author (White, 1971) seems to indicate that infants can probably derive much more pleasure and perhaps developmental gain from the
first months of life than they now do. (Also see Hunt, 1961.) However,
under current practices of child-rearing, whatever infants experience during their first months of life (except for extreme deprivation) does not
apparently lead to important differential achievement by age one. Although
differences in achievement are, of course, present in every group of one-
year-old infants, developmental differences that are indicative of future
educational performance do not appear to emerge until at least 18 months
of age, if then.

We have said that important or predictive developmental divergence
first becomes clear during the second year of life. Amplification of this
key statement is necessary. We do not mean to say that all children test
out as average throughout the first 18 months of life. Nor do we mean to
say that scores for all children between 18 and 24 months of life immediately reflect their levels of ability for the rest of their lives. Between
birth and 18 months of age, for example, a small percentage of children
with serious developmental handicaps will score well below average on
tests of general developmental status such as the Gesell, Griffiths, Bayley,
and so on. An infant who repeated scores below 85 (one standard devi-
ation below the mean in most cases) may indeed be manifesting what we
are calling important developmental divergence. Such children constitute
somewhat less than 17 percent of the population. Of these, some will
ultimately develop normal or even superior ability; others will indeed never
function at normal levels (see Knobloch and Pasamanick). Others will end
up with moderate handicaps. The vast majority of children (over 82 percent) will regularly score above 85 on infant development tests with a
central tendency of 100. However, whether they score 90 or 115 in this
first year of life doesn't seem to tell us much about levels of function at
age three and up.

Turning to the period from 18 months of age on, we suggest that children who will ultimately be exceptional in either direction (talented or of lower-than-average competence) will begin to reveal their direction of development first. Gradually, additional children will reveal predictive divergent advancement levels as a function of the degree to which they are exceptional. The modal child, by definition, will test at an average of 100 not only at 18 months but repeatedly throughout his developmental years, barring special educational experiences, test errors, and other factors that occasionally influence test performance. For some large but not surely identified number of children, then, developmental divergence will never be shown, simply because the average child, by definition, is non-divergent. He does, on the other hand, reveal divergence to some extent at 18 months and increasingly thereafter, in relation to the most exceptional children. By scoring around 100 regularly from 18 months on, he reveals that he is neither particularly precocious nor particularly handicapped.

It seems to us that mothers are obliged to make at least three major sets of choices in regard to child-rearing practices during this period. The first choices become necessary when locomobility emerges (ordinarily in the form of crawling). The resultant potential for self-injury and for destructiveness, creation of clutter, and intrusion on the private domain of older siblings must be coped with by every family. The choices made vary widely and seem to link with subsequent developments in the child.

Some time late in the first year or into the second, mothers make a second important modification of their child-rearing practices. Sooner or later they become aware of their child's emerging capacity for language acquisition. Some choose to feed the growth of language by going out of their way to talk a great deal to their children. Some provide language input effectively by careful selection of suitable words and phrases and by exploiting the child's interest of the moment. Others provide a great deal of input but with considerably less skill and effectiveness. Other mothers show minimal attention to the language interests of their children or for other reasons provide negligible amounts of language input.

The third major shaping of fundamental child-rearing practices during this period appears to be triggered by the onset of negativism sometime after 14 or 15 months of age. The disappearance of the benign, easy-to-get-along-with 12-month-old is very disconcerting to many mothers. Negativistic behavior is usually experienced as stressful to some degree by all mothers. Styles of reaction to such behavior in children vary from the overpunitive all the way to the overacquiescent.

These three emerging phenomena—locomobility and its stressful consequences, language-learning ability, and negativism—force maternal reactions that become fairly fixed in most cases by the time the child is 18 months of age. It is this three-step creation of the early child-rearing styles that underlies our emphasis on the 10- to 18-month period of life.

Families, especially mothers, react to their particular infants in a variety of ways during the 10- to 18-month period. Certainly, few are prepared to react on the basis of training or even reliable advice. This to us constitutes a gross injustice to many children and their parents. How do those families who are currently doing a first-rate job function? What are the characteristics of successful caretakers (usually mothers)?

IMPORTANT CHARACTERISTICS OF PRIMARY CARETAKERS

The responsibility for child-rearing currently rests in the hands of the mother in American society. That situation may change if and when day care for infants becomes more prevalent. We believe the ideas we are espousing will be relevant to good infant day-care practices as well as to home rearing of children. What then can we say in a succinct fashion about optimal characteristics of mothers? We can divide the problem into a few major components.

Attitudes and Values

The performance of a mother derives in part from her attitudes and values. It is also significantly affected by her resources, both material and psychological. We can single out at least the following areas of importance with respect to attitudes and values: life in general, young children, the formative role of infancy, possessions, housekeeping, and safety.

LIFE IN GENERAL.   A woman who is seriously depressed or very angry or unhappy about life probably cannot do a good job of getting her young child off to a good start. None of our successful mothers have such attitudes toward life, while a few of our unsuccessful mothers do.

YOUNG CHILDREN.   Some mothers don't seem to really enjoy their children during the one-to-three age range. They spend as little time as possible with them, and when they interact with them, they don't seem to get much pleasure from the experience. Some of our mothers who do poorly fall into this category, others of them do not; virtually all our successful mothers seem to derive a great deal of pleasure from their children during this age range.

THE FORMATIVE ROLE OF THE ONE- TO THREE-YEAR AGE RANGE. Mothers seem to vary considerably on this dimension. We doubt that many of our C mothers believe strongly that this period of life has profound significance for development. On the other hand, not all A mothers do either. It is our impression that many of our A mothers perform excellently without any measurable degree of commitment to this thesis. They seem to spontaneously grant their infants generous measures of attention and consideration, simply as a part of a natural way of life.

POSSESSIONS. There is a fair degree of incompatibility between a strong desire to preserve the contents of one's home and the normal tendency toward nonmalicious destructiveness in infants. The mother who is very concerned about her possessions is in for trouble. She has basically three routes to take. She can physically prevent her child from contacting many items in the home by the habitual use of playpens, cribs, and gates. We suspect this route produces frustration and stunting of curiosity in infants. She may allow the child the run of the house and attempt to prevent damage by stopping the child with words or actions when he appears about to break something. This route is often unsuccessful because of the child's limited understanding of words and normal development of negativism. At the very best, it results in a mother who is very frequently saying "No, don't touch that" to her child. Another practice is to allow the child to roam, and to accompany him in an attempt at constant supervision combined with gentle redirection. This route is very time- and energy-consuming, and few mothers can afford it.

HOUSEKEEPING. Very few of our A mothers are meticulous housekeepers. Most of them seem to have accepted the idea that an infant and a spotless home are incompatible. The problem is often aggravated by a husband who insists on a spotless home, in part because he doesn't realize how much work is entailed. The paths a mother of an infant may take to maintain a spotless home are similar to those for the preservation of possessions, and the pitfalls are similar.

SAFETY. We have already described the potential for self-injury that every infant has. The danger is very real. Again, mothers vary widely in how they deal with danger. And again, most of the ways that reduce the danger carry with them the real possibility of reducing the child's normal curiosity and development. About all our study tells us so far is that our A mothers are usually more inclined than our C mothers to take risks on this score with their one-year-olds. There is some research that suggests that children have more built-in controls than we give them credit for. The work on depth perception by Gibson and Walk (1960), for example, suggests that by the time children begin to crawl, they can skillfully discriminate depth and furthermore are inclined to avoid moving off safe positions and injuring themselves. There are certain African tribes that allow their infants access to sharp weapons and utensils, with no apparent serious injuries resulting. It is our impression that infants are generally far more careful about protecting themselves than we think. We do not mean to suggest that no caution need be exercised. Earlier, we alluded to the problems of razor blades, broken glass, and so on, but there is a middle ground in the treatment of the problem of safety, and some mothers are markedly overprotective to the point where they seem to interfere too much with good development.

MOTHERING, A VASTLY UNDERRATED OCCUPATION

We will begin with the bold statement that the mother's direct and indirect actions with regard to her one- to three-year-old child, especially during the second year of life, are, in our opinion, the most powerful formative factors in the development of a preschool-age child.

Further, we would guess that if a mother does a fine job in the preschool years, subsequent educators such as teachers will find their chances for effectiveness maximized. Finally, we would expect that much of the basic quality of the entire life of an individual is determined by the mother's actions during these two years. Obviously, we could be very wrong about these declarative statements. We make them as very strong hunches that we have become committed to, as a kind of net result of all our inquiries into early development.

Let us quickly add that we believe most women are capable of doing a fine job with their one- to three-year-old children. Our study has convinced us that a mother need not necessarily have even a high school diploma, let alone a college education. Nor does she need to have very substantial economic assets. In addition, it is clear that a good job can be accomplished without a father in the home. In all these statements we see considerable hope for future generations.

BEST GUESSES ABOUT MOST EFFECTIVE CHILD-REARING PRACTICES

Our A mothers talk a great deal to their children, and usually at a level the child can handle. They make them feel as though whatever they are doing is usually interesting. They provide access to many objects and diverse situations. They lead the child to believe that he can expect help and encouragement most, but *not all* the time. They demonstrate and explain things to the child, but mostly on the child's instigation rather than their own. They prohibit certain activities, and they do so consistently and firmly. They are secure enough to say "no" to the child from time to time without seeming to fear that the child will not love them. They are imaginative, so that they make interesting associations and suggestions to the child when opportunities present themselves. They very skillfully and naturally strengthen the child's intrinsic motivation to learn. They also give him a sense of task orientation, a notion that it is desirable to do things well and completely. They make the child feel secure.

Our most effective mothers do not devote the bulk of their day to rearing their young children. Most of them are far too busy to do so; several of them, in fact, have part-time jobs. What they seem to do, often without knowing exactly why, is to perform excellently the functions of designer and consultant. By that I mean they design a physical world, mainly in the home, that is beautifully suited to nurturing the burgeoning curiosity of the one- to three-year-old. It is full of small, manipulable, visually detailed objects, some of which were originally designed for young children (toys), others normally used for other purposes (plastic refrigerator containers, bottle caps, baby-food jars and covers, shoes, magazines, television and radio knobs, etc.). It contains things to climb, such as chairs, benches, sofas, and stairs. It has available materials to nurture more mature motor interests, such as tricycles, scooters, and structures with which to practice elementary gymnastics. It includes a rich variety of interesting things to look at, such as television, people, and the aforementioned types of physical objects.

In addition to being largely responsible for the type of environment the child has, this mother sets up guides for her child's behavior that seem to play a very important role in these processes. She is generally permissive and indulgent. The child is encouraged in the vast majority of his explorations. When the child confronts an interesting or difficult situation, he often turns to his mother for help. Although usually working at some chore, she is generally nearby. He then goes to her and usually, but *not always,* is *responded to* by his mother with help or shared enthusiasm, plus, occasionally, an interesting, naturally related idea. These ten- to thirty-second interchanges are usually oriented around the child's interest of the moment rather than toward some need or interest of the mother. At times, under these circumstances, the child will not receive immediate attention. These effective mothers do not always drop what they are doing to attend to his request, but rather if the time is obviously inconvenient, they say so, thereby probably giving the child a realistic, small taste of things to come.

These mothers very rarely spend five, ten, or twenty minutes teaching their one- or two-year-olds, but they get an enormous amount (in terms of frequency) of teaching in "on the fly," and usually at the child's instigation. Although they do volunteer comments opportunistically, they react mostly to overtures by the child.

These effective mothers seem to be people with high levels of energy. The work of a young mother without household help is, in spite of modern appliances, very time- and energy-consuming. Yet we have families subsisting at a welfare level of income, with as many as eight closely spaced children, that are doing every bit as good a job in child-rearing during the early years as the most advantaged homes. (A Russian-type "Hero of the People" award ought to go to such remarkable women.)

12

Ramifications for Society

B. L. WHITE

INFORMAL EARLY EDUCATION— CHILD-REARING PRACTICES

We have suggested that the 10- to 18-month period of life is in effect a critical period for the development of the foundations of competence. In addition, we have focused on what we believe is the primary importance of the central caretaker's role in this basic developmental area. To the extent that these admittedly preliminary judgments have validity, we believe that society must pay considerably more attention to child-rearing practices. Few, if any, modern societies make extensive efforts to prepare and assist their families to raise children. Our work suggests that substantial numbers of children and families are being short-changed, and not merely poor families and children.

The interest among parents is clearly great. Witness the commercial effort in the forms of the many articles in the popular press and in magazines. Observe the sales of Dr. Spock's books on child care. Note the rapidly growing sales of educational toys and other products for infants and toddlers. Aside from an occasional home-economics or child-development course in high school, or their counterparts given to a minority of college students, this society is largely mute with respect to training for parenthood. Indeed, a major justification for a new day-care center at Harvard is the strongly felt need among many female undergraduates to gain some firsthand exposure to and knowledge about young children. Clearly, something is fundamentally wrong about this situation.

Shouldn't every family be aware of the steps in the language-acquisition process that begins at 8 or 9 months and culminates in the mastery of most common grammatical constructs and basic vocabulary by age three? Shouldn't the details of the building of the foundations of intelligence be common knowledge? The same question could be asked about the social-attachment process, which seems to be most important during the first three years.

Not all the information we need is currently available. In particular, scientific determination of various effective child-rearing practices has so far only begun for this important age range. Much more research is needed. Nevertheless, we do know much more even now than is available to parents. Furthermore, what little is available is not easily available. It is certainly easier today to learn how to drive a car than it is to get comparable information on how to raise children. Perhaps neighborhood information centers might be established, complete with sample home layouts, audio-visual material, books, and so on, and even materials that could be loaned to families. We might even include courses in child development and child-rearing in high schools for all children, rather than for the minority of students who now study such topics. Finally, could we not utilize the talents of parents now past their child-bearing years, even perhaps older retired people, many of whom would enjoy helping new parents immensely?

INFANT-EDUCATION PROGRAMS FOR CHILDREN LESS THAN THREE YEARS OF AGE

Until the recent budget cutbacks, there seemed to be a growing trend toward formal infant-education programs often associated with the provision of day care for working mothers. Planning the curricula for such programs has been difficult because of inadequate dependable knowledge. Studies such as ours would seem to have potential utility for such activity. The fact that our effective mothers manage to perform a great deal of work while simultaneously doing a superb job of child-rearing has implications for the amount of parent–infant interchange necessary, as well as for the quality of that interchange. In the light of our study, it does not appear that personnel in infant centers ought to hover over their charges, constantly overseeing their every move and pumping a barrage of language into their ears. The fact that well-developing infants initiate the vast majority of their own experiences has implications for practice, as does our observation that television viewing is rare during the first two years of life. What we are suggesting is that in our current state of ignorance about desirable curricula for such programs, we could do worse than emulate successful parents. Over the next few years, ours and other projects, it is to be hoped, will generate more secure information on this and related topics.

PRESCHOOL EDUCATION PROGRAMS FOR THREE- AND FOUR-YEAR-OLDS

There are at least two direct relations between our study and educational programs for three- and four-year-olds. Our information on the characteristics of well-developed three- to six-year-olds relates to the issue of the goals of early education, and our findings about the behaviors of very effective mothers seem to relate to curriculum issues.

For many years, experienced preschool practitioners have objected to the emphasis on cognitive development in certain preschool programs. Our study reinforces those objections, pointing as it does to the remarkable array of social skills exhibited by our competent children. To some extent, of course, by concentrating on children who cope well in all areas, we guarantee the presence of social skills in our picture of the competent child. Nevertheless, we believe that these skills are worthy of direct attention, since, from the earliest years, children acquire cognitive skills within a social matrix. Deficiencies in coping with that social matrix unquestionably make most educational experiences more difficult for children. We would recommend that practitioners considering the problem of specifying particular goals for preschool programs consider the possible relevance of our list of distinguishing abilities of competent children.

As for the relevance of effective maternal practices, we would like to point out that the growing "open education" movement is, in spirit, at least, much more compatible with effective maternal practices than are teacher-centered programs. The skill of the professional for many preschool children might be directed more toward the problems of the design of a suitable physical environment and toward their functions as consultants, rather than toward their functions as the center of activity in a classroom. At the very least, such a reorganization of effort would reduce the disparity felt by three-year-olds as they move from the typical optimal conditions for development in the home to those in the preschool institution.

EPILOGUE

In what we have learned, we find much to be optimistic about. We are convinced that we have witnessed the effective shaping of young lives at the most important formative period. We think we have partially unravelled the process. Finally, it seems to us that most American families want very much to give their children an excellent "early education," and furthermore, that most of them have resources with which to do so.

References

BAYLEY, NANCY. *The California Infant Scale of Development.* Berkeley: University of California Press, 1936.

BEREITER, C., and ENGLEMAN, S. *Teaching Disadvantaged Children in the Preschool.* Englewood Cliffs, N.J.: Prentice-Hall, Inc., 1966.

BING, ELIZABETH. "The Effect of Child-Rearing Practices on Development of Differential Cognitive Abilities." *Child Development* 34 (1963): 631–48.

BLOOM, B. S. *Stability and Change in Human Characteristics.* New York: John Wiley & Sons, Inc., 1964.

CALDWELL, BETTYE M. "A New Approach to Behavioral Ecology." In *Minnesota Symposia on Child Pyschology,* vol. 2. Minneapolis: University of Minnesota Press, 1968.

ESCALONA, SIBYLLE K., and CORMAN, HARVEY. "Albert Einstein Scales of Sensori-motor Development." Ditto report. New York: Yeshiva University, 1968.

GOLDEN, M., and BIRNS, BEVERLY. "Social Class Differentiation in Cognitive Development: A Longitudinal Study." Paper presented at the Society for Research in Child Development at Santa Monica, Calif., March 1969.

HALPERN, FLORENCE. "The Mental Development of Black Rural Southern Children Aged One Week to Thirty-Six Months." Paper presented at the Society for Research in Child Development at Santa Monica, Calif., March 1969.

HARLOW, HARRY F., and KUENNE, MARGARET. "Learning to Think." *Scientific American* 181, no. 2 (August 1949).

HESS, R., and SHIPMAN, V. "Early Experience in the Socialization of Cognitive Modes in Children." *Child Development* 36 (1965): 869–86.

HOLLINGSHEAD, A. B., and REDLICH, F. C. *Social Class and Mental Illness.* New York: John Wiley & Sons, Inc., 1958.

HUNT, J. McV. *Intelligence and Experience.* New York: The Ronald Press Company, 1961.

JENSEN, A. R. "How Much Can We Boost IQ and Scholastic Achievement?" *Harvard Educational Review* 39, no. 1 (1969).

LaCROSSE, E. R.; LEE, P. C.; LITMAN, FRANCES; OGILVIE, D. M.; STODOLSKY, SUSAN, and WHITE, B. L. "The First Six Years of Life: A Report on Current Research and Educational Practice." *Genetic Psychology Monographs* 82 (1970): 161–266.

McCARTHY, DOROTHEA. "Language Development in Children." In *Manual of Child Psychology,* 2nd ed. Edited by Leonard Carmichael, pp. 492–630. New York: John Wiley & Sons, Inc., 1954.

MURPHY, LOIS B. *Personality in Young Children.* New York: Basic Books, 1956.

PIAGET, JEAN. *The Origins of Intelligence in Children,* 2nd ed. New York: International University Press, 1952.

SCHAEFER, EARL S. "Intellectual Stimulation of Culturally Deprived Infants." Excerpted from Mental Health Grant Proposal No. MH-09224-01, Laboratory of Psychology, National Institute of Mental Health, 1968.

SCHOGGEN, MAXINE, and SCHOGGEN, PHIL. "Environmental Forces in the Home Lives of Three-Year-Old Children." In *DARCEE: Papers and Reports.* John F. Kennedy Center for Research on Education and Human Development, George Peabody College for Teachers, vol. 5, no. 2 (1971).

SIEGEL, ALBERTA E. Editorial in *Child Development* 38 (1967): 901–7.

UZGIRIS, I. C., and HUNT, J. McV. "A Scale of Infant Psychological Development." 1964 mimeographed.

WACHS, T. D.; UZGIRIS, INA C.; and HUNT, J. McV. "Cognitive Development in Infants of Different Age Levels and from Different Environmental Backgrounds." Paper presented to biennial meeting of the Society for Research in Child Development, New York, March 29–April 1, 1967.

WHITE, B. L. *Human Infants: Experience and Psychological Development.* Englewood Cliffs, N.J.: Prentice-Hall, Inc., 1971.

WOLF, R. M. "The Identification and Movement of Environmental Process Variables Related to Intelligence." Unpublished doctoral dissertation, University of Chicago, 1964.

appendix I

MEASUREMENT TECHNIQUES: MANUALS AND RELIABILITY STUDIES

A

Auditory Screening Technique

AUDITORY TEST

NAME _____ EXAMINER _____ DATE _____

To test child's hearing:

Examiner begins by occupying child in a nonverbal manner while mother moves quietly out of child's visual range. After child has been successfully occupied for about 15-20 seconds, mother WHISPERS child's name or a simple phrase, such as "Look at me," "Where is Joe," "Raise your hand," etc., three times from each of three different positions. Mother should whisper three times from left side of room, three times from right side, and three times from a middle position roughly in back of child, alternating randomly among the three positions, for a total of nine whispers.

If the child fails to respond 50% of the time or more, repeat entire procedure, but this time mother should speak in a normal voice rather than in a whisper. (*Note*: Preoccupation with object or familiarity with mother's voice will sometimes interfere with child's response, although he may have normal hearing. In such cases, examiner should be flexible in interpreting test results.)

Examiner should watch child's face to record responses; there are three response levels:

0. No response
I. Simple Alerting—child shows sign of attention by interrupting his activity, raising his head, etc.
II. Directionally Accurate Response—child turns toward direction of whisper, looks for whispering person, etc.

TRIALS	LEFT	MIDDLE	RIGHT
1			
2			
3			
4			
5			
6			
7			
8			
9			

April 1970

B

Visual Screening Technique

VISUAL SCREENING OF ONE- AND TWO-YEAR-OLDS

Procedures followed:

1. Case History;

   a. General health
   b. Family eye health history
   c. Pregnancy (full term or premature)
   d. First crawl age (quality)
   e. First walk age (quality)
   f. Coordination
   g. First grasp and manipulate age
   h. Family visual history (e.g., strabismus, myopia, etc.)

2. Observations; examiner's impressions of the child's coordination, and crawling and walking ability.

3. Visual Acuity; distance: Sty Car at 10 feet, near: AO child's chart at 13 inches (when possible).

4. Ocular Pursuits and Near Point of Convergence; using dangle bell when possible; when it is not, use ray gun (red light and clicking noise).

5. Cover Test; penlite and occluder (when possible).

6. Distance Retinoscopy; using loose lenses with research assistant standing 10 feet away holding objects to attract the subject's attention.

7. Stereo Fly; to determine three-dimensional vision ability.

8. Ophthalmoscopy; to investigate eye health.

Prepared by M. Zolot, April 1970

C

Manual for Testing
the Language Ability of
One- to Three-Year-Old Children

Introduction and Description of Tests, *258*

Testing Procedures, *258*

Sample Data Sheets, *263*
  12-24 MONTHS, *263*
  24-36 MONTHS, *269*

Scoring System, *274*

Reliability Studies, *276*

This Manual was prepared by Janice Marmor. Revised April 19, 1971.

INTRODUCTION AND DESCRIPTION OF TESTS

The following procedures have been devised to test the receptive-language ability of children between the ages of 12 and 36 months. In the 12- to 24-month-old group, the tests measure the ability to understand vocabulary words and to follow verbal instructions. The vocabulary items are based on the Pacific Expressive Vocabulary Objects as described by Meyers.* The procedure consists of responding to simple object labels, and also to more difficult labels for classes of objects by identifying their referent objects. The instructions items include the ability to follow simple, familiar commands or to carry out more complex sequences of behavior.

The test battery for the 24- to 36-month-old group is also receptive in nature and includes the Ammons Full-Range Picture Vocabulary Test,† the Pacific Expressive Vocabulary Objects from Meyers, and a grammar test roughly adapted from Bellugi-Klima's Grammatical Comprehension Tests.‡ The Meyers test is used only in the event that the Ammons FRPVT proves to be too difficult.

Procedures and scoring information are contained in the general instructions for each test. Sample data sheets are also included.

I. PROCEDURE FOR LANGUAGE TESTING: 12-24 MONTHS

Adaption Phase

1. Allow about ten minutes to get to know mother and child, and to briefly explain objectives and testing procedure to mother, since she will be serving as examiner with your assistance.

2. Get detailed inventory from mother of child's receptive vocabulary, including names of toys and household objects, foods, body parts, other family

---

*C.E. Meyers, et al., "Four Ability-Factor Hypotheses at Three Preliterate Levels in Normal and Retarded Children" (monograph of the *Society for Research in Child Development*, 1964), 29, (5), 62-68.

†R.B. Ammons and J.C. Holmes, "The Full-Range Picture Vocabulary Test: III. Results for a Preschool-Age Population," *Child Development*, 1949, 20, 5014.

‡U. Bellugi-Klima, "Grammatical Comprehension Tests," mimeographed, March 1968.

members, and so forth. Second, get inventory of instructions that child is likely to be able to understand and follow, including daily activities and games (turn off the light, throw me the ball), chores for mother (bring me a diaper), and grooming activities (brush your hair). A checklist of some common object names and activities is included in data sheet to facilitate this process.

3. Spend several minutes transferring information above to data sheet before beginning testing procedure.

Testing Phase

A. Vocabulary—"Meyers Test"

1. Depending on information procured from mother, begin testing with either item A1, A2, or A3. (This will most likely vary with age of subjects, the 12-14-month-olds starting with A1, and 18-24-month-olds starting with A3.)

2. *When beginning with A1 (simple labeling)*: Arrange the objects listed on data sheet on floor in front of S, and have the mother ask of each item in turn, "Where is the ___ ; show me ___ ; point to the ___ ; " and so forth. Any clear means that S uses to identify the desired object is acceptable. Make use of natural situations as much as possible. For example, if child spontaneously picks up a ball, ask him to "put the ball in the cup" rather than to "show me the cup." (This would illustrate an understanding of the word "cup," but not necessarily "ball," since S was already holding the ball.) Do not upset the child by working against his inclination of the moment. Rather, attempt to utilize these inclinations in the testing situation. For item A1, five objects must be labeled correctly before moving to A2. If A1 is not completed correctly, move on to B1 (simple instructions).

3. *A2 (labelling classes of familiar objects)*: Proceed as for item A1, using S's own toys, but S must be able to identify at least two examples of each object; i.e., a big red ball and a small green ball are both identified by S as "ball." S must know four classes correctly before moving on to item A3. If criterion is not met, move on to either B1 or B2.

4. *A3 (labelling classes of unfamiliar objects)*: Arrange two examples of each of the following items on floor in front of S: ball, cup, keys, glasses, pencil, spoon, toothbrush. Proceed as for item A1. Be sure *not* to remove each object as it is identified, for this will diminish size of object pool, making each subsequent identification easier. However, if S has latched onto a favorite object, which distracts him from the task at hand, try to substitute it for something less troublesome. Four classes must be labelled correctly for full credit. Move on to item B3.

B. Capacity to Understand Instructions

Making use of the home environment and its natural situation is particularly recommended for testing understanding of instructions. For example, if child is standing up, ask him to sit down; if he is thirsty, ask him where the milk is. Lamps can be turned on and off, and doors opened and closed upon request. An onlooking sibling is often an appropriate examiner for certain instructions such as "give me a kiss," "bring me the ball," etc.

1. *B1 (simple familiar instructions)*: Mother asks child to do at least four simple, familiar activities. If these are completed correctly, go on to B2. If not, conclude testing at this point.

2. *B2 (familiar sequence of behavior)*: Proceed as for B1, using more complex instructions, which were indicated on inventory checklist. Four instructions must be correctly followed before moving on to item B3. If B2 is not performed correctly, conclude testing at this point.

3. *B3 (unfamiliar instructions)*: Select two objects that S can identify correctly, and instruct him to carry out two instructions with each item. ("Bring _____ to the door; put _____ on the chair," etc.; see data sheet.) A correct score would mean that S correctly followed four instructions.

4. An uncooperative child might respond to positive reinforcement in the form of raisins or minimarshmallows cut in fourths. These should be used sparingly, however. A note of caution: Be certain not to let child or siblings see these treats before you are ready to use them. The "let's-play-a-game" approach may also prove effective.

5. Although it seems to be easier to begin testing with vocabulary items, the order of testing is not immutable. Some children are more amenable to following instructions and will simultaneously display an understanding of object names while carrying out instructions.

6. Be sure not to test the child beyond the minimum criterion necessary to pass any one item. This will tire child needlessly.

II. PROCEDURE FOR LANGUAGE TESTING: 24-36 MONTHS

Allow five to ten minutes to get to know mother and child, and to briefly explain objectives and procedure of test to mother, since she will be serving as examiner with your assistance. Explain that examiner will set up each testing situation (holding up the Ammons cards, or arranging the props for the grammar test) and will say the vocabulary word or grammatical statement for each item. Each word or statement is then to be repeated, verbatim, by the mother to the child. Be sure the mother understands this. The mother should also be told that two repetitions are allowed. It is sometimes comforting for the child if he sits on mother's lap. Be sure your materials are organized and compartmentalized beforehand and are accessible in the order in which they are to be used.

A. Ammons Vocabulary Test

Begin testing with the Ammons Full-Range Picture Vocabulary Test. Follow the instructions included with the Ammons Plates. For this age range, most plates contain only one or two appropriate items, although occasionally there will be more than two that are appropriate. On the other hand, some plates will have no appropriate items; i.e., Form A, Plate 1: "pie," "window"; Plate 2: nothing appropriate. If S succeeds readily with easiest items, administer item for next age level; i.e., on Plate 1, Form A, if "pie" (1.7) and "window" (1.7) are answered easily, try "seed" (6.5) and "sill" (6.7) before going on to Plate 2. See data sheet for list of items to be administered. Those that are checked (√) should always be given. Words marked with a dash (-) should be given when checked items above are answered correctly.

B. Meyers Vocabulary Test

This test will be used *only* when a score of less than six correct is obtained on the Ammons Vocabulary Test. In administering Meyers Vocabulary Items, arrange two examples of each of following items on floor in front of S: ball, cup, keys, glasses, pencil, spoon, toothbrush. Have the mother ask of each kind of item, "Where is the ___ ," "show me ___ ," or "point to the ___ ," and so forth. In order to receive credit for having identified a class of any particular item, S must identify *both* examples; i.e., when S successfully points to one ball, mother says, "Now show me another one," or "Point to the other ball." Be sure *not* to remove each object as it is identified, for this will diminish the size of the object pool, making each subsequent identification easier. Four classes must be identified correctly for the child to pass the item.

C. Grammar Test

1. Before administering grammar test, read through the items several times and become familiar with the toy props to be used for each item. This is necessary to prevent errors and confusion during testing situation. Make sure equipment is complete and easily accessible during testing session. If possible, E and S should sit at a table or desk, and make use of the table surface for setting up each item. If this is not convenient, the bare floor can be used.

2. If mother is being used as examiner, ask her to repeat each item to S verbatim as E says it after E arranges props. This should be done consistently throughout testing session. Two repetitions are permitted. If an answer is ambiguous but has already been given two trials, mark it as questionable and come back to it later.

3. Follow instructions for each item as described in grammar test and record "+" for correct completion and "0" for incorrect answer, in scoring column to the left of items.

Note: Several items consist of two parts, both of which must be answered correctly for credit to be received. After scoring item, mark its validity (high or low) in the validity column.

4. If at any time during testing three items are failed consecutively, discontinue testing.

5. If at least 24 of the first 26 items are completed correctly, extra-credit items (27-30) should be administered. If less than 24 have been correct, discontinue testing with number 26.

6. Some children are distracted by the toy props, while others are very shy or negative. In these situations, positive reinforcement in the form of raisins or miniature marshmallows cut in fourths may prove useful. Ask the mother's permission first and use these sparingly so that the child is not satiated. A note of caution: Be certain not to let child or siblings see these treats before you are ready to use them.

Name _____   Code _____

Tester _____   Sex _____

Birth date _____/_____/_____   Age _____/_____

Test date _____/_____/_____   Yrs.   Mos.

Score:

Vocabulary _____ Instructions _____

Pass Level _____ Developmental Age _____

Comments:

INVENTORY CHECKLIST

Show following list to mother to help her think of words and expressions her child is familiar with:

Vocabulary Words

____ ball	____ cookie	____ radio	____ brother
____ cup	____ apple	____ record	____ mommy
____ keys	____ carrot	____ music	____ daddy
____ glasses	____ snack	____ picture	____ boy
____ spoon	____ drink	____ book	____ girl
____ toothbrush	____ juice	____ magazine	____ doggy
____ coat	____ pillow	____ newspaper	____ cat
____ hat	____ bed	____ phone	____ kitty
____ jacket	____ blanket	____ telephone	____ pussycat
____ shoe	____ chair	____ soap	____ pony
____ socks	____ highchair	____ washcloth	____ horse
____ water	____ crib	____ towel	____ car
____ milk	____ table	____ doll	____ bus
____ cereal	____ television	____ baby	____ train
____ cracker	____ TV	____ sister	____ stove

(cont.)

INVENTORY CHECKLIST (cont.)

_____ refrigerator	_____ eye	_____ teeth	_____ fingers
_____ brush	_____ nose	_____ tongue	_____ bellybutton
_____ comb	_____ mouth	_____ feet	
_____ blocks	_____ hair	_____ toes	

Instructions

_____ come here	_____ kiss	_____ put away
_____ give me	_____ lie down	_____ get up
_____ bring me	_____ go to sleep	_____ brush, comb hair
_____ get me	_____ walk	_____ do you want a cookie, juice
_____ stand up	_____ run	_____ bring me a diaper
_____ sit down	_____ don't run	_____ open, close the door
_____ put away	_____ listen	_____ sit down on the chair
_____ pull	_____ show me	_____ wave bye-bye
_____ push	_____ where is	_____ stop
_____ hug	_____ fall down	_____ turn on, off (the light)

A. RECEPTIVE-LANGUAGE CHECKLIST AND DATA SHEET

Knows *simple word or label* for own toys; i.e., mama, bottle, cup, show, doggie. Child must know 5 labels.

VALIDITY

object	label	object	label	
				Item 1.
1. _____ : _____		4. _____ : _____		
2. _____ : _____		5. _____ : _____		
3. _____ : _____				

Knows *classes* for *familiar objects* (may be chosen by mother or child). Knows 2 examples of each of own toys but does not know E's toys. Child must get 4 out of 5 correct.

Score (0, +)   *response*

	1.			1.		Item 2.
□	——		□	——		
	2.			2.		

	1.			1.
□	——		□	——
	2.			2.

	1.
□	——
	2.

Knows *classes* for *unfamiliar objects*. (Knows at least some of Meyer's objects and recognizes 2 examples of each.) Child must get 4 correct. Suggested objects: "Point to the. . .; where is the. . .; show me another. . . ."

Score (0, +)   response

		1.			1.		Item 3.
□	BALL			□	PENCIL		
		2.			2.		

		1.			1.
□	CUP		□	SPOON	
		2.			2.

=

		1.			1.
□	KEYS		□	TOOTHBRUSH	
		2.			2.

		1.
□	GLASSES	
		2.

265

B. INSTRUCTIONS

Understands *simple familiar* instructions (requiring only a single discrete change in behavior). Child must respond to 4 instructions that mother indicates are familiar; i.e., wave bye-bye; stop it; kiss me; sit down; get up; come here.

VALIDITY

Item 1.

Score (0, 1, 2)　　　*instruction*　　　　*response*

1. _____

2. _____

3. _____

4. _____

Understands instructions for *familiar sequences of behavior* (requiring more than a single change in activity). Child must respond to 4 instructions that mother indicates are familiar; i.e., get me _____ ; go to your room; give _____ to mommy; put _____ over there; bring _____ here.

Item 2.

Score (0, 1, 2)　　　*instruction*　　　　*response*

1. _____

2. _____

☐ 3. _____

☐ 4. _____

Can carry out matrix of *unfamiliar instructions* using experimenter's *or* child's own toys. Use any 2 toys known to S in carrying out 2 unfamiliar instructions; use each toy in each instruction, for a total of 4 responses.

Sample instructions:

Put keys, ball under the table, on the chair, on Mommy's head, in Mommy's lap, in your bed, on Daddy's desk, etc.

Take/bring ball, keys into the kitchen, to the door, to the chair, etc.   VALIDITY

┌──────────────┐
│ Item 3.   │
│   │
│   │
└──────────────┘

OBJECT score (0, 1, 2)   *instruction*   *response*

         ☐ ——————————————— 1.

1. ____

         ☐ ——————————————— 2.

_____

         ☐ ——————————————— 3.

2. ____

         ☐ ——————————————— 4.

_____

SCORING: VOCABULARY AND INSTRUCTIONS
(Language, 12-24 months)

VOCABULARY

0 = Does not respond to language at all
1 = Knows some names but not classes of own toys
2 = Knows some classes of own or experimenter's toys

INSTRUCTIONS

0 = Unable to follow even simplest instructions
1 = Follows simple familiar instructions
2 = Partially follows instructions calling for familiar sequences of behavior
3 = Completely follows instructions calling for familiar sequences of behavior
4 = Partially follows unfamiliar instructions
5 = Completely follows matrix of unfamiliar instructions

VOCAB. + INSTRUCT.	PASS LEVEL	DEV. AGE	RATINGS 1st Testing	RATINGS 2nd Testing
0 + 0	0	10 mos.	C	C−
1 + 0	I	12 "	C+	C
1 + 1	II	14 "	B	C+
1 + 3	III	*16 "	B+,A−	B
2 + 3	IV	18 "	A−	B+
2 + 4	V	21 "	A	A−
2 + 5	VI	24 "	A+	A

*Scored as 17 months on earlier data sheets (before 9/70).

Name _____   Code _____

Tester _____   Sex _____

Birth date _____   Age _____

Test date _____   Yrs.   Mos.

SCORE:

	Total Score	Pass Level	Devel. Age
AMMONS			
MEYERS VOCAB.			
GRAMMAR			

OVERALL SCORE: _____

COMMENTS:

(Language, 24-36 months)
AMMONS FULL-RANGE PICTURE VOCABULARY TEST
Answer Sheet—Form A

√ = Always include this item
- = Include this item when checked items on plate
have been answered correctly

Plate 1

√pie (1.7)
√window (1.7)
-seed (6.5)
sill (6.7)
transparent (13.3)
rectangular (14.7)
sector (16.0)
illumination (16.0)
culinary (17.2)
egress (A6.3)

Plate 2

athletes (8.6)
competition (15.0)
revelry (A4.0)
ebullience (A6.4)

Plate 3

√counter (4.0)
√pump (4.4)
-clerk (6.4)

Plate 3 (cont.)

sport (7.6)
recreation (10.8)
pugnacity (16.9)
replenishment (A3.1)
retaliation (A4.1)

Plate 4

shrubbery (9.8)
dwelling (11.7)

Plate 5

surf (12.5)
isolation (12.9)

Plate 6

√horse (1.5)
√wagon (2.3)
-insect (6.7)
transportation (8.6)
antiquated (A3.8)

(cont.)

269

AMMONS FULL-RANGE PICTURE VOCABULARY TEST (cont.)

Plate 7

discussion (7.7)
skill (10.9)
amour (13.8)

Plate 8

√firecracker (2.7)
√clothes (3.0)
-explosion (4.9)
clean (5.5)
dehydration (A4.3)

Plate 9

√farm (4.1)
currency (12.2)
tranquility (16.5)
agrarian (A6.2)

Plate 10

√furniture (4.4)
-steel (6.0)
refreshment (6.2)
liquid (7.3)
container (9.5)
centigrade (14.5)

Plate 11

√clock (1.6)
√locket (3.0)
√numbers (3.4)
engraving (9.8)

Plate 12

√hot (5.2)
fear (7.4)
nutrition (10.4)
gorging (12.8)

Plate 12 (cont.)

poverty (13.9)
mastication (A2.6)
itinerant (A4.5)
coercion (A4.6)
corpulence (A5.5)
insatiable (A5.6)

Plate 13

√telephone (2.1)
√crying (2.9)
√accident (3.0)
vehicles (9.5)
destruction (10.0)
portrait (10.2)
communication (10.6)
consolation (13.4)
negligence (14.3)
bereaved (15.4)
deleterious (A6.2)

Plate 14

danger (5.6)

Plate 15

√bed (1.6)
√newspaper (2.5)
anaesthesia (11.7)
immersion (14.6)
displacement (A5.0)
perusing (A5.0)

Plate 16

√propellers (3.7)
harbor (8.1)
locomotive (8.2)
nautical (16.5)

PASS LEVEL		DEVEL. AGE (MONTHS)
0-6	0	18
6-8	I	24
99-11	II	30
12-15	III	36
16	IV	42
17-18	V	48
19-20	VI	54
21+	VII	60

MEYERS VOCABULARY TEST

To be used only when a score of less than 6 correct is obtained on the Ammons Vocabulary Test.

Arrange *two* examples of each of the following items on floor or table in front of S and say,

"Where is the _____," then, "Can you show me another _____." S must identify both examples.

BALL _____

CUP _____

SPOON _____

KEYS _____

PENCIL _____

EYEGLASSES _____

TOOTHBRUSH _____

Total correct _____

GRAMMAR TEST

VALIDITY	SCORING		
		I.	E sits with S at a table or on bare floor; puts out two balls and two cups and places one ball in one cup and says:
	1.		1. Take the ball *out of* the cup.
	2.		2. Put the ball *in* the cup.
	3.		3. Point to *your* head.
			Arrange one cup upside down, the other right side up:
	4.		4. Put the ball *on* the cup (or *on* the chair, etc.).
	5.		5. Stand *in front of* the chair (desk, TV, or any object in room that has a distinct front and back).
			Put out boy, daddy, and girl doll (with fork in hand). Arrange boy and girl in standing position about two inches apart, facing each other:
	6.		6. Show me how the girl feeds the boy.
		II.	
	7.		7. Touch the daddy *of* the boy.
	8.		8. Touch *his* head. (S may touch head of either male doll).
	9.		9. Touch the daddy's boy.

(cont.)

GRAMMAR TEST (cont.)

VALIDITY	SCORING	

10.

10. Show me how the girl feeds *herself*.

Leave dolls in background and bring out cup, box, and balls. Arrange cup and box four inches apart. Place one ball next to cup, the other ball distant from cup and box but still in plain view:

11.

11. Move the ball *toward* the cup; now move the ball toward the box.

12.

12. Stand *behind* the chair (desk, TV, mother, or any object that has distinct front and back).

13.

13. Point to *my* head.

III.

Arrange dolls in two groups: 2 in one group and 1 in the other group:

14.

14. Give me the *doll*.
Give me the *dolls*.

Bring out the two blond dolls and the small boy doll and arrange all dolls in one group in front of S:

15.

15. Point to the doll that *is* sitting.
Point to the doll that *isn't* sitting.

Bring out the two balls, cup, and box:

16.

16. Give the *little* boy the ball.
Give the *big* boy the *little* ball.

17.

17. Give me a cup *and* a ball.

Arrange cup and box about 4 inches apart. Place one ball next to cup and other ball distant from cup and box, but still in plain view:

18.

18. Move the ball *away from* the cup.

19.

19. Give me *either* a cup *or* a box.

Leave balls, cups, and box in background and bring out pictures (on 8″ x 10″ sheet of paper), and 3 pink cards with blue yarn attached. Show S cards first:

20.

20. Show me the one that is *tied*.
Show me the one that is *untied*.

IV.

21.

21. Point to the ones you *can* eat.
Point to the ones you *can't* eat.

Bring out boy doll, girl doll, and daddy doll:

22.

22. Show me how the *doll walks*.
Show me how the *dolls walk*.

Put away dolls, leave out balls, box, and cups and take out bundles of sticks. Hold purple one and arrange others on table:

23.

23. Give me a stick that is *longer and thinner* than this one.

GRAMMAR TEST (cont.)

VALIDITY		SCORING	
		V.	Arrange two cups and one box in a row, each about 2 inches apart. Give S a ball·
	24.		24. Put the ball *between* the cup and the box.
	25.		25. Give me a stick that is *shorter than* this (purple) one.
	26.		26. Give me something that is *neither* a ball *nor* a cup.
		VI.	Ask the following items *only* if at least 24 of the above 26 items have been answered correctly:
			Put out one boy doll and two girl dolls:
	27.		27. Make the boy hit one of the girls. Make the girl that the boy hit run away.
			Put out the doll with the hat and show S how the hat can be taken on and off. E takes off hat and says to make this story:
	28.		28. *Before* she put on her hat, she sat down.
			Show S the cowboy and horse and how they move. E tells S to make this story:
	29.		29. *After* he went for a ride, he took a walk.
			Put out two deer (or two sheep):
	30.		30. Show me how the deer *lies* down. Show me how the deer *lie* down.

GRAMMAR TEST—LEVELS OF DIFFICULTY*
Totals correct per level

I.	II.	III.
1. out	7. daddy of	14. doll/dolls
2. in	8. his	15. is/isn't
3. your	9. daddy's boy	16. little/big
4. on	10. feeds herself	17. and
5. in front of	11. toward	18. away from
6. girl feeds boy	12. behind	19. either, or
	13. my	20. tied/untied
Pass = 5 out of 6 correct	p = 5/7 correct	p = 5/7 correct

*Each level can be passed with a lower score than the criteria listed above IF additional items at a higher level are also passed. For levels I, II, and III, S must pass 2 items at the next highest level OR 1 item that is two levels higher. For levels IV and V, S must pass one additional item at any higher level.

Example:

Susie passes 5 items at level I, but only 4 items at level II. However, she also passes 2 items at level III. Although she doesn't meet the 5-out-of-7 criterion for a level II pass, the additional items passed at level III give her a legitimate level II pass. The same outcome would result if Susie had passed 4 items at level II, none at level III, and one item at level IV.

(cont.)

GRAMMAR TEST—LEVELS OF DIFFICULTY (cont.)

IV.
21. can/can't
22. walk/walks
23. longer and thinner

p = 2 out of 3 correct

V.
24. between
25. shorter than
26. neither, nor

p = 2/3 correct

VI.
27. hit/girl that boy hit
28. before
29. after
30. lies/lie

p = 2/4 correct

	Pass Level		Developmental Age
TOTALS: 0.	_____	=	18 mos.
I.	_____	=	24
II.	_____	=	36
III.	_____	=	42
IV.	_____	=	48
V.	_____	=	54
VI.	_____	=	60
PASS LEVEL	_____	=	

SCORING SYSTEM

12-24 Months

The final score earned on the language test for one-year-olds is based on the combined score for Vocabulary and Instructions. Scores are expressed as developmental age equivalents, in months, ranging from Level I (= 10 months), for the subject who cannot follow any instructions and does not demonstrate a knowledge of any vocabulary words, to Level VI (= 24 months), the score given to subjects who can identify objects from their class label and can completely follow a sequence of unfamiliar instructions. This scoring system is outlined in detail on page 275.

24-36 Months

The final score earned on the language test for two-year-olds is based on an average of the Ammons Vocabulary score (or the "Meyer Test," in the case where this is used instead; see page 261 and the score on the grammar items. On the Ammons Test, the score is based on the total number of words correctly identified, as summarized on page 276.

Scoring of the grammar items is somewhat more complex. The score is based on the highest level of difficulty that the subject can master. For example, to pass Level I, a subject must correctly complete five out of six Level I items. To pass Level V, he must complete two out of three Level V items. Because the test items are arranged in order of increasing difficulty, it is presumed that a child who passes items at Level V can also pass most items in Levels I-IV. A detailed outline of this scoring system is presented on pages 273-74 and summarized on page 276.

The final score on the Language Test for 24-36-month-olds is expressed as a developmental age equivalent based on the average of the development-age scores on the Ammons Vocabulary and on the Grammar Test.

Scoring System—12-24 Months

Vocabulary and Instructions

Scoring Level	Developmental Age	Definition
0	10 mos.	0 = Does not respond to language at all 0 = Unable to follow even simplest instructions
I	12 mos.	1 = Knows some names but not classes of own toys 0 = Unable to follow even simplest instructions
II	14 mos.	1 = Knows some names but not classes of own toys 1 = Follows simple familiar instructions
III	16 mos.	1 = Knows some names but not classes of own toys 2 = Partially follows instructions calling for familiar sequences of behavior
IV	18 mos.	2 = Knows classes of own or experimenter's toys 3 = Completely follows instructions calling for familiar sequences of behavior
V	21 mos.	2 = Knows classes of own or E's toys 4 = Partially follows unfamiliar instructions
VI	24 mos.+	2 = Knows classes of own or E's toys 5 = Completely follows matrix of unfamiliar instructions

Scoring System—24-36 Months

Ammons Vocabulary and Grammar Items

	Pass Level	Devel. Age.	Criteria for Pass
Ammons	0	18 mos.	0-6 words passed
	I	24	6-8
	II	30	9-11
	III	36	12-15
	IV	42	16
	V	48	17-18
	VI	54	19-20
	VII	60	21+
Grammar*	0	18 mos.	Less than 5 items passed
	I	24	5 out of 6
	II	36	5 out of 7
	III	42	5 out of 7
	IV	48	2 out of 3
	V	54	2 out of 3
	VI	60	2 out of 4

See footnote, page 273, for further scoring details.

RELIABILITY RUN—LANGUAGE TEST BATTERY

An interobserver reliability study on the Language Test Battery was run between observers Burton White and Janice Marmor in December 1969. A total of ten subjects were used, five 12-24-month-olds and five 24-36-month-olds. Each subject was seen on two separate occasions, once by Marmor and once by White. An attempt was made to schedule both visits to any one subject at the same time of day, and to balance first-time visits equally between the two observers. All observations were completed within a two-week time period.

Two statistical tests of correlation were used to determine the level of reliability achieved: the Pearson Product-Moment correlation statistic, and the Spearman Rank correlation coefficient. In each case, four correlations were performed: an overall correlation using all ten subjects, and three subtest correlations for the 12-24-month-old group, the Ammons scores, and the grammar test.

Table I lists the results of these tests. In all cases, reliability was found to exceed $r = 0.900$. Raw scores are listed on page 277. All scores are developmental age equivalents, in months.

TABLE I

	SPEARMAN			PEARSON		
	N	r_s	sig.	df	r_p	sig.
Overall correlation	10	0.993	.01	8	0.978	.01
12-24-month-olds	5	0.973	.05	3	0.928	.05
Ammons test	5	0.916	.05	3	0.900	.05
Grammar test	5	0.916	.05	3	0.969	.05

Reliability Run Scores—Language Test Battery
(All scores in months)

Subjects	C.A.	Overall Score		12-24 months		Ammons		Grammar	
	Mos	White	Marmor	White	Marmor	White	Marmor	White	Marmo
1	12	16	14	16	14				
2	12.5	12	14	12	14				
3	19.5	21	21	21	21				
4	20	21	21	21	21				
5	22	18	18	18	18				
6	24	30	33			36	42	24	24
7	25.5	36	45			36	54	36	36
8	29.5	57	54			66	66	48	42
9	33.5	57	57			66	66	48	48
10	34.5	45	51			42	54	48	48

Pearson Product-Moment Correlation

Overall Reliability—10 Subjects—12-36 Months

$$r = \frac{N \, \Sigma \, XY - \Sigma \, X \, \Sigma \, Y}{\sqrt{[N_2 X^2 - (2X)^2]\,[N \, \Sigma \, Y^2 - (\Sigma \, Y)^2]}}$$

S's	X	Y	X^2	Y^2	XY
1	16	14	256	196	224
2	12	14	144	196	168
3	21	21	441	441	441
4	21	21	441	441	441
5	18	18	324	324	324
6	30	33	900	1089	990
7	36	45	1296	2025	1620
8	57	54	3249	2916	3078
9	57	57	3249	3249	3249
10	45	51	2025	2601	2295
	313	328	12325	13478	12830
N = 10	$\Sigma \, X$	$\Sigma \, X$	$\Sigma \, X^2$	$\Sigma \, Y^2$	$\Sigma \, XY$

1. *Overall Pearson*

$$r = \frac{[10(12830)] - [(313)(328)]}{\sqrt{[10(12325) - (313)^2][10(13478) - (328)^2]}}$$

$$= \frac{128,300 - 102,664}{\sqrt{(123,250 - 97,969) \times (134,780 - 107,584)}}$$

$$r = \frac{25,636}{\sqrt{(25,281)(27,196)}} = \frac{25,636}{\sqrt{687,542,076}} = \frac{25,636}{26,221.0} = .978$$

Overall Pearson $r = 0.978$

12-24 Months, Pearson

S's	X	Y	X^2	Y^2	XY
1	16	14	256	196	224
2	12	14	144	196	168
3	21	21	441	441	441
4	21	21	441	441	441
5	18	18	324	324	324
	88	88	1606	1598	1598
$N = 5$	ΣX	ΣY	ΣX^2	ΣY^2	ΣXY

$$r = \frac{[5(1598)] - [(88)(88)]}{\sqrt{[5(1606) - (88)^2][5(1598) - (88)^2]}} = \frac{7790 - 7744}{\sqrt{[8030 - 7744][7790 - 7744]}}$$

$$r = \frac{246}{\sqrt{(286)(246)}} = \frac{246}{\sqrt{70356}} = \frac{246}{265.3} = .928$$

12-24 months Pearson $r = 0.928$

Pearson: *Ammons*

S's	X	Y	X^2	Y^2	XY
6	36	42	1296	1764	1512
7	36	54	1296	2916	1944
8	66	66	4356	4356	4356
9	66	66	4356	4356	4356
10	42	54	1764	2916	2268
	246	282	13068	16308	14436
N = 5	ΣX	ΣY	ΣX^2	ΣY^2	ΣXY

$$r = \frac{5(14{,}436) - (246)(282)}{\sqrt{[5(13{,}068) - (246)^2][5(16{,}308) - (282)^2]}} = \frac{72180 - 69372}{\sqrt{(65{,}340 - 60{,}516)(81{,}540 - 79{,}524)}}$$

$$r = \frac{2808}{\sqrt{(4{,}824)(2{,}016)}} = \frac{2808}{\sqrt{9{,}725{,}184}} = \frac{2808}{3118.5} = 0.9004$$

Ammons Pearson $r = 0.900$

Pearson: *Grammar*

S's	X	Y	X^2	Y^2	XY
6	24	24	576	576	576
7	36	36	1296	1296	1296
8	48	42	2304	1764	2016
9	48	48	2304	2304	2304
10	48	48	2304	2304	2304
	204	198	8784	8244	8496
N = 5	ΣX	ΣY	ΣX^2	ΣY^2	ΣXY

$$r = \frac{[5(8496)] - [(204)(198)]}{\sqrt{[5(8784) - (204)^2][5(8244) - (198)^2]}}$$

$$r = \frac{42{,}480 - 40{,}392}{\sqrt{(43{,}920 - 41{,}616)(41{,}220 - 39{,}204)}} = \frac{2088}{\sqrt{(2{,}304)(2{,}016)}}$$

$$r = \frac{2088}{\sqrt{4{,}644{,}864}} = \frac{2088}{2155.2} = .96882$$

Pearson Grammar $r = 0.969$

Spearman Rank Correlation Coefficients

		Scores		Ranks			
S's	BW	JM	BW	JM	d_i	d_i^2	
1	16	14	2	1.5	.5	.25	
2	12	14	1	1.5	-.5	.25	
3	21	21	4.5	4.5	0	0	
4	21	21	4.5	4.5	0	0	.011 Overall r_s = .993
5	18	18	3	3	0	0	.052 12-24 mos. r_s = .973
6	30	33	6	6	0	0	n.s.3. Ammons r_s = .805
7	36	45	7	7	0	0	.054 Grammar r_s = .913
8	57	54	9.5	9	.5	.25	
9	57	57	9.5	10	-.5	.25	
10	45	51	8	8	0	0	

$N = 10$ $\Sigma d_i^2 = 1.0$

---

(1) *Overall Reliability Using*
Spearman (All 10 S's)

$$r_s = \frac{\Sigma x^2 + \Sigma y^2 - \Sigma d^2}{2\sqrt{\Sigma x^2 \; \Sigma y^2}}$$

$$\Sigma x^2 = \frac{N^3 - N}{12} = \Sigma \left(\frac{t^3 - t}{12}\right)$$

$$\Sigma x^2 = \frac{990}{12} - \frac{6}{12} + \frac{6}{12} = 82.5 - 1.0 = 81.5$$

$$\Sigma y^2 = 81.5 \qquad \frac{81.5 + 81.5 - 1.0}{2\sqrt{(81.5)(81.5)}} = \frac{162}{163}$$

$$\Sigma d^2 = 1.0$$

Overall r_s = .993 sig. at < .01 level

(2) Spearman: *12-24 months*

$$\Sigma x^2 = \frac{(5)^3 - 5}{12} - \left(\frac{2^3 - 2}{12}\right) = \frac{125 - 5}{12} = \frac{6}{12} = 9.5$$

$$\Sigma y^2 + \frac{(5)^3 - 5}{12} - \left(\frac{2^3 - 2}{12} + \frac{2^3 - 2}{12}\right) = \frac{125 - 5}{12} - 1.0 = 9.0$$

$$r_s = \frac{9.5 + 9.0 - .50}{2\sqrt{(9.5)(9.0)}} = \frac{18}{2(9.25)} = \frac{18}{18.50} = .973$$

r_s = .973 12-24 months sig. at < .05

(3) Spearman: *Ammons*

	Scores		Ranks			
S's	BW	JM	BW	JM	d_i	d_i^2
6	36	42	1.5	1	.5	.25
7	36	54	1.5	2.5	−1.0	1.00
8	66	66	4.5	4.5	0	0
9	66	66	4.5	4.5	0	0
10	42	54	3	2.5	.5	.25

$N = 5$ $\Sigma\, d_i^2 = 1.50$

$$r_s = \frac{9.0 + 9.0 - 1.50}{2\sqrt{(9.0)(9.0)}} = \frac{16.5}{18} = 0.9166$$

$r_s = 0.917$ Ammons sig. at $< .05$

(4) Spearman: *Grammar*

	Scores		Ranks			
S's	BW	JM	BW	JM	d_i	d_i^2
6	24	24	1	1	0	0
7	36	36	2	2	0	0
8	48	42	4	3	1	1.0
9	48	48	4	4.5	−.5	.25
10	48	48	4	4.5	−.5	.25

$\Sigma\, d_i^2 = 1.50$

$$\Sigma x^2 = \frac{(5)^3 - 5}{12} - \left(\frac{3^3 - 3}{12}\right) = 10 - 2 = 8.0$$

$$\Sigma y^2 = \frac{(5)^3 - 5}{12} - \left(\frac{2^2 - 2}{12}\right) = 10 - .5 = 9.5$$

$$r_s = \frac{8.0 + 9.5 - 1.50}{2\sqrt{(8.0)(9.5)}} = \frac{16}{(2)(8.72)} = \frac{16}{17.44} = .9174$$

$r_s = .917$ Grammar sig. at $< .05$ level

RELIABILITY RUN—LANGUAGE TEST BATTERY

An interobserver reliability study on the Language Test Battery was run between examiners Janice Marmor and Geraldine Kearse in February and March 1970. A total of ten subjects were seen, five 12-24-month-olds and five 24-36-month-olds. Subjects were seen in their own homes with mother present on two separate occasions, once by each examiner. Testing lasted from 30 to 60 minutes. An attempt was made to schedule both visits to any one subject at about the same time of day, and to balance first-time visits equally between the two examiners. All observations were completed within a three-week time period.

The Pearson Product-Moment correlation statistic was used to determine the level of reliability obtained. Four correlations were performed as follows: an overall correlation using all ten subjects; and three subtest correlations for the 12-24-month-old group, the Ammons scores, and the grammar test.

The table below shows the results of these four correlations. In all cases, reliability was found to exceed $r = 0.88$. Scores, expressed as developmental age equivalents, in months, follow.

Correlations	N	Pearson Coefficient
Overall correlation	10	$r = 0.962$
12-24-month-olds	5	0.888
Ammons test	5	0.887
Grammar test	5	0.960

Scores—Expressed as Developmental Age Equivalents
(All scores in months)

Subjects	C.A.	Overall Score		12-24 Months		Ammons		Grammar	
	Months	J.M.	G.K.	J.M.	G.K.	J.M.	G.K.	J.M.	G.K.
1	12	16	14	16	14				
2	13	16	14	16	14				
3	18	24	18	24	18				
4	18	16	14	16	14				
5	20	18	17	18	17				
6	24	27	27			36	36	18	18
7	27	39	36			42	36	36	36
8	28	27	24			36	24	18	24
9	30	42	44			48	52	36	36
10	32	45	57			48	66	42	48

RELIABILITY STUDY—LANGUAGE TEST
(24-36 MONTHS)

An interobserver reliability study on the Language Test for 24-36-month-olds was run between examiners Janice Marmor and Maxine Manjos in March 1971. Seven subjects ranging in age from 24-35 months were seen twice, over a period of two weeks. Subjects were tested in their own homes with mother present on two separate occasions, once by each examiner. Testing sessions lasted from 20 to 40 minutes. For each child, the sessions were scheduled five to seven days apart, at approximately the same time of day and in the same physical setting (at a table or on the floor). In addition, an attempt was made to balance first-time visits equally between the two examiners. The Pearson Product-Moment correlation of the scores obtained by the two examiners was 0.97.

The scores, expressed as developmental age levels, in months, are listed in the table below.

| | | *Score obtained* | | | | |
Subject	Age at Time of Test	by Marmor X	by Manjos Y	X^2	Y^2	XY
1	24 mos.	27 mos.	27 mos.			
2	26	36	42	1296	1764	1512
3	30	48	51	2304	2601	2448
4	31	39	42	1521	1764	1638
5	31	21	21	441	441	441
6	33	42	39	1764	1521	1638
7	35	54	54	2916	2916	2916
		$X = 267$	$Y = 276$	$\Sigma X^2 = 10971$	$\Sigma Y^2 = 11736$	$\Sigma XY = 11322$

$$r = \frac{N \Sigma XY - \Sigma X \Sigma Y}{\sqrt{[N \Sigma X^2 - (\Sigma X)^2][N \Sigma Y^2 - (\Sigma Y)^2]}}$$

$$r = \frac{(7)(11322) - (267)(276)}{\sqrt{[(7)(10971) - (267)^2][(7)(11736) - (276)^2]}} \qquad r = \frac{5562}{\sqrt{(5508)(5976)}}$$

$$r = \frac{5562}{\sqrt{32,915,808}} \qquad r = \frac{5562}{5737.2}$$

$$r = 0.9694 = 0.97 \qquad r = 0.97$$

RELIABILITY RUN—LANGUAGE TEST BATTERY

An interobserver reliability study on the Language Test Battery was run between examiners A and B in December 1969.* A total of ten subjects were used, five 12-24-month-olds and five 24-36-month-olds. Each subject was seen on two separate occasions, once by Examiner A and once by Examiner B. An attempt was made to schedule both visits to any one subject at the same time of day, and to balance first-time visits equally between the two observers. All observations were completed within a two-week time period.

Two statistical tests of correlation were used to determine the level of reliability achieved: the Pearson Product-Moment correlation statistic, and the Spearman Rank correlation coefficient. In each case, four correlations were performed: an overall correlation using all ten subjects, and three subtest correlations for the 12-24-month-old group, the Ammons scores, and the grammar test.

The table below lists the results of these tests. Following the table are the actual calculations for both the Pearson and the Spearman tests. In all cases, reliability was found to exceed $r = 0.900$.

Table of Results

	N	Spearman r_s	sig.	df	Pearson r	sig.
Overall Corr.	10	0.993	.01	8	0.978	.01
12-24 mos.	5 .	0.973	.05	3	0.928	.05
Ammons	5	0.916	.05	3	0.900	.05
Grammar	5	0.917	.05	3	0.969	.01

$df = N - 2$

Correlation using Spearman r_s and Pearson$_r$

*Two other interobserver reliability studies have been run between two different teams of observers. On a study of the Language Test Battery conducted in March 1970 reliability was found to exceed $r = 0.88$ in all cases. A study of the Language Test (24-36 months) was conducted in March 1971; the Pearson Product-Moment Correlation was 0.97.

Pearson Product-Moment Correlation

Overall Reliability—10   Subjects—12-36 Months

$$r = \frac{N \, \Sigma \, XY - \Sigma \, X \, \Sigma \, Y}{\sqrt{[N_2 X^2 - (2X)^2][N \, \Sigma \, Y^2 - (\Sigma \, Y)^2]}}$$

S's	X	Y	X^2	Y^2	XY
1	16	14	256	196	224
2	12	14	144	196	168
3	21	21	441	441	441
4	21	21	441	441	441
5	18	18	324	324	324
6	30	33	900	1089	990
7	36	45	1296	2025	1620
8	57	54	3249	2916	3078
9	57	57	3249	3249	3249
10	45	51	2025	2601	2295
	313	328	12325	13478	12830
N = 10	$\Sigma \, X$	$\Sigma \, X$	$\Sigma \, X^2$	$\Sigma \, Y^2$	$\Sigma \, XY$

1. *Overall Pearson*

$$r = \frac{[10(12830)] - [(313)(328)]}{\sqrt{[10(12325) - (313)^2][10(13478) - (328)^2]}}$$

$$r = \frac{128,300 - 102,664}{\sqrt{(123,250 - 97,969) \times (134,780 - 107,584)}}$$

$$r = \frac{25,636}{\sqrt{(25,281)(27,196)}} = \frac{25,636}{\sqrt{687,542,076}} = \frac{25,636}{26,221.0} = .978$$

Overall Pearson $r = 0.978$

12-24 Months, Pearson

S's	X	Y	X^2	Y^2	XY
1	16	14	256	196	224
2	12	14	144	196	168
3	21	21	441	441	441
4	21	21	441	441	441
5	18	18	324	324	324
	88	88	1606	1598	1598
N = 5	ΣX	ΣY	ΣX^2	ΣY^2	ΣXY

$$r = \frac{[5(1598)] - [(88)(88)]}{\sqrt{[5(1606) - (88)^2][5(1598) - (88)^2]}} = \frac{7790 - 7744}{\sqrt{[8030 - 7744][7790 - 7744]}}$$

$$r = \frac{246}{\sqrt{(286)(246)}} = \frac{246}{\sqrt{70356}} = \frac{246}{265.3} = .928$$

12-24 months Pearson $r = 0.928$

Pearson: *Ammons*

S's	X	Y	X^2	Y^2	XY
6	36	42	1296	1764	1512
7	36	54	1296	2916	1944
8	66	66	4356	4356	4356
9	66	66	4356	4356	4356
10	42	54	1764	2916	2268
	246	282	13068	16308	14436
N = 5	ΣX	ΣY	ΣX^2	ΣY^2	ΣXY

$$r = \frac{5(14,436) - (246)(282)}{\sqrt{[5(13,068) - (246)^2][5(16,308) - (282)^2]}} = \frac{72180 - 69372}{\sqrt{(65,340 - 60,516)(81,540 - 79,524)}}$$

$$r = \frac{2808}{\sqrt{(4,824)(2,016)}} = \frac{2808}{\sqrt{9,725,184}} = \frac{2808}{3118.5} = 0.9004$$

Ammons Pearson $r = 0.900$

Pearson: *Grammar*

S's	X	Y	X^2	Y^2	XY
6	24	24	576	576	576
7	36	36	1296	1296	1296
8	48	42	2304	1764	2016
9	48	48	2304	2304	2304
10	48	48	2304	2304	2304
	204	198	8784	8244	8496
N = 5	ΣX	ΣY	ΣX^2	ΣY^2	ΣXY

$$r = \frac{[5(8496)] - [(204)(198)]}{\sqrt{[5(8784) - (204)^2][5(8244) - (198)^2]}}$$

$$r = \frac{42{,}480 - 40{,}392}{\sqrt{(43{,}920 - 41{,}616)(41{,}220 - 39{,}204)}} = \frac{2088}{\sqrt{(2{,}304)(2{,}016)}}$$

$$r = \frac{2088}{\sqrt{4{,}644{,}864}} = \frac{2088}{2155.2} = .96882$$

Pearson Grammar   *r = 0.969*

Spearman Rank Correlation Coefficients

	Scores		Ranks			
S's	BW	JM	BW	JM	d_i	d_i^2
1	16	14	2	1.5	.5	.25
2	12	14	1	1.5	−.5	.25
3	21	21	4.5	4.5	0	0
4	21	21	4.5	4.5	0	0
5	18	18	3	3	0	0
6	30	33	6	6	0	0
7	36	45	7	7	0	0
8	57	54	9.5	9	.5	.25
9	57	57	9.5	10	−.5	.25
10	45	51	8	8	0	0
N = 10					$\Sigma d_i^2 = 1.0$	

.011 Overall r_s = .993
.052 12-24 mos. r_s = .973
n.s.3. Ammons r_s = .805
.054 Grammar r_s = .913

(1) *Overall Reliability* Using Spearman (All 10 S's)

$$r_s = \frac{\Sigma x^2 + \Sigma y^2 - \Sigma d^2}{2\sqrt{\Sigma x^2 \, \Sigma y^2}}$$

$$\Sigma x^2 = \frac{N^3 - N}{12} - \Sigma \left(\frac{t^3 - t}{12}\right)$$

$$\Sigma x^2 = \frac{990}{12} - \frac{6}{12} + \frac{6}{12} = 82.5 - 1.0 = 81.5$$

$$\Sigma y^2 = 81.5 \qquad \frac{81.5 + 81.5 - 1.0}{2\sqrt{(81.5)(81.5)}} = \frac{162}{163}$$

$$\Sigma d^2 = 1.0$$

Overall $r_s = .993$ sig. at $< .01$ level

(2) Spearman: *12-24 months*

$$\Sigma x^2 = \frac{(5)^3 - 5}{12} - \left(\frac{2^3 - 2}{12}\right) = \frac{125 - 5}{12} = \frac{6}{12} = 9.5$$

$$\Sigma y^2 + \frac{(5)^3 - 5}{12} - \left(\frac{2^3 - 2}{12} + \frac{2^3 - 2}{12}\right) = \frac{125 - 5}{12} - 1.0 = 9.0$$

$$r_s = \frac{9.5 + 9.0 - .50}{2\sqrt{(9.5)(9.0)}} = \frac{18}{2(9.25)} = \frac{18}{18.50} = .973$$

$r_s = .973$ 12-24 months sig. at $< .05$

(3) Spearman: *Ammons*

	Scores		Ranks			
S's	BW	JM	BW	JM	d_i	d_i^2
6	36	42	1.5	1	.5	.25
7	36	54	1.5	2.5	−1.0	1.00
8	66	66	4.5	4.5	0	0
9	66	66	4.5	4.5	0	0
10	42	54	3	2.5	.5	.25

$N = 5$ $\Sigma d_i^2 = 1.50$

$$r_s = \frac{9.0 + 9.0 - 1.50}{2\sqrt{(9.0)(9.0)}} = \frac{16.5}{18} = 0.9166$$

$r_s = 0.917$ Ammons   sig. at $< .05$

(4) Spearman: *Grammar*

	Scores		Ranks			
S's	BW	JM	BW	JM	d_i	d_i^2
6	24	24	1	1	0	0
7	36	36	2	2	0	0
8	48	42	4	3	1	1.0
9	48	48	4	4.5	−.5	.25
10	48	48	4	4.5	−.5	.25

$$\Sigma d_i^2 = 1.50$$

$$\Sigma x^2 = \frac{(5)^3 - 5}{12} - \left(\frac{3^3 - 3}{12}\right) = 10 - 2 = 8.0$$

$$\Sigma y^2 = \frac{(5)^3 - 5}{12} - \left(\frac{2^2 - 2}{12}\right) = 10 - .5 = 9.5$$

$$r_s = \frac{8.0 + 9.5 - 1.50}{2\sqrt{(8.0)(9.5)}} = \frac{16}{(2)(8.72)} = \frac{16}{17.44} = .9174$$

$r_s = .917$ Grammar   sig. at $< .05$ level

Reliability Run Scores—Language Battery

Observers A and S

Raw Scores in Developmental Age Equivalents
(All scores in months)

Subjects	CA	Overall Score		12-24 mos.		24-36 mos. Ammons		Grammar	
		BW	JM	BW	JM	BW	JM	BW	JM
1	12	16	14	16	14				
2	12 1/2	12	14	12	14				
3	19 1/2	21	21	21	21				
4	20	21	21	21	21				
5	22	18	18	18	18				
6	24	30/2.5	33/2.75			36/3.0	42/3.5	24/2.0	24/2.0
7	25 1/2	36/3.0	45/3.75			36/3.0	54/4.5	36/3.0	36/3.0
8	29 1/2	57/4.75	54/4.5			66/5.5	66/5.5	48/4.0	42/3.5
9	33 1/2	57/4.75	57/4.75			66/5.5	66/5.5	48/4.0	48/4.0
10	34 1/2	45/3.75	51/4.25			42/3.5	54/4.5	48/4.0	48/4.0

Summary: Scoring Schema

12-24 mos. Level	12-24 mos. Vocab.-Instr. Dev. Age	Ammons Points	24-36 mos. mos./yrs. Dev. Age	Level	Grammar Dev. Age	Score
0	10 mos.	6-8	30/2.5	I	24/2.0±	5/6
I	12	9-11	36/3.0	II	36/3.0	5/7
II	14	12-15	42/3.5	III	42/3.5	5/7
III	16	16	48/4.0	IV	48/4.0	2/3
IV	18	17-18	54/4.5	V	54/4.5	2/3
V	21	19-20	60/5.0	VI	60/5.0	2 or 3/4
VI	24+	21	66/5.5			

Average = Overall Score for 24-36 mos.

D

Manual for Testing Abstract Ability

Introduction, *292*

Description of Tests, *292*

Procedures, *292*
  HUNT-UZGIRIS, *292*
  PACIFIC TEST SERIES, *301*
  STANFORD-BINET ITEMS, *306*

Reliability, *307*
  HUNT-UZGIRIS, *307*
  MEYERS PACIFIC TEST SERIES, *308*

Scoring, *308*
  HUNT-UZGIRIS, *307*
  PACIFIC TEST SERIES WITH STANFORD-BINET ITEMS, *315*
  SCORING SHEETS, *316*

This manual was prepared by Bernice Shapiro. Revised March 1971

INTRODUCTION

The following procedures have been devised to test the ability of children between 9 and 36 months to deal with abstractions. In testing infants between 9 and 18 months, the Hunt-Uzgiris Scale, Series 1 and 5, has been used. For the Hunt-Uzgiris Scale, scoring is based on the highest developmental level an infant has reached on the particular series.

In assessing children between 18 and 36 months, the following tests devised by Meyers et al. have been used: Pacific Form-Color-Matching, Pacific Pattern Completion, Pacific Form and Picture Completion.

Children who attain a maximum score on the Pacific test series (41-43 points) will be given additional items selected from the Stanford-Binet Intelligence Scales. These additional items, selected from subtests Year III through Year VI, deal with the capacity to use abstract ability. A detailed description of items and scoring information is contained in the general instructions.

DESCRIPTION OF TESTS

Series 1 and 5 of the Hunt-Uzgiris Scale have been designed to measure the object concept. In the following table, the developmental stages in the evolution of the infant's concept of object are listed:

Stage	Behavior
I & II	Infant recognizes objects as part of own action. No active search for a hidden object.
III	Some permanence associated with objects; finds partly hidden object.
IV	Active search for completely hidden object; searches only where object was last found.
V	Observed displacements of objects are mastered.
VI	Invisible displacements of objects are mastered.

The Pacific Test Series consists of three subtests that contain three-dimensional materials. The child is required to complete various patterns and pictures and to match abstract forms.

PROCEDURES

Hunt-Uzgiris Scale

A child is assigned to a developmental stage based on his performance on the various items of the Hunt-Uzgiris scale, Series 1 and 5.

No.	Description

(Series 1)

3	Finding an object that is partially hidden
4	Finding an object hidden under one screen
5	Finding an object hidden under one of two screens
6	Finding an object hidden under one of two screens alternately
7	Finding an object under one of three screens
8	Finding an object after successive visible displacements
9	Finding an object hidden under three superimposed screens
10	Finding an object hidden in a container that is covered by superimposed screens
11	Following an object through one hidden displacement
12	Following an object through one hidden displacement with two screens
13	Following an object through one hidden displacement with two screens used alternately
14	Following an object through one hidden displacement with three screens
15	Following an object through a series of invisible displacements in sequence (object under last screen)
16	Developing representation of a series of displacements (object under first screen)

(Series 5)

5	Recognizing the reverse side of objects
6	Understanding the relationship of the container and contained
7	Understanding equilibrium
8	Understanding gravity
9	Dropping objects in order to study their trajectories
10	Making detours
11	Recognizing the absence of familiar persons

SERIES I: VISUAL PURSUIT AND PERMANENCE OF OBJECTS

I. Visual Pursuit of a Slowly Moving Object

1. Following an Object Moving Slowly Through an 180° Arc
(Bright Object: Beads)

Place the infant in an infant seat or supine on a flat surface. Take a bright object and hold it about 10 inches in front of the infant's eyes, until he focuses on it. It may be necessary to shake the object slightly in order to attract attention or to vary its distance from the infant's eyes, to find the optimal focal distance. If an older infant tends to focus on the examiner rather than the object, stand behind the infant. A ring of large, plastic beads of various colors may be used as the target object, or a red and white bull's-eye pattern, the latter suggested by B. White. Move the object slowly through an arc of 180° around the infant's head and observe his behavior. Repeat five times.

    a. does not follow the object
    b. follows object through part of arc with jerky accommodations
    c. follows object through part of arc smoothly
    d. follows object through the complete arc smoothly

2. Reacting to the Disappearance of a Slowly Moving Object (Beads)

Place the infant in an infant seat or supine on a flat surface. Take a bright object, such as the multicolored ring, and hold it slightly above the infant's line of vision, about 10 inches from his eyes, shaking it gently until the infant focuses on it. If the infant tends to focus on the examiner, stand behind and to one side of the infant. Once the infant has raised his eyes and focused on the object, move it slowly to one side and away from the infant, making it disappear below the edge of the seat or some other surface on which the infant is lying. Observe the infant's glance as the ring disappears from his sight. Repeat three times, always moving the object to the same side and having it reappear slightly above the infant's eyes.

    a. does not follow object to point of disappearance
    b. loses interest as soon as object disappears (eyes begin to wander and then focus on any interesting object within view)
    c. lingers with glance on the point where the object disappeared
    d. lingers with glance on the point where the object disappeared and returns glance to starting point (above)
    e. searches with eyes around the point where object disappeared

II. Following an Object Through a Partial Disappearance

3. Finding an Object that is Partially Hidden (Doll, Animal)

Have the infant sitting either in an infant seat, on mother's lap* or propped up on the floor. If the infant is in the seat, provide a working surface by putting a writing board, a small table, etc., over the seat. Use an object in which the infant shows interest and one that is unitary, so that a portion of the object cannot be equivalent to the whole object. A small, brightly colored doll or a plastic animal may be used, but an object such as a necklace would be unsuitable. Hold the object in front of the infant and, if he demonstrates interest by reaching for it, place the object on the surface, within the infant's reach, and

*Infant seated on mother's lap is recommended procedure for ease in testing a mobile child.

cover it with a screen in such a way that a small portion of the object would remain visible (the feet of the doll, the tail of the animal, etc.). Use a white, nontransparent scarf as a screen. Observe the infant's reaction. If in his fumblings to obtain the object, the infant covers it up completely, start a new trial. Repeat three times or until the infant's reaction is clear. If the examiner develops doubts as to the infant's desire for the object or the infant's ability to pick up the object, one trial in which the object is placed on the surface in front of the infant without being covered by a screen should be interspersed and the infant's behavior compared.

    a. loses interest in the object once it is covered
    b. reacts to the loss of the object but does not obtain it when it is partially hidden
    c. obtains the object

III. Following an Object Through a Complete Disappearance

Note: It is best to present the next five situations in succession. The object chosen for these situations should be one in which the infant shows strong interest, since otherwise one cannot be sure whether the infant gives up searching for the object because he has lost interest in it, or because he is unable to follow the displacements. It is permissible to change objects at any point. However, it is important to recognize that loss of interest may signify that the task has become too difficult. If the examiner suspects that the infant is losing interest owing to the difficulty of the task, hide the same object in a simpler way (i.e., a way that the infant was previously able to handle) and observe whether the infant will then search for the object. If the infant is still interested in the object, he will usually search for it in the easier situation. Also, the constant disappearance of a desired object often proves frustrating to young infants. When it seems that the loss of interest in an object may be due to frustration, permit the infant to play with the object for a minute without interference and observe whether interest is restored. On the other hand, if the need to relinquish the object after each trial appears to be causing the frustration, it is best to pick up the object as soon as the infant removes the screen and begins to reach for it, without permitting the infant to actually obtain the object each time.

    Since these situations are presented to infants varying considerably in age, certain adjustments in procedure are helpful with younger and older infants. The younger infants tend to become frustrated, and it is necessary to check constantly for their interest in the object being used as well as their attention to the task. For example, failure to follow the successive displacements in the last situation of this series would certainly lead to failure. Since infants often do tend to be impatient and start the search immediately, it is necessary to make sure that they have observed all the displacements. Contrariwise, older infants tend to become bored with the simple hidings, and if their reactions are clear, it is often desirable to cut the number of trials with the simple hidings to a minimum in order to prolong their cooperation. The cooperation of older infants is also secured by helping them see this as a game and permitting them a turn at hiding the object, if they so desire.

Practically any object in which the infant shows a strong interest may be used, as long as it is small enough to be completely covered by each of the screens without bulging too conspicuously. A necklace has been very popular, but a small doll, a red car, a plastic flower, etc., may be used. Food such as cereal or candy may also be used.

The three screens have to be large enough to cover the hidden object. They should be unattractive in themselves, and should differ enough to permit the infant to tell one from the other. A large, white, nontransparent scarf, a piece of cloth printed in a small, pale pattern, a square pillow covered with dull corduroy, and a piece of drably colored cloth have all been used as screens. The cloth has been generally used as the third screen instead of the pillow with younger infants, who often find the pillow too heavy to lift.

It is quite important to work on a sound-absorbing surface in order to make sure that the noise resulting from putting the object down does not serve as a clue. A floor covered by any kind of rug is usually adequate.

4. Finding an Object Hidden Under One Screen (Necklace, Doll, Car, Flower, Food)

Have the infant sitting on the floor or propped in a crib in order to have a flat work area around the infant. Take an object in which the infant shows strong interest and hold it out to him. If the infant starts to reach for the object, place it on the surface within the infant's reach and quickly cover it completely with a screen (before the infant grasps the object). Observe the infant's reaction to the disappearance of the object. Repeat three times. If the infant succeeds in obtaining the object on the first trial, shift the work area to one side of the infant (left or right) and present all the succeeding trials on the same side.

   a. loses interest in the object
   b. reacts to the loss of the object, but does not obtain the object
   c. pulls screen in order to play with the screen
   d. pulls screen and obtains the object

Note: It is important to differentiate search for the hidden object from pulling at the screen out of a desire to play with the screen itself. In general, if the infant has demonstrated a desire for the object before it was hidden and reaches for it either while lifting the screen or immediately after pulling the screen off, one may assume that the infant is searching for the hidden object. On the other hand, if the infant lifts the screen and holds it for a considerable length of time before reaching for the now-exposed object, possibly even directing attention to the screen, one may guess that the infant has lifted the screen for its own sake.

5. Finding an Object Hidden Under One of Two Screens
(Necklace, Doll, Car, Flower, Food)

If the infant obtains the object in two out of three trials when it is hidden under a single screen, place a second screen on the opposite side of the infant during the last trial of hiding the object under the first screen, and then hide the object in the same manner under the second screen. Observe the infant's reaction. To repeat the trial, hide the object under the second screen two more times, and then switch to hiding the object under the first screen and count this last trial as a repeat.

    a. loses interest in the object
    b. searches for the object where it was previously found—i.e., under the first screen
    c. searches for the object where it is observed to be hidden—i.e., under the second screen

6. Finding an Object Hidden Under One of Two Screens
Alternately (Necklace, Doll, Car, Flower, Food)

If the infant searches correctly at least twice in the presence of two screens, hide the object under the first and second screen alternately, three to five times, and observe the infant's behavior.

    a. becomes perplexed and loses interest in object
    b. searches haphazardly under one or both screens
    c. searches correctly under either of the two screens

7. Finding an Object Hidden Under One of Three Screens
(Necklace, Doll, Car, Flower, Food)

If the infant searches correctly in at least three trials when the object is hidden under one of two screens, introduce a third screen in front of the infant and hide the object under each of the three screens in a random fashion, from five to seven times, or until the infant's behavior appears clear.

    a. loses interest in the object
    b. searches haphazardly under some or all screens
    c. searches directly under the correct screen

8. Finding an Object After Successive Visible Displacements
(Necklace, Doll, Car, Flower, Food)

Arrange three screens in front of the infant, all within his reach. Take an object in which the infant shows a strong interest and hold it in such a way that the hand would *not* cover the object. Hide it successively under each of the three screens by moving the hand along the path of the screens; i.e., so that the object becomes hidden under one screen and then reappears in the space between the screens and again becomes hidden as the hand passes under another screen. Leave the object under the last screen. Observe where the infant searches for the object. If the infant finds the object directly under the last screen, change the position of the screens by making the last screen the first, to check for preference for any particular screen. If the infant again searches correctly, on the next trial, change the direction of the path followed by the hand in order to check for a position preference. Repeat the hiding three to five times and note the infant's reaction each time.

    a. does not follow the object through the successive hidings
    b. searches only under the first screen, which hides the object
    c. searches under the screen where the object was found on the previous trial
    d. searches under all screens haphazardly
    e. searches under all screens in the order of hiding
    f. searches directly under the last screen in the series

Note: It is permissible to interrupt the series at this point.

IV. Finding an Object Hidden Under a Number of Superimposed Screens

9. Finding an Object Hidden Under Three Superimposed Screens (Object in Which Strong Interest Shown)

Take an object in which the infant shows a strong interest and place it in front of the infant within his reach. Cover the object with one screen, then take a second screen and cover the first screen with the second, and so on. Arrange the screens in such a way that the infant cannot remove all of them with one swipe of the hand. Observe the infant's behavior, especially at the moment when he removes the topmost screen and faces the second screen, instead of finding the hidden object. Repeat two or three times.

    a. loses interest in the object
    b. lifts one or two screens, but gives up before finding the object
    c. removes all screens and finds the hidden object

10. Finding an Object Hidden in a Container that is Covered by Superimposed Screens (Object in Box Under Screen)

Note: Present this more difficult task to the infant only if he searches correctly when the object is hidden under the three superimposed screens or if he persists in removing all three superimposed screens with a single pull.

Take an object in which the infant is interested and place it inside a box with an easily removable cover, or wrap it in one of the screens, and then proceed to cover the hidden object by stacking the remaining screens over it. Observe the infant's reaction.

    a. loses interest in the object
    b. gives up search after removing one or all of the superimposed screens
    c. persists in searching and obtains the object

Note: It is not only permissible, but desirable, to interrupt the series at this point. If all the situations are presented in sequence, the infant often shows what may be termed a generalization reaction to "lift all screens in sight." This leads to some search behavior among infants who are really unable to handle an invisible displacement. If it is unfeasible to intersperse other test situations, a break for some free play would be desirable.

V. Following an Object Through an Invisible Displacement

11. Following an Object Through One Hidden Displacement (Object in Box Under Screen, Remove Box)

Make sure the work area is covered with some sound-absorbing material. Place a screen in front of the infant. For hiding, use a small object in which the infant shows interest, such as a miniature doll, a small stuffed animal, or a small car. To produce the hidden displacement, use a cardboard box without a cover, deep enough to make the object invisible to the infant once it is lowered into it. While the infant watches, lower the object into the box and then hide the box under the screen. Turn the box over under the screen, to make the object fall out. Let the object remain hidden under the screen, but remove the empty box and show it to the infant. Urge the infant to find the object and observe his behavior. Repeat three times. If the infant seems to lose interest, check on the difficulty of the task by hiding the same object under the screen with a simple displacement.

    a. loses interest in the object
    b. reacts to the loss of the object, but does not search for it
    c. searches only in the box for the hidden object
    d. checks the box and proceeds to search under the screen
    e. searches directly under the screen

12. Following an Object Through One Hidden Displacement With two Screens (Object in Box Under Second Screen, Remove Box)

If the infant succeeds in finding the hidden object at least twice with one screen, place a second screen beside the first one and proceed to hide the object *in the same manner* under the second screen. Observe the infant's search. To repeat, hide the object under the second screen at least three times and then switch back to hiding it under the first screen.

    a. searches only in the box
    b. searches under the screen where the object was previously found
    c. searches under the correct screen

13. Following the Object Through One Hidden Displacement With Two Screens (Object in Box Under Second Screen, Remove Box)

If the infant succeeds in finding the object with two screens at least twice, hide it in the same manner under the two screens alternately. Repeat three to five times.

    a. loses interest in the object
    b. searches haphazardly under the two screens
    c. searches directly under the correct screen

14. Following an Object Through One Hidden Displacement With Three Screens (Object in Box Under One of Three Screens, Remove Box)

If the infant succeeds in finding the object with two screens used alternately, introduce a third screen and hide the object in the same manner under each of the three screens in a random fashion. Repeat five times.

    a. loses interest in the object
    b. searches haphazardly under all three screens
    c. searches directly under the correct screen

VI. Following an Object Through a Series of Invisible Displacements

15. Following an Object Through a Series of Invisible Displacements in Sequence (Object Hidden in Hand Under Last of Three Screens)

Arrange three screens on a sound-absorbing surface in front of the infant. Use an object small enough to be hidden in the closed hand, such as a small doll, a plastic flower, etc., in which the infant shows interest. Use the hand rather than the box to produce the invisible displacement. While the infant watches, hide the object in the closed hand and then hide the hand under each of the three screens in succession, leaving the object under the last of the screens. Make sure the infant is paying attention throughout the whole procedure and that the object is not visible in the hand when the hand appears in the spaces between the screens. Show the infant that your hand is empty after the last displacement. Observe the infant's search for the object. Repeat at least three times, always taking the same path and leaving the object under the last screen.

    a. searches only in the examiner's hand

    b. searches only under the first screen in the series

    c. searches under all screens in the same order as followed by the examiner's hand

    d. searches directly under the last screen

Pacific Test Series

Pacific Form-Color Matching

Materials. Fourteen 3-by-12-inch pieces of 1/8-inch masonite on which have been glued colored forms. On one end is one 1/4-inch plywood figure, the model, surfaced with adhesive-backed shelf paper. On other end are two figures, one of which is the same form and color as the one on the first end. The figures are circles of 2 1/2-inch diameter; rhombuses with sides 1 1/4 inches and angles of 60 degrees and 120 degrees, with a 60-degree angle at the bottom; 2 1/2-inch squares; isosceles triangles with legs of 2 1/2 inches and base of 3 1/2 inches, with the base down; and stars with 2 1/4 inches between alternate points. Below are the shapes and colors of the figures from left to right:

Board Model	Choices	
A red circle	red circle	green rhombus
B red circle	green rhombus	red circle
C yellow rhombus	yellow rhombus	black circle
D yellow rhombus	green circle	yellow rhombus
1 red square	red square	green circle
2 red circle	red circle	green rhombus
3 black circle	black circle	pink star
4 green square	pink rhombus	green square
5 red triangle	red triangle	black circle
6 green star	red circle	green star
7 yellow rhombus	yellow rhombus	black circle
8 pink rhombus	pink rhombus	black circle
9 pink star	pink star	black square
10 black triangle	pink rhombus	black triangle

Procedure. Place the board directly in front of S with the choices (to E's left) covered by a 3 1/2-by-6-inch manila strip. Say, "See this one?" Point to the left figure (to E's right) and say, "Find it over here." Expose the covered choices.

    Use boards A, B, C, and D as demonstrations. If necessary, guide S's hand to the correct choice. Present the series 1 through 10 rapidly and encourage S to choose quickly. Correct each mistake quickly without stopping time. Credit immediate self-corrections. Discontinue after failure on four out of five items.

Score.   Count each identification. One point for each correct response in test series.

Articulation.   None required.

Pacific Pattern Completion

Materials.   Eight colored corrugated boards, 9 by 12 inches, each with a cutout from the middle of a 12-inch side. For each board there are three smaller pieces, one of which is the cutout (having the same form and color and obviously fitting), and two of which are "wrong." S is to fit the correct one. In series A, the correct choice is the only one of the three with both *correct form and correct color*. In series B, one of the "wrongs" has the same form but the wrong color. The mode of 4 inches is observed in the cutouts and choices, as far as possible. That is, each cutout is 4 inches at the outside edge and 4 inches deep, regardless of its form. Forms are squares, semicircles, quarter-circles, triangles, wedges (same as triangles but with 2-inch small end rather than point), and bridges. The bridge is "pi" shaped, made by cutting the main card with the two vertical 4-inch cuts as though to make a 4-by-4-inch square, but leaving a 2-by-2-inch stub in the bottom middle.

Two of the cards, A and B, are for demonstration but are scored if successful response is made after the initial demonstration.

Procedure.   In each case, *place large card with cutout side facing S, and the three choices between S and the large card*. Using sample card A with cutout portion facing S, place response items on same side as cutout section following the number series (1, 2, 3) on back of each response choice. Use numbers for demonstration ("dem.") and after showing the correct response, replace all choices in order required for administration ("adm.") to the subject. Ask S to "put the one that fits here" (point to cutout portion). *Help S to place his choice if he demonstrates some motor difficulty in handling and placing his responses in the large cards. Compliment on making a correct choice when applicable. Correct all errors and explain verbally the reason for choosing the response item.*

Administer items 1 and 2 of series A using number series (1, 2, 3) on back of responses for layout. Demonstrate sample card B by showing approval for correct choice made by S. Follow procedure as in series A. Administer items 1-4.

Allow a reasonable length of time for S to make corrections in his responses, distinguishing carefully between S's trying out and his seeming to have made a final choice. Avoid glances of doubt, or motions of overhesitation that might cue S that his selection was wrong, but avoid also too quick a conclusion of a set, lest he be viewing his results with an eye to correction.

The cards and their associated cutout choices are listed below. Choice numbers (1), (2), and (3) refer to left-right arrangement (to E) of the three choices when placed between the large card and S.

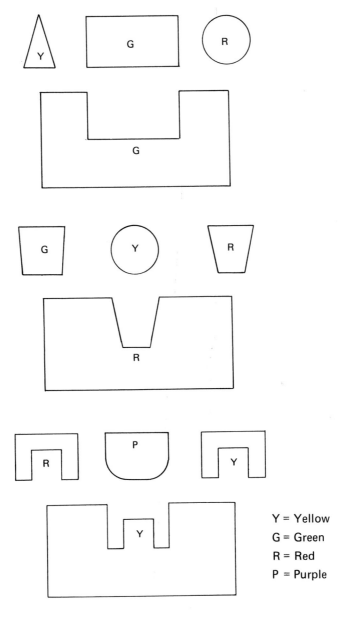

Y = Yellow
G = Green
R = Red
P = Purple

Diagrams based on items A, B, and B3 of Pacific Pattern Completion.

Card A. Green (square):	(1) (dem.) yellow triangle
	(2) (dem.) green square
	(3) (dem.) red circle
	(1) (adm.) green square
	(2) (adm.) red circle
	(3) (adm.) yellow triangle
Card Al. Purple (wedge):	(1) purple wedge (4 by 2 inches at ends, side slightly over 4 inches)
	(2) yellow circle
	(3) red square
Card A2. Pink (triangle):	(1) green circle
	(2) pink triangle
	(3) purple square
Card B. Red (wedge):	(1) (dem.) green wedge
	(2) (dem.) yellow circle
	(3) (dem.) red wedge
	(1) (adm.) red wedge
	(2) (adm.) yellow circle
	(3) (adm.) green wedge
Card Bl. Pink (quarter-circle):	(1) black circle
	(2) blue quarter-circle
	(3) pink quarter-circle
Card B2. Black (triangle):	(1) black triangle
	(2) yellow half-circle
	(3) white triangle
Card B3. Yellow (bridge):	(1) red bridge
	(2) purple half-circle
	(3) yellow bridge
Card B4. Blue (half-circle):	(1) blue half-circle
	(2) purple half-circle
	(3) red rectangle (2 by 4 inches)

In the case of wedges, triangles, half-circles, and quarter-circles, where rotation would affect difficulty, the item is always placed with narrower or curved side toward the large card, as though cut from it and moved away without rotation action.

Score. Give 1 point for correct choice on series A. Give 2 points for selecting proper color and form on series B. Give 1 point when form alone is correct in series B. Maximum score: 13 points. Discontinue after four out of five items have been failed.

Time. No time limit.

Note. It is not necessary for correct response to fit perfectly into cutout portion in order to receive score. If S hands his choice to E, place in cutout position and comment or make correction.

Articulation. None used. Only three normal Ss within age range attained maximum.

Pacific Form and Picture Completion

S is to put two pieces together to form a whole figure or picture.

Materials. Forms A, B, and C consist of pairs of identical geometric shapes. Form A is a pair of red circles, 4 1/4 inches in diameter, each cut in half, hence giving four half-circles. Form B is a pair of blue squares, 4 1/2 inches on each side, each cut exactly in half to provide rectangles, four in all. Form C is a pair of purple squares, each cut in half to provide triangles, the hypotenuse being about 5 3/4 inches.

Pictures I to VIII are pairs of colored pictures mounted on heavy board, each 3 3/4 by 4 1/2 inches. Both of picture pair I are cut in half, with an irregular cut (see pp. 312-13) so as to permit E to demonstrate how S should bring his pieces together to make a complete picture. One member of each of picture pairs II to VI is cut into two pieces, the other left intact as the model for S to produce. One member of each of picture pairs VII and VIII is cut into three pieces, to be put together to make the replica of the respective intact picture. The pictures were cut from the reading-readiness book, *Stories in Pictures* (6). Two books are required, of course, to produce the picture pairs. Pictures I to VIII are: I, a dog; II, a duck; III, a baby; IV, a giraffe; V, a boat; VI, a doll; VII, a clown; VIII, a top.

Procedure. Form A: Place two red half-circles approximately 6 inches apart, with two straight edges on outside in front of examiner. Place the others the same way before S. Demonstrate with E's forms to make a complete circle. Ask S to "make a ball just like mine." If S succeeds, go on to next item. If he fails, place half-circles with curved side outward and demonstrate with E's forms. Indicate to S to make his the same way.

Form B: Show two rectangles and assemble into a square. Place rectangles with shortest sides facing each other, 6 inches apart. Ask S to "make a box just like mine." If S succeeds, go on to next item. If he fails, place rectangles with longest sides facing each other and demonstrate with E's forms.

Form C: Show two triangles and assemble into a square. Place the triangles so the two longest edges (hypotenuses) are to the outside and perpendicular to each other. Request S to imitate E's design. If S succeeds, administer item I. If he fails, reverse position of triangles so longest edges are facing each other (6 inches apart).

Pictures I to VIII: Place segments of picture in front of S, one picture at a time. Demonstrate item I only. On items II to VIII, show E's uncut picture and ask S to make his picture look the same. Make corrections on all errors or noncompletions.

Directions for placement of parts, items I to III: *Place top edge and bottom edge of picture on a horizontal plane* (line) in front of S. Items IV to VI: *Place top and bottom edges approximately 2 inches apart on a vertical plane* (line) in front of S. Items VII and VIII: *Place in random order inside an imaginary 8-inch circle.*

Score. Forms A, B, and C: Give 2 points for correct placement on first trial, on each. Give 1 point for correct placement on second trial, on each. Items I to VI: Give 1 point for each correctly completed picture. Items VII and VIII: Give 2 points for correctly completed picture. Give 1 point for two of three pieces correctly placed together. Maximum score: 16. Discontinue after failure on four out of five items.

Time. No time limit.

Articulation. None required.

Description of Items from Stanford-Binet Intelligence Scale

Stanford-Binet items to be administered when S has attained a maximum of 41-43 raw score points (Developmental Stage V = 32.0 months) on the Pacific Test Series.

See Stanford-Binet Manual (form L-M) for specific instructions on administering the following selected items. Pages 130 to 151 describe the scoring procedure.

Binet Items:

 Year III (pages 72-73 in Binet Manual)
  #3: Block Building: Bridge
  #4: Picture Memories
  Score: If both passed* = Stage VI–36 months

 Year III-6 (page 74)
  #1: Comparison of Balls
  #2: Patience: Pictures
  Score: 42 months–Stage VII

---

*All items in each year level must be passed if subject is to receive credit for passing that year level. However, an item missed at one stage may be credited if an item at any higher level is answered correctly.

Year IV (pages 77-78)

> #3: Opposite Analogies I
> #4: Pictorial Identification
> #5: Discrimination of Forms

Score: 48 months—Stage VIII

Year IV-6 (page 79)

> #1: Aesthetic Comparison
> #2: Opposite Analogies I
> #3: Pictorial Similarities and Differences I

Score: 54 months—Stage IX

Year V (pages 81-83)

> #2: Paper Folding: Triangle
> #5: Pictorial Similarities and Differences II
> #6: Patience: Rectangles

Score: 60 months—Stage X

Year VI (pages 84-85)

> #3: Mutilated Pictures
> #5: Opposite Analogies II

Score: 72 months—Stage XI

Scoring the Stanford-Binet Items

Subjects scoring within the 41-43 point range (Developmental Stage V) will be given the additional items selected from the Stanford-Binet Intelligence Scale. The rules for scoring are as follows:

A. At least two Binet items must be passed to qualify a subject to move up to the next Developmental Stage (VI).

B. Although the number of items per year level varies (two items for Year III, three items for Year V), all items for each year level must be passed to give credit for that year level. However, an item missed at any stage will be credited if an item at a higher level is passed. For example, A subject misses one item at Level IV but passes another at Level IV-6. Credit for the Level IV is then given.

RELIABILITY—ABSTRACT ABILITIES

Hunt-Uzgiris Scale

Five infants ranging in age from 10 to 17 months were examined twice within 24 to 48 hours by two examiners using Series 1 and 5 of the Hunt-Uzgiris Scale. Infants were seen in their own homes with their mothers present, on January 13 and 14, 1970. Their scores, expressed as developmental age equivalents, follow:

	Examiner 1	Examiner 2
Subject A—17 mos. boy	15 mos.	15 mos.
Subject B—10 mos. boy	8 mos.	11 mos.
Subject C—10 mos. girl	15 mos.	15 mos.
Subject D—11 mos. girl	11 mos.	11 mos.
Subject E—12 mos. boy	15 mos.	11 mos.

Test-retest reliability expressed as a Pearson Product-Moment Correlation was .628.

Meyers Pacific Test Series

Five subjects ranging in age from 26 to 35 months were examined twice within 24 to 48 hours by two examiners using the Pacific Pattern Completion Test, the Pacific Form and Picture Completion Test and the Pacific Form and Color Matching Test. Subjects were seen in their own homes with their mothers present, on January 14 and 15, 1970. Their scores, expressed as developmental age equivalents, follow:

	Examiner 1	Examiner 2
Subject A—29 mos. boy	32 mos.	32 mos.
Subject B—31 mos. boy	28 mos.	28 mos.
Subject C—35 mos. girl	28 mos.	28 mos.
Subject D—26 mos. boy	28 mos.	28 mos.
Subject E—26 mos. girl	24 mos.	24 mos.

Test-retest reliability expressed as a Pearson Product-Moment Correlation was 1.00.

For the entire abstract-ability test series, overall test-retest reliability was .786.

Hunt-Uzgiris Score Sheet—Series 1

Item	Score	Item	Score	Item	Score
3	a - 0	5	a - 0	7	a - 0
	b - 2		b - 2		b - 2
	c - 4		c - 4		c - 4
4	a - 0			8	a - 0
	b - 2	6	a - 0		b - 2
	c - 2		b - 2		c - 2
	d - 4		c - 4		d - 2
					e - 2
					f - 4

Hunt-Uzgiris Score Sheet—Series 1 (cont.)

9	a - 0	12	a - 2		15	a - 0
	b - 2		b - 2			b - 2
	c - 4		c - 4			c - 4
10	a - 0		d - 0	d - does not search	16	a - 0
	b - 2	13	a - 0			b - 2
	c - 4		b - 2			c - 4
			c - 4			
11	a - 0	14	a - 0			
	b - 0		b - 2			
	c - 2		c - 4			
	d - 4					
	e - 4					

Hunt-Uzgiris Score Sheet—Series 5

5	a - 0	
	b - 2	
	c - 4	
6	a - 0	
	b - 2	(also 2 pts. for placing objects in but not removing them)
	c - 4	
7	a - 0	
	b - 2	
	c - 4	
8	a - 0	
	b - 2	
	c - 4	
9	a - 0	
	b - 2	
	c - 4	
10	a - 0	
	b - 2	
	c - 4	
11	a - 0	
	b - 2	
	c - 4	

Hunt-Uzgiris Scoring for Children 5-18 months

	ITEMS		Developmental	
Stage	Series I	Series V	Age Range	Midpoint
III	3	5	5-6 mos.	5.5 mos.
IV	4,5,6,7	9,10	7-9 mos.	8.0 mos.
V	8,9,10	6,7	10-12 mos.	11.0 mos.
VI	11,12,13, 14,15,16	8,11	13-18 mos.	15.5 mos.

		Minimum Points Required
Stage	Total points for Stage	to Attain Each Stage*
III	8	6
IV	24	16
V	20	14
VI	32	20

*Based on a percentage of total points for stage; i.e., to attain Stage III the subject must receive 6 out of 8 points.

Pacific Test Series Scoring for Children 18-36 months

Scoring information for the Pacific Test Series subtests

Total Points	Developmental Stage	Age Equivalent	Midpoint
0-20	I	15-18 mos.	16.5 mos.
21-30	II	19-22	20.5
31-36	III	23-26	24.5
37-40	IV	27-30	28.5
*41-43	V	31-33	32.0

Stanford-Binet Items:

Year III	VI		36.0 mos.
Year III-6	VII		42.0
Year IV	VIII		48.0
Year IV-6	IX		54.0
Year V	X		60.0
Year VI	XI		72.0

*Subjects scoring within this range (Developmental Stage V) will be administered selected items from the Stanford-Binet Intelligence Scale.

PACIFIC PATTERN COMPLETION—SCORE SHEET

NAME _____ AGE _____ SCORE _____

Place each large card with cutout side facing S, and the three choices between S and the large card. Don't rotate choices; place as though cut out and moved straight away from card. Say, "Put the one that goes here" (pointing to cutout). Discontinue after failure on four out of five items.

Place sample card A with three choices in numerical order and demonstrate.

1 point each.

Change order of choices to green-red-yellow. Ask S to put the one that fits here—pointing to gap.

		1	0
A.	Green Square	☐	☐

Correct all errors, explaining correct choice. Help S place the form if he shows some motor difficulty but has indicated correct choice.

		1	0
A1.	Purple Wedge	☐	☐
A2.	Pink Triangle	☐	☐

B—Allow one demonstration trial—let S place correct choice—then rearrange the choices.

		2 pts	1 pt.	0
B.	Red Wedge	☐	☐	☐

On B items, credit 2 points for correct choice, 1 point for right form but wrong color.

		2	1	0
B1.	Blue quadrant	☐	☐	☐
B2.	Black triangle	☐	☐	☐
B3.	Yellow bridge	☐	☐	☐
B4.	Blue oval	☐	☐	☐

FORM AND PICTURE COMPLETION—SCORE SHEET

NAME _____ AGE _____ SCORE _____

Forms

A. Place two red half-circles approximately 6 in. apart with the straight edges on outside in front of E. Place others same way before S.

	2	0
Demonstrate with E's forms to make a circle. Ask S to "make one just like mine." If S succeeds, go on to blue square. If S fails,	Circle 1	☐ ☐

Place half circles with curved sides out, demonstrate, and ask S to make one the same.

	1	0
	Circle 2	☐ ☐

B. Show two rectangles and assemble into square. Place with short sides facing, 6 in. apart. Ask S, etc.

	2	0
	Blue square 1	☐ ☐

If S fails, place long sides together, demonstrate, and ask S to make one.

	1	0
	Blue square 2	☐ ☐

C. Place triangles and assemble. Place S's triangles same way, ask, etc.

If S fails, place , demonstrate, ask. . . .

	2	0
Purple square	☐	☐

	1	0
Purple square	☐	☐

Pictures. Correct all errors or incompletions.

1. Dog   Place E's and S's segments. Demonstrate with E's. Ask S to "make yours just like mine."

	1	0
1. Dog	☐	☐

2. Duck   Place uncut pictures in front of E, pieces before S.

	1	0
2. Duck	☐	☐

3. Baby

	1	0
3. Baby	☐	☐

4. Giraffe

	1	0
4. Giraffe	☐	☐

5. Boat

	1	0
5. Boat	☐	☐

6. Doll

	1	0
6. Doll	☐	☐

7. Clown

	1	0
7. Clown	☐	☐
All 3 correct	1 / ☐	0 / ☐
2 pieces	2 / ☐	0 / ☐

8. Top

	1	0
8. Top—all 3	1 / ☐	0 / ☐
2 pieces		

PACIFIC FORM AND COLOR MATCHING

NAME _____ AGE _____ SCORE _____

Place board in front of S, with choices covered by a manila strip. Say, "See this" (uncover choices); "Find it over here." Use the first few as demonstrations and place at the end: Begin when S seems to have the response set. One point for each correct response. Discontinue after failure on four out of five items.

	+ (plus)	– (minus)
○ ○ ◇ A		
○ ◇ ○ B		
◇ ◇ ○ C		
◇ ○ ◇ D		
□ □ ○ 1		
○ ○ ◇ 2		
○ ○ ✡ 3		
□ ◇ □ 4		
△ △ ○ 5		
✡ ○ ✡ 6		
◇ ◇ ○ 7		
◇ ◇ ○ 8		
✡ ✡ □ 9		
△ ◇ △ 10		

Pacific Test Series Scoring for Children 18-36 months

Scoring information for the Pacific Test Series subtests

Total Points	Developmental Stage	Age Equivalent	Midpoint
0-20	I	15-18 mos.	16.5 mos.
21-30	II	19-22	20.5
31-36	III	23-26	24.5
37-40	IV	27-30	28.5
*41-43	V	31-33	32.0
Stanford-Binet Items:			
Year III	VI		36.0 mos.
Year III-6	VII		42.0
Year IV	VIII		48.0
Year IV-6	IX		54.0
Year V	X		60.0
Year VI	XI		72.0

*Subjects scoring within this range (Developmental Stage V) will be administered selected items from the Stanford-Binet Intelligence Scale.

SAMPLE SCORING SHEET

HUNT-UZGIRIS SCALE

NAME _____ AGE ___ DATE _____ EXAMINER _____

Series I: Visual Pursuit and Permanence of Objects

I. Visual pursuit of a slowly moving object

    1. Following an object moving slowly through an $180°$ arc (bright object: beads)

      a. does not follow the object

      b. follows object through part of arc with jerky accommodations

      c. follows object through part of arc smoothly

     *d. follows object through the complete arc smoothly

    2. Reacting to the disappearance of a slowly-moving object (beads)

      a. does not follow object to point of disappearance

      b. loses interest as soon as object disappears (eyes begin to wander and then focus on any interesting object within view)

     *c. Lingers with glance on the point where the object disappeared

     *d. lingers with glance on the point where the object disappeared and returns glance to starting point (above)

      e. searches with eyes around the point where object disappeared

II. Following an object through a partial disappearance

    3. Finding an object that is partially hidden (doll, animal)

      a. loses interest in the object once it is covered

      b. reacts to the loss of the object but does not obtain it when it is partially hidden

     *c. obtains the object

III. Following an object through a complete disappearance

    4. Finding an object hidden under one screen (necklace, doll, car, flower) (food)

      a. loses interest in the object

      b. reacts to the loss of the object, but does not obtain the object

      c. pulls screen in order to play with the screen

     *d. pulls screen and obtains the object

    5. Finding an object hidden under one of two screens (necklace, doll, cat, flower) (food)

      a. loses interest in the object

      b. searches for the object where it was previously found, *i.e.*, under the first screen

     *c. searches for the object where it is observed to be hidden, i.e., under the second screen

    6. Finding an object hidden under one of two screens alternately (necklace, doll, car, flower) (food)

      a. becomes perplexed and loses interest in object

      b. searches haphazardly under one or both screens

     *c. searches correctly under either of the two screens

*Starred items represent correct responses.

7. Finding an object hidden under one of three screens (necklace, doll, car, flower) (food)

    a. loses interest in the object

    b. searches haphazardly under some or all screens

  *c. searches directly under the correct screen

8. Finding an object after successive visible displacements (necklace, doll, car, flower) (food)

    a. does not follow the object through the successive hidings

    b. searches only under the first screen which hides the object

    c. searches under the screen where the object was found on the previous trial

    d. searches under all screens haphazardly

    e. searches under all screens in the order of hiding

  *f. searches directly under the last screen in the series

IV. Finding an object hidden under a number of superimposed screens

9. Finding an object hidden under three superimposed screens (object in which strong interest is shown)

    a. loses interest in the object

    b. lifts one or two screens, but gives up before finding the object

  *c. removes all screens and finds the hidden object

10. Finding an object hidden in a container which is covered by superimposed screens (object in box under screen)

    a. loses interest in the object

    b. gives up search after removing one or all of the superimposed screens

  *c. persists in searching and obtains the object

V. Following an object through an invisible displacement

11. Following an object through one hidden displacement (object in box under screen, remove box)

    a. loses interest in the object

    b. reacts to the loss of the object, but does not search for it.

    c. searches only in the box for the hidden object

  *d. checks the box and proceeds to search under the screen

    e. searches directly under the screen

12. Following an object through one hidden displacement with two screens (object in box under second screen, remove box)

    a. searches only in the box

    b. searches under the screen where the object was previously found

  *c. searches under the correct screen

13. Following the object through one hidden displacement with two screens used alternately (object in box under 1 of 2 screens, remove box)

    a. loses interest in the object

    b. searches haphazardly under the two screens

  *c. searches directly under the correct screen

14. Following an object through one hidden displacement with three screens (object in box under 1 of 3 screens, remove box)

    a. loses interest in the object

    b. searches haphazardly under all three screens

  *c. searches directly under the correct screen

*Starred items represent correct responses.

VI. Following an object through a series of invisible displacements

  15. Following an object through a series of invisible displacements in sequence (object hidden in hand under last of three screens)

    a. searches only in the examiner's hand
    b. searches only under the first screen in the series
    *c. searches under all screens in the same order as followed by the examiner's hand
    *d. searches directly under the last screen

  16. Developing representation of a series of displacements (object hidden in hand under first of three screens)

    a. searches only under the last screen and gives up
    b. searches haphazardly under all three screens
    *c. searches systematically from the last screen to the first in reverse order

Series V: The Construction of the object in Space

I. Development of the notion of a recognizable object

  1. Development of alternate glancing (large plastic flower)

    a. looks in only one direction
    b. looks at both patterns, but switches glance slowly from one to the other (one to two switches per 20 seconds)
    *c. looks at both patterns, switching the glance quickly from one to the other (four to five switches per 5 seconds)

  2. Development of localization of an object by its sound (rattle)

    a. does not turn head to the source of sound
    b. turns head toward the source of sound in one direction only
    c. turns head correctly in the direction of the sound
    *d. localizes the source of sound with his eyes

  3. Understanding the trajectory of a slowly moving object (small object)

    a. loses interest in the object when it disappears
    b. searches for the object in front of him with his eyes
    c. searches for the object at the point of its disappearance or in the direction where it was previously visible
    *d. switches glance to the other side of the screen and anticipates the reappearance of the object

  4. Understanding the trajectory of a rapidly moving object (small light weight object)

    a. does not follow the dropping object and keeps looking at the examiner's hand
    *b. turns eyes to the correct side or follows partly
    *c. follows the trajectory of the object and finds it with his glance
    d. searches with glance for the object at the point where its trajectory was last visible
    *e. leans forward to search for the object in the direction in which it fell even though the last portion of its trajectory was not visible

  5. Recognizing the reverse side of the objects (object with definite reverse side-animal or rattle)

    a. continues to reach and grasp the object.
    b. withdraws hands and shows evidence of surprise at the reversal
    *c. grasps the object, but turns it to the "right" side immediately each time or turns the object over several times looking at it intently

* Starred items represent correct responses

II. Development of understanding of relationships between objects

    6. Understanding the relationship of the container and contained (small beads and container)

        a. does not place the objects into the container

        b. places the objects into the container and takes them out one by one

      *c. places the objects into the container and turns the container over in order to remove the objects

    7. Understanding equilibrium (small blocks)

        a. does not build a tower

      *b. approximates two blocks, but does not leave one on top

      *c. builds a tower of at least two blocks

    8. Understanding gravity (car on incline)

        a. plays with the object without using the incline

        b. guides the object down the incline

      *c. permits the object to roll down the incline

    8. *Alternate*: Understanding gravity when pulling a string

        a. loses interest in the object

        b. pulls string, but not enough to obtain the object from the floor or on the table

        c. pulls string, but not enough to get the object from the floor, while using it successfully on the table

      *d. pulls string and obtains the object

III. Interest in the phenomenon of the fall

    9. Dropping objects in order to study their trajectories (box filled with small objects)

        a. does not drop any of the objects

        b. drops several objects repeatedly but pays little attention to where they fall

      *c. drops several objects repeatedly and looks down to see where they fall

IV. Representation of Objects in space

    10. Making detours (roll toy beneath chair)

        a. loses interest in the object

        b. attempts to crawl directly to the object, following the same path that the object took

      *c. goes around the obstacle and attempts to retrieve the object from behind

    11. Recognizing the absence of familiar persons (ask where familiar person is such as brother or sister)

        a. does not comprehend the question

        b. goes to look for that person

      *c. indicates knowledge of the absence of that person by pointing to the outside, saying "gone," "bye-bye," etc.

*Starred items represent correct responses.

DESCRIPTION OF ITEMS FROM STANFORD-BINET
INTELLIGENCE SCALE

Stanford-Binet items to be administered when S has attained a maximum of 41-43 raw score points (Developmental Stage V = 32.0 months) on the Pacific Test Series.

See Stanford-Binet Manual (form L-M) for specific instructions on administering the following selected items. See pages 130 to 151 for scoring procedure.

Binet Items:

Year III   (pages 72-73 in Binet Manual)
  #3: Block Building: Bridge
  #4: Picture Memories
  Score: If both passed* = Stage VI–36 months

Year III-6   (page 74)
  #1: Comparison of Balls
  #2: Patience: Pictures
  Score: 42 months–Stage VII

Year IV   (pages 77-78)
  #3: Opposite Analogies I
  #4: Pictorial Identification
  #5: Discrimination of Forms
  Score: 48 months–Stage VIII

Year IV-6   (page 79)
  #1: Aesthetic Comparison
  #2: Opposite Analogies I
  #3: Pictorial Similarities and Differences I
  Score: 54 months–Stage IX

Year V   (pages 81-83)
  #2: Paper Folding: Triangle
  #5: Pictorial Similarities and Differences II
  #6: Patience: Rectangles
  Score: 60 months–Stage X

Year VI   (pages 84-85)
  #3: Mutilated Pictures
  #5: Opposite Analogies II
  Score: 72 months–Stage XI

---

*All items in each year level must be passed if subject is to receive credit for passing that year level. However, an item missed at one stage may be credited if an item at any higher level is answered correctly.

SCORING THE STANFORD-BINET ITEMS

Subjects scoring within the 41-43 point range (Developmental Stage V) will be given the additional items selected from the Stanford-Binet Intelligence Scale. The rules for scoring are as follows:

A. At least two binet items must be passed to qualify a subject to move up to the next Developmental Stage (VI).

B. Although the number of items per year level varies (two items for Year III, three items for Year V), all items for each year level must be passed to give credit for that year level. However, an item missed at any stage will be credited if an item at a higher level is passed. For example, A subject misses one item at Level IV but passes another at Level IV-6. Credit for the Level IV is then given.

RELIABILITY—ABSTRACT ABILITIES

Hunt-Uzgiris Scale

Five infants ranging in age from 10 to 17 months were examined twice within 24 to 48 hours by two examiners using Series 1 and 5 of the Hunt-Uzgiris Scale. Infants were seen in their own homes with their mothers present, on January 13 and 14, 1970. Their scores, expressed as developmental age equivalents, follow:

	Examiner 1	Examiner 2
Subject A—17 mos. boy	15 mos.	15 mos.
Subject B—10 mos. boy	8 mos.	11 mos.
Subject C—10 mos. girl	15 mos.	15 mos.
Subject D—11 mos. girl	11 mos.	11 mos.
Subject E—12 mos. boy	15 mos.	11 mos.

Test-retest reliability expressed as a Pearson Product-Moment Correlation was .628.

Meyers Pacific Test Series

Five subjects ranging in age from 26 to 35 months were examined twice within 24 to 48 hours by two examiners using the Pacific Pattern Completion

Test, the Pacific Form and Picture Completion Test and the Pacific Form and Color Matching Test. Subjects were seen in their own homes with their mothers present, on January 14 and 15, 1970. Their scores, expressed as developmental age equivalents, follow:

	Examiner 1	Examiner 2
Subject A—29 mos. boy	32 mos.	32 mos.
Subject B—31 mos. boy	28 mos.	28 mos.
Subject C—35 mos. girl	28 mos.	28 mos.
Subject D—26 mos. boy	28 mos.	28 mos.
Subject E—26 mos. girl	24 mos.	24 mos.

Test-retest reliability expressed as a Pearson Product-Moment Correlation was 1.00.

For the entire abstract-ability test series, overall test-retest reliability was .786.

E

Manual for Assessing the Discriminative Ability of One- to Three-Year-Old Children

Introduction, *324*

Subjects, *324*

Materials, *324*

Procedure, *325*

Testing, *327*

Criterion, *329*

Level at Which to Start, *330*

Choosing the Rewarded and Nonrewarded Members of Each Pair, *330*

The Reliability Study, *331*

This manual was prepared by Barbara Koslowski

INTRODUCTION

This test has been developed by the Harvard Preschool Project as one of a battery of new assessment techniques for children of chronological age (CA) one to three years. A preliminary finding of the project's research is that especially talented three- to six-year-old children are good observers. Such children notice small discrepancies in physical appearances, in the following of rules, in statements of logic, etc., sooner than do their peers. We have developed a simple test of the capacity to note discrepancies in physical appearances that may be used with children of CA one to three years.

SUBJECTS

Within the CA one to three years, we have repeatedly found it most difficult to test children 15 to 20 months of age. During these few months, the normal growth of autonomous behavior very often interferes with the requirements of test situations. Therefore, we do not ordinarily recommend the use of this or similar tests that require the child of this age to perform numerous cooperative acts.

Finally, mention should be made of the examiner's general attitude during testing. The aim is not to present the child with the test and then see how much of it he completes spontaneously. Rather, the examiner should try to induce the child to perform to his full capacity. Some suggestions for eliciting maximum performance from young children can be found in the "Procedure" section under the heading, "Reinforcement."

Materials. Eight pairs of test materials are used. The difficulty of these materials can be ordered on a Guttman scale.

The pairs can be divided into two groups. For the first three pairs—the three easiest—the relevant cues are rather gross differences between two objects. Within this group, the most discriminable pair of objects consists of two containers: a small, bright red, cylinder-shaped container, and a dull-green cup, about three times as large as the red container. The second pair of objects embodies only a size difference and consists of two opaque white plastic cups, one about three times as large as the other. The most difficult of this group of objects consists of two opaque plastic cups, identical except for color. One is white; the other, bright turquoise. In all three cases, the containers are turned upside down so that the positive container can conceal the reward.

The remaining pairs of stimuli present much finer differences. These stimuli consist of pairs of line drawings done in black ink, on white, 3-by-$2\frac{1}{2}$-inch cards about as thick as an index card. Using a ring of cellophane tape, each card is attached to an upside-down, opaque white plastic cup. These drawings are pictured on pages 326-27.

PROCEDURE

The present section deals only with *what* is done. The more involved *why*'s of the procedure are given in the footnotes.

The mother is asked to stay in the same room, although she need not sit right next to the child. In fact, the situation is often less testlike if she goes about her usual activities, providing they are not too distracting.

After rapport is established, the child is given some cereal, or a raisin, etc. (see Reinforcement section). This is done to spark his interest, to ascertain what, if anything, he has a preference for, and to give him the idea that the reward is his—that he is to look for it. After this, each pair of stimuli is presented for a training session, followed immediately by a testing session. If possible the examiner sits across a table from the child. If none is readily available, the box that contains the test materials doubles as a table.

Training. The child is allowed to play with the two test objects for a while. If the objects in question happen to be the cards and if S shows a preference for one of them, that card is the one used to cover the reward. For the rare cases in which the child shows no preference, and for the three easiest pairs, the list on page 330 shows which number of each pair conceals the reinforcement.

If cards are used on a training trial, E points to the drawings on both cards, tracing the general outline with his fingers, and making certain that the child is looking at the *drawings*. To avoid an uncomfortable silence, he usually accompanies the gestures with statements like, "See," "See the picture," "This one goes like this," etc. As a general rule, whenever oral language is used, it is kept to a minimum and consists of simple words: ball, circle, a lot, only one, etc.

Each stimulus pair is presented for three training trials. The right-left position of the positive stimulus is alternated during these three trials. Each trial proceeds as follows. The examiner shows the child the food, points to or outlines the positive drawing, and hides the food under the positive cup. He makes certain that the child looks at the drawing and then at the food, rather than just at the part of the table where the food is placed.*

---

*This is an attempt to make salient the fact that the reward is associated with one particular drawing.

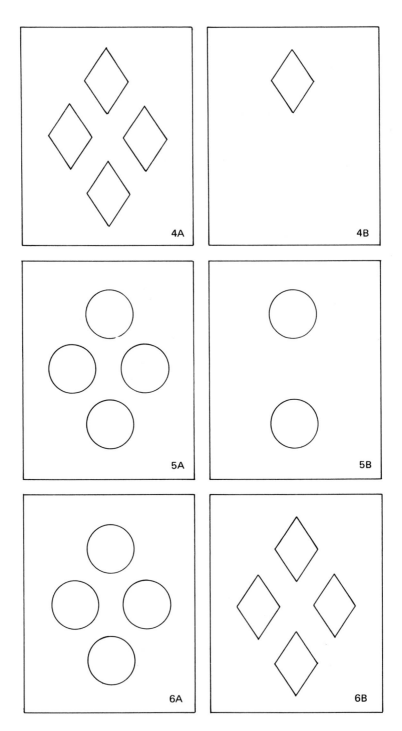

Figure 1A. Three of the five pairs of stimulus cards. These three pairs of cards constitute the fourth, fifth, and sixth pairs of stimuli.

Figure 1B. The remaining two of the five pairs of stimulus cards. These two pairs of cards constitute the seventh and eighth pairs of stimuli.

After the child finds and eats his reward, the examiner makes certain the child continues to watch while he changes the position of the stimuli (saying something like, "Now I'm going to move it," or, "Now it's going over here"), points to the positive stimulus, and hides the reward just as above.

Note that after each training trial, the positions of the test objects are alternated *before* the reward is hidden.*

Testing. During testing, a screen (an 8 1/2-by-11-inch piece of cardboard) is placed in front of the test objects before the reward is hidden.

Two points should be noted here. The first has to do with changing the position of the objects. Before the screen is put in front of the test objects, their

---

*If the examiner hides the reward and *then* alternates the positions of the test objects, some children have a tendency to designate the *place* where they saw the reward hidden; i.e., the place now occupied by the incorrect test object.

R-L position is disrupted. E either holds the positive one while he brings the screen down, or else places one object on top of the other while the screen is brought down.*

The second point has to do with alternating. Within any three consecutive correct trials (i.e., within criterion), one must omit the possibility that the child is responding to an alternation rule. Thus, any three consecutive correct trials place the positive stimulus in one of the following example patterns: R-R-L or R-L-L. After presenting each pair of test objects, the examiner scores the child's performance on the scoring sheet.

Reinforcement.   Three types of edible rewards are used for all children: raisins cut in half; miniature marshmallows cut into quarters; or pieces of sweet, dry cereal, such as Captain Crunch or Apple Jacks.

Two points should be noted here: If the child's attention or enthusiasm seems to be waning, one quite reliable way of increasing it is to change the reinforcement or (if it does not seem likely that the child will lose his appetite) to hide two different types of reinforcement on each trial.

Although many children will work ad infinitum for bits of food, some children require a bit more enticement to show what they can do. These are some suggestions that have worked in the past. They have been used both singly and in combination:

1. The mother may know whether the child has a strong preference for a particular kind of food and can usually be counted on to provide some.
2. Social rewards are often more valuable than any kind of food. To this end, being enthusiastic helps, in that children are particularly responsive to applause, cheers, bursts of "Good!" "Very nice!," pats on the head, and hugs.
3. Some children who find little pleasure in eating the reinforcement find true joy in collecting it. Such children are given a cup and told that they can "save" their raisins, etc., in the cup. The examiner augments this game with statements like, "Boy, you really have a lot in that cup," "That's really good," "Would you like to find some more for your cup?" etc.
4. One little girl who was delighted with her recent proficiency in using language was more than willing to play if each correct choice was followed by a word she did not know: super, groovy, stupendous, etc. A little boy first became excited by the game when each correct choice was followed by a raisin *and* a piece of cereal, a combination that the examiner called a "little breakfast."
5. If all else fails, the examiner might try hiding his or her own jewelry—an earring, bracelet, cuff link, tie clasp, etc.

Feedback.   Whenever S chooses the negative object of a pair, the examiner does the following: He does *not* allow S to lift the positive object. He points to the

*Again, if this is not done, some children automatically choose the *place* at which the reward was last hidden.

table where the negative object was and says, in a mildly woeful voice, "Oh! Too bad. No raisins. See! The raisins are over here, under this one" (as he lifts the positive object and points to the reward). He points to the drawing on the card and to the food, and then covers the reinforcement with the cup a few times to convey the fact that the reinforcement was under the positive object.

If the child then reaches for the reward, the examiner usually shakes his head and says, "No, I have to hide it again." An exception to this rule is made when it is clear that a child who guesses wrong is genuinely trying to learn how to play the game (as opposed to being interested only in getting the reward), and when such a child shows extreme disappointment in not being rewarded for a wrong choice.

CRITERION

Criterion for each pair of test objects is three consecutive correct trials out of seven. A trial ends when the child deliberately designates his choice in any of the following ways: pointing to, labeling, touching, or picking up one of the objects. If he picks up both objects, the trial is scored as incorrect.*

A certain pattern of responding is given special consideration during the testing. This pattern is shown by a child who seems to be using gestures to eliminate the negative object. During training, it is obvious that he is attending closely. Yet on each trial, he *consistently* touches or points to the negative object and then picks up the positive one. During testing, he does the same thing. Since his behavior is consistent, and since he does the same thing during training, the examiner should alter the criterion for the end of a trial to reflect this pattern of responding.

Level at which to start. Stimuli are chosen to ensure that the S is successful with at least the first two pairs he is presented with. The age norms on page 330 provide an approximate guide for this.

If, with seven trials, S is unable to reach criterion on a given stimulus pair, he is given the next most difficult pair, to make certain he has reached his limit. Once the child has failed two consecutive pairs of stimuli, the testing is stopped.

---

*The second special type of child is one who is very unsure of himself. During training, even though he is attending, he consistently designates the correct stimulus and then looks up at E and does not pick up the designated stimulus until E confirms his choice. Since what is involved is his lack of confidence rather than his lack of ability, the usual testing procedure is to continue either nodding or saying, "Yes, that's right," after S points to the correct stimulus. A fairly successful strategy one can try during training with this type of child is to ask her if her dolly, doggy, puppet, etc., can find the raisin. This reduces the level of ego involvement to manageable proportions, and saves the child from blame for a wrong choice. This low-confidence child is distinguished from one who is guessing by his behavior during training. A child who is guessing becomes unsure of himself only during testing. He does not need encouragement during training.

Controlling impulsiveness.* Occasionally, children show a tendency to lunge at random for a stimulus as soon as the screen is raised. To control for this, when E lifts the screen, he sees to it that the stimuli are too far away for the child to reach. After S has had a chance to look at them, E moves both stimuli toward him and allows him to choose one.

If the table area is too small to permit this, E might try lightly holding back the child's arms for a few seconds, or, with a verbal child, E might simply say, "Now wait a minute and look at them before you pick one."

If there is no table area, the surface on which the stimuli are placed can itself be moved, first away from, and then back close to the child.

LEVEL AT WHICH TO START

With any child younger than 24 months, start with stimulus pair #1. By 24 months of age, the first stimulus pair can be omitted, and the training may begin with pair #2. By 30 months, a bright child may be started with pair #3. A dull child, however, could probably benefit from the extra practice gained by starting with pair #2. A 36-month-old can be started with pair #4.

CHOOSING THE REWARDED AND UNREWARDED MEMBERS OF EACH PAIR

Stimulus Pair	Rewarded Member
1	small red container
2	the smaller of the two containers
3	white container
4-8	member A of each pair

(The same small white container is thus the rewarded member of both pair 2 and pair 3. Although this is unorthodox, it was reasoned that in both cases, in order to choose the rewarded container, the child would first have to discriminate it from the unrewarded one—and his discriminative ability is the prime concern of this test.)

In general, children of this age seem to prefer drawings that are either made up of a lot of, as opposed to few, stimuli (e.g., 4 and 5A instead of 4 and 5B), or else stimuli that are complete or consistent rather than those that are not (e.g., 7 and 8A instead of 7 and 8B).

*We realize that the classical studies of discrimination learning do not try to eliminate this variable. Rather, they regard it as one of the many obstacles the child should overcome on his own. However, the present test is aimed at assessing the child's discriminative capacity in the absence of interference.

SUMMARY OF THE RELIABILITY STUDY OF THE
SENSING-DISCREPANCIES INSTRUMENT

In order to determine whether the discrimination-learning procedure yields a measure of the child's discriminative ability that is relatively independent of the examiner, two examiners tested each of ten children. Five of the children were first tested by Examiner A; five were first tested by Examiner B. With one exception, there was a 48-hour interval between the two test sessions. For each child, both sessions occurred at the same time of day and in the same physical setting (either at a table or on the floor). In addition, both examiners started each child at the same level of stimulus difficulty.

The data from one of the originally scheduled children was discarded because her home situation made it impossible to test her reliably. The ten children whose results were used were of the following ages: 11, 11, 12, 22, 23, 24, 26, 27, 31, and 36 months.

The Pearson Product-Moment Correlation of the scores obtained by the two examiners was .9.*

Child	Child's Age in Months	Score Obtained by Examiner A X	Score Obtained by Examiner B Y	X^2	Y^2	XY
1	24	7	4	49	16	28
2	11	2	2	4	4	4
3	11	2	1	4	1	2
4	23	2	3	4	9	6
5	31	8	8	64	64	64
6	12	2	2	4	4	4
7	22	2	3	4	9	6
8	36	8	6	64	36	48
9	26	8	7	64	49	56
10	27	6	6	36	36	36
	$\Sigma =$	47	42	297	228	254

$r = (10 \times 254) - (47 \times 42) = 10 \times 297 - (47)^2 \ 10 \times 228 - (42)^2$

$$r = 0.9$$

*Additional reliability studies have been conducted following the procedures stated above. The Pearson Product-Moment Correlation obtained by two examiners in October 1970 was .92. The Pearson Product-Moment Correlation obtained by two examiners in January 1971 was .81.

F

Manual for Assessing
Social Abilities of
One- to Six-Year-Old Children

Instructions, *334*

Extent of Coverage, *334*

Amount of Scoring, *334*

Independence of Categories, 335

Reliability, 335

Checklist for Scoring Social Behavior, *335*

A. *Categories for Interaction with Adults, 335*
1. Attention of Adult—Positive 2. Attention of Adult—Negative
3. Uses Adult as Resource—Instrumental
4. Uses Adult as Resource—Emotional 5. Controls Adults
6. Compliance with Adult's Directives 7. Noncompliance
8. Expresses Affection 9. Expresses Hostility to Adults

B. *Categories for Interaction Between Peers, 342*
1. Attention of Peer 2. Peer as a Resource—Instrumental
3. Leads in Peer Activities—Positive or Neutral
4. Leads in Peer Activities—Negative 5. Being a Model
6. Follows Lead of Peer—Peer Gives Verbal Directions

This manual was prepared by Daniel Ogilvie and Bernice Shapiro, September 1969. Appended April 1970

7. Follows Lead of Peer—Peer Gives No Direction
8. Refuses to Follow, or Ignores Peer's Directions   9. Imitation of Peer
10. Expresses Affection to Peer   11. Expresses Hostility to Peers
12. Competes with Peers for Adult's Attention   13. Competes for Equipment
14. Pride in Product—Creation
15. Pride in Attribute—Possession, Action, Boasting
16. Imitation of Adult   17. Adult Role Play   18. Child Role Play

Social Behavior Checklist Additional Reliability Procedures, *351*

Checklist for Scoring Social Behavior, *351*

Scoring Social Behavior Checklist, *356*

INSTRUCTIONS

In the process of developing and refining a system for scoring social behavior of children, two checklists have been constructed. The first (Form A) is the complete checklist from which a summary form (Form B) was developed. Form B is used primarily for training purposes, and when satisfactory inter-rater reliability is achieved with Form B, the novice observer "graduates" to the more complex Form A for further training sessions. Since Form B is simply a collapsed version of Form A, the manual describes both.

EXTENT OF COVERAGE

It is important to note that no attempt has been made to score all social actions and interactions of children. As described elsewhere, great care has been taken to select variables that have been known to differentiate well-developed children from poorly developed children. Hence, the observer should not expect to score all social behaviors. Some actions cannot be categorized and should not be "forced" into the checklist.

AMOUNT OF SCORING

Each time subject performs a scorable act, a slash mark is placed in the appropriate cell. For example, if S calls to an adult and the adult does not respond, a slash mark is placed in cell Ic, unsuccessful. If S calls again and A still does not respond, another slash is placed in the same cell. Slash marks are added each time S calls. If A eventually responds (Ic, successful) and S asks for a cracker, a slash mark is placed under IIe (Resource: seeks food). In another example, S is arguing with P. P hits S, and S responds with same (Score: IXB2, responds). Several minutes later, S hits again (Score: B.11 physical), and seconds later throws a block at P (Score: B.11 physical). Acts in sections A.1,2,3,4,5, and B.1,2,3,4,12, and 13 should be scored according to whether they are successful or unsuccessful.

INDEPENDENCE OF CATEGORIES

An attempt has been made to describe each category with sufficient clarity to avoid both misscoring and multiple scoring. In a number of sections of the manual, categories likely to cause confusion are contrasted with related categories in an attempt to delineate category boundaries as carefully as possible. Each scorable act, then, should receive just *one* score. Multiple scoring of a single act should be avoided.

RELIABILITY

Reliability has been assessed by computing correlation coefficients on half-hour paired observations. Although this procedure does not directly determine, for example, if both observers simultaneously observe behavior A and score it in cell Z (only a minute-by-minute scoring breakdown could give that information), consistently high correlations obtained by observing a substantial number of children and by using rotating observers decreases the probability of chance agreements. In its current form, an overall correlation coefficient of .87 was computed on paired half-hour observations of 20 children, aged three to six, in seven preschools.

CHECKLIST FOR SCORING SOCIAL BEHAVIOR

A. Categories for Interaction with Adults

1. Attention of Adult—Positive

    a. Moves toward and stands or sits near A
    b. Touches A
    c. Calls to A
    d. Begins interaction with adult:

        (1) Tells something to A
        (2) Shows something to A

This section is meant to be scored at those times when a child does something designed to get the attention of an adult, whether it be the teacher, his mother, or a stranger. It does not matter for the purposes of this section what the child does once he has obtained the adult's attention. He may have no further end in mind, or he may go on to use the adult as a resource (see Section A.3), attempt to control the adult (see Section A.5), or express affection (see Section A.8).

We have found, after observing children between the ages of one and six, that the techniques children use to obtain the adult's attention can be grouped into six categories. Each of the six may be scored alone, or in combination if S uses more than one technique when trying to get the adult's attention.

a. *Moves toward and stands or sits near A.* Child places himself in the vicinity of an adult and waits or expects to be noticed by the adult. No score should be given if S just happens to be near and shows no attention-seeking behavior.

b. *Touches A.* This is meant to include all instances of a child's touching A or pulling at A's clothing in order to make the adult be aware of his presence and attend to him. Excluded from this definition are those instances in which a child seeks physical contact or comfort from an adult (see Section A.4), as well as those in which a child expresses affection to an adult by touching him in some way (see section A.8).

c. *Calls to A.* Any time a child calls out the adult's name or title ("Teacher"), or calls out "Mama" or its equivalent, he should receive a score here. Calls to A may also include yelling to A, whining, or speaking the adult's name. When a child both calls to an adult and touches the adult, he should receive two scores in this section. Each separate, discrete act is scored.

d. *Begins an interaction with A.*

(1) *Tells something to A*—In this category are included those times when a child initiates a conversation with an adult about things that the adult is not focused on at the moment. For example, in school a child might start to tell the teacher about something that went on at home, or over the weekend, or he might talk about the weather, or something he is doing. Generally, this will happen when an adult is nearby but doing something else; and, in order to get the adult to focus on him, a child might say, "I went to the zoo yesterday." The attempt to start a conversation is then interpreted as an attempt to get the attention of an adult. If the child uses the adult's name or touches her before saying "I went to the zoo," he would get a score for these specific actions as well.

(2) *Shows something to A*—This category is meant to cover those instances when a child shows something to an adult in order to begin an interaction or simply to be noticed. The child can show the adult practically anything; however, when the object is something the child has just made or seems proud of (i.e., new clothes), this behavior should be scored in section B.14, Pride in Product, or B.15, Pride in Attribute. Generally, the technique of showing to an adult to begin an interaction will involve materials in the classroom—i.e., the hamsters, or an interesting picture in a book. The object might also be something of no particular interest but simply used as an excuse for a conversation. If the showing of an object does in fact lead to a conversation, the child should receive two scores.

2. Attention of Adult—Negative

   a. Shows off
   b. Misbehaves

This section is meant to score those times when a child attempts to gain an adult's attention through negative behavior; that is, silliness, exaggerated actions, or misbehavior.

   a. *Shows off.* This phrase should be interpreted in its everyday meaning—namely, silly or exaggerated behavior performed with the specific intent of drawing attention to oneself and—for the purposes of this category—drawing the attention of an adult. Showing off for the benefit of peers would not be scored here.

   b. *Misbehaves.* This should also be interpreted in the everyday sense of the word, with the added feature of purposeful misbehaving in order to draw attention to oneself. Actions falling into this category are closely related to showing off, but they have a more negative character to them, such as making loud noises, pounding on the table, etc.

3. Uses Adult as Resource—Instrumental

   a. Seeks explanation or information
   b. Seeks A's judgment in peer dispute
   c. Seeks help with clothing
   d. Seeks help with equipment
   e. Seeks food

This section is intended to reflect the number of times a child is observed to make use of an adult in order to obtain something by means of a verbal request or demand, or a physical demonstration of his need. His object may be to gain information, assistance, or food, and he may demonstrate this by declaring what he wants, making a request, making a demand, or by gesturing, acting out, or pointing. A request is any statement that can end in a question mark. Behavior in the form of demands or orders to any adult that do not relate to resources are to be scored under section A.5, Controls Adult. Verbal requests or demands may include crying, whining, monosyllabic utterances, babbling, and words or word strings. In scoring resource categories, we assume the child's need for help or assistance in doing something or obtaining something he cannot or will not do alone. We are interested in scoring all attempts made by the child to use the adult as a resource.

   a. *Seeks explanation or information.* S requests clarification; asks T what something is used for, how it works, "What's that?" "When are we leaving?" "When is Daddy coming home?" "Is it my turn now?" "Do I have to clean up?"

   b. *Seeks A's judgment in peer dispute.* S asks T for support in argument with peer concerning whose turn it is to use something. "He won't let me have a turn with the bicycle."

S and P are having a dispute about whether S is her friend or her neighbor; finally, S turns to A as if to ask for some support from her. A says to S, "You can be a friend and a neighbor." This settles the dispute.

c. *Seeks help with clothing.*   In school settings, this behavior is often seen at recess time or at end of school day. S asks for assistance with zipper, hood, boots, etc. S may need help with smock, buttons, or dress-up costumes.

d. *Seeks help with equipment.*   S asks T how to use something; to obtain something for him; S may need help setting up new activity, such as painting; may ask T to fix something, or to write his name on painting.

S asks, "Will you read this to me?" "May I go outside?" (S requires help opening the door.)

"May I hear my records now?" (S requires help operating record player.)

S asks M to separate toy soldiers that are stuck together.

S is trying to erase a picture from his magic-sketch screen. He tries for a while, turns to A, saying, "I can't do it," and then hands the screen to A. A shakes it for him until the picture disappears.

e. *Seeks food or help with food.*   Ordinarily during snack time, S requests more food, or during meal time S needs help with food—opening containers, for example. S may request a drink during the morning. S may ask permission to have a cracker, even though he can obtain it by himself.

4. Uses Adult as Resource—Emotional

This section is intended to reflect the child's emotional dependency on an adult. Scores should be given whenever he demonstrates this dependency either verbally or physically.

Seeks comforting or reassurance.   After a hurt or disappointment, S seeks A's aid, support, or affection: this should be distinguished from situations where S demonstrates affection to A and may require on-the-spot interpretation; general dependency manifested by seeking comforting can be scored in this section. For example, S runs to M when a stranger enters the home.

5. Controls Adults

a. *Directs*

(1) Positive
(2) Neutral
(3) Negative

This section refers to those interactions in which the child attempts to control or influence the behavior of adults. The child's verbal or physical directives to A may be positive, neutral, or negative, depending upon the content of the directives and the style of delivery used. Children may control adults affectionately, naturally (matter-of-factly), or in a hostile fashion. Directives may be verbal as well as nonverbal.

Section A.3, Uses Adult as Resource—Instrumental, precedes Controls Adults, and many behaviors classified under the former section could also be placed under the latter. The command, "Get me some juice," is clearly an attempt to control A, but it is also an attempt to use A as a resource. To avoid double scoring, actions intended to control the behavior of A in order to use as a resource are categorized under section A.3. Aside from very strongly worded commands like "Shut up" or "Go to hell" (statements that would be scored under section A.9, Hostility) all remaining attempts at control are categorized under section A.5.

Examples

"Come play with me."

"Be careful so you won't fall."

Father enters home, and S says, "Come with me." F asks, "What do you want?" S takes him by the hand and enthusiastically leads him to her room to point out a picture that she has drawn that day.

"Sit down."

"Close the door."

"Drink your coffee so we can go."

S dressed herself in slacks and a jersey. Her mother comes downstairs in a dress. S says, "But Mom, you had better wear slacks today because I have some on."

A babysitter is putting away dishes and places a container in the wrong drawer. S shakes his head "No" and points to the correct drawer.

Mother is at the sink, washing breakfast dishes. S crawls toward M and attempts to open the door beneath the sink where some pots and pans are stored. M does not realize she is in S's way and S shoves her leg.

S inadvertently knocks over a glass of water. Mother sponges the area but misses some of the water. S says, "Look, you didn't get some!" in a scolding voice. M returns to complete the job.

S is in nursery school working with Play Doh. He hears P in hallway calling for assistance in opening a door. S yells impatiently to T, "Miss B, you get that door! P is bothering me."

M does not respond to being shoved by S. S pushes harder and screams "Ah!" M moves aside and says, "Oh, I'm sorry. Was I in your way?"

6. Compliance with Adult's Directives

This section is used to score those instances in which S readily complies with A's directive.

a. *Compliance.* Those times when S follows A's directive are scored in this category.

Examples

> Mother says to subject, "Go see if Joe's crying." S runs to living room and sits down by Joe.

> In another example, Mother says to subject, "Want to get Mommy a towel?" S goes into bedroom and returns with a dishcloth. M says, "That's a dishcloth, get me a towel." S returns with a bathroom towel.

> S is in kitchen while M is preparing supper. M says, "Please help Mommy; set the table." S opens silverware drawer and begins placing spoons, etc., on table.

> S and M are in S's room. M says, "Let's put away your blocks." S begins stacking blocks in block wagon.

> T says to S, "You may have only one tray at a time; put one back." S replaces one tray on its shelf.

7. Noncompliance

    a. Resistant—verbal
    b. Resistant—physical
    c. Disobeys or ignores

This section is used to score those times when S refuses to comply with A's directives; scoring is in three categories.

a. *Resistant-verbal.* All verbal noncompliance is scored in this category; for example, when S verbally says he does not want to do something suggested by A or verbally indicates through whining that he does not want to comply, such as in the following situations:

> Mother tries to put S's snowsuit on him. S whines and does not help her.

> Mother tells S it is time for his nap. S says "No" and whines.

b. *Resistant-physical.* This form of noncompliance may occur alone or along with verbal noncompliance. If both verbal and physical resistance occur, they are viewed as two discrete behaviors and warrant two scores under section V.

Examples

> M tries to put S's snowsuit on him; S whines and hides his feet in such a way as to hinder the mother's putting his snowsuit on.

> T tells S to play in another room. S does not move. T comes over to S and takes his hand. S drops to floor and lies limp in T's hands. T must pull S out of the room with no help from S.

c. *Disobeys or ignores.* The most obvious noncompliant behavior occurs when S actively disobeys A's directive by doing something else. Implied disobedience occurs when S ignores A's directive.

For example, T says to S, "Clean up now, S." S then reaches for additional blocks to add on to his building.

8. Expresses Affection

a. Verbal

   (1) Smiles or laughs
   (2) Makes friendly statement

b. Physical

   (1) Touches
   (2) Shares or makes friendly gesture

The four subcategories under this section are intended to measure behaviors that leave no doubt in the observer's mind that affection is being expressed. Friendly statements made by S that attempt to control the behavior of A, such as "Sit next to me," "Play with me," are scored under section A.5, Controls Adult.

a. Verbal

   (1) *Smiles or laughs*—This category is reserved for instances in which S expresses focused pleasure to A in his presence. If A comes over to S and S looks up and smiles at A, S receives a score.

   (2) *Makes friendly statement*—Statements like "I like you," "You're nice," are statements of affection. As stated above, certain friendly statements that are aimed at controlling the behavior of A ("Sit next to me") are scored under section A.5, Controls Adult.

b. Physical

   (1) *Touches*—Expressions of physical affection to A, like hugging, embracing, holding, and patting are scored in this category. T is reading a story to a small group of children. S is standing next to T. As T reads, S puts her arm around T's shoulders.

   (2) *Shares or makes friendly gestures*—This category is used when S offers A a valued object (food, toy, game, etc.) or engages in behavior indicative of concern over the welfare or comfort of A (gets chair for A, retrieves dropped object).

The following form of social behavior is also classified in this category:

A is a guest who has just arrived at S's home. S immediately hands A a doll, paper clip, block, etc. Although one might be tempted to score this behavior in section B.14 (Shows Pride in Product or Possession), we have witnessed this sequence often enough to be convinced that the nature of the behavior is friendly; it is often the child's way of saying: "I'll be your friend." On the other hand, if such behavior persists or if it begins after an extended visit, it is scored appropriately under section B.14 (Pride in Product) or section A.1 (Attention of Adult), depending on other characteristics of the behavior.

9. Expresses Hostility to Adults

   a. Verbal
   b. Physical

      (1) Hits, grabs, throws objects, etc.
      (2) Tantrum
      (3) Rejects physical affection.

The categories under this section are types of behaviors that leave no doubt in the observer's mind that direct or displaced hostility to A is being expressed by S.

Often a thin line differentiates verbal hostility from verbal control of A (section A.5). If the communication is phrased in terms of a demand intended to produce physical action or physical confinement on the part of A ("Leave me alone," "Get out of here," "Move!"), the behavior is scored under controlling (section A.5).

   a. *Verbal*—Forthright statements of personal dislike ("I hate you"), strong and definite vocal rejections of A ("You're bad"), and other firmly stated expressions that betray momentary or long-standing dislike of A are one type of hostility S expresses to A.

   b. *Physical*:

      (1) *Hits, grabs, throws objects, etc.*—Hostile actions that entail direct physical contact (also near misses) are another type of hostility. Hitting, slapping, pulling hair, biting, spitting, kicking, and throwing objects or toys are examples of behaviors that should be scored under section A.9.
      (2) *Tantrum*—More displaced patterns of hostile behavior are tantrums. Head banging, screaming, holding breath, various forms of writhing, and dumping food or objects intentionally and angrily onto the floor are scored here when the observer is convinced that such behavior is an alternative to more direct expression of anger toward A.
      (3) *Rejects physical affection*—When an adult attempts to comfort a child by means of physical affection (hugs, touches, strokes) after a disappointment or mishap and the child withdraws from A or actively rejects the affection, a score for hostility is placed under this section. The physical affection expressed by the adult must be clear and direct, rather than a casual pat or touch.

B. Categories for Interaction Between Peers

1. Attention of Peer

   a. Moves toward and stands or sits near P
   b. Touches P
   c. Calls to P

    d. Begins interaction with P:

        (1) Tells something to P

        (2) Shows something to P

    e. Shows off

This section is meant to score those times when a child does something designed to get the attention of a peer. It does not matter what occurs after the attention has been sought or obtained. The child may have no further end in mind, or he may go on to use the peer as a resource (See Part B, section 2), attempt to lead the peer (See Part B, section 3), or express affection (See Part B, section 10). Each of the following six categories may be scored alone or in combination with others.

    a. *Moves toward and stands or sits near P.* Child places himself in the vicinity of a peer and waits or expects to be noticed by the peer. No score should be given if S just happens to be near P and shows no attention-seeking behavior.

    b. *Touches P.* This is meant to include all instances of a child's touching P or pulling at P's clothing in order to make the peer be aware of his presence and attend to him. Excluded from this definition are those instances in which a child seeks physical contact or comfort from a peer, as well as those in which a child expresses affection to a peer by touching him in some way (see section B.10).

    c. *Calls to P.* Any time a child calls out the peer's name or title, he should receive a score here. Calls to P may also include yelling to P, whining, or speaking the peer's name. When a child both calls to a peer and touches the peer, he should receive two scores in this section. Each separate, discrete act is scored.

    d. *Begins an interaction with P:*

        (1) *Tells something to P*—In this category are included those times when a child initiates a conversation with a peer about things that the peer is not focused on at the moment. For example, in school a child might start to tell another student about something that went on at home, or over the weekend, or he might talk about the weather, or something he is doing. Generally, this will happen when a peer is nearby but doing something else; and in order to get his friend to focus on him, a child might say, "I went to the zoo yesterday." The attempt to start a conversation is then interpreted as an attempt to get the attention of a peer. If the child uses the peer's name or touches him before saying, "I went to the zoo," he would get a score for these specific actions as well.

        (2) *Shows something to P*—This category is meant to cover those instances when a child shows something to a peer in order to begin an interaction or simply to be noticed. The child can show the peer practically anything; however, when the object is something the child has just made or seems to be proud of (i.e., new clothes), this behavior should

be scored in section B.14, Pride in Product, or B.15, Pride in Attribute. Generally, the technique of showing something to a peer to begin an interaction will involve materials in the classroom—i.e., the hamsters, or an interesting picture in a book. The object might also be something of no particular interest but simply used as an excuse for a conversation. If the showing of an object does in fact lead to a conversation, the child should receive two scores.

e. *Shows off.* This phrase should be interpreted in its everyday meaning; namely, silly or exaggerated behavior performed with the specific intent of drawing attention to oneself and—for the purposes of this category—drawing the attention of a peer. Showing off for the benefit of an adult would not be scored here.

2. Peer as a Resource—Instrumental

a. Seeks information or explanation
b. Seeks P's judgment in dispute
c. Seeks help with clothing
d. Seeks help with equipment

This section reflects S's tendency to use peers or siblings as a means of obtaining information or help. It is intended for situations in which S makes a request or poses a question to a peer, makes a demand or statement, or otherwise indicates a need or desire for help or information. Such items should be scored in section B, 3 or 4.

a. *Information or explanation*

"What are you doing?" "Why are you doing it that way?" "Where are my clocks?"

S: "Where's the hammer?" to peer, as they are searching for some toys in a box.

"May I play with that after you?" "Can I sit next to you?"

b. *Judgment*

S brings in peer B when S cannot convince peer A of something. S seeks support for his position. S asks peer A for support during argument with peer B.

c. *Clothing*

S asks peer instead of T to tie shoe, etc. S: "Can you tie my shoe?"

d. *Equipment*

S requests peer's help in obtaining a toy or asks for demonstration of how to work something. S asks peer to put record on phonograph.

S has been trying to erase another picture from his magic-sketch screen. He turns to P and says, "I can't do this, you know." Peer ignores him.

S asks peer to pour juice for him.

3. Leads in Peer Activities—Positive or Neutral

4. Leads in Peer Activities—Negative

These sections refer to those interactions in which the child attempts to control or influence the behavior of his peers. In order to avoid double scoring, actions that are intended to control the behavior of a peer in order to obtain a resource are scored under Part B, section II, Uses Peer as Resource, rather than here; and strongly worded commands that indicate hostility are scored under Part B, Expresses Hostility to Peers.

The child's verbal or physical directive to a peer may be positive, neutral, or negative, depending upon the content of the directive and the affect expressed by the style of delivery or tone of the child's communication; that is, whether the directive given is affectionate, matter-of-fact, or hostile.

Examples:

"Come over to my house after school."

"Sit next to me."

S and P are playing catch in a driveway. Ball goes in street. P starts to go after it. S says, "Be careful! If you go in the street you might get hurt by a car."

"Sit down."

"Close the door."

S and P are playing on the jungle gym. S is sitting at the top and says to P, "Come up here."

"Give him back his truck!"

S says to P, "Get off my blanket!"

5. Being a Model

In addition to verbal and physical directives, a child may exert influence or control over peers through a modeling process. Any attempt to set himself up as a model for peer behavior, when unaccompanied by a directive, is scored under section 5, Serves as a Model for Peer.

Examples:

S and P are playing with blocks while sitting on the floor. S gets up and runs to the piano. He pounds on the keys, and P follows him and also pounds on the keys. S then goes to the clothes corner and selects a fireman's hat, which he puts on his head. P comes after him and says, "I'll be a fireman, too," and he also puts a fireman's hat on his head.

S and P are sitting at a table playing with clay. S says, "I think I'll make an elephant," and proceeds to do so. P watches S and follows his exact procedure as he also makes an elephant.

6. Follows Lead of Peer—Peer Gives Verbal Directions

a. Peer tells S what to do.

   b. Peer tells S how to do something.
   c. S follows but modifies P's directions.

This section is concerned with the instances in which S follows the lead of a peer, including direct imitations and more subtle following behaviors.

We have classified three types of following behaviors:

   (1) *What to do*—This reaction is scored as following P's lead when S responds to a direction given by a peer.

   P: "Let's play ball here." S joins P and plays ball.

   (2) *How do do something*—When S does an activity according to P's directions of *how* to do it, this behavior is scored as following the lead of a peer.

   P: "Throw the ball like this." S does what P directs him to do.

   S is coloring. P walks over to S and says, "Use this crayon now." S follows P's directions.

   (3) *Follows but modifies*—When S follows the basic idea P suggests but modifies it, his behavior is scored under this section.

   P: "Let's play ball here." S: "Let's play ball outside."

   P: "Let's build a house." S: "Let's make it a teepee."

7. Follows Lead of Peer—Peer Gives No Directions

This section lists five possible reactions S may give to P's physical or verbal *behavior* (exclusive of directions scored in Section B.6).

   a. Involved observation
   b. Verbally supports Peer's statement
   c. Follows peer around
   d. Joins peers engaged in specific activity

   (1) *Involved observation*—When S is obviously "caught up" visually with peer's behavior, he gets a score under this section. S watches intently as P paints, for example.

   (2) *Verbally supports peer's statement*—When a peer says something and S verbally supports the P's comment, a score is placed under this section.

P, when listening to a record of "Peter and the Wolf," says, "Oh, this is really scary." S says, "Oh, I'm scared."

P says to P2, "You're scribbling!" P2 answers, "I am not." S says, "You are too!"

   c. *Follows peer around.* S's behavior is scored when he literally follows a peer around inside or outside. There is no additional interaction. S is just a tag-along.

   d. *Joins peers engaged in specific activity.* When S sees peer doing something and joins him in his activity, his behavior is scored as following peer's behavior. He may or may not have been doing something else before he joins the peer or peers.

S sees peers looking at hamsters. He walks over to them and joins them in looking at the hamsters.

8. Refuses to Follow, or Ignores Peer's Directions

This section is used to tabulate S's refusals to follow a peer's directions. Examples:

Peer and S are building with blocks. P says, "Put that block up here, okay?" S says, "No more up there."

S is coloring. P walks over to S and says, "Let's play in the doll corner." S continues to color.

9. Imitation of Peer

We are interested in scoring all immediate peer imitation here, whether it be repetition of words, sentences, gestures, or a sequence of behavior. The model and the behavior copies should be noted as well as the scoring.

Repeats sound or action. When S repeats a sound or action done first by P, his behavior is scored as following peer's behavior. The observer will also score the instances when S slightly modifies P's sound or action.

P says, "Bang, Bang." S a few moments later says, "Bang, bang, bang."

P shakes head in time to music. S, who has been watching P, starts to shake her head and moves her arms in time as well.

10. Expresses Affection to Peer

  a. Verbal:

    (1) Smiles or laughs
    (2) Makes friendly statement

  b. Physical—touches (hugs)
  c. Offers help or shares

This section is intended to measure direct verbal or physical expressions of affection to peers. Criteria for scoring such behavior are very similar to those stated in section A.8, Expresses Affection to Adults; that is, behavior that leaves no doubt in the observer's mind that affection is being expressed. Friendly statements that attempt to control the behavior of a peer, such as "Sit next to me," "Come play with me," are scored in section B.3, Leads in Peer Activities.

  a. Verbal:

    (1) *Smiles or laughs.* When S expresses focused pleasure to a peer in his presence by smiling at him or by friendly laughing with him, the behavior is scored as expressing affection.

    A peer comes over to S, and S looks up and smiles at P.

    (2) *Makes friendly statement*

S and peer are looking at a book together when S says to P, "I like you; you're my best friend."

In another example, S and P are on swings and P says to S, "I like you." S smiles and says, "I like you, too."

b. *Physical—touches and hugs*

S and P are listening to a story, when S puts his arm around P's shoulder. This is scored as physical affection. Behaviors such as hugging, patting, embracing, and holding hands are scored as expressions of affection.

c. *Offers help or shares*

When S offers P a valued object (game, toy, food, etc.) or engages in behavior indicative of concern over the welfare or comfort of P (gets crayons for P, retrieves a dropped object, helps P put on his shoes), this behavior is scored as expressing affection to P.

11. Expresses Hostility to Peer

a. Verbal
b. Physical:

(1) Hits, grabs, spits, etc.
(2) Physically disrupts peer's activity (equipment)
(3) Refuses to share
(4) Rejects physical affection

This section is intended to measure direct verbal or physical expressions of hostility to peers. Criteria for scoring such behavior are very similar to those stated in section A.7, Expresses Hostility to Adults; that is, behavior that leaves no doubt in the observer's mind that hostility is being expressed.

a. *Verbal.* Forthright statements of personal dislike ("I hate you"), strong and definite vocal rejections of a peer ("You're not my friend"), and other firmly stated expressions that betray momentary or long-standing dislike of P are scored as expressions of hostility to peers.

Often a thin line differentiates verbal hostility from negative verbal directing of peers (section B.4). If the communication is phrased in terms of a demand intended to produce physical action or physical confinement on the part of P ("Leave me alone"; "Get out of here"; "You can't play with us"; "Move!"), the behavior is scored as giving directions (section B.4).

b. *Physical:*

(1) *Hits, grabs, spits, etc.*—Hostile actions that entail direct physical contact (also near misses) fall into this category. Hitting, slapping, pulling hair, biting, spitting, kicking, or throwing objects or toys are examples of behaviors scored as physical hostility.

(2) *Physically disrupts peers' activity*—A group of peers is building an

elaborate block structure, when S attempts to join them. P says to S, "You can't play with us," to which S responds by knocking down the structure.

(3) *Refuses to share*—S is coloring at a table, when P arrives with a sheet of paper and asks to share the crayons. S refuses, saying, "I'm using them now; you can't have any."

(4) *Rejects physical affection*—S and P are lining up to go outside. T tells class to choose partners. P takes S's hand; S pulls away.

12. Competes with Peers for Adult's Attention

S's overt competitive behavior is scored in this section. Unlike some of the other sections, this one demands on-the-spot interpretation of the behavior with the aid of situational and behavioral cues. Often competitive behavior can be seen as S and P try to use the same toy or to get A's attention; however, the observer should decide whether or not the competition is overtly present and then score the behavior in the most appropriate section. Often S will compete for A's attention with one or more peers. This can occur in a didactic situation when S wants to say something to the T. Or S can begin a conversation with T who is paying attention to someone else, and this is scored as competition.

> T is reading to the class. She asks, "What happens next?" S and several peers wave their hands trying to get T's attention so they can give the answer. In another example, T is trying P's shoelace and S approaches and says, "He has new shoes on." S receives a score under section 12.

13. Competes for Equipment

A common source of competition is over equipment. This competition may be a silent tug-of-war over a toy, a verbal argument, or a combination of verbal and physical competition. S may or may not have possession of the item at first. Examples:

> S and P both want to ride on a swing in the playground. They run to it and both pull at it. P lets go. S swings.

> P (or S) has a ball. S (or P) tries to take it away; after some words and pulling, S (or P) gains possession of the ball.

14. Pride in Product—Creation

This section is used to score those times when a child is pleased with something he has created and shows it in some way. Expressions of pride in product need not be verbal. The focus of such behavior can be to a peer, to A, to A and peers, or to self. Examples:

> S finishes drawing a picture and holds it up in front of himself and smiles broadly.

> S takes a clay figure he made over to T and shows it to her.

> S says to P, "Look at my picture."

15. *Pride in Attribute—Possession, Action, Boasting*

S may express pride in something he owns or possesses at the moment, (Possession), something he is in the process of doing or has done (Actions), or something he claims he can do (Boasting).
Examples:

"Look at my new car."

"This is a dress my mother made."

If S expresses pride in something he has done, is doing, or claims he can do, a score is placed in this section.

"Yesterday I made a big tower at home."

"Look what I'm doing."

"I can hold six glasses in my hand at once."

"Teacher, I can climb up here."

16. *Imitation of Adult*

    a. Imitates adult's statements
    b. Imitates adult's actions

a. *Imitates A's statements.* When S directly repeats or imitates a statement made by an adult who is present, this behavior should be scored under section B.16.

b. *Imitates A's actions.* When S directly repeats or imitates an action done by an adult who is present, this behavior should be scored under section B.16.
Examples:

T says to class, "It's clean-up time." S repeats, "It's clean-up time."

Mother is sweeping the floor, finishes, places broom against wall. S comes over to the broom, takes it, and sweeps the floor as mother did.

17. *Adult Role Play*

S's role-playing behavior as an adult is scored under this section. Most of these instances will occur during a free-play situation. Sometimes, S might refer to his "growing up" in conversation. Occasionally S may take on the role of an animal that is analogous to a human role, such as Mama or Papa Bear in "The Three Bears." When this occurs, the observer can score S's role as adult role playing.

    a. Dresses up like adult
    b. Plays adult role
    c. Expresses desire to grow up

a. *Dresses like A.* Frequently, adult role playing can be seen when S dresses up like an adult. A subject may put on an old pair of her mother's shoes. In school, a subject may wear a man's coat and hat. No verbal conversation is necessary for S to get a score.

b. *Plays adult role.* When S plays an adult role, such as mother, father, teacher, policeman, or fireman, a score is placed in this section. Usually S will demonstrate an extended behavioral sequence while playing an adult role. That is, the observer may see or hear several cues indicating S is involved in adult role playing.

For example: S and P are in the doll corner. S puts on high heels and a woman's dress. She turns to P and says, "Go make your bed and then we will go to the store."

c. *Expresses desire to grow up.* When S refers to his growing up, getting bigger and older, the reference is scored as an expression of the desire to grow up under section B.16. Such a comment can be made to a peer or an adult.

For example: S to T: "My grandmother gave some earrings to my mother for me." T to S: "When can you wear them?" S to T: "When I get older, my mother says I can have them for my own."

18. Child Role Play

a. Plays immature role
b. Expresses desire to remain a child

S's role-playing behavior as a baby or expressions of a desire to remain young or a child are scored under this section. Occasionally S may take on the role of an animal that is analogous to a human role, such as Baby Bear in "The Three Bears." The observer can score such behavior as immature role playing.

a. *Plays immature role.* When S is playing an immature role, such as a baby, his behavior is scored under section B.18. He may act or verbalize like a baby (crawling, babbling, fake crying) or allow himself to be treated as a baby.

For example: S and P are in doll corner. P is the mother. S pretends to be the baby and allows himself to be wheeled around in the baby carriage.

b. *Expresses desire to remain a child.* This behavior is analogous to section B.16, except for the fact that S says something about being small, young, or a baby. This can occur in conversation with T or P or in role playing.

For example: P says to S, "I'm a big ape." S replies to P, "I'm a little monkey and I'm scared." S says, "I'm little," or "I'm too small to do that."

SOCIAL BEHAVIOR CHECKLIST
ADDITIONAL RELIABILITY PROCEDURES

Interobserver agreement using the Social Behavior Checklist was ascertained by comparing the frequencies for each category of behavior during a series of ten half-hour observations of children one to three years old. The checklist consists of forty categories, half of which pertain to adult-child interaction and the other half of which concern child-child interaction. If a child was seen in a situation involving only himself and his mother, only twenty categories were used to compute reliability; otherwise, forty categories were considered in the calculations. On the basis of these check marks, Pearson Product-Moment correlations were computed on ten paired observations, as explained in an earlier document.

SOCIAL BEHAVIOR-RELIABILITY

In order to ascertain interobserver agreement on the Social Behavior Checklist, simultaneous observations by two observers were carried out on ten subjects between the ages of one and three years. Each observation lasting one half hour took place during the week of December 8, 1970, in the child's home. The following table shows individual and overall Pearson Product-Moment correlations for both one- to two-year-olds and two- to three-year-olds.

Subject	Interobserver agreement	Overall agreement for subjects 1-2 years
A boy 13 mos.	1.00	
B boy 17 mos.	.860	
C girl 15 mos.	.628	.850
D boy 17 mos.	.854	
E boy 13 mos.	.906	

Subject	Interobserver agreement	Overall agreement for subjects 2-3 years
A girl 35 mos.	.868	
B boy 34 mos.	.909	
C boy 26 mos.	.822	.835
D girl 25 mos.	.943	
E girl 29 mos.	.635	

Overall agreement
for subjects 1-3
years

.843

CHECKLIST FOR SCORING SOCIAL BEHAVIOR

NAME   DATE AND TIME

CODE # _____ AGE _____ PLACE OF OBS. _____ OBSERVER _____

A. Categories for Interaction between Child and Adult

1. Attention of Adult—Positive
   (Examples of behavior to be scored; moves
   toward and stands or sits near A; touches A; calls
   to A; shows something to A; tells something to A)

Successful	Unsuccessful

2. Attention of Adult—Negative
   (Shows off; misbehaves)

Successful	Unsuccessful

3. Uses Adult as a Resource—Instrumental
   (Seeks explanation or information; seeks A's
   judgment in peer dispute; seeks A's help with
   clothing, equipment, or food)

Successful	Unsuccessful

4. Uses Adult as a Resource—Emotional
   (Seeks comforting, seeks reassurance)

Successful	Unsuccessful

5. Controls Adult—Positive, Neutral, or Negative
   (Directs A in a positive, neutral, or negative
   manner)

Successful	Unsuccessful

6. Compliance with Adult's Directives
   (Child readily follows A's directives)

7. Noncompliance with Adult's Directives
   (Resistance, either verbal or physical; disobeys,
   ignores)

8. Expresses Affection to Adult
   (Verbal affection—smiles, laughs, makes friendly
   statement; physical affection—touches, hugs,
   shares, makes friendly gesture)

9. Expresses Hostility to Adult
   (Verbal—rejections or expressions of dislike;
   physical—hits, grabs, throws object, tantrum,
   rejects physical affection)

Verbal	Physical

(cont.)

353

CHECKLIST FOR SCORING SOCIAL BEHAVIOR (cont.)

10. Imitation of Adult
    (Direct imitation of adult's statement or action)

11. Pride in Product—Creation
    (Expressions of pride in a creation S has completed; either to self, peer, or adult)

12. Pride in Attribute
    (Expression of pride in possessions or actions; boasting)

13. Adult Role Play (time entire sequence)
    (Dresses up like adult, plays adult role, expresses desire to grow up)

14. Child Role Play
    (Plays immature role, expresses desire to remain a child)

Note: Please list comments about this subject on reverse side.

B. Categories for Interaction between Peers

1. Attention of Peer
   (Moves toward and stands or sits near P; touches P; calls to P; shows something to P; tells something to P; shows off)

Successful	Unsuccessful

2. Uses Peer as a Resource—Instrumental
   (seeks explanation or information; seeks P's help with clothing or equipment)

Successful	Unsuccessful

3. Leads in Peer Activities—Positive or Neutral
   (Directs P in a positive or neutral manner)

Successful	Unsuccessful

4. Leads in Peer Activities—Negative
   (Directs P in a negative manner)

Successful	Unsuccessful

(cont.)

5. Serves as a Model for Peer
(Situations where S is copied by P without having given P any directions to do so)

6. Follows Lead of Peer—Peer gives S Verbal Directions
(Follows P in what to do or how to do something; follows but modifies peer's directions)

7. Follows Lead of Peer—Peer gives No Verbal Directions
(Involved observation; verbally supports peer's statement; follows peer around; joins peer or group engaged in specific activity)

8. Refuses to Follow Peer's Directions
(Resists, refuses, disobeys, or ignores peer's directions)

9. Imitation of Peer
(Repeats sound or action of peer—e.g., word, phrase, sentence, gesture, sequence of behavior in game, etc.)

Who	What

10. Expresses Affection to Peer
(Verbal—smiles, laughs, makes friendly statement; physical—touches, hugs, offers of help or sharing)

11. Expresses Hostility to Peer
(Verbal—hostile or resistant statements; physical—hits, grabs, spits, physically disrupts peer's activity or equipment, refuses to share, rejects physical affection)

Verbal	Physical

12. Competes with Peer for Adult's Attention
(Talks about materials or peers in which A is showing an interest; tries to be picked by A for a specific task)

Successful	Unsuccessful

13. Competes with Peer for Equipment
(Verbal or physical competition over classroom objects or equipment)

Successful	Unsuccessful

SOCIAL COMPETENCE: SCORING INFORMATION

After having collected data on the social behavior of children aged one to three years for the past year, we needed to calculate indices of social competence for each child. Using the original eight dimensions of social competence that formed the basis for the Social Behavior Checklist, we derived a scoring system based in part on raw frequencies and in part on bonuses for favorable ratios of positive to negative and successful to unsuccessful behaviors. To be exact, the following discussion shows, for each dimension, what elements contributed to the overall competence scores.

Each of the eight dimensions of social competence is scored for each subject. One-year-olds' scores are computed separately from two-year-olds'. Raw scores are converted to standard scores, with the maximum score in each age group (ones and twos) receiving 10 points, and the intervening scores proportioned in between 0 and 10. The adult competence score consists of five dimensions: gaining the attention of an adult, using the adult as a resource, expressing affection and hostility to adults, showing pride in product, and adult role play. The peer competence score consists of three dimensions: leading and following, expression of affection and hostility, and competition for equipment and for adult's attention. Peer competence scores were computed only where sufficient interaction warranted their inclusion; that is, if during at least 60 percent of the time a child was observed, he was in the presence of peers, then his peer score was computed. For children with both adult and peer scores, a combined index of social competence is computed based on all eight dimensions.

In summary, scores on all dimensions are converted to standard scores that range from 0 to 10. The maximum adult-competence score is 50; the maximum peer-competence score is 30; the maximum combined score is 80.

SCORING SOCIAL BEHAVIOR CHECKLIST

Getting an Adult's Attention

From a psychological point of view, the ability to get an adult's attention through socially acceptable means is one factor contributing heavily to the social-competence score. The frequency of successful socially acceptable attempts is counted; if success outweighs lack of success on this dimension, a bonus of 2 points is added. The actual ratio of success to lack of success is added to the score (with a maximum ratio of 5); if total frequency of positive attention-getting attempts is greater than total frequency of negative attention-getting attempts, then a bonus of 2 points is added. Finally, the ratio of positive to negative attention-getting attempts is entered into the score. These elements are then added to produce a score on dimension one: getting an adult's attention.

Using an Adult as a Resource

If a child shows success in utilizing an adult as a resource, either instrumentally or emotionally, then the total frequency of such success is added to his competence score and receives greatest weight; further, a bonus of 2 points accrues if success outweighs failure in using an adult instrumentally; next, a 2-point bonus is added for success outweighing failure in using an adult as an emotional resource; then the ratio of success to failure is entered in using an adult instrumentally (with a maximum of 5); the ratio of using the adult as an instrumental vs. an emotional resource is then added to the competence score for dimension two, using an adult as a resource.

Expression of Affection and Hostility to Adults

The child's ability to express *both* affection and hostility is viewed as a manifestation of social competence. The total frequency of affection scores is added if the scores for affection outweigh the hostility scores, then the frequency of hostility scores is added; the presence of hostility scores receives a bonus of 2 points, and the ratio of affection to hostility is entered, with a maximum of 5. This method ensures equal weighting of affection and hostility.

Pride in Product

This dimension of social competence has been weighted equally in the scoring system, despite its lower frequency overall. Expressions of pride in creations, possessions, or actions are added to a subject's score in their raw frequency form.

Adult Role Play

Similar to pride in product in its less frequent occurrence, this dimension is likewise given equal weight in the scoring system, with total frequency of such scores entered into the competence score.

Leading and Following: Peers and Children

The ability to lead and follow other children (under age seven) is another dimension of social competence. The frequency of positive (or neutral) leadership attempts, combined with the frequency of following other children (with or without verbal directions) formed one part of this score and receives greatest weight; further, if successful leadership attempts (positive, neutral, or negative) outnumbered unsuccessful attempts, a bonus of 2 points accrued; the ratio of success to failure in leadership attempts was added (with a maximum of 5); and finally, the subject received a bonus of 2 points if overall leadership attempts outweighed the following.

Expression of Affection and Hostility to Peers and Children

The subject's total affection frequency was entered, followed by a bonus for expression of hostility, and the inclusion of the ratio of affection to hostility. The frequency of hostility scores is entered only if affection scores are present.

Competition with Peers and Children

The score for competition consists of the number of successful attempts at competing for adult's attention and for equipment, added to which is the ratio of success to failure in competition attempts.

COMPETENCE FACTORS

For Col. # headings, see Social Behavior Checklist numbers entered in boxes on following page.

SUBJECT: _____ AGE: _____ CYCLE: _____

Type A (Col 9 = 0 or blank)	Type B (Col 9 = 1, 2, 3, 4, 5)
Col: 10 12 14 16 18 20 22 24 34 36 38 46	Col: 18 20 22 24 28 30 42 44 46 48 50
Total — — — — — — — — — — — —	Total — — — — — — — — — — —
Col: 48 50	Col: 52 54
Total — —	Total — —

(cont.)

COMPETENCE FACTORS (cont.)

$10 \rightarrow$ _____

if $10 > 12, \underline{2} \rightarrow$ _____

$10/12 \rightarrow$ $0 > $ _____ > 5

if $10 + 12 > 14 + 16, \underline{2} \rightarrow$ _____

$10 + 12/14 + 16 \rightarrow$ $0 > $ _____ > 5

A = Attention of Adult   _____

$18 + 22 \rightarrow$ _____

$18 > 20, \underline{2} \rightarrow$ _____

$18/20 \rightarrow$ $0 > $ _____ > 5

if $20 > 24, \underline{2} \rightarrow$ _____

$18 + 20/22 + 24 \rightarrow$ $0 > $ _____ > 5

R = Using Adult as a Resource   _____

$34 \rightarrow$ _____

if $34 - 36 - 38 > 0, 36 + 38 \rightarrow$ _____

if $36 + 38 > 2, \underline{2} \rightarrow$ _____

$34/36 + 38 \rightarrow$ $0 > $ _____ > 5

RA = Expression of Affection
       and Hostility to Adults   _____

PP = 46 + 48   _____
PP = Pride in Product

RP = 50   _____
RP = Role Play

$18 + 20 + 28 + 30 \rightarrow$ _____

if $18 + 22 > 20 + 24, \underline{2} \rightarrow$ _____

$18 + 22/20 + 24 \rightarrow$ $0 > $ _____ > 5

if $18 + 20 + 22 + 24 > 28 + 30, \underline{2} \rightarrow$

   _____

LF = Leading and Following
      Peers and Children   _____

$42 \rightarrow$ _____

if $42 - 44 - 46 > 0, 44 + 46 \rightarrow$ _____

if $44 + 46 > 2, \underline{2} \rightarrow$ _____

$42/44 + 46 \rightarrow$ $0 > $ _____ > 5

RP = Expression of Affection   _____
      and Hostility to Peers and Children

$48 + 52 \rightarrow$ _____

$48 + 52/50 + 54 \rightarrow$ $0 > $ _____ > 5

C = Competition with Peers   _____
     and Children

	A	R	HA	RP	PP	HP	LF	C		Competence
Raw	—	—	—	—	—	—	—	—	=	_____
Weight	—	—	—	—	—	—	—	—		
Corrected	—	—	—	—	—	—	—	—	=	_____

G

Manual for Quantitative Analysis
of Tasks of
One- to Six-Year-Old Children

General Instructions and Definitions, *362*

   I. Definitions, 362
   A. TASKS
   B. MAJOR TYPES OF TASKS—SOCIAL, NONSOCIAL, AND
      COMMUNICATION

   II. Coding Tasks—General Directions, 114
   A. RAW MATERIAL
   B. CODING
   C. REFINING THE CODING
      1. Subsuming short, instrumental tasks   2. Short, non-instrumental tasks
      3. Elevating tasks to the focal level
      4. Coding the same behavior applied to different aspects of the environment
      5. Coding multiple tasks   6. Coding tasks as other-initiated

Summary, 365
Final Coding, 366
Figure 1. Example of Coding, 366

   This manual was prepared by Burton L. White and Barbara Kaban, April 1971. The authors wish to extend their gratitude to Cherry Collins, Kitty Riley Clark, Andrew Cohn, Joan Bissell, and Ingrid Stocking for their contributions.

Social Tasks: Labels, Definitions, and Examples, *367*

   I. Labels and Definitions, 367

   II. Examples and Notes, 368

      1. To Please 2. To Cooperate 3. To Gain Approval 4. To Procure a Service
      5. To Achieve Social Contact; To Gain Attention
      6. To Maintain Social Contact 7. To Avoid Unpleasant Circumstances
      8. To Reject Overtures or Peer Contact; To Avoid Attention 9. To Annoy
      10. To Dominate; To Direct or Lead 11. To Compete; To Gain Status
      12. To Resist Domination; To Assert Self 13. To Enjoy Animals
      14. To Provide Information 15. To Converse
      16. Production of Verbalizations

Nonsocial Tasks: Labels, Definitions, and Examples, *378*

   I. Labels and Definitions, 378

   II. Examples and Notes, 380

      1. To Eat 2. To Relieve Oneself 3. To Dress or Undress Oneself
      4. To Ease Discomfort 5. To Restore Order 6. To Choose
      7. To Procure an Object 8. To Construct a Product
      9. To Engage in Large-Muscle Activity 10. Non-Task Behavior
      11. To Pass Time 12. To Find Something To Do
      13. To Prepare for an Activity 14. To Explore 15. To Pretend
      16. To Improve a Developing Motor, Intellectual, or Verbal Skill
      17. To Gain Information—Visual 18. To Gain Information—Verbal
      19. To Gain Pleasure 20. To Imitate 21. To Operate a Mechanism

Task Instrument Reliability Study, *388*

I. Definitions

A. Tasks

The task is simply whatever a child seems to be trying to do. Taking his cues from the child's behavior and from any environmental stimuli to which the child attends, the observer describes the apparent purpose behind the child's efforts. For example, a child who is ostensibly washing his hands may or may not be trying to clean himself. He may be occupied with making the soap bar slide back and forth through his hands, or with feeling the water. The observer attempts to identify the exact focus of the child's attention at the moment, and then codes the child's action as a type of task. A child in a classroom may or may not have the task the teacher has in mind. The teacher very often wants the child's task to be *to gain information*. If she is successful, the child may indeed be primarily concerned with gaining information. In many instances, however, a child may prefer to orient his efforts elsewhere. If the child is uninterested in the "lesson," his task may be *to pass time*. Another common alternative is social activity, and another is attention-seeking behavior. The clue to the use of the system is to adopt the child's orientation.

Note 1: By definition, all tasks are performed with more than minimal involvement.

Note 2: The manual is recommended for use with children in the age range one through six years. However, the same type of activity must occasionally be coded differently for children of different ages. When this is the case, we have given directions and examples in the notes.

B. Major Types of Tasks—Social, Nonsocial, and Communication

1. Social tasks are those in which a child's primary purpose is to create an effect on another individual or a group of individuals.

2. Nonsocial tasks are all other tasks, except for—

3. Communication tasks, which number three: *to provide information, to converse*, and *to produce a verbalization*. (See later sections for complete definitions.)

Note: A small percentage of behavior does not appear amenable to such classification. For example, aimless fidgeting and desultory wandering is coded as non-task behavior.

II. Coding Tasks—General Directions

A. Raw Material

The observer, standing no closer to the subject than six and no further than ten feet, records what the child appears to be trying to do from moment to moment. A stopwatch is used, but accuracy is attempted only to the nearest five seconds. Events covering less than three seconds are not coded. The raw material is recorded in commonsense terms. We suggest the habit of beginning each entry with the word "to" in order to help maintain the teleological set.

B. Coding

Differentiating the focal task from instrumental tasks. The stream of behavior consists of a series of tasks within tasks; e.g., a child may procure permission (a service) from an adult in order to procure an object, and procure the object in order to construct a product. Assuming each task lasts less than 15 seconds (see below), the ultimate or farthest-removed end in the series (in this case, *to construct a product*) will be coded as the *focal* task, and the preceding tasks (i.e., the series of means) will be subsumed (see below) under this focal task. If there is uncertainty about a particular end being the ultimate one, the next-to-farthest-removed end will be coded as the focal task; e.g., if a child is constructing a product, and there is only a slight possibility that he is constructing this product primarily *to maintain social contact* with the teacher, then the focal task will be *to construct a product*.

Any instrumental task that lasts more than 15 seconds is elevated to the focal level, on the assumption that the young child is limited in his capacity to maintain his focus on more remote tasks.

Note: Often several purposes are served at once. We have arbitrarily decided to code the most essential one; e.g., S tells peers to sit where they are. S leans on the table and repeats message from T importantly. S tells peers to be quiet. In this example, there is a hint of role play when S repeats a message from T; nevertheless, the most essential task is to direct, and his behavior sequence is coded as such.

Immediately after the raw material is obtained, the observer retires to a quiet area to code the protocol.

C. Refining the Coding

The observer, utilizing short-term memory, upgrades the quality of the raw data, making sure that all time is accounted for. He then prepares a molecular chronology with suitable task labels.

Example:

0:00-0:50 *to pass time*
0:50-1:10 *to cooperate*
1:10-2:05 *to pass time*, etc.

1. *Subsuming short, instrumental tasks.* Occasionally, with children two to six years of age, one purpose is clearly present for as long as five minutes. For example, a child may want *to maintain social contact* with a mother, or at least attention from a mother; he may use a variety of procedures to achieve his purpose. When it is clear that diverse procedures are in the service of—i.e., are instrumental to—some overriding purpose, the coder should subsume each of them under this purpose, as long as they last less than 15 seconds.

2. *Short, noninstrumental tasks.* Behaviors that last less than three seconds and that are not instrumental to the focal task are not coded.

3. *Elevating tasks to the focal level.* With the exceptions noted below, a task, to be considered focal, must last at least three seconds and be engaged in with more than minimal involvement.

   a. *An instrumental task may, at times, last 15 seconds or longer.* In such cases, the instrumental task will no longer be subsumed under the end to which it was directed. Instead, it will be coded as a distinct focal task. We are assuming that any task that lasts 15 seconds demands the focal attention of the young child.

   b. *Elevating tasks out of a pass-time or find-something-to-do sequence.* The general 15-seconds rule will apply here also. Since there are a variety of ways in which a child may pass time, any specific task within a pass-time sequence must last 15 seconds or longer and be done with more than minimal involvement in order to be elevated to the focal level. This rule also applies to a find-something-to-do sequence.

   c. *Spanning.* Very often, a child will perform two *momentary* tasks with the same goal (e.g., two attempts to initiate social contact with the same person) within a 15-second period. If the time between these tasks is not devoted to a focal task—i.e., if the child appears purposeless—then the entire 15-second period is coded according to the momentary tasks at each end. (In this case, to initiate social contact.) Do not span when the child is in a *pass time* situation.

4. *Coding the same behavior applied to different aspects of the environment.* Occasionally, a child may, e.g., explore one object for a certain period of time and then explore a second object. This sequence of exploratory behavior directed at two distinct objects will be coded as "*to explore 1*" and "*to explore 2.*"

5. *Coding multiple tasks.* On rare occasions, a child will engage in two distinct behaviors simultaneously, each of which is directed to a distinct end; e.g., a child may be intently putting a puzzle together while at the same time telling a peer that his (the child's) house is better than the peer's. This sequence would be coded as a multiple task: *to construct a product* and *to compete.*

When in doubt, one must consider whether the two tasks might be rapidly alternating, whether one task might be instrumental to the other, or whether both might be directed toward the same end.

One must also be careful to distinguish the case of one behavior serving two ends (in such a case only one end is coded as focal) from a situation in which two behaviors serve two ends. Only the latter situation is coded as multiple.

6. *Coding tasks as other-initiated.* Three behaviors are by definition other-initiated: *to cooperate, to assert self,* and *to pass time.* Three others are by definition self-initiated: *to please, to annoy,* and *non-task behavior.* All other tasks are coded as other-initiated when they are undertaken at the suggestion of another person and last at least 15 seconds, provided the child is not subjected to continual directions and suggestions (in which case the task becomes *to cooperate*). When a child adopts a task at another's suggestion and spends less than 15 seconds in its performance, it is also coded *to cooperate.*

SUMMARY

Duration of task	Purpose it serves.	How to code it
less than 3 sec.	instrumental to focal task	subsume it under focal task
less than 3 sec.	not instrumental to focal task	do not code
3 sec. or more, but less than 15 secs.	instrumental to focal task	subsume it under focal task
3 sec. or more, but less than 15 secs.	not instrumental to focal task	code it as a separate task
15 secs. or more	instrumental to focal task	code all as a separate focal task
15 secs. or more	not instrumental to focal task	code all as a separate focal task
15 secs. or more	part of a pass-time sequence	code all as a separate focal task
twice within 15 secs.	any of those listed	code period between tasks as a focal task if no other focal task intervenes, unless a child is in a pass-time situation.

FINAL CODING

The refined chronology of tasks is transferred onto a coding form. The observer enters information also on the following task characteristics:

a. The source of initiation of the task (i.e., self, adult, etc.)

b. Mother response (encourages, discourages, ignores)

c. The gross level of success that the child seems to attain (i.e., successful, unsuccessful, or irrelevant)

d. Any special comments

Note: Momentary tasks (those lasting less than three seconds) are not coded. (See Example of Coding Sheet.)

Task Data Sheet

Name:		Date: 12/30/71	Setting:	In living room alone with toys,
		Time: 9:50 a.m.		then with M in kitchen.
	John C.	Record #: 1	Observer:	KLW

Time	Focal Task	Other-Initiated	Mother response	Success Yes	No	Irr	Comments
0:00-0:55	To gain information—visual (0)					X	
0:55-1:05	To ease discomfort			X			
1:05-1:20	To gain attention (0)				X		
1:20-2:05	To improve a developing skill			X			Stacks and unstacks plastic saucers
2:05-2:50	To maintain social contact (M)			X			Joins M in kitchen
2:30-2:40	To cooperate (M)	X					M wipes S's nose

Example of Coding Sheet

SOCIAL TASKS: LABELS, DEFINITIONS, AND EXAMPLES

I. Labels and Definitions

1. *To Please*

Def.: To attempt to obtain another's good favor by means of a sustained display of affection, or by offering an object to the other person.

2. *To Cooperate*

Def.: To comply with another's directive when there is little evidence that the compliance is unwilling. To listen, when brief demands are made on one's attention.

3. *To Gain Approval*

Def.: To ask (verbally or nonverbally) for favorable comment on a piece of work or on behavior.

4. *To Procure a Service*

Def: To try to obtain aid from another.

5. *To Achieve Social Contact—To Gain Attention*

Def.: a. to join a group
b. to initiate social contact
c. to maximize the chance of being noticed

6. *To Maintain Social Contact*

Def.: To be absorbed in ensuring that a social contact continues, or to be interested in the social pleasantry rather than in the content of a conversation or other activity.

7. *To Avoid Unpleasant Circumstances*

Def.: To do something for the purpose of evading actual disapproval, possible disapproval, or simply a clash.

8. *To Reject Overtures, Peer Contact; To Avoid Attention*

Def.: To refuse to allow to join one's group or become sociable with oneself. Rarely: to act in order to minimize the possibility of being noticed.

9. *To Annoy*

Def.: To disturb another. To act in a manner designed to displease; to provoke by means of irritating teasing.

10. *To Dominate; To Direct or Lead*

Def.: To play the leader role or to demonstrate a process to others or advise others; in short, to direct a specific activity of others.

11. To Compete; To Gain Status

Def.: To contend for something (e.g., in games involving competition), to make comparisons between own "superior" product (possession, etc.) and other's product (possession, etc.), or to try to elevate one's standing (in one's own eyes or in the eyes of an audience) by appealing to an authority figure.

12. To Resist Domination; To Assert Self

Def.: To oppose any intrusion on one's personal domain, including both:

    a. resistance to demands, orders, or any trampling underfoot, and

    b. protection of property

13. To Enjoy Pets

Def.: Affectionate play with animals.

14. To Provide Information

Def.: To indicate or communicate, in a public way, one's affects, desires, needs, or specific intelligence.

15. To Converse

Def.: Any give-and-take of verbalization, when there is mutual interest in the conversation, rather than a social or some other overtone, or where the communications cannot be heard.

16. Production of Verbalizations

Def.: The actual production of communication. That is, when a child is engaged in the give-and-take of exchanging communications and he is deficient in language skills and cannot get across what he wants to say.

II. Examples and Notes*

1. To Please

a. S and FP are playing with cooking utensils. FP has been looking for some more sawdust. S holds out a tin of sawdust and says, "Do you want one?"

b. S brings a small toy to observer and gives it to her. The action, fairly common, seems to be a way of asking, "Will you be my friend?"

c. S is alone in the kitchen with a baby. She spontaneously hugs and cuddles the baby.

Note: Very brief attempts at pleasing another person are coded *to gain attention*, as long as S does not already have this attention.

To Please vs. To Cooperate. The opposite of *to please* is *to annoy* (these are both self-initiated tasks), while the opposite of *to cooperate* is *to resist domination/assert self* (these are both other-initiated tasks).

---

*Abbreviations used in this manual refer to the following: S = subject; M = mother; T = teacher; AT = assistant teacher; FP = female peer; MP = male peer; O = Observer.

To Please vs. To Cooperate vs. To Restore Order. Whenever a child in a school setting performs the routine, socially prescribed sequences of activities, such as cleaning up after performing a task, the behavior is coded *to cooperate*. Occasionally, however, a child will do more than what is habitually expected of him; e.g., he will do the cleaning up for another person. When this happens, the social context provides the clues for coding his behavior. If the child is socially isolated when he does this, his behavior is coded *to restore order*. However, if he does this in the presence of someone who will be pleased or impressed with his behavior, or if he later calls attention to his behavior, the sequence is coded *to please*, followed in the latter case by *to gain approval*.

2. To Cooperate

a. S has finished lunch and his mother approaches with a washcloth. S puts up minimal resistance as his mother holds his head with one hand and wipes his face with the other.

b. S is busy playing with pots and pans on the kitchen floor while his mother washes the dishes. He looks up and stops his play when his mother turns to him and says, "Your sister should be coming home soon. It's almost time for lunch."

c. AT says that it's story time now and that the blocks must be put away. S begins to stack the blocks that she was playing with in their corner.

d. MP points to building materials on the floor and says, "Pick those up. You dropped those." S picks up the materials and carries them to the table.

Note 1: Cooperation tasks are usually brief. However, if S carries out in a desultory manner a task assigned by another—that is, he neither evades the task nor adopts the task as a goal in itself—then the whole sequence should be coded *to cooperate*. (If it takes him more than 15 seconds to carry out the task, the task itself becomes focal.)

Note 2: If a child cooperates simply by continuing, for example, to sit in a particular place, the cooperation is of such a low degree that it is simply not coded; e.g., S is sitting in a chair; T begins to tie his shoe; S simply continues to sit in the chair. Unless S is watching T (*gain information*), this sequence of behavior is coded *to pass time*.

Note 3: When children in a school setting perform the routine, socially prescribed, habitual sequences of activities, such as cleaning up (oneself, materials, or an area) after performing a task, the sequence will be coded *to cooperate* whether or not S is specifically instructed to perform this activity.

S finishes painting a picture. He then, without necessarily being told to do so, puts the picture in an appropriate place to dry, puts the apron away, and washes his hands. This sequence of activities following the painting is coded *to cooperate*.

Note 4: If a child adopts as his own a task suggested by another, the behavior is coded as other-initiated, provided it lasts more than 15 seconds. When the task lasts less than 15 seconds, it is coded as *to cooperate*. For example, T suggests S might want a paintbrush. S follows T (for more than 15 seconds). This sequence is coded *to procure an object* (teacher-initiated). However, if in the course of obtaining the paintbrush S is subjected to a constant stream of suggestions or directions, then the whole sequence should be coded *to cooperate*.

> Mother and young S (1 1/2 years) are home from the grocery store. They have to walk up three flights of stairs to get to their apartment. M says, "Here we go," and takes S's hand at the bottom of the first flight of stairs. S soon drops his mother's hand and struggles upstairs by himself. He huffs and puffs. The sequence is coded *gross motor activity*, with the notation added, "Mother-initiated and encouraged," if it lasts more than 15 seconds; *to cooperate*, if it lasts less than 15 seconds.

To Cooperate vs. To Gain Information. If a peer begins to talk to S, and S listens for less than 15 seconds, the listening is coded *to cooperate*. If S listens for 15 seconds or longer, it is coded *to gain information.*

To Cooperate vs. To Maintain Social Contact. To maintain social contact is proactive; *to cooperate* is reactive. Look at the source of direction for sustaining the cooperation. If someone else tries to maintain social contact—e.g., if someone else directs S—S's compliant behavior will be coded *to cooperate*. If S initiates the behavior in question without being told to do so, his behavior will be coded *to maintain social contact.*

To Cooperate vs. To Gain Approval vs. To Avoid Unpleasant Circumstances. In tasks in which the child is carrying out the wishes of another, *to cooperate* is the most conservative label and should therefore be used when there is any doubt that more was involved. Don't use *gain approval* unless the child asks for favorable comment when he has completed the task. Don't use *avoid unpleasant circumstances* unless the child clearly shows either reluctance or fear.

To Cooperate vs. To Assert Self. If the child is putting up no resistance in a disagreeable situation, code *cooperate* even though it may be clear to observer that the child would rather assert self; e.g., S proudly displays a necklace she wears. MP tries to take it off her neck and she looks unhappy, but lets him pull at it.

See the *Note* on *To Avoid Unpleasant Circumstances vs. To Cooperate* (page 374).

See the *Note* on *To Prepare for an Activity vs. To Cooperate vs. To Avoid Unpleasant Circumstances* (page 385).

3. To Gain Approval

> a. T is showing FP how to punch a hole in the milk carton and insert a straw. S has managed to do this himself. S pushes his milk carton across the table to T.

> b. S has constructed a "sputnik"-type shape from plastic building pieces. S looks at the shape. S twirls the shape. S walks to AT and holds up the shape. In response to AT's question, S says, "Flying saucer." AT admires the saucer. S comes across the room and holds the saucer up in front of FP.

> c. S climbs up onto her crib, leans over the railing, does a headstand with her feet supported by the crib railing. She says while upside down, "Look at me, mommy, look at me—*look.*"

Note: The demonstration of a skill or the display of a product is essential for the behavior to be scored in this category. Make sure you have clear the distinction between *to gain approval* and both *to cooperate* and *to gain attention* (see notes on these tasks).

See the note on *To Gain Attention vs. To Gain Approval* (page 372).

See the note on *To Cooperate vs. To Gain Approval vs. To Avoid Unpleasant Circumstances* (page 370).

4. To Procure a Service

a. MP is at the sink. S puts on an apron and goes to the sink. MP tells S that she can't play there. S walks across the room to the door and calls to T, "He won't let me wash up." S and T have a conversation about the problem. Eventually T gets up and goes to the sink.

b. S takes her apron, puts it on, then fumbles with the buttons. S goes to T who is helping a peer. S stands by T, then follows T as she walks across the room and stands next to her again. T bends down and buttons the apron.

Note 1: This task is rare at the focal level. Usually a child procures a service in order to carry out some larger task (e.g., help with buttons).

Note 2: If a child asks for aid and waits while aid is procured, the waiting is subsumed under *procure a service*, as long as it takes less than fifteen seconds. If it lasts 15 seconds or longer, it is coded as either *to pass time* or *to gain information*.

Note 3: Procuring a service can encompass all types of emotional behavior, from happy requests to tearful demands.

a. S and P are happily wrestling in a front hall. When they crash to the floor, they squeal and giggle, *to gain pleasure*. P gets up; S follows him and says, "Give me a ride, give me a ride." S tries to get on P's back.

b. Mother is on the phone and S stands at her feet. S holds up her arms in a gesture indicating she wants to be picked up. Mother looks at her but goes on talking. S hangs on to mother's legs and cries, then reaches up again.

Assuming S knows he has the other's attention in both examples, both sequences are coded *to procure a service*.

To Procure a Service vs. To Eat vs. To Gain Attention. If a child asks for something to eat or drink and gets it within 15 seconds, code *to eat*.

If a child asks for something to eat or drink and is ignored, code *to gain attention*.

If a child asks for something to eat and is refused within less than 15 seconds, code *to eat*.

If a child asks for something to eat, mother says yes, and child spends less than 15 seconds waiting for mother to get the food, code *to eat*.

If S waits more than 15 seconds, code *to procure service* followed by *to pass time* or *to gain information*.

5. To Achieve Social Contact—Gain Attention

a. S is sitting at a table, monitoring the room. T sits down at a neighboring table; S gets up and goes to T's table. S stands by T and then sits next to T.

b. S is at the sink, washing clothes. Two peers at the table behind him are discussing birthday parties. S turns around and says, "Can I come to your party?"

c. FP is in the back corner. S goes over to FP and says, "Let's play nurse."

d. S is at a table with five peers, playing with clay. S announces that he is making a cake. S looks at a balloon and calls attention to it. S looks at his clay and calls attention to it.

Note 1: If there is a response to an attempt *to gain attention*, then the coding immediately becomes another task. In *gain attention* and *maintain social contact* sequences, subsume *to gain attention* under *to maintain social contact* when other person attends in less than 15 seconds. If no response is obtained and another attempt at *gaining attention* is made no more than 15 seconds later (and there is no intermediate distracting high-involvement task), then the whole sequence is labeled *to gain attention*.

Note 2: If a three- or four-year-old child is not alone, and is engaging in a verbal redundant naming—i.e., is labeling—and if his labeling appears to serve a social function, it is coded as *to gain attention*. If, however, the child is alone and is labeling, his behavior is considered a form of learning exercise and is coded as *to improve a developing skill*. If a one- or two-year-old child is labeling within a social situation (looking at a book with mother) and his behavior serves both a social and a learning function, code *to improve a developing skill*.

Note 3: Young children at home frequently function in situations where they have some but not all of another's attention: in the kitchen near mother, for example, or in a playroom with a peer. Even though S may have some part of the other's attention all the while, assume that short verbal outbursts on his part are made for the purpose of *gaining attention*.

Note 4: When a young child heads toward a room in which his mother is working, assume he wants her attention and code the time spent in getting to the room *achieve social contact* (assuming it takes him 15 seconds or more to achieve the contact). However, if S is heading for a room in which a peer is playing, code more conservatively; don't assume that what he wants is the peer's attention. He may only want to see what P is doing (*gain information—visual*).

To Gain Attention vs. To Provide Information. When S repeatedly makes informative statements to another who pays no attention, code *to gain attention*.

To Gain Attention vs. To Gain Approval. *To gain attention* includes both positive and negative attention-attracting behavior. Behavior to attract attention to a *product* should be scored under *to gain approval*; *to gain attention* is self-centered rather than product-centered.

See *Note* on *To Maintain Social Contact vs. To Initiate Social Contact* (page 374).

See *Note* on *To Annoy vs. To Gain Attention vs. To Dominate* (page 375).

G. To Maintain Social Contact

a. S follows FP to trash can and watches FP put rubbish in it. Follows FP to table, sits down, and pulls out neighboring chair for FP. S whispers to FP. T asks FP a question and S answers. FP tells whole table T's message. S puts her arm around FP and whispers again.

b. S is sitting in a group. The group leaves and S follows.

c. S is playing on the kitchen floor with tennis ball. It rolls away from him and mother rolls it back. S laughs at M and rolls the ball toward her. The ball playing becomes a game played by S in order to maintain contact with M.

d. S is constructing a product with low involvement in order to maintain social contact with the teacher; *to construct a product* is subsumed under *to maintain social contact*.

Note 1: To code a sequence of behavior *to maintain social contact*, S must be more than passive. He must actively seek to maintain social contact. A state of social contact is defined by the following: active conversation, physical contact, exclusive eye contact. Proximity is not enough. He may do this in a variety of ways: verbally, with clinging behavior, by *procuring a service*, by disruption.

Note 2: If *maintain social contact* attempts occur within a 15-second period and if no other focal task intervenes, then the entire sequence is labeled *to maintain social contact*. See *Spanning*, under General Directions.

Note 3: A child can maintain social contact by allowing another or a group to approach him under certain circumstances; e.g., S can maintain social contact by allowing a group to catch up to him when he has previously run ahead of them.

Note 4: Sometimes it is difficult to determine whether a child's attention is primarily focused on the social pleasantry or the content of a conversation or activity. For example, a child may join a peer who is looking at a book. He may point at a picture in the book with genuine interest. He may give every indication that what he enjoys is looking at the book with a friend. When observer is in doubt whether child's attention is primarily on the book or the friend, he should molecularize his coding: code each five seconds of behavior as minutely as he can.

Note 5: Young children frequently stay near their mothers when they are uneasy. If S hovers near M in order to feel safe due to anxiety over observer's presence, such clingy behavior is coded *to maintain social contact* even if mother is occupied. If S makes some gesture or utterance that indicates he knows he doesn't have mother's attention, behavior is coded *to gain attention*.

To Maintain Social Contact vs. To Converse. In social situations where conversation is taking place, this category must clearly be distinguished from *to converse*. The latter is used when the conversation itself is the center of the child's attention, while *to maintain social contact* is used when the child seems primarily to want to keep the attention and companionship of another. If there is a "small talk" quality to the interchange, code *to maintain social contact*; if there seems to be a high interest in the content of the conversation, code *to converse*.

To Maintain Social Contact vs. To Initiate Social Contact. The distinction between attempts at maintaining social contact and attempts at initiating it, if spaced within 15 seconds, depends upon the response of the other person involved. If the other person attends within 15 seconds, it is coded as *to maintain social contact* and the time spent gaining attention is subsumed; if the other person does not attend, it is coded as *to initiate social contact*.

To Maintain Social Contact vs. To Pass Time. To pass time is the more conservative. *To maintain social contact* cannot be used unless there is high involvement in keeping the social contact.

To Maintain Social Contact vs. To Gain Pleasure. Excited interaction among young peers, such as wrestling and chasing games, are frequently on the border between *to maintain social contact* and *to gain pleasure*. In order for his behavior to be coded *to gain pleasure*, S must have as his primary concern his own state of pleasurable excitement (usually accompanied by signs of hilarity). S must have abandoned as a primary concern the effect he is creating on anyone else.

See *Notes* on *To Cooperate vs. To Maintain Social Contact* (page 370).

7. To Avoid Unpleasant Circumstances

a. S is making cakes with Play Doh and is chewing bits of the dough. T asks in a disapproving voice whether S is eating the dough again. S says "No" and immediately puts down his cake and runs to the bathroom.

b. S is playing with his younger brother's gun. His mother tells him to give it back and he runs down the hall shooting it. Finally M says, "You have until I count to five," and begins counting. S hands over the gun to his little brother.

Note: Under some conditions, S may avoid unpleasant circumstances by leaving the field. For example, MP may say to S, "I'm going to take your toy away." If S now walks away from MP, his behavior is coded as *to avoid unpleasant circumstances*. If he stays where he is, on the other hand, and says "No" and clutches his toy, his behavior will be coded *to assert self*.

To Avoid Unpleasant Circumstances vs. To Cooperate. To cooperate is more conservative. For his behavior to be coded *to avoid unpleasant circumstances*, the child must clearly show either reluctance or fear. If neither of these is present and the child is carrying out another's wishes, the behavior is coded *to cooperate*.

See the *Note* on *To Avoid Attention vs. To Avoid Unplesant Circumstances* (page 375).

See the *Note* on *To Cooperate vs. To Gain Approval vs. To Avoid Unpleasant Circumstances* (page 370).

See the *Note* on *To Prepare for an Activity vs. To Cooperate vs. To Avoid Unpleasant Circumstances* (page 385).

8. To Reject Overtures, Peer Contact; To Avoid Attention

a. FP1 carries her chair to the table where S and FP2 are crayoning. S says to FP1, "We don't like you any more."

b. It is S's birthday and the custom is for the "birthday boy" to sit in the middle of the circle and be feted. S hides.

To Reject Overtures vs. To Assert Self. If a peer asks to join S or S's activity, S's rejection of the peer's attempts is coded *to reject overture*. If a peer takes something away from or infringes upon S, S's rejection of the peer's attempts is coded as *to assert self*. If S tries to get himself and his property away from P because he is afraid P will take his toy or wreck his game, code *to assert self/protect domain*.

To Avoid Attention vs. To Avoid Unpleasant Circumstances. It has been customary to use *to avoid attention* only when the child is avoiding positive attention. The avoiding of negative or possible negative attention should be scored under *to avoid unpleasant circumstances*.

9. To Annoy

a. S is riding a tricycle. MP1 is riding in the fire truck and MP2 is on the small tricycle. S rides in front of MP1. MP1 reverses and S smiles. S bangs into MP2.

b. S and two peers are sitting at a table drawing with crayons. S selects a crayon, leans across the table and draws on FP's paper.

Note: One must distinguish *to annoy* from playful teasing. To be labeled *to annoy*, the behavior must show clear signs of a desire to irritate. In situations where a child is provoking an adult, code *to annoy* unless the situation turns into a game enjoyed by both parties (*to maintain social contact*).

To Annoy vs. To Assert Self. Annoyance behavior is self-initiated, while assertion is other-initiated. A behavior that is initially coded as *to assert self* may turn into *to annoy* if S shifts his attention from his domain to another person.

To Annoy vs. To Gain Attention vs. To Dominate. Annoyance behavior should be scored only when the focus of the task is on hurting or harassing another, rather than instrumental to calling attention to the self (*to gain attention*) or flexing power muscles (*to dominate*).

10. To Dominate; To Direct or Lead

a. S and MP are playing. S's verbalizations are of the following type: "Now we'll play this game. First I'll have a turn, then you'll have a turn. And when we're finished, then we'll build a railroad."

b. MP is playing with a garden hose. S holds MP's hand and thus guides the direction of the hose.

c. MP is riding a tricycle. S says, "It's Ann's turn now," and stops the tricycle.

d. S tells peers to sit where they are. S leans on the table and repeats a message from T importantly. S tells peers to be quiet.

Note: There is an element of role play in this piece of behavior, but the essential task is *to dominate*.

See *Note* on *To Annoy vs. To Gain Attention vs. To Dominate* (page 126).

11. To Compete; To Gain Status

a. FP and S are making cakes with play dough. S says, "I have more than you."

b. The drummer is a coveted position. It is music time and T is about to hand out instruments. S asks, "Can I be the drummer?"

c. The children are playing a game. There is no prearranged sequence of turns. S says, "It's my turn."

12. To Resist Domination; To Assert Self

a. FP1 says to FP2 that she doesn't like S. FP2 agrees. S says, "I don't like you either." S throws crayon into the box, gets up from the table, and walks away.

b. All the children have assigned seats. MP is sitting in S's seat. S says to MP, "That's my seat."

c. The children are playing a game at which they take turns in a prearranged sequence. MP takes S's turn. S says, "That's my turn."

d. S is playing with a music box in her own bedroom. FP looks at it. S clutches it to her chest and walks away, looking at FP defiantly.

e. S is sitting unhappily near FP. Mother suggests a variety of activities she hopes will interest S. S sits and stubbornly whispers, "No, no, no," over a 20-second period.

See *Note* on *To Reject Peer Overture vs. To Assert Self* (page 375).
See *Note* on *To Annoy vs. To Assert Self* (page 375).

13. To Enjoy Animals

Note 1: S cannot simply sit and hold the animal. S must pet or fondle the animal at least twice within each 15-second period.

Note 2: This category was added to avoid the necessity of lumping this behavior under *to gain pleasure*. Other behavior with animals (annoyance, resisting domination, etc.) should be scored in the appropriate social category.

14. To Provide Information

S and FP are playing together with toy dishes. S looks up and says, "I went to the zoo. I saw a lion and an elephant. I saw a tiger."

Note 1: In an ongoing focal task such as *to construct a product*, a one-sentence instance of *to provide information* should be regarded as momentary. If the *to provide information* is 15 seconds, then it may be elevated out; however, if it is relevant to the ongoing behavior and is *not* of 15-second duration, then it must be subsumed. If, however, the *to provide information* is *not* relevant to the ongoing task, lasts more than five seconds and is of high involvement, then it may be raised to focal level. A caution: It is necessary, if this behavior involves any kind of social exchange, not to be too atomistic, but to be cognizant of and characterize the whole sequence.

Note 2: *To provide information* may occasionally be confused with *to direct/dominate*. *To provide information* is the more conservative choice, and should, therefore, be used either if there is question of intent or because of hearing difficulty.

Note 3: *To provide information* may be used when there is appropriate verbalization, whether there is an audience or not. The first sentence of such an outflow would constitute a momentary *to gain attention*.

Note 4: *To gain information* and *to provide information* are distinct categories and should be used only when the exchange is *exclusively* one or the other. In a situation where it appears both are going on, the correct label would probably be *to converse*.

15. To Converse

S is loading plastic toys into a paper bag with fierce concentration. He inadvertently rips the bag.

S: (sadly) I tear it! I tear it! Tear it! Tear it, Mommy.

M: Did you tear the bag? Why?

S: Cause.

M: Cause why?

S: I tear it.

M: I see you're having trouble putting the things into the bag. Can you fix it?

S: I can't.

M: Do you want me to put some tape on it?

S: Tape on it. The tape in the drawer!

Note 1: In a non-task sequence, occasionally there are intermittent "few second" conversations lasting for more than 15 seconds. If there is continuity of topic throughout the verbal exchanges and the conversation covers at least half the total time, then the entire sequence (both the exchanges and the gaps between) may be elevated out as a *to converse* task. If, however, in the exchanges, there is no continuity of topic, the isolated remarks may be subsumed in the non-task category, unless, of course, it is deemed that the child is trying *to maintain social contact* or *to gain attention* or some other task.

Note 2: In an ongoing task such as *to improve a developing motor, intellectual or verbal skill, to construct a product*, etc., if the conversation is related to that task, it is subsumed unless it lasts more than 15 seconds.

Note 3: If two children are engaged in animated conversation and it is difficult to decide if the sequence is a social one or a communication one, the distinction may be made on the basis of conversation content. If there is a "small talk" quality to the interchange and it appears primarily instrumental to the *maintaining of social contact*, it should be designated in that category; if, however, there is a more serious overtone and there seems to be high interest in the content of the conversation, it properly belongs in *to converse*.

16. Production of Verbalizations

S is asking for something, but his mother can not understand what he is saying. He repeats his request several times, getting agitated when she doesn't respond correctly.

Note: To use this category, S must have difficulty producing the verbalization or making himself understood. He must wait for a response or rearrange his output in order to get a response. If this behavior is not observed, then code the output as *to gain attention*.

NONSOCIAL TASKS: LABELS, DEFINITIONS, AND EXAMPLES

I. Labels and Definitions

1. *To Eat*

Def.: To ingest food or drink.

2. To Relieve Oneself

Def.: To void or to eliminate.

3. *To Dress or Undress Oneself*

Def.: Self-explanatory.

4. *To Ease Discomfort*

Def.: Purposeful behavior to alleviate physical or psychic discomfort, in contrast to apparently aimless or habitual behavior.

5. *To Restore Order*

Def.: To return things to a previously acceptable state but not for the purpose of easing discomfort, pleasing another, or preparing for an activity.

6. *To Choose*

Def.: To choose a specific object from an array.

7. To Procure an Object

Def.: To get something, not as an instrumental task for constructing a product, but as a task per se. If procuring an object in order to use it for constructing a product or for any purpose takes longer than 15 seconds, it is coded as focal.

8. To Construct a Product

Def.: Involves the whole complex of behavior of procuring materials and using the materials (e.g., glue, pencils, piece of puzzle), oriented toward the end product as a consequence of the use of the materials.

9. To Engage in Large-Muscle Activity

Def.: To engage in large-muscle activity as an end in itself, not as a means of getting attention, being a member of a group, etc. To use gross motor muscles to propel all or some part of the body, or to perform other motor activities that require unusual physical effort and coordination. Working hard to do something with the body that is out of the ordinary; e.g., bike riding up a hill (after the skill has been mastered).

10. Non-task Behavior

Def.: To remain in place and not dwell on any specific object (e.g., desultory scanning, sitting with eyes closed, or holding a blank stare), or to wander aimlessly from one location to another.

11. To Pass Time

Def.: To occupy oneself with some alternative task in a situation where one is captive (i.e., must remain in the field) and where the prescribed activity holds no appeal for one. To occupy oneself while waiting for a prescribed activity to begin.

12. To Find Something to Do

Def.: To move around, sampling objects and activities in a purposeful fashion but not settling in on anything specific.

13. To Prepare for an Activity

Def.: To perform the socially prescribed activities or sequence of actions that a child carries out almost automatically owing to previous experience and/or practice, in order to prepare for something that the child anticipates.

14. To Explore

Def.: To explore materials, objects, activities, or people. To investigate the properties or nature of materials, objects, activities, or people through touch, taste, vision, etc. Experimenting with an object or a material's possibilities by adding to it or taking something away from it as the primary concern, rather than for the purpose of constructing a product or because of interest in the process per se, as is evident in *to* pretend.

15. To Pretend—Role Play

Def.: To fantasize in any of the following ways: to pretend to be someone or something else; to pretend to be doing something one really isn't; to pretend an object is something other than what it really is; to pretend to be in an imaginary situation.

16. To Improve a Developing Motor, Intellectual, or Verbal Skill

Def.: To improve a developing motor, intellectual, or verbal skill is typically distinguished by the redundancy of S's behavior (i.e., repeats the same sequence of actions again and again) and by less-than-masterful skill in performing the activity in question.

17. To Gain Information—Visual

Def.: Sustained visual inquiry directed toward a specific object or person.

18. To Gain Information—Verbal

Def.: To attend to language from any source. To gain information through listening when the prime interest is on the context of information being made available.

19. To Gain Pleasure

Def.: To engage in a task for no other reason than to achieve a state of gaiety, excitement, or amusement.

20. To Imitate

Def.: The immediate reproduction of the behavior of another person.

21. To Operate a Mechanism

Def.: To attempt to use or manipulate a mechanism. Operating a mechanism is, by definition, instrumental, but becomes focal when it takes 15 seconds or longer to execute.

II. Examples and Notes

1. To Eat

Note 1: A child may be eating and doing something else simultaneously; e.g., *to gain information*. If this occurs, then multiple coding is used for the sequence. However, the observer must carefully note whether the two activities are occurring simultaneously or alternating.

Note 2: Very low-level eating need not be coded. Child's attention must be focused on eating. For example, S may run around house with a stick of licorice in his mouth; this is not considered eating unless he sucks or chews. Similarly, when a baby has a bottle in his mouth, he is considered to be eating only when he is actually taking in fluid.

2. To Relieve Oneself

Eliminating or voiding should be coded in the appropriate category when it is instrumental to some larger task. For example, a child may go to the bathroom in response to an adult threat (*to avoid unpleasant circumstances*). A child may void on the living-room couch in order to irritate his mother (*to annoy*). He may reject adult suggestion that he use the toilet, and eliminate in his pants instead (*to assert self*). If a young child sits on the toilet for a long time without voiding or eliminating, and if he practices an action while he sits there, such as rolling and unrolling toilet paper, code *to improve a developing skill*. If the child proceeds to eliminate, then this sequence is coded as an other-initiated *to relieve oneself*.

3. To Dress or Undress Oneself

The category is used in a similar manner to that of relieving oneself.

When a child spontaneously puts clothes on or takes them off, *to dress oneself*. When a child practices putting on and off an article of clothing, *to improve a developing skill*. When a child dresses himself in response to adult suggestion, other-initiated *to dress oneself*, as long as it takes at least 15 seconds. When a child dresses himself in response to adult threat, *to avoid unpleasant circumstances*. When a child throws on a coat in less than 15 seconds and then runs out the door, *to prepare for an activity*.

4. To Ease Discomfort

a. To rub eyes, to scratch arm, etc.

b. S drops a toy on his foot, begins to cry, and runs to his father for comfort.

c. S patiently tries to make a three-legged chair stand correctly. She tries again and again, and finally, angrily throws the chair down and kicks it.

Note: When S is in a state of obvious discomfort as revealed by crying or whimpering, assume his task is to ease it.

5. To Restore Order

a. To replace items, to pick items up, to pull up socks, to tuck in shirttails, to wipe mouth on sleeve after eating—*without being told to do so*.

b. A fishing line is tangled around the pole. S untangles it.

Note: One must be careful to distinguish *to restore order* from *to ease discomfort*. If a child pulls up his socks, it could be that they had been wrinkled up inside his shoe and had been causing discomfort. If there is no clue that wrinkled socks, for example, have been causing discomfort, and if S adjusts them nevertheless, without being told to do so, then the behavior is labeled *to restore order*. If S adjusted them in response to a specific request, then the behavior is either *to cooperate* or *to avoid unpleasant circumstances*.

Note: When one-year-olds finish examining or using an object, they characteristically drop it and run on to something else. If a young child *starts* to put something away at the end of an activity, code this behavior *to restore order*.

See the *Note* on *To Cooperate vs. To Restore Order* (page 369).

6. To Choose

a. S is standing in the pantry looking up at boxes and cans of food, deciding what he wants.

b. S is looking for something he can saw. He walks around the yard sampling various objects until he finds one that is suitable.

c. S is standing before a shelf full of toys or materials. He spends more than 15 seconds selecting one. (If he had spent less than 15 seconds in procuring one, the behavior would have been coded *to prepare for an activity*.)

7. To Procure an Object

a. S wants a toy that FP has. S asks for it, tries to grab it, etc.

b. S has a piece of hard candy wrapped in cellophane. He spends more than 15 seconds removing the paper. Removing the paper is coded as *to procure an object*, rather than as *to eat* or *to explore*.

Note: If S's overriding task is to construct a product, but if he spends 15 seconds or more in procuring an object to be used in constructing the product, then procuring the object is elevated to the focal level.

8. To Construct a Product

S gets two tins filled with paint and carries them to the easel. S then gets a brush and a piece of paper. She puts the paper on the easel and begins painting. S paints for four minutes, and then announces, "I'm finished." This entire sequence of behavior is labelled *to construct a product*.

Note 1: If S takes 15 seconds to get the materials ready, this preparatory behavior is elevated to the focal level and is labeled *to prepare for an activity*.

Note 2: Common examples of constructing a product are putting a puzzle together, making something out of clay, painting, and digging a hole. A less common example would be burying someone in sand at the beach, as long as S showed enough skill to rule out *to improve a developing skill* and was not interested solely in exploring the properties of the sand.

Note 3: Common indications that S is constructing a product are:

a. Verbal cues ("I'm making a castle"; "Now I need blue paint for the picture").

b. The class as a whole is told to construct a specific object.

c. S calls attention to his product after its completion.

To Construct a Product vs. To Improve a Developing Skill. *To construct a product* is more common in older children, while *to improve a developing skill* is more common in younger children. As long as an end product is involved in the child's activity, his behavior should not be called *to improve a developing skill* unless there is a definite practice (i.e., repetitive) situation involved. Try to determine whether S shows pride in his product (*to construct a product*) or in his skill (*to improve a developing skill*). In a Montessori situation, S is more likely to perceive a situation as a practicing situation. Young children ages one and two are more likely to be thinking about their own action than an end product.

To Construct a Product vs. To Pretend. Younger Ss are more likely *to pretend*, older Ss, *to construct a product.* Imitative behavior is the most salient cue for *to pretend*, e.g., if a child pretends to be "Mommy" baking a pie, the behavior is coded *to pretend* even though the construction of a product (a pie) is an indirect result of the pretending.

To Construct a Product vs. To Explore. Younger Ss are more likely to explore; older Ss to construct a product. Exploratory behavior is usually marked by a variety that is not essential to the construction of an end product. While the child may be exploring only one object, he will typically look at it from different angles, turn it around, manipulate it in many different ways.

9. To Engage in Large-Muscle Activity

To climb a jungle gym, to jump, to run, to ride a bike up a hill (after the skill has been mastered), to swim vigorously, to run very quickly after a ball, or to climb a tree.

Note: Watch for large-muscle activity that turns into something else; e.g., running that becomes pretending to be an airplane.

To Engage in Large-Muscle Activity vs. To Improve a Developing Skill. *To improve a developing skill* is more conservative. As long as an activity that requires much physical exertion is not yet perfected, it is labeled *to improve a developing skill*. Thus, swimming by a beginner will be coded *to improve a developing skill*, while a good swimmer's behavior will be labeled *large-muscle activity*.

10. Non-Task Behavior

a. S stands still, looking around the room at nothing specific.

b. S lies across his chair, gazing blankly at the floor.

c. S wanders from the living room to the kitchen, and then out into the hall.

11. To Pass Time

a. T is instructing class how to make Christmas cards. S is looking around the room and playing with his shoe, rarely attending to T.

b. S fingers his napkin while waiting for juice and cookies to be distributed for snack time.

c. S is in playpen. He looks around the room, fingers a toy momentarily, changes position of his feet. He does not devote his attention to any specific task for as long as 15 seconds.

Note 1: The actual behavior seen in categories 10 and 11 may be the same, but the difference in coding will be determined by the specific situation. If it is obvious that S cannot leave the field or T has made an explicit statement about an impending activity, the behavior is coded as *to pass time*.

Note 2: The criteria for coding an activity as a focal task during a *pass time* sequence are that it must take place for at least 15 seconds, with more than minimal involvement.

Note 3: One can never have a multiple task with *to pass time*. If the second is performed with more than minimal involvement, only it is coded. If it is done with minimal involvement, it is not elevated out of the *pass time* sequence.

Note 4: For the sake of their own safety, very young children are frequently placed in *pass time* situations. The following are the most common: crib, playpen, diaper table, grocery cart, car seat, high chair. If the child is confined to one room indoors by means of a locked gate, or if he is placed in a large pen outdoors, his situation is also defined as *to pass time*. If he has access to more than one room, or if he plays in an enclosed yard, he is not considered a captive; i.e., he is not in a *pass time* situation.

See the *Note* on *To Maintain Social Contact vs. To Pass Time* (page 374).

12. To Find Something to Do

S moves around the room, purposefully and carefully inspecting the puzzles, books, and toys T has placed on the tables.

Note 1: S must actively sample different objects for the sequence to be coded *to find something to do*. Apparent visual sampling is not an adequate criterion for using this category.

Note 2: The criteria for coding an activity as a focal task during a *find something to do* sequence are that it must take at least 15 seconds, with more than minimal involvement.

13. To Prepare for an Activity

When the child decides to do something (painting), all the things he does in preparation for the activity (i.e., getting the apron, getting paper, brushes, etc.) are instrumental to doing that activity. Therefore, they are not coded as distinct preparatory tasks. When a group of preparatory actions totals less than 15 seconds, they are subsumed under the subsequent focal task; when they take more than 15 seconds, they are labeled *to prepare for an activity*.

Note 1: When preparatory activities are cut off before 15 seconds but not by the consummatory activity, they are coded as *to prepare for an activity*.

Note 2: In keeping with the general 15-seconds rule, if any particular task (e.g., *procuring an object*) within the *prepare for activity* sequence lasts 15 seconds, it, too, is elevated to the focal level.

Note 3: Any type of consummatory behavior (e.g., painting, eating, etc.) is usually a hint to look for preceding behavior that will be coded as *to prepare for an activity*.

To Prepare for an Activity vs. To Cooperate vs. To Avoid Unpleasant Circumstances. If the child wants very much to engage in the activity in question, his preparatory activities are coded *to prepare for an activity*. If the child feels neutral about the activity and is preparing for it only at the request of another, his preparation is coded *to cooperate* (unless it takes longer than 15 seconds). If the child is opposed to the activity that will follow, his preparation is labeled *to avoid unpleasant circumstances*.

14. To Explore

Clay and flour are on a nursery school table. S moves the flour around the table.

S is playing with mud. He squeezes it through his fingers, tastes it, adds water to it so that it pours easily, saws it with a comb, etc.

15. To Pretend

a. A child pushes a stroller while wearing his mother's high-heeled shoes.

b. A child pretends to eat someone's nose.

c. A child pretends a piece of cardboard is a hat.

d. A child pretends to be asleep.

A distinguishing feature of *to pretend* is often some sort of deferred imitation; e.g., a $2\frac{1}{2}$-year-old leafs through her mother's address book, and occasionally licks her fingers as adults do when they want to turn pages easily. When questioned, her mother says this is a gesture she herself frequently makes.

To Pretend vs. To Improve a Developing Skill. Occasionally, behavior that would ordinarily be coded *to pretend* (e.g., a child is pushing a buggy) will be coded *to improve a developing motor skill* because the child's young age makes it very unlikely that he is imitating an adult's behavior. If an older child were to engage in this same activity, or if a young child made it quite clear (for example, by putting a baby in the buggy) that he was imitating adult behavior, the situation would be coded as *to pretend*.

16. To Improve a Developing Motor, Intellectual, or Verbal Skill

a. S practices how to tie his shoelaces, how to write the letter *A*, how to use cuisinier rods to learn a number concept, or how to draw a circle.

b. A child is riding a tricycle, walking, climbing a ramp in a less-than-masterful way.

c. S scribbles with a crayon, using a rapid redundant motion.

d. S works on a formboard puzzle, attempting to fit circular shapes into circular openings. When he achieves success, he takes the circular piece out and tries to fit it in again.

e. S practices how to sing "Twinkle, Twinkle, Little Star."

f. If a child is alone, and is engaged in a verbal, redundant naming—i.e., is labeling—his behavior is considered a form of learning exercise and is coded as *to improve a developing skill.* If the child is not alone, and if the labelling appears to serve a social function, it is coded as *to gain attention,* provided he is old enough and has sufficient skill with words to use them easily. If a very young child labels in a social situation, and his behavior serves both a social and a learning function, it is coded *to improve a developing skill.*

To Improve a Developing Skill vs. To Explore. This distinction can best be made in terms of repetitiveness. While the "practicing" aspect of *to improve a developing skill* requires a fair amount of repetition, exploratory behavior is usually marked by variety. While the child may be exploring only one object, he will typically look at it from different angles, turn it around, manipulate it in many different ways.

In addition, in exploratory behavior, the child's main concern is the object itself. In *to improve a developing skill,* on the other hand, he is more concerned with the process than the specific object.

To Improve a Developing Skill vs. To Pretend. The distinction is usually between practice and redundancy vs. imitation. See the *Note* on *To Construct a Product vs. To Pretend* (page 383).

17. To Gain Information—Visual

Young children in the home spend much of their time engaged in steady looking.

a. S watches as his mother makes a bed.

b. S watches observer.

Note 1: To distinguish between sustained visual inquiry (*to gain information*) and a blank stare (*non-task behavior* or *to pass time*), carefully note behavioral cues. If S is in place and staring steadily but shows no signs of attending to the object, or if S appears to be sleepily staring into space, label it *non-task behavior* or *to pass time.*

Note 2: When a child scans a room or outdoor scene without dwelling on any one object or person for at least three seconds, code this scanning behavior *non-task* or *to pass time.* Sustained regard is defined as a gaze that does not travel more than five degrees in any direction. (If a child is looking straight ahead and his arms are spread-eagled sideways, the plane made by his arms is 180 degrees and the plane of his gaze is 90 degrees. Gaze may stray no more than five degrees away from the line of sight; this enables observer to determine whether child is looking at one object or at more than one.)

If child is looking out the window, code *to gain information–visual* only when observer can see that child's eyes are steadily focused on a particular object or happening outside; otherwise, code *non-task* or *to pass time*. If child gives some clue that he is looking toward something specific (pointing, showing signs of excitement while looking out the window, running to the window when he hears a horn), code *to gain information–visual*.

To Gain Information–Visual vs. To Improve a Developing Skill. Sometimes a child makes something happen in order to watch the results. He may roll a stick, push a button, kick a piece of snow, and then steadily look at what happens. If the action itself is momentary and if the looking is sustained, then the sequence is coded as *to gain information–visual*; e.g., a two-year-old flicks a stick with her finger and watches it roll across the tabletop.

If the action itself lasts as long as or longer than the looking, the sequence is coded *to improve a developing skill*; e.g., a two-year-old winds a mechanical car with a key and watches the axle spin as he turns the key. Code *to improve a developing skill*, because winding is difficult and it takes as long to make the axle spin as to watch it move. The child's attention must be on his own action.

18. To Gain Information–Verbal

a. S watches a TV program. "Sesame Street," "Captain Kangaroo," "Superman," "Lucy," "Beverly Hillbillies."

b. S listens to M read a story.

c. S listens to a conversation in which he is not involved.

In school situations the child is considered to be *gaining information* only when the prime interest is on the content of the information; i.e., S is hooked on the content of the instructions, and is not oriented toward pleasing T, etc.; e.g., S listens for 15 seconds or more to T, who is giving instructions about how to do something. (If he listens less than 15 seconds, it is coded as *to cooperate*.)

19. To Gain Pleasure

a. S is being pushed on a swing and is laughing.

b. S and MP are engaging in small talk and are giggling.

c. S and FP are throwing food in the air and finding the activity hilarious.

Note: One could conceivably maintain that almost anything a child does (e.g., *to construct a product, role play, to ease discomfort*) is in some sense pleasurable or else the child would not engage in it. To keep *to gain pleasure* from becoming an all-encompassing category, the same rule of more than minimal involvement will be applied to the behavioral indices of pleasure before a behavior will be coded in this category. S must display definite signs of pleasure, most obviously by laughing and giggling.

See *Note* on *To Maintain Social Contact vs. To Gain Pleasure* (page 374).

20. To Imitate

S is sitting on floor with FP. FP hits a toy drum several times. S hits the toy drum several times.

To Imitate vs. To Cooperate. In *to imitate*, the immediate reproduction of the behavior of another is totally initiated by S, with little or no attention paid to the response of the other person. In *to cooperate*, the task would be other-initiated.

To Imitate vs. To Pretend. Deferred imitation is coded as *to pretend*; immediate reproduction of another's behavior is coded as *to imitate*.

21. To Operate a Mechanism

Note: Operating a mechanism is by definition instrumental, but it becomes focal because it takes so long to execute; e.g., getting a radio to go on. In order to distinguish this category from *to explore*, S must obviously begin operating the mechanism for a definite purpose (e.g., to hear the radio make a noise). If he is simply feeling the radio, or looking at it from different angles, the sequence is coded as *to explore*. If he turns it on and off redundantly, the sequence is coded *to improve a developing skill*. If he gets it on in less than 15 seconds and listens to someone talking on the radio, the sequence is coded *to gain information–verbal*.

TASK INSTRUMENT RELIABILITY STUDY

In March 1970, a reliability study on the task instrument was conducted by observers I and II. Five subjects (three girls, two boys) ranging in age from 12 to 32 months were observed.

Procedure:

Three ten-minute protocols were recorded simultaneously for each child by the two observers and then coded separately. Percent of time agreed upon by the two observers was calculated for each protocol.

Results:

The mean percent agreement for the five subjects (15 protocols) was 70.7%. The median was 70%.*

Name/Age	Prot. #	% Agreement
Subject 1	1	80
(7/6/67)	2	68
	3	67.5
		Mean: 71.8
Subject 2	1	82
(3/3/69)	2	79
	3	69
		Mean: 76.6
Subject 3	1	61
(3/10/68)	2	70
	3	91
		Mean: 74
Subject 4	1	79
(2/9/68)	2	76
	3	60
		Mean: 70.1
Subject 5	1	37.5
(3/9/68)	2	66
	3	74
		Mean: 59.1

*Additional reliability studies have been conducted. In October 1969, two observers observing six children achieved a mean percent agreement of 65.6%. In December 1970, two observers observing six children achieved a mean percent agreement of 70.2%.

appendix **II**

INDIVIDUAL SUBJECT DATA

SUBJECT #2

SUBJECT #2 IS A TWO-YEAR-OLD middle-class A boy. He is the younger of two children (sister aged four) of well-educated parents. The family lives in a large, comfortable apartment in an urban area.

S's mother is an affectionate, gentle woman who is very aware of her child's interests and abilities. Often, she will offer suggestions and help him set up a particular activity (e.g., doing puzzles). Although she is usually busy with household chores, she is always available to S and ready to answer his questions or help him.

There are many interesting and appropriate toys available for S. He makes extensive use of the materials, often engaging in very sophisticated activities. However, at other times he will be observed wandering around the house holding his favorite blanket.

Summary of Test Scores

S: Subject No. 2   Group: 2-year A

Tests	S's Score	Group Median	S's Rank	No. of S's Tied at that Rank
Bayley (MDI) 24 mos.	137 IQ	105 IQ	2/12	—
Stanford-Binet 36 mos.	140 IQ			
Language Test				
at 24 mos.	42 mos.	36.0 mos.	1/7	—
at 27 mos.	54 mos.	40.5 mos.	1/9	—
at 30 mos.	51 mos.	51.0 mos.	1/4	6
at 36 mos.	57 mos.			
Abstract Abilities				
at 24 mos.	28.5 mos.	20.5 mos.	1/9	—
at 27 mos.	32.0 mos.	24.5 mos.	1/9	—
at 30 mos.	32.0 mos.	24.5 mos.	1/8	—
at 36 mos.	54.0 mos.			
Discrimination				
at 24 mos.	Level 7	Level 3	1/6	—
at 27 mos.	Level 7	Level 4	2/6	—
at 30 mos.	Level 7	Level 7	2/5	3
at 36 mos.	Level 8			
Social Competence				
with Adults	20.1	16.7	3/12	—
with Peers	7.4	6.2	5/12	—
Overall	27.5	22.5	5/12	—

Summary of Test Scores Tables were prepared by Janice Marmor, April 1971.

```
                              SOCIAL COMPETENCE FOR SUBJECT 2 (2A)

GAIN        0                          AC
ADULT       OXXXXXXXXXXXXXXXXXXXXXXXXXXXXXXXXXXXXXXXXXXXXXX
ATTENTION   OXXXXXXXXXXXXXXXXXXXXXXXXXXXXXXXXXXXXXXXXXXXXXX
            0
USE         0                     C      A
ADULT       OXXXXXXXXXXXXXXXXXXXXXXXXXXXXXXXXXXXXX
RESOURCE    OXXXXXXXXXXXXXXXXXXXXXXXXXXXXXXXXXXX
            0
HOSTILITY   0               C A
AFFECTION   OXXXXXXXXXXXXXXXXXXXX
TO ADULT    OXXXXXXXXXXXXXXXXXXX
            A0C
ROLE PLAY   0
            0
            0
            0
PRIDE IN    0        A
PRODUCT     0XXXXXXXX
            0XXXXXXXX
            0
COMPETES    0
WITH        0A C
PEER        0| |
            0
HOSTILITY   0     C A
AFFECTION   OXXXXXXXXXXXXXXXXXXXXX
TO PEER     OXXXXXXXXXXXXXXXXXXXXX
            0
LEADS AND   0      C   A
FOLLOWS     OXXXXXXXXXXXXXXXX
PEER        OXXXXXXXXXXXXXX
            0
            0   1   2   3   4   5   6   7   8   9   10
```

SUBJECT NUMBER 2   SUBJECT CLASS 2A   91.8 % OF OBSERVED TIME REPRESENTED

SOCIAL TASKS

```
TO PLEASE                                          O=
TO COOPERATE                                       O
TO GAIN APPROVAL                                   C
TO PROCURE A SERVICE                               O===
TO GAIN ATTENTION                                  O==
TO MAINTAIN SOCIAL CONTACT                         C=======
TO AVOID UNPLEASANT CIRCUMSTANCES                  O
TO ANNOY                                           O
TO DIRECT                                          O=
TO ASSERT SELF (PROTECT DOMAIN)                    O
TO PROVIDE INFORMATION                             O
TO COMPETE                                         O
TO REJECT OVERTURES                                O
TO ENJOY PETS                                      O
TO CONVERSE                                        O==
TO PRODUCE VERBALIZATIONS                          O
                      NON-SOCIAL TASKS
TO EAT                                             O===
TO GAIN INFORMATION - VISUAL                       O===========
TO GAIN INFORMATION - VISUAL AND AUDITORY          O=====
NON-TASK                                           O===========
TO PASS TIME                                       C==
TO FIND SOMETHING TO DO                            O=
TO PREPARE FOR AN ACTIVITY                         O=====
TO CONSTRUCT A PRODUCT                             O=====
TO CHOOSE                                          O
TO PROCURE AN OBJECT                               O=
TO ENGAGE IN LARGE MUSCLE ACTIVITY                 O=
TO GAIN PLEASURE                                   O=====
TO IMITATE                                         O
TO PRETEND (ROLE PLAY)                             O
TO EASE DISCOMFORT                                 C=
TO RESTORE ORDER                                   C=
TO RELIEVE ONESELF                                 O
TO DRESS/UNDRESS                                   O
TO OPERATE A MECHANISM                             C
TO EAT AND TO GAIN INFORMATION (VISUAL)            O====
TO EAT AND TO GAIN INFORMATION (VISUAL AND AUDITORY) O=======
TO EXPLORE                                         O======
TO IMPROVE A DEVELOPING SKILL (MASTERY)            O
```

```
C1234567890123456789012345678901234567890123456789 0
0          10         20         30         40        50
```

TASK DATA (% OF TOTAL TIME)

SUBJECT #5

SUBJECT #5 IS A TWO-YEAR-OLD middle-class A boy. He is the youngest of three children (a brother is 5, a sister is 3 1/2). Both parents are professional people; the mother works part time.

Subject lives in a large, lovely home (at least 15 rooms) close to the city. Although the home is furnished with valuable antiques, the children have access to all areas of the house. They are frequently observed in the living room using the furniture for climbing and imaginative play.

Next to the subject's bedroom there is a large playroom in which he spends a great deal of time watching television. When his mother is at home, the subject will often be observed playing word games with her or including her in his activities. She takes part in these activities willingly and will often expand and encourage the games.

Summary of Test Scores

S: Subject No. 5   Group: 2-year A

Tests	S's Score	Group Median	S's Rank	No. of S's Tied at that Rank
Bayley (MDI) 24 mos.	97 IQ	105 IQ	11/12	—
Stanford-Binet 36 mos.	142 IQ			
Language Test				
at 24 mos.	37.5 mos.	36.0 mos.	3/7	—
at 27 mos.	51.0 mos.	40.5 mos.	2/9	2
at 30 mos.	51.0 mos.	51.0 mos.	1/4	6
at 36 mos.	57.0 mos.			
Abstract Abilities				
at 24 mos.	20.5 mos.	20.5 mos.	6/9	2
at 27 mos.	24.5 mos.	24.5 mos.	5/9	—
at 30 mos.	34.0 mos.	24.5 mos.	5/8	—
at 36 mos.	54.0 mos.			
Discrimination				
at 24 mos.	Level 3	Level 3	4/6	6
at 27 mos.	Level 5	Level 4	4/6	2
at 30 mos.	Level 8	Level 7	1/5	3
at 36 mos.	Level 2			
Social Competence				
with Adults	19.7	16.7	4/12	—
with Peers	13.0	6.2	2/12	—
Overall	32.7	22.5	2/12	—

SOCIAL COMPETENCE FOR SUBJECT 5 (2A)

```
GAIN            O
ADULT           OXXXXXXXXXXXXXXXXXXX  A C
ATTENTION       OXXXXXXXXXXXXXXXXXXX  | |
                O
USE             O                C        A
ADULT           OXXXXXXXXXXXXXXXXXXXXXXXXXXXXXXXXXXXXXXXXXXXXXX
RESOURCE        OXXXXXXXXXXXXXXXXXXXXXXXXXXXXXXXXXXXXXXXXXXXXXX
                O
HOSTILITY       O              C A
AFFECTION       OXXXXXXXXXXXXXXXXXXXXX
TO ADULT        OXXXXXXXXXXXXXXXXXXXXX
               A?C
ROLE PLAY       O
                OXXXXXXXXXXXX
                OXXXXXXXXXXXX
                O
PRIDE IN        O      A
PRODUCT         O      |
                O
                O
COMPETES        OA C
WITH            OXXXXXXX
PEER            OXXXXXXX
                O
HOSTILITY       O      C A
AFFECTION       OXXXXXXXXXXXXXXXXXXXXXXXXXXXXXXXXXXXXXXXXXXXXXXXXX
TO PEER         OXXXXXXXXXXXXXXXXXXXXXXXXXXXXXXXXXXXXXXXXXXXXXXXXX
                O
LEADS AND       O      C   A
FOLLOWS         OXXXXXXXXXX
PEER            OXXXXXXXXXX
                O
                O   1   2   3   4   5   6   7   8   9   10
```

SOCIAL TASKS

```
TO PLEASE                                          0=
TO COOPERATE                                       0=
TO GAIN APPROVAL                                   0
TO PROCURE A SERVICE                               0==
TO GAIN ATTENTION                                  0======
TO MAINTAIN SOCIAL CONTACT                         0
TO AVOID UNPLEASANT CIRCUMSTANCES                  0
TO ANNOY                                           0
TO DIRECT                                          0
TO ASSERT SELF (PROTECT DOMAIN)                    0=
TO PROVIDE INFORMATION                             0=
TO COMPETE                                         0
TO REJECT OVERTURES                                0
TO ENJOY PETS                                      0
TO CONVERSE                                        0
TO PRODUCE VERBALIZATIONS                          0

                  NON-SOCIAL TASKS

TO EAT                                             0=======
TO GAIN INFORMATION - VISUAL                       0==========
TO GAIN INFORMATION - VISUAL AND AUDITORY          0==================================
NON-TASK                                           0=======
TO PASS TIME                                       0==
TO FIND SOMETHING TO DO                            0=
TO PREPARE FOR AN ACTIVITY                         0=
TO CONSTRUCT A PRODUCT                             0
TO CHOOSE                                          0
TO PROCURE AN OBJECT                               0
TO ENGAGE IN LARGE MUSCLE ACTIVITY                 0
TO GAIN PLEASURE                                   0=
TO IMITATE                                         0
TO PRETEND (ROLE PLAY)                             0=
TO EASE DISCOMFORT                                 0=
TO RESTORE ORDER                                   0
TO RELIEVE ONESELF                                 0
TO DRESS/UNDRESS                                   0
TO OPERATE A MECHANISM                             0==
TO EAT AND TO GAIN INFORMATION (VISUAL)            0=
TO EAT AND TO GAIN INFORMATION (VISUAL AND AUDITORY) 0====
TO EXPLORE                                         0=
TO IMPROVE A DEVELOPING SKILL (MASTERY             0====

  1234567890123456789012345678901234567890123456789 0
  0        10        20        30        40        50
```

TASK DATA (% OF TOTAL TIME)

SUBJECT #6

SUBJECT #6 IS A ONE-YEAR-OLD lower-class C girl. She has four older siblings ranging in age from 6 to 19. The family lives in a run-down two-family house in a suburban area. However, their apartment is well kept at all times.

There are few toys available or appropriate for a one-year-old. The subject's mother tries to interest the subject in books or watching television with little success. The subject is particularly oriented toward her mother and demands to be carried by or close to her mother at all times.

Summary of Test Scores

S: Subject No. 6   Group: 1-year C

Tests	S's Score	Group Median	S's Rank	No. of S's Tied at that Rank
Bayley (MDI) 12 mos.	82 IQ	99 IQ	3/4	—
Stanford-Binet 24 mos.	109 IQ			
Language Test				
at 12 mos.	13 mos.	11.5 mos.	2/3	—
at 15 mos.	16 mos.	16.0 mos.	2/3	—
at 21 mos.	24 mos.	25.5 mos.	2/2	—
at 24 mos.	30 mos.			
Abstract Abilities				
at 12 mos.	15.5 mos.	9.5 mos.	1/4	—
at 15 mos.	11.0 mos.	11.0 mos.	2/3	—
at 21 mos.	16.5 mos.	18.5 mos.	2/2	—
at 24 mos.	16.5 mos.			
Discrimination				
at 12 mos.	Level 1	Level 0	1/2	—
at 15 mos.	Level 3	Level 3	1/2	2
at 21 mos.	Level 3	Level 4	2/2	—
at 24 mos.	Level 4			
Social Competence				
with Adults	13.3	10.6	9/14	—
with Peers	0.0	24.3	6/6	9
Overall	13.3	30.7	10/14	—

SOCIAL COMPETENCE FOR SUBJECT 6 (1C)

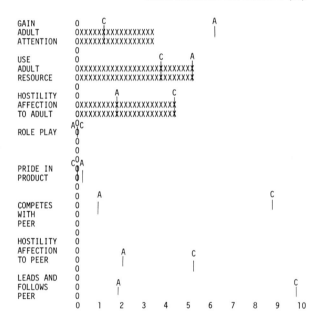

SUBJECT NUMBER 6   SUBJECT CLASS IC   97.0 % OF OBSERVED TIME REPRESENTED

SOCIAL TASKS

TO PLEASE   0=
TO COOPERATE   0====
TO GAIN APPROVAL   0==
TO PROCURE A SERVICE   0=
TO GAIN ATTENTION   0==
TO MAINTAIN SOCIAL CONTACT   0======
TO AVOID UNPLEASANT CIRCUMSTANCES   0==
TO ANNOY   0=
TO DIRECT   0===
TO ASSERT SELF (PROTECT DOMAIN)   0
TO PROVIDE INFORMATION   0
TO COMPETE   0
TO REJECT OVERTURES   0
TO ENJOY PETS   0
TO CONVERSE   0
TO PRODUCE VERBALIZATIONS   0

NON-SOCIAL TASKS

TO EAT   0=======
TO GAIN INFORMATION - VISUAL   0===============
TO GAIN INFORMATION - VISUAL ANDAUDITORY   0==============
NON-TASK   0==============
TO PASS TIME   0
TO FIND SOMETHING TO DO   0
TO PREPARE FOR AN ACTIVITY   0======
TO CONSTRUCT A PRODUCT   0
TO CHOOSE   0
TO PROCURE AN OBJECT   0=
TO ENGAGE IN LARGE MUSCLE ACTIVITY   0
TO GAIN PLEASURE   0
TO IMITATE   0
TO PRETEND (ROLE PLAY)   0==
TO EASE DISCOMFORT   0=
TO RESTORE ORDER   0=
TO RELIEVE ONESELF   0
TO DRESS/UNDRESS   0
TO OPERATE A MECHANISM   0=
TO EAT AND TO GAIN INFORMATION (VISUAL)   0==
TO EAT AND TO GAIN INFORMATION (VISUAL AND AUDITORY) 0=
TO EXPLORE   0===========
TO IMPROVE A DEVELOPING SKILL (MASTERY   0=

                                                 0123456789012345678901234567890123456789012345678 90
                                                 0   10   20   30   40   50

                                                 TASK DATA (% OF TOTAL TIME)

SUBJECT #8

SUBJECT #8 IS A ONE-YEAR-OLD middle-class A boy who is the only child of a graduate-student couple. He is a bright, assertive, active child, exposed to unusually frequent interaction with his mother, who engages his attention with a variety of interesting learning experiences ranging from books to live animals. She is a mother who manages to extract a learning experience from the most mundane task and make it come to life. Subject #8 has access to all parts of the home which, although small, has been arranged to provide the maximum in enjoyment for the child. The mother is totally child-centered in philosophy and very devoted to shaping the child's interests and awareness of the world around him. The home is fairly well equipped with toys suitable to the subject's age and interest level.

Summary of Test Scores

S: Subject No. 8   Group: 1-year A

Tests	S's Score	Group Median	S's Rank	No. of S's Tied at that Rank
Bayley (MDI) 12 mos.	106 IQ	103 IQ	5/10	—
Stanford-Binet 24 mos.	123 IQ			
Language Test				
at 12 mos.	18 mos.	16 mos.	2/7	2
at 15 mos.	24 mos.	17 mos.	1/5	2
at 21 mos.	36 mos.	36 mos.	3/4	3
at 24 mos.	36 mos.			
Abstract Abilities				
at 12 mos.	15.5 mos.	15.5 mos.	2/5	4
at 15 mos.	15.5 mos.	15.5 mos.	2/6	3
at 21 mos.	20.5 mos.	22.5 mos.	4/7	—
at 24 mos.	20.5 mos.			
Discrimination				
at 12 mos.	Level 3	Level 2	1/4	2
at 15 mos.	Level 3	Level 2	1/4	2
at 21 mos.	Level 3.50	Level 3.25	4/6	—
at 24 mos.	Level 6			
Social Competence				
with Adults	33.8	17.3	2/14	—
with Peers	0.0	7.9	6/6	9
Overall	33.8	20.1	3/14	—

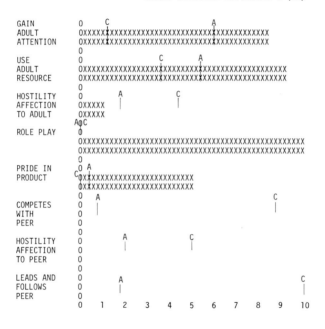

SOCIAL COMPETENCE FOR SUBJECT 8 (1A)

SUBJECT NUMBER 2   SUBJECT CLASS 1A   97.7 % OF OBSERVED TIME REPRESENTED

SOCIAL TASKS

```
TO PLEASE                                          0=
TO COOPERATE                                       0====
TO GAIN APPROVAL                                   0=
TO PROCURE A SERVICE                               0=
TO GAIN ATTENTION                                  0==
TO MAINTAIN SOCIAL CONTACT                         0=
TO AVOID UNPLEASANT CIRCUMSTANCES                  0
TO ANNOY                                           0
TO DIRECT                                          0
TO ASSERT SELF (PROTECT DOMAIN)                    0=
TO PROVIDE INFORMATION                             0
TO COMPETE                                         0
TO REJECT OVERTURES                                0
TO ENJOY PETS                                      0
TO CONVERSE                                        0
TO PRODUCE VERBALIZATIONS                          0

                            NON-SOCIAL TASKS

TO EAT                                             0=
TO GAIN INFORMATION - VISUAL                       0=================
TO GAIN INFORMATION - VISUAL ANDAUDITORY          0=================
NON-TASK                                           0======
TO PASS TIME                                       0=
TO FIND SOMETHING TO DO                            0
TO PREPARE FOR AN ACTIVITY                         0==
TO CONSTRUCT A PRODUCT                             0
TO CHOOSE                                          0
TO PROCURE AN OBJECT                               0===
TO ENGAGE IN LARGE MUSCLE ACTIVITY                 0
TO GAIN PLEASURE                                   0=
TO IMITATE                                         0
TO PRETEND (ROLE PLAY)                             0
TO EASE DISCOMFORT                                 0
TO RESTORE ORDER                                   0
TO RELIEVE ONESELF                                 0
TO DRESS/UNDRESS                                   0
TO OPERATE A MECHANISM                             0
TO EAT AND TO GAIN INFORMATION (VISUAL)           0=====
TO EAT AND TO GAIN INFORMATION (VISUAL AND AUDITORY) 0====
TO EXPLORE                                         0=========
TO IMPROVE A DEVELOPING SKILL (MASTERY            0============
                                                  0123456789012345678901234567890123456789012345678 90
                                                  0        10        20        30        40        50
```

TASK DATA (% OF TOTAL TIME)

SUBJECT #9

SUBJECT #9 IS A TWO YEAR OLD middle-class A child who lives in a comfortable, modern home in a woodsy, suburban setting. She is an only child, but spends a great deal of time in the company of a two-year-old playmate.

Her parents are college educated and are often away from the home. The subject's mother has an active career and works several days a week. During her absence, subject is cared for by several regular babysitters, usually along with her two-year-old girl friend (Subject #10). This setup (with the girl friend) was carefully arranged by subject's mother, who feels that it is in the best interest of her child's development. Subject's father also takes part in his daughter's care when he is at home. He has a warm and affectionate relationship with her that contrasts somewhat with his wife's cooler but active approach. The mother often both directs and takes part in subject's play, setting up games and puzzles or reading to subject. She also treats her daughter in an adult-like manner.

The subject herself is a mature child who gets along well with adults. She tends to dominate her playmates and is pushy and stubborn, insisting on getting her own way. She spends a great deal of time playing outdoors, riding a bicycle and playing on her backyard jungle gym.

Summary of Test Scores
S: Subject No. 9   Group: 2-year A

Tests	S's Score	Group Median	S's Rank	No. of S's Tied at that Rank
Bayley (MDI) 24 mos.	109 IQ	105 IQ	5/12	—
Stanford-Binet 36 mos.	150 IQ			
Language Test				
at 24 mos.	30 mos.	36.0 mos.	6/7	—
at 27 mos.	36 mos.	40.5 mos.	7/9	3
at 30 mos.	51 mos.	51.0 mos.	1/4	6
at 36 mos.	51 mos.			
Abstract Abilities				
at 24 mos.	20.5 mos.	20.5 mos.	5/9	—
at 27 mos.	24.5 mos.	24.5 mos.	6/9	2
at 30 mos.	24.5 mos.	24.5 mos.	3/8	2
at 36 mos.	54.0 mos.			
Discrimination				
at 24 mos.	Level 3	Level 3	4/6	6
at 27 mos.	Level 3	Level 4	5/6	4
at 30 mos.	Level 3.5	Level 7	3/5	—
at 36 mos.	Level 8			
Social Competence				
with Adults	10.0	16.7	10/12	—
with Peers	12.5	6.2	3/12	—
Overall	22.5	22.5	6/12	—

SOCIAL COMPETENCE FOR SUBJECT 9 (2A)

```
GAIN          O
ADULT         OXXXXXXXXXXXXXXXXXXXX   A C
ATTENTION     OXXXXXXXXXXXXXXXXXXXX   | |
              O
USE           O                C
ADULT         OXXXXXXXXXXXXXXXXXXX      A
RESOURCE      OXXXXXXXXXXXXXXXXXXX      |
              O
HOSTILITY     O
AFFECTION     OXXXXXXXXX     C A
TO ADULT      OXXXXXXXXX     | |
             AOC
ROLE PLAY     O
              O
              O
              O
PRIDE IN     CO      A
PRODUCT       O      |
              O
              O
COMPETES     OA  C
WITH          OXXXXXXXXXXXXXXXXXXXXXXXXXXXXXXXXXXXXXXXXXXXXXXXXXXXXXX
PEER          OXXXXXXXXXXXXXXXXXXXXXXXXXXXXXXXXXXXXXXXXXXXXXXXXXXXXXX
              O
HOSTILITY     O     C A
AFFECTION     OXXXXXXX |
TO PEER       OXXXXXXX |
              O
LEADS AND     O
FOLLOWS       OXXXXX C   A
PEER          OXXXXX |   |
              O
              0   1   2   3   4   5   6   7   8   9   10
```

```
SUBJECT NUMBER 9          SUBJECT CLASS 2A          96.3 % OF OBSERVED TIME REPRESENTED

          SOCIAL TASKS

TO PLEASE                                            0===
TO COOPERATE                                         0==
TO GAIN APPROVAL                                     0==
TO PROCURE A SERVICE                                 0===
TO GAIN ATTENTION                                    0===
TO MAINTAIN SOCIAL CONTACT                           0===
TO AVOID UNPLEASANT CIRCUMSTANCES                    0==
TO ANNOY                                             0==
TO DIRECT                                            0==
TO ASSERT SELF (PROTECT DOMAIN)                      0==
TO PROVIDE INFORMATION                               0==
TO COMPETE                                           0
TO REJECT OVERTURES                                  0==
TO ENJOY PETS                                        0=
TO CONVERSE                                          0===
TO PRODUCE VERBALIZATIONS                            0
          NON-SOCIAL TASKS

TO EAT                                               0=========
TO GAIN INFORMATION - VISUAL                         0==============
TO GAIN INFORMATION - VISUAL AND AUDITORY            0==================
NON-TASK                                             0===
TO PASS TIME                                         0==
TO FIND SOMETHING TO DO                              0
TO PREPARE FOR AN ACTIVITY                           0====
TO CONSTRUCT A PRODUCT                               0
TO CHOOSE                                            0
TO PROCURE AN OBJECT                                 0=====
TO ENGAGE IN LARGE MUSCLE ACTIVITY                   0==
TO GAIN PLEASURE                                     0
TO IMITATE                                           0==
TO PRETEND (ROLE PLAY)                               0====
TO EASE DISCOMFORT                                   0
TO RESTORE ORDER                                     0
TO RELIEVE ONESELF                                   0
TO DRESS/UNDRESS                                     0
TO OPERATE A MECHANISM                               0
TO EAT AND TO GAIN INFORMATION (VISUAL)              0=
TO EAT AND TO GAIN INFORMATION (VISUAL AND AUDITORY) 0====
TO EXPLORE                                           0====
TO IMPROVE A DEVELOPING SKILL (MASTERY)              0

          0123456789012345678901234567890123456789012345678901234567890
          0         10        20        30        40        50

          TASK DATA (% OF TOTAL TIME)
```

SUBJECT #10

SUBJECT #10 IS A TWO-YEAR-OLD middle-class A girl, the youngest of three children, including an eight-year-old sister and a six-year-old brother. Her family lives in a comfortable, warmly furnished home in an attractive suburban neighborhood. The home has a well-equipped playroom, a piano that subject often uses, and an enclosed backyard complete with swing set and bicycles.

Subject #10 is an outgoing and friendly child with a generally sunny disposition. She gets along well with peers and has grown up in frequent contact with a girl friend of the same age. Her older siblings are very affectionate toward subject and often include her in their play. When they are at school, subject plays well by herself.

Subject #10's parents are well educated and show concern for their children's development, particularly subject's mother. She is a busy, efficient woman dedicated to interests outside the home as well as to the upbringing of her children. She frequently takes subject along on errands, but spends much time away from the home, with subject being cared for by several regular babysitters, usually together with her two-year-old playmate. The subject's mother has gone to some trouble to set up an arrangement so that her child can be cared for in the company of her little friend.

When at home, subject's mother does not set up or participate in subject's play, as a rule, but encourages her independence, frequently checking on her and praising her activities. The mother provides comfort and affection when subject shows a need for this.

Summary of Test Scores

S: Subject No. 10   Group: 2-year A

Tests	S's Score	Group Median	S's Rank	No. of S's Tied at that Rank
Bayley (MDI) 24 mos.	106 IQ	105 IQ	6/12	—
Stanford-Binet 36 mos.	135 IQ			
Language Test				
at 24 mos.	33 mos.	36.0 mos.	5/7	2
at 27 mos.	45 mos.	40.5 mos.	4/9	—
at 30 mos.	51 mos.	51.0 mos.	1/4	6
at 36 mos.	51 mos.			
Abstract Abilities				
at 24 mos.	20.5 mos.	20.5 mos.	7/9	—
at 27 mos.	28.5 mos.	24.5 mos.	4/9	2
at 30 mos.	24.5 mos.	24.5 mos.	6/8	—
at 36 mos.	54.0 mos.			
Discrimination				
at 24 mos.	Level 3	Level 3	4/6	6
at 27 mos.	Level 2	Level 4	6/6	2
at 30 mos.	Level 7	Level 7	2/5	3
at 36 mos.	Level 8			
Social Competence				
with Adults	14.8	16.7	9/12	—
with Peers	6.2	6.2	6/12	—
Overall	20.9	22.5	9/12	—

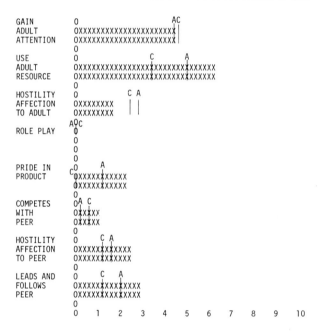

SOCIAL COMPETENCE FOR SUBJECT 10 (2A)

SUBJECT NUMBER 10   SUBJECT CLASS 2A   98.8 % OF OBSERVED TIME REPRESENTED

SOCIAL TASKS

TO PLEASE   0=
TO COOPERATE   0===
TO GAIN APPROVAL   0=
TO PROCURE A SERVICE   0====
TO GAIN ATTENTION   0==
TO MAINTAIN SOCIAL CONTACT   0==
TO AVOID UNPLEASANT CIRCUMSTANCES   0
TO ANNOY   0
TO DIRECT   0=
TO ASSERT SELF (PROTECT DOMAIN)   0=
TO PROVIDE INFORMATION   0=
TO COMPETE   0
TO REJECT OVERTURES   0
TO ENJOY PETS   0
TO CONVERSE   0
TO PRODUCE VERBALIZATIONS   0

                        NON-SOCIAL TASKS

TO EAT   0===========
TO GAIN INFORMATION - VISUAL   0============
TO GAIN INFORMATION - VISUAL ANDAUDITORY   0============
NON-TASK   0====
TO PASS TIME   0==
TO FIND SOMETHING TO DO   0==========
TO PREPARE FOR AN ACTIVITY   0====
TO CONSTRUCT A PRODUCT   0
TO CHOOSE   0
TO PROCURE AN OBJECT   0
TO ENGAGE IN LARGE MUSCLE ACTIVITY   0
TO GAIN PLEASURE   0=
TO IMITATE   0
TO PRETEND (ROLE PLAY)   0=
TO EASE DISCOMFORT   0=
TO RESTORE ORDER   0=
TO RELIEVE ONESELF   0
TO DRESS/UNDRESS   0
TO OPERATE A MECHANISM   0
TO EAT AND TO GAIN INFORMATION (VISUAL)   0=
TO EAT AND TO GAIN INFORMATION (VISUAL AND AUDITORY)   0====
TO EXPLORE   0====
TO IMPROVE A DEVELOPING SKILL (MASTERY   0==========

                                                 0123456789012345678901234567890123456789012345678890
                                                 0   10   20   30   40   50

                        TASK DATA (% OF TOTAL TIME)

SUBJECT #11

SUBJECT #11 IS A ONE-YEAR-OLD middle-class A girl. She has one older sister, aged five. The family lives in an airy, pleasant, five-room apartment in an academic area. The father does research and teaches at the college level and the mother, although active in volunteer activities, spends much of her time at home with the children.

The subject spends each morning at home alone with her mother while her sister attends school. She is a physically mature child and enjoys climbing on furniture and exploring household objects. Her mother does not restrict her in these pursuits but does keep a watchful eye on the subject to make sure she does not get into trouble. The subject's mother is easily accessible to the subject and will often make suggestions to her. In addition to household objects, there are many toys, books, and dolls that the subject is encouraged to play with.

Summary of Test Scores

S: Subject No. 11   Group: 1-year A

Tests	S's Score	Group Median	S's Rank	No. of S's Tied at that Rank
Bayley (MDI) 12 mos.	119 IQ	103 IQ	2/10	—
Stanford-Binet 24 mos.	119 IQ			
Language Test				
at 12 mos.	18.0 mos.	16.0 mos.	2/7	2
at 15 mos.	21.0 mos.	17.0 mos.	2/5	—
at 21 mos.	39.0 mos.	36.0 mos.	2/5	—
Abstract Abilities				
at 12 mos.	15.5 mos.	15.5 mos.	1/5	—
at 15 mos.	15.5 mos.	15.5 mos.	1/6	—
at 21 mos.	24.5 mos.	22.5 mos.	1/6	—
Discrimination				
at 12 mos.	Level 2	Level 2	2/4	5
at 15 mos.	Level 2	Level 2	2/4	6
at 21 mos.	Level 4	Level 3.25	3/6	—
Social Competence				
with Adults	13.9	17.3	6/14	—
with Peers	11.0	7.9	3/6	—
Overall	24.9	20.1	5/14	—

SOCIAL COMPETENCE FOR SUBJECT 11 (1A)

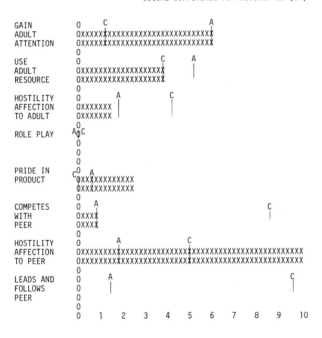

SUBJECT NUMBER 11   SUBJECT CLASS 1A   99.3 % OF OBSERVED TIME REPRESENTED

SOCIAL TASKS

```
TO PLEASE                                          0=
TO COOPERATE                                       0=
TO GAIN APPROVAL                                   0=
TO PROCURE A SERVICE                               0=
TO GAIN ATTENTION                                  0====
TO MAINTAIN SOCIAL CONTACT                         0=
TO AVOID UNPLEASANT CIRCUMSTANCES                  0=
TO ANNOY                                           0=
TO DIRECT                                          0=
TO ASSERT SELF (PROTECT DOMAIN)                    0===
TO PROVIDE INFORMATION                             0=
TO COMPETE                                         0=
TO REJECT OVERTURES                                0=
TO ENJOY PETS                                      0=
TO CONVERSE                                        0=
TO PRODUCE VERBALIZATIONS                          0=
```

NON-SOCIAL TASKS

```
TO EAT                                             0==
TO GAIN INFORMATION - VISUAL                       0==============================
TO GAIN INFORMATION - VISUAL ANDAUDITORY           0=========
TO PASS TIME                                       0==============
NON-TASK                                           0==
TO FIND SOMETHING TO DO                            0==
TO PREPARE FOR AN ACTIVITY                         0
TO CONSTRUCT A PRODUCT                             0
TO CHOOSE                                          0
TO PROCURE AN OBJECT                               0==
TO ENGAGE IN LARGE MUSCLE ACTIVITY                 0==
TO GAIN PLEASURE                                   0==
TO IMITATE                                         0
TO PRETEND (ROLE PLAY)                             0==
TO EASE DISCOMFORT                                 0
TO RESTORE ORDER                                   0
TO RELIEVE ONESELF                                 0
TO DRESS/UNDRESS                                   0
TO OPERATE A MECHANISM                             0
TO EAT AND TO GAIN INFORMATION (VISUAL)            0=
TO EAT AND TO GAIN INFORMATION (VISUAL AND AUDITORY) 0
TO EXPLORE                                         0=====
TO IMPROVE A DEVELOPING SKILL (MASTERY             0=====
                                                   0123456789012345678901234567890123456789012345678 90
                                                   0    10    20    30    40    50
```

TASK DATA (% OF TOTAL TIME)

SUBJECT #12

SUBJECT #12 IS A TWO-YEAR-OLD middle-class A boy. The family lives in a spacious home in a suburban area close to the city. The subject has three siblings, a sister (five years old) and two brothers (one four years old, and an infant three months old). Both parents are well educated. Although the mother does not work, she is out daily, and the children are left in the care of the live-in maid.

The subject is a lively child who enjoys playing with vehicles: trikes, wagons, cars, trucks. He has free access to most areas of the house and is encouraged to play outside as well.

Although subject's home is well equipped with toys, the atmosphere is not particularly child-centered. Subject's mother is usually busy with her own activities and restricts her interactions with subject to checking up on what he is doing.

Summary of Test Scores

S: Subject No. 12   Group: 2-year A

Tests	S's Score	Group Median	S's Rank	No. of S's Tied at that Rank
Bayley (MDI) 24 mos.	102 IQ	105 IQ	8/12	2
Language Test				
at 24 mos.	36.0 mos.	36.0 mos.	4/7	4
at 27 mos.	36.0 mos.	40.5 mos.	7/9	3
at 30 mos.	42.0 mos.	51.0 mos.	2/4	—
at 36 mos.	51.0 mos.			
Abstract Abilities				
at 24 mos.	20.5 mos.	20.5 mos.	6/9	2
at 27 mos.	24.5 mos.	24.5 mos.	6/9	2
at 30 mos.	24.5 mos.	24.5 mos.	3/8	2
Discrimination				
at 24 mos.	Level 2	Level 3	5/6	2
at 27 mos.	Level 3	Level 4	5/6	4
at 30 mos.	Level 7	Level 7	2/5	3
Social Competence				
with Adults	7.1	16.7	12/12	—
with Peers	0.8	6.2	10/12	—
Overall	7.9	22.5	12/12	—

SOCIAL COMPETENCE FOR SUBJECT 12 (2A)

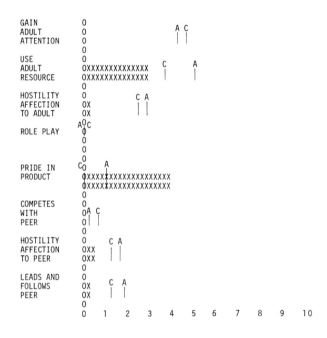

SUBJECT NUMBER 12   SUBJECT CLASS 2A   98.4 % OF OBSERVED TIME REPRESENTED

SOCIAL TASKS

```
TO PLEASE                                              0===
TO COOPERATE                                           0==
TO GAIN APPROVAL                                       0==
TO PROCURE A SERVICE                                   0==
TO GAIN ATTENTION                                      0=
TO MAINTAIN SOCIAL CONTACT                             0====
TO AVOID UNPLEASANT CIRCUMSTANCES                      0==
TO ANNOY                                               0
TO DIRECT                                              0==
TO ASSERT SELF (PROTECT DOMAIN)                        0==
TO PROVIDE INFORMATION                                 0
TO COMPETE                                             0
TO REJECT OVERTURES                                    0
TO ENJOY PETS                                          0
TO CONVERSE                                            0
TO PRODUCE VERBALIZATIONS                              0
                     NON-SOCIAL TASKS

TO EAT                                                 0===
TO GAIN INFORMATION - VISUAL                           0===================
TO GAIN INFORMATION - VISUAL ANDAUDITORY               0===================
NON-TASK                                               0=
TO PASS TIME                                           0
TO FIND SOMETHING TO DO                                0==
TO PREPARE FOR AN ACTIVITY                             0
TO CONSTRUCT A PRODUCT                                 0==
TO CHOOSE                                              0==
TO PROCURE AN OBJECT                                   0==
TO ENGAGE IN LARGE MUSCLE ACTIVITY                     0====
TO GAIN PLEASURE                                       0==
TO IMITATE                                             0
TO PRETEND (ROLE PLAY)                                 0
TO EASE DISCOMFORT                                     0==
TO RESTORE ORDER                                       0==
TO RELIEVE ONESELF                                     0
TO DRESS/UNDRESS                                       0
TO OPERATE A MECHANISM                                 0
TO EAT AND TO GAIN INFORMATION (VISUAL)                0====
TO EAT AND TO GAIN INFORMATION (VISUAL AND AUDITORY)   0
TO EXPLORE                                             0====
TO IMPROVE A DEVELOPING SKILL (MASTERY                 0=========
                      01234567890123456789012345678901234567890
                      0         10        20        30        40        50

                           TASK DATA (% OF TOTAL TIME)
```

SUBJECT #13

SUBJECT #13 IS A TWO-YEAR-OLD middle-class A boy. His family lives in a lovely, spacious home in an affluent suburban area close to the city. Subject is a middle child, the only boy, with two sisters, a six-year-old and a one-year-old baby. Both parents are well educated. Although subject's mother does not work, she is very busy at home and goes out on frequent errands, usually bringing the subject along.

When at home, she usually lets the subject occupy himself with his many toys and books rather than participating in or directing his play. Subject's mother particularly encourages gross motor activities and shows concern for the healthy physical development of her children. An indoor exercise bar for the children's use and a jungle gym set outdoors reflect this interest.

Subject #13 tends to seek out his mother for emotional support; perhaps his position as a middle child, with a new baby in the home and an older sister who often excludes him from her play, encourages this "babyish" behavior. At such times, subject's mother is quite willing to cuddle him and allow him to tag along after her with his blanket in hand.

Summary of Test Scores
S: Subject No. 13   Group: 2-year "A"

Tests	S's Score	Group Median	S's Rank	No. of S's Tied at that Rank
Bayley (MDI) 24 mos.	102 IQ	105 IQ	8/12	2
Stanford-Binet 36 mos.	128 IQ			
Language Test				
at 24 mos.	36 mos.	36 mos.	4/7	4
at 27 mos.	39 mos.	40.5 mos.	6/9	—
at 30 mos.	36 mos.	51 mos.	3/4	—
at 36 mos.	48 mos.			
Abstract Abilities				
at 24 mos.	20.5 mos.	20.5 mos.	4/9	—
at 27 mos.	20.5 mos.	24.5 mos.	8/9	—
at 30 mos.	20.5 mos.	24.5 mos.	7/8	—
at 36 mos.	48 mos.			
Discrimination				
at 24 mos.	Level 3	Level 3	4/6	6
at 27 mos.	Level 8	Level 4	1/6	—
at 30 mos.	Level 8	Level 7	1/5	3
at 36 mos.	Level 8			
Social Competence				
with Adults	21.9	16.7	2/12	—
with Peers	0.0	6.2	12/12	—
Overall	21.9	22.5	7/12	—

SOCIAL COMPETENCE FOR SUBJECT 13 (2A)

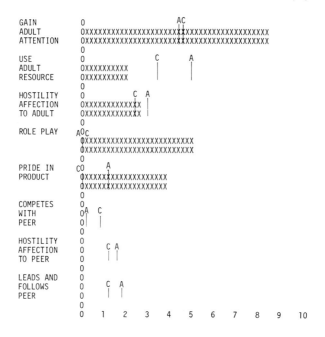

SOCIAL TASKS

Task	
TO PLEASE	0====
TO COOPERATE	0
TO GAIN APPROVAL	0==
TO PROCURE A SERVICE	0=====
TO GAIN ATTENTION	0====
TO MAINTAIN SOCIAL CONTACT	0======
TO AVOID UNPLEASANT CIRCUMSTANCES	0
TO ANNOY	0
TO DIRECT	0=
TO ASSERT SELF (PROTECT DOMAIN)	0
TO PROVIDE INFORMATION	0
TO COMPETE	0
TO REJECT OVERTURES	0
TO ENJOY PETS	0
TO CONVERSE	0
TO PRODUCE VERBALIZATIONS	0

NON-SOCIAL TASKS

Task	
TO EAT	0=
TO GAIN INFORMATION – VISUAL	0==============
TO GAIN INFORMATION – VISUAL AND AUDITORY	0==============
NON-TASK	0====
TO PASS TIME	0===
TO FIND SOMETHING TO DO	0=
TO PREPARE FOR AN ACTIVITY	0=
TO CONSTRUCT A PRODUCT	0
TO CHOOSE	0
TO PROCURE AN OBJECT	0==
TO ENGAGE IN LARGE MUSCLE ACTIVITY	0=
TO GAIN PLEASURE	0
TO IMITATE	0
TO PRETEND (ROLE PLAY)	0======
TO EASE DISCOMFORT	0=
TO RESTORE ORDER	0
TO RELIEVE ONESELF	0
TO DRESS/UNDRESS	0
TO OPERATE A MECHANISM	0=
TO EAT AND TO GAIN INFORMATION (VISUAL)	0
TO EAT AND TO GAIN INFORMATION (VISUAL AND AUDITORY)	0
TO EXPLORE	0======
TO IMPROVE A DEVELOPING SKILL (MASTERY	0=========

```
0123456789012345678901234567890123456789012345678901234567890
0         10        20        30        40        50
```

TASK DATA (% OF TOTAL TIME)

SUBJECT #14

SUBJECT #14 IS A TWO-YEAR-OLD lower-class C boy who lives in a three-family apartment in a rather stark working-class neighborhood. The home is fairly roomy, nicely furnished, and kept spotlessly clean. Subject #14 has his own small bedroom apart from his 5 1/2-year-old sister and 6-month-old baby brother.

He is a very active and vigorous child who causes much mischief for his often overwrought mother. She finds him to be a difficult child to handle and often refers to how much easier his more docile sister was to raise. He, in turn, is frustrated by the restrictions put on his activities (the neatness of the home is important to subject's mother) and also by the fact that he is usually excluded from his sister's "girlish" games. Sex-role differences are a recurring issue in this home. The subject's father is sometimes home during the day. At these times, he sides with his wife in restricting subject's activities and admonishing him to behave.

The subject has few appropriate toys of his own and is encouraged to play outdoors on a small back porch or on the backyard swing set. He seems to be bored and frustrated, and subsequently takes his energies out in "mischief."

Summary of Test Scores
S: Subject No. 14   Group: 2-year C

Tests	S's Score	Group Median	S's Rank	No. of S's Tied at that Rank
Bayley (MDI) 24 mos.	86 IQ	86 IQ	3/5	—
Stanford-Binet 36 mos.	92 IQ			
Language Test				
at 24 mos.	30 mos.	18 mos.	1/3	—
at 27 mos.	36 mos.	27 mos.	1/5	—
at 30 mos.	42 mos.	27 mos.	1/3	—
at 36 mos.	39 mos.			
Abstract Abilities				
at 24 mos.	16.5 mos.	16.5 mos.	all 16.5	—
at 27 mos.	16.5 mos.	16.5 mos.	2/2	3
at 30 mos.	16.5 mos.	16.5 mos.	1/2	2
at 36 mos.	24.5 mos.			
Discrimination				
at 24 mos.	Level 4	Level 3	1/3	—
at 27 mos.	Level 3	Level 2	2/3	2
at 30 mos.	Level 3	Level 3.5	4/5	—
at 36 mos.	Level 6			
Social Competence				
with Adults	24.6	11.7	1/6	2
with Peers	2.0	4.7	5/7	—
Overall	26.6	17.6	2/7	—

SOCIAL COMPETENCE FOR SUBJECT 14 (2C)

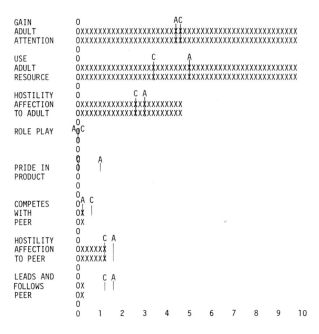

SUBJECT NUMBER 14   SUBJECT CLASS 2C   98.2 % OF OBSERVED TIME REPRESENTED

SOCIAL TASKS

```
TO PLEASE                                              0==
TO COOPERATE                                           0==
TO GAIN APPROVAL                                       0==
TO PROCURE A SERVICE                                   0=====
TO GAIN ATTENTION                                      0====
TO MAINTAIN SOCIAL CONTACT                             0===========
TO AVOID UNPLEASANT CIRCUMSTANCES                      0==
TO ANNOY                                               0
TO DIRECT                                              0==
TO ASSERT SELF (PROTECT DOMAIN)                        0===
TO PROVIDE INFORMATION                                 0
TO COMPETE                                             0
TO REJECT OVERTURES                                    0
TO ENJOY PETS                                          0
TO CONVERSE                                            0==
TO PRODUCE VERBALIZATIONS                              0

                      NON-SOCIAL TASKS

TO EAT                                                 0====
TO GAIN INFORMATION - VISUAL                           0=========
TO GAIN INFORMATION - VISUAL ANDAUDITORY               0=============
NON-TASK                                               0
TO PASS TIME                                           0
TO FIND SOMETHING TO DO                                0==
TO PREPARE FOR AN ACTIVITY                             0
TO CONSTRUCT A PRODUCT                                 0
TO CHOOSE                                              0
TO PROCURE AN OBJECT                                   0==
TO ENGAGE IN LARGE MUSCLE ACTIVITY                     0==
TO GAIN PLEASURE                                       0
TO IMITATE                                             0
TO PRETEND (ROLE PLAY)                                 0==
TO EASE DISCOMFORT                                     0==
TO RESTORE ORDER                                       0==
TO RELIEVE ONESELF                                     0==
TO DRESS/UNDRESS                                       0
TO OPERATE A MECHANISM                                 0==
TO EAT AND TO GAIN INFORMATION (VISUAL)                0==
TO EAT AND TO GAIN INFORMATION (VISUAL AND AUDITORY)   0=
TO EXPLORE                                             0====
TO IMPROVE A DEVELOPING SKILL (MASTERY                 0============

                      01234567890123456789012345678901234567890123456789012345678990123456789 0
                      0        10        20        30        40        50

                              TASK DATA (% OF TOTAL TIME)
```

SUBJECT #16

SUBJECT #16 IS A ONE-YEAR-OLD lower-class A boy. He has two older sisters, aged three and four. The family lives in a five-room apartment in an urban area. The father is at present attending college at night, and the mother hopes to go back to college to get her degree.

The subject is an active, curious child. Although there are few toys appropriate for a one-year-old, the subject keeps himself busy exploring household objects. However, his activities often get him into trouble, since he is usually one step behind his mother, undoing what she has just straightened.

The subject's mother is a warm, affectionate person who often finds herself exasperated by this active, assertive little boy.

Summary of Test Scores

S: Subject No. 16   Group: 1-year A

Tests	S's Score	Group Median	S's Rank	No. of S's Tied at that Rank
Bayley (MDI) 12 mos.	102 IQ	103 IQ	7/10	3
Language Test				
at 12 mos.	16 mos.	16 mos.	3/7	2
at 15 mos.	18 mos.	17 mos.	3/5	2
at 21 mos.	27 mos.	36 mos.	4/5	2
Abstract Abilities				
at 12 mos.	15.5 mos.	15.5 mos	2/5	4
at 15 mos.	15.5 mos.	15.5 mos.	4/6	2
at 21 mos.	24.5 mos.	22.5 mos.	2/6	2
Discrimination				
at 12 mos.	Level 2	Level 2	2/4	5
at 15 mos.	Level 2	Level 2	2/4	6
at 21 mos.	Level 3	Level 3.25	5/6	2
Social Competence				
with Adults	13.8	17.3	7/14	—
with Peers	1.4	7.9	5/6	—
Overall	15.2	20.1	8/14	—

SOCIAL COMPETENCE FOR SUBJECT 16 (1A)

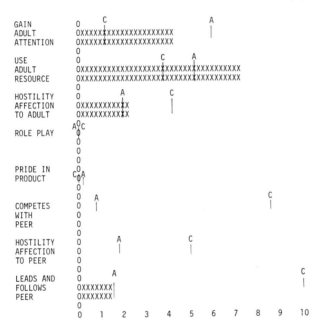

SUBJECT NUMBER 16   SUBJECT CLASS 1A   97.3 % OF OBSERVED TIME REPRESENTED

SOCIAL TASKS

```
TO PLEASE                                             0
TO COOPERATE                                          0===
TO GAIN APPROVAL                                      0
TO PROCURE A SERVICE                                  0==
TO GAIN ATTENTION                                     0====
TO MAINTAIN SOCIAL CONTACT                            0===
TO AVOID UNPLEASANT CIRCUMSTANCES                     0
TO ANNOY                                              0
TO DIRECT                                             0
TO ASSERT SELF (PROTECT DOMAIN)                       0==
TO PROVIDE INFORMATION                                0
TO COMPETE                                            0
TO REJECT OVERTURES                                   0
TO ENJOY PETS                                         0
TO CONVERSE                                           0
TO PRODUCE VERBALIZATIONS                             0
```

NON-SOCIAL TASKS

```
TO EAT                                                0=========
TO GAIN INFORMATION - VISUAL                          0==============
TO GAIN INFORMATION - VISUAL ANDAUDITORY              0============
NON-TASK                                              0==
TO PASS TIME                                          0==
TO FIND SOMETHING TO DO                               0==
TO PREPARE FOR AN ACTIVITY                            0==
TO CONSTRUCT A PRODUCT                                0
TO CHOOSE                                             0
TO PROCURE AN OBJECT                                  0========
TO ENGAGE IN LARGE MUSCLE ACTIVITY                    0
TO GAIN PLEASURE                                      0
TO IMITATE                                            0
TO PRETEND (RULE PLAY)                                0
TO EASE DISCOMFORT                                    0==
TO RESTORE ORDER                                      0==
TO RELIEVE ONESELF                                    0
TO DRESS/UNDRESS                                      0
TO OPERATE A MECHANISM                                0
TO EAT AND TO GAIN INFORMATION (VISUAL)               0====
TO EAT AND TO GAIN INFORMATION (VISUAL AND AUDITORY)  0=
TO EXPLORE                                            0=======
TO IMPROVE A DEVELOPING SKILL (MASTERY                0=======
                                                      0123456789012345678901234567890123456789012345678901234567890
                                                      0    10        20        30        40        50
```

TASK DATA (% OF TOTAL TIME)

SUBJECT #17

SUBJECT #17 IS A ONE-YEAR-OLD middle-class A girl. She has an older sister, aged four. Both parents are college educated. The subject's mother continues her interest in art in a home studio. The family lives in a comfortable one-family home in an academic area.

The subject is a shy, watchful child whose early physical development was fairly slow. She spends most of her time with her mother, who is warm but reserved; verbal interaction between mother and child is not very high.

The subject has the run of the house. There are a fair number of manipulative toys available to her, such as small blocks, puzzles, and dolls. Both parents are at home a good deal of the time, and they are consistently affectionate and available to the subject, although they are not inclined to didactic interaction with her. In nice weather much of her playtime takes place outdoors, with mother gardening nearby.

Summary of Test Scores

S: Subject No. 17   Group: 1-year A

Tests	S's Score	Group Median	S's Rank	No. of S's Tied at that Rank
Bayley (MDI) 12 mos.	100 IQ	103 IQ	8/9	—
Language Test				
at 12 mos.	12 mos.	16 mos.	6/7	—
at 15 mos.	14 mos.	17 mos.	5/5	—
at 21 mos.	27 mos.	36 mos.	4/5	2
Abstract Abilities				
at 12 mos.	15.5 mos.	15.5 mos.	3/4	2
at 15 mos.	15.5 mos.	15.5 mos.	3/6	—
at 21 mos.	18.5 mos.	22.5 mos.	5/6	—
Discrimination				
at 12 mos.	Level 1	Level 2	3/4	—
at 15 mos.	Level 2	Level 2	2/4	6
at 21 mos.	Level 6	Level 3.25	2/6	—
Social Competence				
with Adults	10.1	17.3	10/14	—
with Peers	0.0	7.9	6/6	9
Overall	10.1	20.1	11/14	—

SOCIAL COMPETENCE FOR SUBJECT 17 (1A)

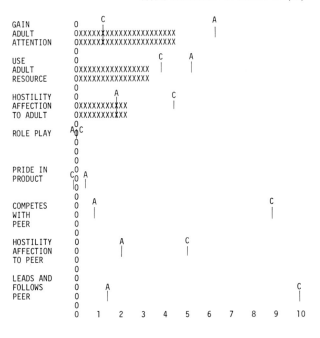

SOCIAL TASKS

```
TO PLEASE                                              0
TO COOPERATE                                           0
TO GAIN APPROVAL                                       0
TO PROCURE A SERVICE                                   0=
TO GAIN ATTENTION                                      0======
TO MAINTAIN SOCIAL CONTACT                             0===
TO AVOID UNPLEASANT CIRCUMSTANCES                      0
TO ANNOY                                               0
TO DIRECT                                              0
TO ASSERT SELF (PROTECT DOMAIN)                        0=
TO PROVIDE INFORMATION                                 0=
TO COMPETE                                             0
TO REJECT OVERTURES                                    0
TO ENJOY PETS                                          0
TO CONVERSE                                            0
TO PRODUCE VERBALIZATIONS                              0
```

NON-SOCIAL TASKS

```
TO EAT                                                 0====
TO GAIN INFORMATION - VISUAL                           0==================================================
TO GAIN INFORMATION - VISUAL ANDAUDITORY              0=====
NON-TASK                                               0============
TO PASS TIME                                           C
TO FIND SOMETHING TO DO                                0
TO PREPARE FOR AN ACTIVITY                             0
TO CONSTRUCT A PRODUCT                                 0
TO CHOOSE                                              0
TO PROCURE AN OBJECT                                   0=
TO ENGAGE IN LARGE MUSCLE ACTIVITY                     0
TO GAIN PLEASURE                                       0=
TO IMITATE                                             0
TO PRETEND (RULE PLAY)                                 0=
TO EASE DISCOMFORT                                     0
TO RESTORE ORDER                                       0
TO RELIEVE ONESELF                                     0
TO DRESS/UNDRESS                                       0
TO OPERATE A MECHANISM                                 0
TO EAT AND TO GAIN INFORMATION (VISUAL)                0=======
TO EAT AND TO GAIN INFORMATION (VISUAL AND AUDITORY)   0
TO EXPLORE                                             0=============
TO IMPROVE A DEVELOPING SKILL (MASTERY                 0

                                       0123456789012345678901234567890123456789012345678901234567890
                                       0         10        20        30        40        50
```

TASK DATA (% OF TOTAL TIME)

SUBJECT #18

SUBJECT #18 IS A TWO-YEAR-OLD lower-class A girl. She is the youngest of seven children ranging in age from two to twelve years. The family lives in a run-down, sparsely furnished house in an urban area. Both parents are very educationally oriented and spend a great deal of time interacting with their children.

Subject spends each morning alone with her mother while all the other children are in school. Mrs. C is totally available to subject and serves as a playmate as well as a teacher. Most of the activities are centered around storybooks and coloring books. Other than books, there are very few toys available for subject to play with.

Summary of Test Scores

S: Subject No. 18   Group: 2-year A

Tests	S's Score	Group Median	S's Rank	No. of S's Tied at that Rank
Bayley (MDI) 24 mos.	100 IQ	105 IQ	10/12	—
Language Test				
at 24 mos.	18 mos.	36.0 mos.	7/7	2
at 27 mos.	27 mos.	40.5 mos.	9/9	—
at 30 mos.	18 mos.	51.0 mos.	4/4	—
Abstract Abilities				
at 24 mos.	16.5 mos.	20.5 mos.	8/9	—
at 27 mos.	20.5 mos.	24.5 mos.	9/9	—
at 30 mos.	20.5 mos.	24.5 mos.	8/8	—
Discrimination				
at 24 mos.	Level 2	Level 3	5/6	2
at 27 mos.	Level 3	Level 4	5/6	4
at 30 mos.	Level 0	Level 7	5/5	—
Social Competence				
with Adults	16.2	16.7	7/12	—
with Peers	0.4	6.2	11/12	—
Overall	16.6	22.5	10/12	—

SOCIAL COMPETENCE FOR SUBJECT 18 (2A)

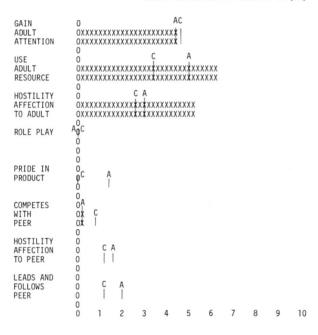

```
                                                AC
GAIN        0
ADULT       OXXXXXXXXXXXXXXXXXXXXXXX|
ATTENTION   OXXXXXXXXXXXXXXXXXXXXXXX|
            0
USE         0                    C       A
ADULT       OXXXXXXXXXXXXXXXXXXXXXXXXXXXXXXXXXXX
RESOURCE    OXXXXXXXXXXXXXXXXXXXXXXXXXXXXXXXXXXX
            0
HOSTILITY   0                C A
AFFECTION   OXXXXXXXXXXXXXXXXXXXXXXXXXXXX
TO ADULT    OXXXXXXXXXXXXXXXXXXXXXXXXXXXX
            0
ROLE PLAY   A0C
            0
            0
            0
PRIDE IN    0
PRODUCT     0C       A
            0        |
            0
COMPETES    0A
WITH        0X   C
PEER        0X   |
            0
HOSTILITY   0
AFFECTION   0    C A
TO PEER     0    | |
            0
LEADS AND   0
FOLLOWS     0    C   A
PEER        0    |   |
            0
            0
            0  1  2  3  4  5  6  7  8  9  10
```

SUBJECT NUMBER 18   SUBJECT CLASS 2A   95.9 % OF OBSERVED TIME REPRESENTED

SOCIAL TASKS

```
TO PLEASE                                              )
TO COOPERATE                                           )===
TO GAIN APPROVAL                                       0
TO PROCURE A SERVICE                                   0===
TO GAIN ATTENTION                                      0===
TO MAINTAIN SOCIAL CONTACT                             0=========
TO AVOID UNPLEASANT CIRCUMSTANCES                      )
TO ANNOY                                               )
TO DIRECT                                              )
TO ASSERT SELF (PROTECT DOMAIN)                        0==
TO PROVIDE INFORMATION                                 )
TO COMPETE                                             0=
TO REJECT OVERTURES                                    0
TO ENJOY PETS                                          0
TO CONVERSE                                            0
TO PRODUCE VERBALIZATIONS                              0

                          NON-SOCIAL TASKS

TO EAT                                                 0===========
TO GAIN INFORMATION - VISUAL                           0==============
TO GAIN INFORMATION - VISUAL ANDAUDITORY               )===========
NON-TASK                                               0===
TO PASS TIME                                           0
TO FIND SOMETHING TO DO                                0=
TO PREPARE FOR AN ACTIVITY                             0
TO CONSTRUCT A PRODUCT                                 0
TO CHOOSE                                              0
TO PROCURE AN OBJECT                                   0=
TO ENGAGE IN LARGE MUSCLE ACTIVITY                     0
TO GAIN PLEASURE                                       0
TO IMITATE                                             0
TO PRETEND (ROLE PLAY)                                 0===
TO EASE DISCOMFORT                                     0
TO RESTORE ORDER                                       0=
TO RELIEVE ONESELF                                     0=
TO DRESS/UNDRESS                                       )
TO OPERATE A MECHANISM                                 0======
TO EAT AND TO GAIN INFORMATION (VISUAL)                0=====
TO EAT AND TO GAIN INFORMATION (VISUAL AND AUDITORY)   0=====
TO EXPLORE                                             0========
TO IMPROVE A DEVELOPING SKILL (MASTERY                 0===

                                                       0123456789012345678901234567890123456789012345678901234567890
                                                       0         10        20        30        40        50
```

TASK DATA (% OF TOTAL TIME)

SUBJECT #19

SUBJECT #19 IS A ONE-YEAR-OLD middle-class A girl who is the youngest of three children. She has two sisters, aged five and seven. The family lives in a comfortable seven-room house in the suburbs of Boston. Both parents are professionally trained, although the mother does not work.

The subject is an attractive child who is under strict supervision much of the time, either in a playpen or gated off in one room. When allowed access to other areas of the house, she is watched rather closely by her mother when there is any likelihood of her "getting into" things.

Summary of Test Scores

S: Subject No. 19   Group: 1-year A

Tests	S's Score	Group Median	S's Rank	No. of S's Tied at that Rank
Bayley (MDI) 12 mos.	102 IQ	103 IQ	7/9	3
Language Test				
at 12 mos.	13 mos.	16 mos.	5/7	—
at 15 mos.	16 mos.	17 mos.	4/5	4
at 21 mos.	36 mos.	36 mos.	3/5	3
Abstract Abilities				
at 12 mos.	11.0 mos.	15.5 mos.	4/5	2
at 15 mos.	15.5 mos.	15.5 mos.	4/6	2
at 21 mos.	16.5 mos.	22.5 mos.	6/6	—
Discrimination				
at 12 mos.	Level 2	Level 2	2/4	5
at 15 mos.	Level 1	Level 2	3/4	—
at 21 mos.	Level 2	Level 3.25	6/6	—
Social Competence				
with Adults	0.7	17.3	14/14	—
with Peers	0.0	7.9	6/6	9
Overall	0.7	20.1	14/14	—

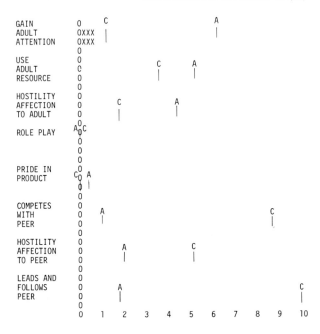

SOCIAL COMPETENCE FOR SUBJECT 19 (1A)

SUBJECT NUMBER 19   SUBJECT CLASS 1A   99.8 % OF OBSERVED TIME REPRESENTED

SOCIAL TASKS

```
TO PLEASE                              0=
TO COOPERATE                           0=
TO GAIN APPROVAL                       0
TO PROCURE A SERVICE                   0
TO GAIN ATTENTION                      0=
TO MAINTAIN SOCIAL CONTACT             0==
TO AVOID UNPLEASANT CIRCUMSTANCES      0
TO ANNOY                               0
TO DIRECT                              0
TO ASSERT SELF (PROTECT DOMAIN)        0
TO PROVIDE INFORMATION                 0
TO COMPETE                             0
TO REJECT OVERTURES                    0
TO ENJOY PETS                          0
TO CONVERSE                            0
TO PRODUCE VERBALIZATIONS              0
```

NON-SOCIAL TASKS

```
TO EAT                                              0===
TO GAIN INFORMATION - VISUAL                        0=================================
TO GAIN INFORMATION - VISUAL ANDAUDITORY            0=======
NON-TASK                                            0===========
TO PASS TIME                                        0
TO FIND SOMETHING TO DO                             0==
TO PREPARE FOR AN ACTIVITY                          0
TO CONSTRUCT A PRODUCT                              0
TO CHOOSE                                           0
TO PROCURE AN OBJECT                                0===
TO ENGAGE IN LARGE MUSCLE ACTIVITY                  0
TO GAIN PLEASURE                                    0=
TO IMITATE                                          0
TO PRETEND (ROLE PLAY)                              0
TO EASE DISCOMFORT                                  0
TO RESTORE ORDER                                    0=
TO RELIEVE ONESELF                                  0
TO DRESS/UNDRESS                                    0
TO OPERATE A MECHANISM                              0
TO EAT AND TO GAIN INFORMATION (VISUAL)             0=
TO EAT AND TO GAIN INFORMATION (VISUAL AND AUDITORY) 0================
TO EXPLORE                                          0
TO IMPROVE A DEVELOPING SKILL (MASTERY              0=======

                                                    0123456789012345678901234567890123456789012345678901234567890
                                                    0         10        20        30        40        50
```

TASK DATA (% OF TOTAL TIME)

SUBJECT #20

SUBJECT #20 IS A ONE-YEAR-OLD middle-class A girl. She has a three-year-old sister and a 4 1/2-year-old brother. The family owns their own home in a suburban area, but they have moved twice in the duration of the study.

The subject is a chubby little girl whose motor development was slow. She is growing up in a household devoted to supplying children with interesting things to do. The playroom is a beautifully stocked room, better equipped than many nursery schools. There are many materials that invite exploration—e.g., a large rack of wooden formboard puzzles, blocks of many types, mechanical toys, a large collection of sewing materials suitable for young children, a large collection of picture books. In addition, the subject's mother spontaneously takes part in many of subject's activities, frequently explaining, expanding, naming, or counting for the subject.

Summary of Test Scores

S: Subject No. 20   Group: 1-year A

Tests	S's Score	Group Median	S's Rank	No. of S's Tied at that Rank
Bayley (MDI) 12 mos.	134 IQ	103 IQ	1/10	—
Stanford-Binet 24 mos.	132 IQ			
Language Test				
at 12 mos.	21 mos.	16 mos.	1/7	—
at 15 mos.	24 mos.	17 mos.	1/5	2
at 21 mos.	42 mos.	36 mos.	1/5	—
Abstract Abilities				
at 12 mos.	15.5 mos.	15.5 mos.	3/5	2
at 15 mos.	15.5 mos.	15.5 mos.	5/6	2
at 21 mos.	24.5 mos.	22.5 mos.	3/6	—
Discrimination				
at 12 mos.	Level 3	Level 2	1/4	2
at 15 mos.	Level 2	Level 2	2/4	6
at 21 mos.	Level 3	Level 3.25	5/6	2
Social Competence				
with Adults	21.1	17.3	4/14	—
with Peers	0.0	7.9	6/6	9
Overall	21.1	20.1	6/14	—

SOCIAL COMPETENCE FOR SUBJECT 20 (1A)

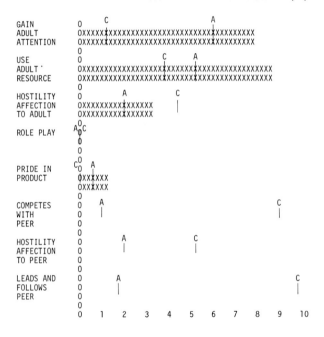

SUBJECT NUMBER 20   SUBJECT CLASS 1A   99.8 % OF OBSERVED TIME REPRESENTED

SOCIAL TASKS

```
TO PLEASE                                              0
TO COOPERATE                                           0=
TO GAIN APPROVAL                                       0
TO PROCURE A SERVICE                                   0===
TO GAIN ATTENTION                                      0===
TO MAINTAIN SOCIAL CONTACT                             0=====
TO AVOID UNPLEASANT CIRCUMSTANCES                      0
TO ANNOY                                               0
TO DIRECT                                              0
TO ASSERT SELF (PROTECT DOMAIN)                        0
TO PROVIDE INFORMATION                                 0
TO COMPETE                                             0
TO REJECT OVERTURES                                    0=
TO ENJOY PETS                                          0
TO CONVERSE                                            0
TO PRODUCE VERBALIZATIONS                              0
```

NON-SOCIAL TASKS

```
TO EAT                                                 0===
TO GAIN INFORMATION - VISUAL                           0=================================
TO GAIN INFORMATION - VISUAL ANDAUDITORY               0==============
NON-TASK                                               0==
TO PASS TIME                                           0===
TO FIND SOMETHING TO DO                                0=
TO PREPARE FOR AN ACTIVITY                             0
TO CONSTRUCT A PRODUCT                                 0
TO CHOOSE                                              0=
TO PROCURE AN OBJECT                                   0
TO ENGAGE IN LARGE MUSCLE ACTIVITY                     0===
TO GAIN PLEASURE                                       0
TO IMITATE                                             0
TO PRETEND (ROLE PLAY)                                 0=====
TO EASE DISCOMFORT                                     0=
TO RESTORE ORDER                                       0=
TO RELIEVE ONESELF                                     0
TO DRESS/UNDRESS                                       0
TO OPERATE A MECHANISM                                 0
TO EAT AND TO GAIN INFORMATION (VISUAL)                0=====
TO EAT AND TO GAIN INFORMATION (VISUAL AND AUDITORY)   0=
TO EXPLORE                                             0=========
TO IMPROVE A DEVELOPING SKILL (MASTERY                 0====

          01234567890123456789012345678901234567890123456789 0
          0        10        20        30        40        50
```

TASK DATA (% OF TOTAL TIME)

SUBJECT #24

SUBJECT #24 IS A ONE-YEAR-OLD middle-class A boy. The family lives in a large, comfortable house in a prosperous suburban area. Subject has three older siblings ranging in age from three to eight. Both parents are physicians, but at present the mother is not practicing.

Subject's mother is a warm, energetic woman who is usually busy with household chores. Although the household is loosely organized from the adult point of view, for a child it is a lovely place to grow up. Every room on the first floor contains play equipment suitable to subject's level of development. A hardwood ramp in the living room, propped against a table, is a challenge to climb on. Blocks and a well-stocked toy shelf in the dining room invite exploration. There is a variety of challenging toys in the kitchen (boxes with different-shaped holes for different-shaped objects; stacking toys; mechanical toys that require dexterity to operate). There is also a playpen in the kitchen that is full of toys, but subject usually plays on the floor.

Subject #24 is a friendly child who goes about his business slowly and with deliberation. Once he starts to do something, he rarely gives up. He responds with great interest to his environment (his mastery score is the highest of all one-year-olds). His mother does not spend a lot of time in didactic type of interaction with him, but she is tuned in to the type of activities and materials that interest him. She invites exploratory behavior such as finding out what's inside the kitchen cabinets, or playing with water and dishes in the kitchen sink. When S tries very hard to do something and runs into trouble, he receives ready attention and help from his mother, whether he needs assistance with a torn paper bag, or with folding a paper bag and putting it away in the proper cupboard, or with unfolding the paper liner from a box of animal crackers. Childish enterprises that might appear meaningless or inconsequential to many busy mothers receive ready support from this mother.

Summary of Test Scores

S: Subject No. 24   Group: 1-year A

Tests	S's Score	Group Median	S's Rank	No. of S's Tied at that Rank
Bayley (MDI) 12 mos.	107 IQ	103 IQ	4/9	—
Language Test				
at 12 mos.	10 mos.	16 mos.	7/7	—
at 15 mos.	18 mos.	17 mos.	3/5	2
at 21 mos.	24 mos.	36 mos.	5/5	—
Abstract Abilities				
at 12 mos.	8.0 mos.	15.5 mos.	5/5	—
at 15 mos.	15.5 mos.	15.5 mos.	5/6	2
at 21 mos.	20.5 mos.	22.5 mos.	4/6	2
Discrimination				
at 12 mos.	Level 0	Level 2	4/4	2
at 15 mos.	Level 2	Level 2	2/4	6
at 21 mos.	Level 2	Level 3.50	6/6	2
Social Competence				
with Adults	35.7	17.3	1/14	—
with Peers	0.0	7.9	6/6	9
Overall	35.7	20.1	2/14	—

SOCIAL COMPETENCE FOR SUBJECT 24 (1A)

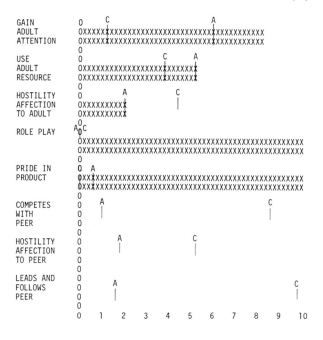

SUBJECT NUMBER 24   SUBJECT CLASS 1A   97.6 % OF OBSERVED TIME REPRESENTED

SOCIAL TASKS

```
TO PLEASE                                              0
TO COOPERATE                                           0=
TO GAIN APPROVAL                                       0
TO PROCURE A SERVICE                                   0=
TO GAIN ATTENTION                                      0==
TO MAINTAIN SOCIAL CONTACT                             0==
TO AVOID UNPLEASANT CIRCUMSTANCES                      0
TO ANNOY                                               0
TO DIRECT                                              0
TO ASSERT SELF (PROTECT DOMAIN)                        0
TO PROVIDE INFORMATION                                 0
TO COMPETE                                             0
TO REJECT OVERTURES                                    0
TO ENJOY PETS                                          0
TO CONVERSE                                            0
TO PRODUCE VERBALIZATIONS                              0
```

NON-SOCIAL TASKS

```
TO EAT                                                 0=====
TO GAIN INFORMATION - VISUAL                           0=============
TO GAIN INFORMATION - VISUAL ANDAUDITORY               0=============
NON-TASK                                               0
TO PASS TIME                                           0
TO FIND SOMETHING TO DO                                0===
TO PREPARE FOR AN ACTIVITY                             0
TO CONSTRUCT A PRODUCT                                 0
TO CHOOSE                                              0
TO PROCURE AN OBJECT                                   0====
TO ENGAGE IN LARGE MUSCLE ACTIVITY                     0
TO GAIN PLEASURE                                       0
TO IMITATE                                             0
TO PRETEND (ROLE PLAY)                                 0
TO EASE DISCOMFORT                                     0
TO RESTORE ORDER                                       0=
TO RELIEVE ONESELF                                     0
TO DRESS/UNDRESS                                       0
TO OPERATE A MECHANISM                                 0=
TO EAT AND TO GAIN INFORMATION (VISUAL)                0=======
TO EAT AND TO GAIN INFORMATION (VISUAL AND AUDITORY)   0=
TO EXPLORE                                             0==============
TO IMPROVE A DEVELOPING SKILL (MASTERY)                0===================
                                                       0123456789012345678901234567890123456789012345678901234567890
                                                       0         10        20        30        40        50
```

TASK DATA (% OF TOTAL TIME)

SUBJECT #27

SUBJECT #27 IS A TWO-YEAR-OLD lower-class C boy who is the youngest of three children. His parents are divorced and he lives with his mother and two sisters in a sizable but somewhat run-down two-family house on a dead-end street. The child is allowed access to all parts of the house and is allowed to go outside to play by himself. There are many toys available both in and outside the house, although they are usually broken or missing some essential part. Subject is left unsupervised for long periods, during which time he may be playing, watching other children, or interacting with his sisters. His mother sporadically displays some interest in the child and occasionally speaks to him, but her reactions are erratic and unpredictable and her moods are likely to shift markedly in the space of a short time.

Summary of Test Scores

S: Subject No. 27   Group: 2-year C

Tests	S's Score	Group Median	S's Rank	No. of S's Tied at that Rank
Bayley (MDI) 24 mos.	88 IQ	86 IQ	2/5	—
Language Test				
at 24 mos.	18 mos.	18 mos.	3/3	3
at 27 mos.	30 mos.	27 mos.	2/5	—
at 30 mos.	27 mos.	27 mos.	2/3	2
Abstract Abilities				
at 24 mos.	16.5 mos.	16.5 mos.	all 16.5	—
at 27 mos.	16.5 mos.	16.5 mos.	2/2	3
at 30 mos.	18.0 mos.	16.5 mos.	1/2	2
Discrimination				
at 24 mos.	Level 2	Level 3	3/3	2
at 27 mos.	Level 2	Level 2	3/3	2
at 30 mos.	Level 3.5	Level 3.5	2/4	—
Social Competence				
with Adults	11.2	11.7	4/6	—
with Peers	4.3	4.7	4/7	—
Overall	15.5	17.6	4/7	—

SOCIAL COMPETENCE FOR SUBJECT 27 (2C)

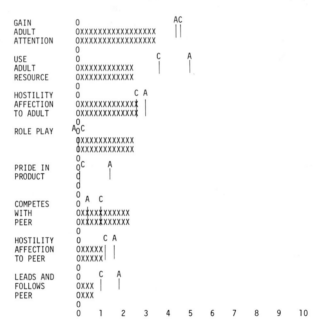

SUBJECT NUMBER 27   SUBJECT CLASS 2C   97.1 % OF OBSERVED TIME REPRESENTED

SOCIAL TASKS

```
TO PLEASE                                                      0
TO COOPERATE                                                   0=
TO GAIN APPROVAL                                               0=
TO PROCURE A SERVICE                                           0==
TO GAIN ATTENTION                                              0==
TO MAINTAIN SOCIAL CONTACT                                     0====
TO AVOID UNPLEASANT CIRCUMSTANCES                              0=
TO ANNOY                                                       0
TO DIRECT                                                      0
TO ASSERT SELF (PROTECT DOMAIN)                                0===
TO PROVIDE INFORMATION                                         0
TO COMPETE                                                     0
TO REJECT OVERTURES                                            0
TO ENJOY PETS                                                  0
TO CONVERSE                                                    0
TO PRODUCE VERBALIZATIONS                                      0
                          NON-SOCIAL TASKS
TO EAT                                                         0==
TO GAIN INFORMATION - VISUAL                                   0===========
TO GAIN INFORMATION - VISUAL ANDAUDITORY                       0===
NON-TASK                                                       0===============
TO PASS TIME                                                   0
TO FIND SOMETHING TO DO                                        0==
TO PREPARE FOR AN ACTIVITY                                     0
TO CONSTRUCT A PRODUCT                                         0
TO CHOOSE                                                      0
TO PROCURE AN OBJECT                                           0==
TO ENGAGE IN LARGE MUSCLE ACTIVITY                             0=====
TO GAIN PLEASURE                                               0
TO IMITATE                                                     0
TO PRETEND (ROLE PLAY)                                         0==
TO EASE DISCOMFORT                                             0=
TO RESTORE ORDER                                               0==
TO RELIEVE ONESELF                                             0
TO DRESS/UNDRESS                                               0=
TO OPERATE A MECHANISM                                         0
TO EAT AND TO GAIN INFORMATION (VISUAL)                        0=
TO EAT AND TO GAIN INFORMATION (VISUAL AND AUDITORY)           0
TO EXPLORE                                                     0=============
TO IMPROVE A DEVELOPING SKILL (MASTERY                         0==========================
                          0123456789012345678901234567890123456789012345678901234567890
                          0         10        20        30        40        50
```

TASK DATA (% OF TOTAL TIME)

SUBJECT #30

SUBJECT #30 IS A TWO-YEAR-OLD lower-class C girl. She is the youngest of eight children ranging from two to nine years of age. Neither parent completed high school. The family owns their home, a large, comfortable one-family house in a suburban area. The house is always impeccably clean and neat.

The subject is a dark-haired pretty child who is socially adept. The parents and children are very warm and affectionate with each other, and most interactions between the mother and the subject are affectionate teasing.

There are very few toys available for the subject to play with. Each morning she spends most of her time watching television or following her mother around while she does the household chores.

Although the social atmosphere in this household is remarkably pleasant, the subject's time is devoid of interesting activities, aside from those of a social type.

Summary of Test Scores

S: Subject No. 30   Group: 2-year C

Tests	S's Score	Group Median	S's Rank	No. of S's Tied at that Rank
Bayley (MDI) 24 mos.	77 IQ	86 IQ	4/5	—
Language Test				
at 24 mos.	18 mos.	18 mos.	3/3	3
at 27 mos.	21 mos.	27 mos.	4/5	1
at 30 mos.	21 mos.	27 mos.	3/3	2
Abstract Abilities				
at 24 mos.	16.5 mos.	16.5 mos.	all 16.5	—
at 27 mos.	16.5 mos.	16.5 mos.	1/2	3
at 30 mos.	20.5 mos.	16.5 mos.	1/2	2
Discrimination				
at 24 mos.	Level 3	Level 3	2/3	2
at 27 mos.	Level 4	Level 2	1/3	—
at 30 mos.	Level 7	Level 3.5	1/5	—
Social Competence				
with Adults	24.6	11.7	1/6	2
with Peers	20.7	4.7	1/7	—
Overall	45.3	17.6	1/7	—

```
                    SOCIAL COMPETENCE FOR SUBJECT 30 (2C)

GAIN            0                        A C
ADULT           OXXXXXXXXXXXXXXXXXXXXXXXXXXXXXXXXXXXXXXX
ATTENTION       OXXXXXXXXXXXXXXXXXXXXXXXXXXXXXXXXXXXXXXX
                0
USE             0                   C        A
ADULT           OXXXXXXXXXXXXXXXXXXXXXXXXXXXXXXXXXX
RESOURCE        OXXXXXXXXXXXXXXXXXXXXXXXXXXXXXXXXXX
                0
HOSTILITY       0              C A
AFFECTION       OXXXXXXXXXXXXXXXXXXXXXXXXXXXXXXXXXXXXXXXXXXXXXXXXX
TO ADULT        OXXXXXXXXXXXXXXXXXXXXXXXXXXXXXXXXXXXXXXXXXXXXXXXXX
                0
ROLE PLAY     A C
              0
                0
                0
                0 C      A
PRIDE IN        O|      |
PRODUCT         0
                0
                0
COMPETES        0A C
WITH            OXXX
PEER            OXXX
                0
HOSTILITY       0     C A
AFFECTION       OXXXXXXXXXXXXXXXXXXXXXXXXXXXXXXXXXXXXXXXXXXXXXXXXX
TO PEER         OXXXXXXXXXXXXXXXXXXXXXXXXXXXXXXXXXXXXXXXXXXXXXXXXX
                0
LEADS AND       0    C  A
FOLLOWS         OXXXXXXXXXXXXXXXXXXXXXXXXXXXXXXXXXXXXXXXXXXX
PEER            OXXXXXXXXXXXXXXXXXXXXXXXXXXXXXXXXXXXXXXXXXXX
                0
                0   1   2   3   4   5   6   7   8   9   10
```

SUBJECT NUMBER 30   SUBJECT CLASS 2C   94.9 % OF OBSERVED TIME REPRESENTED

SOCIAL TASKS

```
TO PLEASE                              0 =====
TO COOPERATE                           0 ======
TO GAIN APPROVAL                       0 ===
TO PROCURE A SERVICE                   0 ====
TO GAIN ATTENTION                      0 =======
TO MAINTAIN SOCIAL CONTACT             0 =========
TO AVOID UNPLEASANT CIRCUMSTANCES      0
TO ANNOY                               0
TO DIRECT                              0 ===
TO ASSERT SELF (PROTECT DOMAIN)        0 ===
TO PROVIDE INFORMATION                 0 =
TO COMPETE                             0
TO REJECT OVERTURES                    0
TO ENJOY PETS                          0
TO CONVERSE                            0
TO PRODUCE VERBALIZATIONS              0
                      NON-SOCIAL TASKS

TO EAT                                         0 =====
TO GAIN INFORMATION - VISUAL                   0 ==============
TO GAIN INFORMATION - VISUAL AND AUDITORY      0 =========
NON-TASK                                       0 =====
TO PASS TIME                                   0
TO FIND SOMETHING TO DO                        0 =
TO PREPARE FOR AN ACTIVITY                     0 =
TO CONSTRUCT A PRODUCT                         0
TO CHOOSE                                      0
TO PROCURE AN OBJECT                           0 =
TO ENGAGE IN LARGE MUSCLE ACTIVITY             0
TO GAIN PLEASURE                               0 ==
TO IMITATE                                     0
TO PRETEND (ROLE PLAY)                         0 ==
TO EASE DISCOMFORT                             0 ==
TO RESTORE ORDER                               0
TO RELIEVE ONESELF                             0
TO DRESS/UNDRESS                               0
TO OPERATE A MECHANISM                         0
TO EAT AND TO GAIN INFORMATION (VISUAL)        0 ====
TO EAT AND TO GAIN INFORMATION (VISUAL AND AUDITORY)  0 =========
TO EXPLORE                                     0 ====
TO IMPROVE A DEVELOPING SKILL (MASTERY         0
                                               0123456789012345678901234567890123456789012345678901234567890
                                               0        10        20        30        40        50
```

TASK DATA (% OF TOTAL TIME)

SUBJECT #31

SUBJECT #31 IS A ONE-YEAR-OLD middle-class A boy who is the youngest of three boys. The family is composed of his parents and siblings, plus grandparents who live in the same building, as well as a babysitter who lives there too and appears to take almost full charge of the child. Although his parents are well educated and generally loving and interested in the subject, he is often in the care of the babysitter, who at best provides good caretaking but little stimulation. The child is rarely engaged in play but generally follows people (child or adult) from room to room, or looks for long periods out the window. The home atmosphere is quiet and controlled, and there are few, if any, available toys for the subject to play with. He is confined generally to one or two rooms, since there are unsafe stairways between various floors of the house.

Summary of Test Scores

S: Subject No. 31   Group: 1-year A

Tests	S's Score	Group Median	S's Rank	No. of S's Tied at that Rank
Bayley (MDI) 12 mos.	112 IQ	103 IQ	3/10	—
Language Test				
at 12 mos.	14 mos.	16 mos.	4/14	2
at 15 mos.	16 mos.	17 mos.	4/5	4
at 21 mos.				
Abstract Abilities				
at 12 mos.	15.5 mos.	15.5 mos.	2/5	4
at 15 mos.	15.5 mos.	15.5 mos.	2/6	3
at 21 mos.				
Discrimination Test				
at 12 mos.	Level 2	Level 2	2/4	5
at 15 mos.	Level 3	Level 2	1/4	2
at 21 mos.				
Social Competence				
with Adults	4.2	17.3	13/14	—
with Peers	5.1	7.9	4/6	—
Overall	9.4	20.1	12/14	—

SOCIAL COMPETENCE FOR SUBJECT 31 (1A)

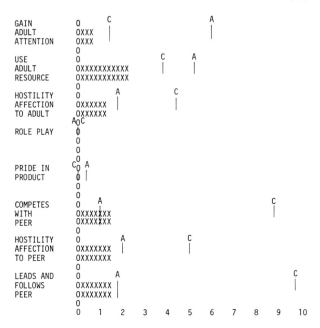

SUBJECT NUMBER 31   SUBJECT CLASS 1A   97.4 % OF OBSERVED TIME REPRESENTED

SOCIAL TASKS

```
TO PLEASE                                      0
TO COOPERATE                                   0
TO GAIN APPROVAL                               0
TO PROCURE A SERVICE                           0=
TO GAIN ATTENTION                              0=
TO MAINTAIN SOCIAL CONTACT                     0==
TO AVOID UNPLEASANT CIRCUMSTANCES              0
TO ANNOY                                       0
TO DIRECT                                      0
TO ASSERT SELF (PROTECT DOMAIN)                3=
TO PROVIDE INFORMATION                         ?
TO COMPETE                                     0
TO REJECT OVERTURES                            0
TO ENJOY PETS                                  0
TO CONVERSE                                    0
TO PRODUCE VERBALIZATIONS                      0
```

NON-SOCIAL TASKS

```
TO EAT                                         0===========
TO GAIN INFORMATION - VISUAL                   0===============
TO GAIN INFORMATION - VISUAL ANDAUDITORY       0==================
NON-TASK                                       0=====
TO PASS TIME                                   0==
TO FIND SOMETHING TO DO                        0
TO PREPARE FOR AN ACTIVITY                     0
TO CONSTRUCT A PRODUCT                         0
TO CHOOSE                                      0
TO PROCURE AN OBJECT                           0=====
TO ENGAGE IN LARGE MUSCLE ACTIVITY             0
TO GAIN PLEASURE                               0=
TO IMITATE                                     0
TO PRETEND (ROLE PLAY)                         0==
TO EASE DISCOMFORT                             0
TO RESTORE ORDER                               0
TO RELIEVE ONESELF                             0
TO DRESS/UNDRESS                               0
TO OPERATE A MECHANISM                         0=
TO EAT AND TO GAIN INFORMATION (VISUAL)        0=====
TO EAT AND TO GAIN INFORMATION (VISUAL AND AUDITORY) 0
TO EXPLORE                                      0===========
TO IMPROVE A DEVELOPING SKILL (MASTERY)

                     0123456789012345678901234567890123456789012345678900
                     0         10        20        30        40        50
```

TASK DATA (% OF TOTAL TIME)

SUBJECT #35

SUBJECT #35 IS A TWO-YEAR-OLD lower-class A girl. She is the youngest child with four brothers and one sister, the next oldest of whom is two years older than subject. They live in a working-class section just outside the urban area in an eight-room house. The most striking aspect of subject #35's family life is the devotion and interest toward her children displayed by her lively and energetic mother. She participates actively in their daily lives, even to the extent of watching "Sesame Street" with her children and folding laundry nearby so as to interact fully with them. There is open communication among the family members, promoting a desirable atmosphere for nurturing a developing child to his utmost potential.

Summary of Test Scores

S: Subject No. 35   Group: 2-year A

Tests	S's Score	Group Median	S's Rank	No. of S's Tied at that Rank
Bayley (MDI) 24 mos.	104 IQ	105 IQ	7/12	—
Language Test				
at 24 mos.	36 mos.	36 mos.	4/7	4
at 27 mos.	42 mos.	40.5 mos.	5/9	—
at 30 mos.				
Abstract Abilities				
at 24 mos.	28.5 mos.	20.5 mos.	2/9	3
at 27 mos.	28.5 mos.	24.5 mos.	2/9	—
at 30 mos.				
Discrimination				
at 24 mos.	Level 6	Level 3	2/6	—
at 27 mos.	Level 6	Level 4	3/6	2
at 30 mos.				
Social Competence				
with Adults	8.9	16.7	11/12	—
with Peers	2.3	6.2	9/12	—
Overall	11.2	22.5	11/12	—

SOCIAL COMPETENCE FOR SUBJECT 35 (2A)

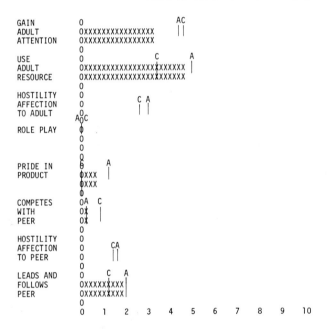

SUBJECT NUMBER 35   SUBJECT CLASS 2A   95.8 % OF OBSERVED TIME REPRESENTED

SOCIAL TASKS

```
TO PLEASE                                          0
TO COOPERATE                                       0=
TO GAIN APPROVAL                                   0
TO PROCURE A SERVICE                               0==
TO GAIN ATTENTION                                  0
TO MAINTAIN SOCIAL CONTACT                         0
TO AVOID UNPLEASANT CIRCUMSTANCES                  0
TO ANNOY                                           0
TO DIRECT                                          0=
TO ASSERT SELF (PROTECT DOMAIN)                    0
TO PROVIDE INFORMATION                             0
TO COMPETE                                         0
TO REJECT OVERTURES                                0
TO ENJOY PETS                                      0
TO CONVERSE                                        0
TO PRODUCE VERBALIZATIONS                          0
```

NON-SOCIAL TASKS

```
TO EAT                                             0======
TO GAIN INFORMATION - VISUAL                       0=============
TO GAIN INFORMATION - VISUAL ANDAUDITORY           0=======================
TO PASS TIME                                       0====
NON-TASK                                           0======
TO FIND SOMETHING TO DO                            0
TO PREPARE FOR AN ACTIVITY                         0====
TO CONSTRUCT A PRODUCT                             0
TO CHOOSE                                          0
TO PROCURE AN OBJECT                               0===
TO ENGAGE IN LARGE MUSCLE ACTIVITY                 0
TO GAIN PLEASURE                                   0==
TO IMITATE                                         0
TO PRETEND (ROLE PLAY)                             0
TO EASE DISCOMFORT                                 0
TO RESTORE ORDER                                   0
TO RELIEVE ONESELF                                 0
TO DRESS/UNDRESS                                   0
TO OPERATE A MECHANISM                             0
TO EAT AND TO GAIN INFORMATION (VISUAL)            0=
TO EAT AND TO GAIN INFORMATION (VISUAL AND AUDITORY) 0=========
TO EXPLORE                                         0========
TO IMPROVE A DEVELOPING SKILL (MASTERY             0===========

0123456789012345678901234567890123456789012345678901234567890
0         10        20        30        40        50
```

TASK DATA (% OF TOTAL TIME)

SUBJECT #36

SUBJECT #36 IS A TWO-YEAR-OLD lower-class A boy who is the younger of two boys in his family (brother is aged five). The family lives in a well-kept, small, four-room apartment in a working-class urban area. Subject has access to most areas of the apartment and is frequently engaged in play activities with his many toys, especially when his brother is at home.

Subject spends each morning alone with his mother while his brother attends school. He stays close to her, following her around as she does her household chores.

Subject's mother is a warm person who is concerned about her children's development. Although her interaction with her children is limited, she keeps a close watch on their activities, disciplining them frequently with verbal reprimands.

Summary of Test Scores

S: Subject No. 36   Group: 2-year A

Tests	S's Score	Group Median	S's Rank	No. of S's Tied at that Rank
Bayley (MDI) 24 mos.	119 IQ	105 IQ	3/12	—
Language Test				
at 24 mos.	33 mos.	36.0 mos.	5/7	2
at 27 mos.	36 mos.	40.5 mos.	7/9	3
at 30 mos.				
Abstract Abilities				
at 24 mos.	24.5 mos.	20.5 mos.	3/9	—
at 27 mos.	20.5 mos.	24.5 mos.	7/9	—
at 30 mos.				
Discrimination				
at 24 mos.	Level 4	Level 3	3/6	—
at 27 mos.	Level 2	Level 4	6/6	2
at 30 mos.				
Social Competence				
with Adults	18.0	16.7	5/12	—
with Peers	3.3	6.2	8/12	—
Overall	21.2	22.5	8/12	—

SOCIAL COMPETENCE FOR SUBJECT 36 (2A)

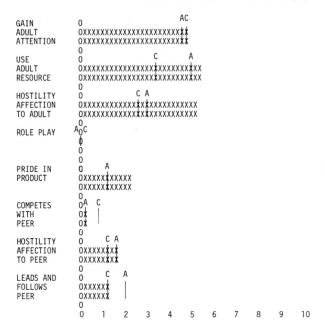

```
          SUBJECT NUMBER 36          SUBJECT CLASS 2A          96.7 % OF OBSERVED TIME REPRESENTED

          SOCIAL TASKS

TO PLEASE                                         0
TO COOPERATE                                      0====
TO GAIN APPROVAL                                  0==
TO PROCURE A SERVICE                              0====
TO GAIN ATTENTION                                 0====
TO MAINTAIN SOCIAL CONTACT                        0=
TO AVOID UNPLEASANT CIRCUMSTANCES                 0==
TO ANNOY                                          0==
TO DIRECT                                         0==
TO ASSERT SELF (PROTECT DOMAIN)                   0
TO PROVIDE INFORMATION                            0
TO COMPETE                                        0
TO REJECT OVERTURES                               0
TO ENJOY PETS                                     0
TO CONVERSE                                       0
TO PRODUCE VERBALIZATIONS                         0
                     NON-SOCIAL TASKS

TO EAT                                            0======
TO GAIN INFORMATION - VISUAL                      0========
TO GAIN INFORMATION - VISUAL ANDAUDITORY          0=========
NON-TASK                                          0==========
TO PASS TIME                                      0
TO FIND SOMETHING TO DO                           0====
TO PREPARE FOR AN ACTIVITY                        0=
TO CONSTRUCT A PRODUCT                            0
TO CHOOSE                                         0
TO PROCURE AN OBJECT                              0==:
TO ENGAGE IN LARGE MUSCLE ACTIVITY                0
TO GAIN PLEASURE                                  0=
TO IMITATE                                        0
TO PRETEND (ROLE PLAY)                            0=
TO EASE DISCOMFORT                                0
TO RESTORE ORDER                                  0====
TO RELIEVE ONESELF                                0
TO DRESS/UNDRESS                                  0
TO OPERATE A MECHANISM                            0
TO GAIN INFORMATION (VISUAL)                      0===
TO EAT AND TO GAIN INFORMATION (VISUAL)           0===
TO EAT AND TO GAIN INFORMATION (VISUAL AND AUDITORY)  0==
TO EXPLORE                                        0===
TO IMPROVE A DEVELOPING SKILL (MASTERY            0===
                              0================================
                              0123456789012345678901234567890123456789012345678901234567890
                              0        10        20        30        40        50

                                    TASK DATA (% OF TOTAL TIME)
```

SUBJECT #37

SUBJECT #37 IS A ONE-YEAR-OLD lower-class C boy. He has two older siblings, aged two and five. The mother raises the children alone, since she is divorced. The family lives in rather modest circumstances, in a four-room apartment in a low-income housing project that is poorly kept; and the apartment is equipped in a meager fashion to suit the needs of three young children. The subject, who is physically immature for his age, is kept in a playpen or jump seat for long periods, with the TV playing nearby. Interaction with his mother is of a playful and affectionate nature. Despite the meager physical surroundings, the child displays real interest in objects and toys, manipulating them for long periods when left to himself.

Summary of Test Scores

S: Subject No. 37   Group: 1-year C

Tests	S's Score	Group Median	S's Rank	No. of S's Tied at that Rank
Bayley (MDI) 12 mos.	50 IQ	99 IQ	4/4	—
Language Test				
at 12 mos.	10 mos.	11.5 mos.	3/3	2
at 15 mos.				
at 21 mos.				
Abstract Abilities				
at 12 mos.	8.0 mos.	9.5 mos.	3/4	—
at 15 mos.				
at 21 mos.				
Discrimination				
at 12 mos.	Level 0	Level 0	2/2	3
at 15 mos.				
at 21 mos.				
Social Competence				
with Adults	13.4	10.6	8/14	—
with Peers	0.0	24.3	6/6	9
Overall	13.4	30.7	9/14	—

SOCIAL COMPETENCE FOR SUBJECT 37 (1C)

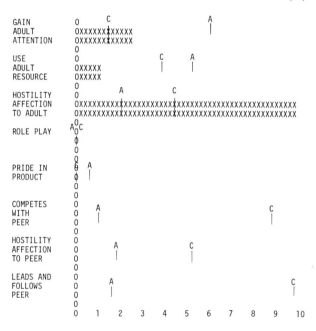

SUBJECT NUMBER 37   SUBJECT CLASS 1C   98.9 % OF OBSERVED TIME REPRESENTED

SOCIAL TASKS

```
TO PLEASE                                              0
TO COOPERATE                                           0=====
TO GAIN APPROVAL                                       0
TO PROCURE A SERVICE                                   0
TO GAIN ATTENTION                                      0=
TO MAINTAIN SOCIAL CONTACT                             0=
TO AVOID UNPLEASANT CIRCUMSTANCES                      0
TO ANNOY                                               0
TO DIRECT                                              0
TO ASSERT SELF (PROTECT DOMAIN)                        0
TO PROVIDE INFORMATION                                 0
TO COMPETE                                             0
TO REJECT OVERTURES                                    0
TO ENJOY PETS                                          0
TO CONVERSE                                            0
TO PRODUCE VERBALIZATIONS                              0
```

NON-SOCIAL TASKS

```
TO EAT                                                 0=
TO GAIN INFORMATION - VISUAL                           0==================
TO GAIN INFORMATION - VISUAL ANDAUDITORY               0=======
NON-TASK                                               0=========
TO PASS TIME                                           0=======
TO FIND SOMETHING TO DO                                0
TO PREPARE FOR AN ACTIVITY                             0
TO CONSTRUCT A PRODUCT                                 0
TO CHOOSE                                              0
TO PROCURE AN OBJECT                                   0===
TO ENGAGE IN LARGE MUSCLE ACTIVITY                     0
TO GAIN PLEASURE                                       0=
TO IMITATE                                             0
TO PRETEND (ROLE PLAY)                                 0
TO EASE DISCOMFORT                                     0
TO RESTORE ORDER                                       0
TO RELIEVE ONESELF                                     0
TO DRESS/UNDRESS                                       0
TO OPERATE A MECHANISM                                 0
TO EAT AND TO GAIN INFORMATION (VISUAL)                0=
TO EAT AND TO GAIN INFORMATION (VISUAL AND AUDITORY)   0==
TO EXPLORE                                             0==========
TO IMPROVE A DEVELOPING SKILL (MASTERY                 0=====================
           0123456789012345678901234567890123456789012345678901234567890
           0        10        20        30        40        50
```

TASK DATA (% OF TOTAL TIME)

SUBJECT #38

SUBJECT #38 IS A TWO-YEAR-OLD lower-class A boy who is the youngest of six children ranging in age from two to eight years. He lives in a small, somewhat disheveled apartment, in a run-down building in a working-class urban area. The home is not well equipped with toys, although there are some suitable objects for a child his age to use. However, subject #38 spends most of his time attending to his mother and her activities, occasionally imitating her household chores.

The subject's mother is a warm, energetic woman who seems able to cope with the many demands of a large family. She organizes the group activities such as eating and playing rather well, considering her limited resources.

Summary of Test Scores

S: Subject No. 38   Group: 2-year A

Tests	S's Score	Group Median	S's Rank	No. of S's Tied at that Rank
Bayley (MDI) 24 mos.	94 IQ	105 IQ	12/12	—
Language Test				
at 24 mos.	18 mos.	36.0 mos.	7/7	2
at 27 mos.	30 mos.	40.5 mos.	8/9	—
at 30 mos.				
Abstract Abilities				
at 24 mos.	16.5 mos.	20.5 mos.	9/9	—
at 27 mos.	20.5 mos.	24.5 mos.	8/10	
at 30 mos.				
Discrimination				
at 24 mos.	Level 0	Level 3	6/6	—
at 27 mos.	Level 3	Level 4	5/6	4
at 30 mos.				
Social Competence				
with Adults	17.1	16.1	6/12	—
with Peers	14.4	6.2	1/12	—
Overall	31.6	22.5	3/12	—

```
                                    SOCIAL COMPETENCE FOR SUBJECT 38 (2A)

GAIN           0                              AC
ADULT          OXXXXXXXXXXXXXXXXXXXXXXXXXXXXXXXXX
ATTENTION      OXXXXXXXXXXXXXXXXXXXXXXXXXXXXXXXXX
               0
USE            0                    C       A
ADULT          OXXXXXXXXXXXXXXXXXXXXXXXX
RESOURCE       OXXXXXXXXXXXXXXXXXXXXXXX
               0
HOSTILITY      0             C A
AFFECTION      OXXXXXXXXXXXX|  |
TO ADULT       OXXXXXXXXXXXX|  |
              A O C
ROLE PLAY      0 
               OXXXXXXXXXXXXXXXXXXXXXX
               OXXXXXXXXXXXXXXXXXXXXXX
               0
PRIDE IN       0    A
PRODUCT        0    |
               0
               0
COMPETES       0A C
WITH           OXXXXXXXXXXXX
PEER           OXXXXXXXXXXXX
               0
HOSTILITY      0    C A
AFFECTION      OXXXXXXXXXXXXXXXXXXXXXXXXXXXXXXXXXXXXXXXXXXXXXXXXXX
TO PEER        OXXXXXXXXXXXXXXXXXXXXXXXXXXXXXXXXXXXXXXXXXXXXXXXXXX
               0
LEADS AND      0    C   A
FOLLOWS        OXXXXXXXXXXXXX
PEER           OXXXXXXXXXXXXX
               0
               0   1   2   3   4   5   6   7   8   9   10
```

SOCIAL TASKS

```
TO PLEASE                              0
TO COOPERATE                           0====
TO GAIN APPROVAL                       0
TO PROCURE A SERVICE                   0==
TO GAIN ATTENTION                      0====
TO MAINTAIN SOCIAL CONTACT             0=======
TO AVOID UNPLEASANT CIRCUMSTANCES      0
TO ANNOY                               0
TO DIRECT                              0
TO ASSERT SELF (PROTECT DOMAIN)        0==
TO PROVIDE INFORMATION                 0
TO COMPETE                             0
TO REJECT OVERTURES                    0=
TO ENJOY PETS                          0
TO CONVERSE                            0
TO PRODUCE VERBALIZATIONS              0
                   NON-SOCIAL TASKS
TO EAT                                 0===
TO GAIN INFORMATION - VISUAL           0================
TO GAIN INFORMATION - VISUAL AND AUDITORY  0============
NON-TASK                               0================
TO PASS TIME                           0
TO FIND SOMETHING TO DO                0
TO PREPARE FOR AN ACTIVITY             0
TO CONSTRUCT A PRODUCT                 0
TO CHOOSE                              0
TO PROCURE AN OBJECT                   0==
TO ENGAGE IN LARGE MUSCLE ACTIVITY     0==
TO GAIN PLEASURE                       0============
TO IMITATE                             0=
TO PRETEND (ROLE PLAY)                 0
TO EASE DISCOMFORT                     0
TO RESTORE ORDER                       0
TO RELIEVE ONESELF                     0=
TO DRESS/UNDRESS                       0
TO OPERATE A MECHANISM                 0===
TO EAT AND TO GAIN INFORMATION (VISUAL)  0
TO EAT AND TO GAIN INFORMATION (VISUAL AND AUDITORY)  0
TO EXPLORE                             0
TO IMPROVE A DEVELOPING SKILL (MASTERY  0=====

0123456789012345678901234567890123456789012345678901234567890
0        10        20        30        40        50
```

TASK DATA (% OF TOTAL TIME)

appendix

ENVIRONMENTAL INSTRUMENTS

AND

SUPPLEMENTARY TABLES

A. Manual for Human Interaction Scale, *467*
B. Manual for Object Interaction Scale, *505*
C. Typical Day Questionnaire, *510*
D. Preliminary Interview, *511*
E. First Home Interview, *512*
F. Final Home Interview, *524*
G. Supplementary Tables, *533*

A

Manual for Human Interaction Scale

I. Definition of Dimensions, *468*

   1. Activities

   2. Initiation Index

   3. Encouragement Index

   4. Interaction Techniques

   5. Compliance Index

II. Guidelines of Using the Interaction Scale, *490*

   Recording Raw Data

   Coding Steps

   Phase Units

   Other Guidelines

   Sample Protocol

III. Reliability, *505*

This scale was developed by Jean Carew Watts (Project Director), Itty Chan Barnett (Assistant Director), Nancy Apfel, Christine Halfar, and Geraldine Kearse (former staff member).

PART I: DEFINITION OF DIMENSIONS

The following five dimensions will be defined and described with examples:

1. Activities
2. Initiation Index
3. Encouragement Index
4. Interaction Technique
5. Compliance Index

Dimension 1—Activities

The Activity dimension refers to the behavior of the child. For purposes of this scale, "behavior" includes the following:

The child's actual ongoing behavior
Behavior that is being prepared for and is likely to occur
Behavior that is suggested but that may or may not occur

Cluster I: (Highly Intellectual Activities	1 = Verbal and Symbolic Learning
	2 = Perceptual, Spatial, and Fine Motor Learning
	3 = Concrete Reasoning
	4 = Expressive Skills
	5 = Executive Skills
Cluster II: (Moderately Intellectual Activities)	6 = Exploration of and Play with Household Items
	7 = Play with Toys
	8 = Exploration of Nature
	9 = Gaining General and Routine Information
Cluster III: (Nonintellectual Activities)	10 = Basic Care
	11 = Gross Motor Activities
	12 = Unspecific Behavior
Cluster IV: (Social-Emotional Activities)	31 = Positive Social-Emotional Behavior
	32 = Negative Social-Emotional Behavior
	33 = Neutral Social-Emotional Behavior

In assigning the Activity dimension of an interaction, an attempt is made to answer this question: What opportunity does the behavior present for the child's development? The identification of activity is based on a consideration of several observable components: the quality of the child's behavior, the characteristics of material objects involved, and the behavior of the other person in interaction with the child. A brief description of the clusters of activities and some introductory examples will now be presented.

Cluster I activities are situations that are likely to lead to intellectual gain for the child. The nonspecific way in which these activities are defined permits their application to a variety of situations. Thus, opportunities for learning are seen as occurring both in the structured use of "educational materials" and "lessons," (e.g., looking at books, using a shape-sorting box, painting a picture) and in the less formal events that mother or child may elaborate into situations for learning (e.g., labeling pictures on boxes, using kitchen utensils as materials for classification, designating a row of chairs as an imaginary train).

The following are three examples of activities from Cluster I:

a. Mother reads the child a story. Child looks at the pictures in the book. (Activity 1—Verbal or Symbolic Learning)

b. Mother is dressing the child for bed and labels the pictures printed on the fabric of the child's pajamas. Child repeats the labels after mother. (Activity 1—Verbal or Symbolic Learning)

c. Child stacks several tin cans in decreasing order of size. Mother notices and comments, "Oh, you've found the cans." (Activity 2—Spatial, Perceptual, or Fine Motor Learning)

In the first example, the mother's behavior, the child's behavior, and the nature of the material all point to learning for the child. In the second example, the material, the child's pajamas, is not designed for use in connection with intellectual experience, but the behavior of both mother and child indicate that, in fact, the routine event of being dressed has become an opportunity for learning. In the third example, the child's behaviors of stacking and ordering are the indicator of a learning experience, although neither the mother's response nor the qualities of the objects involved would in themselves indicate the likelihood of learning for the child.

The activities in Cluster II are situations of generalized experience that are not readily related to cognitive acquisition. In behaviors involving material objects, it is the undifferentiated use of the objects, rather than their particular qualities, that indicates an only moderate likelihood of intellectual gain.

The following two examples illustrate the quality of Cluster II activities:

a. Child is chewing on the corner of a book. Mother takes the book away. (Activity 7—Play with Toys)

b. Mother opens a cupboard door in the kitchen and tells the child, "Here are some things to keep you busy." Child begins taking boxes and cans from the shelves. (Activity 6—Exploration of and Play with Household Items)

In the first example, the material, a book, is designed for intellectual activity, but the child is using it inappropriately with respect to cognitive learning. In the second example, neither the materials, mother's behavior, nor the child's behavior present clear indications of this situation as an intellectual activity for the child.

The activities in Cluster III are routine situations that have little likelihood of promoting cognitive gain for the child. Material objects and the behavior involved in Cluster III activities are relevant only to the care of the child's physical needs and his large motor development.

The activities in Cluster IV are situations in which the primary focus is emotional expression or social behavior. Each will be defined and described, with examples given.

1. Verbal and Symbolic Learning

This activity indicates that the main focus of the child is the *acquisition* of *verbal skills*, such as building of receptive vocabulary, mastery of articulation and expressive speech, and use of language materials (e.g., picture books, children's records, and educational TV programs that promote verbal skills). In this activity, the child is often engaged in labeling objects or pictures, putting words together grammatically, counting, reciting, or attending to books, educational TV, or other media for language skills. This activity may be suggested or elicited by another person. The following are some common examples typifying this activity for children aged one to three:*

a. M touches S's eye and says "eye." S repeats. M asks, "Where is Mommy's eye?" S touches M's eye. M asks, "Where is Mommy's nose?" S touches M's nose.

b. S points at a balloon on his pajamas and says, "Red." M corrects: "No, *blue*. It is a blue balloon." S says, "Blue." M says, "Can you find another blue balloon?" S points correctly.

c. M and S are getting ready to read a picture book. S says, "Good Night, Moon" (title of the story) and points at a balloon on the floor: "Moon?" M laughs, "No, that is a *balloon*. That is different from *moon*." S says, "Loon?" M says, "That is right." S says, "Moon?" M says, "That is a balloon." M points at the moon picture in the book, then at the balloon, and says, "Moon and balloon." S repeats, "Moon, loon."

d. S feels his soup bowl and says to M, "Hot." M says, "No, it is not hot. It is *warm*. See, Mommy's tea is *hot* [M moves her cup over for S to touch]. Joe's soup is warm."

e. Sister teaches S to recite "Humpty Dumpty sat on a wall . . ." etc.

Exclusion:

a. S is eating soup at the lunch table and says to M, "Hot." M says, "Hot? Let me put some cold milk in," and pours some milk in S's soup. (Basic Care)

b. Sister directs S to sit on the chair, and says, "You are Humpty Dumpty." S complies. Sister says, ". . . Humpty Dumpty falls down." S jumps down and curls up on the floor. (Expressive–Role Play)

c. M stops in the middle of a story and asks S, "Can you find the mouse?" S looks for the mouse imbedded in the details of the picture. (Spatial and Perceptual Learning)

d. S and M are pulling a belt. M teases, "My belt." S echoes, "My belt." M says, "It is mine." S echoes, "Mine." M echoes back, "Mine." S and M chant "Mine" over and over, and they laugh. (Enjoyment of Social Game)

*In all the following examples, S = subject child, M = mother, F = father.

2. Perceptual, Spatial, and Fine Motor Learning

This activity indicates that the main focus of the child is differentiation in visual perception and spatial orientation, or acquisition of skills for perceptual and fine motor coordination. In this activity, the child is often involved in visually sorting or matching colors and shapes (when the main focus is not on verbal labeling); in understanding size, distance, angle, and spatial perspective of objects; in fitting, stacking, molding, or pasting tasks; or in using those materials that are designed to promote skills in perceptual and fine motor learning, such as a magnifying glass, binoculars, puzzles, a shape-sorting box, nesting cups, Tinker Toys, Lego blocks, stacking blocks, scissors, and crayons. This activity may be suggested or elicited by another person. The following are common examples typifying this activity for children aged one to three:

a. M shows S how to stack three graded mixing bowls on the floor.

b. S concentrates in putting the button through the buttonhole. S accomplishes it. M praises.

c. S looks through the binoculars. M says, "Can you see Mommy?" S looks and says, "Yes, I see you, Mommy."

S fits shaped blocks into the shape-sorting box. M looks on.

Exclusion:

a. S makes spaghetti with Play Doh. M says, "Mm . . . Yummy." (Expressive—Role Play)

b. S asks M to button up his shirt. M complies. (Basic Care)

c. M directs S in putting blocks away on the toy shelf. (Executive Skill)

3. Concrete Reasoning

This activity indicates that the main focus of the child is concrete reasoning and the formation of concepts such as object permanence, differentiation of means and ends, classification, dissonance, causality, and scientific law of momentum. In this context, the child often engages in "hide and seek" situations, or is involved in experimenting with gravity, equilibrium, weight, etc., in categorizing similarities and differences, in investigating the reflection of images or the reverse side of an object, in exploring the operation of mechanical or electrical equipment, or in revealing foresight in planning, anticipation, or understanding of means-end relationships. This activity may be suggested or elicited by another person.

For this particular activity, there are subcategories. They are listed below with their assigned numbers:

(1) object permanence (which includes peek-a-boo games and searching for a lost object)
(2) differentiation of means and ends
(3) scientific laws and principles (which include the laws of gravity, momentum, buoyancy, trajectory phenomena, shadow phenomena, reflection, equilibrium, and the relationship of cause and effect)

(4) abstract categorization and classification

(5) miscellaneous (which includes the recognition of dissonance, the ability to dual-focus, dumping objects from a container, high-level exploration, recognition of the reverse side of an object, originality in problem solving, interesting associations of uses of an object)

The following are some examples typifying each subcategory:

(1) Object Permanence:

a. S pulls the bedspread over her head. M says, "Where is Veda?" S unveils her face. M says, "Peek-a-boo. There she is!"

b. S is eating raisins in a high chair. S drops some and they disappear from view. M asks, "Where did they go?" S looks and finds them under M's chair.

(2) Differentiation of Means and Ends:

a. S's ball rolls under the washer. M suggests that S use a track from his train set to get it out. (Means/Ends)

b. S wants to go into the dining room, but there is a big toy box blocking the doorway. M watches as S goes through the kitchen and pantry and enters the dining room through the other door. (Detour)

(3) Scientific Laws and Principles:

a. S throws little wooden dolls out of his playpen one by one and watches them fall. M puts the toys back into S's playpen. (Gravity)

b. S turns the light switch on and off. M tells her to stop. (Causality)

c. S looks at his own reflection on the metal bottom of a toy box. M asks, "See the baby?" (Reflection)

(4) Abstract Categorization and Classification:

a. S takes out some rubber animals from a box and lines them up on a low table. M looks on and says, "You have many *animals*." (Categorization)

b. S helps M put the silverware away. M says, "Put the big spoons here and the little spoons there." S sorts the spoons and puts them into two piles. (Classification)

c. M and S are looking at a picture book. M points and says, "Here is the Daddy cat, here is the Mommy cat, here is the Sister cat, here is the Brother cat, and here is the Baby cat. That is a nice *cat family*." (Categorization)

(5) Miscellaneous:

a. S puts shoes on the wrong feet. Then she realizes it and corrects it. M praises. (Dissonance)

b. S is busy lining up beans on the bench. M walks by S's back and goes into the bathroom. Sister comes and calls M. S tells sister, "Mommy is in the bathroom." S has not moved his eyes away from his beans all this time. (Dual Focus)

Exclusion:

a. S eats raisins and drops some in front of him, in full view. S picks them up and eats. M looks on. (Basic Care—food behavior)

b. S throws toy out of playpen and cries, wanting to get out. M ignores. (Negative Social and Emotional Expression)

c. M gives S a box of kitchen equipment. S puts cake-decorating tubes in and out of the flour sifter one by one. (Play with Household Items)

4. Expressive Skills

This activity indicates that the main focus of the child is the expression of imagination and fantasy or the creation of representational products. Often, the child is involved in pretending to be someone or something (role play), in assigning roles to symbolic toys or objects in his play, in portraying an imaginative role in fantasy play, in telling make-believe stories, or in creating representational products, such as painting "a monster," constructing a block "garage," or building a sand castle. The following are some common examples typifying this activity for children aged one to three:

a. S and older sister are playing with dolls. S rocks her "baby" in her arms and gives her "baby" a toy bottle. (Expressive—Role Play)

b. S and peer are playing doctor. S examines peer's belly with a small block. (Expressive—use of make-believe object in Role Play)

c. M folds handkerchief to make twin dolls and hands it to S: "Here are Jackie's twin babies." S hugs the twins. (Expressive—Role Play)

d. S scribbles lines with red crayon and tells M, "Fire." (Expressive—Creative Work)

e. S and older sister have a "tea party" with S's toy tea set. (Expressive—Role Play)

f. S puts on a pair of "spaceman shoes," turns the knobs on an airconditioner, and talks into its electric cord: "1, 2, 3, Go!" Peer starts to run. (Expressive—Role Play)

Exclusion:

a. S concentrates in dialing the play phone with his index finger, obviously trying to master the fine motor coordination. M praises. (Fine Motor Learning)

b. S takes a doll to her sister. (Play with Toys)

5. Executive Skills

This activity indicates that the main focus of the child is the acquisition of practical, executive skills that call for patterned steps to accomplish an end goal. Often, the sequential task also involves fine motor learning and concrete reasoning, but sequencing of execution is the prominent aspect. In this activity, the child may be involved in carrying out instruction, in following sequential steps in games, in doing little errands such as fetching the newspaper, or in participating in household chores, such as picking up toys, sponging the table, or unloading dishes. These activities may be suggested or solicited by another person. The following are common examples typifying this activity for children aged one to three:

a. S unloads the dishwasher for M and puts the dishes on the table.

b. M, S, and brother are raking leaves on the terrace. S is using a small rake to gather leaves into a pile.

c. S carries a bag of rubbish to the incinerator with M. M lifts S up for S to drop the bag into the incinerator.

d. M puts a clean sheet on S's crib and hands S the dirty one, saying, "Put it in the cellar for Mommy." S carries the sheet to the kitchen, opens the cellar door and throws the sheet down the stairs.

e. S plays ring-around-the-rosy with sibs. S flops down when sib says, "All fall down!"

Exclusion:

a. S pulls the dishwasher in and out, repeatedly. M stops S. (Explore Household Item)

b. S gets the key from M and tries to fit the key in the keyhole. (Fine Motor Learning)

c. S smells the leaves he raked. M watches. (Explore Nature)

d. M suggests S pick up toys. S sorts out all the matchbox cars and puts them in a special box. (Concrete Reasoning—Categorization)

6. Exploration of and Play with Household Items

This activity indicates that the main focus of the child is the investigation of places and objects in the household (here, household is extended to include also any manmade dwellings, structures, and objects). Through such investigations, the child is presumed to gain a certain amount of undefined cognitive input. (If the input could be more clearly defined and could be coded as an activity at the higher level, it would be elevated to an activity included in Cluster I.) In this activity, the child is often involved in getting into places and nonplaythings, in inappropriate use or abuse of property, or in unsafe situations. Going places and playing with household objects may be suggested and solicited by another person. The following are some common examples typifying this context for children aged one to three:

a. M pulls out her kitchen drawer for S. S takes out pots, pans, cooking utensils, aprons, potholders, etc.

b. S hesitates about going up the back stairs leading to neighbors on the second floor, and says "No, no" to himself. Finally S goes up. Father comes to get S down and scolds S.

c. S puts her hands in the toilet bowl and splashes the water inside. M stops S.

d. S tries to poke her finger into the electric outlet on the wall. M removes S.

e. S gets into M's handbag, taking out bits of paper, a hairbrush, and some bobby pins. M says, "No, Vera." S ignores M and takes out more things.

Exclusion:

a. M opens kitchen drawer for S. S takes out pots and pans. S tries to fit a lid on the right pot. (Spatial and Fine Motor Learning)

b. S turns the switch of the television on and off. M says "No" and carries S to the kitchen. (Concrete Reasoning—Causality)

c. S plays with M's handbag, carrying it on her arm and walking around, assuming an important air. (Expressive—Role Play)

d. S gets on the coffee table, then jumps down. Repeats. M cautions S to be careful. (Gross Motor—Jumping)

7. Play with Toys

This activity indicates that the main focus of the child is the use and examination of playthings. Through "play" the child is presumed to gain a certain amount of undefined cognitive input, in addition to enjoyment. (If the input could be more clearly defined and coded as an activity at a higher level, the play would be elevated to an activity included in Cluster I.) In this activity, the child is often engaged in manipulating or transporting toys, in using toys in an unspecified manner, such as moving a toy truck back and forth, or in inappropriate use or the abuse of toys. Play with toys is frequently suggested and solicited by another person. The following are some common examples typifying this context for children aged one to three:

> a. S is in a jumper chair. M hands S a Playplax piece. S holds it, bangs it on the tray and mouths it.
>
> b. M suggests Play Doh. S pounds on it and squeezes it.
>
> c. S lines up some rubber animals on the table and moves them around. M watches S.
>
> d. S rips a picture book. M says, "No, that's a no-no."
>
> e. M puts a song record for children on the phonograph. S listens to "Skip to my Lou" and other songs.

Exclusion:

> a. S lines up toy animals on the table. M says, "Stephanie has many *animals.*" (Concrete Reasoning—Categorization)
>
> b. S lines up some stuffed animals on the big bed and puts a blanket on them. S tells M, "They go night-night." (Expressive—Role Play)
>
> c. M hands S some Play Doh and demonstrates how to roll it out with a rolling pin. (Fine Motor Learning)
>
> d. M and S listen to a story record—"The Little Engine That Could." (Verbal Learning)

8. Exploration of Nature

This activity indicates that the main focus of the child is the exploration of living things—plants and animals. Through such exploration, the child is presumed to gain information about the world of nature and/or acquire skills in caring for and handling living things. (If the cognitive gain from such explorations could be more clearly defined and could be coded as an activity at the higher level, the exploration would be elevated to Cluster I.) In this activity, the child is often involved in examining plants and flowers, watching birds, fish, or other small animals, taking walks in woods and parks, or playing with pets and caring for them. These may be suggested or solicited by another person. The following are common examples typifying this activity for children aged one to three:

> a. M asks, "Who would like to see the fish?" S says "Me" and watches M sprinkle some fish food into the aquarium.

b. S and M pat a kitten together.

c. M pushes S in her stroller and goes around the block for a walk. M points at some flowers and says, "Look, Stephanie." S looks at the flowers.

d. M suggests S go look for some ants. S squats down and watches the ants crawling around on the ground.

e. S crumbles a rose. M says, "Don't break it. Smell it." S smells the roses in the vase.

Exclusion:

a. S is patting a kitten. M labels for S: "Kitty." S babbles in response. (Verbal Learning)

b. S crumbles a rose. M tells S to sweep up the petals and hands S a brush and a dustpan. S tries to sweep up the petals. M helps. (Executive Skills)

c. S puts a long stick across his chest under his overall bib and runs around the room, flapping his arms and saying to himself, "I am a big bird." M watches and laughs. (Expressive—Role Play)

9. Gaining General and Routine Information

This activity indicates that the main focus of the child is gaining general information about his daily routine life and the wider world around him. Through such general information, which is often trivial, the child is presumed to gain knowledge of the world that may lead to further cognitive inquiries and input. (If the cognitive input from this general information were more clearly defined and could be coded as an activity at the higher level, it would be elevated to an activity in Cluster I.) In this activity, the child is often involved in requesting routine information, seeking feedback in his factual knowledge, giving statements of obvious facts, or watching children's entertainment programs or adult programs on television. These may be suggested or solicited by another person. The following are some common examples typifying this activity for children aged one to three:

a. M and S are at the mailbox in the main lobby. Someone goes out the door. S asks, "What, Mommy?" M informs, "That was the storeman. He just went out the door."

b. S questions M: ". . . Tina home?" M says, "Not yet, in the afternoon." S repeats, "Tina home in the afternoon?" M says, "Right."

c. S asks M, "Where is Mark?" M informs, "Mark is in the playroom."

d. M tells S, "I am going down to put the laundry in the washer." S says, "OK." M leaves for downstairs.

e. M asks, "Where are your sister's shoes?" S says, "Here," and points under the table.

Exclusion:

a. M is getting S's party clothes ready. S points at her patent leather shoes and asks, "My party shoes are black?" M says, "Yes. They are black." (Verbal Learning—labeling color)

b. M tells S she is going downstairs. S goes down with M and follows M around while M does laundry. (Neutral Social Behavior—maintaining social contact)

10. Basic Care

This context refers to the activity or behavior contents in which the child's focus is satisfaction of biological needs and adjustment to social norms in meeting those needs. Here, the child is often involved in eating, bathing, using the toilet or being diapered, dressing, and keeping clean and neat. These activities are frequently suggested or solicited by another person. Some common examples for children aged one to three are listed below:

a. M serves S a hot dog and potato chips for lunch.

b. M asks S if he is wet. S says, "No."

c. S and brother are taking a bath together in the tub.

d. S asks for another cookie. M provides.

e. M powders S and dresses her.

Exclusion:

a. S tries to cut his hot dog with knife and fork. M holds the hot dog steady for S. (Fine Motor Learning)

b. S is on the diapering table, being changed before her nap. S and M label the colors of the balloons on S's pajamas. (Verbal Learning)

c. S and his brother are bathing together. S imitates his brother in squeezing the soap into pieces. (Play with Household Items)

d. S wants the baby powder. M says, "Let Mommy show you." M shakes some powder on S and rubs it in. S tries to do the same. (Executive Skill)

11. Gross Motor Activities

This activity indicates that the main focus of the child is the acquisition of skills for gross motor coordination or the use of equipment that promotes coordination of the large muscles. Here the child is often engaged in crawling, walking, climbing, running, pulling, pushing, or tossing behavior; or he is involved in balancing his body, as in kneeling, squatting, tiptoeing and whirling around; or he is involved in the use of certain playthings or playground equipment that promote gross motor coordination, such as bouncing seats, rocking horses, pushcarts, swings, slides, tricycles, jungle gyms, rope ladders, or jumpropes. (If the child uses his body for high-level exploration of physical phenomena, the activity coded would be appropriate to the intellectual content involved. For example, pedaling on a tricycle and then watching how long it takes for the tricycle to come to a stop would be elevated from a Gross Motor Activity to Concrete Reasoning—Momentum, in Cluster I.) The following are some common examples typifying this activity for children aged one to three:

a. M holds S's hands and helps him to learn to walk.

b. S is sitting on the swing. Babysitter instructs S how to bend her knees and pump herself on the swing.

c. S pedals his tricycle around on the playground. M looks on.

d. S does a somersault. Aunt looks on and claps her hands.

e. S takes a roller skate to M. M puts it on S's foot, and holds S's hand as he walks around on it.

Exclusion:

a. S approaches a downhill slope on his tricycle. S calls to M. M says, "Use your feet and go down slowly." S uses his feet as a brake and goes down the slope slowly on his tricycle. (Concrete Reasoning—Gravity)

b. S and her sister pretend they go shopping for cereal on their tricycles. (Expressive—Role Play)

c. S plays pool with M, taking turns hitting the ball with the cue. (Fine Motor Learning)

12. Unspecific Behavior

This activity encompasses the pass-time or purposeless behavior of the child, and all other activities or behaviors that cannot be coded in the other contexts because of unspecified situations, ambiguity of behavior, or unclear protocols. Some examples typifying this are:

a. S wanders around aimlessly, then sits down with a blank look on her face. M asks, "What are you going to do?" (Purposeless Behavior)

b. M calls S and says, "Let's go downstairs." S complies. (Unspecific situation)

c. S babbles something to M. M looks at S. S walks away. (Ambiguity of Behavior)

d. S whispers something in M's ear. M whispers back—observer can't hear what they say. (Unclear Protocol)

31. Emotional and Social Expression—Positive

This activity indicates that the main focus of the child is the expression of positive emotional feelings, such as affection, joy, pleasure, or contentment; or gestures of social kindness, such as respect, thoughtfulness, empathy, sharing, and offering help. Here, the child often demonstrates such feelings through facial expression, gestures, or actions, such as smiles, kisses, jumping up and down for joy, offering help to someone, comforting someone who is crying; or he reveals his feelings by statements ("I love you, Mommy") or by verbalizing his concern ("Cookie for Jimmie [peer] too"). He may also engage in pleasure-seeking activities, such as being entertained, roughhousing with someone, or playing spontaneous social games. These behaviors are often likely to be suggested or solicited by another person. The following are some common examples typifying this behavior for children aged one to three:

a. Father carries S in his arms, hugs and tickles S, and playfully pretends to bite S's belly. S laughs.

b. S tells her brother, "Close your eyes." Her brother complies. S tickles her brother's eyelid. Her brother laughs and rolls over in the chair. S gets on top of her brother and they roll and laugh together.

c. S's sister makes funny faces at S. S laughs.

d. S offers her half-eaten banana to her brother, who says "No" and shows S his own banana.

e. Peer crawls behind chair and gets stuck. Peer cries. S tries to pull peer's feet to get her out and calls M to help.

f. M pulls on a belt S is playing with and teases, "That's mine." S says, "Mine." M echoes, "Mine." S echoes, "Mine." M and S chant "Mine" back and forth. (Verbal Game)

Exclusion:

a. S stands near M for her attention. (Seeking Attention—Neutral Social Behavior)

b. S and sister hold hands and try to do ballroom dancing. (Expressive—Adult Role Play)

c. S sits on babysitter's lap and they swing on the swing together. (Gross Motor Learning)

d. M gives S a lollipop. M says, "What do you say?" S says to M, "Thank you." (Socialization to Polite Forms—Neutral Social Behavior)

e. S and her sister play peek-a-boo behind a curtain. (Concrete Reasoning—Object Permanence)

f. S falls and cries. M holds S and pats his back. (Crying—Negative Emotional Behavior)

32. Emotional and Social Expression—Negative

This activity indicates that the main focus of the child is the expression of negative emotional feelings, such as hostility, anger, sadness, distress, fear, or jealousy; or negative social behaviors such as aggression, tantrums, rejection of another, selfishness, or destructiveness. Here, the child often demonstrates such feelings through facial expressions, gestures, or actions, such as an angry look, whining or crying, tantrums, hitting or pushing someone, throwing or destroying things; or he reveals such feelings by verbalizing how he feels ("I don't like you!" or "I am scared"). Some examples typifying this behavior for children aged one to three are:

a. S bumps his head and cries. M picks S up and comforts him.

b. S snatches two bowling pins away from peer, who protests. S runs away with the pins.

c. S hears a man with a deep voice on television. S tells M, "I am scared," and lays his head on M's lap.

d. S is crying. Brother goes to him. S shouts, "Go away!" (Rejection)

e. S lies on the floor crying and kicking. M threatens to give S's bottle to her stuffed bear if S doesn't go upstairs for her nap. S cries, M carries S upstairs.

f. S's brother wouldn't give S his lollipop and ran out the door. M explains to S that it is her brother's candy. S pouts and tells M in an angry tone, "You hit me." M laughs and says, "No, I did not," and hugs S.

Exclusion:

a. Some visitors come into the house. S follows close behind and sucks his thumb. (Emotional Security—Neutral Emotional Behavior)

b. S hits her doll "for being naughty." M looks on and smiles. (Expressive—Role Play)

33. *Emotional and Social Expression—Neutral*

This activity indicates that the main focus of the child is the expression of emotional need for security, social contact, or attention; or the compliance with certain culturally prescribed neutral social behaviors such as gestures and modes of speech. Here, the child may be engaged in seeking emotional reassurance by sucking his thumb, using a "security object," seeking attention or social contact as an end in itself, competing with others; or he may be involved in saying greetings or waving, addressing someone politely, using polite forms such as "thank you" and "please." These behaviors may be suggested by another person. The following are some examples typifying this behavior for children aged one to three:

a. S gets up from playing with cards and walks to the kitchen where M is working. M says, "I am here." S smiles and goes back to her cards in the dining room.

b. S walks near M, who is busy helping S's sister with arithmetic problems. S pulls M's dress. M doesn't respond. S climbs on the table and throws sister's crayons at M and sister. M puts S down on the floor and tries to distract S with a puzzle.

c. S sucks his thumb. M says, "Don't." S doesn't comply. M tries to shame him, saying, "Look at Joseph with his finger in his mouth. Laugh at him—Ha, Ha." S continues sucking his thumb.

d. M is putting a bandage on S's brother's hurt finger. S shows M her finger and says, "Boo-boo, too." M looks and says, "No, there is no boo-boo." S asks for a bandage. M says, "No, you can't have any." M leaves the room.

e. S sits in the playpen and babbles to M. M looks up at S and says "Hi."

Exclusion:

a. S goes into the kitchen and asks M for a glass of water. (Basic Care)

b. S babbles to M, who looks out from behind the newspaper and says "Hi, peek-a-boo." (Concrete Reasoning—Object Permanence)

c. M puts S in her crib for a nap. S sucks her thumb as she lies down. (Basic Care)

d. S picks up two crayons from the table where her sister and M are working. M takes the crayons back from S. (Play with Household Items—not S's playthings)

Dimension 2—Initiation Index

This dimension simply keeps track of who initiates an activity:

1 = mother or the principal caretaker
2 = the subject child
3 = another adult (over 7 years of age)
4 = another child (for age 1 subject, 2-7 years; for age 2 subject, 4-7 years)
5 = peer (for age 1 subject, peer under 2 years; for age 2 subject, peer under 4 years)
0 = doesn't apply or don't know

The following are some examples:

a. S goes to pull off a pillowcase. (S initiates)

b. M offers S a cookie. S takes it. (M initiates)

c. Sib bounces her body to the music. S imitates. (Sib initiates)

Dimension 3—Encouragement Index

This dimension notes the other person's attitude concerning the child's behavior, according to the following codes:

1 = The other person encourages the child's behavior.
2 = The other person discourages the child's behavior.
0 = The other person's attitude to the child's behavior is neutral.

The following are some examples that illustrate the use of this dimension:

a. S goes to show M a spool of thread. M says "See" and demonstrates how to roll it on the floor. (M encourages play with household item by suggestion and demonstration)

b. Sib and S play tea party with a toy tea set. (Sib encourages role play by active participation)

c. S falls and cries. F picks S up and says, "Where is the doggie?" (F discourages crying by distraction)

d. S pulls at the cat. M says, "No, no. Be nice to the kitty." (M discourages S's behavior by restriction)

e. S puts a block under the doormat repeatedly. M peeks in briefly. (M is neutral toward S's play)

Dimension 4—Interaction Techniques

This dimension is an account of the techniques (or types of behavior) used by the other person when he is interacting with the child.

There are fifteen techniques distinguished in this scale. Originally they were defined as the "Maternal Behavior Techniques," but subsequently have been modified and expanded to become "Interaction Techniques" that may be used by any other person: the mother, another adult, an older child, or a peer (playmate close in age). The fifteen interaction techniques are grouped into the following seven categories:

Category I:	21	Didactic Teaching
(Teaching)	25	Justification or Statement of a Rationale
	40	Active Participation
Category II:	22	General Information Giving
(Informing)		

Category III:	23	Suggestion or Command
(Directive)	31	Positive Reinforcement or Affection
	37	Focusing on a Task
Category IV:	24	Restriction or Prohibition
(Restrictive)	32	Negative Reinforcement or Hostility
	34	Distraction or Ignoring
	36	Refusal to Help or Comply
Category V:	35	Providing Service or Assistance
(Help)		
Category VI:	38	Providing Materials
(Preparatory)	39	Changing Location
Category VII:	33	Observing or Interpreting
(Neutral)		

These techniques will be defined and described with examples below.

21. Didactic Teaching

This technique indicates that the focal effort of the other person is to instruct the child. Teaching may be accomplished by labeling, reading, explaining, demonstrating, assessing what the child knows, providing feedback, imparting specific knowledge, or relating experiences for the purpose of concept formation. Teaching is often proactive* and is always coded as encouraging. (See the Encouragement Index, page 481.) The following are some common examples of this technique used with children aged one to three:

a. S and her sister are looking out at the window. Sister says, "See the doggie? Doggie. It goes bow-wow." (Labels and expands)

b. S points at a balloon on his pajamas and says, "Red." M corrects: "No, *blue*. It is a blue balloon." (Provides feedback)

c. M shows S how to hold a toy rolling pin to roll out Play Doh. (Demonstrates)

d. M reads a picture book to S. ". . . Good night, room. Good night, room. . . . Good night, cow jumping over the moon. . ." (Reads)

e. S has been pointing out a tiny mouse in the illustrations of a picture book. M turns to another page and asks, "Can you find the mouse here?" It is imbedded in the details of the illustration. (Assesses S's spatial perception)

f. M, pouring some cold milk in S's soup, says, "The cold milk will cool off your hot soup." (Imparts facts about physical phenomenon)

25. Justification or Statement of a Rationale

This technique indicates that the focal effort of the other person is to provide explanations or reasons to the child. He may make "because" statements, answer "why" questions, or provide justification to his directives or control over the child. It may be used in proactive or reactive situations, and

---

*A "proactive" situation is one in which the other person is initiating an activity. In a "reactive" situation, the other person is responding to the child's behavior.

may be either encouraging or discouraging with respect to the behavior of the child. The following are some common examples of this technique used with children aged one to three:

a. M tells S, "Put on your shoes; *it is cold in here."* (Justification for directive)

b. M cautions S, "Don't touch the iron. *It is hot; you will get hurt."* (Justification for restriction)

c. S asks, "Why Gary cries?" Brother answers, "Because he feels angry." (Gives reason)

d. M says, "If you don't go to bathroom now, you'll have to wait until we get to Janie's house." (Rationale for option)

40. Active Participation

This technique indicates that the focal effort of the other person is to engage actively in behavior with the child. Another person may join in the child's play or tasks, dramatize for the child, or entertain him by roughhousing with him or through playful teasing. Usually this technique is used to promote the child's interests in tasks and his enjoyment of life. It may be used in proactive or reactive situations. The following are some common examples of this technique used with children aged one to three:

a. M and S are playing pool, taking turns to hit the balls. (Joins in play)

b. S hands diapers one by one to M for her to fold. (Includes S in household task)

c. S talks to sister on the play telephone and then they have a tea party with toy tea set. (Joins in role play)

d. Sister makes funny faces at S. S laughs. (Entertains S)

e. S and brother roll around and roughhouse on the couch. (Social game)

f. Father tickles S and pretends to bite S's belly playfully. (Affectionate game)

g. S calls M's attention to her belt and says, "Mine, mine." M echoes, "Mine." They chant "Mine" back and forth and laugh. (Verbal game)

h. M imitates the roaring of a lion as part of a story she is reading to S. (Dramatizes)

i. S asks for milk. M teases by pretending to drink S's milk before handing it to S. (Playful teasing)

22. General Information Giving

This technique indicates that the focal effort of the other person is to inform the child about routine matters. He may make comments on routine facts, such as, "It is a nice sunny day"; or set rules, such as, "We eat at the table"; or simply engage in low-level social conversation. This technique may be used in proactive or reactive situations and is usually neutral in tone. The following are some common examples used with children aged one to three:

a. Someone goes out the lobby door. S asks, "What, mommy?" M informs, "That was the storeman. He just went out the door." (Statement of fact)

b. S pats a kitten. M says, "That is a nice little kitty." (Comments)

c. Sister tells S, "Mommy said we can't play at Daddy's desk." (Comments)

d. Babysitter says, "It is almost time for 'Sesame Street.' " (Statement of future event)

e. M is dressing S for a birthday party, and chats: "Remember the birthday party you went to at Amy's house? There were lots of little children. You all had party hats on. . ." (Chatting about past experience)

23. Suggestion or Command

This technique indicates that the focal effort of the other person is to direct the child to do a certain task or to behave in a certain way. He may request, beg, urge, or command the child to do something; or he may suggest by a physical gesture, such as handing a suggested toy to the child; or he may give the child a choice, as in, "You want to drink juice or water?" This is an encouragement technique and is usually used in proactive situations. It may also be used in reactive situations when the other person consents to the child's request for permission. The following are some common examples of this technique for children aged one to three:

a. M says to S, "Will you pick up all the toys now?" (Requests)

b. M serves soup and says to S, "Please eat it all up—for Mommy." (Urges)

c. M yells at S, "Go out to play. *Out!*" (Orders)

d. Sister says to S, "Let's dance." (Suggests)

e. Sister hands a toy bottle to S and says, "You feed the baby." S pretends to feed her doll. (Physical suggestion and command)

f. Grandmother asks S, "Would you like to read *Peter Rabbit* or *Curious George?*" (Suggests reading by offering choice)

g. M asks S, "Will you get Mommy a tissue?" (Requests to do an errand)

h. S reaches for a hairbrush. M says, "All right." (Permits)

i. S takes a book to M and says, "Read." M says, "OK." (Consents to reading)

31. Positive Reinforcement or Affection

This technique indicates that the focal effort of the other person is to actively promote the child's endeavors in an ongoing task or behavior, or to demonstrate his affection and liking for the child. He may encourage the child by praising, rewarding, or promising a reward (can be affection or material); by showing approval and pleasure; or by favorably comparing the child to others. He may express his liking for the child by demonstrating affection and enjoyment, or by verbal statements, such as "I like you." This technique is also used when the other person defends the child by protecting him against someone or something, or by making excuses for his behavior. This is an encouragement technique and is often used in reactive situations. The following are some common examples used with children aged one to three:

a. S does a somersault. Aunt claps her hands and says, "Yea, yea!" (Praise)

b. S correctly fits a block into the shape-sorting box. M says, "Good for you, Brenda." (Verbal praise)

c. At lunch table, M says to S, "You eat up your sandwich and then I will give you a cookie and potato chips." (Promise of reward)

d. S carries a pile of folded clothes into brother's room for M. M hugs S and says, "Thank you." (Rewards with affection)

e. S walks around with a maple pod on her nose; peer chuckles. (Approval)

f. Father tosses S in the air and hugs and kisses S. (Affection)

g. S bumps his head and cries. M picks S up, rubs his head and pats him. (Comforts)

h. S tells M, "I love you, Mommy." M smiles, "I love you too." (Verbal affection)

i. S picks up a doll and sister tries to take it away. M moves S away from sister and tells her, "Let him play with the doll." (Defends)

37. Focusing on a Task

This technique is fairly self-explanatory. It indicates that the focal effort of the other person is to concentrate the child's interests and attention on an ongoing task. It is often in the form of a suggestion. It is an encouragement technique and is usually used in reactive situations. Some common examples are listed below:

a. S and M are reading a picture book. S is distracted by the fast-moving advertisement on television. M says, "Let's find out what happens to Curious George." S looks at the book. M continues reading the story.

b. S and sisters are fooling around at the lunch table. M says to them, "Eat your sandwiches."

c. S stacks rings, then looks away. M puts another ring in S's hand. S stacks it on the cone. (Physical focusing)

24. Restriction or Prohibition

This technique indicates that the focal effort of the other person is to verbally prohibit or restrict the child's behavior. He often states, and sometimes implies, "No's" and "Don'ts." He may ask or beg the child not to do something or he may strongly prohibit the child. He may also refuse or postpone the child's request for permission. Usually this technique is used in reactive and restrictive situations, but sometimes it may also be used proactively in warning or cautioning circumstances, such as "Don't climb so high, or you'll fall." The following are some common examples used for children aged one to three:

a. S pulls out records from the hi-fi cabinet. M says, "No, Brenda." (Commands)

b. S chews on pen. M says, "You don't eat pens, young man." (Restricts by statement)

c. S fiddles with television knobs. M yells at S, "Stop fooling with the television." (Forceful command)

d. S says, "I am done," and starts to get down from his high chair. M says: "Wait, let me get your bib off first." (Implied "Don't get down yet" in "Wait")

e. S and sister are yelling. M says, "Please be quiet." (Implied "Don't be noisy")

f. S asks for milk. M says, "I will give you milk at bedtime." (Postponed permission)

g. S is climbing on a chair. M cautions, "Be careful. That chair may tip." (Warning)

32. Negative Reinforcement or Hostility

This technique indicates that the focal effort of the other person is to forcefully restrain the child's endeavor in a given ongoing task or behavior; or to express hostility or aggression to the child. He may attempt to stop the child by blocking or removing him from an activity; taking away the object he is involved with; punishing him by scolding, spanking, isolating, withholding privileges and the like; threatening to punish; employing harsh criticism; or expressing disapproval, displeasure, or rejection. He may display his hostility toward the child by making pejorative or derogatory comments to him; assaulting him offensively; engaging in aggressive or defensive fights; teasing him maliciously; or showing dislike for him through rejection or avoidance. When the other person is an adult, this technique is usually used in reactive and restrictive situations. When the other person is a child, this technique may often be used in proactive situations. The following are common examples of this technique used with children aged one to three:

a. S mouths a matchbook. M takes it away. (Removes object)

b. S pokes his finger in an electric outlet. M moves S away from the outlet. (Removes child)

c. S bites M. M spanks S's hand and says "No." (Spanks)

d. S gets into sister's bag again. M yells, "Go to your room!" (Punishes by isolation)

e. S lies on the floor kicking and crying. M says, "If you don't stop now, I am going to give your bottle to Teddy [bear] " (Threatens)

f. S soils her diapers. M yells at her, "You are a pig! Why didn't you tell me?" (Makes pejorative remark)

g. S and other children are running around outside. Peer (aged five) pushes S down. (Assaults)

h. S tries to take his brother's dump truck. S's brother pushes him away. (Defensive fight)

i. Sister and her peer walk into sister's room with dolls. S tries to follow. Sister blocks S and shuts the door, saying, "Not you." (Rejects)

j. S sucks his thumb. M shames S: "Look, look at Joseph with his finger in his mouth. Laugh at him, Ha-Ha!. . . Everybody come to look and laugh at Joseph. . ." (Derogatory remark)

34. Distraction or Ignoring

This technique indicates that the focal effort of the other person is to divert the child's attention and interest from a given task or behavior to a more desirable task or behavior. He may do so by providing alternatives, by suggesting a new activity, or by talking about something else in order to distract the child. This technique is usually used in reactive and restrictive situations. It may also be used when the other person is obviously aware of the child's seeking for attention or approval but deliberately ignores him in order to discourage such behavior, or because of other reason, such as being occupied in a phone conversation. The following are some common examples of this technique used with children aged one to three:

a. S whines. M distracts: "We are going bye-bye soon." (By talking about something else)

b. S tries to take sister's Playplax. M distracts S with another Playplax. (By providing substitute)

c. S pulls dishwasher door up and down, repeatedly. M shows S a donut and tries to distract: "Want a donut, Scott?" S ignores M. (By suggesting new activity)

d. S asks M for soda. M says, "How about some milk instead?" (By suggesting alternative)

e. M has refused to give a bandage to S, who says she has a cut on her finger. S follows M to kitchen and insists that she has a "boo-boo" on her finger. M ignores S. (By deliberately ignoring her request)

f. S calls M and then stands near M when M does not respond. M is busy talking on the phone. (Because of preoccupied situation)

36. Refusal to Help or Comply

This technique indicates that the focal effort of the other person is to discourage the child's request for help by refusing it, by postponing it to a later time, or by suggesting that someone else help. Here, the *motive* is not necessarily discouragement of the child in a given task, but may be inconvenience to the other person at the time of the request, or a desire for the child to help himself. Nevertheless, it has a discouraging tone at the time it is used. This technique may also be used when the other person refuses to comply with the child's directives or demands and in that way restricts him. It is usually used in reactive situations. The following are some common examples of this technique used with children aged one to three:

a. S tries to spin a top, and goes to sister for help (she helped S before). Sister says "Uh-uh" (no), and runs out to the telephone, which is ringing. (Refuses help—because of inconvenience)

b. S goes to show M a truck with a broken door. M is busy with laundry and says to S, "I'll fix it for you later." (Postpones help)

c. S, riding on a tricycle, approaches a downhill slope and calls to M for help. M says: "You can do it. Use your feet and go down slowly." (Refuses help—in order to encourage S to help himself)

d. S tries to unwrap a piece of candy and goes to M for help. M is busy and says, "Ask Mary to help you." (Suggests that someone else help)

e. S tries to open the door to sib's room (sib and peer are playing inside and don't want S to go in). S looks to M and babbles as she tries to turn the door knob. M shakes her head and says, "No, Brenda, I can't help you." (Refuses help)

f. S demands to go out and tries to put on his jacket. S goes to M for help with his jacket. M shakes her head. (Refuses to comply)

35. Providing Service or Assistance

This technique indicates that the focal effort of the other person is to offer or perform services for the child, or to assist him when he is in difficulty. This is usually an encouragement technique and may be used in proactive or reactive situations. It may also be used when the other person yields unwillingly to the child's demands. In such cases, it is a technique of "giving in." The following are some common examples of this technique used with children aged one to three:

a. M diapers and dresses S. (Provides service)

b. S is struggling to eat some soup with a spoon. M says, "Want Mommy to feed you?" (Offers service)

c. Babysitter pushes S on the swing. (Provides service)

d. S is working on a puzzle and has some trouble fitting a piece in. Visiting adult, who has been looking on, turns the puzzle piece around and places it right next to where it should go. (Provides help)

e. S tries to reach for a toy car on the table. M hands it to S. (Provides help. *Note*: If M initiates this, it would be coded as Physical Suggestion)

f. S struggles to push a stroller up a slope. M asks, "Want Mommy to help?" (Offers assistance)

g. M has refused S's request to reach toy, but S keeps whining for toy. M gives in and hands S the toy. (Yields to S's demand)

38. Providing Materials

This technique indicates that the focal effort of the other person is to prepare the child for a given activity by providing materials or setting up the activity. Usually this is an encouragement technique and may be used in proactive or reactive situations. The following are some common examples used with children aged one to three:

a. M puts a pegboard set on the table, and gets S settled in the chair to play with it. (Prepares for play)

b. S asks for milk. M pours milk in a glass and hands it to S. (Provides food)

c. Sister, who has suggested playing with carriage, gets the carriage out for S. (Prepares for play)

d. M gets S ready for her nap by putting a blanket on S, handing S her bottle, and pulling down the shades. (Prepares for nap time)

39. Changing Location

This technique is also self-explanatory. Its focal effort is to change the child's location. The other person may suggest that the child move or he may carry or lead him. Often it is used in proactive situations. It may be an encouragement technique in preparing for a desired activity, it may be for the convenience of the other person, or it may be for reasons unclear to the observer. (*Note*: If M changes S's location in order to terminate an undesired activity or behavior, then it would be coded as Negative Reinforcement—to remove child.) The following are some common examples of this technique used for children aged one to three:

a. M takes S out of his jumper chair and puts S on the floor. (Transports S)

b. S goes to M and says, "Pee-pee." M rushes S to the bathroom. (Leads to another location)

c. M calls S, "Come on, Jackie, we are going inside [the house]." (Suggestion for change of location)

d. S is playing outdoors with sibs and peers. M calls S from inside, "Go play in the backyard." (Change of location for play)

e. M carries S to her room to put S down for a nap. (Transports S)

f. Sister whispers something to S, then takes S's hand and leads him to the parlor. (Leads to another location)

33. Observing or Interpreting

This technique indicates that the focal effort of the other person is to attend to the child by observing him, checking up on him, listening to him; or by trying to interpret what he wants, what he says, or how he feels. This technique is usually used in reactive situations and is usually neutral in tone. The following are some common examples of this technique used with children aged one to three:

a. S is drinking his bottle. M peeks in, then leaves. (Checks in)

b. M watches S, who is playing with nutshells. (Observes)

c. M listens to S, who says, "I am scared of the man [on television]." (Listens)

d. S tries to open food-cabinet door. M questions, "What do you want? Strawberry?" (Interprets what S wants)

e. S whines and rubs her eyes. M questions, "Are you tired and sleepy?" (Interprets how S feels)

f. S says to M, "Up, up." M questions, "What is up?" S says, "Lady up"—referring to the observer, who has followed S upstairs. (Questions what S says)

g. S comes out of the bathroom and says to M, "Pants up." M is puzzled: "Your pants *are up*. What do you want?" S says, "Pee-pee." M says, "Oh! You meant pants down!" and rushes S to the bathroom. (Questions what S wants)

h. S comes back from putting a shirt away for M. M questions, "Did you put it in the dresser?" S nods. (Checks up on S)

Dimension 5—Compliance Index

The child's response to a directive or restrictive technique is noted according to the following codes:

1 = S complies.
2 = S does not comply.
0 = Not relevant or unknown.

PART II: CODING STEPS AND GUIDELINES

Recording Raw Data

This scale is applied to continuous dictated observational records. The observer follows the subject child with a small portable tape recorder and a stopwatch. He times and records the child's behavior and surrounding events, in a way similar to that of a commentator who reports a ball game. For each ten-minute observation protocol (or observational record), the observer also notes the following background information:

1. the subject child's identification code and age (number of days from the first birthday)
2. observation and protocol number, and observer code
3. date and time (rounded to the nearest hours)
4. weather and temperature
5. place (indoor, outdoor, or mixed)
6. principal caretaker
7. people present
8. television or radio program, or type of records being played, if any

For each observation, three continuous observational records (with a ten-minutes break following each) are taken. The first and last records are then coded directly from the tape, and the second one is coded from a written transcription.

Coding Steps

1. Fill in the background information for each ten-minute observation protocol on the coding sheet.
2. From the taped dictated record or its transcript, time exactly the duration of each interaction between the subject child and another person that occurs in the context of a distinct activity. The duration of an interaction comprises the basic coding unit.

   a. S pulls the wastebasket (0:00-0:03 sec.), then touches the hot oven; M says, "No, don't touch it" (0:03-0:11 sec.), S complies. (Here, the interaction duration, 0:03-0:11, is the coding unit.)

   b. M reads a picture book to S (0:00-0:58 sec.), then M and S look for the mouse embedded in the illustration (0:58-1:20 sec.). (Here, the activity duration for reading, 0:00-0:58, is one unit; the activity duration for spatial learning, 0:58-1:20, is another unit.)

   The duration of a given unit is recorded in two ways. The first is to note the time as closely as possible, as in the examples above. The duration is also recorded by rounding off the time to the nearest five-second intervals. Thus, in example *a* above, the exact duration is eight seconds (time 0:03-0:11), and the rounded-off duration is five seconds (time 0:05-0:10).
3. For each coding unit, note the person who is interacting with the child. Interactions are classified according to the following five types, on the basis of the particular person involved in the interaction.

   (1) mother
   (2) the subject child only
   (3) another adult (over seven years of age)
   (4) another child (for age one subjects, 2-7 years; for age two subjects, 4-7 years)
   (5) peer (for age one subjects, peer under two years; for age two subjects, peer under four years)

These types of interaction are defined below:

   (1) *Mother*: This refers to the principal caretaker, usually the mother, who has the primary responsibility of caring for the child during a given observation.
   (2) *Subject*: This refers to the subject child who is being observed. (See step 8 for special cases of coding subject child's behavior when he is alone.)
   (3) *Another Adult*: This refers to any person who is not the principal caretaker and who is over seven years of age. It could be the father, a grandparent, another adult male or female, a sibling, or a peer who is seven or older. This could also be the mother when she is *not* the principal caretaker in a given observation.

(4) *Another Child*: This refers to another child who is not the principal caretaker, and who is between two and seven years of age for subjects age one, or between four and seven years of age for subjects age two. It could be a sibling, a playmate, or someone who happens to come into contact with the subject.

(5) *Peer*: This refers to another child who is close in age to subject—less than two years of age for subjects age one, and less than four years of age for subjects age two; and who is not the principal caretaker of the subject child. It could be a sibling or a playmate or anyone who comes into contact with the subject.

In the case where there is more than one person interacting with the child, use the arrangement above as a hierarchy. Thus, Type 1 will take precedence over Type 3, Type 3 over Type 4, Type 4 over Type 5.

4. Once the duration of the coding unit and the type of interaction is decided, enter the activity code in the appropriate type column on the coding sheet. Then code horizontally the other dimensions: the Initiation Index, the Encouragement Index, the technique used by the other person, and the subject child's compliance to it (if relevant).

Example:

M suggests, "Let's read *Good Night Moon*." S complies.

Act.	Init.	Enc.	Tech.	Compl.
1	1	1	23	1

Here the activity is reading, initiated by M, who encourages with suggestion, and S complies.

5. If more than one technique is used, list the several techniques as they first occur. Fill in the other dimensions for each technique listed, so there may be several coding statements for the same activity.

Example:

M reads "Good Night Moon" to S and dramatizes.

Act.	Init.	Enc.	Tech.	Compl.	Coding Statement
1	1	1	21	0	1
1	1	1	40	0	2

6. When more than one coding statement is used in a given unit, choose a *summary coding statement* by selecting the coding statement that contains the predominant technique (usually the one having the longest duration within the interaction). Thus, the example above may be:

Act.	Init.	Enc.	Tech.	Compl.	Coding Statement
1	1	1	21	0	1-1 (summary code = 1)
1	1	1	40	0	2-0 (secondary code = 0)

For most analyses, the summary code is used to represent the entire coding unit; e.g., the technique in the summary statement is considered to have lasted for the entire duration of that interaction. It is indicated by a 1 following the coding statement number. All secondary codes are indicated by 0.

7. If no one technique is predominant in an interaction unit that includes several techniques that are in the same class, add a summary coding statement and use the code for the class in the technique column. Thus, the example above may be:

Act.	Init.	Enc.	Tech.	Compl.	Coding Statement
1	1	1	21	0	1-0
1	1	1	41	0	2-0
1	1	1	01	0	0-1 (summary code)

8. For "Type 2 Interaction" (the subject child), the child is actually alone, and there is no interaction with another person. It is used to record those behaviors of the child that fall into Activity Category #2 (Spatial and Fine Motor Learning) and Activity Category #3 (Concrete Reasoning). We have a special interest in learning more about these two types of activities in the intellectual development of children aged one to three, and for this reason we keep an account of these two activities as they occur, even if the child is alone. Only the Activity dimension is coded here. For Activity Category #3, the subcategories are also coded, immediately following the activity.

Example:

S fits puzzle pieces.

Act.	Subcategory	Coding Statement
2	0	1-1

Example:

S looks at his own reflection in a mirror.

Act.	Subcategory	Coding Statement
3	3	1-1

Phase Rule in a Given Activity

A long activity episode may have two or more distinguishable phases. These phases are coded separately, provided that within each phase, a given technique or a different initiation lasts 15 seconds or more. The several phases of a long activity episode are timed separately, and each has its own summary coding statement.

The following is an example of a long activity episode with several phases and their corresponding codes and summary statements:

Time	Activity Episode	Phase	Act.	Init.	Enc.	Tech.	Compl.	Coding Statement
0:00-0:05	M: "Let's read a story." S complies.		1	1	1	23	1	1-0
0:05-0:20	M and S find a book, then get settled on couch.	(I) 20 sec.	1	1	1	38	0	2-1
0:20-1:00	M reads and labels.	(II) 40 sec.	1	1	1	21	0	1-1
1:00-1:10	S looks away, M focuses S on the book.	(III) 30 sec.	1	2	1	37	0	1-0
1:10-1:40	M reads and labels and dramatizes.		1	1	1	21	0	2-0
			1	1	1	40	0	3-0
			1	1	1	01	0	0-1
1:40-1:45	S labels, M praises.		1	1	1	31	0	1-1
1:45-1:55	S looks at pictures, M looks on and smiles.	(IV) 15 sec.	1	1	0	33	0	2-0
1:55-2:00	S points at bookcase and says, "Put it away."		5	2	1	23	0	1-0
2:00-2:10	M lifts S up, S puts the book in the bookcase.	15 sec.	5	2	1	35	0	2-1

Other Guidelines

1. *Intermittent Interaction.* If the interval between two interactions focused on the same activity is more than 15 seconds, code the two interactions separately. If the interval is less than 15 seconds, code the sequence as one continuous interaction.

Example:

0:00-0:10   M reads a picture book to S.
<u>0:10-0:30</u>   M attends to baby sib.

0:30-0:55   M reads to S.
<u>0:55-1:00</u>   M attends to baby sib.

1:00-1:35   M reads to S.

Here, the activity is reading, and there are two intervals in which M attends to the baby. The first separates the activity of reading by 20 seconds, and the second by five seconds. Thus, for the latter case, two interactions are coded for the activity of reading:

0:00-0:10   Activity #1
0:10-0:30   No interaction
0:30-1:35   Activity #1

2. *Interruption.* If an interruption in the form of interaction within a different activity context occurs and lasts 15 seconds or longer, time and code the interruption as a separate interaction. If the interruption lasts less than 15 seconds, code the sequence as one continuous activity, omitting the coding that would apply to the interrupted interaction.

Example:

```
0:00-1:10   M reads a picture book to S.
1:00-1:20   M and S look for the mouse embedded in the illustrations.
1:20-2:00   M continues reading to S.
```

Here, the focal activity is reading and the interruption is an activity of spatial learning. Since the interruption lasts 20 seconds, it will be coded separately.

```
0:00-1:00   Activity #1
1:00-1:20   Activity #2
1:20-2:00   Activity #1
```

If the activity of looking for the embedded mouse lasts less than 15 seconds, the entire sequence will be coded as one continuous reading activity.

```
0:00-2:00   Activity #1
```

3. *Directive and Restrictive Techniques.* When a directive or a restrictive technique (#23, 24, 32, or 34) appears in a focal activity more than once, code each occurence separately only if there were different outcomes as indicated in the compliance dimension.

Example:

```
Sib suggests play "going to the grocery store." S says, "No."
Sib suggests play "going to a picnic." S complies.
```

Act.	Init.	Enc.	Tech.	Compl.
4	1	1	23	2
4	1	1	23	1

Here, the activity is imaginative play, and there are two suggestions, with different outcomes. Thus, both will be coded. (If S complies to both suggestions, then only Technique #23 with a positive outcome will be coded).

4. *Repetition of Techniques #23 or #24.* If Technique #23 or #24 is repeated before S responds to it, the repetition of the technique is not coded. If Technique #23 with a positive outcome is repeated, code the repetition as a focusing technique (#37).

Example:

```
S chews on a pen. M says, "Don't." S looks at M with pencil in his mouth. M repeats,
"You don't eat pens, young man." S takes the pen out of his mouth.
```

Act.	Init.	Enc.	Tech.	Compl.
6	2	2	24	1

Here, the activity is play with household item, and M discourages it by restriction, which is repeated before S responds to it with compliance.
Example:

Sib (aged six) says, "Let's dance." Sib and S stand facing each other and holding hands—in the position for ballroom dancing. Sib repeats, "Let's dance," and they start to dance.

Act.	Init.	Enc.	Tech.	Compl.
4	4	1	23	1
4	4	1	37	1

Here, the activity is adult role play. Sib repeats the suggestion after S agrees to it, so the repetition is coded as focusing (Technique #37).

5. *Unclear Compliance to Directive or Restrictive Technique.* In the case when S reacts to the directive or restrictive technique in contradictory ways by (a) contradiction between verbal response and action, or (b) contradiction over time within a given coding unit, code an action rather than a verbal response, and a positive rather than a negative response.
Examples:

S climbs on the banister on the stairs. M tells S to get down. S says, "No," but comes down. (Here, S complies in action, and compliance will be coded as his response to the restrictive technique.)

M suggests ginger ale for S. S says, "No," but then changes her mind. M hands the cup to S. (Here, the positive response for compliance will be coded.)

6. *Unclear behavior of S.* When the subject child's unclear behavior in an interaction becomes clear later on, code it as it is coded later.
Example:

S opens the kitchen-cabinet door. M asks, "What are you doing? Want a cracker?" S nods. M gets a cracker for S.

Act.	Init.	Enc.	Tech.	Compl.
10	2	0	33	0
10	2	1	38	0

Here, M questions the unclear behavior of the child in the beginning of the interaction, then provides food for S. The entire interaction is coded as Activity 10 (Basic Care).

7. *Overlapping Interaction.* When more than one person is interacting with the subject child simultaneously or intermittently, code the person who is ranked higher (see the listing on page 491). If the persons are in the same group (or Type), code the behavior of the person who interacts most with the child.

Example:

M dresses S. F comes to help.

Here, the mother, who is in Type 1 interaction, is coded; the father, who is in Type 3, will not be coded.

Example:

Sister (age nine) is labeling pictures in a book for S. Another sister (age ten) joins in briefly and praises S.

Here, both sisters are in Type 3 interaction. The behavior of the first sister, who is the principal person interacting with the child, will be coded, and the other will not be coded.

RELIABILITY STUDIES

Two reliability studies were conducted. The first was done before the study reported in this book was undertaken, and was limited to the Activity dimension of the Human Interaction Scale. The second was done after the study was in progress and included all five dimensions of the scale.

Study Number 1 Procedure

The children who participated in this reliability study were five one-year-olds (two girls and three boys, ranging from 11 to 16 months), and seven two-year-olds (three girls and four boys, ranging from 25 to 28 months). Each child was visited by one of four pairs of observers, who observed him for three 5-minute sessions. Each five-minute observation was timed and taped simultaneously by the pair of observers, and was later coded independently. Percent of coding agreement by the paired observers was calculated for each protocol in the following two ways:

1. *Protocol Agreement.* Total seconds of coding agreement, including time in which no interaction is taking place.

2. *Interaction Agreement.* Total seconds of coding agreement, excluding time in which no interaction is taking place. Disagreement is counted when observer 1 and observer 2 code the same interaction differently, or when one codes an interaction and the other does not. Three steps were followed in calculating interaction agreement:

   a. The timing of each interaction was rounded to the nearest five-second intervals.
   b. A five-second "displacement" in timing was allowed.
   c. Momentary interactions that lasted less than three seconds were considered as lasting five seconds.

Sample Protocol, Coded Directly from Taped Continuous Record

Subject _____ Date _____ Time _____ Observer _____

Observation # _____ Protocol # _____

Code   1-9   ID _____ 11   Observer _____ 12-13   Observation # _____

14   Phase _____ 15-17   Days _____ 18-19 Prot. # _____ 21-22   Time _____

23   Weather: 1=snow   2=rain/unsettled   3=fine   24   Temperature: 1=cold   2=mild   3=hot

25   Place   1=outdoor   2=indoor   3=mixed

27   Caretaker: 1=M   2=F   3=Other > 7, Who? _____ 4=Child. Who? _____

5=peer. Who? _____ 0=none.

28   Other > 7 present?   0=no   2=yes, no interaction   3=yes, interaction. Who? _____

29   Other child present?   0=no   2=yes, no interaction   4=yes, interaction. Who? _____

30   Other peer present?   0=no   2 yes, no interaction   5=yes, interaction, Who? _____

31   TV, Radio on?   0=no   2=yes, not attended to   3=yes, attended to.   Program? _____

34-35	37-39	41-43	(1) MOTHER 45-54								(3) OTHER > 7 45-54								(4) CHILD 1 = 2-7 2 = 4-7 45-54							
Int. #	Exact time	Rounded time	Ty	C	I	E	T	S	#	M	Ty	C	I	E	T	S	#	M	Ty	C	I	E	T	S	#	M
1	0:08-0:15	0:10-0:15	1	0	9	/	/	2	2	0	/	/															
2	0:15-0:22	0:15-0:20																								
3	0:22-0:54	0:20-0:55																								
4	1:05-1:10	1:05-1:10																								
5	4:44-4:48	4:45-4:50																		4	3	2	2	2	3	2	/	/
6	4:52-5:03	4:50-5:05	1	3	2	2	2	3	4	/	/	/															
			1	3	2	2	2	3	8	0	2	0															

498

Sample Protocol (cont.)

REMARKS: _____

	(5) PEER 1 = < 2 2 = < 4							(2) SELF (Piaget)							
	45-54								45-54						NOTE
Ty	C	I	E	T	S	#	M	Ty	C	Sub Cat.			#	M	
															m informs S that she is going downstairs to do laundry
								2	0 3	0 3	–	–	–	/ /	S winds up music box
								2	0	2	– –	–	– –	/ /	S opens & shuts the tiny door of a toy bus
								2	0 3	0 5	–	–	–	/ /	S dumps small wooden figures out of toy bus
															S takes a postcard from sib, sib grabs it back
															S cries M says "Here is one for you" and Hands
															S another postcard S stops crying

Sample Protocol (cont.)

Column code ranges — Int.# = 34-35, Exact time = 37-39, Rounded time = 41-43, each behaviour section = 45-54.

Sections: **(1) MOTHER** | **(3) OTHER > 7** | **(4) CHILD** (1 = 2-7, 2 = 4-7)

Int.#	Exact time	Rounded time	Ty	C	I	E	T	S	#	M			Ty	C	I	E	T	S	#	M	Ty	C	I	E	T	S	#	M
7	5:19–5:45	5:20–5:45	/	/	0	/	/	3	5	0	/	/																
			/	/	0	/	/	2	3	/	2	0																
8	5:45–6:09	5:45–6:10	/	/	0	/	/	3	/	0	/	0																
			/	/	0	/	/	3	5	0	2	/																
9	6:10–6:27	6:10–6:25	/	0	/	/	/	2	3	/	/	/																
			/	0	/	/	/	3	3	0	/	/																
10	6:27–6:39	6:25–6:40	/	/	0	2	/	3	3	0	/	0																
			/	/	0	2	/	3	5	0	2	/																
11	6:56–7:11	6:50–7:10	/	0	/	/	/	3	8	0	/	/																
12	7:11–7:44	7:10–7:45	/	0	/	2	/	2	/	0	/	/																
13	7:44–9:30	7:45–9:30	/	0	/	/	/	2	/	0	/	/																
			/	0	/	/	/	4	0	0	2	0																
14	9:30–9:45	9:30–9:45	/	0	2	/	/	2	3	/	/	/																
			/	0	2	/	/	3	3	0	2	0																
15	9:45–10:00	9:45–10:00	/	0	/	/	/	2	/	0	/	0																
			/	0	/	/	/	4	0	0	2	0																
			/	0	/	/	/	0	2	0	0	/																

Sample Protocol (cont.)

(5) PEER 1 = < 2 2 = < 4							(2) SELF (Piaget)						NOTE
45-54							45-54							
Ty	C	I	E	T	S	#	M	Ty	C	Sub Cat.			#	M	
															M wipes S's nose & suggests ginger ale for S. S says no but then reaches for the cup
															M hugs S on her lap & holds the cup for S to drink
															M suggests reading a story. S goes to find a book as M looks on
															S wants more water, M questions & holds cup for S to drink more
															M & S get settled down in a chair for the story
															S questions. M labels "moon" & "balloon" for S
															M reads the book "Good Night Moon" to S & dramatizes
															M suggests S look for the imbedded mouse in the illustration, S finds it.
															M resumes reading the story & dramatizes squeak of mouse

The following is an example of how these steps are applied:

	Obs. 1	Obs. 2
Interaction time	3:34-3:36	3:30-3:32
Expanded to 5-second duration	3:34-3:39	3:30-3:35
After rounding	3:35-3:40	3:30-3:35
After displacement	3:30-3:35	3:30-3:35

In this example, the actual duration of the momentary interaction is two seconds. However, for purposes of reliability calculations, it is expanded to five seconds. Then the timing is rounded to the nearest five-second intervals. Finally, the displacement rule is applied for adjusting the clocked timing of the interaction. Thus, depending on whether or not the observers agree on the coding for the activity, their total agreement or disagreement *time* is five seconds for the example above.

Results.

For the one- to two-year-olds, agreement calculated over total observation time was high–85%, 85%, and 82%, with an average agreement of 84%. Reliability based on interaction time only was lower, but still acceptable, relative to standards of other, comparable studies. The weighted average was 54%, 82%, and 84%, with an overall agreement of 73%. Results for the two- to three-year-olds were very similar to those for the one- to two-year-olds. Agreement on total observation time was 85%, 83%, and 85%, with an average agreement of 84%, while the weighted average for agreement on interaction time only was 84%, 80%, and 73%, with an overall agreement of 79%.

It should be noted that in most cases, low agreement occurred when the proportion of interaction time in an observation was low. This may probably be explained by the fact that protocols with short interaction times tended to contain a higher number of small units, which increased the possibility of error from overload. Also, with small units, it is usually more difficult for the observer-coder to define the activity, owing to its momentary nature.

Study Number 2 Procedure

Six children were involved in the second reliability study, three one-year-olds and three two-year-olds. Three ten-minute observations were made on each child.

The procedure differed from that of Study Number 1, in that agreement was checked for each of the dimensions of the Human Interaction Scale: Activity, Initiation, Encouragement, Technique, and Success in Control, not just for the Activity dimensions alone. Also, instead of checking agreement on a statement-by-statement basis, each observer's total for each item cluster of a dimension was compared to the other observer's total. Thus, if observer 1 coded 100 seconds spent on highly intellectual activities in a given set of three ten-minute observations on one child, and the other observer coded 80 seconds on highly intellectual activities, then item agreement was calculated as 80% (80/100). Average agreements on each item cluster, or on single items where appropriate, was then calculated by averaging over observer pairs. Agreement for each dimension as a whole was calculated by averaging agreement over individual items or clusters and over observer pairs.

Results.

Findings from this study are given in the table on page 504. The table shows that agreement for each of the five dimensions was 86% for Activities, 78% for Initiation, 85% for Encouragement, 76% for Techniques, and 87% for Success in Control. Details of agreement for specific items or item clusters may be found in the table.

Average Agreement on all Dimensions of the Human Interaction Scale

	Interactor	Activity	Initiation	Encouragement	Technique	Success in Control
Mean	95	86	78	85	76	87
Range	80-100	78-95	57-98	78-95	71-79	68-93
Median	95	84	89	85	77	91

Average Agreement on Specific Items of Each Dimension

Activity

	Highly Intellectual	Moderately Intellectual	Nonintellectual
Mean	89	88	82
Range	73-95	76-97	10-100
Median	90	88	76

Initiation

	Mother	Subject
Mean	85	72
Range	52-100	42-96
Median	94	87

Encouragement[a]

	Encourages	Discourages	Neutral
Mean	93	52	74
Range	82-99	0-75	30-97
Median	95	36	77

Techniques

	Involvement	Information	Direct	Restrictive	Help[b]	Preparation	Observation
Mean	83	89	82	65	78	60	67
Range	38-100	0-100	70-91	0-92	45-90	0-79	46-92
Median	85	92	84	50	64	46	76

Success in Control

	Yes	No	Don't Know
Mean	77	66	91
Range	48-99	0-100	75-96
Median	78	59	95

[a]Most errors were in judging "discouragement" versus "neutral" categories.
[b]Most errors were in judging "help" versus "preparation" categories.

B

Manual for Object Interaction Scale

I. Introduction
II. Definition of Dimensions
III. Coding Guidelines
IV. Reliability Check

This scale was developed by Jean Carew Watts (Project Director) Itty Chan Barnett (Assistant Director), Nancy Apfel, Christine Halfar, and Geraldine Kearse (former staff member).

I. INTRODUCTION

This scale assesses the subject child's interaction with the material aspects of his environment. At present, it is being refined and expanded for a more detailed and complete assessment of the child's use of his environment.

This is a preliminary manual. It contains the following dimensions:

1. Room
2. Restriction
3. Human Stimulus
4. Object Stimulus
5. Description of Object Quality
6. Description of the Child's Activity

The first four dimensions were used in the preliminary data analysis (page 000), and they will be defined and discussed in the following pages. The last two dimensions are being expanded and are not included in the data analysis.

II. DEFINITION OF DIMENSIONS

Dimension 1—Room

This dimension notes the room occupied by the child:

1 = living room
2 = dining room
3 = kitchen, including pantry and breakfast area
4 = playroom
5 = the child's bedroom
6 = other bedroom
7 = bathroom
8 = stair or hall
9 = study
10 = den, sunroom, or inside porch
11 = balcony or outside porch
12 = basement or attic
13 = public place—indoors
99 = open air

Dimension 2—Restriction

This dimension notes the barriers and restrictions imposed upon the child:

0 = not restricted
1 = restricted to crib
2 = restricted to high chair, car seat, etc.
3 = restricted to playpen (also car ride, etc.)
4 = physical restraint, such as being held and carried
5 = psychological restraint, such as "Eat in the dining room or kitchen, not in the living room."

Dimension 3—Human Stimulus

This dimension notes the person who is attended to by the subject child. The person is coded according to the following categories:

1 = mother or principal caretaker
2 = the subject child
3 = another adult (over seven years of age)
4 = another child (for age one subjects, 2-7 years; for age two subjects, 4-7 years)
5 = peer (for age one subjects, peer is under two years; for age two subjects, peer is under four years)
6 = television
9 = observer

The person categories are defined below:

1. *Mother*: This refers to the principal caretaker, usually the mother, who has the primary responsibility of caring for the child during a given observation.
2. *Subject*: This refers to the subject child who is being observed when he is attending to his own body.
3. *Another Adult*: This refers to any person who is not the principal caretaker and who is over seven years of age. It could be the father, a grandparent, another adult male or female, or a sibling or peer who is seven or older. This could also be the mother, when she is *not* the principal caretaker in a given observation.
4. *Another Child*: This refers to another child who is not the principal caretaker, and who is between two and seven years of age for subjects aged one, and between four and seven years of age for subjects aged two. It could be a sibling, a playmate, or someone else who happens to come into contact with the subject.
5. *Peer*: This refers to another child who is close in age to the subject—less than two years of age for subjects aged one, and less than four years of age for subjects aged two—and who is not the principal caretaker of the subject child. It could be a sibling or a playmate or anyone who comes into contact with the subject.

Dimension 4—Object Stimulus

This dimension notes the *size* of the object that is attended to by the subject child, and its *portability* for the child:

1 = small, portable object
2 = small, nonportable object
3 = large, portable object
4 = large, nonportable object

III. CODING GUIDELINES

This scale is based on a fifteen-second-unit time sampling. The observer, using a stopwatch, observes the child's interaction with his surroundings for fifteen seconds, and then for the next 15 seconds the observer codes or records on the coding sheet information pertaining to the six dimensions. Each observed fifteen seconds is a unit. There are twenty units in each ten-minute protocol.

For each fifteen-second unit, code directly or describe the following dimensions:

1. *Room*: Code according to the location of S in a given unit. If there is more than one, code the room in which the child spends the longest time.

Example:

S walks out of the *kitchen* and goes to look for a toy in the *living room*.

Here, the child's presence in the living room is of a longer duration and hence will be coded. Kitchen will not be coded.

2. *Restriction*: Code according to the restriction used. If there is a change in restriction, code the restriction having the longest duration in the unit.

Example:

M takes S out of the *playpen*; S crawls around on the floor.

Here, absence of restriction (0) has the longer duration, and hence no restriction will be coded. Restriction in the playpen (3) will not be coded.

3. *Human Stimulus*: Note the person or persons attended to by the subject in a given unit. If the child attends to more than one category of person, code each category. If the child attends to none, use "0" code.

Example:

S is at the lunch table, and looks on as sister (aged six) hands her a spoon and M serves hot soup in her bowl.

Here, both the sister (category 4) and the mother (category 1) will be coded in the same unit.

4. *Object Stimulus*: Note the object(s) attended to by the subject child in a given unit. If the child attends to more than one object and they are in different categories in terms of size and portability, code each category. If the child attends to none, indicate so with "0" code.

Example:

S scribbles on the bookcase with a crayon.

> Here, both the large, nonportable bookcase (4) and the small, portable crayon (1) will be coded in the same unit.

5. *Description of Object*: Describe in as much detail as possible the properties and nature of the material object(s) attended to by the subject child in the 15-second unit.

6. *Description of the Child's Activity*: Describe in as much detail as possible the child's interaction with his surroundings in the fifteen-second unit.

IV. RELIABILITY CHECK

In February 1970, a simple reliability check on this preliminary scale was conducted by two pairs of observers. Each pair of observers noted and coded the four dimensions (Room, Restriction, Human Stimulus, and Object Stimulus) in three ten-minute observational protocols. Agreement was checked by simply noting whether or not both observers in each pair agreed on the codes in a given unit. The resulting agreement between observers was close to 100 percent for each of the dimensions.

C

Typical Day of the Week

A. I'd like you to tell me as much as possible about your activities and those of X* yesterday. We have found that we can learn a great deal about a child if we follow his activities closely for one whole day. It will also help us choose the most convenient time to visit your house. So try to remember everything you and X did yesterday, starting from about this time yesterday to the time X went to bed and from the time he got up this morning to now. Take it hour by hour and try to remember.

Time	Where was X?	With whom?	What was X doing?	Where were you?

B. Would you say yesterday was a pretty typical day for X? _____
_____

C. When did X spend time with his father yesterday? _____

What were they doing? _____

D. When did X spend time with his sister(s) and/or brother(s) yesterday? _____
_____

What were they doing? _____

E. When did X spend time with other children yesterday? _____

What were they doing? _____

F. When did X spend time with other adults yesterday? _____

What were they doing? _____

G. I'd like you to tell me about your activities during this last weekend. _____
_____

What did you do that was different? _____

H. When did X spend time with his father? _____

What were they doing? _____

*X indicates child.

510

D

Preliminary Home Interview

Name of the Child _____   Date of Interview _____

Birthdate _____   Interviewer _____

1. Who is primarily responsible for the care of the child during the day?

   _____mother _____father _____sibling _____babysitter

   _____other (please specify) _____

2. General schedule of S:

   awakes_____   lunch_____

   breakfast_____   nap (aft.)_____

   nap (morn.)_____   dinner_____

3. How many siblings does S have? (name and age) _____

4. What time do siblings usually arrive home? _____

5. Does mother have to leave house to get them?

   _____yes   _____no

6. Does S usually go with her?

   _____yes   _____no

7. Are there any *regular* times/events when S is not available for observation? When?

   _____no   _____yes _____

8. Is there any usual time for vacations? When? _____

9. I hereby give the Preschool Project the permission to view my children's school records.

   _____

E

First Home Interview

    I. Basic Care Routine, *513*

   II. Typical Day, *510*

  III. Health of Child, *510*

  IV. Mobility, *514*

   V. Significant Family Events, *515*

  VI. Demography, *517*

 VII. Favorite Playthings, *520*

VIII. Topography, *520*

  IX. Residence Rating, *520*

   X. Demographic Chart, *528*

This questionnaire was developed by Jean Carew Watts (Project Director), Itty Chan Barnett (Assistant Director), Nancy Apfel, Christine Halfar, and Geraldine Kearse (former staff member).

Child's Name_____Age (months)_____ Sex_____ ID _____

SES _____ ETH _____ REL _____

Address _____

Telephone _____

Date of Interview _____

Interviewer _____

I. BASIC CARE ROUTINE

A. Sleep

  1. When does X* usually awake? _____

  2. Go to bed? _____

  3. Does X have a regular time for naps? _____ No _____ Yes

     If yes, when? _____

B. Meals
  1.
     (a) When does X usually have breakfast? _____

     (b) lunch _____ (c) supper _____

     (d) snacks _____

  2. Does he ever have a bottle? _____

  3. Does X feed himself? _____

  4. Does he get himself a glass of water or a snack when he wants? _____

C. Toilet

  1. Is X toilet trained? _____

  2. When did you finish toilet training him? _____

  3. Does X dress himself (except for shoes)? _____

  4. Does X wash his hands by himself? _____

  5. Does X brush his teeth by himself? _____

D. Chores

  1. Are there any little chores he usually helps you with? _____

*X indicates child.

SECTION II of the Home Interview is a Typical Day of the Week Questionnaire, identical to the one shown on page 510.

III. HEALTH OF CHILD

A. Is X healthy? _____

B. Does X have any difficulty in seeing or hearing? _____

C. Any other physical difficulties? _____

D. Has he had any important medical or surgical experience? _____

E. Has there been anything unusual in X's development? _____

F. Has anyone, including you and your husband, had any health problems since X was

born? _____ No _____ Yes _____
If yes, has this person had to be away from home, or has this affected your

routine? _____

IV. MOBILITY/SUPERVISION/RANGE OF EXPERIENCE

A. Are there any rooms in the house into which X must not go unless an adult is with

him? _____

B. Any parts of rooms (e.g., closet)? _____

C. Any equipment he must not touch? _____

D. Any furniture he must not climb on? _____

E. Any furniture he must not sit on? _____

F. Is there any special room or part of a room where X is supposed to play when he's

indoors? _____

G. Where may X play when he is out of the house? _____

    1. Private or semiprivate yard   2. Open space available on grounds or in building

    3. Park within walking distance   4. Vacant lot or space

    5. None available   6. Other _____

H. How many times during the week do you take X out with you, such as errands, visits, trips? Where do you usually take him?

        1 2 3 4 5 6 7 or more _____

How many times during the weekend do you take X out with you? Where do you usually take him?

      1 2 3 4 5 6 7 or more _____

I. Do you let X play outside the house when you are not with him?
   0 = No
   1 = In the yard or on porch only
   2 = At neighbor's or relative's house

J. Do you usually plan X's playtime for him? Or do you leave it up to him? _____

K. Do you usually take part in any of X's activities? 0 = No; 1 = Yes

   If yes, which ones? _____

L. How much time per day do you spend reading to X? _____

M. How much time does X spend watching TV? _____

   What program(s) does he watch? _____

V. SIGNIFICANT FAMILY EVENTS

Interviewer: "Now I would like to get some idea of how many family changes have occurred since X was born." (Ask the following questions.)

A. Since X's birth, has the family had any major difficulty, such as divorce, death, separation, remarriage?

      0 = No   1 = Yes _____ (Specify)

B. Have you worked full time or part time since X was born?

      0 = No   1 = Yes

   1. If yes, when did you start that job? How long did you continue? Who took care of X during that time?

	Start	Stop	Caretaker
a.			
b.			
c.			

   2. If not, how many different caretakers have you had to take care of X on a regular basis since X was born?

	Start	Stop	Caretaker
a.			
b.			
c.			

SIGNIFICANT FAMILY EVENTS (cont.)

C. Have there been any other family events that you think might have had some influence on X's behavior or development?

        0 = No   1 = Yes _____ (Specify)

D. Do you have babysitters from time to time? Yes _____ No _____

If so, how often? _____

Is this usually the same person, or does it vary? _____

VI. DEMOGRAPHIC INFORMATION, QUESTION FORM:

Use a separate question form for each individual. Start with children, doing oldest to youngest, then do mother and father. Ask all questions, and write in *exact response* in the space provided on left. After interview, consult *key* on right and enter code on chart on Page 3.

Name: _____   Relationship to the subject: _____

Interviewer: "I would like to ask you some background information. You must not feel obliged to answer these questions if you want to keep the information private."

A. *Sex:* (Ask only when it is necessary.)

B. *Age:* How old are you (is X?) _____

When is X's (children) birth date? _____

C. *Where grew up:* Where did you (X) grow up? _____

D. *Urban:* Is it a large city? etc. _____

Key:

A. *Sex:* 1 = male; 2 = female

B. *Age:* Fill in

C. *Where grew up:*
1 = Greater Boston
2 = East Coast, D.C. to Maine
3 = Midwest
4 = West Coast
5 = South and Southwest
6 = Foreign

D. *Urban:*
1 = Large city (e.g., N.Y.C., Boston);
2 = Small city (less than 100,000 population)
3 = Near metropolitan area (e.g., Cambridge)
4 = Suburban
5 = Small town
6 = Farm country

517

DEMOGRAPHIC INFORMATION, QUESTION FORM (cont.)

E. *Education:*
   For Adults: What is the last grade you completed in school? _____

   What education have you had since high school? _____

   For Children: Where is X going to school, and what grade is he in now? _____

F. *Occupation:** Do you have a job outside the house? _____

   What is your husband's work? _____
   (Find out responsibilities involved in his job)

   Does X (other adults or children) have a job? _____

G. *Ethnic:* (Do not ask this question. Guess your answer, and write down information on which your guess is based.) _____

E. *Education:*
   1 = Graduate professional training
   2 = Standard college or university graduation
   3 = Partial college/junior college/vocational school
   4 = High school graduation (12th G.)
   5 = Partial high school (10th-11th G.)
   6 = Junior high school (7th-9th G.)
   7 = Elementary school graduation (6th G.)
   8 = Less than six years of school

F. *Occupation:**
   1 = Executive (large firm) and upper professional
   2 = Executive (small firm) and lower professional
   3 = Technical and supervisory
   4 = White-collar worker
   5 = Skilled blue-collar worker
   6 = Semiskilled
   7 = Unskilled
   8 = Unemployed

G. *Ethnic:*
   1 = Afro-American
   2 = Afro-West Indian
   3 = Afro-Latin American
   4 = Chinese and other Oriental
   5 = Irish; 6 = Italian; 7 = Jewish; 8 = Portugese;
   9 = Spanish American; 10 = Other Caucasian;
   11 = Other

H. *Religion*: Would you mind telling me what your (X's) religion is?

H. *Religion*:
1 = Catholic
2 = Jewish
3 = Protestant
4 = Other
5 = None

_____

I. *Family Income*: Would you mind telling me your family income?
(1) Is it under $3,000?
(2) Is it between $3,000 and $7,000?
(3) Is it between $7,000 and $12,000?
(4) Is it between $12,000 and $20,000?
(5) More than $20,000?

I. *Family Income*:
1 = Under $3,000
2 = $3,000 to $7,000
3 = $7,000 to $12,000
4 = $12,000 to $20,000
5 = Over $20,000

J. *Language at home*:

Do you (X) speak only English at home? _____
Does X speak English to his babysitter, etc.? (if appropriate)

_____

J. *Language spoken at home*:
1 = English only
2 = English and Chinese equally
3 = Chinese mostly, and some English
4 = Chinese only
5 = English and European languages equally (German, French, Spanish, Italian, etc.)
6 = European mostly and some English
7 = European only

K. *Marital status*:

Are you married? _____

K. *Marital status*:
1 = married
2 = separated
3 = divorced
4 = widowed

_____

*See the Hollingshead Scale. In deciding between 1 and 2, take into account S's education and job responsibilities; e.g., chemist or stockbroker can be classified 1 or 2.

VII. FAVORITE TOYS AND PLAYTHINGS

Would you please tell me what are X's favorite toys and playthings? _____

_____

VIII. TOPOGRAPHY

(Make a map, including approximate size and location of rooms and major pieces of furniture. Number the rooms.)

IX. RESIDENCE RATINGS

This section to be rated after the interview.

IMPORTANT: Do not ask these as questions.

A. Home (Rate the following):

    1. Type: (1) Single-family house   (2) Two-or three-family house

              (3) Apartment in apartment house   (4) Apartment over store

              (5) Public housing   (6) other

    2. Ratio of rooms to people _____

    3. Quality of building in which the family lives:

        (1) Excellent = well built, well kept, expensive

        (2) Good = well built, well kept, modest

        (3) Fair = evidence of upkeep, but not enough

        (4) Poor = inadequate upkeep, inadequate building

        (5) Deteriorated = extremely poor building quality

    4. Quality of Interior of Home:

        (1) Excellent = clean, good condition, well furnished

        (2) Good = generally excellent, but very modest, or some inadequacies

        (3) Fair = generally fair, some items poor

        (4) Poor = everything poor, or some fair and some very inadequate

        (5) Deteriorated = very poor, extremely inadequate

    5. Appliances available:

Washing machine _____	Freezer _____	Car _____
Dryer _____	Dishwasher _____	Television _____
Stove _____	Vacuum cleaner _____	Phonograph _____
Refrigerator _____	Telephone _____	Radio _____

B. Neighborhood (Rate the following):

    1. What is the mixture of business, industry, and residential in this block?

        (1) entirely residential   (2) mostly residential and a few stores

        (3) mostly commercial—many stores   (4) mostly industrial—factories

    2. What type of housing is there in the block?

        (1) mostly one-family houses   (2) one-family and multiple-family houses

        (3) one-family houses and apartment buildings   (4) almost no one-family houses

3. Quality of housing in neighborhood:

    (1) Very good = large houses in top repair; exclusive apartment buildings

    (2) Good   = medium to large single-family houses in good repair, but little ostentation in house or on grounds; apartment houses with medium to large flats, well kept, but no fancy display

    (3) Average   = small and neat single-family houses (six rooms or less); the best quality two-family houses with adequate yard space; small apartments in clean but plain buildings—strictly utility

    (4) Fair   = small houses in poor condition; average two-family houses, not much yard space; apartments in deteriorated buildings (often converted from large homes)

    (5) Poor   = run-down building but repairable (semi-slum)

    (6) Very poor = building beyond repair, unhealthy and unsafe, area very unattractive—broken windows, trash about.

C.

1. Describe the home in terms of size, maintenance, furnishings, status, etc.

_____

2. Describe the immediate neighborhood in terms of size and maintenance of homes on the street, presence of commercial establishments, trees and open

spaces, status, etc. _____

X. DEMOGRAPHIC CHARACTERISTICS—After interview, transfer information from *Demographic* to this chart.

A. Individuals:

Adults	Sex	Age	Where Grew Up	Urban	Education	Occupation	Ethnic* Group	Religion*	Income**	Language Spoken at Home
1. Mother										
2. Father										
3. Caretaker (specify)										
4. Other adults (specify)										
5.										
6.										
7.										

Children (list in birth order, starting with the oldest)

	Sex	Age in Months	Birth Date	Where Grew Up	Grade in School	Ethnic*	Religion**	Language
8.								
9.								
10.								
11.								
12.								
13.								
14.								

* Do not ask
**Stress this question as optional

F

Final Home Interview

I. Responsibility for Child, *525*

II. Toys and Equipment Inventory, *526*

III. Toys and Household Objects, *529*

IV. Training, 529

V. Self-Care, Security Objects, Eating, Etc., *530*

VI. Reading, *530*

VII. TV Viewing, *531*

VIII. Intellectual Development, *531*

IX. Personality Development, *532*

X. Mother—Personal, *532*

XI. Demographic Information, *532*

This questionnaire was developed by Jean Carew Watts (Project Director), Itty Chan Barnett (Assistant Director), Nancy Apfel and Christine Halfar.

This interview is given to mothers of children who have reached the age of three years (at which time observations and testing are concluded) and who have been participating in the study for at least one year.

The interview is conducted in an informal conversational style, with the following questions serving as a guide to the interviewer, who may elaborate or vary the phrasing or the placement of these questions, and add or eliminate questions, at her discretion. The interview is intended to function as an outline to help the interviewer elicit from the mother her opinions and attitudes about her three-year-old and about child-rearing. With the mother's consent, the interview is tape-recorded.

RESPONSIBILITY FOR CHILD

1. Who is regularly responsible for taking care of [child's name] when you are out, or are not taking care of him/her yourself?

   How often does this person take care of _____ ?
   For how long?

2. Could you tell me what types of things your husband does with _____ ?
   For example, how often might he:
   a. bathe him/her
   b. put him/her to bed
   c. feed him/her
   d. dress him/her
   e. play with him/her
   f. discipline him/her
   g. take him/her out with him

3. How much time on the average does your husband usually spend with _____
   on a weekday? weekend?

4. Do you and your husband have different approaches to _____
   at times? For instance, do you handle certain situations differently?

TOYS AND EQUIPMENT INVENTORY

For this section, the interviewer asks if she may see the child's playthings, explaining that we have seen _____ play with different things and we would like to have a more complete description of these.

The interviewer uses the following checklist to record the toys seen. Then the questions in the following section, Toys and Household Objects, are asked of the mother to determine which toys are regularly used, which are favorites, how the child plays with each type of toy, and what the mother thinks the child "gets out of playing with them."

1. Books, approximate number, titles of a few favorites.

2. Records, approximate number, titles of a few favorites.

Toy	Star if a Favorite	Check if Owned	Used Regularly?	How Played with?
Category I				
1. Lotto				
2. Number games				
3. Alphabet, letter, and word games				
4. Others (list)				
Category II				
1. Puzzles				
2. Tinker Toys				
3. Blocks				
4. Lego, Lincoln logs (intricate construction)				
5. Beads				
6. Pegboard				
7. Snapping/zipping/ buttoning toys				
8. Nesting, stacking toys				
9. Others (fine motor)				

Category III

1. Household objects
   played with (list)

_____ _____

_____

Category IV—Specify cognitive potential (e.g., moving parts)

1. Cars, trucks
_____

2. Animals, stuffed toys
_____

3. Dolls
_____

4. Pull toy
_____

5. Music box
_____

6. Other
_____

Category V

1. Telephone
_____

2. Dress-up clothes, hats
_____

3. Puppets
_____

4. Doctor/nurse kit
_____

5. Filling station, barn,

   etc., with small figures
_____

6. Tea set
_____

7. Guns
_____

8. Others (imaginative

   props)
_____

Category VI

1. Crayons
_____

2. Paints and brushes
_____

3. Others (expressive)
_____

Toy	Star if a Favorite	Check if Owned	Used Regularly?	How Played With?
Category VII (mobile)				
1. Pedal, push carts				
2. Wagon				
3. Skates				
4. Bicycle				
5. Others (gross motor)				
Category VIII (stationary)				
1. Playhouse				
2. Slide				
3. Sandbox				
4. Others				
Category IX (13)				
1. Wind-up toys				
2. Filter glass				
3. Magnet				
4. Gravity-operative toys				

To be completed after the interview:

Describe play area—size, order, arrangement (in child's reach). Small map.
     Child-size table and chairs?

Describe outside play area—equipment, size, grass, etc.

TOYS AND HOUSEHOLD OBJECTS

Toys

1. What are _____ 's favorite toys?

   a. How does _____ play with them? (Describe S's activity with each.)
   b. What does she/he get out of playing with this?

2. *Toys seen*—We'd like to know which ones _____ plays with, how, and what you think he/she gets out of playing with them in each case. (Refer to inventory classes and mention some specific toys.)
   a. Is it used?
   b. How played with?
   c. What she/he gets out of playing with this?
   d. (when applicable) What he/she might get from toy in future?

Household Objects

1. Are there any things around the house other than conventional toys that you allow

   _____ to play with?
   a. Which?
   b. How used?
   c. What does he/she get out of playing with this?

2. Are there other things he/she would like to play with that you don't permit him to play with?

TRAINING

There are stages of normal "growing up"—things that most children learn by age five. But children reach these stages at different ages. Take bowel training, for example. Can you tell me:

1. When did you start bowel training with _____ ?
2. How did you go about it?
3. How did he react?
4. When actually did this get to be a regular habit?
5. When did you start bladder training?
6. How did you go about this?
7. How did he react?
8. When actually did this get to be a regular habit?

SELF-CARE, SECURITY OBJECTS, EATING, ETC.

1. Does _____ dress himself? How much does he do by himself? (Tie shoes, buttons, snaps, zippers?)

2. Did you teach him or did he learn by himself? When did he start?

3. Does _____ wash his hands by himself?

4. Does _____ brush his/her teeth by self?

5. Comb hair?

6. Are there any little household care tasks that _____ does regularly? Do you expect him to do certain things, such as putting toys away, hanging up his pajamas?

7. Feed himself with spoon? Other utensils?

8. Does _____ have a bottle in addition to meals sometimes? Regularly?

9. Does _____ give any trouble with eating?

10. Does he/she have any objects (like dolls, blankets, pacifiers) that he likes to hang onto?

11. Did _____ play in a playpen or jump chair? How long would he/she stay in there in a day?

12. Does _____ have any regular playmates beside his/her brothers and sisters? How often do they play together?

READING

1. Do you and _____ look at books together?

2. a. Is this a regular part of your schedule, or isn't _____ that interested yet?
   b. If not, then magazines, newspapers?
   c. How long a session?

3. Is it mostly looking at pictures or what do you do?
   a. Story line and/or labels?

4. Is it just you and _____, or do siblings and/or father join in?

5. If siblings present, is reading primarily directed toward the older children or toward

   _____ ?

6. Does _____ ever look at books alone? What does she/he do with them?

TV VIEWING

1. Does _____ watch certain TV programs regularly? Which ones?
2. What do you think he/she gets out of watching "Sesame Street"?
3. Do you think he/she will be still watching and learning from it next year?
4. What does he get out of other children's programs, like "Mister Rogers," Miss Jean, "Hodge Podge Lodge"?
5. Does _____ watch any adult programs? Which ones?
6. What do you think she/he gets from these adult shows?
7. How many hours a day does _____ watch TV?
8. Does he usually sit through a whole program, or wander in and out, looking up now and then?
9. a. Do you regulate which shows _____ watches?
   b. How much he watches?

INTELLECTUAL DEVELOPMENT

1. Each child is unique, of course, and each has different skills or some things he does better than other things. What is _____ like as far as different skills are concerned?
   a. His language (speech) development?
   b. How he reasons things out?
   c. Is he good with his hands (building or making things work)?
   d. Drawing, expressive play?
   e. Social skills: Does he get along well with adults? with peers?
2. Is he like siblings in regard to these skills? How?
3. What do you think he'll be like by age five? Changed or not?
4. With regard to skills and abilities, whom do you think he'll be like in the family when he grows up?
5. a. Are you trying to develop certain skills in _____?
   b. How are you trying to do this?
6. To what extent do you think these first three years are important to developing certain skills?
7. What's important for a parent to do for a child in this respect?

PERSONALITY DEVELOPMENT

1. What is _____ like as a person now; I mean, is he: (allow M to comment before suggestions)
   a. Outgoing or shy?
   b. Easygoing? Irritable or anxious?
   c. Does he/she play by him/herself (independent)? Clinging or whiney?

   d. Would you describe _____ as aggressive? as cooperative?

   e. When _____ plays with other children his age, does he/she often suggest the games and things to play?

2. Is _____ like his/her brothers/sisters? In what ways?

3. What do you expect _____ to be like as a person when he's five?

4. In what ways will he have developed, changed, or not changed, by age five, do you think?

5. Whom in the family do you think he'll be like when he grows up?

6. a. Are you trying to develop/encourage certain qualities in _____?
   b. How are you trying to do this?
   c. What about qualities you aren't too pleased about? (Have any? What?)
   d. How do you deal with these?

7. a. To what extent do you feel that what parents do in the child's first three years of life is important to a child's personality?
   b. What are the most important things a parent should do for a child in this respect?

8. Have there been any specific events or circumstances that have had an effect on

   _____'s personality?

MOTHER—PERSONAL

1. Do you belong to any civic, religious, social, political organizations?
   Which?
   Attend frequently?
   Type of work involved?

2. Do you have a job or do you do volunteer work?
   Full or part time?
   What sort of work?

DEMOGRAPHIC INFORMATION

1. Is the composition of home same?
2. Has your husband's job changed?
   Description of job:
3. Have there been family income changes:

G

Supplementary Tables

Comparison of Age Groups Among A and C Children on Percentage of
Observation Time:

Table 1   Spent with others on different types of activities, *534*

Table 2   Others use each technique in Human Interaction Scale, *535*

Table 3   During which mother was the main caretaker, *536*

Table 4   Spent with mother on different types of activities, *537*

Table 5   Mothers use each technique in H. I. Scale, *538*

Table 6   Mothers encourage, initiate, and are successful in controlling the child's
          activities, *539*

Table 7   Spent interacting with different classes of people, *540*

TABLE 1. Comparison of Age Groups Among "A" and "C" Children on Percentage of Observation Time Spent with Other People, Including Mother, on Different Types of Activities[a]

Activities[c]	Class I and II A's				Class III and IV A's				All A's[b]				All C's			
	Months				Months				Months				Months			
	12-15	18-21	24-27	30-33	12-15	18-21	24-27	30-33	12-15	18-21	24-27	30-33	12-15	18-21	24-27	30-33
Highly Intellectual	9.3	14.4	5.8	14.4	4.6	9.9	8.7	28.5	8.3	13.9**	7.0**	17.6**	6.6	4.9	1.7	6.6
Moderately Intellectual	19.2	16.5	18.2	13.4	24.3	10.0	14.0	8.7	20.2	15.6	16.4	12.4	20.1	18.9	15.3	12.9
Non-intellectual	15.1	12.5	14.8	11.5	11.3	11.8	15.6	7.8	14.3*	12.4	15.0	10.6	8.7	12.7	11.9	6.6
Social	3.0	1.6	2.8	3.7	3.3	2.8	1.7	0.7	3.1	1.8	2.3	3.0	1.4	0.4	2.5	2.6
All Inter-action	46.6	45.0	61.6	43.0	43.5	34.5	40.0	45.7	45.9**	43.7*	40.1**	43.6**	36.8	36.9	31.4	28.7
No. of Subjects	8	7	7	7	2	1	5	2	10	8	12	9	3	2	6	4

[a]Each entry is a mean of percentages of total observation time during which other people, including mother, engage with the child in the listed activities. For each subject, the total amount of time spent with other people on an activity is summed over the five observations of a 3-month phase, and the percentage of total observation time (9,000 secs.) is calculated.

[b]Means of all A subjects considered as one group. This method of calculation was used because the n's for the working-class groups were too small for their means to be taken as reliable.

[c]Highly Intellectual Activities include activities likely to promote verbal, spatial, reasoning, expressive, and executive skills (categories 1-5 of the Activities dimension of Human Interaction Scale); Moderately Intellectual Activities include unstructured play with toys, household objects, and living things, and routine conversation (categories 6-9); Nonintellectual Activities include basic care, gross motor activity, and nonspecific activity (categories 10-12); Social Activities include interactions concerning negative and positive social behavior (categories 31-33).

*p .05 **p .01. Two-tailed "t's" are calculated on the difference between the means of all A children versus all C children in the same 3-month phase.

534

TABLE 2. Comparison of Age Groups Among "A" and "C" Children on Percentage of Observation Time Other People, Including Mother, Use Each Technique in the Human Interaction Scale[a]

Techniques[c]	Class I and II A's				Class III and IV A's				All A's[b]				All C's			
	Months				*Months*				*Months*				*Months*			
	12-15	18-21	24-27	30-33	12-15	18-21	24-27	30-33	12-15	18-21	24-27	30-33	12-15	18-21	24-27	30-33
Teaching	3.8	7.7	3.0	4.1	1.4	1.8	1.5	14.4	3.3	7.0**	2.4	6.4*	1.0	1.5	0.7	2.0
Facilitation	28.0	22.6	25.5	23.0	23.0	17.6	27.2	21.1	27.0	21.9	26.2**	22.6**	24.1	22.5	15.9	14.7
Routine Talk	5.1	4.1	6.2	5.3	5.3	3.3	4.6	3.4	5.1	4.0**	5.5	4.9	7.5	8.2	7.5	6.6
Observation	7.0	8.1	5.3	5.1	7.3	4.8	4.4	3.8	7.0	7.7	4.9	4.8	4.4	7.1	5.6	3.6
Restriction	5.3	5.0	5.3	5.3	10.5	7.7	4.6	4.1	6.3	5.4	5.0	5.1*	6.7	4.1	7.7	8.0
No. of Subjects	8	7	7	7	2	1	5	2	10	8	12	9	3	2	6	4

[a]Each entry is a mean of percentages of total observation time during which other people, including mother, use the listed techniques. For each subject, the total amount of time other people use a technique is summed over the five observations of a 3-month phase, and the percentage of total observation time (9,000 secs.) is calculated.

[b]Means of all A subjects, middle-class and working-class, considered as one group.

[c]Teaching is category 21 of the Technique dimension of the Human Interaction Scale; Facilitation includes all techniques that generally promote the activity in an interaction (categories 23, 25, 31, 35, 37, 38, 39, 40 and class-codes 1, 3, 5, 6); Routine Talk is category 22; Observation includes category 33; Restriction includes all attempts to inhibit the child's activity (categories 24, 32, 34, 36 and class-code 4).

* $p < .05$ ** $p < .01$.   Two-tailed "t"s" are calculated on the difference between the means of all A children versus all C children in the same 3-month phase.

TABLE 3. Distribution of Subjects on Varying Percentages of Observations During Which Mother Was the Main Caretaker

% Observations in Which M Is Caretaker	Class I, II A's				Class III, IV A's				All C's			
	12-15	18-21	24-27	30-33	12-15	18-21	24-27	30-33	12-15	18-21	24-27	30-33
100%	5	7	4	4	2	1	4	2	3	2	5	4
80%	2	0	0	0	0	0	1	0	0	0	1	0
50%	1	0	3	3	0	0	0	0	0	0	0	0

TABLE 4. Comparison of Social Class Groups Among "A" and "C" Children on Percentage of Observation Time Spent with Mother on Different Types of Activities[a]

Activities[d]	Class I and II[c] A's				Class III and IV A's				All A's[b]				All C's			
	Months				Months				Months				Months			
	12-15	18-21	24-27	30-33	12-15	18-21	24-27	30-33	12-15	18-21	24-27	30-33	12-15	18-21	24-27	30-33
Highly Intellectual	8.9	12.3	3.2	11.9	3.5	8.6	4.5	26.9	7.8	11.8**	3.8*	15.2**	4.5	3.8	1.5	4.8
Moderately Intellectual	17.0	13.5	11.4	9.3	19.5	8.1	9.2	7.4	17.5	12.8	10.5	8.9	11.7	12.0	10.3	9.5
Non-intellectual	14.5	10.8	13.2	9.3	10.1	9.6	13.5	5.6	13.6*	10.7	13.3*	8.5	8.0	10.8	8.6	5.4
Social	2.0	1.3	2.6	3.1	2.7	2.1	1.0	0.4	2.2	1.4	1.9	2.5	1.3	0.4	1.7	1.5
All Interaction	42.4	37.9	30.4	33.6	35.8	28.4	28.2	40.3	41.1**	36.7**	29.5*	35.1**	25.5	27.0	22.1	21.2
No. of Subjects	8	7	7	7	2	1	5	2	10	8	12	9	3	2	6	4

[a]Each entry is a mean of percentages of total observation time during which mothers engage with their children in the listed activities. For each subject, the total amount of time spent with mother on an activity is summed over the five observations of a 3-month phase, and the percentage of total observation time (9,000 secs.) is calculated.

[b]Means of all A subjects considered as one group. This method of calculation was used because the n's for the working-class groups were too small for their means to be taken as reliable.

[c]Classification according to Hollingshead and Redlich (1958).

[d]Highly Intellectual Activities include activities likely to promote verbal, spatial, reasoning, expressive, and executive skills (categories 1-5 of the Activities dimension of Human Interaction Scale); Moderately Intellectual Activities include unstructured play with toys, household objects, and living things, and routine conversation (categories 6-9); Nonintellectual Activities include basic care, gross motor activity, and nonspecific activity (categories 10-12); Social Activities include interactions concerning negative and positive social behavior (categories 31-33).

*p .05 **p .01. Two-tailed "t's" are calculated on the difference between the means of all A children versus all C children in the same 3-month phase.

537

TABLE 5. Comparison of Social Class Groups Among "A" and "C" Children on Percentage of Observation Time Mothers Use Each Technique in the Human Interaction Scale[a]

	Class I and II[c] A's				Class III and IV A's				All A's[b]				All C's			
	Months				Months				Months				Months			
Techniques[d]	12-15	18-21	24-27	30-33	12-15	18-21	24-27	30-33	12-15	18-21	24-27	30-33	12-15	18-21	24-27	30-33
Teaching	3.7	6.4	1.8	3.7	1.3	1.5	0.9	13.3	3.2	5.8*	1.5	5.8*	1.0	1.5	0.7	1.6
Facilitation	24.8	19.1	17.7	17.1	17.2	13.4	19.3	17.7	23.3*	18.4	18.4**	17.2**	15.4	15.2	10.9	10.7
Routine Talk	2.7	1.9	2.2	4.0	0.8	1.7	2.0	1.5	2.3	1.9	2.1	3.5*	1.1	2.5	0.8	0.5
Observation	6.9	7.7	4.9	4.7	7.0	4.7	4.0	3.7	6.9	7.4	4.7	4.5	4.4	5.8	4.4	3.1
Restriction	4.7	3.6	4.1	3.7	9.4	6.2	2.4	3.5	5.7	3.9	3.4	3.6	4.2	2.8	5.3	6.1
No. of Subjects	8	7	7	7	2	1	5	2	10	8	12	9	3	2	6	4

[a] Each entry is a mean of percentages of total observation time during which mothers use the listed techniques. For each subject, the total amount of time mother uses a technique is summed over the five observations of a 3-month phase, and the percentage of total observation time (9,000 secs.) is calculated.

[b] Means of all A subjects, middle-class and working-class, considered as one group.

[c] Classification according to Hollingshead and Redlich.

[d] Teaching is category 21 of the Technique dimension of the Human Interaction Scale; Facilitation includes all techniques that generally promote the activity in an interaction (categories 23, 25, 31, 35, 37, 38, 39, 40 and class-codes 1, 3, 5, 6); Routine Talk is category 22; Observation includes category 33; Restriction includes all attempts to inhibit the child's activity (categories 24, 32, 34, 36 and class-code 4).

*p .05 **p .01. Two-tailed "t's" are calculated on the difference between the means of all A children versus all C children in the same 3-month phase.

TABLE 6. Comparison of Social Class Groups on Frequency with Which Mothers Encourage, Initiate, and are Successful in Controlling the Child's Activities[a]

	Class I and II[c] A's				Class III and IV A's				All A's[b]				All C's			
	Months				Months				Months				Months			
	12-15	18-21	24-27	30-33	12-15	18-21	24-27	30-33	12-15	18-21	24-27	30-33	12-15	18-21	24-27	30-33
Encourages	59.0	61.5	57.8	58.6	45.6	48.1	64.1	71.9	58.3	57.6	60.9**	60.9**	59.1	56.6	47.2	46.3
Discourages	18.8	21.7	18.1	24.4	35.0	40.5	20.2	9.7	24.3	21.5	22.6***	76.2**	22.7	18.1	35.1	35.8
M Initiates	35.6	44.5	33.4	30.2	29.2	27.2	32.2	46.8	41.4*	34.6	31.0**	36.4***	32.6	30.0	23.9	27.8
S Initiates	57.3	52.5	55.1	53.9	62.9	67.4	54.9	44.9	54.6	58.5	54.3***	52.8***	51.0	56.8	69.3	64.4
Success in Control	20.0	22.2	21.9	23.2	23.4	26.3	22.5	18.5	22.6	20.8	22.9	21.2	22.5	20.2	24.7	26.6
Failure to Control	6.5	7.2	9.7	10.3	14.1	13.0	8.1	4.6	8.6	7.3	9.4	8.6*	8.5	10.0	13.2	13.4
No. of Subjects	8	7	7	7	2	1	5	2	10	8	12	9	3	2	6	4

[a]For each subject, the total number of mother-child interactions was found for the five observations of a 3-month phase and percentages calculated of interactions that were encouraged by the mother, discouraged by the mother, etc. Entries are means of these individual percentages.

[b]Means of all A subjects, middle-class and working-class, considered as one group.

[c]Classification according to Hollingshead and Redlich.

*p .05 **p .01 Two-tailed "t's" are calculated on the difference between the means of all A children versus all C children in the same 3-month phase.

TABLE 7. Comparison of Social Class Groups Among "A" and "C" Children on Percentage of Observation Time Spent Interacting with Different Classes of People

| | Class I and II[b] A's | | | | Class III and IV A's | | | | All A's[b] | | | | All C's | | | |
| | Months | | | | Months | | | | Months | | | | Months | | | |
	12-15	18-21	24-27	30-33	12-15	18-21	24-27	30-33	12-15	18-21	24-27	30-33	12-15	18-21	24-27	30-33
Mother[a]	43.0	40.4	30.8	35.7	36.0	28.6	30.7	40.4	41.6	38.9	30.8	37.5	26.4	27.8	22.2	25.4
Adults	1.6	3.3	1.7	1.2	5.5	2.1	4.4	0.3	2.4	3.2	2.8	1.0	0.5	3.4	5.8	3.8
Children	2.3	3.9	6.6	5.9	2.0	4.1	6.4	5.0	2.2	3.9	6.5	5.7	9.2	6.9	3.4	3.1
Peers	0.3	0.1	2.9	2.4	0.0	0.0	1.0	0.0	0.2	0.1	2.1	1.9	2.3	0.0	0.3	0.9
No. of Subjects	8	7	7	7	2	1	5	2	10	8	12	9	3	2	6	4

[a]*Mother* refers to the child's true mother or main caretaker; other "Adults" are people over 7 years of age; other "Children" are children 4-7 years old (for the two-year-old subject), or 2-7 (for the one-year-old subject); "Peers" are children 0-4 (for the two-year-old subject), or 0-2 (for the one-year-old subject).

[b]Classification according to Hollingshead and Redlich.

Index

Index

A

Abstract abilities tests, 291–322
  procedures, 292–307
  reliability studies, 307–8
Abstract thinking capacity, testing for, 26
Abstract thought; capacity: 2–3 years
  comparison data (table), 62
  results, 61–65
  tests, 60–61
Achievement level, as indicator of child-
  rearing practices, 39–40
Active participation, as interaction technique, 483
Activity preparation
  frequency analysis; one–two years, 101
  as nonsocial task, 82
Adult role-playing, as social ability, 13,
  42
Affection/hostility to adults, as social
  ability, 12, 42
Age, as grouping factor, 29
Agency, development of sense of, 235,
  236, 237–38
Ames, Louise Bates, 6

Ammons Full-Range Picture Vocabulary
  Test, 48, 53, 258, 260–61, 274,
  275
  answer sheet, Form A, 269–70
Ammons, R. B., 258n
Annoyance, as social task, 81
Apfel, Nancy, 159n, 180n
Attentional ability—dual focus, as non-
  social ability, 16
Attitudes of mother, as performance in-
  fluence, 240–42
Auditory screening technique, test pro-
  cedure, 254
"Average" mother, basic behavior, 183,
  186, (tables) 184, 185
Avoidance of unpleasant circumstances,
  as social task, 69

B

Banks, Ellen C., 61n
Bank Street College of Education, 6
Barker, Roger, 68
Barnett, Itty Chan, 159n, 180n

Basic care, as activity dimension, 477
Bayley DQ Test, 38, 40, 65
Bayley Infant Development Scale, 134
Bayley IQ Test, 26
Bayley Mental Developmental Index, 112,
    115, 123, 126–27, 145, 148
Bayley, Nancy, 238
Behavioral protocols, as technique, 7
Bellugi-Klima, Ursula, 49, 258, 258n
Bereiter, Carl, 5, 8
Biber, Barbara, 6
Bing, Elizabeth, 173
Birns, Beverly, 20
Bloom, Benjamin, 5
Brackbill, Yvonne, 6
Brown University, 6

C

Caldwell, Bettye M., 68n
Capacity for receptive language, develop-
    ment of, 237
Carmichael, 47
Case studies: one-year-olds
  "A" boys
    background, 122–23
    nonsocial tasks, 131, (tables), 129–
        30
    social competence, 124–25, 403, 425,
        441, 450
    social task data, 128, 131, (tables),
        129–30, 404, 426, 442, 451
    task initiation data, 131–34, (tables),
        132
    test performance, 123–24
    test scores, 402, 424, 440, 449
  "A" girls
    background, 114–15
    nonsocial tasks, 117, 120, (tables),
        118–19
    social competence, 116, 413, 428,
        434, 437
    social task data, 116–17, (tables),
        118–19, 414, 429, 435, 438
    task initiation data, 120–21, (tables),
        122
    test performance, 115–16
    test scores, 412, 427, 433, 436
  "C" boys
    background, 126
    nonsocial tasks, 131, (tables), 129–
        30
    social competence, 127–28, 459
    social task data, 128, 131, (tables),
        129–30, 460

Case studies: one-year-olds (Cont.)
  "C" boys (Cont.)
    task initiation data, 131–34, (tables),
        133
    test performance, 126–27
    test scores, 458
  "C" girls
    background, 111–12
    nonsocial tasks, 117, 120, (tables),
        118–19
    social competence, 112–13, 400
    social task data, 116–17, (tables),
        118–19, 401
    task initiation data, 120–21, (tables),
        121
    test performance, 112
    test scores, 399
Case studies: two-year-olds
  "A" boys
    background, 146–47
    nonsocial tasks, 149–50, (tables),
        153–54
    social competence, 149, 394, 397,
        416, 419
    social task data, 149, (tables), 151–
        52, 395, 398, 417, 420
    task initiation data, 154–55, (tables),
        153
    test performance, 147–48
    test scores, 393, 396, 415, 418
  "A" girls
    background, 134
    nonsocial tasks, 142
    social competence, 135–36, 406, 410,
        431, 453
    social task data, 139, 142, (tables),
        140–41, 407, 411, 432, 454
    task initiation data, 142, (tables),
        143
    test performance, 134–35
    test scores, 405, 409, 430, 452
  "C" boys
    background, 143–45
    nonsocial tasks, 149–50, (tables),
        153–54
    social competence, 146, 422, 444
    social task data, 149, (tables), 151–
        52, 423, 445
    task initiation data, 154–55, (tables),
        154
    test performance, 145–46
    test scores, 421, 443
  "C" girls
    background, 137
    nonsocial tasks, 142
    social competence, 138–39, 447

Case studies: two-year-olds (Cont.)
  "C" girls (Cont.)
    social task data, 139, 142, (tables), 140–41, 448
    task initiation data, 142, (tables), 144
    test performance, 137–38
    test scores, 446
Changing location, as interaction technique, 489
Child Development, 7, 258n
Child development
  critical period of, 234
  one year; conclusions, 234–36
  special importance of 10–18-month period, 237–40
  two years; conclusions, 236–37
Child-rearing practices
  effective, 242–44
  projected informal early education, 245–46
Choice, as nonsocial task, 82
Clark, Kitty Riley, 69n
Cognitive abilities, 6
Cohn, Andrew, 69n
Collins, C. W., 69n
Colorado, University of, 6
Communication, as social task, 81
Comparison tables, "A" and "C" children, 534–40
Compensatory education, 8
Compensatory preschool programs, 5
Competence (*See also* Social competence)
  assessment techniques, 19, 19n
  development of; quantitative methods, 40–41
  divergence by age, 2–3
  etiology of, in young children, 18–20
  growth of, 19
  ratings, as grouping factor, 29
  as variable in sample, 10
Competence and task data (*See* Case studies)
Competence dimensions: two–three years
  capacity for abstract thought, 60–65
  capacity to sense dissonance, 54–60
  development of social competence, 41–47
  general intellectual development, 65–67
  receptive language development, 47–54
Competition
  as behavior classification, 42
  as social task, 81
Comprehension of instructions, as language test: one–two years, 48
Concept, definition, 14

Conceptual basis of scales, as source of error, 182
Concrete reasoning, as activity dimension, 161, (fig.), 166, 471–72
Cooperation, as social tasks, 69
Cooperation tasks; increase at age three, 90
Core abilities, in disadvantaged six-year-olds, 6
Corman, Harvey, 61
Curiosity, as hallmark of one-year-old, 234–35

D

Day-care programs, 6
Deutsch, Martin, 5
Developmental divergence, 20
  factors in, 20–22
  indicators of, 238–39
Developmental status, tests of, 238–39
Didactic role, of mother, 186n
Didactic teaching, as interaction technique, 482
Diffuse role, of mother, 159, 174, 201
Direct, nonparticipatory roles, 162
  of interactor, 162
  of mother, 186n
Direct roles, of mother, 162–63, 201
Discriminative ability assessment; one–three-year-olds, 323
Discriminative ability assessment: one–three-year-olds (Cont.)
  choosing rewarded and unrewarded members, 330
  criterion, 329–30
  level of starting, 330
  procedure, 325–27
  reliability study, 331
  subjects, 324–25
  testing, 327–29
Discriminative ability, early, 55
Dissonance, assessing capacity to sense; two–three-year-olds
  comparison data (table), 58
  results, 56–60
  test for measuring, 55–56
Distraction, as interaction technique, 487
Domination and resistance, as social tasks, 81
  one–two years, 91
  as social tasks, 81
Dressing/undressing, as nonsocial task, 81
Dual-focusing ability, 19n

E

Early education program
  goals described, 18
  pioneers and professionals in, 5–6
Early experience, evaluative basis for,
    16–17
Early human development
  approach characterized, 3–5
  environmental factors, 25–26
  theoretical orientations toward, 4
Easing discomfort, as nonsocial task, 81
Eating, as nonsocial task, 81
Educability
  development of, 4
  divergence by age two–three, 21
Emotional and social expression, as activity dimensions, 478–80
Empathization, as behavior classification, 42
"Empty" behavior, 171
Engelman, S., 5
Environment
  and competence, 156
  definition, 157
Environmental observation
  case study: Sandra, a one-year-old "A" girl
    commentary, 206–207, 208, ˙209, 210–11
    human environment, 203–204
    observations, 204–206, 207–208, 208–209, 209–10
    physical environment, 202–203
  case study: Cathy, a one-year-old "C" girl
    commentary, 215–16, 217, 218–19, 220–21
    human environment, 212
    observations, 212–15, 216–17, 217–18, 219
    physical environment, 211–12
  case study: Nancy, a two-year-old "A" girl
    commentary, 224, 225
    human environment, 222
    observations, 222–23, 224–25
    physical environment, 221–22
  case study: Robert, a two-year-old "C" boy
    commentary, 228, 229
    human environment, 226–27
    observations, 227–28, 228–29
    physical environment, 226
Environment comparison data, 176–200
  observation method: observers, 180–81

Environment comparison data (Cont.)
  observation schedule, 177, 179–80, (tables), 178, 179
  possible sources of error, 181–82
  preliminary analysis, 182–86
  tentative nature of, 182
Environment scales, 159–75
Escalona, Sibylle K., 61
Ethnicity, as variable in sample, 10
Executive skills
  as activity dimension, 161, (fig.) 165, 473–74
  as nonsocial abilities, 16
Experience patterns: one–two years
  "A" versus "C" children, 91, 94–95
  categories, 85
  comparative task data (tables), 92–93, 96–97
  frequency analyses, 100–2, (table), 101
  initiation data, 102–3
  language, 95, 98
  live vs. mechanical language experience, 95
  mastery experience, 98–100
    comparison data (tables), 99, 100
  predictions of difference, 85–86
  social vs. nonsocial tasks, 103–4
  specific nonsocial tasks, 105, 107, (tables), 106, 108
  specific social tasks, 104–5
  statistical analysis of hypotheses (table), 109–10
  task data (table), 94
Experience patterns: two–three years, 84–110
  variables in experiment, 84–85
Experience, related to environment, 157
Exploration and play with household items, as activity dimension, 474
Exploration
  as nonsocial task, 82
  of objects; one–two years, 90
Expressive/creative activity, (fig.), 165
Expressive skills, as activity dimension, 473

F

Facilitative techniques, mothers' use of, 192–93
Final Home Interview, 524–32
  demographic information, 532
  intellectual development, 531
  mother—personal, 532
  personality development, 532

Final Home Interview (Cont.)
  reading, 530
  responsibility for child, 525
  self-care, 530
  toys and equipment inventory, 526–28
  toys and household objects, 529
  training, 529
  TV viewing, 531
Finding something to do, as nonsocial task, 82
Fine motor/spatial activity, (fig.), 164
First Home Interview
  basic care routine, 513
  demographic information
    characteristics, 522–23
    questionnaire form, 517–19
  favorite toys and playthings, 520
  health of child, 514
  mobility/supervision/range of experience, 514–15
  residence ratings, 520–21
  significant family events, 515–16
  topography, 520
  typical day questionnaire, 514
Focusing on task, as interaction technique, 485
Freud, S., 4n

G

Gain attention: one–two years; frequency analysis, 100–101
Gain information
  audio and visual: one–two years, 91
  audio and visual, as nonsocial task, 83
  visual, as frequent activity: one–three years, 90
Gaining approval, as social task, 69
General and intellectual development: two–three years
  comparison data (table), 66
  results, 65–67
  tests for, 65
General information giving, as interaction technique, 483–84
Gesell, 238
Gesell Institute, 6
Getting and maintaining attention of adult, 18, 42
Gibson, 241
Golden, M., 20
Grammar, testing in two–three year olds, 49
Grammatical Comprehension Tests, 258, 261–62

Grammatical Comprehension Tests (Cont.)
  sample, 271–74
  scoring system, 274–76
Grey, Susan, 8
Griffiths, 238
Gross motor learning, as activity dimension, 160, 477–78
Guttman scale, 324

H

Halfar, Christine, 159n, 180n
Halpern, Florence, 20
Harlow, Harry, 55
Harvard Preschool Project, 3, 4, 6
  major goal, 156
  plan of, 22
  preliminaries to, 5–8
Harvard University School of Education, 5
  Research and Development Center, 3, 4
Head Start, 8 (*See also* Project Head Start)
Hearing screening procedures, 38, 38n
Hess, R., 173
Hollingshead, A. B., 29, 37, 197, 197n
Holmes, J. C., 258
HOME Scale (*See* Human or Material Environment Scale)
Human competence; six-year-olds, 10–16
Human Infants' Experience and Psychological Development, 4n
Human Interaction Scale, 174, 176, 180, 183
  activities, criteria for judging, 159, 168–72
  activities dimensions, 160–62, 468–80
  advantages of, 163
  coding guidelines, 494–97
  coding steps, 491–93
  compliance index, 490
  dimensions, 468
  dimensions connections, example, 163, 167–68
  encouragement index, 481
  general dimensions, 160
  initiation index, 480–81
  interaction techniques, 481–90
  interactive quality of, 172
  phase rule for activities, 493–94
  recording raw data, 490
  reliability studies
    agreement on all dimensions (table), 504

Human Interaction Scale (Cont.)
  reliability studies (Cont.)
    procedures, 497, 502–3
    sample protocol, 498–501
  technique dimensions; features, 162–63
Human or Material Environment Scale,
    173n
Hunt, J. McV., 6, 20, 61, 173, 238
Hunt-Uzgiris Object Scale, 61, 64
  description, 292–301
  reliability, 321
  sample scoring sheets, 316–19
  score sheets, 308–10
  scoring, 307–8

I

Ilg, Frances, 6
Illinois, University of, 6
Imitation, as nonsocial task, 83
Index of Social Position, 29, 197
Infancy
  adaptive abilities, 4, 4n
  development of intelligence in, 4n
Infant-education programs, projected,
    246–47
Infantile sexuality, 4n
Information gaining, as activity dimen-
    sion, 476 (*See also* Gain informa-
    tion)
Initiation data, social and nonsocial tasks,
    102–10
Intellectual activities, scale of, (fig.), 171
Intellectual and social competence, 176
Intellectual competence, as nonsocial abil-
    ity, 14–15
Intellectual development
  hierarchy of activities, 168, 170–72,
    (table), 169
  structured vs. unstructured use of ma-
    terials, 172
Intellectual gain, of child, 170
Interaction
  effect of socioeconomic factors on, 195,
    197
  intellectual activity comparisons, 187–
    89
  low interaction value activities, 189
  moderate intellectual promise activities,
    188
  mothers' use of techniques, 192–93
  with others: "A" and "C" differences,
    195, (table), 196
  with physical environment, 197–99,
    (table), 198
  quality and quantity differences, 187–88

Interaction data
  differences: "A" and "C" children;
    one–two years, 186–99, (figs.),
    187, 188, 189, 190, 191, 192, 193,
    194, 196, 198
  environmental comparison study, 182–
    86
Interactor, roles of, 162–63
Interobserver reliability, 83
Interpersonal dimensions, classification of,
    42
Intervention work, 8
Interviews, as source of information on
    mother, 174, 175

J

Justification or statement of rationale, as
    interaction technique, 482–83

K

Kaban, Barbara, 69n
Kearse, Geraldine, 159n, 180n, 282
Knobloch, 238
Koslowski, Barbara, 55n

L

Laboratory of Human Development, 5
LaCrosse, E. R., 4, 7
Language, as barrier to testing, 40
Language ability
  degree of language exposure as factor,
    21
  testing for, 26
Language ability tests, 257–90
  procedure: 12–24 months, 258–60
  procedure: 24–36 months, 260–73
  reliability studies, 276–90
  sample data sheets, 263–67
  scoring schema, 289–90
  scoring procedures, 268–69
Language acquisition, development of,
    239
Language development: one-year-old, 235,
    236
Language experience: one–two years, 95,
    98
Large-muscle activity, as nonsocial task,
    82
Lesser, Gerald, 5
Limited interest, as factor in testing, 54

Linguistic abilities, 6 (*See also* Language ability)
Linguistic competence
"confounding variables," in testing, 53–54
high-achievement children: 1–1½ years, 50, 52
as nonsocial ability, 13–14
one–two-year-old test, 47–48
two–three-year-old test, 48–49
Lipsitt, Lewis, 6
Locomotor ability
development of, 237, 239
response to, as factor in development, 21
Longitudinal natural experiment
case studies: competence and experience data, 111–55
competence dimensions, 39–67
data gathering: protocols, 27
design of, 25–26
experience patterns analysis, 84–110
ongoing experience analysis, 68–84
screening instruments, 38
subject age as factor in testing, 26–27
subjects, 27, 29
subject sample description, 29, 32, 37, (tables), 30–31, 33–36
testing schedule, 26–29
Lorenz, Konrad, 9

M

McCarthy, Dorothea, 47
McNeil, David, 48n
Maintaining adult attention, as social ability, 10–11
Managerial role, of mother, 158–59, 201
Manjos, Maxine, 283
Mann-Whitney U Test, 43, 45n, 46, 50, 56
Marmor, Janice, 38n, 48n, 276, 282, 283
Mastery behavior: one–two years, 90
Mastery experience: one–two years, 98–100
Maturational status, as screening instrument, 38
MDI (*See* Bayley Index)
Mechanism operation, as nonsocial task, 83
Meyer, C. E., 61, 258, 258n, 292
Meyer's Pacific Test Series, 48, 61, 64 (*See also* Pacific Test Series)
MIH study, 47
Minnesota, University of, 6
Mobler, Mary Meader, 48n

Moore, Shirley, 6
Mother
attitudes and values: influence on performance, 240–42
didactic role, 186n
diffuse role, 159, 174, 201
direct role, 162–63, 201
managerial role, 158–59, 173–74, 201
and one-year-old, 235
participatory and nonparticipatory roles, 157–58
role in child's activity, 193, 195, (table), 194
role in early social experience, 18
style of behavior with child, 186
Mothering, as an occupation, 242
Murphy, Lois, 17

N

Nature exploration, as activity dimension, 475–76
Negative reinforcement, as interaction technique, 486
Negative social activity, (fig.), 166
Negativism
as factor in testing, 41, 53–54
and maternal reactions to, 239–40
Neutral role, 162, 163
Nimnicht, Glen, 8
Nonparticipatory, facilitative role, of mother, 186n
Nonparticipatory roles, in child's environment, 157–58, 162, 163
Nonsocial abilities: six-year-olds, 13–16
Nonsocial competencies; differences: one–two-year-olds, 47
Nonsocial tasks: one–two years, 87, 90, (tables), 87, 88–89
Non-task behavior, 82
one–two years, 90

O

Object Interaction Scale, 160, 172–73, 175, 180, 181
coding guidelines, 508–9
dimensions
human stimulus, 507
object stimulus, 508
restriction, 507
room, 506
experiences coded, 173
reliability check, 509

Object-labelling, as language test: one–two years, 48
Object procurement
   frequency analysis: one–two years, 101–2
   as nonsocial task, 82
Observation: two–three years (*See* Competence dimensions)
Observational technique, 7
Observer effects
   on data: source of error, 181
   problems associated with, 85
Observing, as interaction technique, 489–90
"Oddity" test, 55–56
Ogilvie, Daniel, 41n, 332n
Ongoing experiences: one–six years
   development of analytic instrument for, 68–69
   illustrations (figs.), 70–80
   nonsocial tasks categories, 81–83
   social tasks categories, 69, 81
"Open education" movement, 247
Other-initiated tasks, 102–5, 107

P

Pacific Expressive Vocabulary Objects (Meyers), 258, 259, 261, 274, 275
   sample, 271
Pacific Form and Picture Completion Test, 292
   description, 305–6
   score sheet, 312–13
Pacific Form-Color-Matching Test, 292
   description, 301–2, 314
Pacific Pattern Completion Test, 292
   description, 302–5
   score sheet, 311
Pacific Test Series (*See also* individual tests)
   overall scores, 308, 310, 315
   reliability, 321–22
Parent-child centers, 4
Participatory roles, in child's environment, 157–58
Pasamanick, 238
Passing time, as nonsocial task, 82
Pearson Product-Moment Correlation statistic, 276, 282, 283, 284, (tables), 277–79, 285–87, 308, 321, 322
   discriminative ability, 331
Peer-related activities, 42
   as social abilities, 12–13

Perceptual, spatial and fine motor learning, as activity
   dimension, 470–71
Pet enjoyment, as social task, 81
Physical environment, the child's interaction with, 197–99, (table), 198
Physical maturity: one-year-old, 236
Piaget, Jean, 4, 4n, 20, 55, 60, 218
Piaget's theory of intelligence, 4, 4n
Play with toys, as activity dimension, 475
Pleasing, as social task, 69
Pleasure gain, as nonsocial task, 83
Positive reinforcement, as interaction technique, 484–85
Positive social activity, (fig.), 167
Preliminary Home Interview, sample, 511
Preschool education programs, projected, 247
Pretending, as nonsocial task, 82
Primary caretakers, characteristics of, 240–42
Procuring aid
   one–two years, 91
   as social task, 69
Product construction, as nonsocial task, 82
Productive language, 47
Project Head Start, 4, 20, 160
Providing materials, as interaction technique, 488–89
Providing service, as interaction technique, 488
Purpose, compared to task, 170, 170n

Q

Questionnaires, on child's environment, 173–74

R

Receptive language, 21
   ability: 21–36 months, 52–53
   assessing development: two–three years, 41, 47–54
   comparison data, (table), 49
Redlich, F. C., 29, 37, 197, 197n
Refusal to help, as interaction technique, 487–88
Rejection of peer contact, as social task, 69
Reliability of scales, as source of error, 181

Reliability study, of social competence, 43

Relieving oneself, as nonsocial task, 81

Residence, as variable in sample, 10

Resisting distractions, as behavior classification, 42

Restoring order, as nonsocial task, 81

Restriction or prohibition, as interaction technique, 485–86

Restrictive techniques, mothers' use of, 192–93

S

Schaefer, E. S., 20

Schoggen, Maxine, 68n

Schoggen, P., 68n

School/home settings, differences, 161

Self-initiated tasks, 102–105, 107

Self praise and pride, as social ability, 13, 42

Sensing discrepancies, testing for, 26

Sensorimotor intelligence, scales for assessment of, 60–61

Sensory-discrimination capacity, 5

SES (*See* Socioeconomic status)

Sex, as grouping factor, 29

Shapiro, Bernice B., 41n, 332n

Shipman, V., 173

Siegel, Alberta, 7

Sizer, Theodore, 5

Skill improvement, as nonsocial task, 83

Social abilities: six-year-olds, 10–13

Social abilities assessment: one–six-year-olds

  additional reliability procedures, 351–52

  amount of scoring, 334

  categories

    interaction with adults, 335–42

    interaction with peers, 342–51

  checklist for scoring, 353–55, 356–58

  checklist for scoring social behavior, 335–51

  extent of coverage, 334

  factors in social competence, 358–59

  independence of categories, 335

  reliability, 335

Social Behavior Checklist, 42–43

Social Class and Mental Illness, 197n

Social competence, 19n

  one-year-olds, 43–45

  two-year-olds, 45–47

  two–three-year-olds

    assessment techniques, 41–43

Social competence (Cont.)

  two–three-year-olds (Cont.)

    behavior classes, 42

    comparisons (table), 44

    group medians (table), 45

    results and discussion, 43–47

    scoring instructions, 42–43

Social contact

  one–two years, 91

  as task, 69

Social development

  activities, 168

  one-year-old, 235

Social vs. nonsocial tasks: one–two years, comparative data (table), 90

Socioeconomic factors, effect on interaction patterns, 195, 197

Socioeconomic status

  characteristics in subject sample, 29–38

  as variable in sample, 10

Spatial, perceptual and fine motor learning, as activity dimension, 160, 161

Spearman Rank Correlation coefficient, 276, 284, (tables), 280–81, 287–89

Spock, Benjamin, 245

Stanford-Binet Intelligence Scales, 17, 18, 64, 65, 134, 145, 148, 292

  description, 306–7, 320

  scoring, 321

Suggestion or command, as interaction technique, 484

Symbol, definition, 15

T

Task analysis: one–six-year-olds, 360–89

  coding; general directions

    coding, 363–64

    raw material, 363

    refining coding, 364–66

  definitions: tasks, 362–63

  final coding, 366

  instrument reliability study, 388–89

  nonsocial tasks

    examples, 380–88

    labels and definitions, 378–80

  social tasks

    examples, 368–78

    labels and definitions, 367–68

Task scales, 68–83, 159

Taylor, Jolinda, 41n

Teacher opinion, as information source, 17

Tennican, Kathy, 38n

Test data, problems in using, 17
Test-taking ability, as indicator of competence, 54
Three-year-olds, focus of study narrowed to, 19–20
Tinbergen, 9
Typical Day Questionnaire, 173–74, 175, 180, 181
   sample, 510

U

Unspecific behavior, as activity dimension, 478
Use of adults as resources, as social ability, 11, 18, 42
U.S. Office of Education, 3
Uzgiris, I. C., 20, 61, 173

V

Values, of mother: influence on performance, 240–42
Verbalization, as social task, 81

Verbal symbolic learning, as activity dimension, 160, 162, (fig.), 164, 470
Vision screening procedures, 38, 38n, 256
Vocabulary, testing in two–three-year-olds, 48–49

W

Wachs, T. D., 20, 173
Walk, 241
Watts, Jean Carew, 23, 159n, 180n
Wechsler test, 10
Weckart, David, 5, 8
White, Burton L., 4, 4n, 6, 23, 48n, 55n, 61n, 69n, 238, 276
Wolf, Richard M., 5, 173
Wright, Herbert, 68

Z

Zolot, Melvin, 38n